Reader Series
in Music Librarianship

Published *Readers* in the series are:

Reader in Library Administration. 1969.
Paul Wasserman and Mary Lee Bundy.

Reader in Research Methods for Librarianship. 1970.
Mary Lee Bundy and Paul Wasserman.

Reader in the Academic Library. 1970.
Michael M. Reynolds.

Reader in Library Services and the Computer. 1971.
Louis Kaplan.

Reader in American Library History. 1971.
Michael H. Harris

Reader in Classification and Descriptive Cataloging. 1972.
Ann F. Painter.

Reader in Technical Services. 1973.
Edward L. Applebaum.

Reader in Medical Librarianship. 1973.
Winifred Sewell.

Reader in Government Documents. 1973.
Frederic J. O'Hara.

Reader in Science Information. 1973.
John Sherrod and Alfred Hodina.

Reader in Library Cooperation. 1973.
Michael M. Reynolds

Reader in Music Librarianship. 1973.
Carol June Bradley.

Reader in Music Librarianship

Edited by

Carol June Bradley

1973

Library of Congress Catalog Card Number: 73-82994
ISBN: 0-910972-48-6

Published by Indian Head Editions
901 26th Street, N.W.
Washington, D.C. 20037

Printed in the United States of America

Dedicated to the Memory
of
CATHARINE KEYES MILLER
1905–1966

Foreword

Unlike many other academic disciplines, librarianship has not yet begun to exploit the contributions of the several disciplines toward the study of its own issues. Yet the literature abounds with material germane to its concerns. Too frequently the task of identifying, correlating, and bringing together material from innumerable sources is burdensome, time consuming or simply impossible. For a field whose stock in trade is organizing knowledge, it is clear that the job of synthesizing the most essential contributions from the elusive sources in which they are contained is overdue. This then is the rationale for the series, *Readers in Library and Information Science.*

The *Readers in Library and Information Science* includes books concerned with various broad aspects of the field's interests. Each volume is prepared by a recognized student of the topic covered, and the content embraces material from the many different sources from the traditional literature of librarianship as well as from outside the field in which the most salient contributions have appeared. The objectives of the series are to bring together in convenient form the key elements required for a current and comprehensive view of the subject matter. In this way it is hoped that the core of knowledge, essential as the intellectual basis for study and understanding, can be drawn into focus and thereby contribute to the furtherance of professional education and professional practice in the field.

Paul Wasserman
Series Editor

Contents

III

BIBLIOGRAPHIC SERVICES WITHIN A MUSIC LIBRARY

A. The Bibliographic Description of Musical Editions, to the End of Establishing Their Printing Dates, Variants, Sequence, and Inter-relationships

SELECTED BIBLIOGRAPHY

B. Cataloguing and Classification

SELECTED BIBLIOGRAPHY

C. Thematic Indices

SELECTED BIBLIOGRAPHY

D. Application of Data Processing Techniques

SELECTED BIBLIOGRAPHY

E. Copyright and Music

SELECTED BIBLIOGRAPHY *Harry Kownatsky*, comp.

F. Exhibitions

SELECTED BIBLIOGRAPHY

IV

MECHANICAL PROCESSES OF A MUSIC LIBRARY

A. Acquisitions

B. Binding

V

PHONOGRAPH RECORDS, TAPES, ETC., WITHIN THE MUSIC LIBRARY

VI

BUILDINGS AND EQUIPMENT APPROPRIATE FOR THE MUSIC LIBRARY

VII

MUSIC LIBRARIANSHIP

Preface

The literature of American music librarianship dates from 1887—W. A. Bardwell's description of the Brooklyn Public Library's circulating music collection,[1] the first in an American public library. Ten years later, James Duff Brown, probably the earliest English writer on music librarianship, published an open letter to *The Library* on the cataloguing and classification of music [reprinted in subdivision III. B. below, pp. 143–145. These and other early components of what has become the literature of music librarianship were written by both musicians and librarians; they were published in the literatures of music, librarianship, bibliography, and printing. Many classic articles, the cornerstones on which American music librarianship is built, appear in sources which are long out-of-print, or otherwise unavailable in music libraries and library school libraries. The independent American literature of music librarianship began in 1934, date of the first issue of *Notes,* the journal of the newly-formed Music Library Association.

This diffusion and unavailability of the historical foundations of our profession became very apparent to me during my work on the manuscript of the Music Library Association's *Manual of Music Librarianship.*[2] That volume, the first specifically designed for American music librarians, depended heavily on bibliography, its individual chapters written to bring up-to-date, augment, and expand the appropriate bibliographic references.

Although at that time I was working in a well-established academic music library—one in which the professional staff had always been actively involved in the work of the Music Library Association and had consistently collected the source materials of music librarianship—I was obliged to use several general libraries and the privilege of interlibrary loans to gather and consult many of the sources quoted in the MLA *Manual* chapters. As my collection of xeroxed articles grew, it occurred to me that a companion volume to the MLA *Manual,* reprinting in one place the scattered, less-generally available articles, would be desirable. It would also create a fine source book for newly-established music libraries, young music librarians, and library school students.

Beginning with the bibliographies in the MLA *Manual,* then Nicewonger,[3] Baldwin,[4] and Wagner,[5] I worked backwards to collect and group—by contemporary librarianship's subdivisions—as much of the literature of music librarianship as I could secure. Although my emphasis was always on English-language literature, especially as it reflected American practices, three non-English language articles were ultimately included. Those articles, which should be more widely known to American music librarians, were translated especially for this *Reader.* One, Lesure's "Bibliothècaires et musicologues," was translated by Dr. Rita Benton for *Notes*[6] after I had completed my selection of articles for this *Reader* and Dr. Isabelle Cazeaux had made the translation printed here. The other two articles have not been published in English before.

Although we are frequently unaware of our factual historical background and the evolutionary stages by which we have attained our contemporary realities, a purely retrospective *Reader* would be of limited appeal and utility. Instead, I have selected articles to reprint which are difficult to locate, out-of-print, and/or were originally published in sources which cannot normally be expected to be available, *en toto,* in either a music library, a library school library, or the average general library. Prior to this *Reader,* persons seeking to examine the articles cited in the MLA *Manual* were obliged to collect the music ones in a music library, those from library literature in a library school library, and those from the literatures of bibliography and printing in a fine general library.

Working forward from the date of the MLA *Manual* to the present, I have used the standard periodical indexes, i.e., *Library Literature, Music Index,*[7] the *Music Article Guide,*[8] and the *Brio* "Index of articles published in selected musical periodicals."[9] For many of the bibliographic citations I have provided annotations. If an annotation mentions bibliography as a feature of the cited source, I have attempted to exclude all the citations of that bibliography in this *Reader;* only those required to complete a subject's coverage are included. Persons interested in pursuing the subject of the annotated article should consult its bibliography for further information.

The use of bibliography in this *Reader* is designed to bring together in one volume as much information as possible. It is somewhat unusual, and may appear to create a like bibliographical circumstance to that of the MLA *Manual.* That circumstance is not, however, repeated. It is impossible to reprint, in its entirety, the literature of a profession. It seems appropriate, therefore, to provide comprehensive bibliographic control of that literature. The key to the distinction between the two bibliographical situations is: The MLA *Manual* built on existing literature; this *Reader* reprints the classic articles which made up that literature and, in addition, annotates those historical items which it does not reprint. Unless an individual is doing in-depth research in the specific subject of an annotated article, he should be spared the necessity of consulting it by using the annotation. Thus this *Reader* provides, for the first time, a carefully-organized, fully-indexed overview of the literature of music librarianship.

In the introductory paragraph I quoted the beginnings of the English-language literature of music librarianship. Subsequent discussion has mentioned only the MLA *Manual* as basic literature on which this *Reader* builds. Actually, both the MLA *Manual* and this *Reader* are built on:

1. Wallace, Ruth, ed. *The care and treatment of music in a library.* American Library Association. Committee on Cataloging. Contribution, no. I. Chicago: American Library Association, 1927.
2. McColvin, Lionel R. and Reeves, Harold. *Music libraries; their organization and contents, with a bibliography of music and musical literature.* London: Grafton, 1937. 2v.
3. McColvin, Lionel R. and Reeves, Harold. *Music libraries, including a comprehensive bibliography of music literature and a select bibliography of music scores published since 1957.* Completely rewritten, revised and extended by Jack Dove. London: A. Deutsch, 1965. 2v.
   See annotations in MLA *Manual,* p. 55 and Duckles 2nd ed., 1350.
4. Bryant, Eric Thomas. *Music librarianship: A practical guide.* London: J. Clarke; New York: Hafner, 1959.
   See annotations in MLA *Manual,* p. 50 and Duckles 2nd ed., 1323.
5. Duckles, Vincent, ed. "Music libraries and librarianship," *Library Trends,* 8 (April, 1960), 495-617.
   The individual articles are cited in their appropriate places throughout this *Reader.* See also the annotation in Duckles 2nd ed., 1339.
6. *Music, libraries and instruments.* Papers read at the Joint Congress, Cambridge, 1959, of the International Association of Music Libraries and the Galpin Society. Hinrichsen's Eleventh Music Book. London: Hinrichsen Edition, 1961. "Section two: Music librarianship": pp. 40-99. "Section three: Record libraries": pp. 99-126. "Towards a definition of certain terms in musical bibliography": pp. 147-155.
7. Redfern, Brian L. *Organizing music in libraries.* London: Bingley, 1966.
8. *Notes,* no. 1-15, July, 1934—December, 1942; series 2, v. 1, December, 1943- Washington, D.C., etc.: Music Library Association, 1934-
   Journal of the Music Library Association.
9. *Notes: Supplement for Members,* no. 1, September, 1947- Washington, D.C.: Music Library Association, 1947-
10. *Fontes artis musicae,* v. 1, 1954- Kassel: Bärenreiter-Verlag, 1954-
   Journal of the International Association of Music Libraries.
11. *Brio,* v. 1, Spring, 1964- London: United Kingdom Branch of the International Association of Music Libraries, 1964-
   Journal of the United Kingdom Branch of IAML.

There are several articles reprinted from *Notes,* articles so crucial to the adequacy of this volume that they could not be merely cited even though *Notes* itself is generally available. [Its First Series and early issues of the Second Series are accessible since they were reprinted by the AMS Reprint Company.]

Fontes artis musicae cannot be considered generally available and therefore, quite a few articles are reprinted from its pages. IAML's recent promotional campaign may increase its American circulation, but it is questionable if many individuals or institutions will buy the back issues which contain the reprinted articles. For their generosity in contributing to the very existence of this *Reader* by allowing articles to be reprinted without permission fee, I am deeply grateful to the International Association of Music Libraries and M. Vladimir Féderov, editor of *Fontes.*

No articles are reprinted from *Library Trends,* all back issues of which are and—according to the publisher—will remain in print. Users of this volume may reasonably be expected to have immediate access to, or to purchase for themselves, the special issue on music librarianship [**5** above] and the issues containing the two articles cited elsewhere [**22**, 4, **71**, 74].

To gain maximum effectiveness from the selection process used in preparing this *Reader,* the student of music librarianship is expected to have on his shelf the *Library Trends* issue [**5**], the MLA *Manual,* this *Reader,* and ready access to *Notes.*

Many of the items included in this collection were originally read as papers at professional meetings. Rather than subject them to the indignities of truncation and de-personalization, I have allowed them to stand essentially as read—including the usual introductory and closing remarks.

A *Selected Bibliography* appears at the head of most subdivisions throughout the *Reader;* each item therein is numbered and referred to throughout the *Reader* by that number. In those references, the item number is in boldface type within square brackets; the second number, in roman type, is the page on which the item is cited.

In addition to the original notes of the reprinted articles, there are Editor's Notes written especially for this *Reader.* Both sets of notes are arranged in a single numerical sequence; those supplied by the Editor are clearly labelled.

"Duckles 2nd ed., 1053" refers to item 1053 in [**59**, 73] below. Rather than duplicate his bibliographical information and annotations, I have quoted the item numbers in the latest edition of Duckles available to me now (a third edition is imminent).

The *Index* comprehends concepts, subjects, library names, personal names and titles of the reprinted articles, as well as the bibliographic citations throughout the volume.

* * * * *

One of the most pleasant duties, at the end of a four-year project, is to formally thank those institutions and individuals who have contributed to its completion. The staff of the Vassar College Library, especially the Interlibrary Loan Department personnel, was very helpful during the initial stages of document collection. The Vassar College administration very graciously allowed an inordinate amount of xerox copying at a time in the chronology of photocopying that it was quite expensive. The Interlibrary Loan Department of the University Libraries, State University of New York at Buffalo, was most cooperative. Mme. Kathi Meyer-Baer translated her article on publishers' use of plate numbers from its original German for publication in this *Reader.* Dr. Isabelle Cazeaux translated both the Clercx-Lejeune and Lesure articles from their French editions. Mr. Harry Kownatsky, Curator of the Edwin A. Fleisher Collection of Orchestral Music, prepared the bibliography and introduction to the section on copyright in relation to music, III. E. Ms. Lenore Coral very graciously revised portions of her thesis for publication here. Ms. Elizabeth Murray conducted the voluminous correspondence necessary to obtain reprint permissions from copyright owners and authors. Professor James Coover, who wrote the summary statement on acquisitions, IV.A, also read the entire manuscript and made substantive suggestions for its improvement.

CJB
Buffalo, New York
December 29, 1971

NOTES

[1] W. A. Bardwell, "A library of music," *Library Journal,* 12 (April, 1887), 159.

[2] Carol June Bradley, ed., *Manual of music librarianship* (Ann Arbor, Michigan: Music Library Association, 1966).

[3] Harriet Nicewonger, "A selected bibliography on music librarianship in the United States," *Library Trends,* 8 (April, 1960), 614-617.

[4] Margaret I. Baldwin, "Music librarianship; an annotated bibliography of periodical literature 1942–June 1952" (M.S.L.S. thesis, Drexel Institute of Technology, 1952).

[5] Marjorie K. Wagner, "Music librarianship in the U.S. 1876-1955; an annotated classified bibliography" (M.S.L.S. thesis, Catholic University of America, 1958).

[6] "Librarians and musicologists," *Notes,* 24 (June, 1968), 665-669.

[7] *Music Index.* (Detroit: Information Service, 1949-). Monthly, with annual cumulations. Indexes *Notes, Fontes,* and *Brio.*

[8] *Music Article Guide.* A comprehensive quarterly reference guide to signed feature articles in American music periodicals (with a capsule description of each article). (Philadelphia: Music Article Guide, 1965-).

See especially headings "Library collections" and "Library practices." Indexes by title, author, subject and major subject headings. Indexes *Notes.*

[9] Christel Wallbaum, comp., "Index of articles published in selected musical periodicals," *Brio,* 1 (1964-).

Indexes British music periodicals. A regular feature of each issue.

I

A GENERAL SURVEY AND OVERVIEW OF MUSIC LIBRARIES

A. The Scope, Organization and Function of Music Libraries as Well as Their Inter-relationship With Musicology and Musicologists

SELECTED BIBLIOGRAPHY

12. Apel, Willi. *Harvard Dictionary of Music.* Cambridge: Harvard University Press, 1947. "Libraries": pp. 398-404.

The first section of the article is a history of American music libraries and librarianship. Includes many bibliographic citations.

13. _____ . *Harvard Dictionary of Music.* 2nd ed. Cambridge: Belknap Press of Harvard University Press, 1969. "Libraries": pp. 468-480.

Although the historical essay is not reprinted, more American music libraries and their catalogues are included than in the original edition. The two articles complement, not supersede, each other.

14. Grove, Sir George. *Grove's Dictionary of Music and Musicians.* 5th ed. Edited by Eric Blom. London: Macmillan; New York: St. Martin's Press, 1954. "Libraries and collections": v. 5, pp. 160-223.

Description of American music libraries, pp. 207-220; special collections and holdings of particular strength are mentioned for the individual libraries.

15. Hopkins, Julia A. "Music in libraries," *Wisconsin Library Bulletin,* 3 (November/December, 1907), 89-93.

A brief description of some techniques of providing music in libraries in 1907.

16. Duncan, Barbara. "Music from the library point of view," *ALA Bulletin,* 21 (1927), 331-332.

Abstract of her paper read at the 4th annual Art Reference Round Table, ALA Conference, Toronto, June 24, 1927.

17. Strunk, William Oliver. *State and resources of musicology in the United States, a survey made for the American Council of Learned Societies.* American Council of Learned Societies . . . Bulletin no. 19, December 1932. Washington, D.C.: American Council of Learned Societies, 1932. "Part II: Musicological equipment of libraries:" pp. 52-68; "Music Library Association (1931)": p. 76.

18. Moor, Arthur Prichard. *The library-museum of music and dance; a study of needs and resources, leading to suggestions for an educational program.* Teachers College, Columbia University, Contributions to education, no. 750. New York City: Teachers College, Columbia University, 1938.

19. Grout, Donald J. "The music library and musicology," *Notes,* 1st series, no. 11 (August, 1941), 3-12.

20. Music Library Association. *Music and libraries; selected papers of the Music Library Association, presented at its 1942 meetings.* Edited by Richard S. Hill. Washington, D. C.: Music Library Association, 1943.

Contents: "The Carnegie music sets," Florence Anderson.—"Materials for the study of Latin American music," Gilbert Chase.—"Music in wartime and post-war America," Edwin Hughes.—"The Music Library Association and the United Service Organizations," Raymond Kendall.—"The music library in the college of the future," Jerrold Orne.—"The relation between the music librarian and the music publisher," Gustave Reese.—"The army library service," Major R. L. Trautman.—"Early American publications in the field of music," W. T. Upton.

21. Smith, Carleton Sprague. "Musicology and the library," *Music Journal,* 4 (November/December, 1946), 13, 44-46.

22. Duckles, Vincent H. "Musical scores and recordings," *Library Trends,* 4 (October, 1955), 164-173.

A bibliographic essay on music in American libraries written for a *Trends* issue entitled "Special materials and services." Very good background study, especially for library school students.

23. Appel, Richard Gilmore. "The American music library, past, present, and future." In *One hundred years of music in America,* edited by Paul Henry Lang, pp. 245-256. New York: G. Schirmer, 1961.

24. "American music libraries and information agencies," *Fontes artis musicae,* 16 (1969/3), 108-150. Preface by Thor E. Wood.

Includes descriptions of eight collections, as well as several less specific articles which are cited elsewhere in this *Reader.*

25. Watanabe, Ruth T. *Introduction to music research.* Englewood Cliffs, N. J.: Prentice-Hall, 1967. "The music library": pp. 7-13.

26. Davies, John H. *Musicalia: Sources of information in music.* Oxford: Pergamon Press, 1966. "The music librarian": pp. 93–105; "Printing, publishing and copying": pp. 138–145.

See annotation in Duckles 2nd ed., 1382.

27. ——. *Musicalia: Sources of information in music.* Second edition, revised and enlarged. Oxford: Pergamon Press, 1969. "The music librarian": pp. 72–78; "Printing, publishing and copying": pp. 107-113.

Davies also contributes a quarterly survey, "Musicalia," to *The Library World.*

28. Gerboth, Walter. "The publics of the music library," *Fontes artis musicae,* 18 (1971/1-2), 19-21.

Music in our Libraries

by O. G. Sonneck

Oscar George Theodore Sonneck, 1873–1928, was the first Chief of the Music Division of the Library of Congress. During his tenure, 1902–1917, he formulated Class M *of the LC classification scheme; and he developed a music library unequalled in its holdings of American publications, and especially outstanding in its facilities for the study of opera history. His rôle in the coming-of-age of American musical scholarship and bibliography is documented by Carl Engel in the introduction to Sonneck's posthumously-published, autobiographical essay "99 Pacific Avenue; or, In search of a birthplace" [*The Musical Quarterly*, 19 (October, 1933), 456–465]. Twenty-five years after Sonneck's death, Otto Kinkeldey wrote of his contributions to music librarianship in the United States [*Notes*, 11 (December, 1953), 25–32]. The bibliography of his publications is included in the Sonneck entry written by Nathan Broder for the German encyclopedia,* Die Musik in Geschichte und Gegenwart, *v. 12.*

Sonneck made this eloquent plea for intellectual and financial support of the fledgling music libraries of the United States in 1917, while he was still at the Library of Congress. His persuasions for the acquisition of esoterica and his justifications for acquisition monies are equally valid today.

Poets and other generous souls have extolled the charms of music until the emotional superiority of music over other arts has become a dogma too venerable for doubt. Possibly the emotional appeal of music *is* more intense than that of other arts, but the account is squared by several obstructions in the path of that appeal. Chief among these (with all the inherent consequences) is the inordinately complex and costly apparatus required for performance of musical works in the larger forms, such as symphonies, oratorios, operas. The composer faces a second disadvantage in the necessity of recording his thoughts with the help of symbols which can reach the sense appealed to, the ear, only by way of another sense, the eye. Furthermore, comparatively few music-lovers possess the imagination or the training to transform such visual impressions into the corresponding aural impressions. The accomplishment of "reading the score" of a modern opera, for instance, is an accomplishment indeed, and of truly deterring difficulty. Yet on this very accomplishment of those interested in him every composer sooner or later depends for his intercourse with contemporaries or posterity whenever the performer, the intermediary between composer and public, chooses not to perform a composer's works.

A minimum of reflection will show how under the circumstances, without the hospitality of libraries, composers are in danger of being shut off from posterity. But there his musical thoughts lie practically buried alive, encapsuled in books of mute hieroglyphics. It is the best the world can offer him until that time when we shall have not merely musical libraries but "museums" of music, where in sundry feasible ways the public appeal of works of musical art will be made to endure, in effect similar to the permanent and ever-direct appeal of paintings, sculptures, etc., in museums of the Fine Arts. A fantastic dream? Not at all; but my present purpose does not permit of unfolding my ideas on this solvable problem of art-conservation and presentation.

If works of musical art, then, must fall back gradually on the hospitality of libraries—from the

SOURCE: First published in *The Art World,* II (1917); reprinted in O. G. Sonneck *Miscellaneous studies in the history of music* (New York: Macmillan, 1921), pp. 287–295.

very nature of music virtually the hospitality of a mausoleum—has the best been made of the situation? Hardly. Musical libraries that are reasonably representative of the mighty growth of musical culture in our country, culture that springs from tender but healthy roots two hundred years old, are too few and far between to suggest a different answer. Perhaps the librarian profession still hesitates to recognize in music intellectual elements not less worthy of attention than genealogy or fiction. Perhaps we suffer from a dearth of expert musical librarians whose authority might compel a more hospitable attitude of mind. Perhaps musicians and music-lovers in musical communities are still too indifferent, or too unaware of their power of concerted action to have the rights of music as a cultural and therewith civic factor more adequately respected in libraries. Perhaps American libraries are richer in good will than in funds; perhaps the cost of music, comparatively much greater than that of literature, works as a handicap. Whatever the reason or reasons, the fact remains that music is deplorably underfed in the great majority of our libraries. Otherwise cities like New York, Philadelphia, Chicago, St. Louis, Cincinnati, San Francisco, Minneapolis and half a dozen others of our musical centres would not lag so far behind Boston in the possession of a municipal musical library of which all citizens may feel proud. They would not be able to emulate certain unique features of the late Mr. Allen A. Brown's munificent gift to the city of Boston, but if they had started in time and had persevered, they would now, as they ought, possess musical collections fairly equal to his in extent and merit.

In any ambitious community a library without the complete works of Shakespeare, Goethe, Dickens, Ibsen, Molière, Balzac, Dante, Longfellow, Poe—or without various serial works published to embrace a comprehensive selection of representative and historically important literary masterpieces, such as Johnson's 75-volume edition of English writers, would very properly invite scornful criticism. Apply a similar test with reference to the great masters of music. Does your local library contain the more or less complete editions of the works of Palestrina, Orlando di Lasso, Bach, Händel, Purcell, Rameau, Grétry, Haydn, Mozart, Beethoven, Schubert, Schumann, Mendelssohn, Berlioz, Liszt, Wagner, Verdi? Does it contain such historical publications as the *Denkmäler der Tonkunst* in Austria and Germany, the *Paléographie musicale, Les Archives de Maîtres de l'Orgue, L'arte musicale in Italia, Les maîtres musiciens de la Renaissance française,* the series of volumes of the Musical Antiquarian Society or the other similar undertakings designed to rescue from oblivion and to revive, at least for the student, masters of the past? If by way of excuse the answer be that there is no demand in a particular, supposedly musical community for such publications; that too much of the music is of "purely antiquarian interest" and of too little "musical interest to modern ears," then my counter-argument is: first, that the community is not yet as musically cultured as it thinks it is, or ought to be; second, that the tendency to appoint prevalent fashion or taste a complacent judge of art-values of the past is damnable and is more likely than not to lead to a conservatism hostile toward pioneers of the future; third, that "purely antiquarian interest" is not more of a crime and not less of a virtue in music than in other fields of human endeavor represented for that very reason in libraries. My fourth is, that much, very much music pleasing to the modern ear is already too dead even for antiquarian interest, hence might be denied asylum in libraries on special principles; my fifth, that a librarian ought not to content himself with giving to the public what it happens to want, but ought to help create a demand for what the public needs; my sixth, that no self-respecting library can afford to be without certain cultural documents, whether they be consulted frequently or seldom. Do you ask for more? then my seventh: that the needs of one solitary scholarly specialist should weigh with librarians just as heavily as the wants of a hundred "general" and generally superficial and unproductive readers.

After all, it is not the frequency of use that counts, but the use to which a book is put. A costly and rare book consulted only once in ten years, but then by a man of far-reaching research or codification of research, has justified its acquisition just as much as an inexpensive, commonplace book consulted every day for mere receptive information.

If the absence of works of "antiquarian" or "modern" interest be explained on the grounds of expensiveness, the explanation will carry weight. For it is a regrettable fact that chamber music, orchestra music, opera scores and so forth entail an expenditure which acts as a barrier to the comprehensive acquisition of meritorious music. And when the prices of foreign works of musical art are Americanized, a librarian may well despair of his ability to satisfy the needs of a musical community. When scores of the type mentioned above run in cost anywhere from four to two hundred and fifty dollars, the difficulty of assembling a representative collection of music becomes obvious, not to mention a moderate indulgence in bibliographical rarities or in autograph scores.

On the other hand, however, by no means all desirable and necessary music is beyond reach of even poor institutions. In every country music publishers have sought to meet the situation by issuing the standard works by standard composers for a moderate price. By surveying such editions any librarian with a modicum of expert knowledge may assemble a collection of indispensable works of musical art and of books on music. Indeed, respectable publishers have tried to facilitate his task by forming for him just such collections at a price which, of course, keeps pace with the character, extent and scope of the purchases *en bloc* suggested. Strange to say, either for lack of confidence in the interested disinterestedness of publishers—or for lack of interest or knowledge or ability to resist the temptation of wasting one's meagre funds on favored composers and alluringly advertised expensive publications—or for other reasons, it would appear that the movement has not been an unqualified success. True, many small libraries have embraced the opportunities offered, but just as many have neglected them, with the result that the number of reasonably well-equipped public musical libraries seems to be abnormally small in our country.

There is something fundamentally wrong somewhere in the situation if, for instance, a prominent publisher could sell to private music-lovers many thousand single volumes, but to public libraries only about fifty complete sets of a remarkable publication (now nearing the hundredth volume) which will form a comprehensive musician's library in itself, costs less than two dollars a volume, and for merit belongs to that type and class of publication which ought to be not in fifty, but in a thousand public libraries.

Precisely such serial publications, in a way encyclopedic publications, ought to form the basis of every public collection. It is the centre from which the concentric method of library development can best find its outward impetus; and no other method, provided it be not employed too rigidly or pedantically, will produce equally satisfactory results. Without it the collections will soon become unbalanced; they will suffer from obesity here and from anemia there. Nor is this all. Such publications, planned as libraries within libraries, lend themselves to bibliographical treatment for reference purposes more readily and more fruitfully than collections formed by picking out this or that work from catalogues. And paradoxical as it may sound, small libraries, with contents of such publications analytically catalogued, will often be in a better position to supply a sudden demand for specimens of work by an out-of-the-way composer than large libraries with an operating force too small or administrative machinery unsuited for proper analysis of collective publications.

Occasionally I have been asked to estimate the annual outlay necessary to form a good musical working library satisfactory to readers esthetically and historically as well as pedagogically inclined.

The question is a rather dangerous one to answer, because such estimates are hardly ever better than guesses or expressions of personal judgment not necessarily in harmony with that of colleagues. Having thus invited criticism of my estimates, I would say that an annual appropriation of three hundred dollars[1] for the purchase of good music and good books on music is the *minimum* expenditure from which to expect results of substantial benefit to even small musical communities. This estimate applies merely to reference libraries, not to circulating libraries with branch offices. Moreover, it takes into account only the acquisition of printed music and does not concern itself with a collection of talking-machine records or player-piano rolls, so useful and desirable for purposes of *vulgarisation,* as the French would say. The larger a community is, or the more it bubbles over with musical activities, the more inadequate such a small annual appropriation as the above naturally becomes. If we pass on to our musical centres, or would-be musical centres, even one thousand dollars[2] will prove insufficient if music really is meant to find a place in the public library in keeping with the community's interest in music.

In my humble opinion the public libraries in cities like those mentioned above would deserve no *ordre pour le mérite* for exceptional services rendered, if their annual appropriation for music and books on music reached or exceeded two thousand dollars. They would really be doing their duty only (and not more) toward music and its devotees by spending that sum every year. Even so, they would soon discover that the intelligent annual expenditure of two thousand dollars[3] will not nowadays cover the field of legitimate ambition and that their musical collection will retain at that rate the characteristics of a good "working library" on a fairly large scale, but will never develop into a really first-class library of international importance for antiquarian research or the study of modern music.

These estimates will come as a shock to hard-pressed librarians and library trustees. I tender my sympathy; yet I must adhere to my estimates, since they are based on our experiences at the Library of Congress. There we have spent each year since 1902 vastly more than two thousand dollars on music and books on music. In fact, in one year necessity or opportunity, as one might prefer to call it, compelled us to spend not very far from ten times that amount. Nor do the more than 80,000 "pieces" (so-called in bibliographical jargon) purchased since 1902—and representing about one-tenth only of the entire collection—tell the whole story. The other nine-tenths consist of the American musical copyright deposits that have accumulated since about 1820 and the European deposits since 1891. Blessèd are they who do not come into contact with the bulk of this music; but of the about 25,000 publications drawn from the Copyright Office at the Library of Congress into its Music Division every year, perhaps one-fifth is music which any library might care to purchase if it could afford it. If one considers that these 5000 publications include hundreds of scores of expensive chamber and orchestra music, and opera scores by composers of standing or promise, the estimate of a market value of five thousand dollars[4] certainly must be conceded to be very conservative.

With such a steady influx of material by way of copyright deposits or purchase (not to mention valuable gifts or autograph compositions by American composers) the collections in the custody of the Music Division of the Library of Congress *in their totality* cannot help surpassing not only in quantity (mere numerical superiority would be of little moment) but in quality and scope all other American collections by far and, within certain limits, rivaling and even excelling the foremost collections abroad. But this is not the deduction from the above excursion into statistics here intended. The plea is for a very much more enlightened, for a very much less philistine and stingy consideration of musical art in American libraries. Perhaps the financial burden suggested will be borne more cheerfully and more willingly if it be considered that even the unprecedented financial support that music finds in the Library of Congress does not by any manner of means put us in possession of "all the music published in the world," as vocal Baedekers have it on sight-seeing automobiles. We do not harbor the ambition to suffer from such a horrible affliction. The few library experts who really know how much or how little music cast in certain forms of art is preserved in famous libraries, also know the difficulty of assembling enough of the entire literature to form a collection of preëminent importance and usefulness.

The Library of Congress may have reason to believe that it now houses collections of operatic music, orchestral music, chamber music, books on music old and new, and so forth, second to none for purposes of serious art-study; that it can now place on exhibition an accumulation of musical rarities sufficient to force the blush of emotion in even the most blasé of connoisseurs; but no more than any other library can it claim completeness for special fields. While it may claim absolute superiority in some respects over all other institutions, on the other hand it must acknowledge an inferiority in other respects to certain institutions abroad that is pathetic; for instance, in the matter of autograph scores of great masters or of codices illustrating medieval music. Their cost and scarcity simply prohibit any attempt at rivalry. Hence it was the part of easy wisdom to curb ambition where ambition would have been ludicrous.

Which is a convenient way of insisting that even the Library of Congress is too poor for rendering a national service musically on a scale befitting the National library of the United States. Advisedly I say "a national service," because many visitors still entertain the strange belief that the Library of Congress is a local institution for the exclusive benefit of Washington! In that case its musical collections would have become by this time a grotesque anomaly.

NOTES

[1] According to the U.S. Department of Labor, Consumer Price Index, $300 in 1917 would have been the purchasing power of $760.41 in July of 1966—the latest date for which purchasing power measured on a continuum with the 1917 dollar is available.—*Editor.*

[2] The purchasing power of $2534.70 in July, 1966.—*Editor.*

[3] The purchasing power of $5069.40 in July, 1966.—*Editor.*

[4] An estimated market value of $12,673.50 in July, 1966.—*Editor.*

Forms and Functions of the Music Library

by Manfred F. Bukofzer[1]

We all know the feeling of frustration that befalls us whenever the particular item in which we are interested cannot be found in the catalog. It is some comfort in such cases to lay the blame on the shoulders of the music librarian, provided there is one, or on the person in charge of the buying or collecting policy, provided there is such a policy. But we should not bestow our criticism too liberally, since obviously we cannot expect to find items that may lie outside the scope of the particular library. This paper is concerned with putting the various functions of music libraries clearly before you in an effort to classify existing libraries and their policies, and to give directives for the building of new ones.

If I make in the following the distinction between five forms or types of music libraries, it should be well understood that in reality none of these represent self-contained units that adhere slavishly to any one form. But although actually in practice they may overlap, they represent five pure types that should be kept distinct in principle in order to see more clearly what the field of concentration should be in each case. Let me start with the music division of the public library, designed to supply in the field of music what the public library in general is supplying to the community. The second form is represented by the music collection of a music school or conservatory, primarily serving the teaching needs in these institutions. The third form is the music section of a university library, essentially interested in music as a field of humanistic and historical studies. Many of our larger universities have not only a representative collection but contain treasures that make them unique in many respects. The fourth category is the centralized repository like the Music Division of the Library of Congress, where the aim is to collect everything printed relating to music, and where by virtue of the copyright law a mass of music finds its permanent quarters. The fifth type consists of a great variety of libraries which may all be designated as specialized collections. What I have in mind are collections of music resulting from the specialty of the institution. The Huntington Library, for example, with its emphasis on early English literature, contains, more or less incidentally, a most valuable collection of 16th and 17th century English music. I say "incidentally," because the main object was the collection of texts rather than music. Among similarly specialized libraries we may mention the Clark Memorial Library in Los Angeles, the Folger Shakespeare Library with some extremely rare items, the Hispanic Society, the Drexel Collection of the New York Public Library, the Newberry Library, the Morgan Library, and many other private collections; then there are the collections of sacred music in the Union Theological Seminary and the Hebrew Union College; and finally special music libraries, like the Isham Memorial Library at Harvard which concentrates on keyboard music. The latter is an especially attractive and modern type of library, the holdings of which consist almost entirely of photostats collected from all over Europe. To the fifth type also belongs a new form of library that has come into being recently as a functional part of broadcasting stations and motion picture studios. In addition to a great deal of standard, printed material, they contain many musical manuscripts of works composed for their own use and available nowhere else. Possibly fifty years hence, this may be regarded as the most characteristic music of the 20th century.

The five types are all associated with certain institutions and from these they derive their primary function. The first forms part of the Public Library, the second is associated with the Conserva-

SOURCE: Reprinted from Manfred F. Bukofzer, "Forms and functions of the music library," *Notes: Supplement for Members,* No. 3 (March, 1948), 3–9, by permission of the Music Library Association.

tory or Music School, the third with the University, the fourth with a legislative body, and the fifth with agencies or institutions the aim of which may or may not be musical.

If we analyze the five types, we find that practically none of them is restricted exclusively to its main function and that, on the contrary, circumstances may have forced the institution to devote a great part of its efforts to other pursuits. Let us take a concrete example of the first type, especially apposite at this meeting, the Music Division of the San Francisco Public Library. Aside from having a particularly well-rounded collection of music and literature on music, it serves also as an information center for musical activities in general, organizes concerts of recorded music drawn from its record collections, collects programs of the region, and keeps a complete date-book for concerts in order to avoid overlapping and duplication in concert schedules. Other features can only be understood through its local history. For example, its holdings of vocal scores of operas is especially noteworthy—a reflection of the long tradition of opera in this city. And it can only be called a fortunate accident that the library can pride itself not only on a fair set of musicological periodicals dating from the end of the 19th century, but also of a number of monumental complete editions of great composers—Bach, Handel, Beethoven, Mozart, and the like. These cannot often be found in the music division of the run-of-the-mill public library, since being historical editions they are not supposed to be used for performance.

In fact, most of these services, functions, and attributes are not things one can count on finding in the average public library, although the San Francisco Public Library is probably not unique in respect to any one of them, and other libraries may have different ones. The New York Public Library acts as concert agent and music publisher. It has given concerts of music drawn from its own collections and has brought out certain of its rare items in black-line print, a most praiseworthy undertaking. Similarly, the Clark and Newberry Libraries have arranged concerts of old music contained in their holdings.

If these are exceptions that prove the rule, the primary function of a public music library is probably to satisfy the demand for music and books on music in the standard fields. In doing this, we often find that the repertory of both preclassic and modern music is being neglected. Both do belong to the repertory and ought to find adequate representation. What a music library should include has been outlined by McColvin and Reeves, a book that unfortunately, in spite of its merits, was antiquated before it came out. Its sins of omission and commission are too numerous to be discussed here; suffice it to say that its main fault lies in the fact that its limits are drawn at once too narrow and too wide.

One aspect of music collecting for which the public libraries are best fitted is that of local and regional material. If they do not preserve it, nobody will, and it will disappear forever. The music of the missionaries and the gold rush period that has been prepared for this convention give a good idea of unique regional material, and similar material should be collected in other parts of the country. Furthermore, such rare, early material should not be collected to the exclusion of similar, but contemporary documents. Public libraries can well afford to maintain a file of clippings from local newspapers, and collections of pictures and programs of local musical events. Such documents come under the heading of "cheap material" because it does not tax budgets which are habitually too small.

The function of a music school library is very closely defined by the demands of the school. While the public library can and should make miniature scores of standard works serve most purposes, a music school will have to have large scores and complete sets of parts—and such materials for performance run into considerable money. The average librarian does not realize how much money can disappear in parts for symphonic and chamber music. Unfortunately, the teaching requirements in many music schools are restricted to a small number of works in the standard repertory, and we may find numerous editions of these to the detriment of less-known, less-studied, and less-taught works of equal or even superior merit.

The University Library serves primarily the music historian and musicologist, and aims at giving the undergraduate historical orientation. In accordance with this function, it must have the literature about music, a full representation of the scholarly, complete editions, and the periodical literature. To expect holdings of this sort in a public library would be unrealistic, although there are such exceptional cases as the Cleveland, San Francisco, and especially, the New York Public Library. Many universities, however, are at once conservatories and institutes for humanistic training, and often they have to have both study and performance editions. An attempt to supply materials for both fields obviously presents difficulties which can only be resolved in those rare instances where unlimited funds are available. At my own university, I am sometimes presented with the dilemma of whether to spend thirty dollars on a set of parts for a symphony of which we have at least five other editions, on some musicological book or historical edition, or possibly even on five sets of all the Beethoven string quartets for class use; and however biased one may be in favor of his own special interest, the decision has to be made for the benefit of the department as a whole.

There can be no question, however, that it is absolutely essential that an institution bestowing a Ph.D. degree in music must have a comprehensive library, since wherever this condition is not met, the degree is worth only as much as the library. If a comprehensive collection can not be assembled otherwise, it must be done through extensive purchases of microfilms. At present, microfilms are also indicated for other than financial reasons, since many books can no longer be purchased in their original form. The checklist of music publications prepared by Miss Heyer[2] will give you an idea of some of the things a musicological library must contain, although it is necessarily incomplete, and what is worse, it lists identical publications as different works. The faulty cataloging which produced this result ought to have been recognized by anyone who had had the benefit of professional training. Furthermore, these lists include only periodicals and historical collections. A standard has never been set up for minimum library holdings in the vast field of musicological literature. The setting of such a standard would be an invaluable project for the future.

The function of the fourth type, the centralized repository, need not concern us here, because by its very nature there will only be one library of the kind in any country. The Music Division of the Library of Congress has assumed the leadership in so many musical activities that it would be impossible to discuss it adequately in a short paper. It is no secret that its holdings are not complete even in the fields of modern publications of music and its literature. It contains, on the other hand, many specialized collections, such as the Schatz collection of opera libretti and a fine collection of opera scores, that go beyond the responsibilities of a repository.

The function of special libraries is circumscribed by its definition, although here improvements could also be made by the full realization of the scope of their musical holdings and the formulation of a buying policy in the field of music. One of the greatest drawbacks of the specialized library is the fact that usually there is no printed catalog. In fact, often there is insufficient musically trained personnel to prepare a catalog that meets musicological standards.

This survey of the functions of different types of libraries brings me to the constructive suggestions I would like to make. The recognition of distinct functions also entails, in my opinion, certain obligations. Here as always the motto is *noblesse oblige,* or in other words, he who has property or large holdings also has responsibilities. The first responsibility is that for proper cataloging. The cataloging problem is a serious one. Possibly, the music division of a public library or the collection of a music school could be cataloged with the aid of existing catalogs by personnel that had only a smattering of music, but the need for musicologically trained staffs in the other three types of libraries is becoming increasingly apparent. I am not trying to promote musicology here, as I may be accused of doing for obvious reasons. The whole question is simply one of efficiency and lowest costs, since I believe that a competent and efficient person is the one for the job. This was different forty years ago when musicologists were rare and music librarians practically an unbegotten species, except for Sonneck. The cataloging of special libraries which sometimes have the only extant copy of a book for which no LC card exists calls for a complete set of all the printed music catalogs available—a condition I do not find realized in many libraries. The situation with regard to manuscript music is especially bad. More often than not, we must have recourse to general catalogs of manuscripts, and even these are not as completely represented as they should be. I must mention, however, some positive signs of attempts to mend the situation: the new edition of Vogel's bibliography of printed secular Italian music, revised by Professor Einstein, and appearing now in installments in NOTES; the English union catalog of printed music before 1800, in which Mr. Besterman is so interested, and in which it is hoped American institutions will also participate; and the catalog of the holdings of the Isham Library, now appearing in the *Journal of Renaissance and Baroque Music.*

The second point is that a library should formulate a definite collecting policy. In order to have one, the librarian in charge must be able to assess the strength and the weakness of his collection, and have a conception of what constitutes—as the saying goes—a "well-rounded" collection. Public libraries have the duty of collecting local regional records and of seeing that in the buying policy the repertory and the books on historical orientation go hand in hand rather than against each other. I see the future of the music division of a public library not merely in the establishment of a miniature imitation of a big music library. While there always must be the essential minimum of basic editions, the music division could specialize not only in their regional collections in which they will or ought automatically to lead, but also they can specialize in other fields, as the San Francisco Music Division does in the field of opera. There are untold fields for concentration: national schools are favorites, even if by now they are a little hackneyed, or certain musical forms, such as chamber music or song literature. The type of concentration I have never seen as yet is the one on an historical period—the Middle Ages, Renaissance, Baroque, or Modern, to name only the most neglected ones.

The collecting policy of a university library is, by and large, dictated by its purpose, but even here fields of specialization do offer themselves. Comprehensive representation of the literature is naturally the first and never quite completely realized responsibility, but this can be complemented by emphasis on theory, as we have it at the University in Berkeley, on 16th century music, as we find it at the Eastman School, and similarly with other concentrations at other places. Purchases would be simpler for university libraries if the music holdings of collections like that of the Huntington Library were accessible in catalog form. This would be advantageous not only because it would make the collection itself more easy to use, but also because it would help to avoid unnecessary duplication. The specialized libraries might lead the way in bringing out catalogs, since their holdings of music are not so vast and would not present the problems that the compilation of catalogs would for libraries like the New York Public or the Library of Congress with their more comprehensive collections.[3]

The third point can be stated briefly. It is "decentralization" as a means of "intensification" or "decentralized concentration." It has become fashionable in our atomic age to advocate decentralization for external, pragmatic reasons. Aside from these, however, there are intrinsic reasons. Obviously, the Library of Congress cannot grow at the same pace it has over the past fifty years. Big libraries cannot continue to be active in all fields at once, and the delegation of responsibility in certain fields or subjects to other institutions will come sooner or later. The decentralization would bring an intensification or concentration in that field at the new institution, and only in this way can the high standards of the libraries concerned be insured.

The fourth point—which is related to the third—would be the foundation of new specialized libraries in the music field, such as we have seen, on the one hand, in the radio and the motion picture library, and on the other, in the Isham Library. More than two years ago I laid plans for an archive of manuscript music before 1500—that is, a complete collection of mediaeval and Renaissance music transmitted to us only in manuscript form. The original manuscripts would be photographed, indexed, and cataloged. It would automatically lead to a census of early music manuscripts, the need for which has been felt for years. The urgency for such an archive is obvious to anyone who has worked in the field and who knows the dirth of mediaeval and renaissance source materials in this country. Such a large scale collection could be made only with the aid of federal institutions and the State Department. It would have the advantage of not costing an impossibly large sum, and it could be duplicated photographically for relatively little. Other libraries could select similarly circumscribed fields, such as Gregorian chant, folk song, primitive music, and so forth.

My fifth and last point is the relative weakness of even our best libraries with regard to reprints of old music. These materials should also interest the music divisions of public libraries, since they are usually inexpensive, performing editions. European editions of old music have never been systematically collected in this country, and since there are an immense number of them, the existing gaps are very large and probably will never be completely filled.

The five types of libraries will naturally be affected differently by the five points, but they are all affected in some fashion. I have left mechanical and technical problems (microfilms, recordings) aside, since they only complicate the issue, but do not fundamentally alter it. Each type of library must decide what its primary and secondary function is, and only if that decision is made can a clear division of responsibilities be effected.

None of the functions is superfluous and none should be disregarded, but the vagueness of direction and the failure to recognize the various functions invites costly and unwanted duplication of effort, and prevents the efficient realization of what I consider to be the essential future direction of the growth and development of music libraries: decentralized concentration.

NOTES

[1]This paper was read by the author on Monday, June 30th, 1947, at the luncheon in The Sun Room of the Alexander Hamilton Hotel during the joint ALA-MLA meeting in San Francisco.

[2]Anna Harriet Heyer, *A check-list of publications of music* (Ann Arbor, Michigan: School of Music, University of Michigan, 1944).–*Editor.*

[3]The catalogues of many of these libraries have been published since Dr. Bukofzer wrote this; see Duckles *Music reference and research materials,* "Catalogs of music libraries and collections," pp. 195-268 [59, 73].–*Editor.*

The Scope of the Music Research Library[1]

by Alexander Hyatt King

Something of a composite because it describes both the contents or materials of a music library and its aims as a research facility, this paper is reprinted here for the stunning importance it ascribes indices and location files prepared within individual research libraries. Too long considered both old-fashioned and exhorbitantly expensive, the provision of those permanent tools which assure maximum utility of an individual library's holdings is surely the essence of professionalism.

To the best of my knowledge, the literature concerning music libraries, which is admittedly not very extensive, contains nothing that sets forth the scope of the research library in this field. If I may risk a definition, by "scope" I refer in general terms to the contents and aims of this type of library. More particularly, I mean how its bibliographical resources should be organized in order to face special problems of cataloguing; what facilities for research it should offer; what kind of reference work it ought to be able to undertake, both in the field of pure music and in the vastly wider one of cognate subjects. But at the outset, I must admit that most of my remarks are unashamedly chimerical because I know that these aims, however desirable, are only very partially realized today even in the best-equipped and best-staffed music libraries in the world. Later perhaps, I can suggest some reasons why this flight of fancy may not be wholly futile. For the moment, however, I must ask your indulgence for taking you on an excursion in a "Celestial Omnibus" through realms where musical research could be pursued in ideal conditions, unhampered by shortages of any kind.

So many peculiar problems are posed by the acquisition of manuscript and printed music for purposes of research, that they can only be outlined here. All early MSS., whether in modal or mensural notation, are so very rare and important that they should be secured without hesitation. But the nearer we approach modern times the greater becomes the flow of manuscripts into the market, although even so, they are not changing hands as freely today as they did a century ago. Then only a few musical research libraries existed, owners had less need to turn their treasures into money, and competition among purchasers was much less keen. It is perhaps rash, in present circumstances, to try to lay down any rigid principles, but some policy of representative selection seems best. Once a good collection of autographs of foreign composers has been built up on these lines, the librarian can most profitably turn his attention to those of his own country. By all the means at his command he should persuade composers to preserve also their sketch-books, and, if possible, proof sheets, for the benefit of posterity, or else arrange for photographs of them to be made before they are sold or lost. It may be noted that excellent work in this field is now being done by the Donemus Institute of Amsterdam. For the complete study of the relation between composers and publishers, the archives of the firms are essential, and should be acquired by purchase or deposit, under restrictive covenant, if necessary.

The pursuit of manuscript material should be co-ordinated with the acquisition of the printed text, which will, in any country with a respectable legal and musical tradition, come within the range of copyright deposit, although there may, of course, be some difficulty in persuading publishers to understand their obligations under this process and to appreciate the benefits they derive from it. The purchase of current foreign music poses some special problems. Although the choice of standard editions of the classics and old music generally is fairly obvious, it is not easy to deal with the prolific modern composer. Given unlimited money, the librarian may endeavour to buy every work

---

SOURCE: Reprinted from A. Hyatt King, "The scope of the music research library," *Library Association Record*, 54 (April, 1952), 126-131, by permission of The Library Association and the author.

indiscriminately, whether or not its quality is likely to make it useful to the researcher. But such a vast accumulation might quite well produce more bother than time saved. On the other hand, selection requires evaluation, and even if the librarian can obtain on approval the nth symphony of Myaskovsky or the latest of Villa Lobos' voluminous series of Brazilian folk song settings, or his newest 'chorôs,' he will have to be a prodigiously good score-reader to assay their merits quickly. It should not, however, prove impossible to enlist the advice of disinterested critics and rely partly on them. Thus, the only remaining obstacle will be the actual purchase of the music, a process that is made unnecessarily protracted and difficult by the chronic lack of organization in the foreign music trade. The intending purchaser will also find—to his exasperation—that standard foreign lists often include, as being printed and for sale, compositions that exist in MS copies on hire only.

The field of so-called antiquarian music is so wide, with so many pitfalls, that it would require almost a whole paper to itself for an adequate statement of policy in acquisition. In all research libraries, the gaps in past publications are enormous. It is difficult to give any logical reason why a work issued in 1925 or 1895, and now out of print, should be deemed any more or less antiquarian than one of 1685, assuming that all three represent the only source available. Obviously the indigenous product must have priority. The librarian should learn all he can about the publishers of his own country, about the rarity and relative importance of score and parts, size and points of issue. But there is so much to learn that he must not be afraid of making mistakes. If he is presented with a choice of several rare items of which only one can be purchased, the criterion of musical excellence and interest in performance must surely be the final arbiter. For classical composers, such as Weber, who have not been published in a complete edition, no opportunity should be lost of buying all original and early editions. In view of the scanty amount of music listed in American *Book Prices Current* and in *Book Auction Records,* a useful guide to value and rarity can be built up in the form of a slip-index based on entries in the catalogues of all second-hand dealers of repute and continuity.

There remains the acquisition of programmes which, though often containing many musical examples, are not music, and even when copiously annotated are, with few exceptions, hardly literature. Yet as a record of performance and taste, not to mention their glossy portraits and exotic advertisements, they contain vital material for the researcher. Since they are apparently not covered by the copyright act and, except for a few long-established series, never have been, every day, everywhere, hundreds of programmes are vanishing. Not only those of the nineteenth century, but even those published barely thirty years ago are so elusive and, sometimes, illusory that the whole genus might be called the flying saucers of the musical universe. Yet they must be caught by hook or by crook.

It is one thing to acquire printed music of both past and present in unlimited quantities; to catalogue it is quite another matter. For music presents two problems peculiar to itself, first the identification of selections, extracts and arrangements, and secondly, the dating of the vast amount of material issued without a date between, roughly, 1700 and 1900. To grapple with the former, the cataloguer needs a wide knowledge of sources, standard editions and bibliographies, eked out by a good deal of luck. He may, for instance, search for several days to identify a so-called song by Wagner and then, weary with exasperation, stumble upon the melody in an inner part of *Götterdämmerung* on which some gem of modern American poetry has been superimposed. The arranger is, with few honourable exceptions, loth to disclose his source, presumably lest another poach profitably on his preserve. So the cataloguer may sometimes never find the source at all; and the piece is relegated to the catalogue section marked "unidentified excerpts," a veritable graveyard of lost causes through which the researcher stumbles cursing the incompetence of librarians.

In any large catalogue this problem is very serious though, perhaps, less so than the absence of dates, which it is now almost fashionable to emphasize, and for which the reasons are as inscrutable as the ways of music publishers themselves. Accurate dates are essential to the clarification of arrangement in large headings, unless the researcher is to waste time in guessing the order of priority in editions of works whose autograph has been lost. Therefore information from every possible source must be collated.

The simplest way to date a work is undoubtedly to be able to turn it up in a slip index of advertisements copied from both the daily and musical press of the eighteenth to the mid-nineteenth century. To compile such an index is laborious but is really a *sine qua non* of cataloguing, and needed by both librarian and researcher alike. But even this index would not be comprehensive for certain countries. The gaps and the inevitable shortcomings must be made good from a collection made, if possible, of music publishers' catalogues of all periods. These, whether printed as a bibliographical part of a musical composition or as a separate book, are indispensable. They must be hunted out patiently and systematically even in the most unlikely places such as an edition of Suetonius's *Histoire des empereurs romains,* published by Roger of Amsterdam in 1699, with which was issued as an advertisement a sixteen-page list of the firm's musical products. These catalogues must be supplemented by lists of plate numbers, with changes of address culled from directories. Although these sources contain many pitfalls, they can, if used with caution, form a valuable complement.

Hampered by the total lack of any comprehensive and historically accurate history of music-printing, the cataloguer will need a bibliography of all articles on the subject, which are scattered in technical and musical journals. The information they contain is particularly vital for the dating of what may be called the incunable period of lithographic music printing–namely from 1796, the year of Senefelder's revolutionary laundry list, to about 1825, which may be taken as an arbitrary equivalent of the year 1500. The dating of lithographed music is still hazardous, but is as essential for the "incunable" period as for the early products of transfer printing, namely from about 1850 onwards. Further assistance in dating can be derived from changes of currency which can generally be fixed from the time of legislative and political action, from the evidence of dedications, and from the study of the re-drawing of title page illustrations by successive artists. The names of the music engravers also may help to close a chronological gap, especially in France between 1740 and 1820 when this profession was followed with outstanding success by women. Information from any or all of these sources should enable the cataloguer–if he has the leisure–to reduce the margin of error in dating to a maximum of two years. It may not be out of place to remark that this method of dating music is sometimes apt to introduce the style of bibliography into descriptive cataloguing–which is dangerous. What the researcher requires to know is the date of the earliest issue of, for instance, a series of quintets by Boccherini, of which the manuscripts are lost. He does not want to have the date obscured by clouds of bibliographical verbiage. Problems of transcription, issue in parts and the like, can usually be surmounted without recourse to that.

By means of added entries, subsidiary catalogues can be compiled, giving not only classified lists of vocal and instrumental works, but also song titles and a full list of the authors of vocal texts, specifying as far as possible the source of all poems, if not made clear in the title. A much needed tool for the researcher is a series of indices on the lines of Day and Murrie's *English Song Books 1651-1702* (1940), carrying the work up to 1800 for all important collections not only in English but in French and German as well. There are not so many of these as might be expected. In instrumental music a most useful index would be one to military marches, many of which are of great antiquity and very complicated bibliographically through changes of title. Here, too, the number of collections is not overwhelmingly large, and such an index would satisfy even the most importunate type of military musicologist.

Having, then, equipped himself as comprehensively as possible to face the problem of cataloguing music, the librarian must consider the range of special and general reference material. One of the commonest group of questions asked is "what did the musicians of the past look like? How did they sing or play? What instruments, separately or in combination, have been used at different times?" Since no books give a complete or satisfactory answer, here, too, the librarian will need to compile his own indices. First, let us take personal iconography. It is true that the great composers are tolerably well covered by special articles and an occasional pamphlet, but the portraits of the not so great, the Interesting Historical Figures–as Tovey depreciatively dubbed them–are much harder to come by. One turns hopefully to the A.L.A. *Portrait Index,* but in most cases it is almost useless. Far too many of its scanty references for musicians lead to nineteenth century collections containing vile steel engravings libellously re-drawn from third-rate lithographs. The Crosby Brown Collection of Musicians' Portraits in New York is obviously important, but its catalogue contains only biographical chatter, without a single word on the date, style or artist of any portrait. The only index of this sort worth compiling must be based on originals, for which the librarian must amass his material from many sources. Apart from paintings he will draw primarily on the title pages and frontispieces of early editions, musical almanacs and dictionaries of the nineteenth century: secondary sources will lead him to the catalogues of collections of prints and drawings published by libraries all over the world, in which he may or may not find an index of subjects.

For performance, his net must be cast infinitely wider, though there are a few books such as Kinsky's *Geschichte der musik in Bildern* to serve as a basis. Scheurleer's intention in compiling and publishing his card index *Iconographie des instruments de musique* (1914), was excellent, but it was only part of a much larger scheme, and was practically confined to paintings in Dutch collections. The number of other European paintings of musical interest is enormous. A selection is given in Sauerlandt's *Die Musik in fünf Jahrhunderten der europaischen Malerei* (1922) and in H. H. Ewer's *Musik im Bild* (1913). Apart altogether from paintings, title pages (which have been strangely ignored), paints and drawings, musical performance is represented in the whole field of plastic art all over the world. Vases, porcelain, ivories, metal work, engraved gems, carvings in stone and wood, and tapestries, of every country and period, preserve the image, often unique, of some musical performance. To co-ordinate and classify even in card indices the graphic with the plastic arts would yield material to satisfy almost every enquiry, including perhaps even such a teaser as "how did the Romans play their trumpets on the walls of Verulamium?" To add to such an index photographs, wherever possible, would double its value and lead to fascinating juxtapositions; a picture of the roaring hydraulus of Nero's time might rub shoulders with the moaning Wurlitzer of our own day.

Together with works on history and theory, books on biography are perhaps the easiest class of musical material to assemble in quantity. But there are large gaps. Many an Interesting Historical Figure has never enjoyed a book to himself, but has had to be content with an essay in some collective volume. These are particularly common in French and German publications of the late eighteenth and early nineteenth century, and a card index to them is an essential means of supplementing full biographies. Perhaps the largest in scope of all special subjects is the literature bearing on opera. It is true that up till the late nineteenth century it is practically confined to Europe, but this does, after all, mean a coverage of more than three centuries and a half in over a dozen languages. In addition to the literary associations of libretti, research into operatic history involves the study of architecture, structural engineering, illumination, costume, design and painting of scenery, and interior decoration. Here again the accurate dating of music is vital, because illustrated title pages often afford the only evidence of the décor of a particular production, and its identification may turn entirely on the margin of error in supplying the date. By compiling a check-list of all historically important illustrations of opera, the research librarian can help to influence its staging in his own time. For from such a list it will be possible to refute the grotesque and inaccurate eclecticism affected by most modern producers and costume designers in their approach to any work between Monteverdi and Meyerbeer. With opera, we must presumably include ballet, as having musical pretensions and affinities.

One of the most neglected topics in musical literature is the history of the concert hall, a fascinating study which is bound to come into its own in time, and, when it does so, much of the literature relating to opera will be found relevant and indispensable. For until about the mid-nineteenth century, few halls were properly designed for concerts, which were usually given in theatres or other buildings. From places of performance, it is a natural step to the history of instruments, to the representation of whose outward form and use I have already alluded. Although at present organology is in its infancy, or at best, adolescence, the potential and necessary literature is vast. The study of innumerable processes of manufacture will call for books on the working of metal, wood and glass over many centuries. Keyboard instruments of all periods and countries, with their rich decoration, have affinities with painting, and so pose many problems which the librarian will find hard to answer without access to the literature of fine and applied arts. Problems in organology are bound also to call for a wide range of books on acoustics. For modern developments, the science of electronics will be much in demand. There is also an increasing interest in the history and construction of mechanical instruments, which have taken on many strange guises in the last four centuries. The researcher in this field will demand books on automata and mechanics, with special reference to the construction of clock-works.

The last few decades have seen the growth of a new and grimly specialized branch of psychology—namely the use of its processes and techniques to assess various manifestations and degrees of musical talent. It seems that this is something quite separate from musical aesthetics, which, from roughly 1860 to 1910, contained a good deal of rather confused psychological speculation. It is not unlikely that the literature of pure musical psychology may expand very quickly, particularly in its bearing on education. This is something for which the research librarian will have to make due allowance.

It is probable that the literature covering the music and instruments of early civilizations and of the so-called primitive peoples should be brought together as a unit for reference purposes rather than separated and grouped with their European counterparts. For though this music is commensurate in scope with the surface of the globe, it has certain broad bases of similarity in technique and theory. But, rather curiously, complete books on this subject are comparatively few. By far the largest source for the researcher is to be found in periodical literature, mainly in the journals of geographical, anthropological and antiquarian societies. Here the librarian is faced with a difficult problem, for it is plainly uneconomical of space and money to purchase a set of fifty or sixty volumes of transactions for the sake of the few which contain articles of musical interest, often with long appendices of the melodies of songs and dances. On the other hand, odd volumes of such sets are very hard to find. He may, therefore, have to fall back on the rather unsatisfactory course of compiling a card index of reference to the relevant volumes in special libraries to which the musical researcher may be referred. It will be a very large index indeed, and, in its arrangement will need to strike a nice balance between the claims of purely geographical divisions and those based on linguistic or ethnographical groupings which outlast and confound the cartographers and politicians. But whatever its shortcomings, it will be invaluable, and will help speedily to locate material for photographic copying when necessary.

With characteristic pungency, Prof. E. J. Dent has remarked[2] that the first forty years of this century were the age of musical archaeology *par excellence.* Now since such archaeology must depend, partly at least, for its success upon research in libraries, it follows that the special music library may be aiding the growth of a dangerous thing—the pursuit of the various branches of research as ends in themselves. The amount of fine music from all ages of the past still to be discovered or rediscovered is immense, and all the complex apparatus of musical bibliography can, really, only justify itself if related to the proper aims of research, which are, briefly, either to study musical history (in the widest possible sense) as the background of performance, or to provide the actual material for it.

With this end in view, it will be a great advantage if the research library is in constant and active touch with all organizations concerned with scholarly performance, because there is a widespread and increasing demand for performances of old music given either from original editions or from new scores prepared from the best possible text. For works composed up to about 1700, it is most important that the original instruments should be used as far as possible, and this practice is, or should be, inseparable from reference to the original editions. Here the librarian can render good service by keeping in close touch with any institution or society concerned with the preservation, restoration and use of old instruments, and by acquiring the relevant early editions from which performing copies can be made. It is true that at present this field for correct performance is limited to chamber music, but there is a growing desire among music lovers to hear larger works played as nearly as possible as the composer wrote them. The discerning public does not wish to hear their phrasing and harmony altered by some distinguished modern composer, conductor or virtuoso, to suit what are sometimes curiously called "modern ears." Still less are the classics acceptable when wholly re-arranged in a style in which it is presumptuously imagined that their authors might have written had they been alive today. There is, mercifully, no real analogy in the other arts to these gross musical perversions, which may in time be reduced to a minimum. For it is as true in music as in literature and coinage, that the good will in time drive out the bad. In acquiring the good musical text and in spreading the knowledge of it, the librarian has an important and urgent duty.

I have left till the last the part which recorded sound should have in the library for musical research. Let it not for one moment be doubted that the gramophone record, though barely sixty years old, is both a worthy subject of research in itself and can make a unique contribution to the study of musical performance. But I venture to think it problematical whether an extensive library of gramophone records could or should be administered as an integral part of a research collection of printed and manuscript material. Both the method of cataloguing records, whether on disc, strip, wire or tape, and the problem of their storage and preservation, are totally different from anything in a library proper, except possibly microfilms. Hence to attempt to coalesce the two might be unwise. But there would certainly be a great deal to be gained from general co-operation between two independent organizations. The research librarian could, for instance, learn something from records in the matter of acquiring scarce and little known editions relating to the singing of the Golden Age. Conversely, the record librarian might be able to use the research library in elucidating problems in the very early history of phonographic machines, in tracking the sources of obscure arrangements and excerpts and perhaps in dating records. I must admit that, at least in the British Isles, this relationship is at present hypothetical, but one hopes that in time the recently inaugurated British Institute of Recorded Sound may fulfil all the archival functions of a truly great collection, and meet an urgent need long since recognized in many other countries.

In talking of music in any of its wider applications and affinities, it would be tempting to conclude by quoting Pater's hard-worked apothegm apparently borrowed from Schopenhauer, that "all art constantly aspires towards the condition of music" and leave it at that. But the more one considers what precisely the literary man of the 1800s meant by "the condition of music," the harder it is to justify the use of this dictum to clarify the relation between music and the other arts. Nevertheless, these words can I think be interpreted at least in a secondary sense, to emphasize something of the universality of music, a quality which it does not wholly lose, even as a special branch of librarianship. If less extensive than other subjects, the scope of musical research is related to a remarkable variety of arts and crafts. But, besides, music is a science and, as I have tried to show, appertains to many branches of science and technology.

But it is time for our "Celestial Omnibus" to descend from the thin air of imagination to the oppressive atmosphere of hard facts. The conductor has for some time been making disapproving noises. He is a man of few words, rather unimaginative, and with a marked tendency to say "no." And now he has finally emphasized his negative attitude by using that device found some thirty years ago on the open-top omnibus. It was a brass knob bearing the legend "Strike once only: Use both hands," which was nearly anticipated by Milton when he wrote:

> But that two-handed engine at the door,
> Stands ready to smite once and smite no more.

Such is the ineluctable guillotine of economy which ever threatens the pursuit of an ideal.

My excuse for having indulged in a fanciful adumbration of what the scope of the library of musical research should be, is this: with such an immense range of desirable objects, it is only possible to decide on practical priorities when that range is fully grasped in theory. The librarian must find the leisure to think, to arrange a system of priorities, and select. He should co-operate as far as possible with others in order to avoid duplication. In the unspecifiable future, it is to be hoped that the recently formed International Association of Music Libraries may be able to coordinate a programme of work aimed at improving the service and resources provided for the researcher. But meanwhile, the special librarian must justify his individual existence by selecting his priorities as imaginatively and usefully as possible. Otherwise, he may find his functions gradually usurped by some vast technical library with more staff and greater pretensions, but less real knowledge. Unless he is alive to this danger, within a few decades the librarian covering a special field of research may be as dead as any of the smaller dinosaurs, and a good deal less decorative as a museum piece.

NOTES

[1] Paper read at the Week-end Conference of the University and Research Section held at Nottingham, September, 1951.

[2] In Chapter I of the second edition of his *Mozart's Operas,* 1947.

B. Discussion of Music Libraries by Type: Public Libraries

SELECTED BIBLIOGRAPHY

29. Bardwell, W. A. "A library of music," *Library Journal,* 12 (April, 1887), 159.

A description of the first circulating collection of music in an American public library, that of the Brooklyn Public Library.

30. Marling, Frank H. "Music books for public libraries," *Musician,* 8 (December, 1903), 443.

An annotated bibliography of 100 books, for $100, to be a nucleus music collection in a public library.

31. Hooper, Louisa M. *Selected list of music and books about music for public libraries.* Chicago: American Library Association, 1909.

Music in the Brookline Public Library, including the classification tables and subject headings used there.

32. "[Symposium on music in American public libraries]" *Library Journal,* 40 (August, 1915), 561-594.

A unique description of the rôle of "American public libraries in the collection and promotion of good music." Includes an interesting article by Otto Kinkeldey, "American music catalogs," pp. 574-578.

33. Bostwick, Arthur Elmore. "Popularizing music through the library," Music Teachers' National Association *Proceedings,* 13 (1918), 209-220.

The rôle of music in public libraries.

34. Meyer, Amy. "Development and use of a circulating music collection," *ALA Bulletin,* 14 (July, 1920), 182-186.

Detroit Public Library Music Room.

35. Wenzel, Florine. "Music in the small communities," California State Library *News Notes of California Libraries,* 15 (April, 1920), 153-159.

The library as center and coordinator of music in the community.

36. Hays, Dorothy C. "Placing a music collection in a small library," *Illinois Libraries,* 6 (April, 1924), 32-33.

Description of the classic acquisition and processing procedures used repeatedly in the U.S. to begin music collections in public libraries. (Hinsdale, Illinois, Public Library)

37. Riddle, Charles. "Music in public libraries. With special notes on the 'John B. M. Camm music reference library' and a comparison of the classifications of music," *Library Association Record,* 16 (January, 1914), 1-10.

Both a history of music in English librarianship to 1913 and a how-it-might-be-done guide. Historically interesting.

38. McColvin, Lionel Roy. *Music in public libraries; a guide to the formation of a music library, with select lists of music and musical literature.* London: Grafton & Co., 1924.

British; see also [**2 & 3**, xiv].

39. Bostwick, Arthur Elmore. *The American public library.* 4th ed., new and enlarged. New York: Appleton, 1929. Pp. 83, 370–373.

Bostwick, an eminent public library administrator, argues for circulating music in public libraries to increase musical literacy, i.e., the ability to read music as well as to play it.

40. Wilder, Luna. "Music in the library," *Library Occurrent,* 11 (April/June, 1934), 170–172.

Historically interesting. An early rationale for music in libraries. Includes practical suggestions for processing music.

41. Posell, Elsa Z. "The music division as a factor in adult education," *Notes,* 1st series, no. 6 (November, 1938), 5-9. Also in *Library Journal,* 63 (October 15, 1938), 769–772.

A description of services of the public library music department which will benefit the non-musician as well as the musician. Includes lists of services a public library can provide, many of which are still relevant.

42. Wadsworth, Robert Woodman. "Notes on the development of music collections in American public libraries." M. A. thesis, University of Chicago, 1943.

Excellent historical summation to 1943. Bibliography: *ll.* 125–140.

43. Fredericks, Jessica. "Building a music department in the public library," *Music Journal,* 4 (May-June, 1946), 17, 59–64.

Some practical suggestions for beginning and building a public library music department.

44. Millen, Irene. "Patterns of growth in public music libraries," *Library Trends,* 8 (April, 1960), 547-555.

45. Stevenson, Gordon. "Music in medium-sized libraries: Some facts and attitudes," *Library Journal,* 90 (March 15, 1965), 1255–1258.

Results of a questionnaire surveying music materials and services which was mailed to 310 public libraries in the United States serving communities of 50,000 to 100,000 population.

46. Lowens, Violet E. "The public library music division; a glimpse of past, present, and future," *Fontes artis musicae,* 16 (1969/3), 129–133.

47. Myers, Kurtz. "The public library and the musical community," *Fontes artis musicae,* 16 (1969/3), 133–135.

Music Materials and the Public Library; A Report to the Director of the Public Library Inquiry: Conclusions

by Otto Luening

"The American Library Association proposed to the Social Science Research Council, in 1946, that the Council 'conduct a thorough and comprehensive study of the American free public library.' The proposal further defined the nature of the study as 'an appraisal in sociological, cultural and human terms . . . of the extent to which the libraries are achieving their objectives' and of the library's 'potential and actual contribution to American Society.' "[1] *This is the report of the investigation into "the actual uses of music records, scores, and books on music in the service of the whole enterprise of music in American society. And the center of study has been community music activity from which the author has looked from the outside into the public library as an instrument, rather than using the public library as a center and looking out at the world of music."*[2]

Luening's conclusions and ten steps by which public libraries can make their most meaningful contribution to American musical activities are reprinted below. The review by Scott Goldthwaite in The Library Quarterly *[20 (April, 1950), 153–154] discusses the entire report, as well as summarizing Luening's findings.*

CONCLUSIONS

In this report to the Director of the Public Library Inquiry an attempt has been made not only to describe what the public libraries in the United States are doing in the field of music, but to emphasize the role that the library, as a public service agency, may play in the future as an influential factor in developing the nation's musical culture. As has been said, public libraries have been active in the music field for many years. Since the invention of modern media of communication made it possible to reproduce the written word cheaply and in quantity and since the phonograph record was popularized and the radio spread music over the world new demands have been made upon the library. Before all this happened there were some libraries which had on their shelves limited stores of music materials for those who searched them out. Now some libraries not only serve as the storehouse of musical knowledge but also, and increasingly, are a potential force in the promotion of our musical culture.

Although for this study only thirty-four music libraries were analyzed, they were selected from a scientifically selected national sample of communities representing a cross-section of the country and divided into groups by size of population. The facts and figures supplied by the libraries serve, therefore, to give us an approximate picture of what is being done musically in the public libraries in this country today.

Whether or not the public library should try to broaden its scope of activities and assume responsibility to provide services revolving around the newer media of communication, such as films and music materials, is a question on which members of the library profession have not themselves

SOURCE: Reprinted from Otto Luening *Music materials and the public library; a report to the director of the Public Library Inquiry* (New York: Social Service Research Council, 1949), pp. 75–79.

agreed. And in most public libraries there are problems of insufficient funds, space, and personnel to carry on their traditional functions, let alone try to take on new ones. Certainly the small libraries cannot be expected to provide the same facilities as those in large cities.

General Findings

Few libraries in the United States have today what might be called well-rounded collections of music materials: books on music, scores, and records. The libraries in which these collections are to be found are located in large cities and they usually have better selections in communities which enjoy a variety of musical activities with which the library cooperates. Most libraries have insufficient funds, space, and personnel to implement their plans. It is very difficult to get qualified music librarians because salary scales are so low that only those with an idealistic concept of public service remain in the field.

The content of most of the music collections in public libraries centers around standard classics, folk music and "popular" music, with relatively few works by less well-known composers, either contemporary or old. Books about music also center around a core of standard titles with less emphasis on basic scholarly and theoretical works or significant contemporary fields. Unimportant works in existing collections might well be weeded out, and other pieces might be transferred to the departments in which they would be more useful than the one in which they are at present. In some communities the expert advice of professional musicians and musicologists might be needed.

The Role of the Public Library in Contemporary Music Culture

The music industry is keenly aware of the vast machinery operating for the publication, production, distribution, and audience development for music. This promotional energy is channelled mainly into the fields of popular music and standard serious music of the "Hundred Best Pieces" type. There is a very important growth of listeners to, and students of, music resulting from the commercial and school music exposure and instruction. This increase in the musically interested population means an increase in the number of people—especially younger people—who can and do use serious musical materials: records, scores, and books.

This tremendous music development of the twentieth century, largely commercial, is a result of inventions which have made mass communication possible. It leaves a number of gaps in musical service not easily, naturally, or probably performed by the commercial music media and agencies. These gaps include the publication and recording of serious contemporary and out-of-the-way older music, performance of such works, and provision of such materials for general use. It also includes a considerable need for materials of value, not easy or cheap to buy or store.

The public library has, therefore, an important and distinctive role to play in supplying the needs of contemporary music culture. The following ten steps are suggested as the means through which the public library might make its greatest contribution to the musical world.

1. Leave the current popular music field to commercial agencies (where it is now well organized), except for two or three research collections for historic record. One of these would be the Library of Congress, where there is the advantage of automatic assembly of the current output under copyright law.
2. Provide for broad and balanced collections of the world's serious music materials including books, scores and records (other than the "Hundred Best Pieces"), and folk music. (This sounds like a formidable task, but a well balanced collection need not necessarily be all-inclusive and can vary considerably in size.)
3. Place the music collection under the direction of a music librarian with the background and qualifications described for the ideal music librarian.
4. Collect manuscripts and published compositions of composers of the community, along with such items as programs, program notes, reviews, and so forth which record the serious musical life of the community.
5. Cooperate with musical groups in the community and serve them in their non-commercial study and performance efforts. Provide a home for such study and performance, if such facilities are not available elsewhere. Such services tend to tie in the music department of the library with the community and adequate appropriations often follow as a result. For public and musical leaders are likely to raise their voices in support of the public library.

6. Allocate to a few large libraries (Library of Congress, The New York Public Library, and network radio libraries) the task of inclusive storage and preservation for use of the world's serious and folk music output, and making this available to other libraries through photostat, microfilm, and inter-library loan. Tie in by union catalogue or other device the contemporary manuscript music and local folk music collections of the community libraries with the Library of Congress, so that in effect, the world's music materials are available by one means or another to the serious student of music or the music lover wherever he may be.

7. Cooperate with other types of libraries in the community: college, university, and any other music libraries that may exist, so that development of these collections may avoid duplication of materials.

8. Provide music services to the smaller communities through the organization of regional or other library units with adequate resources and professional supervision to supplement the work of the smaller libraries.

9. As the number of adequate public library units are organized, develop a uniform, efficient system of shelving, filing, storage, cataloguing, and indexing.

10. Establish in a few large libraries reference collections of tape or wire recordings of music and other programs played on the radio. This would, of course, involve cooperation with the American Federation of Musicians and knowledge of the copyright laws.

NOTES

[1] Luening *Music materials and the public library,* p. [iii]

[2] *Ibid.*, p. [1]

The Rôle of the Public Library in Modern Musical Education

by Vincent H. Duckles

[PRELIMINARY REPORT]

The *public library,* in its broadest sense, may be taken to refer to all public or government supported institutions in the library field including such diverse types as the great national libraries, the state and county libraries, and the municipal libraries concerned with providing library services to the people in cities, towns and smaller communities. Common usage has restricted the term, 'public library', to institutions of the latter kind (municipal libraries) and it would seem reasonable to accept the same restriction in our consideration of the rôle of the public library in modern musical education. We are concerned, therefore, with an important aspect of the musical services of libraries at the community level. Even with such restrictions the subject remains wide in its scope. The great city libraries, such as are found in New York, Boston, Philadelphia, Cleveland, Detroit and San Francisco, possess music collections which are of far more than local interest. Furthermore, they are faced with administrative problems and service opportunities of a kind unknown to the smaller city and town libraries. Any discussion of the library's rôle in musical education must make an initial distinction between the responsibilities of the large city library and those of the small community institution. Once this distinction has been made, there are at least three lines of approach to the important subject of the public library's rôle in modern musical education:

1. *How can the public library contribute to the effectiveness of those institutions, or individuals, directly concerned with the teaching of music?*

There are numerous ways in which the library can assist the public school, or the special music school, in its program of music instruction. There are even greater services which the library can perform on behalf of the private teacher of vocal or instrumental music. The patterns of such service will vary widely depending upon local conditions, but some effort to describe and expand the possible relationships between the library and the music teaching profession would be of value to all concerned.

2. *In what ways can the public library take the initiative in the field of music education?*

It is important to remember that the public library can play a direct, not merely an auxiliary rôle in musical education. It is part of the library's purpose to function as a teaching institution. One of the most fruitful lines of activity in this field has been in adult education. Classes in music appreciation have been organized; concerts of recorded music have been planned. Some libraries have gone so far as to conduct concert series using library facilities and materials from their own collections. Others have developed music appreciation classes for children, often in connection with local musical events. The potentialities in this field are unlimited and call for further investigation.

3. *How can the public library meet the needs of the student in his individual pursuit of musical knowledge and skill?*

The answer to this question lies close to one of the fundamental purposes of the library as an institution; namely, to provide the means for personal development in a chosen field of interest. All education, in the last analysis, is self-education. What may begin as idle curiosity can grow, under the right conditions, into a compelling desire for mastery in a given field. The public library is eminently fitted to provide the right conditions for musical growth, whether it be in the service of the performing musician who needs an opportunity to enlarge his knowledge of the literature, or in the service of the musical scholar seeking

SOURCE: Reprinted from V. H. Duckles, "The rôle of the public library in modern musical education," *Fontes artis musicae,* 3 (1956), 37–38, 140–143, by permission of the International Association of Music Libraries.

more information of a biographical or historical nature.

The strength of the public library as a force in the musical education of a community lies in direct proportion to the strength of its music collection. But it would be unrealistic to expect every public library to maintain a collection comprehensive enough to meet every possible need on the part of its clientele. The answer lies in a well organized system of intercommunication, and in cooperative collection building, two factors which more than justify the interest of the *International Association of Music Libraries* in the special problems of music in public libraries. Three principles of cooperative endeavor may be suggested briefly for further consideration:

1. Every public library should have a collection of basic reference works in music, as well as the minimum essentials of a working collection of books, scores and possibly recordings. What those 'minimum essentials' are can best be determined by a committee of music librarians from public libraries.
2. Exchange relationships, and the production of union lists of music materials should be initiated by public libraries in the same geographical area. Cooperative acquisition should be undertaken so that there will be no needless duplication of rare or expensive items.
3. Each library should assume primary responsibility for collecting the musical resources of its own particular region. It should be the depository for local musical archives and the source of information on local musical history.[1] It can thus become the means by which the community gains knowledge of itself musically—certainly one of the most significant rôles the public library can play in modern musical education.

AN AMERICAN APPRAISAL

The library is traditionally a conserving institution whose function it is to assemble and preserve that part of the heritage of human culture which exists in the form of written records. The school, on the other hand, is an institution primarily concerned with the transmission of that heritage from one generation to another. In actual practice the functions of these two institutions, library and school, can never be separated. They are concerned with somewhat different aspects of the same thing, the perpetuation of knowledge, and they must work closely together in the realization of their aims. Two years ago here in Brussels, at an International Congress of Music Educators, our colleague, Mr. Alfons Ott of the public music library at Munich, addressed himself to the same topic we are considering today; namely, the role of the public library in modern musical education. It is altogether appropriate that an International Congress of Music Librarians should find a place in their program for a discussion of the topic already considered by the educators. A subject of this kind needs to be treated from both points of view because it is as important to see the limits which mark the functions of school and library as it is to recognize their common ground in the matter of musical education.

Thanks to Mr. Ott's admirable statement,[2] recently published by UNESCO in the proceedings of the International Congress on Music in Education *(La Musique dans l'Education,* 1955*)* the foundations of our topic have already been well established. We do not need to take time here to justify the existence of the public music library or question the importance of its educational role, particularly as it applies to the non-professional level of musicianship. Mr. Ott shows very clearly how the public music library, by making music play a vital role in the lives of the people, can give them a greater knowledge of themselves and of their world, and thus contribute to international understanding. In fact, his concept of the public music library as a place where active music-making can be carried on, where local music groups can find materials for their use, where regional archives are developed, contemporary music encouraged, and where collections of books, pictures, musical instruments, are skillfully coordinated for the enjoyment and instruction of the people—this is a picture which would make an ideal program for almost any music library to strive for. But the subject under consideration here is not *any* music library, but the *public* music library and how it can best fulfill its educational role. My contribution to the discussion will take the form of a description of what this particular type of music library means to an American librarian, and some of the practical problems which seem to arise out of his own provincial point of view.

I must confess that to an American librarian the distinguishing features of the "public music library," as set forth by Mr. Ott, are a little hard to discern. American librarianship from its beginnings has been identified thoroughly with the public library viewpoint. This is not a matter of conjecture, it is an historical fact relating to the way in which libraries developed in my country. Even our institutional libraries in schools, colleges and universities are directly influenced by a public service concept, so much so that the specialized, semiprivate, scientific or research libraries, such as the Henry E. Huntington Library at San Marino, or the Folger Shakespeare Library in Washington, are the exceptions rather than the rule. Our international cooperation in the public music library group will be influenced by the fact that the scientific libraries are the late-comers in America—just the reverse of forms take their departure. The same spirit which produced our public libraries produced our public schools, people's schools in every sense of the word, supported by public funds and open to all from the elementary to the university level. Thus, schools and libraries have found a natural meeting point in their character as public institutions. The recognition of their common purpose is exemplified in a recent statement issued by the *California Public Library Standards Workshop:*

> It is the function of libraries to assemble, preserve and make easily available all materials that will assist people to educate themselves continuously; be more capable in their daily occupations; develop their creative and spiritual capacities; appreciate and enjoy works of art and literature; make such use of leisure time as will promote their personal and social well-being; and contribute to the growth of knowledge. (from "Proposed Public Library Service Standards for California," in *News Notes of California Libraries,* July, 1953.)

When an American librarian considers the role of the public library in modern musical education, he thinks of the nearly 40,000 library outlets, central libraries, branches and sub-branches, which serve American communities, large and small, from the Atlantic to the Pacific. Each of these is a potential avenue through which music can be brought into the lives of the people. Do not mistake me here; I am not suggesting that America has some 40,000 music libraries. I am talking of public library outlets, each one of which is capable of sustaining at least the elements of a music library if the conditions are right. *Music in a public library* is, of course, not the same thing as a *public music library.* A self-contained music library must have a substantial collection of music books, scores and recordings, and be placed under the direction of a music library specialist. It is natural that the true music libraries in America should have developed first in the large municipal library systems where a concentration of music materials, accumulated over a long period of time, called for special handling. In this fashion have developed the great public music libraries which are the pride of such cities as Boston, New York, Detroit, Cleveland, Los Angeles and San Francisco. These are, of course, the cream among public music libraries in America. They have the specialized staff, the resources, the respect of the community. Yet because they belong to large urban systems they are in ever present danger of losing that intimate contact with the people which is the mark of true public library service. There are things which can be done at the small community level which cannot be accomplished on a large municipal scale. The educational effectiveness of a public library is determined not by its size, or even by the strength of its collection, but by the kind of relationship it has to its community. The librarian in the small public or branch library is in the best possible position to know the musical resources and interests of his community: the amateur orchestras and choral societies, the chamber groups, the local private music teachers, the music program of the local schools. These are the channels through which the library must work in fulfilling its role in modern musical education. Its effort should be to assist, to supplement and to invigorate those agencies already established in the community for the purposes of music education, and also to provide a place where the interested individual can pursue his own line of self-education in the music field.

But it is rare to find the small public library in the average community of from 10,000 to 50,000 inhabitants equipped to provide such services. Either it will suffer from the lack of a well planned music collection, or from the lack of a musically trained or interested staff. We are confronted here with a basic problem in this field of librarianship: what can be done to help the public library in the smaller community to realize its educational potentialities in the music field. It is too much to expect such a library to become a center of musical knowledge and activity on its own, but here is a place where help can be offered from a higher organizational level. Like the schools, most of our small public and branch libraries are part of a larger county or state system. But while it is fairly common to find a state or county music supervisor in the schools to assist the smaller institutions, no one has ever heard of a state or county supervisor of music in the libraries. Such an officer could help local librarians select materials in the music field, prepare bibliographies and lists of music reference works, give advice in the handling of record collections, organize circulating exhibits of musical interest, and, in general, awaken the local librarian to the possibilities of enlarging his service to the community through music. There would be no virtue in seeking for uniformity of practice throughout a given system; in fact the more diverse the approaches the better. This is one respect in which the library has an advantage over the school in its educational method. It need not confine itself to a single line of approach, but must be prepared to meet all learners at whatever their level of need.

One place where a regional rather than a local service would be helpful is in the matter of supplying materials for large-scale performances: sets of orchestra parts or multiple copies of choral music. Such materials are expensive, far beyond the means of most local libraries, yet they are vita for promoting that active experience which we all recognize as central to musical education of any value. The central or regional library is the place to develop collections of this kind, designed to circulate freely to the smaller public libraries in a particular area. We are beginning to take steps in this direction in America; for example, the *Association of American Choruses* at Princeton[3] supplies chorus parts to member groups throughout the country, but we need a great many more such centers of distribution. I was interested to find that the public music library at Amsterdam has long maintained, a service of this kind, and there is further inspiration for libraries in the work which the organization, *Donemus,* is carrying on in behalf of contemporary composers in Holland.

The national and international music library associations may seem far removed, at first glance, from the public library in the small community, yet our purpose in meeting today is to see what such associations can do to make practical our concept of what a public music library should be. We all recognize that education, to be effective, must grow out of the needs and interests of a particular community; it cannot be imposed from above. But the comprehensive organizations can serve first of all as sources of information, of communication, and thus help local librarians to recognize needs and opportunities when they meet them, and, secondly, establish a community of spirit, an esprit de corps, among those concerned with common problems of music, librarianship and education. The American Music Library Association, the first and largest group of its kind, has not been entirely successful in meeting its obligations to the public music library. It has allowed itself, perhaps unavoidably, to become transfixed on the horns of a dilemma which besets all organizations which are concerned with music. Music is an art in which specialists flourish, yet it is also an art which has a wide popular appeal. To bring the layman and the professional musician together on a plane of mutual respect and understanding (and I include the musicologists among the professionals) is one of the most difficult things to accomplish. Witness the gulf which separates our so-called high quality music journals from those which are designed for popular consumption, or the dichotomy which exists between academic music instruction and the kind of music teaching too often carried on in lower schools or teacher training institutions. Perhaps Europeans are not plagued with this divergence of viewpoint to the extent that we are in America, but I suspect that one of the impulses behind the formation of a separate Commission on Music in Public Libraries within the International Music Library Association was a concern that the vital responsibility of the music library to the layman would be neglected in favor of more specialized clientele.

Anything which serves to break down the barrier between those who devote themselves to music as specialists and those who enjoy it as amateurs will be all to the good. There must be continuous communication between the two or the specialist becomes sterile and isolated and the amateur uninformed and superficial. This leads to the consideration of another problem, which I believe to be one of the central problems of the public music library. It is the problem of *standards,* which, translated into library practice, becomes the problem of *selection.* In the scientific or music research library this problem is not a critical one. The librarian may make himself unhappy trying to stretch a limited budget to purchase all of the important material in his field, but he is never in any real doubt as to the content of that field. If he is a college or university music librarian the scope is defined for him by the kind of instruction offered by the faculty of music. A conservatory is even more circumscribed as to its library needs. Not so the public music library. Who is to decide what books, music and records belong on its shelves? The obvious answer to this question might be: *the public,* but that would be a vast over-simplification of the problem. A cynical observer might reply that water never rises higher than its own source, and that left to its own impetus public taste would fill our libraries with musical trash, just as it has, in effect, killed the broadcasting of good music on the American radio. It is frequently maintained that the public library, which owes its existence to public demand, and is supported by public funds, is therefore obligated to give the public what it wants. But that abstract entity which we call "the public" is seldom very articulate about its needs; some individual always has to make up his mind what it is that the public wants, and all too often the person faced with that decision is lacking in courage or insight. He is inclined to make his selection in line with the lowest common denominator of public taste. We find the same situation existing in our schools because teachers and administrators are afraid to adjust their values too high. I doubt that European librarians and teachers find this threat as ominous as we do in America. It is one of the consequences of a civilization which, as I suggested earlier, is thoroughly committed to the public service point of view. Perhaps this is one respect in which the new world can teach the old, by pointing out some of the dangers and weaknesses inherent in a public centered institution if it does not take steps to safeguard itself from mediocrity. The only safeguard in this instance is an informed and experienced librarian. By informed and experienced I mean one who has a wide knowledge of music and its place in past and present society, and who has experienced some of the delights of making it or participating in it himself. Such a librarian will owe as much allegiance to the art of music as he does to the potential music lover and will be in a position to bring the two into fruitful combination. This, after all, is the essence of the teaching-learning process, and when we have properly qualified librarians in charge of our public music libraries we need have no fear that they are failing to perform an effective role in modern musical education.

NOTES

[1] See also Johnson, pp. 90–96 below, and [**212 & 213,** 224].–*Editor.*

[2] Alfons Ott, "The role of popular libraries in music education," in *Music in education,* Proceedings of the International Conference on the Role and Place of Music in the Education of Youth and Adults, Brussels, 29 June to 9 July 1953 (UNESCO, 1955), pp. 212–217.–*Editor.*

[3] The collection to which Dr. Duckles refers is the Drinker Library of Choral Music, owned by the Association of American Choruses, but–since 1957–housed and administered by The Free Library of Philadelphia. For more detailed information see Bernice B. Larrabee, "The Music Department of The Free Library of Philadelphia," p. 581 [*Library Trends,* 8 (April, 1960)]. A catalogue was published in 1957; see Duckles 2nd ed., 1052.

Of even greater significance to Dr. Duckles' discussion is The Edwin A. Fleisher Collection of Orchestral Music, owned by The Free Library of Philadelphia. The Fleisher Collection is the world's largest, as well as most complete, library of compositions in sets of parts and full score suitable for performance. It began originally as a library for Mr. Fleisher's Symphony Club, a training orchestra founded in 1909. In 1929, Mr. Fleisher presented the Collection to The Free Library. During the U. S. Work Projects Administration, a Music Copying Project employing many copyists greatly expanded the contemporary holdings of the Collection.

The music may be borrowed, except for archival materials which must be protected because of their physical condition, as follows:

1. orchestrations may be lent for performance if the music is in the public domain;
2. copyrighted music may be lent for performance upon permission of the copyright owner;
3. manuscript (unpublished) music may be lent for performance upon permission of the composer or his accredited agent;
4. scores which are otherwise unavailable may be lent through the interlibrary loan network.

The two volume catalogue of the Collection was first published in 1933 and 1945; a revised edition was published in 1965 [see Duckles 2nd ed., 1053]. The catalogue is classified by performance media and includes–for each composition–the dates of the composer, the date of the composition, its first performance, instrumentation, performance time, publisher, title in both its original language and an English translation.–*Editor.*

Reference Demands on the Music Librarian in the Public Library

by Edward E. Colby

The subject, Reference Demands on the Music Librarian in the Public Library, is as large and as diverse as the public which the library serves, whether at the desk, by telephone, by messenger, by mail, or in cooperation with one or more of the other departments of the Library. An inquiry relative to the theoretical writings of Praetorius may be followed, as it often is these days, by the simple and direct question, "What *is* the name of the Mystery Tune?" and from a request for critical material on Beethoven's last string quartets one may be called to turn to "Orpheus in the Underworld," a state of affairs which requires an agile mind capable of leaping from the sublime to the subterranean at a moment's notice.

Before we begin our investigation of music reference work in the public library, we should perhaps decide just what we mean by a reference demand as distinguished from other demands which may be made on the time and energies of the music librarian from day to day. Questions which may be answered by a quick glance at the author or composer and title entries in the card catalog are hardly to be called reference questions, but when we suggest another volume to take the place of the one requested, when we make use of indexes, encyclopedias, and other reference tools, whether in print or in the mental storehouse of the librarian, we are meeting a reference demand, in that we are making use of previously acquired knowledge. From the standpoint of the library user, we may say that the reference problem begins when the borrower's personal choice and personal knowledge can take him no further, and when through the knowledge and choice of the librarian, he is put in a position where he himself can again make a choice, the reference demand has been satisfactorily answered.

By this time it will be realized that what is being said is just as applicable to library reference work in general as it is to music library work, and of necessity a substantial part of the remainder of this discussion will likewise be applicable to either special or general reference service. It must also be realized that there is not always a hard and fast line between a reference demand and a demand for a book *per se*. Finding the right book for a borrower to take home may involve considerable reference work, and for those who keep count on reference questions as well as circulation, there may be occasions on which a tally in both columns is in order.

Music reference demands will, of course, be controlled to some extent by general library policy, on which score there is a close relation with the overall selection policy of the library. If a library specializes in Californiana, or San Franciscana, or Berkeleyana, or any other of the many possible -anas, individuals with reference questions in the field of local music will tend to converge on the library whose resources are best equipped to provide answers to their questions. Other phases of library policy in relation to service to the public may influence the type of material the music department purchases, and hence the types of reference demands which are likely to be received. A public library situated near a large university, for example, may draw the line when it comes to providing reference material for students at the university who prefer to use the public library for geographical or other reasons. The purchase of reference materials for private music teachers or for public school music teachers may be debatable if the school system has a library of its own. The music department of a public library may, of course, deviate from

---

SOURCE: Reprinted from Edward Colby, "Reference demands on the music librarian in the public library," *Notes: Supplement for Members,* No. 8 (June, 1949), 21–26, by permission of the Music Library Association.

general policy, but usually not without serious repercussions from both public and staff. In practice, there are compromises in dealing with various groups of patrons, and I believe we may consider all special groups members of a public to be provided with library reference services in more or less adequate quantities. We have simply tried to point out that over a period to time, even a well-rounded music collection acquires a reputation for strength in some quarters and weakness in others, and that reference demands are likely to gravitate to some extent to the strong points rather than the weak ones.

Up to this point, we have spoken in terms which demonstrate the common ground occupied by music reference and general reference work. We should now like to indicate the individual nature of music reference service. It lies in the fact that the musical score, whether consisting of one staff or 25, is written in a rather complicated language of signs and symbols which require special training for interpretation. It may be protested that anyone who asks for a musical score will certainly know what he wants. What a carefree life music librarians might live were this the case! Actually, we are often called upon to recommend music according to specifications which are not consistently specific—easy music for piano, music of medium difficulty for voice, compositions in certain keys, and so on. This becomes especially involved in the field of choir music, where all four or more voices must be considered. One choir director knows that her tenor will never reach that A-flat, and another would like to have an anthem that can be sung in unison, if she finds that four parts are too much for her charges to handle.

All of these questions require at least some ability to decipher a musical score, and although there are ways of answering them without such ability, these ways are usually devious and costly in time and energy.

It is, of course, a dangerous practice to classify library users as various "types," since in doing so we are likely to develop preconceived ideas about the importance of their questions. We should, rather, meet each question with as little bias as may be possible to human beings, and with an interest in finding the right answer for everyone, whether he be a follower of John Sebastian, the 18th century organist and composer, or John Sebastian, the 20th century harmonica player. It would be rather illogical, however, to formulate a reference service policy based on the demands of the nondescript and indescribable average music department patron, and we shall therefore take the liberty of grouping our reference service users into several categories.

Among the general public, there are first those with a lasting interest in music. Their reference questions are often concerned with biographical, historical, and critical data, though they may range into more specialized fields. One of the most rewarding services one can render such an individual is the compilation of a special reading list on some composer, some form, or some period in musical history. The library always keeps a copy of the list, as Miss Fredricks suggested yesterday,[1] to serve as the basis for a more comprehensive bibliography of the subject. I should include in this class those to whom music in general is an avocation, and those who may be engaged in some highly specialized field of music, such as organ building, but only as a hobby.

Representatives of the second section of the general public are those with a passing, or very ephemeral interest in music. This is in no way meant to be disparaging. Some of them are widely read in many fields, and wish to inform themselves in music as well as gardening, others continually pursue the best sellers, and when the pursuit brings them into the music room for such books as "The Other Side of the Record," they may be encouraged to look further into the lives of various well-known and spectacular artists. This calls for a subtle type of reference work, scarcely a demand, which may be entirely voluntary on the part of the librarian. Others of the "passing interest" group seem to have a peculiar affinity for old songs, especially those sung under sentimental circumstances by some departed relative, and which go da-de-ah-dee-um, or something like that.

Concerning other classes of library users who have some special (and lasting) interest in music, I suppose that the student should top our list. He may be a private student, a public school student, or a university student. If a private student, his teacher may have recommended some supplementary reading in connection with the music he is studying. If a public school student, he may encourage the librarian to do his homework for him. If a university student, he may have a specific assignment, or he may have a reference question quite beyond the scope of the resources of the public library, especially if he asks for something which is available only in an expensive foreign edition.

One can hardly mention the students without next referring to the teachers. In some ways, their demands may be even broader, since they often wish to make a survey of all, or at least most of the available material, literary or musical, in a given field, before making assignments, or before recommending books to be purchased for the school library.

Certain types of professional musicians are steady reference patrons of the music library. Performers are, or so we hope, always on the lookout for new material with which they may enlarge their repertories, and for authentic editions of older masterworks. They too, may require background reading to assist their understanding of compositions on which they are working. Chorus and orchestra directors are looking for new material, and for information on which they can base program notes for their printed concert programs. There is one case on record in which the music librarian himself was asked to provide the program notes for the concerts of the local symphony orchestra. This is reference work which reaches into the field of public relations, inasmuch as the library is supposed to be mentioned with the author of the notes.

Directors of club musicals and pageants often come to the Music Department seeking suggestions for music to be used in historical plays, or in pageants dealing with certain countries or continents. Here it is advisable to determine whether the director wants something authentic or something just for "local" color. Both types exist in quantity. Speaking of clubs, a clubwoman came in not long ago asking that the music librarian provide a complete course in music appreciation, or at least recommend a book that would fill that requirement. In many types of reference work, it is not only the individual who is benefited by diligence on the part of the librarian.

As a very special class, I should mention novelists who are looking for authentical musical references to use in their writings. Some of them have rather unusual ideas about music, and the music librarian has here an opportunity to collaborate in the production of what may be a best seller.

How are we to meet these numerous and diverse demands? We have open to us at least three sources of reference materials. The first is the collection in our own department, not only the reference books, the encyclopedias, biographical dictionaries, and so forth which members of the public are not allowed to take home, even if they are strong enough to carry them, but the collection as a whole which may serve as reference material. The department must have, of course, a good basic collection of reference books, for the building of which I refer you to the excellent lists provided by Miss Fredricks[2] and by the staff of the Music Branch of the University Library.[3] A music department can never have a large enough collection of bibliographies, both of music and of books about music, of discographies, or extensive lists of phonograph records. As supplements to these, catalogs of music publishers, or record manufacturers, and of other libraries, are to be sought after. Bibliographies made up in answer to requests should be kept and expanded. Newspaper and magazine clippings should be kept and indexed. Even the cheap song sheets, containing the words of 20 or 30 hit tunes, can be of value in answering reference questions. Programs, concert notices, musical magazines, bulletins of such organizations as the local chapter of the American Guild of Organists, or the local chapter of the Music Library Association all have their place in contributing to reference material resources, provided they are properly indexed. While it must be admitted that this is a time-consuming work, its rewards are a hundredfold.

Not all authors, we have learned, are classification conscious. They are not especially interested in Dewey or LC. Because of this perversity, they often include valuable material about music in books of folklore, travel, religion, science, the social sciences, history, discussions of art in general, and engineering. Of course, a sympathetic classifier in the catalog department can sometimes tip the scales in favor of the music room in classifying a book, but where only one chapter dealing with music can be found in a book, even the sympathetic classifier must maintain her integrity. This one chapter, however, may contain the story of a popular song unavailable anywhere else in the library. This means that since the books will not always come to the music librarian, the music librarian must go to the books, even if it means leaving his own department. Subject cards can be made for any book in any department, and the inquiring patron may be referred to the proper location through the call-number. In the interest of good intra-library relations, it is well to have an understanding with the heads of other departments concerning this type of activity.

We have seen that we may base our reference service on a solid foundation in our department, and expand it by seeking out music reference materials in books housed in other departments. Our third source of supply lies in other libraries in the same area. I shall omit mention of the Library of Congress and the State Library here, because the very nature of reference work often makes it desirable to consult several volumes rather than one or two, and the question of time presents problems in handling books by mail. At present our inter-library loan facilities are valuable chiefly for the borrowing of individual books, and for that reason are not entirely suitable for reference work. If our music reference facilities are to approach adequacy, we must have a means of knowing immediately what resources exist in the immediate area. In 1947 the Northern California Chapter of the Music Library Association initiated a project which, when completed, will constitute a survey of all resources of music and musical literature in Northern California, and may well serve as a basis for a union catalog of music in this area. This is, at any rate, the goal toward which we are striving, and if carried to successful completion, the project will enlarge the reference facilities of all Northern California music libraries almost beyond present comprehension.

There is little reason to dispute the fact that music reference work on any but an extremely small scale requires personnel trained in music as well as librarianship. Many precious moments may be wasted unless the librarian has ascertained by skilful questioning just what it is that the library patron would like to know. There is a definite tendency on the part of some library users to open the conversation with the most general remarks. He may ask, Do you have any books on European composers? and admit only after detailed cross-examination that he is really searching for a discussion of the manner in which Debussy employed the whole-tone scale in many of his compositions. Questions as to the relative difficulty of certain pieces of music can best be answered by someone who has at least a speaking acquaintance with vocal or instrumental technique. What is most important, perhaps, is the feeling of confidence inspired in the patron by the knowledge that he is talking to someone who understands his subject.

If the foregoing material accomplishes nothing else, it suggests the real need for a positive and active reference policy in the music library. While you treat your patrons as human beings, you have in your mind the resources at your command to answer this or that particular question, and unless the question is very specific, you can point out the possibilities for more or less extended answers. If an answer cannot be given, the patron may be directed to other possible sources of information.

If the music department of the public library is to fulfill its part in the library's general role of educational institution, it must prepare itself for reference service on the broadest possible basis.

NOTES

[1] In her paper "The music library: Development of collection and services," read October 29, 1948, and printed in *Notes: Supplement for Members,* No. 8 (June, 1949), 10–14.–*Editor.*

[2] An otherwise unidentified list, no copy of which has been located, not even in Miss Fredricks' own music library–the San Francisco Public Library.–*Editor.*

[3] *A guide to music reference books,* distributed at the Institute on Music Librarianship which was held at the School of Librarianship, University of California, October 29–30, 1948. That *Guide* was followed by *A guide to reference materials on music,* compiled by Vincent H. Duckles and Harriet S. Nicewonger (Berkeley: University of California Press, 1949), a predecessor of [**58 & 59,** 73].–*Editor.*

Maintenance Costs

by Dorothy Tilly

Can a music department be run on a shoe string? The answer is, emphatically, "No!" Faced with such an apparently nonsensical question it may be argued that *no* library department can be run on a shoe string, but few people other than library administrators realize that in a large, departmentalized library certain subjects are more expensive to maintain than others. Maps, films, fine prints, are examples of types of material which, on account of their format, need special provision for working space, storage, and display. The departments in whose subject fields they occur therefore need special appropriations for their handling, to say nothing of their original cost. Music is another case in point; much of its effectiveness as library material would be lost if suitable equipment were not provided for it. But equipment is only one item on the expense account. In making plans for the organization and financing of music services in a public library, several points must be considered.

In budgeting funds for a music department's book stock it has to be remembered that a large proportion of this stock will consist of music scores and recordings, both notably expensive items. It is frequently necessary to stock several different editions or recordings of the same title, in order to exemplify differences in interpretation. Replacement costs are high in a music department. On account of its constant use for rehearsal, and the speed with which pages have to be turned during performance, the normal wear and tear on music is much greater than on books. Phonograph records are easily damaged, and will stand only a limited number of playings before having to be discarded.

PROCESSING IS EXPENSIVE

Processing costs figure largely in a music department's budget. Cataloging can be done satisfactorily only by a person who is a trained musician *and* cataloger and who has also studied the special technique of music cataloging. Such persons are still rare in the library field. Bindery costs might be estimated, roughly, to be about double those of a department handling only books of the usual circulating type. Whereas the average book circulates many times before it is rebound, practically every piece of music comes in paper, and has to be bound before it can be placed on the shelves. As music is useless unless it opens flat on the music stand and *stays* open, it must be sewn by hand. Special provision has to be made for the processing of music with parts, and anthems need to be "Gamblized"[1] and provided with some durable type of container for storage and for circulation. Sheet music requires protective covering for circulation, with special boxes or files for storage.

The third major expense item is the equipment. Certain standard items of library furniture and equipment can be used as well in a music department as elsewhere, but many special items are needed if the department is to function efficiently. Standard shelving can be used for books, miniature scores, and one or two other classes of music, but the bulk of the music will require at least twelve-inch shelving. It is difficult to hold heavy bound music upright on the shelves, so plenty of built-in supports are advisable. Records need shelving deep enough to take the largest albums, with built-in supports, or locked

---

SOURCE: Reprinted from *Library Journal,* November 1, 1951. Published by R. R. Bowker (a Xerox Company).

cabinets with glass doors. The circulation desk requires a wide enough counter top to allow for the opening and spreading out of record albums, and large portfolios of music; lack of elbow room here can be a great hindrance to quick and efficient handling. Up-to-date record service necessitates the addition of phonographic equipment. This may consist of table model instruments with ear phones, for listening in a public reading room; small models for the workroom, for cataloging and testing damaged records; comfortably furnished sound proof booths or small club rooms for group listening; or an elaborate sound installation for concert use, in the library's auditorium.

A piano is essential for a music department. Ideally, there should be two: a concert grand for the auditorium, for concerts; and a smaller grand or an upright for the use of music borrowers, housed in a small sound-proofed room adjoining the music department. Reading machines for use with microfilm and microprint scores, will be necessary as soon as the department begins to stock scores in these forms.

MUSIC TAKES MORE TIME

In addition to these three major items—book stock, processing, and equipment—there are other points on which the handling of music differs from that of books. It is a fact, well-known to experienced music librarians but not, perhaps, to anyone else, that music is slower to handle than books. For instance, on account of the narrow spines a large proportion of the music has to be lettered and numbered on the front cover instead of on the spine, so that every piece standing on the shelf has to be pulled out before it can be identified. This slows down the processes of shelving and of finding a desired item considerably, and is a factor in determining the amount of page help needed by a department. Loan procedures are slower and more complicated for music than for books because of the necessary collation of orchestral parts, of popular opera scores, and of multiple copies of choral music. Moreover records need careful examination for scratches or other damage. So much music is borrowed for group use that there is likely to be frequent loss of single parts, or of single copies of anthems, and dealing with these complications slows down work at the loan desk. In general, too, music librarians feel that they must work very stubbornly on follow-ups and unreturned volumes, because of their relatively heavy initial and binding costs.

MORE PERSONNEL

Publishers of reference tools have not paid as much attention to music as to some other subjects, and there is still need for the staffs of music departments to furnish some of their own tools. Within recent years the appearance in print of the Music Index[2] has relieved staffs of the necessity of indexing their own magazines, but it is still necessary, in order to give quick and efficient service, to provide some guide to the many anthologies which are an important part of a department's material. Interest in contemporary composition and performance makes it essential that information on current events in the musical world should be provided more promptly than is possible in book form, and the clipping and program files are of the utmost importance to a music library. These files, and the indexes to anthologies, are examples of the type of material which a staff must supply for itself, and in planning for adequate personnel the amount of time to be allotted to these tasks should be considered.

Users of a music collection inevitably include many an authentically ear-minded individual—the type to whom the order of the alphabet and the logic of the decimal system present little more than annoying irrelevancies. He derives, or so it seems, little benefit from stumbling around through catalog cards or shelves of scores that fail to produce the one title he wants with a special editor, arranger, and publisher. Unlike the artist-reader to whom things visual are of the essence he cannot content himself during the searching process with the by-products which it yields. Library mechanics stand as a barrier between him and the desired objective. The meaning of all this to libraries is obvious: the need for a clearly organized catalog with enough staff to encourage and help with its use; in short, higher cost per unit of circulation.

Part of the difficulties with the catalog center upon the high percentage of foreign language publications. Another lies in its involved filing problems. Still another lies in the encouragement of talented youngsters to use the collection.

They may be advanced aurally-speaking, but are frequently helpless at the catalog.

One could say much more as to what is entailed in setting up and maintaining a music department in a public library, but this brief discussion may serve to draw the attention of librarians and budget directors to a few of the problems ahead.

NOTES

[1] A process invented by William M. Gamble early in the 1900's which hinges unattached middle pages of sheet music to prevent their falling out. There is an interesting account of Mr. Gamble's invention and subsequent success in William Arms Fisher *One hundred and fifty years of music publishing in the United States; an historical sketch with special reference to the pioneer publisher, Oliver Ditson Company, Inc., 1783-1933* (Boston: Oliver Ditson, 1933), p. 135. –*Editor.*

[2] See Preface, n. 7, p. xvi.–*Editor.*

C. Discussion of Music Libraries by Type: Academic Libraries

SELECTED BIBLIOGRAPHY

48. Thompson, Lawrence. "The historical background of departmental and collegiate libraries," *Library Quarterly,* 12 (1942), 49-74.

Well-researched study of the origins of departmental libraries within the academic context. Thompson reviews causes, goals, and limitations of library decentralization. Appropriate reading for the academic music librarian.

49. Perkins, Evelyn. "Some impressions concerning recent developments in music libraries in colleges and universities," *Peabody Journal of Education,* 6 (January, 1949), 232-236.

A 1948 state of the art summary.

50. Johnson, Eugene M. "Music libraries in music departments and conservatories." A.M.L.S. thesis, University of Michigan, 1949. "Bibliography": *ll.* 67-75.

51. Fardig, Elsie B. "Music collection of the university library: A study of its organization." M.S. thesis, Florida State University, 1958. "Bibliography": *ll.* 80-82.

A study of the methods of organization and administration of music materials in American university libraries serving accredited music departments which have graduate programs.

52. Shepard, Brooks, Jr. "Paper: The music librarian and his public," *Fontes artis musicae,* 11 (1964/1), 70.

The music librarian in a university music library.

53. Watanabe, Ruth. "The music collection and the college library," *Notes,* 27 (September, 1970), 5-11.

Shall the music materials remain within the college library building, be shared between the library and the music department, or go entirely to the music department? A statement of pros and cons, as well as some compromise solutions.

54. Brazell, Troy V., Jr. "Comparative analysis: A minimum music materials budget for the university library," *College and Research Libraries,* 32 (March, 1971), 110-120.

An attempt to create a statistical model for minimum acquisition monies essential to adequately support faculty and student music library needs.

* * * * *

55. Gleason, Harold. "Music libraries in the school of music," Music Teachers' National Association *Proceedings,* 35 (1940), 132-139.

A summary of the 1940 conservatory situation. Now primarily of historical interest.

55[bis] Watanabe, Ruth. "Problems of a music library in a school of music," Music Teachers' National Association *Proceedings,* 44 (1950), 233-235.

As one of the special problems of the music library housed in the music school's building, Dr. Watanabe points out the ambiguous status of one or two professional music librarians within the composite of a music school faculty. She also mentions the ever-increasing size of the music collections because nothing is discarded; normally music is withdrawn only for its poor physical condition—and even then it may merely be transferred to a non-circulating or Treasure Room collection rather than actually withdrawn and discarded.

56. Ostrove, Geraldine. "Conservatory libraries in the United States," *Fontes artis musicae,* 16 (1969/3), 136-143.

A superb philosophical statement.

Problems of Music Library Administration in the College or University

by Brooks Shepard, Jr.[1]

Last summer in Los Angeles, a committee of the ALA made its especial concern the relationship of the so-called departmental library to the central library of a University. Two quite conflicting philosophies were defined in the course of that conference, reflecting two opposed tendencies in American universities today. Both have arisen from the familiar crises of limited space for rapidly expanding central collections. Both agree on the futility of make-shift architectural additions or compromises, emergency measures of limited duration which only delay a permanent solution.

One philosophy endorses a kind of decentralization: the creation or building up of specialized libraries in physical proximity to the teaching departments making most use of them. These would become the "research centers" in their field, while the central library would become at once the general reference center, primarily for undergraduates, and the storehouse for little used materials in the various classes of books.

The opposing philosophy would place scholarly materials in the central library, making it the research center for the University at large. In those departmental libraries which were maintained (or in their united equivalent, the undergraduate library building), a small *working* collection only would serve for reference and routine use. Implied in this scheme is the centralization of processing functions for all classes, from accessions through cataloging and binding.

I hope I may be forgiven if I have oversimplified, for the sake of brevity, a pair of highly complex formulas. My thumbnail résumé has ignored a third suggested solution, the regional storage library for little-used books of several co-operating libraries. However plausible an ultimate solution this may be for university collections in general, it still appears too remote to solve the immediate pressures of space.

At Yale the administrators and committees concerned with music were urged to consider these two possible alternatives for the disposition of the University's collection of musical material. Their recommendations were to take into account not only the anticipated utility of each program, but also its comparative economy for the University. The following are some of our conclusions concerning a music collection which serves a professional school, a college department of music, and a graduate school department of musicology.

Point 1: *It is impossible, in any but the most arbitrary and illogical fashion, to distinguish a "working" collection from a "research" collection in music.* The distinction cannot be between music proper and literature, obviously, since much music is to be found buried in the middle of textual material, and nowhere else. Conversely, the most satisfactory scholarly treatment of a subject may be located in the prefatory apparatus to a piece of music.

If, to test another approach, we are to attempt separation of materials likely to be used exclusively by the undergraduate in the college or professional school from those the unique intellectual property of the graduate or faculty scholar, the distinction will be no less implausible. At Yale, the *Denkmäler* sets, for example, are given heavy use by Music School students in search of interesting material for programs. The graduate musicologist, if he is a smart one, keeps up with *Opera News* as well as with the *Acta musicologica.*

A ready rejoinder to these last arguments could be: "Why can't your students move freely be-

SOURCE: Reprinted from Brooks Shepard, Jr. "Problems of music library administration in the college or university," *Notes,* 11 (June, 1954), 359-365, by permission of the Music Library Association.

tween the two collections, consulting each?" The answer is: "They could, but they are not likely to." It is not merely unforgivable snobbery to isolate the more challenging sources from the general reference and performing collection; it removes the ready stimulus for intellectual curiosity among those who browse casually in the library. It denies the mentally lazy student the chance to discover for himself some major elements in musical creativeness. And in dividing their principal professional tools, it would sharpen the unhappy distinction between the "practical" musician and the scholar or musicologist.

Point 2: *The unique nature of musical material requires a specialized staff to process it and to serve its users.* Of course, I am aware that this is a claim which most subject librarians will make for the materials they supervise. I think that the claim can be borne out, however, for music. Eva O'Meara, whom I succeeded as music librarian at Yale, once estimated that seven pieces out of ten which passed through her hands raised unique problems not covered by conventional cataloging procedures. My own experience bears out the validity of this figure. Specimens of early music printing may be claimed as the province of a rare book specialist, but when their value to the institution is primarily musical and only secondarily antiquarian, as is generally the case, they should properly go through the hands of a person experienced in cataloging music.

In binding, similar problems are peculiar to our library field which a general library binding staff could not be expected to recognize. That the several instrumental parts of an ensemble piece are to be bound separately is probably not the profoundly obvious axiom to the general binder that it is to us. At the same time, it can easily escape the attention of the non-specialist in binding that a substantial portion of music published today has far from generous margins, and that trimming—if practiced at all on these pieces—must be conservative.

The reference assistance which a library can furnish its readers is surely one of its most useful functions. The undergraduate seldom uses a catalog properly; someone should be on hand to show him how. I don't mean to malign the inexperienced; we have a faculty member of over twenty years incumbency who will pace the perimeter of our reading room like a caged animal, then stand in the middle of the room bellowing, "*Where* do you keep the Beethoven sonatas?" A full time reference staff is not indispensable in the smaller music libraries of the country in order to help guide the reader to the information he requires. What *is* important is the accessibility of musically informed members of the library staff who can save the reader countless minutes without pampering him and who can save the library some wear and tear as well as stalled traffic in its passage ways.

I have been distressed to observe that some financially pinched libraries have lighted upon their reference departments as a suitable area for economy. Were music to be concentrated in a central library, with its reduced and overworked reference staff, it would be one of the principal sufferers among the various categories of books. The manifold peculiarities of musical bibliography would most likely be beyond the experience of the general reference assistant. To my mind, the resulting impersonality of the musical material, as an amorphous block of books, difficult of access and subject to the same treatment as that of books in quite unrelated fields, will enormously reduce their value to an institution of higher learning. It will be a sorry day when a preoccupation with illusions of economy blinds the universities and colleges of this country to the human aspects of books.

Point 3: *The utility of a musical collection depends largely on the reader's freedom to co-ordinate various types of material in conjunction with the special equipment peculiar to musical study.* Here is perhaps the most irrefutable argument for the integrity of a music library in its own quarters, and yet it is one of the most difficult to explain to those unfamiliar with the subject matter. At this stage of our culture, printed music still serves only as an abstraction in symbols of the art itself. A score is "read" in association with a recorded performance of a work; another score is taken to a piano to be played. Few readers will peruse the transcribed edition of the Old Hall Manuscript without Prof. Bukofzer's essay on the table beside them. To cite an extreme, but by no means unique case, I once observed a student trot off to a record listening room carrying under his arm the record of a Brandenburg Concerto, the Bach-Gesellschaft score to the work, the volume of Tovey analyzing it, and the Spitta *Bach* for historical reference. When I commented that he appeared sufficiently equipped for studying all aspects of the work, he complained at our having no pianos in the listening rooms, so that he could stop the record occasionally to play over passages from a piano reduction.

Obviously this desirable and frequently indispensable juxtaposition of widely differing materials would be seriously handicapped if the materials were scattered among two or more locations. It would be virtually impossible if the bulk of the collection were not situated in a building which also contained the appropriate audio equipment and pianos. I will neglect for the moment the teaching problem if classrooms, as well, are not located in this same building.

One large University in this country has a remarkable collection of music: in aggregate, probably one of the finest in America. This collection is dispersed among a number of buildings: a "working collection" in the music building; a research collection in another building; the rare books in still another; and, unaccountably, a most respectable reference collection associated with the women's division of the University, and duplicating material elsewhere in the University. There may be only malice behind the report that the men of the University use this latter library whenever possible in preference to their own scattered collection. The obstacles to convenient musical study in this University, however, are widely criticized. Only one aspect of a University-wide policy, it strikes me as a depressing demonstration of the kind of generalized planning which is unable to grasp the particular problem. What may be demonstrated as suitable for an art library, for example, is by no means equally suitable for a music library. At Yale, to return to examples most familiar to me, an experiment locating scholarly monographs on art in the central library, in order to relieve pressure on the reference and picture-book collection in the Art School, appears to have been successful. One of the art faculty members responsible for the move told me, however, that the decision to separate the materials was based upon the particular methods of art study and research; it would be folly, he felt, to regard the move as proper precedent for other fields.

The same generalized planning which arbitrarily estranges books of fundamentally the same character is often applied to rare books. I have already criticized the misguided assignment of early musical publications to the rare book cataloger, instead of to the music cataloger. May I open fire now on the decision banishing musical rarities to the remote vaults of the general library. Rare musical books have much the same character as new musical books, and certainly share problems of cataloging and of co-ordinated use with other materials. They may cost more to buy or to replace, but not necessarily. They may be more fragile, but not necessarily. If cost should put a book behind iron bars, let us remove some of our Playfords from behind grills and lock up the new Sartori bibliography of Italian instrumental music. Or if fragility is to be the test, the original printing of Hawkins' history of music will outlast on the open shelves its nineteenth century reprint.

I do not mean to propose that the Yale music library, for example, paste a date slip in the back of its Bach manuscript and start it circulating. What I criticize is the point of view which finds the rarity or antiquity of a book more impressive than its contents, and which tries to justify its distant isolation from the body of books of which it is properly a part.

Naturally, a book of staggering value must be protected against the risks which any library faces, and which are provided for only in a stouter vault than our smaller libraries can afford. But I am convinced that even the enticement of temperature and humidity controls seldom offsets the injury done a collection split wide on the basis of rarity and non-rarity.

The principle has been voiced that the book treasures of a university should be amassed and hoarded in a single place, both for the prestige such an arrangement brings to the university and for the appeal it theoretically makes to a donor. There are serious flaws in either thesis. Those of you who have viewed the amassed English Crown Jewels in the Tower of London know that you are unable to see any beauty because their aggregate glitter hurts the eyes. The real prestige of a collection is in its unity or possibly its size, not in the isolation of its rarities. The rich and interested donor, if I can possibly put myself in his place, will be considerably more impressed at seeing the treasures of his field of interest assembled with others of their kind. A particular treasure assumes importance in relation to others of its genre, not to unrelated pieces. But in this, I will accept challenge.

You will have gathered by now that those of us concerned with the future of music in my University were decidedly in favor of the program promoting a research center for music, with the musical materials concentrated in a single building appropriately equipped for their use. I emphasize that our conclusions concerned music specifically; in fact, they went counter to a general policy for the University approved about a year ago. It is to the credit of the promulgators of the centralized policy that they came to recognize the singularity of music library problems, and agreed that the present integrity of the collection should be maintained.

Although I believe that many of these arguments apply to all music libraries, I should like to repeat that they were elaborated particularly in regard to the music collection in a college or university. In such an institution, the whole of the collection, circulating or not, is essentially a reference collection. I understand that elsewhere, as at Yale, students are expected to purchase music to be used for extensive study and performance. In the public library where the greatest use may be of materials borrowed for performance, rather than for study on the spot, I can believe that different emphases would obtain.

While accepting the arguments for maintaining the integrity of a music collection, research scholars may protest the arbitrary removal of musical material from a central building housing the books in related fields. The inconvenience of co-ordinating studies between buildings separated perhaps by several blocks can be not only irritating to the mature scholar, but misleading to students being trained in techniques of research. In an independent research library, where a few sound-proofed rooms may be fitted into the music division, this separation is as unnecessary as it is inadvisable. In a large teaching institution, it is virtually inevitable. The late Andrew Keogh once described the ideal university library as a central storehouse of books with radiating wings housing all of the university's departments of study. Although the growth of our modern universities has destroyed the practicability of Mr. Keogh's vision, the principles behind it are of course as valid as ever. The librarians of special collections must share with the teaching faculty of an institution the responsibility for reminding students of the essential unity of learning, which has been obscured but not invalidated by the compartmentalization of fields of study.

In tackling this major administrative problem, I have dealt only with the physical location of a university's music collection and the staff handling it. The no less weighty matters of administrative organization, library personnel, and budget I have neglected, not merely because of the limitations of time, but because in my experience, they have not been so problematic, and consequently were less on my mind. At Yale, the music library staff is responsible, through an interested and sympathetic faculty committee, to the Dean of the School of Music. Our budget is part of the School budget, and has somehow escaped the truncations recently affecting most other University departments. With the University library administration a close association is maintained on matters of policy and procedure. This is less a matter of obligation or courtesy than of common sense; our microcosm in Sprague Hall is unequipped to deal without assistance in certain broad matters of personnel classification, salaries, appointments, and the like. The library technologists since the war have developed splendid devices of equal service to the small library as to the large, but it is only the mother institution which can afford them and make them available to her brood.

There are many who contemplate with alarm the alternative of a *centralized* library administration, even when the music collection is housed as a physical unit in the music building, and when the staff which handles it is trained for that specific purpose. The shift of authority from the powers responsible for music in a college to those responsible for its books would, the reasoning goes, inevitably result in reduced appropriations and decreased attention to particular musical requirements.

Certainly much depends on the receptiveness of the university librarian to the appeals placed before him by the music librarian and his faculty. Without an interested and co-operative faculty, in fact, the most grandiloquent music librarian will have difficulty winning favor or even a proportionate consideration for his province. This is generally true whether the library is virtually an autonomous department in the college, vying with other departments for consideration, or if it is merely a corner of the college's general collection of books.

But to regard centralized library authority as inherently menacing is to forget a prime responsibility of the music librarian himself, or to deprecate one of his essential aptitudes. A lamentable fact which most of us face is that the college or university librarian is seldom a musical enthusiast. In our Eastern colleges, he is often a connoisseur of English literature: as likely as not, of the eighteenth century. Frequently, he is a business man, which is not a bad thing in the long run. But he needs to be told, and reminded periodically, of the importance of music in the university, of the prestige which a selective and well managed music collection brings to it, of the problems particular to musical material which defy generalized planning about books, and of the counterpoise which these arguments offer to those of economy.

It is on the success of this campaign that an effective college music library program may depend, be it within a centralized or decentralized administrative scheme. The campaign is worthy of a substantial part of a music librarian's energy, even if it should become his major administrative problem.

NOTE

[1]This paper was read at the Winter Meeting of the Music Library Association in Boston on February 6, 1954.

The Living Library

by George Sherman Dickinson[1]

George Sherman Dickinson, 1888-1964, was educated at Oberlin College where he subsequently taught for six years. In 1916, he was appointed Assistant Professor of Music at Vassar College. For the next thirty-seven years, Prof. Dickinson provided impetus and direction to the Vassar College Department of Music.

As professor of Music, Dickinson directed a gradual shift of emphasis away from "Appreciation" and the factual history of music to the historical study of music as a literature in aesthetic and critical terms. He developed an introductory course, Music as a literature, *which first appeared–by that title–in the 1923-24 Vassar College catalogue.*

As Acting Chairman and then Chairman of the Music Department, Dickinson presided over the construction of its new building, occupied in 1931. In the center of that building is the library–its reading room two stories high, with three tiers of open stacks on the inside wall, and a tower. Adjoining the reading room are individual listening rooms, each equipped with piano, record playback equipment, reserve records, shelves for reserve music and books, and the comfortable furnishings appropriate to long hours of study.

It was in his capacity as first Music Librarian at Vassar (1927-1953) that Dickinson developed his Classification of Musical Compositions *(Poughkeepsie, New York: Vassar College, 1938); cf. also [***141***, 141] and C. J. Bradley, "The Dickinson Classification for Music; An Introduction," to be published in* Fontes artis musicae, *19 (1972/1).*

In 1961, the Vassar College Music Library was named The George Sherman Dickinson Music Library to honor his years as Professor of Music, 1916–1953, and as Music Librarian, 1927–1953.

Dickinson's conception of the library as the heart of the music department is exemplified by his location of the library in the center of the Music Department's building; by his article "The living library," in which he describes his 'ideal' music library; and by his classification scheme for the systematic organization of music.

Whatever our professional titles may be, we are all in various capacities engaged in the serious undertaking of education. In ways of which we are not necessarily conscious, our affairs overlap and our activities intertwine. Whatever we bring into the range of experience of the student–from the kind of music he learns to the intellectual (and Fahrenheit) temperature of the room in which he learns it–has to do with education.

Even the quiet place called the library has a part which, if thoughtfully played, is far from the unassertive and sometimes static role which the library is accustomed to accept. For the library is not only a place where *things* are kept; it is still

SOURCE: Reprinted from George Sherman Dickinson, "The living library," *Notes*, 3 (June, 1946), 247–255, by permission of the Music Library Association.

more a place where *ideas* are kept. The things which you draw out of the library must be returned or you will be fined. The ideas, on the contrary, may be retained. Without realization that the library is a boundless source, we and the library are both the poorer. The only significant conception of the music library is, in truth, one which acknowledges it as a fundamental, comprehensive center of materials of all sorts for the teaching and learning of music.

If the library is to claim the organic place in education just set forth, it is imperative that it be developed in the particular institution in ways completely functional to the education maintained there. The living library will hence take on an individuality of its own, growing out of the special services which it has to perform and out of the personalities who administer them.

There will thus be many kinds of library, every one of them obligated to develop a conscious viewpoint indicative of its native character. But, important as the immediate character of the library may be, what the library is becoming is still more so. Decisions are reached every day which will be only fully felt a decade hence. For the young library is the direct ancestor of its future older self and is likely to pass on the family traits. Not only must the library have an individual view of immediate effect; it must have a long view as well. No library has ever been known to command enough money for materials or for carrying out processes. A constant, shrewd power of selection must therefore preside over every operation, avoiding wastage and coupling as fully as possible the practical and the ideal in the interests of the present and the future. The directions toward which a library should grow and the activities in which it should engage thus depend upon deep insight into its potential responsibilities.

The materials which a generous conception of the educational function of the library assigns to it are more numerous and varied than would commonly be supposed. Let us first go over in a general way the scope of the ideal institutional music library.

The staples are, of course, printed music, books and periodicals, manuscripts and prints. In these days, also, there are other forms of reproduction: the photo-offset, the photostat, the microprint, the glass slide, the microfilm slide, the film strip, and the animated film. These all have their place in the library under certain circumstances.

The proper scope of the music library includes not only music to see, but music to hear. Hence recordings of various sorts also demand a place—some, like the disc, belonging to the present; others, like the metal tape recording, belonging to the future,—a future in which recorded music, through foreseeable technical advances, will unquestionably establish its artistic and educational validity.

It is evident that the inclusion in the library of materials which the reader cannot pick up and scan with the natural eye requires specialized projection equipment, and that the presence of recordings calls for reproduction equipment. In both cases it must be such as the reasonably intelligent person can manage successfully and of a sort which will stand up under use.

Not only is such equipment indicated, but suitable places in which it may be individually used are necessary. Viewing rooms and acoustically effective, insulated listening rooms accordingly take their place along with the usual reading rooms, seminar rooms, and study cubicles, as indispensable parts of the library establishment.

Associated with the library, if not an actual part of it, is also the museum. Its contents may be anything pertinent to music and suitable to display.

Whether the library ought to assume the responsibility for concerts of infrequently heard music, and to possess facilities for the purpose, including the proper instruments, depends on whether such music may be heard in authentic performances under other local auspices.

We may now look into the contents of the library more closely and inquire first what the range of its holdings should be in order to give it claim to high standing. Into the fabric of these holdings can be inflected whatever individual characteristics are to mark the library's special institutional function.

As its backlog of music the library must have the collected works of the greater number of significant composers whose music has been so issued. The parallel in the field of literature is a rigid one, where no library could be regarded as sound without authentic and complete editions of the works of the great literary figures. In music, more than in literature, the library must depend upon musicological and other collections and anthologies, and hence must possess most of the *Denkmäler* type of series. For composers not particularly well covered in these ways the library must collect separate works in sufficient quantity so that even lesser composers of historical significance are intelligibly represented. Contemporary materials in good proportion must be acquired currently while they can be had, so that the future library shall not suffer. As a part of and in supplementation to such a basic collection, the library must have in the cheap editions every-day, working copies of as much as possible.

If the library serves an institution where specialists instruct in performance in the various branches of music literature, separate unit collections of these literatures are in the long run an economy as well as a convenience.

Music itself is thus the center of gravity of any music library. After that, in high coordination, come the books and periodicals which represent what is known and thought about the music, its context, and the persons in all capacities connected with it. Here the materials vary deeply in significance and greatly overlap. Much of ephemeral value need not be taken seriously into account. Of unique importance are the essential works of many epochs which give the basic record of and commentary on the music of their times. Each generation likewise has its reflections on the past which may or may not be valuable in themselves, but which are a necessary aid to interpreting the time which produces them. There are also the constantly renewed researches of later times which bring to light, as best may be, the hidden and partially dismembered records of the past. Whether the form taken be that of history, criticism, aesthetics, theory, biography, anecdote, bibliography, lexicography, or what not, the clue to the library's needs is found in the light thrown on the music itself and on the circumstances which have made it what it is. In supplementation of this range of material, many nonmusical works are also essential. Some of them are indispensable in the music library itself; others may be consulted in or be borrowed from the general collection.

In many libraries it is obvious that manuscripts and prints are a luxury, somewhat limited in direct usefulness. Specimens of such material are nevertheless of educational consequence, though they need not be acquired with the systematic devotion required in other fields. Except as a token of pride, the facsimile is for the most part as useful as the original.

The same principle, which calls for a full representation of the significant literature in printed music, applies, at least ideally, to the repertory of recorded music. The acquirement of a wide range of records, as they come out, whether they have immediate practical application or not, is, in general, far-sighted. Only in the fact that recordings suffer a somewhat early obsolescence, in the fast-moving technology of sound reproduction, do record collections occupy a less secure place than corresponding printed versions of the same music.

The museum which most libraries will be able to develop will consist in opportunistically acquired pieces, forming no very representative or homogeneous whole. They nevertheless have educational value in their representation of assorted types. The obtainment of instruments made in this country is in itself worth while and not very difficult. The instruments acquired need not be old or valuable to serve a useful purpose. While instruments merely on display, especially obsolete ones, offer their own special interest, instruments kept in playing condition are still more to the point. In this day of revived interest in the harpsichord and clavichord and in their music, when good reproductions may be had, these two instruments, at least, could be acquired by most library museums.

Out of these various possessions of the library, concerts of unique educational usefulness can with imagination be shaped. It is certainly not inappropriate that the library, as the custodian of treasures, should possess the facilities and provide occasions for bringing listener and unfamiliar music together.

In the course of acquiring the varied possessions which have been enumerated in the foregoing paragraphs according to general principle, the library must at the same time individualize itself according to its own principle. This it must not do accidentally or casually, but as the result of profound consideration of its institutional function. It is easy to buy what members of the faculty ask for and to keep up with the best advertised listings, on the supposition that a satisfactory library is being built,—a library balanced by natural forces and serving effectively an immediate practical purpose. This benevolent *laissez-faire* accounts sufficiently well for some of the libraries in which we try to work today.

An approximate basis of individualization among libraries lies along the lines indicated in the title of this session—the lines of the music school, the college, the university.

Although some of the more comprehensive music schools have spread their contacts over the field of music so as to touch all or nearly all of its parts, there remain, at the undergraduate level at least, certain characteristic emphases. These are created to a considerable degree by the plain facts of time distribution. In the music school, therefore, where performance bulks large, the library should have a performance division, as extensive and diversified and full of duplicates as the pedagogy and registration of the institution require, and as freely usable as the policy of subsidizing the individual student with practice music permits. Such a collection demands special treatment in every way and would best be brass-bound, riveted, and disinfectable. In the college, if such a division of the library exists, it will scarcely be as extensive as in the music school.

In the music school it is probable that chamber, choral, and orchestral groups will be promoted more intensively than in the college. Collections of scores and parts suitable to these repertories can therefore afford to be somewhat more elaborately developed.

In the province of music and books called for in support of the study of theory as a pedagogical branch, the distinction between music school and college need not be great. As the subject is likely to be taught, the teacher will, as a matter of fact, use the library in marked disproportion to its use by the student (though this is not as it should be). With reference to theory in the broader sense of technical and aesthetic formulation of musical principles, the libraries of music school and college would tend to diverge from one another, with the college library leaning toward a musicological content. In the music school especially, works of pedagogical import called for in connection with teachers' training studies are essential.

The place of music history and criticism in most music schools is subordinate to that of other studies and notably inferior to the position given them in the college. Their respective libraries of music and books may therefore properly reflect this fact, not only in the range of material but in its degree of advancement. In the case of the college the distinction may be made, however, that enough of its faculty are likely to be engaged in historical research to warrant a library which in some particulars at least approaches the graduate standard fixed by the university in these subjects.

Throughout the above commentary there will be seen to run the general distinction between a performance collection and a reference collection. As a matter of fact, the music school or college library partakes of both characteristics, each in its own degree. There remains, however, in both cases the practical consideration of protecting valuable, often irreplaceable, bound volumes, intended chiefly for reference, from the abuse which music used intensively for performance, even by classroom teachers, is certain to suffer. The wise library will lay down the principle that expensive material required for such uses will be duplicated in a cheap edition or the necessary pages (if not copyrighted) will be reproduced in some suitable manner. Only by the well understood establishment of such a principle of distinction between performance and reference materials will costly items in the library be protected.

The proper status of the library of the music school or college within the university does not differ enough from its status when they exist as independent institutions to call for remark. It is at the graduate level that the university library takes on its more individual qualities. Its character is now further conditioned by the requirements of genuine research and its boundaries reach out for those of the ideal library. In spite of the ideal of comprehensiveness, the way is still open to the university library to individualize itself through special collections of unique character or completeness, through the unusually elaborate development of certain divisions, through the possession of some well known treasures, or even through distinctive facilities and services in the use of its materials.

As a special phase of its individuality, every American library has a peculiar obligation, touching upon holdings of all types. It is to accept the responsibility for collecting, preserving, and making accessible musical materials of every sort from the locality in which the library is situated. Only through such regional activity can we expect the record of musical culture in this country to be kept unbroken.

Each one of us may now conduct a ceremonial inventory of his own library's shortcomings. For it is obvious, under the standards here laid down, that many institutional libraries are in their infancy. The next generation should see unprecedented expansion. In one sense this is an agreeable prospect, assuming that such expansion will be judiciously guided. In another sense it is a less promising prospect, since it is certain that there will not be enough to go around. In the field of new publications each library can take care of itself in proportion to its judgment and financial resources. It is in the field of desirable or indispensable material which has gone out of print that the pinch comes.[2] In further aggravation, present conditions in the world at large make for unprecedented scarcity.

Since there is nothing as satisfactory as the

original item itself, we shall doubtless continue to compete with one another for what is left. But this is not the intelligent or at least the entire answer to the problem, especially for undeveloped libraries and for those of modest resources. The answer lies in the promotion of some of the methods of reproduction which improved technical processes now afford or can be made to afford in the promising future which lies before them.

Through photography the library of whatever size may expand, multiply the number of its duplicate copies, remove the pressure from its more valuable holdings, acquire items of rarity. This has long been possible at considerable expense through the photostat copy. It has become increasingly common at moderate cost through the photo-offset, by which facsimile editions of uncopyrighted material may be produced in commercial quantities. Valuable as this method is, its results have been cheapened in too many cases by poor workmanship, scant margins, overreduction, and inferior paper. With care in manufacture the products of this process can take their place in the library beside its orthodox holdings.

A less expensive process is found in the microprint, which calls for production in moderate quantities to be economical. As described in Fremont Rider's *The Scholar and the Future of the Research Library,* 100 book pages may be confined to the space of a single 3 x 5 card and filed as both its own catalog card and the text itself. The application of this method to music would call for a larger card to each 100 pages, or for fewer pages to the card. Not only is the process itself comparatively inexpensive, but replacement and duplication are cheap and the storage space required is phenomenally reduced. It is evident that an efficient and flexible reading machine is called for, which will afford selection of any one of the pages on the card without the necessity of passing through all the intervening pages, as is required by the film roll. Such a machine should be made adaptable to the reading of music for keyboard performance.

Though less easy to manipulate, the microfilm is also a cheap method and can be used by the individual in a reading machine, or if desired can be projected on the screen for an individual viewer or for a group. Any number of positive copies can be made from the master negative, which may be stored as a future source of supply. The satisfactory projection of film upon a screen calls for the production of a bright image under mild daylight conditions. This requires brilliant illumination of the film, which in turn calls for heat-proof glass, or quiet ventilation, or both, to protect the film. Ideal projection also provides for remote control of the film frame by frame, forward or backward. All these conveniences are practicable, though not so far incorporated in any one machine. The microfilm as a common library convenience awaits the mounting of each film in a cartridge, which can be slipped into the viewer or projector interchangeably without the tedious process of threading the film into the machine. Storage for the microfilm is economical though of course not as compact as for the microprint.[3]

We have so far been speaking of *reproducing* existing material and have accordingly remained more closely within the accepted boundaries of library activity. As an educational agency, however, the library may be conceived as well to have the prerogative of *producing* material. In the fast-advancing field of visual education the library is offered opportunity of collaboration with the teacher in devising varied and ingenious visual aids to learning. The library is the appropriate custodian of such materials and should make itself the authority on reproducing them for or projecting them in the classroom. This benevolent invasion of the classroom should supplant, or at least supplement, the labors of the music professor who draws his own charts or prepares his own material for slide or film photography. Bright ideas for class illustration have faded before the technical task of realizing them. Bright ideas have never emerged at all because music educators are not yet fully sensitive to the potentialities of parallel visual instruction. Music as an art of audible motion can profit the more, because of its evanescent quality, from the educational support of concrete visual devices. The library should assume to be the center of all materials and apparatus useful to this end.

The library should also assume, in the field of sound recording and reproduction, analogous educational duties to those set forth for the visual field. It should initiate recordings of educationally significant unrecorded music, and should possess the equipment for doing so. Since the library must solve the problems of convenient and musically effective phonographic reproduction in its own listening rooms, it is in a position to transfer its knowledge and experience to the classroom.

Much thought remains to be put into equipment for sound reproduction in the library listening rooms and in the classroom. Beyond the obvious requirement of fidelity of tone, the phonograph which teacher and student alike can use effortlessly must be equipped in a number of special ways. It should have a device for cushioned lowering and raising of the needle by the movement of a lever, so that playing may be stopped and resumed again at the exact point. It should have a locating device with a numbered scale so that predetermined passages in the music may be found instantly for study. Quick, quiet, automatic, selective record changing may well be included, but should not interfere with free manual operation. Since records differ in fidelity and in the amount of scratch, there must be graduated frequency controls. The speaker should be located across the room from the listener, even in the case of fairly small listening rooms, and certainly in the case of classrooms. The cabinet which houses the apparatus should be of table height, and should incorporate an extension shelf for writing or should be placed beside a table of the same height as the cabinet. A rack for records should be provided as an integral part of the assembly. All controls should lie within easy reach. Ideally an entire phonograph-table work center might well be built as a single unit. We shall long be dependent on the musical repertory of discs, but if metal tape should replace discs, the same conveniences of manipulation for the purpose of study should be provided.

The library listening room also calls for a truck, with vertical compartments for records, which shall serve as the equivalent of a reserve shelf to contain the recorded material set aside for and assigned to a class for study. Reserve shelves for the scores corresponding to the music of the records should be provided, and if film or microprint material is employed a reading machine must be incorporated. The listening room fully equipped for study also requires a piano.

Implied in all the above specifications is the principle that the library should develop visual and auditory materials in full coordination with one another as a contribution to the technic of education. Under the leadership of the library, the same principle deserves to be carried into the classroom, lecture room, and even the studio.

This paper has abounded in enough "should's" and "must's" to arouse suspicions of theorization. *Who* will actually do these things? *How* can they be done? one may ask.

The candidate for this assignment is unmistakably the specialist music librarian, without one or more of whom no library can expect to advance in the days to come. Besides being a library technician, he would also best be a musician, scholar, and business man. If in addition he should turn out to be a human being, with the instincts of a teacher as well, you are fortunate indeed. It is he who will do much to give the library its individuality and its look toward the future. There are such persons and there will be more as the profession develops.

But except in the case of the few great libraries it is becoming less and less advantageous to steer one's own way alone. The answer to the question of how the things we covet may be accomplished is concentrated in the word *collaboration.* In the following examples we shall have to be satisfied to do little more than scratch the surface of desirable collaboration on the part of institutional libraries.

Cooperative cataloging already exists but should be expanded. Exchange of work is also profitable in such fields as bibliography, analytics, indexing. Exchange of information concerning comparative holdings, especially the spread of mutual knowledge concerning holdings in regional and other individual collections, is an obligation. How to start and elaborate such collections should be shared. One of the most pressing and profitable undertakings would be studies, surveys, and listings of the most suitable materials to correlate with various types of curricular needs. Discriminating listings of reference works for different conditions are called for. Investigations are required to show what materials are obtainable in these difficult times, and what measures may gradually be taken to fill the vital gaps through joint arrangements for reprints. Exchange of methods, including safe shortcuts, solutions of the care of special materials, of the problems peculiar to the binding of music, and the like, is desirable. Every library every so often needs a survey of policy and practice. At such times thought from the outside is beneficial. A new or modified blueprint may result from sympathetic collaboration.

If group thought and action are desirable in these largely operational matters, they are actually imperative in facing the business world and getting what we want in materials and equipment. That we are too often content to buy what we can get and make the best of it is shown by the shortcomings summarized below.

The music reproduced in photo-offset by the commercial houses is not necessarily what we need most. The reissue of the collected works and the *Denkmäler* type of material will be slow and uncertain unless joint initiative is taken to underwrite such issues by subscription. In the field of the microfilm most music libraries go their own way or take what they can find. Thus, films or slides of the scores corresponding to such record series as *L'Anthologie Sonore* would be welcome. In reverse, recordings of such an anthology as Schering's *Musikgeschichte in Beispielen* would warm the heart of every history and literature teacher. There are no microprints of musical materials. There is no projection machine ideally suited to listening room and classroom use. Even before the war shortages, the best system for housing discs had been off the market for several years. No phonograph satisfactory for educational purposes exists or promises to appear soon. Very little special furniture for music library and listening room use has been devised.[4]

While some of these things which we want will come along of their own accord in *tempo lento,* institutional music libraries by combined pressure could accelerate the pace many fold. The individual promotion of new undertakings and the development of special equipment are for the most part prohibitive in cost. By acting jointly, we could commission many of the things we want. Only through the pooling of resources, and of ingenuity as well, can we get exactly what we need, get the most for our money, and get it before most of us are dead.

It is not the part of this paper to presume to lay down the methods of collaboration. The persuasive establishment of the principle is the cardinal point. It is, however, pertinent to say that the Music Library Association, though still in its infancy, is evolving as fast as the times, knows some of the answers, and assumes that it exists in large measure for the purpose of supporting collaboration in music library affairs.

All of these various thoughts are based on the conviction that a healthy music education is not seriously possible without a healthy library; and that the time is ready for the music library to take its place consciously in the world of music education, to make itself real and indispensable, to become in fact the living library in the service of a living education.

NOTES

1 An address given before the National Association of Schools of Music Detroit, Michigan, February 19, 1946.

2 The ever-expanding reprint industry is making it possible for all libraries to acquire copies of out-of-print basic materials. See [**205–209,** 223].–*Editor.*

3 See Watanabe, pp. 107–114, in MLA *Manual* for a recent summary of microtext materials in the music library.–*Editor.*

4 See *VI. Buildings and equipment appropriate for the music library* below.–*Editor.*

The Library in a Music School

by Richard M. Murphy[1]

The library of a school of music usually serves three disciplines of study: 1) the training of professional musicians, 2) the training of teachers of music for the public schools, 3) the training of humanists. The symbols of these fields are the Bachelor of Music, the Bachelor of Music Education, and the Bachelor of Arts. Just as each of the disciplines requires its special pedagogics, so each requires particular library resources and services. At the same time, the various disciplines are interdependent because the final goal of all music study is the same: to learn something about the art of music.

Manifestly, our discussion of some of the problems of the library in a school of music is confined to the library needs of the undergraduate. Graduate study, especially that towards the degree of Doctor of Philosophy, introduces an entirely new set of requirements which can usually be furnished only by university and large reference libraries, not by the modestly endowed liberal arts college or music school.

Although they do not exhaust the various types of materials normally found in a music school library, the discussion here will largely be limited to four broad categories of materials which seem to call for special treatment: 1) Manuscripts, 2) Complete Editions, 3) Periodicals and Books about Music, and 4) Recordings. No one can deny the importance of the first category: music manuscripts. There is nothing quite so valuable, truthful, and direct as those materials that supply the ultimate sources of our music. But the purchase of original and rare manuscripts is not the duty of the music school library operating on a limited budget. Such luxuries must always remain the prerogative of old or heavily endowed institutions. Indeed, financial restrictions usually preclude even any fond meditations on this category, since the purchase of a single Bach autograph or 16th century tablature would devour at one gulp the year's working budget of most music libraries.

Nevertheless, there are certain undergraduate needs which can be satisfied only through manuscripts or facsimiles thereof. This is true especially for the study of musical paleography, a study which is invaluable for all the disciplines. The undergraduate, of course, does not study the evolution of notation to become a specialist in this field, but to understand the inherent intellectual problems—the possibilities and limitations—of any system of musical notation. He also studies notation as the reflection and vehicle of musical styles. Musical notations are peculiarly appropriate for the styles they represent: they afford an insight into techniques, transcription, and performance which can be gained in no other way. The manuscript needs of the undergraduate are, therefore, chiefly pedagogical; they are not the research needs of the specialist. Usually, the faculty will include a certain number of specialists working in their chosen fields, and herein lies one of the most difficult problems of library procurement. The music library is indeed obligated to provide the faculty with all the resources it can muster, but the task of accommodating both student and professor in this regard often calls for the exercise of careful judgment. The concept of the library existing primarily for the undergraduate student should always be kept at the forefront. Whenever a difficult choice must be made, it should without exception favor the student. For the student, over-emphasis on facsimile source material is of limited value. The undergraduate is learning the techniques of working with source materials. He can do no more. Too great a multiplicity of sources simply overwhelms him with materials which can have little meaning for him until his training suffices to cope with them.

Despite the fact that source materials must

SOURCE: Reprinted from Richard M. Murphy, "The library in a music school," *Notes,* 10 (September, 1953), 537-545, by permission of the Music Library Association.

therefore play a relatively minor role in the undergraduate library, the category has been discussed here because of the problems it presents. Throughout the discussion, the term facsimile source has been used to cover both printed facsimile editions and microfilms. The best of the substitutes for manuscripts are the printed facsimile editions. With the growing emphasis on historical studies in music, more and more of these editions have appeared each year. They are invaluable in affording the student an insight into source materials. They are more inviting, easier to work with, and more serviceable than microfilms. It is an unfortunate circumstance that most libraries provide what seems to be a ratio of one microfilm reader to each five hundred potential readers. The general inaccessibility of microfilm readers is sufficient reason to purchase printed facsimile editions whenever possible. There is one drawback: some of the editions are expensive. A good example of this is the Rokseth edition of the Montpellier manuscript. It is, of course, a facsimile, transcription, and commentary on a large manuscript, all in one, and thus the price of approximately $200 is not perhaps unreasonable. But fortunately there are a number of other facsimile editions which are quite as useful for the students and yet can be purchased for about $20 each. Although careful selection is clearly necessary, the limited requirements of the undergraduate can usually be fulfilled. In those cases, however, where a library budget will not accommodate facsimile editions, the cheapest substitute is microfilm. Certainly facsimiles intended solely for faculty use may well be on microfilm.

The heart of the music library is in its holdings of complete editions of the works of various composers and in the large historical collections. There is no substitute for the music itself, and there is no substitute for a careful scholarly edition of that music. Only the complete works of a composer can provide a proper perspective on his place in history. Complete editions provide the foundation of all the disciplines associated with the study of music. Of all library purchases, the complete editions should have top priority, and all of them should be purchased as soon as possible wherever and whenever they appear. Virtually every library manifests the same tragical story. In 1910, someone neglected to order an edition which is now out of print. Recently, the longstanding inaccessibility of the older series has been remedied somewhat through the Edwards reprints, but many problems still remain, particularly in regard to the very limited number of reprints undertaken and their very considerable prices. Printing costs in the United States are the highest in the world; in no other country is the output of scholarly investigations in any field so limited by cost. It is no accident that most of the recent complete editions are printed in Europe, since even with the excessive mark-ups charged by most importers, the foreign editions can still be sold here cheaper than they can be produced in this country.

It is a curious fact that many libraries are rather unconcerned about their complete editions. There are few libraries which do not have gaps in some of their sets. Sometimes these discontinuities were present when the volumes were originally purchased; sometimes they are the result of excessive use. Whatever the cause, the gaps could easily be bridged by ordering microfilms of the missing volumes, but almost always there seems to be a strange inertia in this regard. Libraries are prone to continue the search, year after year, for a few miscellaneous volumes of a complete edition which has been out of print for fifty years, although the chances of finding the volumes are practically zero. Admittedly, remedial measures through microfilms are a stop-gap operation, but it is certainly better to have the total edition in some form than an incomplete set. If the volumes turn up later, the films can be discarded with no great financial loss.

To my knowledge, there is no remedy for some of the difficulties inherent in the acquisition of complete editions, but nevertheless their purchase remains the first order of business of any music library. In several instances, the recent editions cannot be microfilmed or photostated because of copyright restrictions, which, lest it be forgotten, protect the original owners or their heirs for 56 years in the United States. A printed copyright claim must appear in all volumes so protected, and thus it is easy enough to determine whether or not the work is restricted in this country. The Liszt edition includes claims only for a few specific works, and these must not be reproduced, but a number of the older editions have no claims at all, and may be microfilmed or photostated in their entirety. A file of negative microfilms of most of these sets is maintained at the Library of Congress, and positive microfilm prints can be made from these negatives at relatively low cost. Whenever a more serviceable reproduction is available, it should be chosen, but at any rate *some* photographic reproduction should be purchased as a substitute for inaccessible complete editions.

In addition to the general holdings of music, two special services of the library of a school of music must be taken into account, since both of them necessitate the collecting of specific types of materials which are directly associated with certain disciplines of study. The first of these has to do with the library, or division of the library, which is intended for the conservatory student: the applied musician. The musician must know and study the technical details of the various editions offered by successful performers and editors, in order to evolve his own performance. If an organist intends to perform a Bach work, for example, he should be familiar not only with the *Bach Gesellschaft* edition, but also the Dupré, Schweitzer-Widor, and other editions as well. For the competent performer, the same critical approach is necessary for all types of music, be it solo, ensemble, or orchestral. Apart from the critical function of the performers' library, there is the primal need of practical editions for applied musicians, since obviously the miniature scores of the general collection cannot serve the school orchestra.

The performers' library poses certain problems of administration. Clearly, it is not the duty of such a library to provide music for private instruction, although just where rehearsal ends and private instruction begins is sometimes difficult to establish. Ideally, the performer should return to the library a clean copy, devoid of all markings. Since this idyllic state is unlikely to be realized very often, common sense administration simply requires that the damage and defacement be held to a minimum.

The other field which requires a special, functional library service is that of music education. The student of music education needs the various editions of the graded types of materials used in public schools. Without extreme care, this can turn into a prodigal operation, since it is standard policy among textbook publishers to alter the collections frequently in the competitive race to sell books. One should bear in mind that, while such collections are necessary and desirable, and while every effort should be made to accommodate the music education student, these collections do not particularly enhance the general quality of any library. What is almost worse, it is also necessary to purchase a substantial number of duplicate copies for class use. Duplications should be held to the absolute minimum required for the practical operation of the department. This is not to imply that the purchase of duplicates is limited to the Department of Education. All departments seek to accommodate their students in so far as it is practical to do so, and the purchase of duplicates is one of the commoner methods employed. One fundamental economic fact should serve, however, as a guiding principle, and this is that every dollar spent for duplicates is a dollar lost in the extension of the total collection.

The third category—periodicals and books about music—embraces all types of writings about music, including theoretical works. In this area, the contentions of faculty and student are revived. The professor normally has a working knowledge of several languages, and quite rightly feels that he should have access to information available only in publications in other languages than English. The student, on the other hand, is usually an apprentice at linguistics. We Americans have an almost naive unawareness of foreign languages and their value, and the American undergraduate in particular is likely to approach his studies with inadequate language qualifications. The student, however, should not be coddled at this point. If everything is made easy for him during his student days, he is likely to have cause to regret it throughout all of his subsequent career. Our musical heritage is primarily European, and a genuine comprehension of that heritage is impossible without some understanding of the languages, ideas, and cultures from which it evolved. In any case, too much of the basic literature on music simply is not available in English. Naturally, where it is available the music school librarian will give it preference. Every effort should be made to document the entire field as thoroughly as possible with books in the English language. No one could possibly wish to proceed on an unrealistic or esoteric basis merely for the sake of collecting original editions. But whenever a really important encyclopedia, catalog, biography, or history comes along that is not available in an English translation, it should not be disqualified on the basis of its language alone. The sooner a student realizes that he cannot hope to become an accredited music scholar without reasonable facility in foreign languages, the better it will be for him, and there is nothing that will bring him to this realization more quickly than the sight of famous classics in his field prominently displayed on the shelves of the library.

The budgets of most school libraries will easily permit purchase of all the worthwhile books in English—unfortunately there are not too many of them. But when the range is increased to include publications in foreign languages, considerable care must be exercised in their selection. The services of a fully trained music librarian or a specialist in musical bibliography is desirable, but when arrangements for such an ideal state of affairs can not be realized, it is safer to leave the selection to a faculty committee. The basic scholarly publications must usually be picked up as opportunities present themselves, since many of them have been long out of print. They represent the hard core of knowledge which is the most treasured heritage of the library, and every effort should be made to find copies of as many of them as possible. After all, there are no substitutes—and no translations—for a long series of basic studies from Jan's *Musici Scriptores Graeci,* through Gerbert's and Coussemaker's editions of the writings of the medieval theorists, down to such relatively common things as Professor Einstein's edition of Köchel.

Monuments such as these in the grand tradition of musical scholarship are fundamental for any music library, and every student should have a chance to become familiar with them. Most of them have withstood the test of time so well that to choose them is usually infinitely easier than to find copies that may be bought. Often, it is much more difficult to appraise and assess the new books. Here the scholarly music magazines, many of them containing extensive sections of reviews of recent publications, render a notable service and make possible an informed selection. Most of the more important books will be reviewed in more than one journal, and it is sometimes wise to compare duplicate reviews. The reviewers are normally selected because they are specialists working in the same or related fields. Although in general this gives their opinions special value and authority, it can also on occasion introduce elements of personal bias which can best be sifted out through the comparison of more than one review. Taken as a whole, however, the book reviews in periodicals serve very well as the basis for a discriminating choice. For most purposes, the reviews in journals in English are alone sufficient—*The Musical Quarterly, Notes, The Journal of the American Musicological Society, Music and Letters,* and so forth —although further reference to the lists of books appearing in some of the magazines is often advisable, and naturally reviews of the foreign books will ordinarily appear earlier in the foreign journals. The quality of the reviewing medium is of the utmost importance; great caution indeed must be exercised in regard to critical opinions on books about music in the daily newspapers. In many cases, such reviews are no more than the blurbs on the book jackets. Even special departments like *The New York Times Book Review,* while competent enough in other fields, scarcely ever offer sound reviews on music books, especially books of scholarly character. The reason for this is that the reviews are usually written by music journalists, who often miss the whole point of a scholarly work. On occasion the writers betray a lack of information necessary for a fair appraisal. Apparently with the belief that a strong offense is the best defense, they adopt a hostile attitude and distort the meaning and accomplishment of a really informative author.

Both to aid in the selection of a well-rounded collection of books and also in their own right as well, a representative group of the scholarly music periodicals of all Western countries should be included in the well-planned library of a school of music. Taken as a whole, such a group will require only a very modest proportion of the library budget, and it will more than repay the expenditure by furnishing an account of the latest research in music that will be international in scope. The steady cumulation of music periodicals means the gradual augmentation of information in the library, and hence this is one area where the faculty and the more advanced students should be fully accommodated. The advantages of following such a policy are immeasurable, and whenever it is not outside the realm of practicality, music libraries should subscribe to every scholarly music journal available, irrespective of language.

The acquisition of music periodicals presents one serious problem. Many of the more important journals have been appearing for years, and few libraries were in business in time to start their subscriptions with the Vol. I of all of them. Worse still, when the publisher's stock of back issues is exhausted, it is difficult, not to mention expensive, to pick up a complete set secondhand. Most of the better magazines issued in the United States are registered for copyright, and thus microfilms of recent runs cannot be made of them. Copyright restrictions, however, rarely introduce as serious a problem as with other forms of publication. Few foreign periodicals are protected in the United States, and relatively few publishers anywhere renew the copyright after the first period of 28 years. The chief difficulty therefore is the almost prohibitive cost of a negative microfilm of a long run of any of the major journals. Co-operative action of a number of libraries, with the cost of the negative shared between them and each taking a positive microfilm print for their collection, seems essential. A microfilm edition of a group of older periodicals has already been issued commercially on this same general pattern, and if the experiment proves successful, it is possible that other sets will be reproduced in this form. In the meantime, perhaps the solution for most libraries is to place the chief emphasis on the current periodicals and, leaving the past to take care of itself, to make sure that the apologies now necessary with regard to the early periodicals do not have to be repeated later for the post-1953 collection.

The fourth category to be discussed here is that of phonograph records. For a variety of reasons, the record library can often be best administered as a separate division of the music library. In some instances it may be found preferable to operate it as an independent, self-contained unit with separate quarters, its own budget, and a staff of specialists. Its increasingly complicated equipment and its many distinctive problems suggest such a separation. At the same time, the function of the different sections of a music school library are all fundamentally identical, and a close liaison between the record section and the collection of music must always be maintained. Serious students of music benefit particularly from being able to follow an orchestra score while listening to a recording of the composition, and no physical barriers should be permitted which tend to hinder the procedure. Indeed, whenever possible, the music catalog should indicate which compositions may be heard as well as seen. The reverse indication in a record catalog is usually less important, since the availability of a score for most recorded compositions can generally be assumed. The cross references might reasonably be limited to works, such as many of those in the *Anthologie Sonore,* where the student might have difficulty in locating the music.

The first problem of the record library remains, in spite of all that has been said on the subject, a purely mechanical one. The battle royal of the record producers between the three speeds seems to have ended with a victory for the $33\frac{1}{3}$ rpm microgroove discs. The shift to a slower turntable speed has been under consideration for years, and only the fact that it would make so much equipment obsolete has delayed its introduction. Now that it has been introduced, the music schools are slowly recovering from the body blow. In spite of the fact that the LP discs have made possible the recording of many large works which would have been much too costly on the old shellac records, there still remains a substantial portion of the record repertoire available only on 78 rpm records. These 78 rpm records grow scarcer and more difficult to obtain hourly. Eventually, of course, most of those that still serve a useful purpose will be dubbed at the slower speed, but in the interim music schools are faced with the difficult necessity of operating at both speeds simultaneously. A new library would be well advised to avoid the problem by temporarily doing without the repertoire available only on the older discs and concentrating on the LP discs and equipment, but the established record library could hardly throw away all of its 78 rpm records, and therefore has had to convert its turntables at considerable expense to accommodate both speeds. The necessity for acquiring new machines and turntables has aggravated the old, perplexing problem of finding sufficient physical space for housing the apparatus and servicing the listeners. Where loud-speakers are used, each machine must have its own compartment, and this means that one machine in one room serves only one listener, or at best, a group of listeners who agree to listen to the same selections. Individual choice is severely limited. The problem of physical space can be partially solved by the use of earphones, but this is usually accompanied by a loss in the verisimilitude of the sound. Nevertheless, the earphones can be attached to the machines either separately or in groups, and thus provide maximum flexibility within a minimum of space. No attempt can be made here to deal with specific types and makes of equipment, but it seems wise to point out that in general durability of equipment is to be preferred to subtle reproduction of sound. The record library in a school of music should be regarded as a pedagogical device, not as the ornament of the connoisseur.[2]

The second main problem a record librarian must face is that of selection. In former days before the vast accumulation of recorded performances, it was possible to listen to all of the recordings of a particular work and select the best. This was a happy situation and one which was, for a time, much encouraged by the record distributors. Obviously, these circumstances no longer prevail. With the overwhelming number of recorded performances, records, like books, must be selected on the basis of the critical opinions of professional reviewers. Their reviews appear everywhere—in newspapers, journals, popular magazines, and special record magazines. The diversity of the sources guarantees widely varied competence and reliability. In addition, all music reviews are subject to the personal predilections of the reviewer, so that even the best of the reviewing mediums should not be trusted implicitly. In this respect, the *Index of Record Reviews,* published by the Music Library Association in *Notes* and cumulated annually, can serve as a remarkably useful guide, since it not only indicates where a substantial number of reviews by responsible commentators may be found, but through a system of symbols attempts to summarize the commentator's opinion on the quality of the performance and recording. The *Index* is one of the finest services offered by the Association, and can serve as a very responsible guide in the selection of phonograph records.

Although this brief discussion by no means covers all of the problems met with in the record section of a music library, the growing length of this paper forces me to proceed to a few final remarks summarizing the general administrative problems in the library of a school of music. Clearly, the most basic questions are budgetary. No other matter could be quite so important, since it is the factor that delimits the procurement possibilities of the entire year. There is no reason why a music library should attempt to operate without as large an annual budget as it can persuade the authorities to grant, and there is still less excuse for the library not spending every dollar allotted to it. To insure the continuance of satisfactorily large allotments, careful planning of an acquisitions program is essential. This planning includes a close study of the institution represented, since obviously the first duty of the library is to fulfill the pedagogical requirements of the faculty and students. These requirements will vary to some extent depending on the character of the institution. A close liaison between faculty and library has been effected in different ways in different schools. Many schools operate under the committee system, with a library committee made up of interested members of the faculty. This committee meets with groups representing the various departments of the school to formulate a general budget. Often, one member of the departmental committee is chosen as library representative ultimately responsible for the purchases recommended. The actual purchases are effected through the central order department of the library, since centralized purchasing is a necessary protection of the budget against duplicate requests, but such mechanical considerations must always remain subsidiary to the far more important function of the planning committee.

Indeed, if any one single element is to be selected as the most important in the building of a valuable music library, that element must surely be the judicious selection of materials according to a well-defined purpose. The goal of the institution as a whole and the quality of the over-all collection should always be kept firmly in mind and ever temper the judgment of immediate exigencies.

NOTES

[1] This paper was read at the joint MTNA-MLA meeting in Cincinnati on February 22, 1953.

[2] See Colby and Johnson, pp. 76-98, in the MLA *Manual* and *V. Phonograph records, tapes, etc., within the music library* below for more up-to-date discussions about music library record equipment.–*Editor.*

The Music Teacher and the Library

by Otto Kinkeldey

Otto Kinkeldey, 1878–1966, music librarian at both The New York Public Library and Cornell University, was also an eminent scholar-musicologist. The first Chair in Musicology in the United States was established for him at Cornell in 1930.

In 1915, while Chief of the Music Division of The New York Public Library, Kinkeldey wrote a detailed evaluation of America's first published book catalogues for music—those by Sonneck of various parts of the Library of Congress' music collection and that of the Allen A. Brown music collection in the Boston Public Library ["American music catalogs," Library Journal, *40 (August, 1915), 574–578]. Kinkeldey praised Sonneck for including plate numbers in his bibliographical description of music and for providing typographical variation within entries to help the reader's eye locate the individual elements of the entry. And as early as 1915, long before the days of conventional or uniform titles, Kinkeldey was concerned about the arrangement of cards for music and books within the card catalogue: Should they be interfiled in a single alphabet as at The New York Public Library or in two alphabets as in Boston and the Library of Congress. For the music of a single composer, he pointed out that it was more appropriate to file cards by opus number than alphabetically by composition title.*

*Carleton Sprague Smith wrote a fine appreciation of Kinkeldey as American music librarian and first President of the Music Library Association to honor Kinkeldey's seventieth birthday [*Notes, *6 (December, 1948), 27–38]. An earlier essay by George Sherman Dickinson had recognized the profound influence of Kinkeldey's activities as librarian and teacher on the development of serious American musical scholarship [*The Musical Quarterly, *24 (October, 1938), 412–418].*

*In the following essay, Kinkeldey describes the ideal use of a conservatory library in combination with performance instruction to broaden the student's knowledge of the literature concurrently with his concentration on specific compositions to improve his technical facility. Ms. Ostrove's paper [***56**, *40], complements Dr. Kinkeldey's discussion.*

The process of education in music as in every other field is not restricted solely to what the pupil receives directly from the teacher in the classroom or in the studio. In fact, no system of education which does not train the student in some method of acquiring new knowledge by his own unaided effort, which does not encourage him to increase his intellectual stature without the direct supervision of a teacher, can be considered a satisfactory system of education.

We generally assume that this type of intellectual progress is accomplished by independent reading, and we often speak of the well-educated man as a well-read man; and this process of self-education should, and often does, extend well beyond the years of systematic school education and tutelage. It would be safe to assume that very few men who have made their mark in the field of letters, of art, or of the sciences have reached their eminence without more of this self-education than of school learning.

Many of our colleges have in recent years made

SOURCE: Reprinted from Otto Kinkeldey, "The music teacher and the library," Music Teachers' National Association *Proceedings,* 42 (1948), 81–86, by permission of the Music Teachers National Association.

an effort to encourage this kind of activity in their students by luring them into an attractive "browsing room" in which an incipient desire to learn by independent reading may be fostered and stimulated. The problem of education in music presents a number of special phases or aspects which do not fit so easily into this general picture of self-education. Music, as an art of living sounds, cannot dispense entirely with the actual acoustic reality of its sound forms. A browsing room in a music school or conservatory, like a browsing room in an ordinary college, may try to entice the student to read books about music, and there can be no question that a certain amount of reading in such books is a primary requirement for the well-educated or the well-read musician. But in dealing with the actual work of musical art a certain amount of living sound is a necessity.

It would be impossible to provide each reader in such a room with a piano or a phonograph. Music is an obtrusive art. It forces its manifestation upon all within the range of hearing, whether they care to listen or not. Our neighbor's radio or phonograph, however delightful it may be to him, can drive us to distraction. Phonographs with earphones in a browsing room might be a solution, but they are not attractive to the student brought up on the modern radio and phonograph. Incidentally, the practice of reading and *hearing* music without the aid of actual sound should be encouraged to the utmost limit. The increasing excellence of mechanical reproduction instruments is having, alongside of the many undoubted benefits which these instruments have brought to the musician, one effect which may prove deplorable. The growing musician may lose the power of inward musical hearing and imagination. Before the advent of the phonograph, the player piano and the radio, the student was compelled to train his imagination and his inner ear so that he could derive a real musical impression from the reading of the printed page of music. No real artist composer can create his work without an active exercise of his musical imagination. No present-day music student should be allowed to finish his course without close attention to the development of this inner sense of hearing. The use of the reproducing instruments may be turned to great advantage in the training of this faculty, but in the end the musical imagination must stand entirely upon its own foundation and must be taught to function without a mechanical aid. The practice of keyboard harmony should not be an end in itself. It should look beyond the fingers to the inner sense. It would be a calamity if our music students, no matter what their special instrument or their special field, should not learn to read an orchestra score well enough to derive some sort of an impression of the actual sound of the work from the mere reading of the printed or written page.

But where is the music student to find the material for training himself in this direction, and how can he find the time? In the ordinary course of music teaching as practiced in most of our music schools the mechanical problem, the question of technique, of necessity, looms very large. Not only the player or the singer, but even the composer, must devote much of his time to the acquisition of a technique. The composer's theory training is largely a matter of technique. For the performer especially (and even for the composer) this must be so, for upon his technical proficiency depends his ability to secure a position and to make a livelihood in the face of competition. And so our prospective musicians must devote most of their time and effort to this kind of training.

Herein lies the danger for the broader development of those parts of a musician's constitution which make him a true artist as well as a well-educated man. To foster artistic growth is more difficult than to teach technique. To increase the student's artistic stature the teacher must arouse in the student a desire to do something for himself outside of the classroom or the studio. Much can be done by the earnest student through reading, and a little guidance by a shrewd teacher will go far. The piano student, the singer, or the violinist should be made aware of the fact that the minute knowledge of, and technical excellence in, the relatively few pieces that he or she must learn for recital programs, is not enough to make a real, broadly-educated artist. And for the prospective teacher in particular a broad knowledge of the literature of his field is an unqualified prerequisite. For the piano student it is not enough that he shall have learned half-a-dozen Beethoven sonatas or a dozen pieces by Chopin or Brahms for concert performance. He should be encouraged to take home, volume by volume, the complete piano works of Beethoven, Chopin, or Brahms or any other great composer, and he should be encouraged to take home works by modern composers. He should "play at" them for better or for worse on his piano, and he should in this manner cultivate that sense of musical imagination and hearing which will give him a much broader understanding of his art and a much sounder judgment. His interpretation of his concert pieces can only benefit by such a procedure.

It should be the task of the conscientious teacher to guide the student into these paths. Of course, there are students who are endowed by nature with the inquiring mind, and they need little or no urging to broaden their outlook. But this is not the character of the average music student. After the beginner has once found his stride and has settled down to the regular performance of his weekly assignment of real practice and careful technical preparation, it should be quite feasible for the wise teacher to encourage with a few judicious suggestions every student to indulge in his leisure hours, almost by way of relaxation, to read over a wide territory which he can never expect to master with complete technical perfection, but which is still a part of his actual musical education. The student will be fortunate who falls into the hands of a teacher who is himself endowed with this desire for breadth and culture, and who is anxious to cultivate such a desire in his pupils.

In order to indulge in this reading for culture the student must have access to a reasonably good collection of such cultural material. He cannot be expected to purchase all the works he would like to read. He must have some sort of a circulating library at his disposal. None of the solid music departments in our large colleges or universities are without resources of this kind. And most of our large conservatories, particularly those that are well endowed, have excellent music libraries attached to the school. It is the teacher in the smaller conservatory who is most likely to run upon difficulties in this matter.

But whether the institution be large or small the establishment and the growth of a collection of such material for cultural reading, both of books about music and of practical compositions, depends to an overwhelming extent upon the activity, the advice and the demands of the teacher. Librarians and Library Committees who watch over the expenditure of library funds rarely take the initiative. It is almost always the actual practical teacher who must make the beginning. Here again the teacher in the smaller conservatory is at a disadvantage. The librarians of the larger institutions grow up in this method of building and expanding. Rarely will they fail to lend a sympathetic ear to well-founded requests for aid from the music teacher, especially when these requests are made systematically, after serious consideration on the part of the teacher of needs and possibilities, and not in a haphazard, sporadic fashion.

It is to the teacher in the smaller conservatory that I should like to proffer a word of advice. The library idea has not yet permeated the small conservatory world. And yet the smaller conservatory is under just as serious an obligation to do something for the broadening of the student's cultural and artistic outlook as the large school. How can this be accomplished where financial resources are limited? Once again, it is the actual teacher and not the director or the president of the board of trustees who must take the initiative. There are few directors who could or who would want to withstand rational and well founded requests for a new departure in this direction.

A college or a university library may spend from $10,000 to $200,000 and even more for yearly book accessions, and the university music school or the music department is entitled to draw upon a fair share of this sum for its own needs. No ordinary conservatory can build a library at this rate. But this does not mean that it should neglect this aspect of music education entirely. If earnest teachers in a small conservatory could persuade their director to spend even twenty to fifty dollars annually on the purchase of scores and books for a library, it would make a sum of two hundred to five hundred dollars in ten years. And with such sums it is quite possible to build up a useful nucleus for such a library as we have been discussing.

The Music Teachers National Association has come to the aid of those who may be interested in such a development by publishing an annual list of the better books about music published during the year. But more important for the kind of reading which has been here advocated is the availability of the works of the great masters and of good modern composers. One would hardly expect the small conservatory to own the large but very expensive editions of "Complete Works" of the great masters. But good, reasonably reliable and cheap editions of the piano works, the violin works, the songs of the masters from Bach to Brahms can be bought for comparatively small sums. Any music librarian in a public library or any honest music dealer can put you on the track of these. Debussy, Ravel, Richard Strauss, Hindemith and the like are not so easily available. For most modern composers, particularly of American composers, purchases would have to be made piecemeal and at higher prices than the classics. The classics in chamber music and symphonic music, which of course should be fairly well represented in a conservatory library, are available in miniature or pocket edition scores that are not nearly so expensive as the scores intended for practical performance. But they serve the purpose of study and cultural reading perfectly well. Well-made series of selected works like the "Musicians Library" published by Ditson forty years ago can render valiant service in a conservatory.

I repeat—a useful conservatory library is not beyond the resources of even a small conservatory. All that is needed is a wide-awake teacher or a group of teachers who will ask for it and who will, after they have secured it, see that they inspire their pupils to use it. So that in addition to the necessary technical training, even a small conservatory may give the pupil something which may justly entitle him to the name of a well-educated or a well-read musician.

D. Discussion of Music Libraries by Type: Radio Music Libraries

Little is known, even among other music librarians, about radio and television music libraries; they are frequently overlooked altogether in professional meetings and in the literature. The best known, the Central Music Library of the British Broadcasting Corporation, doubtless owes some of its renown to the quantity and quality of the published writings of its Music Librarian, John Howard Davies. Although Mr. Davies writes about all phases of music librarianship (see Index), he is certainly a world-recognized expert on radio music libraries. One of his more philosophical papers is reprinted below, his examples drawn from BBC practices. The catalogue of the Central Music Library is in the process of being published; the volumes are arranged by medium: *Chamber music catalogue* (1965), *Piano and organ catalogue* (1965), *Song catalogue* (1966) [see Duckles 2nd ed., 610].

In the United States, radio and television music libraries are not very different from Mr. Davies' descriptions, but there is little published American literature. The larger network music libraries are described briefly in *Groves 5th,* V, p. 214. There is also an early article by W. Perceval-Monger entitled "Music Library of the National Broadcasting Company" in *Special Libraries* [20 (1929), 109-111]; a few miscellaneous articles are quoted in *Music Index* under the subject heading "Radio stations–Libraries."

The Training of the Music Librarian: Radio Music Librarian

by Helge Petersen

In the following I should like to give a short survey of how the music librarian is trained for *radio,* and this, I think, is best done by first outlining the radio music librarian's most important functions.

These functions are not the same, of course, in all broadcasting organizations, but at any rate it is not too much to say, that our work differs a good deal from that of music librarians in general, as it is exclusively intended to serve the radio orchestras of our broadcasting house.

The best and simplest way of describing this service is by saying: It is the music librarian's duty to see that any music broadcast is supplied with all necessary materials in correct editions and in such shape and condition as desired by the conductor in question—all this with the purpose of keeping down rehearsing hours and thus, of course, expenses. And this goes for any kind of music broadcast whether a symphony concert, an opera, a concert of popular music, chamber music, light music, a choral concert or dance music and so on.

As the music broadcasts take up several hours of the daily programmes, it is evident that quite a few materials are needed every day. How are all these materials procured and how are they made fit for use?

In the course of time the broadcasting organizations have invested enormous amounts in materials, and are still improving and extending their libraries. How big these libraries are is not so easy to say. Their size varies from enormous (needing 50 or more people to handle them) to quite small (needing staffs of only two or three).

A typical medium-sized one is that of Danish Radio founded in 1924 by Mr. A. K. Jersholt, needing a staff of eight to ten. Most radio libraries find themselves having to meet a phenomenal range of very old and very new music outside the normal repertory. Much of it has to be transcribed, edited or copied, all manual and mechanical techniques being used. Again most large-scale modern orchestral music has to be hired. All this pre-supposes the most accurate and comprehensive knowledge of publishers' catalogues, changes of copyright ownership, agencies etc.

Orchestral scores and parts, whether library or hired items, soon become a battleground of personal markings—often reflecting the confusion arising from the idiosyncracies of conductors and players. To steer a clear course through all these daily complexities and to present materials which minimise rehearsal time is the daily lot of the radio music librarian. He may also be responsible to orchestral managements for orchestration details involving the engagement of players, besides the inescapable financial side of buying, hiring and copying. Add to this maintenance of the library as a library, with its problems of accommodation, cataloguing and staffing.

Now it is obvious that the professional staff of a radio music library moves in perhaps the most demanding and sophisticated section of the musical profession and must handle both men and materials with full professional assurance. He can save literally thousands of hours of expensive rehearsal time by his foresight and care—or can risk prompt dismissal by simple lack of these attributes. Should he be musician or librarian, or rather which should he be first? There have been examples of musicians and musicologists who have failed lamentably as radio music librarians—and equally, cases of non-professional musicians who have been extremely efficient.

SOURCE: Reprinted from Helge Petersen, "Paper: The training of the music librarian," *Fontes artis musicae,* 11 (1964), 55–57, by permission of the International Association of Music Libraries.

Speaking of the average-sized radio library, where essential work can be managed by three or four trained people, I would, in choosing new staff, opt for those showing evidence of practical musicianship supported by a naturally precise and orderly mind. The one without the other invites disaster. Now the orderly mind which makes a potential librarian reveals itself fairly readily in the first few days. If meticulous attention to detail is not immediately apparent it is unlikely to be learned.

Practical musicianship, on the other hand, can and must be learned. It will normally come through learning an instrument thoroughly or through choral training. Orchestral "know-how" will normally best come from extensive orchestral playing.

I am saying, in fact, that in radio, the development of an all-round musical faculty which enables one to handle scores and parts with authority and assurance (instead of having to take title-pages for granted) is paramount. Formal library qualifications, though useful and even desirable, must take second place. Training and experience which bear directly on servicing musical performances must come before bibliographical and musicological expertise. One cannot expect all these (at high professional levels at least) in one person—the marvel is that occasionally one gets it—to the great advantage of our profession.

It is surely because I.A.M.L. tries to reflect and combine the various specialist and marginal aspects of music librarianship that it becomes a valuable "post-graduate" activity. Nothing, however, can replace musical training and actual day to day experience in the work of servicing a wide range of musical performances. The library training for a musician, comes simply and solely by day to day experience.

The Contribution of Radio Music Libraries to National and International Musical Life

by John Howard Davies

The first need, in considering the contributions which radio music libraries are making or might make to musical life, nationally and internationally, is to establish some perspectives, and to visualise such libraries against the background of a) other music libraries and b) musical life and music-making of various kinds. I shall try to treat the matter as internationally as I can, but it will be readily understood if I incline to base my arguments and quote my examples from British practice, in the belief that musical life is fundamentally much the same anywhere.

Radio music libraries are as old as broadcasting, i.e. very young in comparison with most libraries—thirty years old at most.[1] Those countries which began broadcasting services at the time of Marconi's first commercial enterprises soon found that music was to form the backbone of their work. As had happened somewhat earlier with the first gramophone recordings, artists of all kinds, and all sorts of orchestral combinations were brought into the studios. Almost every month saw exciting technical advances which were reflected in the capacity to transmit musical programmes to a rapidly-growing public. Each radio organization, in its turn, found itself, by *force majeure* in the position of having to provide for live music-making on an unprecedented scale. Impresarios and concert-giving organizations had hitherto hired orchestral music *ad hoc* from publishers, libraries, individuals, orchestral managements, opera houses, musical academies and so forth. The scale of their music-making was, however, soon to be far surpassed by the sheer amount of broadcast music which poured from the Old World and the New. All countries were breaking fresh ground, and some took a more serious view than others of their new and weighty responsibility towards music. From 1922 onwards, the B.B.C. (doubtless others, too,) began to build its own music library, acquiring every bit of important music, particularly full scores and orchestral parts, to meet the incessant demand created by hundreds of hours of monthly musical output. The libraries which have thus come into existence were, therefore, created in the first place by a new and especially urgent need. The present scope and richness of these libraries make some of them unique. Where performing materials of music are concerned, as distinct from source-materials and the literature of music, there is good evidence that the radio music libraries in some European countries are by far the best repositories in their own countries. This is certainly true for Great Britain, France, Belgium, Holland and Sweden, and possibly for others.

Which other libraries are similarly concerned with providing music for performance? The teaching institutions and their student orchestras and chamber-groups; the university music faculties to some extent; the libraries of the established orchestras of the world, so far as their own repertory is concerned; finally, certain public libraries, notably the larger ones of Great Britain, the U.S. and the Scandinavian countries maintain collections of music for performance though very few of these latter attempt to provide orchestral materials.

These observations will suffice to show radio music libraries in perspective with other music libraries. In some countries the radio may need to rely on other organizations for service to its orchestras but more generally it will have developed to a point where it is the envy and

SOURCE: Reprinted from J. H. Davies, "The contribution of radio music libraries to national and international musical life," *International Congress of Libraries and Documentation Centres, Brussels, 1955,* v. I, pp. 178–183, by permission of the publisher. Also published in *Fontes artis musicae,* 3 (1956), 62–67.

frequently the court of appeal of other music-making bodies in the same country.

Now let us consider these libraries in relation to musical life. In the main countries of Europe, with one or two feudal exceptions, the radio takes pride of place among music-making agencies. The reasons are fundamental: a) the radio is the richest impresario normally to be found in any country, b) it broadcasts many tens of times as much music as any other single organization, and c) its unseen audiences are likely to be some hundreds of times greater than even the largest of 'live' audiences. The broadcast repertory is, generally speaking, enormous—it needs to be so if the most tiresome repetition of acknowledged masterworks is to be avoided. Besides bearing the admitted responsibility to "the main stream" of music, most radios, unless they are commercially sponsored, act as the principal *Maecenas* of contemporary creative talent. Very frequently it falls to the radio to initiate revivals of long-forgotten works of musical and historical importance, and, generally speaking, since such works are frequently out of copyright, the radio concerned must establish its own new performing materials. Thus it comes about that the radio music libraries possess many sets of costly and unique materials of orchestral, vocal and chamber music.

What do these materials consist of, and what is their value to musical life? Take the first point. The data I have is in my hands as a result of the decision in 1952 of the Radio Section of A.I.B.M. to exchange lists of materials thought to be rare or unique. The lists vary in size and scope from radio to radio, but between them they cover a very great deal of fine music. In them are to be found the 'little' masses of J. S. Bach and the majority of the church cantatas, the early Mozart and Haydn symphonies, the less-known masses of Haydn and Mozart, items such as *Zaïde, Idomeneo, Titus,* of Mozart and *Serse, Admetus, Hamon, Orlando, Sosarme, Theodora* and *Giulio Cesare* of Handel. These are but token examples drawn at random from the unsuspected riches of European radio libraries. The choral, chamber and instrumental items are legion. Wherever a radio organization has embarked upon a series of historical programmes (the U.K., France and Italy, for example, have launched major projects of this kind) most of the necessary MS. materials are lying in the radio libraries, because, for the most part, such materials did not exist in adequate performing state before the radio revived them, and new materials had to be edited and copied. The idea of a "connoisseur's" programme is not new nor peculiar to the B.B.C. but the bold conception and wide scope of the B.B.C.'s Third Programme, inaugurated in 1946, make it unique. It is, I believe, the only permanent radio programme which is specially planned to cater primarily for highly-developed and critical tastes, both in music and in the other arts and sciences. The Third Programme offers more liberal opportunity both for revival of older music and for supporting modern and new works than the two other B.B.C. programmes which cater for average tastes. It is prepared to pay for this service, not as a luxury but as a national cultural and educational investment.

One of the direct results of this widening of the horizons of broadcast music is a library overflowing with unique or rare materials. The majority of the music of the 13th to the 16th centuries was only to be found in rare editions or old anthologies such as those of Expert, Torchi, Proske and the various Denkmäler series. Much of it now exists in performing form in the B.B.C.'s music library. Numerous sets of Dunstable, Dufäy, Monteverdi, Gabrieli, etc. have been specially prepared in MS., often anticipating "publishers" initiative. Many items now enshrined in *Musica Britannica* first were heard in B.B.C. performances. Two major series of historical programmes account mainly for these possessions: the *Foundations of Music series* (prewar) and the *History of Music in Sound* (1948–50) and the actual materials thus engendered are in steady but increasing demand for non-broadcasts throughout my own country and occasionally abroad. The recorded "History of Music in Sound" now in progress as a 'live' supplement to the new "Oxford History of Music," is being produced to a very large extent from B.B.C. library resources, and forms a direct example of the fertilising quality of such a broadcast concept.

The stimulus given by such enlightened musical policies among broadcast organizations is seminal in various ways. It undoubtedly results in a higher standard of musical awareness, considered over a period of 20 or 30 years; it encourages a fresher and bolder policy from national orchestras and choirs, who having heard attractive new works on the radio, wish to perform them themselves; this in turn sometimes emboldens publishers to meet the new demands by special printings of full scores, band parts, vocal scores, etc. It is of particular interest to me to watch the reactions of British musical organizations outside the B.B.C. to broadcasts of new works or of revivals of old works, and, as the B.B.C.'s Music Librarian, I find myself in a strategic position for this. Of the many new works broadcast in the course of a year, I receive outside enquiries regarding availability of materials for possibly ten per cent. Our materials have gone all over Europe and the Commonwealth and have even penetrated the Vatican.

This brings me to a crucial question regarding the extent to which radio libraries may or ought to help outside bodies. Insofar as non-commercial, state-run radios are concerned, the music stocks, like the whole radio service, are a national possession, but they are naturally reserved, in the first place, for broadcasting purposes, and could, in any case, only be lent or hired externally providing that broadcast programmes did not suffer in any way. Recondite works, after their christening in broadcasts, are likely to be free for months or years before they are needed for further broadcasts, and thus the primary obstacle to their use outside does not apply. There are other obstacles, however. In the case of orchestral materials, editors' and conductors' markings and orchestral-leaders' bowings should not lightly be subjected to the danger of wanton alteration by others. In such cases it is possible to help outsiders by making available negatives and transparencies for cheap running-off of further copies. This help sometimes renders a performance possible by reducing the cost to about one sixth of that of establishing completely new materials. The same applies to making available transparencies of chorus parts, where the actual copies themselves cannot readily be spared externally. Good opera materials are rare, and complaints are frequently heard from opera companies and amateur operatic societies about the poor state of such materials available from publishers or hire-libraries. Any radio, such as the B.B.C., which has fostered studio-opera to any extent, and therefore has had to make new or to improve existing materials is likely to receive requests for help from other opera companies, professional or amateur. Again, since such operas are only very occasionally broadcast, there are large stretches of time when the materials can safely be passed to others without prejudice to broadcast programmes. The question of copyright needs careful consideration in each case. Claims of composer, editor, arranger, librettist, publisher must not be evaded. In my experience, however, I have found that any practical difficulties are small and easily overcome where proper approaches are made to the relevant authorities. Should legal decision or support be exceptionally found necessary, radio music librarians can always apply to their own copyright officials.

Frequently radio organizations hold, by purchase or on permanent loan from publishers, materials which, under contract, may only be used for broadcasts. Again, the B.B.C. often finds that, to ensure a broadcast on an imminent date, it must itself be responsible for making materials of modern works, even, occasionally, those already newly assigned to publishers, who may find that they cannot keep to a particular schedule. Yet again, publishers may not always be willing to face the expense of the alterations, cuts, etc. to materials which are often inevitable in broadcasts, particularly of studio-produced opera. Again permission is usually given to make and hold the necessary scores and parts. It is such broadcasts, currently assessed by outside music-giving bodies for their own purposes, that engender requests for material. As I have indicated, the difficulties regarding proprietary interests, where they exist in such works, are rarely troublesome, since all concerned are genuinely anxious to secure follow-up public performances after broadcasts, and would prefer modest or entirely-waived fees to none at all. At the same time, no responsible music librarian, however sympathetic he may be to penurious music-societies, would wish to embarrass publishers by lending or hiring what can cheaply be bought or hired, and I wish to make it clear that the foregoing remarks regarding possible contributions by radio music libraries to outside music-making, apply primarily to further exploitation of materials completely controlled by the radio. In other cases friendly co-operation with publishers is indicated. It is not to be expected that the present cordial relations between publishers and radios should be strained by unprofessional practices.

Where radio libraries are well-developed, the librarian is probably the best-equipped person for outsiders to approach regarding material ways and means for music-making outside the normal repertoire. Insofar as his radio organization ranges over the musical libraries of his country for source-materials, he should have his fingers on the available national resources and the most useful contacts. This aspect was developed by my radio colleagues, when they reported, on Wednesday, on their national resources.[2]

Experience in radio library work is highly useful and not readily gained elsewhere, at least as intensively, in a short time. This means that good assistants may be sought there by outside bodies. The B.B.C. has in the past few years lost some good library assistants to publishers, recording companies and to other music libraries.

The contribution of radio to musical life in general is, as we have seen, crucial and cumulative. The libraries' share in this is fundamental, and is increased insofar as they are individually willing and able to go beyond their official function and put their knowledge, expertise and (with due safeguard), their resources at the disposal of non-broadcasters who can make proper use of them. I have had in mind throughout this paper active and corporate music-making, which surely lies at the very roots of a healthy musical life. The radio and the gramophone have their rich blessings, but these carry with them certain very real dangers, *viz,* that the musical public could become largely one of supine listeners, content passively to accept the cornucopia of sound which the loudspeaker presents. Television, (a potent force for many things but not for music) accentuates these dangers. Fire is said to be a good servant but a bad master and this is equally true of the increasing panoply of technical contrivances which serve both to stimulate and to debilitate the arts. Technological ingenuity can no more be curbed than the tides, but the price of virility in any art is permanent watchfulness lest the machine be allowed to triumph over personal creative or recreative effort. Only thus will music, in face of the challenge of the machine, flower healthily rather than exotically. Paul Hindemith, in his recent book, "A Composer's World," sets out this argument very forcibly. Its relevance to my thesis is that the contribution of radio to music is not complete unless broadcasts engender local effort, and this, in turn, may sometimes devolve upon the radio library to help with materials.

I have shown that such aid must be very carefully considered *vis-à-vis* publishers. There is, however, a growing section of a new potential repertory which lies outside publishers' interests at present and it is here that radio libraries can make the most specific contribution. Musicological findings are frequently being translated from the library shelf to the concert-hall and recitalroom through the radio's financial and artistic resources. The chain which begins, possibly, with a microfilm from an academic library is not fully forged until performing materials are made by the radio library and broadcasts follow. Even then, it is not finally complete until such broadcasts kindle practical enthusiasms to repeat them locally. With the goodwill of the librarian an attractive broadcast may sometimes become a point of departure instead of, as so often happens, a terminus.

As between radio and radio I have already said that the nucleus of an inventory of interloanable materials completely controlled by the respective organizations is in being. The logical extension of this is that each country's rare and unique musical resources in the form of performing materials should be listed, as completely as possible, probably with the aid of the radio, and collated to form an international inventory as a practical counterpart in the field of music-making to the new 'Eitner' which is in process of being recreated for the benefit of scholarship in the field of pre-1800 music.[3] There is no doubt that a *performer's* 'Eitner' to complement the *scholar's* 'Eitner' could be an important contribution to musical activity over a very large field.

Librarians are usually *"hommes de bonne volonté,"* friendly and helpful people who are anxious both to take the best care and to make the best use of the collections they administer. Music librarians are no exception, and the radio music libraries often find themselves the bridgehead between musicological research and its practical initiation in performance. This gives the potential measure of their contribution to musical life. Although music is an international language, and, as such, one of the few cohesive forces among nations, it does not altogether escape international frictions and misunderstandings. The inter-necine strife and recriminations which sometimes unfortunately characterise musicological effort are, however, unknown in the library field. The five-year growth of this International Association, the useful and practical ground already covered, together with plans for future useful work show, on the contrary, that the liveliest spirit of co-operation and mutual help prevails. In this the radio music libraries fully share, and it forms a healthy augury for the future.

NOTES

[1] See his "Radio music libraries: Historical development and basic policies," *Fontes artis musicae,* 4 (1957), 85–88.–*Editor.*

[2] Papers read earlier at the Fourth Congress of the International Association of Music Libraries, September 11–18, 1955, in Brussels.–*Editor.*

[3] The International Inventory of Musical Sources, generally abbreviated as RISM from its French title, Répertoire International des Sources Musicales [**84, 85**; 75]. The published and/or announced volumes are:

Series A, I: Aarts-Byrd.
II: Cabezón-Eyre.
Series B, I: Recueils Imprimés XVIe-XVIIe Siècles.
II: Recueils Imprimés XVIIIe Siècle.
III: Theory of music from the Carolingian Era up to 1400. 2v.
IV: Manuscripts of polyphonic music, 11th–14th century. 2v.
V: Tropen-und Sequenzenhandschriften.
VI: Ecrits imprimés concernant la musique. 2v.
VII: Lauten und Gitarrentablaturen.

See also Duckles 2nd, 774–776.–*Editor.*

II

BIBLIOGRAPHY: THE MATERIALS OF A MUSIC LIBRARY

This subdivision reprints only those pertinent articles which amplify a single area or genre which music libraries should collect, excluding records (see subdivision V. below). The best general statement of the materials which belong in a music library is by James B. Coover in the MLA *Manual*, pp. 1-6. Many of the articles printed above as descriptive of public or academic music collections and services detail quite precisely what materials should be in those libraries. The three articles which follow discuss 1) the quality of the musical editions acquired for any type music library (Krummel); 2) the ephemera with which America's musical history will be written, but which is all too frequently ignored by harried music librarians (Johnson); and 3) the great benefits which accrue to the music library which collects dealers' catalogues, especially those of music antiquarians (Rosenthal).

The *Selected Bibliography* includes more general discussions of music bibliography vis-à-vis the music library.

SELECTED BIBLIOGRAPHY

57. Chitwood, Julius R. "Development of music bibliography in the United States." M. A. thesis, University of Chicago, 1954. "Appendix IV: Bibliography of bibliographies of music literature separately published in the United States before 1951": *ll. 57-63.*

A discussion and analysis of the music bibliographies published in the United States prior to 1951.

58. Duckles, Vincent, comp. *Music reference and research materials; An annotated bibliography.* New York: The Free Press of Glencoe, 1964.

59. ——. *Music reference and research materials; An annotated bibliography.* Second edition. New York: The Free Press, 1967.

60. Pruett, James, comp. *A checklist of music bibliographies and indexes in progress and unpublished.* 2nd edition. Ann Arbor, Michigan: Music Library Association, 1969.

61. Krummel, Donald W. and Coover, James B. "Current national bibliographies, their music coverage," *Notes*, 17 (June, 1960), 375-388.

See annotation in Duckles 2nd ed., 1347.

62. Heyer, Anna Harriet, comp. *Historical sets, collected editions. . .*

See n. 1, pp. 151-155.

63. Coover, James. *Gesamtausgaben; A checklist.* n.p.: The Distant Press, 1970.

64. Flandorf, Vera S. "Music periodicals in the United States: A survey of their history and content." M. A. thesis, University of Chicago, 1952. "Appendix I: Chronological list of periodicals": *ll.* 110-182; "Appendix II: Check list of music periodicals in the United States, 1786-1951": *ll.* 183-219.

65. Wunderlich, Charles Edward. "A history and bibliography of early American musical periodicals, 1782-1852." Ph.D. dissertation, University of Michigan, 1962. [Available on microfilm or Xerox from

University Microfilms.] "Chronological and descriptive bibliography of early American musical periodicals, 1782-1852": *ll.* 304-655; "Appendix A: Alphabetical index of American musical periodicals, 1782-1852": *ll.* 656-663; "Appendix B: Geographical index of American musical periodicals, 1782-1852": *ll.* 664-668; "Appendix C: Register of publishers, printers, engravers, editors, composers, and authors connected with early American musical periodicals, 1782-1852": *ll.* 669-783.

66. Weichlein, William J. *A checklist of American music periodicals, 1850-1900.* Detroit Studies in Music Bibliography, 16. Detroit: Information Coordinators, 1970.

Includes bibliography.

67. Watanabe, Ruth. "Current music periodicals for libraries," *Notes*, 23 (December, 1966), 225-235.

A periodicals buying guide for music libraries.

* * * * *

68. Krohn, Ernst C. "The bibliography of music," *The Musical Quarterly*, 5 (April, 1919), 231-254.

See annotation in Duckles 2nd ed., 1346.

69. King, A. Hyatt. "Recent work in music bibliography," *The Library*, 26 (September-December, 1945), 99-148.

See annotation in Duckles 2nd ed., 1344.

70. Coover, James B. "The current status of music bibliography," *Notes,* 13 (September, 1956), 581-593.

See annotation in Duckles 2nd ed., 1326.

71. Duckles, Vincent. "Music literature, music, and sound recordings," *Library Trends*, 15 (January, 1967), 494-521.

Trends issue was entitled: "Bibliography: Current state and future trends. Part I."

72. ——. "Music bibliography in the United States (1960-1970)," *Fontes artis musicae*, 18 (1971/1-2), 35-40.

73. Coover, James B. "Reference bibliography in the music library," *Library Trends*, 8 (April, 1960), 519-528.

Trends issue was entitled: "Music libraries and librarianship."

* * * * *

74. Clark, J. Bunker and Clark, Marilyn S. "A music collection for the high school student," *Notes*, 25 (June, 1969), 685-691.

A unique list.

75. National Association of Schools of Music. *A basic music library for schools offering undergraduate degrees in music.* Washington, D. C.: 1967.

76. Grout, Donald J. "Requirements for a research music library," *New Notes*, Bulletin of the Texas Library Association, 20 (April, 1944), 7-11.

Grout enumerates the materials of a music research library, but his statistics are out-of-date.

77. Shepard, Brooks, Jr. "Building a collection to meet the needs of research scholars in music," *Library Trends*, 8 (April, 1960), 539-546.

Trends issue was entitled: "Music libraries and librarianship."

78. ——. "Secondary report: Documentation as it pertains to the music library," *Fontes artis musicae*, 12 (1965/2-3), 108-109.

Shepard defines musical documentation as locating, recording, and arranging—systematically—the information contained in documents. He believes it to be especially appropriate for localia and ephemera, albeit expensive and time-consuming for music libraries.

79. Krohn, Ernst C. "On classifying sheet music," *Notes*, 26 (March, 1970), 473-478.

The care and nurture of sheet music in libraries. Extended discussion on dating by graphic analysis as well as by plate numbers.

80. Hess, Albert G. "The cataloging of music in the visual arts," *Notes*, 11 (September, 1954), 527-542.

Dr. Hess describes the *Archive of Music Representations in the Visual Arts* located at the Duluth Branch of the University of Minnesota which collects reproductions of visual art works depicting musical subjects. He explains the Archive's acquisition and processing techniques as well as its unique cataloguing and classification scheme. Includes bibliographical footnotes.

* * * * *

81. Altmann, Wilhelm. "The trials of a musical bibliographer," *The Musical Times*, 90 (January, 1949), 9-10.

A brief description of Altmann's attempts to create an international catalogue of music.

82. King, A. Hyatt. "The International Inventory of Musical Sources," *Journal of Documentation*, 17 (September, 1961), 137-142.

The history and plan of RISM.

83. Duckles, Vincent. "The International Inventory of Musical Sources," *Notes*, 18 (September, 1961), 558-559.

84. Shirley, Wayne D. "RISM: A report on U. S. activities," *Notes*, 23 (March, 1967), 477-497.

Basic; a description of the project with emphasis on America's activities.

85. Schlager, Karlheinz. "RISM, Series A: A progress report," *Notes*, 25 (December, 1968), 209-210. Translated by Joscelyn Godwin.

Recognizing that there must be international control of music source materials, a joint committee of the International Musicological Society and the International Association of Music Libraries met in Paris in 1952 to plan and coordinate activity. The result, the jointly sponsored *International Inventory of Musical Sources* (which is usually referred to as RISM from its official French title, *Répertoire International des Sources Musicales*) is intended to accomplish cooperatively what Eitner began single-handedly. RISM is conceived as two major series of volumes. One will be devoted to the systematic-chronological coverage of particular categories of sources (e.g., printed collections of the sixteenth, seventeenth and eighteenth centuries; manuscripts of tropes and sequences; of medieval and Renaissance polyphony; of early theoretical works, etc.). The other will be a multi-volume inventory of compositions arranged alphabetically by composer. Ten volumes of the systematic-chronological series have been published or announced (see note 3, page 71). No volumes of the alphabetical sequence have yet been published; the national inventory offices of the individual countries are still reporting holdings to the central editorial offices of RISM in Paris and Kassel. As the alphabetical sequence cannot be established until all the information is received and processed, there is no realistically predicted date by which this series will be published.

* * * * *

86. Baron, Hermann. "The music antiquarian of today," *Brio,* 1 (Autumn, 1964), 4-6.

Continues Rosenthal's historical essay on music antiquarians (pp. 81-89) by listing the contemporary antiquarian's services to scholarship:

1. assess the rarity of individual items;
2. publish the results of his research in his catalogues;
3. register unique copies with RISM;
4. inform appropriate scholars or libraries of newly-acquired items which may contribute to their research or round out their collections;
5. restore and preserve damaged materials; and
6. provide complete bibliographical description of post-1800 imprints.

For additional information on antiquarian music dealers, see [**203**, 223].

Bibliography's Stepchild: The Printed Note

by Donald W. Krummel

This report is concerned with publications devoted primarily to musical notation—texts which preserve musical rather than verbal ideas, their symbols being not words but black and white notes, together with stems, flags, accidentals, and clefs, all superimposed on the five-line stave. Inevitably such publications find their way into a library, and happily they are doing so in such quantity as to make them a problem to librarians.

A long-standing question of terminology greets us at the outset. Strictly speaking, a part of what we are talking about is neither "printed," "published," nor "practical" music. Not all of it consists of "scores"; much of it is more substantial than "sheet music"; and in truth, a good share hardly deserves even to be called "music." The problem of nomenclature is quite apart from the bibliographical matters we shall discuss here; but it does reflect on our failure to provide for wise and competent handling of this material. For present purposes, we shall use the term, "musical editions," broadly distinguishing them from recordings and from books about music.

The menagerie of musical editions is inhabited by a variety of bibliographical animals. Noblest of them all are the great historical series and sets, issued by societies and foundations, handsomely executed and bound, definitive and expensive. Close beside them are the large scores for symphonies, concertos, major chamber works, operas, and oratorios, the product of specialized music publishers, in large full scores for conductors or in minature scores for study. From the same publishers come performance materials—ensemble parts and solo editions, intended to be used, worn out, and retired from service, and which for this reason have often been wrongly thought not to belong in a library. Also present are arrangements and other less ambitious works for bands, large amateur choruses, and church choirs, mostly sold and distributed for group performances requiring many copies. More personalized are the song sheets, timely and ephemeral; they come both from reputable firms and from the "song sharks" who prey on the thousands of tautophonous tyros who feel compelled to express themselves in music. Anthologies come next, ranging from collections of hit tunes and old favorites to hymnals and songbooks, and emanating from a wide variety of sources, from the book trade and music publishers to fraternal, religious, and political organizations. Etudes, exercises, tutors, and instructors for student use, typically produced by music publishers, form still another category. Last but not least come the music education materials, including "basic series" for the classroom, which concentrate on rudimentary skills and are generally issued by specialized educational firms.

These various musical editions form the heart of a library's music collection. They are the medium necessary to the creative musical experience; in comparison, their cousins, recordings and books about music, are passive and petrified, for they are *post hoc* manifestations of the world of original musical sound. Composers and scholars look forward to musical editions as the end product of their labors, and performers refer back to them as the basis of their artistry.

Throughout history, however, musical editions have been slighted in our book-oriented libraries. Churches and monasteries, once having presented performances from these materials, either discarded them or relegated them to an organ loft or wine cellar. Universities and learned societies commonly regarded music as unworthy of the intellectual character of their libraries. Our great retrospective bibliographies generally ignored them altogether, and most current national bibliographies have formulated arbitrary and often elaborate rules for excluding as many of them as possible.

SOURCE: Reprinted from *Library Journal*, March 15, 1965. Published by R. R. Bowker (a Xerox company).

Such library classification schemes as Dewey and Cutter casually acknowledged their existence by dumping them with the books which discuss them.

In the broadening span of today's cultural life, music has become a larger, brighter, and more clearly defined segment of our intellectual spectrum. Enlightened librarians, recognizing this situation, have been quick to accept a responsibility for expanded library service. As with other bibliographical media, the librarian's problems have increased with an information explosion. Crying out for attention are the endless problems of matching a burgeoning bibliographical supply with a rising and more varied demand from users. Three aspects of this problem are the basis for this report: in ascending order of importance, the need for special treatment; the need for bibliographical control; and the need for qualitative standards.

I. THE NEED FOR SPECIAL TREATMENT

In many ways, musical editions resemble printed books; but for a variety of reasons, a line of distinction between the two has often been found convenient. Much confusion has resulted from the different lines that have been drawn—by publishers, distributors, librarians, bibliographers, and performers; along various historical, national, and practical lines; and in each instance with a large number of inconsistencies and clouded areas. The result, at worst, is a minor nuisance. In moments of impatience, however, it has been all too common a practice to overlook the practical reasons for the distinction, laying the blame instead at the feet of the irresponsible, uneducated, and capricious musician whose stereotype we have never completely forgotten. We therefore mention the matter for purposes of suggesting that most difficulties come not from an inherent irrationality in the medium of musical editions, but from a general lack of understanding of its characteristics.

The problem is no simple one, perhaps least of all within the complex operations of a modern library. As an example, an opera vocal score may in many ways be regarded as the text to a dramatic work. It is a book, for all intents and purposes, to the library's accountant who pays for it; to the craftsmen who bind and stamp it; to the circulation librarian who hands it out; and to the stacks man who refiles it. Searchers, however, will not find it listed in the *Cumulative Book Index* (CBI) or *Publishers' Weekly*. Acquisitions librarians will probably save trouble by ordering it from a music supplier rather than through the usual book-trade channels. Catalogers will assign a main entry to the writer of the music, not the words. Amateur performance groups and photoduplication departments will need to study carefully its copyright status, insofar as its protection will be slightly different from that covering most literary texts.

There is, I suspect, a high correlation between a rich, solid musical diet in a library and the incidence of ulcers in the library's internal mechanism. Most operations have developed rules of thumb for telling what is and what is not music; but few realize that a one-to-one basis for definition won't always work where other operations are concerned. Catalogers wonder what could be simpler and more painless than following a "half-or-more" rule, defining "music" as anything in which half or more of the text is made up of musical notation. The reference librarian can hardly agree when he discovers many of his hymnbooks classed as religion, most of his songsters as literature, and a few of his ballads and folksongs in the geography (e.g. folklore) class.

The status of musical editions in a library has also been influenced by the varied functions of music subject-specialists within the total library operation. Many European institutions have followed the administrative practice of segregating all operations involving musical editions, placing their acquisition, cataloging, circulation, and reference work under one administrative unit, but locating elsewhere those operations as they involve books about music, musical manuscripts, and recordings. Music specialists in American libraries are more frequently found behind a special reading-room desk, servicing related materials along with musical editions but calling on other operating units of the library for the various processing operations. Some of our more sohpisticated institutions, meanwhile, appear to be adapting a practice of military organizations which distinguishes between "line" and "staff." The music specialist, by being relieved of direct responsibility for any of the library's "line" operations, is able to make greater use of his subject training; but he does so as an advisory "staff" member, working only indirectly through the units which handle the actual workload. Successful implementation of this plan, as with other arrangements, depends on a favorable climate of cooperation and on a masterly administrator—both of which require an awareness of the diverse problems of dealing with musical editions.

II. THE NEED FOR BIBLIOGRAPHICAL CONTROL

Less than half of the world's output of musical editions is listed in national bibliographies, which originate from scarcely more than a dozen of the world's nations.[1] Fortunately our best lists—the *Deutsche Musikbibliographie* from Leipzig and the *British Catalogue of Music*—cover two of the most productive countries. Eastern European lists are surprisingly adequate, more so generally than those from Italy, France, and most of the smaller Western European nations. In comparison with any of these, the United States fares miserably indeed. Our Copyright Office lists, however immense, are poorly cataloged, incomplete, not felicitously arranged, and next to useless for most library purposes. The Library of Congress's *Music and Phonorecords*, while fairly well cataloged, is highly selective and intermixed with other of the Library's acquisitions. The *Notes* lists cover only publications received.

The cause of music in our national bibliographical network has been hampered by a rather arbitrary exclusion of the output of music publishers from such trade lists as the *CBI* and the *Publishers' Trade List Annual*. Music publishers, in turn, have never succeeded in getting together to assemble a list of their own. In all fairness we should note that the American music publishing industry is extremely diffuse (as noted above) and its output immense (as reflected in the fact that the number of copyright registrations in this country for music annually equals that for books, although much of the music is unpublished). Economically, our music publishing industry is also chronically depressed. Engraving and printing are expensive, distribution costs are high, competition for high-quality work is keen, especially from Europe, and sales are usually low. Furthermore, ambitious editions always seem to be the ones that lose the most money; and this being the case, we should be thankful every time a firm decides to subsidize a deserving musical edition rather than a national music bibliography.

In our changing music world—that totality of musical operations involving composer, performer, listener, and a variety of commercial and intermediary agents—a new function for the musical edition may be anticipated. The physical objects themselves will surely relinquish their virtual stranglehold on our musical repertoire—as new copying techniques are developed, as performance-rights concepts become increasingly sophisticated, and as relationships between various musical participants become realigned and perhaps simplified. But so long as the performer stands between the composer and listener, musical editions will remain the primary means of communicating the art-work itself.

Meanwhile, our total musical repertoire grows as new works are written and old ones are rediscovered; and musicians are constantly searching for new experiences that appear to be better, broader, or just different. The pressure of such needs is forcing the music library to expand and to assume a more important role. Instead of preserving a minimum stock of musical editions and an uneven assortment of lists and guides, the library can expect to become nothing less than the central agency in a systematic dissemination of the entire repertoire. This task will presuppose an adequate bibliographical control of musical editions; and, as with book materials, the most sensible approach to the problem involves covering current publications first, and older ones later.

III. THE NEED FOR QUALITATIVE STANDARDS

Current bibliographies, or their equivalents, generally answer three questions: they tell us what is new, what is available, and what is (by various criteria) good. Covering the American book trade, for instance, *PW* and the *CBI* tell us what is new, as the *PTLA* tells us what is available. In music, the *Notes* and copyright lists cover new publications, while such a guide as Margaret Farish's forthcoming *String Music in Print* (Bowker)[2] will tell us what, in one medium, is available. Answering the third question—what deserves to be acquired—the American book trade is covered by a network of selective lists and reviewing media, reflecting subject areas, degrees of specialization, and levels of interest.

In contrast, musical editions are poorly covered by reviewing media. *Notes* is gallantly fighting for a broad, library-oriented coverage in the face of a serious space problem. A few foreign publications and several American repertoire magazines complete the picture. Newspaper criticism of concert performances may be flourishing; but such journalism, like the observations of analysts and theorists, is to the music librarian at best nothing more than a basis for a triangulation of sorts regarding a musical edition.

The vast profusion of musical editions makes the need for qualitative distinctions especially timely; but more critical are the frequent assertions that our entire music publishing industry has been hopelessly corrupted by commercialism. Composers complain that they are condemned to obscurity because their music is not published. Publishers regretfully cite their sales records to prove that the composers' music will not sell. Judging from the immense quantity of musical inanity coming from the industry, and the fine works by even our best composers which are condemned to no better existence than photocopies, the problem is a real one indeed. The library, permeating our cultural life as it does, is clearly in a position to improve this situation. Its music holdings, published, manuscript, or in photocopy, are exempt from commercial implications except as may be involved in performance rights. Furthermore, the individual editions, having been selected on qualitative grounds and provided with expensive processing treatment, are to this extent endorsed by a library as deserving a performer's attention.

Few of our librarians, however, are well enough trained, or have enough time, to do any more than rely on other people's advice on what is worth placing in a library; and competent advice is too seldom available. The most important need in music librarianship today is for an expanded base of criticism of musical editions.

Together with better reviewing media should go studies of how musical editions are used in a library. In what ways, and to what degree, can an acquisitions program encourage new and ambitious music? Is the library obligated to provide materials for all of the performers numbered among its clientele—on all instruments and at all levels of ability? Librarianship's ancient "value versus demand" controversy still plagues us when we decide between chord-organ manuals and historical sets; but are the libraries with the highest percentage of historical editions necessarily either the best or the most effective? How can a "readers' advisory" service in music be developed? The finest tributes our music libraries receive come from performers who recall their first acquaintance with an exciting but obscure work, in a library or through the suggestion of a librarian. The possibilities are immense for expanded library service through musical editions; but we have given little attention to studies of how this can be done.

The library has gained an enviable reputation for supporting the cause of intellectual freedom, and for championing fine literature rather than pulp publications; but culturally it is lagging badly in promoting the cause of good music. The mandate of the library can certainly be expected to expand to include a wider range of efforts in promoting music. Matching the right performer with the right edition is but part of this task. It is not inappropriate for the library to become an impresario, especially when individual concerts can involve an intensive study of one or two unusual works, with repeated hearings interspersed with commentary and criticism from composers, performers, and listeners. The library's responsibility also involves the documentation of local music history—especially insofar as that history may reflect an enlightened contempt for the packaged series filled with box-office favorites, concentrating instead on the more vital and ambitious events which may take place in schools, churches, neighborhood centers, and private homes.

It is both trite and necessary to add concluding remarks that better music libraries are not built by solving bibliographical problems—that what is needed is a library staff combining musical knowledge and taste with earnest efforts But it is only reasonable to suggest that the work of this staff will be more productive and more rewarding when we are aware of the special problems posed by musical editions; when the available resources are better identified; and when better guidelines are set up for determining which of these resources deserve to benefit from the services offered by the library.

NOTES

[1] See [**61**, 73].—*Editor.*

[2] Margaret K. Farish, *String music in print* (New York: Bowker, 1965); *Supplement* (New York: Bowker, 1968).—*Editor.*

The "Music Antiquarian"

by Albi Rosenthal

Of the innumerable hours music librarians spend reading dealers' catalogues, none are more profitable than those spent in reading the bibliographical information presented in music antiquarians' catalogues. Many times the research which was involved in preparing the bibliographical and historical description of an item cannot be duplicated in the music library which buys the item; music librarians frequently rely on the research of reputable dealers for their catalogue card information.

Rosenthal's bibliographical essay is a fine introduction to the history of music antiquarians, as well as an appreciation of the rôle booksellers have played in the compilation of great music collections, especially in the 19th and 20th centuries.

Since Roman times, when "antiquarius" was used first to describe a writing master, later an official in charge of copying codices, the term "antiquarian" has appeared in a variety of shapes and meanings. In Italian, "antiquario" was synonymous with art collector, more rarely also with art dealer, until most recent times, similar to "antiquaire" in France. Murray's New English Dictionary defines the word "antiquarian" thus: "*adjective and noun; a) of, or connected with the study of antiquities b) applied to a large size of drawing paper*". The term is only rarely used as a noun. In German, French, and Italian the word is now generally understood to mean someone dealing commercially in old objects or books.

The fact that the definition itself is elusive, not to say dubious, has its historical causes, which may become apparent when we try to look into the origin of the species and its evolution a little closer. A Music Antiquarian is, for our present purpose, one who deals commercially in music books, music editions, or music manuscripts which are out of print, or otherwise unobtainable, and, by implication, objects originating in earlier periods.

In attempting to outline the Music Antiquarian in his social function and historical significance we shall try to investigate to what extent he mirrors, follows, or influences certain trends in musical taste, musical scholarship, and collecting standards. For long periods his contours merge with those of the general bookseller, publisher, auctioneer, or even art dealer: it is for this reason, perhaps, that no one has ventured to enquire into his remoter ancestry up to now.

There have been many retrospective periods in history which sought inspiration and spiritual nourishment from the artistic creations of earlier ages. It is in these periods that antiquarians flourish, and may first have established themselves. One of the earliest, if not the earliest reference to such dealers is contained in the following edict of the year 832 A.D.—a period, we may observe, which is characterised by its revival of interest in classical art forms. This 9th-century edict[1] warns bishops and abbots to "*watch their ecclesiastical treasures very carefully, lest some of the jewels, vases, or other valuable objects may disappear through the perfidy or negligence of their custodians, because it has come to our ears that dealers, both Jewish and non-Jewish, boast that they can buy from them anything that takes their fancy.*"

In the 14th century, Richard de Bury (1281-1345) made some wise and amusing observations about booksellers in his famous *Philobiblon.*

The Renaissance and Humanism produced booksellers like Vespasiano da Bisticci in Florence, and others who are the first fully recognisable ancestors of their modern counterparts.

Music could play only an incidental rôle in the revival of classical studies, and in the activities of

SOURCE: Reprinted from Albi Rosenthal, "The "Music Antiquarian'," *Fontes artis musicae*, 5 (1958), 80–89, by permission of the International Association of Music Libraries.

such booksellers: apart from learned speculations about Greek and Roman music, the only tangible classical monuments that could exercise the humanist's curiosity were the theoretical works of Ptolemy and a few others, and some later ones such as Augustine and Boethius.

The first music item ever to figure on a printed catalogue may be found on that remarkable broadside printed in Nuremberg in 1474, in which Regiomontanus, an outstanding humanist, lists his completed and forthcoming publications. Among the latter is *Musica Ptolemei cum Expositione Porphyrii.*[2]

Organised bookselling on an important scale really began with the bi-annual Book Fairs at Frankfurt am Main and Leipzig in the middle of the 16th century. New publications from all over Europe were exhibited, and the catalogues published in connection with these Fairs from 1564 onwards are a bibliographical source of the first order. They contain, on the whole, only newly published works. As early as 1572, however, Georg Willer's catalogue of the new publications at the Frankfurt Fair mentions on the title the inclusion of some older editions.

A retrospective catalogue covering the publications of the past twenty-eight years was issued by George Willer in 1592. There are no fewer than twenty pages of *LIBRI MUSICI VARIAEQUE CANTIONES LATINAE POTISSIMUM TAM SACRAE QUAM PROFANAE . . . alphabetico ordine nominibus autorum.* Part II of this great catalogue comprises a further nine-page section of *Teutsche Music Bücher,* Part III a similar section of Italian, Spanish and French music books which had been exhibited at the Fair from 1568 to 1592.[3]

A facsimile of the music sections of two similar catalogues, compiled by George Draudius in 1611 and 1625 respectively, was recently published by Konrad Ameln.[4] Both these catalogues contain, the title says, *"Music Books printed almost as many years ago as we may remember, and many of which are still to be found in Bookshops."*

An English counterpart to these catalogues—but one not connected with a Trade Fair—is the *"Seconde Parte of the Catalogue of English Printed Books: Eyther written in our own tongue, or translated out of any other language: which concerneth the Sciences Mathematicall as Arthmetick, Geometrie, Astronomie, Astrologie, Musick, the Arte of Warre and Navigation . . . by ANDREW MAUNSELL Booke-seller, London, James Roberts for Andrew Maunsell, 1595."* (STC 17669.)

This is the first printed English Catalogue containing books on music and music-editions. While not in the strict sense a bookseller's catalogue, it is—like the catalogues of Willer and Draudius mentioned above[5]—a catalogue by a bookseller, and, to some extent, for booksellers. In the preface addressed to the *"Master, Wardens and Assistants of the Companie of Stationers and . . . Bookesellers in generall,"* Maunsell says: ". . . *seeing also many singuler Bookes, not only of Divinitie, but of other excellent Arts, after the First Impression, so spent and gone, that they lie even as it were buried in some few studies: that men desirous of such kind of Bookes, cannot aske for that they never heard of, and the Booke-seller cannot shew that he hath not: I have thought good in my poor estate to undertake this most tire-some businesse . . . thinking it is as necessarie for the Bookseller (considering the number and nature of them) to have a catalogue of our English Bookes: as the Apothecarie his Dispensatorium, or the Schoolemaster his Dictionarie."*

The section *"Of Musicke"* begins with *"A Brief Instruction to Musicke, collected by P. Delamote Frenchman, Prin. by Tho. Vautrollier. 1574. 8."* William Bathe's *Introduction to . . . Musicke,* Oxford, 1584, the *Service book* printed by John Day (in 1560), the *Psalmes* of 1563 and 1579, and those of John Wolfe and Thomas Este (East) of 1585 and 1594 respectively are also listed. There are three items under: "Lute" (Adrian Le Roy, translated by F. Ke. Gentleman. *A briefe and plaine Instruction to set all Musicke . . . in Tableture for the Lute . . .* James Rowbothum. 1574); "Gitterne." *A brief . . . instruction . . . to learne . . . the Gitterne.* Pri. for James Rowbothum in 4. (n.d.) and "Citterne." *A new booke of Citterne lessons . . .* Pri. for William Barley. 1953. 4.

The catalogues quoted so far are an indication of the better organisation and the expansion of the general book trade in the countries of Western Europe. Even when they list publications considerably earlier than their date, they nevertheless are designed to give as complete a picture as possible of the new output, including what we would term "second-hand" or out-of-print publications. No really "antiquarian," retrospective trend can be read into these catalogues: for the reader of 1595 a lute manual of 1574 was as contemporary as a theoretical treatise of 1569, or a song book of 1571.[6]

It is not until the 17th century that we come

across evidence of music collecting, and of a definite antiquarian interest in old music and music books. We may assume that scholars like Christopher Simpson or Thomas Mace in England, Athanasius Kircher or, earlier still, Vincenzo Galilei, Mersenne, and others, gathered round themselves music and music treatises of the past which they used for, and quoted in, their works.

One of the greatest music libraries that ever existed was the marvellous collection assembled by King João IV of Portugal (1604-1656), at Lisbon. One copy only of the catalogue, printed in 1649, survives (Bibliothèque Nat., Paris). Its 525 pages are eloquent proof of the unbelievable wealth of that music library, without any doubt the richest in the world at the time. The first volume of the catalogue—two more were planned but never printed—is, alas, all that survives:[7] the whole collection was swallowed up by the earth in the great Lisbon earthquake of 1755. Two months before his death, on September 4th, 1656, the King concluded the acquisition of an entire music collection for which his librarian had negotiated with the Amsterdam bookseller Blaeu. The King himself had studied and annotated the lists submitted by the bookseller, and agreed to the very large purchase price. (In his Will, the King left detailed instructions concerning the future preservation of the music library.)

According to O. E. Deutsch (his article on Music Collections in Grove, 5th edition), the earliest English music collection is that of Samuel PEPYS (died in 1703), preserved in Magdalene College, Cambridge. Both Pepys and Evelyn wrote of their frequent visits to London bookshops, among them Playford's Music Shop. It would not be surprising if evidence of even earlier music collections in Britain could be found.

However, for information on the availability of early music books and editions we have to look mainly to Auction Sale catalogues: the system of book auctions seems to have originated in Holland —one of the earliest was held by Ludwig Elzevir at Amsterdam in 1604—and soon spread to England, where the first book auction was held by William Cooper, bookseller, in 1676. Sale catalogues were only rarely collected systematically, even by libraries, but the British Museum and Bodleian Library have a large number of them, going back to the late 17th century. A most useful list of the English Auction Catalogues containing Music, compiled by Mr. Wakeling, is available in the Music Room of the British Museum.

Apparently the earliest English Music Auction took place at Dewing's Coffee-House in Popes Head Alley, near the Royal Exchange, on December 17th, 1691. A copy of the 16-page 8vo catalogue is preserved in the British Museum *(A Catalogue of Ancient and Modern Musick Books, both Vocal & Instrumental, with divers Treatises about the same, and several Musical Instruments, as also of a Collection of Books in History Divinity and Physick.)* There is no indication of the original owner of that collection nor of the auctioneer, but a prominent advertisement in the catalogue for the *"newly printed the 2d Book of Apollo's Banquet . . . sold by Henry Playford . . ."* makes it probable that the collection was assembled by the elder Playford, who had died a few years earlier (there are also several lots of 20 sets each of music books printed by him in the 1660's and 1670's). The collection here offered for sale is extraordinarily rich, both in English and foreign 16th and 17th century music. Among the latter the works of most of the great Italian madrigalists, Peri's *Euridice,* Monteverdi's *Lamento d'Arianna,* and similar treasures are listed. Among French works we find French songs for four voices by Ronsard, editions of Claude Lejeune, etcetera, and there is also *"an old Spanish Book that Treats about and is full of Musick, di Antonio de Cubicon"* (Cabezon).

Even more important for our purpose is a 4-page 4to catalogue, printed in 1690, of which only one copy appears to survive, according to Wing's Short Title Catalogue (P2428): that preserved in the Bodleian Library, Oxford: it is, I believe, the earliest antiquarian music catalogue printed in England. While Playford's catalogue of 1691 discussed above was an auction catalogue, the present one has all the elements of a bookseller's catalogue.[8] Though fairly long, it will be worth quoting the title of this 1690 catalogue in full *"A Curious Collection of Musicke-Books both Vocal and Instrumental (and several rare copies in Three and Four Parts, fairly prick'd) by the Best Masters, Formerly designed to have been sold by way of Auction: But the reason of its beeing put off, was, that several Gentlemen, Lovers of Musick, living remote from London, having a desire for some of this Collection, and could not be there, they are here set down in order, with the rates, being lower than could be afforded otherwise. The collection is to be sold by Henry Playford, at his house at the lower end of Arundel Street in the Strand; where the Collection may be viewed four Days after the Publication in the Gazette. All Gentlemen and Ladies that desire any of these*

Collections, sending in time the number and the price, may have them delivered, they being designed to be sold off in a Fortnight . . . Catalogues may be had graits of Mr. Knight Bookseller . . . Mr. Carr at his Shop . . . (etc.) . . . at Mr. Henry Playford's . . . and of Mr. Dolliff, Bookbinder in Oxford."

The copy in the Bodleian Library has a ms. note on the title: *Donum Fr. Dolliff, XI Jun. 1690.*

Originally designed to be auctioned, the 121 lots are now offered, as the title informs us, at their affixed prices, to the Gentlemen and Ladies that may buy them. (The custom of fixing a time limit within which orders should be sent is a feature encountered in booksellers' catalogues throughout the 18th century: the period varies with the size of the catalogue). Thus, the modern antiquarian music catalogue was, one is tempted to speculate, born through the inability of gentlemen residing in the country to attend the auctions held in town: we certainly have the title of Henry Playford's catalogue to suggest the point. Nor is it a surprising one: it is in this period and the following century that art and book collections were formed, and flourished in the country houses of the aristocracy.

The catalogue lists a collection of mostly English printed and manuscript music of the 17th century, and a few music books, including a few 16th century items. The earliest is item 93 *"GLARINIA, a large Treatise on Musick in Latin, 4 shillings"* which is, no doubt, a copy of Glareanus, *Dodekachordon,* Basle, 1547. The bulk is made up of vocal and instrumental part books by Morley, Tomkins, Campion, Lawes, Wilbye, Locke, Ferabosco, and many others. Such a catalogue, and the auction catalogues mentioned before, prove that music collecting and dealing in music was by then an established custom. Henry Playford's antiquarian music catalogue did not, however, start a fashion: in spite of his pioneering example we are forced to consult auction and general booksellers' catalogues in our search for old music throughout the 18th century. It is also certain that since the 16th century music publishers carried stocks of old music editions, and that much of the antiquarian music trade was a by-product of their activities.

Towards the middle of the 18th century several firms of antiquarian booksellers are established in London. Their main ambition appears to have been to amass enormous numbers of books from private libraries, and to offer them in catalogues often containing 20, 30, or 40,000 items.

The well-known firm of T. OSBORNE, of Gray's Inn, issued *"A Catalogue of the Libraries of the late Dr. Cromwell Mortimer Secretary to the Royal Society, Edm. Pargiter, Esq., and many others too tedious to mention; all purchased this last summer . . . the whole together being a much larger collection than any ever yet sold by any bookseller in England which will begin to be sold . . . on 26 November 1753 and for the conveniency of the Nobility and Gentlemen who live at a distance will continue selling every day till November 1754."* The catalogue contains under the sections *"Antiquities, Inscriptions, Medals, Mathematicks and other Arts and Sciences"* a number of old music books, valued at a few shillings.

Osborne & Shipton's *Catalogue of near two hundred thousand volumes* issued five years later, 1758, contains a copy of Caroso, Il Ballarino, Venice, 1581, for 5 shillings, and others on music.

Later in the century Thomas Payne & Son issued similar catalogues, among whose lots are listed some music items, with prices; the highest figure, in 1790, is affixed to "Burney's Present State of Music in Germany and Italy, 3 volumes, neat and gilt, 1775–12 shillings." *"The Dancing Master, 2 volumes, 1686,"* on the other hand was to be had for 5 shillings, and William Bathe's *Brief Introduction to the Skill of Song, 1597,* for two shillings–indeed for a song!

It is not surprising that these booksellers failed to price items according to their rarity: on looking through some of these enormous catalogues one is struck by the uniformity of the prices, and their uniformly low level. This was, indeed, a kind of whole-sale bookselling which must, on the other hand, have attracted discriminating buyers.

The manner of distribution of these catalogues is described in a note in Osborne & Shipton's two-volume catalogue of 1754: *"Notwithstanding these two large volumes of the catalogue are attended with a great Expence, they are, as usual, sent to the most eminent Coffee-Houses in and near Town, for Gentlemen's perusal, who are earnestly desired not to take them away; and if taken away, a fine laid upon the landlord or landlady of the House; for, as this Sale will continue for two years, they will always be an amusement to Gentlemen."*

Although several notable music collections were formed in England at this time, there was, as it seems, no bookseller who made a special point of offering more music material than his rivals. It may be significant to remember that this was the era of the encyclopaedists: an epoch still far removed from the trends toward specialisation, which was to alter the picture so decisively in the ensuing century.

It is the period in which Dr. Burney and others, such as Dr. Pepusch, William Boyce, and Hawkins built up their music collections. The autograph MS of Dr. Burney's Journal, mostly portions not included in the published version, contains some revealing passages concerning his collecting methods and relations with booksellers: *"Went out book hunting at stalls, old shops, &c.,"* he writes soon after his arrival in Paris in the summer of 1770. *"I went into La rue St. Jacques (a long street filled with booksellers) not so much to purchase books as to collect catalogues to examine at my leisure. However, I purchased so many books of Canto Fermo, such as Offices, Graduals, Missals, Rituals, Antiphoners, &c., in order to get a thorough knowledge of the Romish Church Music, that at my return to England I shall perhaps be taken up at Dover for a Jesuit come over to propagate the papal doctrines."* . . . *"At last, after several vain attempts, I met with Lacombe, Garrick's bookseller; performed my commissions to him from my friend and made some purchases for myself. I found him an intelligent conversible man . . . I gave him a list of books and pamphlets relative to Music to procure for me which Nourn's correspondent had sought in vain. Lacombe promised me to find more during my absence in Italy. Some of them on musical controversy he furnished me with, bound up together for his own use."* . . . *"Met with the Abbé Roussier at La Chevardière's Music Shop and we were soon made acquainted and had a great deal of musical talk . . . This Abbé has a great collection of books on Musick. I shewed him my catalogue which seemed to make his mouth water. "Ah, Monsieur," (he said) "vous êtes bien riche!"*

In Milan Dr. Burney writes: *"Tuesday, 17th. Spent in hunting after source books . . ."*. In Venice: *"There are no music shops nor is any music engraved stampt or printed with types . . . But the number of booksellers in the fine street called La Merceria is very considerable. I found in no one place so many old Treatises and authors on the subject of music as here . . . The principal booksellers in Venice at present are Pasquali, Raimondini, Bettinelli, Occhi, & Antonio di Castro."*

In Florence: *"Mr. Joseph Molini from whom I have received much assistance . . . at Florence, has been so kind as to undertake to send the books which I collected here and at Bologna to England, directed to his brother. They began a second time to be too much for my trunk and would have been a horrible embarrassment at the entrance into the Pope's territories . . . where they say all books are examined by the Inquisition."*

Burney's notes are both amusing and illuminating. He is surely the first music scholar who admits that he visits bookshops not so much to purchase books, as to collect catalogues! On the other hand, he was a substantial and discriminating customer, and his beloved Library, which was auctioned in London in 1814, proves it: the sale catalogue, partly with prices reached at the auction, is preserved in the British Museum. The sale of music took seven weekdays. The books on music which were to be auctioned a few weeks later were withdrawn and sold en bloc to the British Museum in the following year (1815).

It may be useful to sum up at this point what the evidence so far adduced means in terms of the story of the Music Antiquarian. The personalities we have so far encountered behind the counter were either auctioneers, general booksellers, or music publishers. Music editions of the past are often met with, even listed in separate sections in bookseller's catalogues, but they rarely assume more than incidental importance. Their largely haphasard and uneven prices prove that no definite trends in antiquarian music dealing and collecting had crystallised up to the end of the 18th century.

The great music historians of the century, however, paved the way for a new appreciation of old music. While the works of Dr. Burney, Hawkins, and comparable continental scholars made facts and perspectives of music history accessible and intelligible to a wide public, the musical monuments of the past assumed living shape in their own right only with the romantic revival towards the turn of the century and after. The musical revivalist movements—we need only mention the name of Palestrina as an example—led to what we might call musical historicism—a development which had a profound effect on musical outlook and scholarship. It brought in its train an unprecedented interest in the music of earlier ages, and all the resources of ever more exact and exacting methods of research were brought to bear on the interpretation of its surviving monuments. The provision of source books, the extension of bibliographical exploration to the field of music books and editions, the search for hitherto neglected music of earlier centuries became more and more vital to scholars, libraries, and the newly founded Faculties of Music History.

On the Continent, above all in Germany, this

trend is reflected in the appearance of booksellers' catalogues devoted entirely to old music. The Berlin booksellers R. Friedländer & Sohn, established in 1828, compiled a catalogue of the music collection of A. Westrow, which was auctioned in 1853. The firm of L. E. Lanz in Weilburg issued a music catalogue in 1854 entitled *Verzeichnis einer Sammlung antiquarischer Musikwerke* (Catal. II). Similar ones followed in 1860 and 1861. In 1859 L. F. Maske's Antiquariat, Breslau, issued their catalogue 44, containing the fine collection of Johann Theodor Mosewius. J. D. Class of Heilbronn issued a whole series of music catalogues between 1860 and 1865. Richard Zeune compiled three remarkable music catalogues for the Berlin antiquarian bookseller E. Mecklenburg in 1860 and 1861. (Nos. 10, 12, and 13). Several antiquarian music catalogues were issued by Kirchhoff & Wigand in Leipzig between 1860 and 1865. Others were issued by Asher & Co. of Berlin (specially catals. 68 and 74 of 1862 and 1863) and, notably, by the house of List & Franke of Leipzig.

The catalogues of that firm are well suited to illustrate some aspects of the antiquarian music trade of that period. Within a few years of its Catalogue One of 1862, this firm offered for sale a number of distinguished private music libraries: those of H. Schellenberg of Leipzig, Landsberg of Rome, Strauch of Ernstthal, Kieber of Oederan, and others. The mere fact that such private collections could now be purchased and offered for sale by music antiquarians, is undoubtedly a measure of their growing importance: the sale of similar collections was previously entrusted without exception to auction houses.

The catalogues of List & Francke contain other features worthy of note: the descriptive notes, for instance, are mostly in French, although the catalogues were issued in Germany. The practice of issuing catalogues in foreign languages became widespread in the German-speaking countries. Ludwig Rosenthal writes in the Foreword to his music catalogue in 1880: *"A cause de l'intérêt universel des matériaux nous sommes forcés à donner ce catalogue en français, quoique notre connaissance de cette langue internationale ait bien des lacunes. Nous sommes prêts à donner des explications éventuelles sur ce qui pourra paraitre obscur."* The use of an international language is an indication both of the growing international connections of the antiquarian bookseller and, of course, of the fact that buyers were increasingly to be found in France and the Anglo-Saxon countries.[9]

In England, too, greater prominence is given to music in booksellers' catalogues even in the first half of the 19th century. Thomas Thorpe's catalogue of 1834, for instance, refers on the cover to "an extraordinary assemblage of MSS . . . of the late William Radcliffe, including collections of Elizabethan Madrigals with Music." (The descriptions also are becoming more elaborate, lists of Incipits are given in full, and short biographical notes on the composers are added.) Thomas Kerslake, bookseller at Bristol, underlines music prominently on the cover of one of his catalogues about the same time. The firm of Bernard Quaritch, established in 1847, soon begins to include music in its catalogues. While catal. 24, issued in 1851, contains under the heading Games, Sports & Music only four items, three on music and one on shooting, catalogue 50, October 1852, comprises 120 music items under the heading *"MUSIC, SONGS. The most curious collection of Old English Songs and Ballads ever offered for sale."* In England, especially, the antiquarian music market continued to be further stimulated by auction sales of important music collections.

Perhaps the very existence of a parody of a music catalogue may be taken as a sign that such catalogues were well established and widely known. As early as 1862 such a parody was printed by R. Lonsdale, aimed at Dr. Rimbault and his library, under the title *Catalogue of the Extensive Library of Dr. Rainbeau FRS, FSA, ASS, which Messrs Topsy Turvy & Co. will put up for public competition on Saturday, October 1862.*[10] Here are a few samples chosen partly for their relevance to music dealers and their catalogues:

Lot 1 Doctor Rainbeau's handkerchief, spectacles, and case (much soiled).

Lot 13 "HOW CAN I LIVE?" or, The poor Musick Professor's outcrie against his rich brethren for taking the allowance on Musick from him and dealing at the cheap shoppes by which he and his family are like to be ruined. 8vo. 1862.

Lot 50 DUFFIN's ART OF PUFFING, or the Music Seller's Day Book.

Lot 92 Beethoven's Works, Moscheles edition, the most correct.

Lot 93 Beethoven's Works, Bennett's edition, the most correct.

Lot 94 Beethoven's Works, Benedict's edition, the most correct.

Lot 95 Beethoven's Works, Liszt's edition, the most correct.

Lot 96 Beethoven's Works, Hummel's edition, the most correct.
and so on and so forth.

The antiquarian Music Catalogues now reflect the most conspicuous feature of 19th-century scholarship: that of specialisation. The generation of Fétis, Coussemaker, Bellermann, Jacobsthal, and others, had opened new perspectives to musical research, and had established musicology as a discipline in its own right. Within a short time its literature and range became so vast that the bookseller had to specialise in this field, if he was to serve the expanding circle of customers adequately.

The process was a gradual one, and music buying lagged behind the achievements of musical scholarship. This may be deduced from the following words written by Johannes Wolf: *"Is it not extraordinary that at a time when Heinrich Bellermann and Philip Spitta were occupying Chairs in Music History, when Robert Eitner was active with bibliographical research, when Chrysander was doing his brilliant work, that Leo Liepmannssohn was offering one of the earliest German organ tablatures, the MS of Ileborgh von Stendal of 1448, for 40 marks without finding a buyer in Germany—so that the precious MS was sold abroad?"* Wolf also points out that even the extraordinarily low prices were no inducement to librarians at a time when music was studiously overlooked even in the cataloguing of libraries, with the sole exception, as far as Germany was concerned, of the Berlin Staatsbibliothek.

The name of Leo Liepmannssohn just quoted provides an opportunity for referring briefly to this remarkable personality, who did so much to create the very conception of the Music Antiquarian in the current sense of the word. *"Small and round in stature,"* wrote Prager in his little booklet *Silhouettes of Antiquarian Booksellers, "suffering from asthma in his later years, but nevertheless smoking incessantly—clever, vivacious eyes set in a pink face with short beard, the high dome of his head framed by short white hair. An amusing talker, fond of telling stories, he could sometimes be prevailed upon to disply his mastery of the piano. I have heard him play Chopin with perfect technique while at the same time keeping his beloved cigar going. An extremely learned and friendly man, in spite of his pronounced sarcasm."*

Leo Liepmannssohn first established himself in Paris in 1866, in the rue des Saints-Pères. One of his early catalogues, No:33 of 1870 contains 1141 items, many of them of outstanding rarity. The hallmark of the specialist bookseller is clearly discernible even in his first catalogues. Titles are fully given, collations are added to the more important items. There is a far greater diversity of prices—a much wider and at the same time more solid scale of values, based on intimate knowledge of the music reference works, music history, and current collecting tastes. He notes not only references to existing literature, but indicates results of his own research. In his description of Froberger's *Diverse ingegnosissime . . . Partite, Toccate, Canzone, &c.,* he points out that this work was not printed in 1714, as Fétis had it, but in 1693. He also says that, as the edition speaks of Froberger as *"nunc piae memoriae,"* he must have died in or before that year, not in 1695, as Fétis had stated.

Liepmannssohn, especially after reopening in Berlin in 1873, became the leading specialist in antiquarian music, and the firm retained its preeminence after it had been taken over in 1903 by Otto Haas, on whom this Association bestowed an Honorary Membership in 1953. The long series of almost 250 catalogues issued by that firm is, perhaps, quite apart from being a veritable encyclopaedia of musical literature, the most continuous and reliable record of the trends in music buying, and the availability of material over a period of almost ninety years. Great private collections were being formed in that period—the names of Matthew, Ecorcheville, Wolffheim, Cortot, Hirsch, may alone suffice to illustrate the point. Collections are now built and organised primarily on the lines demanded by musicology. In an article on *Musik-Bibliophilie, Aus den Erfahrungen eines Musik-Sammlers,* 1927, Paul Hirsch gives the six guiding points which governed his acquisitions. Number one is: "Wissenschaftliche Bedeutung." Preservation, rarity, typographical merit, binding, and illustrations come after this consideration.

Public and University Libraries continued in increasing measure to buy systematically to satisfy the rapidly and universally growing need for source material and specialised literature. It is this need which provided the stimulus for music antiquarians in several countries to keep abreast with research in the descriptions and composition of their catalogues. In England, the house of Reeves issued its first music catalogue in 1875, and thus inaugurated a long series of astonishingly rich catalogues. R. Legouix became a wellknown music specialist in Paris. Several of the leading general antiquarian booksellers issued important and well-edited music catalogues: Ludwig Rosenthal's catalogue 26 *Bibliotheca Musica* issued in 1880 in Munich comprises well over 2,000 music items, Jacques Rosenthal's catalogue I, 1895, is entirely devoted to music. Many of its numbers were acquired by the British Museum. Martin Breslauer issued his scholarly and finely produced catalogue "Das deutsche Lied" in 1908, L. S. Olschki in Florence, Quaritch in London, and others, published similar special music catalogues of value. Between the two world wars, and later, new and important firms established themselves both in England, on the Continent, and in America, whose names will be familiar to you—I hope for unimpeachable reasons.

The antiquarian bookseller knows very well that no printed or other matter gravitates more automatically, more powerfully towards the waste-paper basket than his catalogues. Only by giving them bibliographical and typographical thrust in the opposite direction can he achieve the ideal result: namely that not only the goods offered therein should be sold, but that the catalogues themselves should become the faithful satellites of the music-bibliographer, -librarian, and -historian.

"Booksellers' catalogues," as Mr. C. B. Oldman wrote in *Collecting Musical First Editions,* 1938, *"contain some of the fullest and most reliable information on the subject of musical first editions that (the collector) is likely to find anywhere. In particular some of the catalogues recently issued . . . are models of careful research and invaluable as works of reference."*

The usefulness of music dealers' catalogues as sources of bibliographical information was recognised by Petzhold, who gave a list of those he thought noteworthy in his 'Bibliotheca Bibliographica,' 1866. Eitner's Quellenlexikon contains innumerable references to copies of music books in booksellers' catalogues. One wishes sometimes that certain bibliographies should not be quite so adamant in excluding copies held or listed by dealers when enumerating known copies: their editors may rightly point to difficulties arising from quoting from such transient sources, but they have only themselves to blame if the music antiquarian then writes "only one copy in X's bibliography," although it is a book of which several copies may have been prominently described in dealers' catalogues within most recent memory.

Music antiquarians' catalogues were perhaps for the first time collected systematically by Paul Hirsch, and will figure under the names of the firms in the forthcoming part of the Hirsch Library Accessions Catalogue of the British Museum.[11] In some public libraries antiquarian booksellers' catalogues are still, by tradition, consigned not, perhaps, to the "Enfer," but certainly to the Purgatory of the stacks. Their rescue from this anonymous and uncatalogued twilight is a labour of love which is not without reward to music historians and -bibliographers alike.

An enquiry into the nature of music antiquarians' catalogues in the last 100 years might well yield interesting information. If I have been able to draw the attention of music librarians to this somewhat neglected branch of musical literature—and by neglect I do not mean that they have neglected to order from these catalogues—this sketchy and tentative survey may have served a useful purpose.

NOTES

[1] Monumenta Germaniae Historica, Legum Tomus III, p. 364 § 23.

[2] Regiomontanus died before work on the book was put in hand, and Ptolemy's treatise on music was not published for almost another hundred years.

[3] A bibliography of the music books listed in the Frankfurt Fair Catalogues was published by Albert Göhler in 1902 ("Die Messkataloge im Dienst der musikalischen Geschichtsforschung," *Sammelbände d. IMG, & Verzeichnis der in den Frankfurter und Leipziger Messkatalogen 1564–1759 angezeigten Musikalien,* Leipzig, 1902).

[4] Bärenreiter-Verlag.

[5] See also their Italian prototype, Antonio Francesco Doni's *La Libraria* (first edition 1550).

[6] It may be worth recording that the earliest known register of books exported to the New World, listing a consignment of books shipped by the Seville bookseller Diego de Montoya to Pedro de Ochoa *de Ontegui* in Mexico in the year 1586, contains one copy of *Musica de Cabeçon, in pergamino,* price 14 Reis. (Printed in 1578). Two further copies were contained in another case in the same shipment. The first book-sale in the Americas was held in Mexico in 1576. On this occasion several copies of Martin de Tapia's *Bergel de Musica* (1570), and Alonso de Castillo's *Arte de Canto Llano* were sold. These are the earliest music books to become known across the Atlantic.

[7] The catalogue was reprinted in 1874, and a biographical volume added by Joaquim de Vasconcellos in 1900. This volume includes numerous documents relating to the growth of the music library.

[8]See also Wm. C. Smith's article "Playford. Some hitherto unnoticed catalogues of early music," *Musical Times* (July/August, 1926).

[9]Some of the voluminous English 18th-century catalogues had Prefaces and Selling Conditions in French and English.

[10]Published in a facsimile edition, with Preface, by James B. Coover (n. p.: The Distant Press, 1962).–*Editor.*

[11] British Museum. Department of Printed Books. Hirsch Music Library. *Books in the Hirsch Library, with supplementary list of music.* Catalogue of printed books in the British Museum. Accessions, 3rd series–Part 291B (London: The Trustees of the British Museum, 1959).–*Editor.*

Notes on Sources of Musical Americana

by H. Earle Johnson

Although this editor had long known Mr. Johnson's somewhat out-of-sorts indictment of music libraries and librarians for their neglect of musical localia, I guess I thought the situation had improved. But recently I have begun correspondence with music libraries all over the United States in search of brochures, bibliographies, and other ephemera issued years ago by those libraries or their librarians. Unfortunately we, as professional music librarians, have not profited by past errors! Too frequently the reply to my letter is:

> *There are some typewritten sheets here, undated, with no compiler or author indication on them. Miss X, who might know something about them, retired 25 years ago and now lives abroad.*

Or:

> *The library issued many mimeographed bibliographies but no systematic, chronological, or even complete file of them has been kept.*

If, indeed, a former music librarian is still living, it usually requires another exchange of letters with the library to acquire her present address. The former librarian's response to my query is, all too often:

> *I destroyed all my personal files when I retired because they were too bulky and expensive to bring with me.*

Or:

> *I left my personal files, as well as copies of everything I wrote while at the library, in the library. Perhaps the present music librarian will be able to help you.*

From a state library I received a response to the effect that although answers may have been received by Miss X as a result of her query in a 1904 library periodical, her work had apparently not been considered worthwhile enough to keep. A prolonged search, under both her married and maiden names, never turned up even a box of miscellaneous correspondence. If that librarian's correspondence could be located, it might well contain the earliest known report of music holdings in American libraries!

As music librarians we must do better! Although we all buy and catalogue the same published materials, only one or two of us have the privilege, as well as obligation, to collect and preserve in a manner appropriate for posterity's use, the unique documentation of our city, school, or university's musical history. [See also 212 & 213, 224].

Mr. Johnson's article enumerates many of the materials which should be preserved, some successful methods of serving the researcher, and several past errors of non-historically-minded individuals which must not be repeated.

SOURCE: Reprinted from H. Earle Johnson, "Notes on sources of musical Americana," *Notes*, 5 (March, 1948), 169–177, by permission of the Music Library Association.

Before the broad field of Music in America has been adequately analysed and presented, there are source materials still undiscovered which must be hunted down, and subjects as yet untouched which must be studied. Able scholars of the field have been few in number, and they have not exhausted any single corner of it or of its implications, while local surveys by amateurs show plainly that there is need for competent direction in organizing and presenting the material they have so earnestly sought.

Musicological activity by Americans began many years ago, but we may not take much comfort in the record of our encouragement of it. Alexander Wheelock Thayer's monumental biography of Beethoven had to wait fifty-five years for publication in English; Sonneck's "Concert Life in America" found its publisher in Germany and is not yet owned by many of our music libraries. We have gone far enough in our scholarship, however, to recognize that the works—the books, counsels, and collections—of Oscar Sonneck are a firm foundation on which to build. There is further reaping to be done in some of the fields in which he labored, but there will be no need to revise his conclusions or correct his errors, for he was a scholar of irreproachable integrity and enviable skill. Within a decade signs have appeared of a genuine movement toward an accurate and extended appraisal of our musical past from the perspective of the entire country. These signs give urgency to the need for discovering and classifying source materials wherever they may exist.

Sonneck, too, was conscious of this need. One of his first steps was to tour the country in a search for basic materials. He believed, with the historian J. B. McMaster, that newspapers are an unexcelled repository of local history. Sonneck was the first musical scholar to travel in America—although he confined himself largely to the Eastern seaboard—with a perceptive mind for actual documentation as compared with the autobiographical method—first or third-hand—of F. L. Ritter or W. S. B. Matthews. The amount of dust he stirred up in historical societies and music libraries can be appreciated only by one who makes a similar tour today.

Lack of awareness of the location of source materials is a handicap often difficult to overcome. The great libraries of Washington, Boston, and New York are first resorts; beyond them one hesitates. I have recently turned up a few locations and take pleasure in pointing them out, refraining from any attempt at bibliography, a subject so large and so irregular in scope and merit that another and more critical survey would be required to do it justice.

The problem of availability within a library is of great concern to the efficient researcher. Institutions that refuse accredited scholars all privileges except the use of imperfect catalogs and require detailed filling out of hundreds of call-slips ("so that we may count our circulation, you see, and ask the Trustees for more personnel") are bypassed when possible. Scholars generally recognize the obligation of taking care of valuable documents. True, men of great renown have in the past used penknives on newspapers and rare books, but this is not very likely to happen now. The best service ensues when scholars have access to shelves housing special collections in a restricted field. Often a dustcloth is useful since some libraries still scorn the vacuum-cleaner. In this respect of free access (not of dust) the smaller private libraries are often the most satisfactory. I have found infinitely greater satisfaction in historical societies than in public music libraries; in the former the researcher is left free to pursue his own way, while in music libraries he must often explain his entire thought-processes and channel his work through an intermediary. When the subject of music in America is mentioned to music librarians, chances are that the answer will be an enthusiastic, "Yes, indeed! We have ever so much on Stephen Foster and Edward MacDowell. And"—this with a culminating shout—"we have a program of Jenny Lind!"

Source materials, like museum collections, often take surprising forms (e.g., Chicago Art Institute's "Collection of European Shoes"!) and researchers are accustomed to the 'run-around'; it's all a part of the game for the first things wanted are invariably found in the place of last resort. To newspapers will be added pamphlets, tune-books, sheet-music, letters, diaries, programs, scrapbooks, city directories, scores, books of local history, music-instruction books, etc. I am especially concerned at the slight value put upon concert programs; especially is this noticeable in comparison with carefully arranged files of theatrical memorabilia.

Why save programs? There are several reasons which make them valuable. Most theatrical programs represent touring attractions, but an early concert program may be evidence of resident culture; it records the events, not of a week's run, but of one breathless evening. Unlike the theatrical program, its like cannot be found in every city with only a change of date and place. The local taste, the homely talents, the evidences of awakening culture through the presence of an Overture by Beethoven or Mozart—or Kalliwoda—a song by Schubert, or a symphony by Schumann in first performance by an orchestra comprised of resident musicians, doctors, provision-merchants, bank-clerks, all met as 'amateur gentlemen' freed from the commercialism of the touring attraction, form a significant occasion worthy of preservation through this slight tangible evidence of a printed record. The initial performance of "The Creation" or "Elijah" draws "a respectable and fashionable auditory" which fairly bursts with civic pride. What these events lack in glamour by the absence of great performers, they make up in substance of great music; in many cases the glamorous presence will also be there. As a chronicle of cultural progress such events are unsurpassed. The program of a concert by Ole Bull playing "The Echoes of Norway" is far less treasurable than one of Hans Balatka's Musical Society essaying two movements from the Fifth Symphony, or of Herold's Philharmonic struggling with Mendelssohn's "The Tranquility of the Ocean and a Happy Voyage" for the first time in California.

Librarians understandably shudder at the mention of scrapbooks, equipment neither fish nor fowl to the card catalog. But scrapbooks (sans pressed flora) are invaluable to the researcher whether with indexes and critical notices tipped in, or unadorned like those of the Philharmonic Society of Cincinnati which are sole evidence (apart from an incomplete record laboriously deducible from newspapers) of early musical life in that city. Oftentimes handwritten comments on the margins are worth the price of admission.

In Boston the best source materials will be conveniently found in the Allen A. Brown Collection of the Public Library whose scope, careful indexing, and completeness will delight the scholar. Here, skillfully tipped in, are reviews of performances the world over. But in Baltimore the Music Division of the Public Library will consider a request for evidence of the city's musical history passing strange; all such things, including newspapers, are in the Maryland Department which has a useful 'vertical' file with much local material on such things as the national anthem.

It is difficult to say precisely what the New York Public Library owns except that the overwhelmingly large system of card catalogs indicates a great deal. Mr. John Tasker Howard has supervised a serviceable listing of all musical works performed before 1830 according to composer and title, and assembled a section of local histories for quick reference. No one is permitted to examine the stacks. Odell's "Annals of the New York Stage" is a mine of reference material, of course, for Professor Odell and Clarence Brigham of the American Antiquarian Society are two of the world's great newsboys. The Museum of The City of New York, as a new institution, will not be in a position to furnish much to the musician, nor will the Brander Matthews Collection at Columbia University; a small amount of material relating to opera and to Emma Thursby sums up the holdings of the New York Historical Society, but newspapers are well represented, and they have a remarkably choice collection of early songsters. A call on Director Robert W. Vail can be pleasantly productive of ideas. The Long Island Historical Society, on the other hand, is utterly uncoöperative.

The Library Company of Philadelphia owns a comprehensive survey of theatrical bills and a file of early programs by the Musical Fund Society of which Madeira apparently knew nothing when writing his "Annals of Music." These include fine lots on minstrelsy and on family concert companies (e.g., Hutchinsons, Rainers, Barkers); as for opera, no city in America has been more consistently opera-conscious than Philadelphia. How those plain Quakers and pre-destinated Presbyterians loved the sound of the human voice! A large collection of early Philadelphia newspapers, including some not found elsewhere (e.g., The Pennsylvanian) is available. A few manuscripts, hosts of first editions of Beethoven, scores both foreign and American in origin, and other treasures of which neither the Library nor this researcher are fully aware promise a field day for the experienced hand in estimating their value. Now administered by the city, the Library Company (founded by Benjamin Franklin in 1764) maintains its collections intact, but distributed among several locations.

The Pennsylvania Historical Society offers scrapbooks combining musical with theatrical programs, but it also owns the official books of the Academy of Music from time of building in 1867. Manuscripts, biographical notes, and local history of the 17th and 18th centuries are plentiful and well-cataloged. A trained staff gives the visitor confidence that whatever is in its collections is sought out for his examination and that, I assure you, is a comfortable feeling. Their eighty-odd volumes of early American sheet music were finally cataloged a year or two ago. The University of Pennsylvania Library houses an exhaustive theater collection assembled by Professor Quinn, but the musician will find no grist for his mill, and may confine his labors to the institutions mentioned above, plus the Free Library for newspapers of the 19th century, the collection of William Henry Fry's autographs and memorabilia (recently described in a booklet by Professor Upton), and some outstanding sheet music. A German historical society maintains a library of its own, open on application, and the Drexel Institute has the library of the eminent pianist, Charles Jarvis (1837–1895).

Baltimore will provide a pleasant experience since collections are well-housed and within a stone's throw of Washington monument. First I cite the Maryland Historical Society for matters of local background and a collection known as 'Dielman's Morgue.' Louis H. Dielman writes that "The Morgue came into being about 1904 in a small way and had no plan other than to be an 'omnium gatherum' but especially to make a record of the 'little man' of Maryland who never got into the biographical dictionaries. In date it ranges from about 1632 up to yesterday and contains births, marriages, and deaths, compiled from hundreds of newspapers throughout the State, long extracts from Parish records, and Probate records including many wills in extenso; anything was fish that came to my net. In bulk it covered a hundred drawers of 3/5 cards; no close estimate can be made as to the real number of names, but my guess is that it contains 150,000 to 200,000. I have been adding about 1,000 cards a month in my retirement but dwindling eye-sight will soon close that chapter." An example may be cited in Asger Hamerik, director of the Peabody Conservatory from 1872 to 1898, for here Mr. Dielman includes several translated articles from Norwegian periodicals, articles full of interest for their account of earlier friendships with Berlioz and Rossini.

The Peabody Institute offers general information from standard collections. In Baltimore one must turn to two authorities whose kindness will leave the researcher happily in debt. Dr. Dieter Cunz of the University of Maryland is a musically-minded historian of the Germans in the State, and Prof. Otto Ortman, former head of the Peabody Conservatory, owns the largest collection of miscellaneous programs in the city. For the student of 19th century musical life his collaboration is essential.

The Library of Congress is not greatly concerned with the Nation's local history, but it would be unwise to undertake a local study without consulting the Music Division's collection and staff. Items turn up quite casually in this amazing place which are conspicuously lacking in Boston, New York, or Philadelphia, a fact particularly true of early publications, including sheet music, copyright records, and instruction books. At the Library of Congress one may never anticipate where the lightning has struck with a brilliant flash.

I acknowledge a special gratitude for facilities of the Carnegie Library of Pittsburgh which is ably supervised by Miss Irene Millen. Most notable are scrapbooks of the Evens Collection with detailed information on musical life beginning in the 'forties, but there are other materials as well. Pittsburgh has been well served by Dr. Edward Baynham whose dissertation, "The Early Development of Music in Pittsburgh," awaits publication. Exhaustive and documentary, this is close to the final word on the subject of music in that city, and I know of no regional history of music more ably told than that which Dr. Baynham completed in 1944.

The naïve idea that musical progress has been exclusively confined to the northeast will be quite shaken when one examines the story of music in Cincinnati. The river town which gave Theodore Thomas free reign has passed through a long preparatory schooling in good music. Records are not always easy to come by, for Cincinnati's Public Library adheres to a custom of the middlewest (I might say Middle Ages) which combines music and the fine arts in a single department, thus hindering both, I suspect, in attaining full scope in the matter of collections. Several published accounts of early musical life in this city are available here, and nowhere else; sheet music published in Cincinnati is especially worthy of study by reason of its topical nature and for the names of composers, publishers, and lithographers working in this 'show-boat' town nearly a century ago. Mrs. Alice Plaut is enthusiastically aware of these factors and gives willing assistance. The prize, for my purposes, was a small volume in the Historical and Philosophical Society housed at the University, containing full programs of the earliest concerts (1855–65) by a symphony orchestra at which major works by Beethoven, Haydn, Mozart, and contemporary composers were introduced, one concert interrupted by an announcement that war was declared between the States.

St. Louis acquired its early fame largely because

of the presence of Eduard de Sobolewski, pupil of Carl Maria von Weber and a "Davidsbündler." Ernst C. Krohn is the only person in the city today who is aware of this splendid past. His private library of general musicological literature is assuredly one of the finest in the country, and his published brochures on music afford outlines of local history which could easily be expanded into a completer story. The arts division of the public library has the only complete file of Kunkel's *Musical Review,* and the Missouri Historical Society recently fell heir to more than a thousand early programs, but the musicologist will begin and end with private citizen Krohn, his collections and his advice, delightfully given and all-embracing. An odd quirk, however, will send one elsewhere for St. Louis orchestral history, since in 1938 a local dealer sold to the Music Department of Louisiana State University the scores of the St. Louis Philharmonic Orchestra (1860–70) and, presumably, some scores belonging to the St. Louis Oratorio Society (1846–?). The Philharmonic library contained all music performed by that organization in the sixty-two concerts that it gave. Some of this music was in manuscript, the majority of scores and parts in early 19th century European editions.

In the presence of a library of world-renown, there is an inclination to disregard others in the same sector. This must be guarded against in Chicago where the Illinois Historical Society and Chicago Public Library have local items of interest, and make up in willing service what they lack in comparison with the magnificent Newberry Library. First stop in the Newberry should be made at the desk of John T. Windle whose enthusiasm for music gives the student a special advantage of communing with one whose knowledge goes beyond Foster and Gottschalk. In respect to efficient operation the Newberry is unsurpassed in the exactness with which it produces your slightest wish. Is it programs? The Frederick Grant Gleason collection of scrapbooks (1875–1905) is too huge, but there it is; also on call is a series of English scrapbooks covering the third quarter of the century which contains occasional commentary by American correspondents. Theodore Thomas' own scrapbooks, consisting of more than forty volumes, are there; G. P. Upton did not exhaust their possibilities. The Newberry Library owns a Bay Psalm Book, Hans Gram items, and autographs by many composers which are being increasingly consulted by artists for comparison with published scores. Heifetz called recently. There are broadsides and hymn books, and a larger store of materials relating to the entire country than is generally known.

The early musical life of Milwaukee was brilliant beyond our present knowing. Most of our present information is gained from "Der Musikverein von Milwaukee" by Oskar Burckhardt. The Wisconsin Historical Society is in Madison, but it is reported that a local historian is assembling such items regarding music as he can find in a small room at the top of the courthouse. Other than this slight hint, however, I can offer nothing from my two days of investigation there.

Several mid-western cities, including St. Louis, Detroit, and Pittsburgh had a promising early musical life but declined in the late 'sixties owing to the Civil War. The earlier affluence is quite unknown today. Cleveland is a case in point. One must take his cue from the "Annals of Cleveland 1818–1935; a Digest and Index of Newspaper Records of Events and Opinions," a project completed only through the mid-'eighties by WPA. In these volumes are brief entries on which to work for a fuller establishment of early musical life, aided perhaps, by a dissertation, "Musical Developments of the Western Reserve 1803–1880," by William Harvey Porter (Western Reserve University, 1946). This is obtainable at the Historical Society. For newspapers, the *Cleveland Leader* at times approached the status of a musical magazine, and *Brainard's Musical World* will be helpful. By and large any sense of awareness of musical past will be lacking in the libraries of Cleveland.

The entire library of band music which belonged to John Philip Sousa is at the University of Illinois, and is said to be the finest collection of its kind in the United States. It is indexed and arranged in a satisfactory manner for the researcher.

If these findings are rough on music libraries *per se,* I can only say that I am powerless to alter the story as I see it. The following rich collections to be found elsewhere, and which I set down with enthusiasm, are likewise apart from the professional habitat of musicians.

None but the musician will be surprised to know that the American Antiquarian Society in Worcester, Mass., finds a place for music in its concerns. Under the careful supervision of Miss Emma Forbes Waite, over 35,000 pieces of sheet music are arranged and cataloged in many ways. There are listings according to publisher, subject, region, period, composer, author, lithographer, title, or other significant factor, in a manner to serve the investigator more readily than any other similar collection in the country. The Society's collection of hymn and tune books is also notable, but it is in the field of newspapers that all other libraries, including that of Congress, bow in flushed respect. Would you read a New Orleans paper of 1818, or a Chicago paper dated before the fire? Would you go back into the Revolution to see how Bostonians were doing in music? (Esther Forbes did so for her "Paul Revere.") Texas, Sacramento, Portland (Oregon or Maine), Salt Lake City–their papers are here, with advertisements of concerts, of teachers, of births and deaths, of the latest sheet music and instruments locally made or imported, plus tempting 'ads' of turtle soup, rum and brandy, midwives, and apartments to rent. One must remember that Chicago, San Francisco, and Boston each had its 'melancholy fire' in which many things were destroyed, making the researcher's life difficult. But here, saving some of us the expense of travel, rest more California papers than are available in any library of that State. In New Orleans there is only one complete file of the *Times-Picayune,* I understand; it is in possession of an individual who does not allow it to be used by others; consequently, the Antiquarian Society issues are welcome. Of these distant cities current files are not maintained; as the Society's name implies, collections are of the past, often tapering off after 1850. The recently-published "History and Bibliography of American Newspapers 1690–1820," compiled over many years by the Society's Director, Clarence S. Brigham, and published last year, is the most monumental survey of its kind ever attempted, and musicologists will find it invaluable.

Several years ago I visited the Essex Institute in Salem, a dignified place still haunted by dreams of Hawthorne's boyhood and of world commerce carried on in view of its windows. I worked patiently at a few books selected from the catalog, sensing, with that gift of premonition common to researchers and old ladies, that there were good things to come if I could get at them. At length, Miss Tapley, who had observed my reading habits and found them good, invited me to the nether regions of the Institute. There I remained for days among the most amazing assortment of early publications–sheet music, hymn books, scores and parts, programs, broadsides, and church records, all relating to New England–that I have ever seen gathered together in one place. I momentarily expected to come upon an unused pile of Bay Psalm Books, but was well-satisfied with a quantity of William Billings' items.

In the field of sheet music, libraries are customarily alert to sorting and indexing, and there are a dozen important private collections in specialized subjects. Mention should be made of the early Von Hagen imprints at the John Carter Brown Library in Providence, and the early editions of scores and parts, vocal and instrumental, in the library of the influential Handel and Haydn Society of Boston; these include Dr. G. I. Jackson's own set of Arnold's edition of Handel. There is a miscellaneous collection at the Harvard Musical Association in Boston and thousands of uncataloged early imprints are in the Harvard University Library. Starting with no backlog accumulated during the ages, Mrs. Mott has assembled at the Grosvenor Library in Buffalo one of the most diversified collections of sheet music, early and late, in the country.

The fullest prepared story of musical progress in America is to be found in periodicals. Few libraries have yet made a serious attempt to gather musical magazines or to coorelate articles on music from non-musical periodicals. The latter begin irregularly at an early date, and become important, I believe, with the *North American Review* (1815), and later *The Dial, The Harbinger,* the early *Harper's* and *Atlantic Monthly, Saroni's,* and a score of magazines now resting with the dodo bird. The Union List of Serials notes only four entries under *Dwight's Journal of Music;* there are other sets in the East, however, which seem not to have strayed into the historical societies. One day we shall discover that the supply of this great source-book is not large enough to meet the demand and there may be a reprinting on the scale of the ambitious Bach Gesellschaft project now under way.[1] There was no lack of musical periodicals after 1839, but the extent and value of their coverage varies exceedingly, with *Dwight's Journal* and Mason Brothers' *New York Musical Review* setting the highest standard. Music libraries have made no real attempt to deploy these periodicals, but the wise will have an eye to the future and count those collections fortunate which contain them, as well as local histories, publisher's catalogs, musical directories, local publications, and early instruction books, particularly for piano, and for flute.

I have by no means exhaustively covered resources of libraries with respect to their musical Americana. A frequent reaction of librarians is that they do not know what they have in charge. In some instances (such as that of the Library Company of Philadelphia) I consider it urgent that some effort be made to ascertain the importance of holdings in music. Likewise, Harvard University has in its open stacks programs and brochures on music which belong in the safekeeping of the Houghton Library. Universities have a responsibility in these matters now neglected by music departments which still look down the nose at America's musical past except as it concerns their own participation. At the Houghton Library, by the way, there is an unpublished file of Jenny Lind correspondence, but it is more concerned with theology than with music. Yale University School of Music owns Lowell Mason's library which embraces that of Dr. Rinck.

The musicologist's materials are often integrated with collections on American history, thereby inviting consideration of the social picture now regarded as a mark of broad scholarship and a point of view constantly exemplified by Sonneck in his writings. In the next few years the Music Library Association, the American Musicological Society, or other appropriate agency is faced with the rewarding opportunity of making a study of musicological materials in American libraries. This paper is restricted to facilities for the study of Music in America, a subject broad enough to warrant such a survey, and one often isolated by force of circumstances from the larger field of general musicology. It is no secret that a researcher in this subject often gains greater understanding and encouragement in the company of American historians than in that of musicologists. This is to be sincerely regretted, for he knows that he should not be segregated any more than German, Italian, French, or English musicology should be segregated, and that it was the same Bach, Mozart, Haydn, or Beethoven heard in Minneapolis as in Leipzig.

That a survey of musicological materials will be heartily welcomed by historical societies and general libraries I have no doubt after discussing the possibilities with some of them. Direction will be required, however, for untrained curators to determine the relationship and value of their musical holdings to their own community and to the nation-wide, or the world-wide, picture of an over-all musical culture.

NOTES

[1] *Dwight's Journal of Music; a paper of art and literature.* v. 1–41, April 10, 1852–September 3, 1881 (New York: Johnson Reprint Corp., 1968).—*Editor.*

III

BIBLIOGRAPHIC SERVICES WITHIN A MUSIC LIBRARY

A. The Bibliographic Description of Musical Editions, to the End of Establishing Their Printing Dates, Variants, Sequence, and Inter–relationships

A most appropriate introduction to this area of musical research has already been written by Prof. Jan LaRue of New York University ["Musical exploration: The tasks of research bibliography," *Library Trends,* 8 (April, 1960), 510-518]. LaRue divides research bibliography (a term essentially interchangeable with Shepard's musical documentation [78, 74]) into three subdivisions: (1) that concerned with locating and making available hitherto unknown biographical information; (2) with comparative bibliography for the identification and authentication of music; and (3) with the establishment of dates and chronological sequence, especially of musical editions.

The reader is urged to consult LaRue's article before reading further here.

* * * * *

Six similar essays, each overlapping another somewhere while contributing uniquely elsewhere, present a difficult problem of logical precedence. I have finally decided that the most abstract discussion of early music printing practices, unencumbered by minute bibliographical examples, may best prepare the reader for the more detailed Oldman and Deutsch papers. Although Hopkinson's discussion proceeds another step along the road to the standard bibliographical description of musical editions, the irresolution reflected there—as well as that of the later IAML discussion—may soon be resolved by a publication of the IAML Commission for the Dating of Music: *Guide for dating early music,* edited by Donald W. Krummel. Dr. Krummel recently described the scope of the forthcoming volume in his "Guide for dating early music: A synopsis," *Fontes artis musicae,* 18 (1971/1-2), 40–59.

SELECTED BIBLIOGRAPHY

87. Marco, Guy A. "The music manuscript period; a background essay and bibliographical guide," *College & Research Libraries,* 26 (January, 1965), 7-16, 48, 60.

An introduction for the humanities or general reference librarian who has no musical background. Also, a good summary for quick reference.

88. Meyer, Kathi and O'Meara, Eva Judd. "The printing of music, 1473-1934," *The Dolphin* [New York: Limited Editions Club] (1935), 171-207.

Although included in both Duckles and Walker below, it is especially valuable for the beginning student of music printing.

89. Walker, Arthur D. "Music printing and publishing: A bibliography," *Library Association Record,* 65 (May, 1963), 192-195.

A very fine bibliography of English language articles to be used in combination with those in Duckles 2nd ed., items 1186-1255, and the following Addenda to both:

90. Marco, Guy A. "A history of music printing in Italy, France, Germany and the Low Countries, 1473-1600." M.A. thesis, University of Chicago, 1955. "Bibliography": *ll.* 53-62.

90bis. Smith, William C. and Humphries, Charles. *A bibliography of the musical works published by John Walsh during the years 1721-1766.* London: The Bibliographical Society, 1968.

Continues the coverage begun by Smith's *A bibliography of the musical works published by John Walsh during the years 1695-1720* (Duckles 2nd ed., 1239).

91. King, Alexander Hyatt. *Four hundred years of music printing.* 2nd ed. London: British Museum, 1968. "Bibliography": pp. 31-32.

92. Fraenkel, Gottfried Samuel, comp. *Decorative music title pages; 201 examples from 1500 to 1800.* New York: Dover Publications, 1968.

93. Pogue, Samuel F. *Jacques Moderne; Lyons music printer of the sixteenth century.* Geneve: Librarie Droz, 1969.

94. Heartz, Daniel. "Typography and format in early music printing, with particular reference to Attaingnant's first publications," *Notes,* 23 (June, 1967), 702-706.

95. ———. *Pierre Attaingnant: Royal printer of music; a historical study and bibliographical catalogue.* Berkeley: University of California Press, 1969.

"Bibliographical catalogue" contains a listing of 174 items printed by Attaingnant. Includes bibliographical references.

96. Hixon, Donald L. *Music in early America: A bibliography of music in Evans.* Metuchen, N.J.: Scarecrow Press, 1970.

Music entries from Charles Evans *American bibliography; A chronological dictionary of all books, pamphlets and periodical publications printed in the United States of America from the genesis of printing in 1639 down to and including the year 1800, with bibliographical and biographical notes.* Evans completed 12 volumes—through the letter M for the year 1799. Clifford K. Shipton finished 1799 and 1800 in v. 13, published in 1955. Several other bibliographers continued the work and prepared indexes to it. For more information, see the Prefaces of Shipton's v. 13; Bristol's *Index,* v. 14; and the Supplement.

97. Ross, Ted. *The art of music engraving and processing; a complete manual, reference and text book on preparing music for reproduction and print.* Miami: Hansen Books, 1970.

See especially Chapter I, pp. 1-54.

* * * * *

98. Krummel, Donald W. "Graphic analysis; Its application to early American engraved music," *Notes,* 16 (March, 1959), 213-233.

In addition to plate numbers, publishers' addresses, newspaper advertisements, published catalogues, etc., analysis of the printing characteristics of the actual page of music may aid a bibliographer attempting to date undated printed music.

99. Lenneberg, Hans. "Dating engraved music; The present state of the art," *Library Quarterly,* 41 (April, 1971), 128–140.

In his discussion of the descriptive bibliography of printed music, Lenneberg assumes a position midway between that of Hopkinson, the collector ["The fundamentals of music bibliography" reprinted below] and Richard S. Hill, the librarian [see his reviews of Hopkinson's bibliographies, *Journal of the American Musicological Society,* 6 (Spring, 1953), 77–84; and *Notes,* 16 (June, 1959), 385–387]. Bibliographic notes.

* * * * *

100. "Plate number information: A bibliography of sources," In Bradley, C.J. *The Dickinson Classification; A cataloguing & classification manual for music,* pp. 124–125. Carlisle, Pa.: Carlisle Books, 1968, and the following Addenda:

101. "Cotages d'éditeurs antérieurs à c. 1850: Liste préliminaire," *Fontes artis musicae,* 14 (1967/1-2), 22–37.

The beginning of an international history of printers and lists of their plate numbers. The eight countries reported are: Germany, Denmark, France, Italy, The Netherlands, Poland, Sweden and the United States. The U.S. entry, by Donald W. Krummel, is an extensive list of American firms, their dates, and some plate numbers.

102. Heck, Thomas F. "Ricordi plate numbers in the earlier 19th century: A chronological survey," *Current Musicology,* No. 10 (1970), 117–124.

103. Musikantiquariat Hans Schneider. *200 Jahre B. Schott's Söhne, Historisch-bibliographische Schau in 300 ausgewählten Titeln.* Katalog Nr. 153. Tutzing: Musikantiquariat Hans Schneider, 1970.

"Nachwort [Plattennummern]": pp. 69–77.

* * * * *

104. Heawood, Edward. "The position on the sheet of early watermarks," *The Library,* Series 4, 9 (1928–29), 38–47.

105. Stevenson, Allan. "Watermarks are twins," *Studies in Bibliography,* 4 (1951–52), 57–91, 235.

See pp. 57–72 as background for the following LaRue articles.

106. LaRue, Jan. "Watermarks and musicology," *Acta Musicologica,* 33 (1961), 120–146. "Bibliography": pp. 144–146.

107. ———. "Abbreviated description for watermarks," *Fontes artis musicae,* 3 (1957/1), 26–28.

108. ———. "Classification of watermarks for musicological purposes," *Fontes artis musicae,* 13 (January-April, 1966), 59–63.

109. ———. "Specialized lights for watermark readers," *Notes,* 26 (March, 1970), 479–481.

110. Hudson, Frederick. "Concerning the watermarks in the manuscripts and early prints of G. F. Handel," *The Music Review,* 20 (1959), 7–27.

Includes many bibliographic citations.

111. Tuttle, Stephen D. "Watermarks in certain manuscript collections of English keyboard music," In *Essays on music in honor of Archibald Thompson Davison,* pp. 147–158. Cambridge: Department of Music, Harvard University, 1957.

112. Oldman, C.B. "Watermark dates in English paper," *The Library,* Series 4, 25 (June-September, 1944), 70–71.

113. LaRue, Jan. "British music paper, 1770–1820: Some distinctive characteristics," *Monthly Musical Record,* 87 (September-October, 1957), 177–180.

* * * * *

114. Wroth, Lawrence C. "Formats and sizes," *The Dolphin* [New York: Limited Editions Club] 1 (1933), 81–95.

Are There Musical First Editions?

by Kathi Meyer-Baer

Dr. Kathi Meyer-Baer, musicologist-bibliographer, is probably best known to American music librarians for her work in the Paul Hirsch Music Library. She collaborated with Hirsch in the compilation of the four volume catalogue of that Library, published between 1928 and 1947 (see Duckles 2nd ed., 1135). Throughout her long and distinguished career, Dr. Meyer-Baer has been interested in music printing and publishing, as well as aesthetics–her most recent book is Music of the spheres and the dance of death *(Princeton University Press, 1970). In addition to her work on the Hirsch* Katalog, *she compiled the catalogue of the International Exhibition, "Music in Folk Life" held at Frankfort in 1927 (see Duckles 2nd ed., 902) and* Liturgical music incunabula, a descriptive catalog *(London: The Bibliographical Society, 1962). For additional biographical information and a more complete list of her publications, see* Groves 5th, *V, p. 730.*

What is a musical first edition? This question has become quite a problem since bibliophiles started, about forty years ago, to collect musical first editions. Several catalogues of rare book dealers have been devoted to this field: those by Heck in Vienna, Lengfeld in Cologne, Liepmannsohn in Berlin, and the First Edition Shop in London. This topic has been discussed several times in the magazine *Philobiblon.*[1] Primarily the works of the great masters, Bach and Händel; of the Classics, Haydn, Mozart and Beethoven; and the early Romantics, especially Schubert, have attracted attention.

The bibliographical difficulties are especially great with the editions which appeared at the end of the 18th and the beginning of the 19th centuries–the decades between 1790 and 1830–the epoch of the classics. These compositions had certain specific printing conditions which make their dating and bibliographical description intricate. To verify the year of publication–the general basis of bibliography–we are forced to look for additional information.

It is customary to speak of first print and reprint. But we must keep in mind that the publications in question are almost without exception either engraved or lithographed. This restriction is so important because the publication technique of these copies is the reason they are not dated.

The making of a book required a large supply of type, which represented great material value and therefore had to be used again and again. After the printing of the book, the composition (trays of type) was laid aside to be used for another work. The process of engraving was different. The copper and zinc plates used here also represented a costly material. But more costly was the process of engraving, which in a way corresponds to the punching technique (*Stempelschnitt*), for the labor of engraving had to be done individually on each plate of a new work.

Engraving took so much time and was so expensive that the engraved plates were preserved over long periods of time for re-use. To be able to identify the stored plates and to have them ready at a moment's notice for printing a new copy, it became customary to mark the plates belonging to one composition with one number, the so-called plate number (*Plattennummer*). They are also called *Verlagsnummern,* publishers' numbers; however, there is a difference between the two. In the latter case, to the numbers were added the initials of the publisher. These numbers, generally found in the middle of the lower

Source: Reprinted from Kathi Meyer, "Was sind musikalische Erstausgaben?" *Philobiblon,* Jahrg. 8 (1935), Heft 4, 181–184, by permission of Herbert Reichner. Translated by Dr. Kathi Meyer-Baer.

margin of the sheet of music, serve as recognition of a certain edition of a particular publishing house. Therefore, when we know the publishing house and have the plate number before us, we should be able to exactly identify the publication.

The question is, is this number absolutely reliable in identifying an edition? Generally yes, but there are a number of limitations to consider. (1) In that period, very often the whole stock of plates of one publishing house was taken over by another. There then exist two possibilities. Either the new publishing house retained the old plate number and replaced only the title-page; this was easy because the compositions of the period were not bulky and therefore were generally not hardbound, but in soft covers. Or the new publisher changed, in addition to the title-page, the plate number, but retained intact the engraving of music. In this case, the significance of the changed number is clear.

On the other hand, the question arises, is it not now a new edition?

This uncertainty exists also in the first case. The taking over of an old plate number by a new publisher can easily lead to confusion because in one and the same publishing house two different compositions may have the same plate number.

(2) For other reasons, too, one and the same publishing house could use the identical number for entirely different compositions. We must keep in mind that the plate numbers were not introduced as bibliographical aids, but to find the plates in stock quickly, as often as they were needed. Repeated use of a plate number for different works by one publishing house has not been sufficiently considered heretofore. It is this custom which I would like to discuss, as I have been permitted, through the courtesy of the Messieurs Streckers, to examine the old documents of the publishing house of Schott's Söhne in Mainz.

This publishing house still owns a series of stock books (*Plattenbücher*), narrow folio volumes, which list the published works in numerical sequence of the plate numbers. The Schott catalogues have been kept since the year 1802; the entries go back to 1787. Therefore the date 1802 in the entries is valid as a synopsis of the years 1787–1802. Following are a few examples which prove the use of the same plate number for different compositions:

No. 1

1802–1805	Hoffman: Allemande
1816	Grünberger: Neue Orgelstücke nach der Ordnung unter dem Amt der h. Messe zu spielen. Heft 1.

No. 2

1802	Sterkel: Erinnerung des 15ten May 1793.
no date	Mozart: Don Juan.
1816	Grünberger: Neue Orgelstücke, Heft 2.
no date	Agamemnon, ein Ballet (Copy in Stadtbibliothek Frankfurt a.M.)

No. 3

1802–1803	Le Reveil du peuple.
1805	Ouverture de l' opera le Mariage de Figaro.
no date	Sterkel: 6 Lieder. 7te Sammlung.
1813	(N.B.: "this work has been melted down")

No. 40

1811	Sterkel: Recueil de petites pieces a 4 mains.
1827	Mozart: Finale I. Akt. Don Juan als Quartett arrangiert (also in the *Verlagskatalog*).

Such entries of different compositions with the same plate number occur repeatedly up to the number 500. Looking through the stockbooks, the number 501 seems to be the last double entry:

1811	Duetto aus Semiramis mis p. clav. [Duet from Semiramis arranged for pianoforte]
no date	Opferfest pr. P. et V. [Offering for pianoforte and violin]

What can we deduce from these entries? That it was customary, at the turn of the century, to abrade worn out plates or plates that were not needed any more and use their numbers again not only for new editions of the same work, but also for other works in the same publishing house.

As the entries under No. 1 and No. 2 show, the numbers 1, 2, 3, etc., were readily used for the parts (*Hefte*) of serial publications. In this way, also, it was possible to affect double use of the same plate number.

It follows that the numerical sequence of the plate numbers is not always indicative of the chronological order of the publications of a publishing house. Cecil B. Oldman has already referred to this possibility in his most valuable article, "Musical first editions," in *New paths in book collecting,* published in 1934 [reprinted below, pp. 107-116]. He comes to his conclusion for other reasons. He surmises that plate numbers could be reserved in advance for certain publications.

The publishing house of Schott's Söhne—and we may indeed suppose that a number of other publishers used the same method—after voiding and obliterating an engraving, used its number later for another work. A publication which appeared years later [than the numerical sequence of its plate number would indicate] could have a very low number. Here we have the second proof that the plate number is not an unequivocal identification of the works of one publishing house.

A still more important conclusion can be taken from the stock books of Schott, a fact that makes the definition of musical first editions illusory. Here, too, Oldman has advised caution. First of all, one must define exactly what the term musical first edition really means. Oldman, then, differentiates between First edition, Reprint, and New edition, as he had done together with Otto Erich Deutsch in his indispensable essays on early Mozart editions (*Zeitschrift für Musikwissenschaft,* 14, 1931-1932).

I should like to elaborate further on this point. In the stock books we find, for the first numbers, additional remarks—for the later plate numbers this information was apparently entered in other books. Beside the entries of title and plate number there is the added information of the number, as well as date, of the copies made from the plates. As one example we quote the number 23. The short title is given first:

Kreuzer: Ouverture Lodoiska

Jan.	1802	6 copies
Jan.	1802	3 copies
July	1802	24 copies
Sept.	1802	24 copies
Feb.	1803	12 copies
May	1803	36 copies
May	1804	12 copies
Sept.	1804	24 copies
May	1805	12 copies
Sept.	1805	12 copies
Jan.	1806	6 copies
Sept.	1806	6 copies
Jan.	1807	6 copies
Feb.	1807	1 copy
Jan.	1808	12 copies
Sept.	1810	24 copies
May	1812	25 copies
May	1813	25 copies
Nov.	1814	26 copies
April	1816	50 copies
May	1818	50 copies
Aug.	1820	50 copies

This example, chosen at random, seemed especially appropriate because the entries are so copious. There are few examples with such continuous dates and exact information on quantities. It should be noted that the number of copies does not refer to the sold but to the manufactured items. Only as many copies were made—at least by the publishing house of Schott—as were needed at one time, that quantity varying from a minimum of 1 to a maximum of 100. Generally the numbers 6, 12, 24 or 25 and 50 predominate, units perhaps related to the sizes of the paper.

Is it feasible to speak of a new edition for each date [of impression]? This differentiation would certainly go too far. But where should we begin, where stop? Here too, I would agree with Oldman's explanation, but I'd like to go further by posing the question: Is it at all possible to speak of musical first editions at the time in question? Is it not more appropriate to evaluate copies in the manner of graphics—where one speaks of an earlier or later 'state' according to the quality of the copy? Is it not better to identify the items "as one of the first ten copies?" If copies were made over a span of time, naturally differences in the clarity of the engraving can be recognized. The stems of the notes become less distinct, exact; they get blurred. These distinctions I would like to discuss another time.

Now let us investigate some other consequences. Is it really so important to know the number of copies made at one time? Let us clarify that question by an example. A composition of which 12 copies were made, is two years later transferred, along with the whole stock of the original publisher, to another publisher. As mentioned previously, these compositions were not bulky; the few sheets or double sheets were not yet bound. Thus the title-pages could easily be replaced by new ones with the name and address of the new publishing house. The name of the old publisher was erased, the new name engraved over it. This can be recognized in many cases by the deeper tone of ink. Do these changed copies represent a new edition?

Or another case! The publisher remains the same as before, but he has taken a new partner, he has separated from the one with whom he previously worked, or the publishing house has changed its address and so re-engraved its title-pages. Does this represent a reprint? There should be some rules for the terms. It's doubtful, though, that this problem can be solved in every case. Sometimes we will call an edition a 'new edition' if the changes are considerable. But what are the limits? Sometimes the changed copies have to be listed as one and the same edition. Before establishing fixed rules for these definitions and questions, it would be advisable to examine the practices of the early publishing houses more closely. Even the knowledge of the ways of one publisher has taught us many important facts:

1. The same plate number can be used for different compositions.
2. The numerical sequence of the plate numbers is not authoriative throughout for the chronology of the editions.
3. The actual order [sequence] of the editions can only be established with the help of the plate books or journals of the engraver.
4. Sometimes only a few copies at a time were made from the plates.

It would be very gratifying if these few remarks would induce other scholars to thoroughly research the documents of the publishing houses. Archives and stock surveys still exist in a number of early publishing houses. How much easier could the bibliographical task in the area of musical first editions—we will use this expression for the time being—be made by knowing the workshops and their methods and by a compilation of their publications and their peculiarities.

Author's note, 1968: This article was written in 1935. Since then many articles and books have been published on this topic, but as far as I know, not one of them has looked into the stock books. Probably some of the archives of the publishing houses were destroyed during the second World War, especially in Germany. Many should have survived, either with their original owners or in public libraries. The task still awaits scholars in musicology, not only for the purposes of bibliography, but to inform us of the taste and demands of music lovers of that period, as well.

NOTES

[1] G. Kinsky, "Beethoven Erstdrucke bis zum Jahr 1800," 1930; *ibid.*, "Signierte Schubert Erstdrucke," 1931; *ibid.*, "Erstlingsdrucke der deutschen Tonmeister der Klassik und Romantik," 1934.

Musical First Editions

by Cecil B. Oldman

This pioneer essay by Cecil B. Oldman of the British Museum [see A. Hyatt King, "C. B. Oldman: A tribute," Brio, *7 (Spring, 1970), 1-3] discusses various ways of dating undated musical editions. The original bibliography is now so out-of-date and incomplete that I have omitted it. To help the reader, though, I have inserted several notes and vital bibliographical additions to the footnotes.*

Although Oldman apparently intended his words for the private collector, they are very welcome in the literature of music librarianship.

For most music-lovers music is synonymous with music in performance; music as printed matter is for them simply the material which makes performance possible. There have, however, always been a few for whom this material itself has possessed an independent interest; who have collected it for its own sake and valued it as much for its outward form as for its content. But if these have always been a small minority, the number of those who have interested themselves in one special class of printed music—the first editions of the works of the great masters—has been smaller still. It is only in recent years that a growing recognition of the importance of these editions, both as historical documents and as primary sources for the establishment of a correct text, has led to their systematic collection by an ever-growing number of enthusiasts. Unfortunately this growth of interest has not yet called forth any corresponding body of literature to which the novice can turn for guidance. The present paper is, to the best of my knowledge, the first attempt of the kind in English. As a piece of pioneer work I hope it will not be judged too harshly. It does not aim at covering the whole ground, or even at recording the more notable first editions of the chief composers, but endeavours rather to indicate the main problems that confront the would-be collector and to show him how he can best set about to solve them.

At bottom all these problems resolve themselves into one—that of establishing priority of issue. This problem is not peculiar to musical bibliography; it is the fundamental problem for the collector of every sort of printed matter. But for the collector of music it is often particularly difficult to solve, and that for a variety of reasons of which I can only note the most important here. In the first place music hardly ever bears a date. Whether or not it was Handel's publisher John Walsh who was the first to discover the advantage of suppressing this tell-tale piece of information—he is said to have remarked that "women and music should never be dated"—or whether the practice originated in the Netherlands, as others claim, are questions for the curious historian. What is certain is that from about the middle of the eighteenth century a dated piece of music is a very rare exception.[1] Secondly, the fact that music, whether type-set, lithographed or engraved, is generally reproduced by a stereotype process[2] has always made it easy for later impressions from the same plates, with or without correction and from the same or different publishers, to be confused with the original issues. Thirdly, the absence of any real copyright protection for musical publications until about the middle of the nineteenth century,[3] put a premium upon piracy, with the result that within a very short interval after the appearance of a new work by any composer of note there were generally several unauthorised editions upon the market. Certain firms, indeed, seem almost to have specialised in this questionable traffic. Thus, towards the end of the eighteenth century, the German publishers Götz of Mannheim and Hum-

SOURCE: Reprinted from Cecil B. Oldman, "Musical first editions," in *New paths in book collecting,* edited by John Carter, pp. 95-124 (London: Constable, 1934), by permission of Constable Publishers.

mel of Berlin, seem at once to have snapped up all the attractive novelties of their competitors. The collector will be well advised to regard all their publications with suspicion. It is not to be wondered at that composers often felt themselves justified in entering into separate negotiations with several publishers at once. This is the explanation of many curious transactions recorded by the biographers of Haydn and Beethoven which have often shocked their latter-day admirers.[4]

It is obvious that there are two main sources of information at the collector's disposal: external evidence of various kinds and the evidence of the music itself. The first is to be found not only in the detailed bibliographies which are the collector's chief stand-by, but which are, unfortunately, very rare in the field of music, but also in the standard biographies of the composer, in editions of his correspondence, in thematic or other catalogues of his works, in critical editions of the works themselves, in contemporary advertisements or reviews, in publishers' or trade lists, and even in booksellers' catalogues. In all of these, to say nothing of the more general works of reference, the collector may find more or less detailed information that will either solve his problem straight away, or at any rate give him something on which to work. It is, therefore, convenient to discuss them first. For the moment I will confine my attention to the most obvious sources, reserving all reference to the others till I come to examine the evidence afforded by the music itself. The last in my list will be one of the first to engage the collector's attention and fortunately for him it is also one of the best. Booksellers' catalogues contain some of the fullest and most reliable information on the subject of musical first editions that he is likely to find anywhere.[5] In particular, some of the catalogues recently issued by certain German and Austrian dealers are models of careful research and invaluable as works of reference. I only hope that those which I have singled out for special mention in the bibliography at the end of this article are still obtainable, for there is very little else that is specially designed to meet the collector's needs. It is true that for most composers of any importance there exist thematic catalogues in which everything that they wrote is carefully listed—generally in chronological order or in order of opus numbers—and that nearly all of these catalogues contain some information about the earliest printed editions of each work. It is, however, often very meagre and not always accurate. Often nothing is given beyond the name of the original publisher and the date of publication. The fullest, and on the whole the most reliable, are those of Weber by Jähns and of Beethoven and Schubert by Nottebohm, though all three are now badly out of date.[6] Köchel's famous Mozart catalogue,[7] on the other hand, is the despair of the collector: it lumps together editions of varying date and authenticity in no apparent order, and, even so, often refers to them so vaguely that it is impossible to identify them with any certainty. I may remark, parenthetically, that this carelessness has done Mozart himself in ill service. A recent attempt to supplement Köchel's deficiencies[8] has shown how this vagueness of his has led writers on Mozart to draw quite erroneous conclusions as to the popularity (or unpopularity) of his music during his lifetime. So far from his having been a neglected composer, it is now certain that at least seventy of his works were published before his death and many of them in more than one edition. This is only one example of the services that musical bibliography can render to the musical historian.

But to return. More useful to the collector than any of these general catalogues are the few specialised lists dealing exclusively with the printed editions of a composer's works. It is unfortunate that one of the most complete of these is devoted to a composer who is hardly likely to make much appeal to him. O. G. Sonneck's *Catalogue of First Editions of Edward MacDowell* (Washington, 1917), like everything which he undertook, is a masterly piece of work and a mine of information on the curiosities of music publishing. Up to the present [1934] none of the great composers has received such thorough treatment. A good bibliography of printed editions of Bach by Max Schneider was published in the *Bach-Jahrbuch* for 1906, but as it attempts to record all editions up to the date of the commencement of the "Gesamtausgabe" in 1851 it is not able to devote any special attention to the few editions that are of any interest to the collector. Better in this respect is A. Dörfell's *Literarisches Verzeichnis der in Druck erschienenen Tonwerke von Robert Schumann,* published as a supplement to Jahrg. I. of the *Musikalisches Wochenblatt* (Leipzig, 1870), but this, unfortunately, is very difficult to come by. Two composers only have as yet been studied in any detail. The first editions of Beethoven's early works (up to 1800) have been described by Dr. G. Kinsky in an article in *Philobiblon* (Jahrg. III., Heft 9) and Professor O. E. Deutsch has dealt exhaustively with his settings of Goethe in the

Kippenberg-Jahrbuch for 1930. The same two writers have also done valuable pioneer work on the first editions of Schubert. The former has published a short study on the early editions which bear the composer's signature (*Philobiblon,* Jahrg. IV., Heft 5) and the latter has devoted a monograph to his Goethe compositions and edited the very full catalogue of early editions of the composer's works, which was issued by the Vienna firm of V. A. Heck to celebrate his centenary.

On the other great composers little work has yet been done: such sources as are available are set out in the bibliography which I give at the end of the chapter. It is all the more important, therefore, that the collector should familiarise himself with a few general works of reference that contain information on the subject of musical first editions. By far the most useful of these is Robert Eitner's *Biographisch-bibliographisches Quellen-Lexikon der Musiker und Musikgelehrten der christlichen Zeitrechnung bis zur Mitte des 19. Jahrhunderts* (ten volumes, 1899-1904) to which the *Miscellanea musicae biobibliographica* issued under the editorship of Hermann Springer, Max Schneider and Werner Wolffheim (1912-1915) form a rather inadequate sequel. This aims at giving full lists of the works, both in print and in manuscript, of all the composers who fall within its period, and, though it is by no means complete and not always reliable, provides a good starting-point for further researches and is invaluable for rapid reference. It is supplemented to some extent by the many catalogues of public and private collections that have been printed since its publication. In the former category those of the early printed music in the British Museum, of the music in the Royal Collection also housed there, and of the printed music in the Library of the Royal College of Music (all the work of the late W. Barclay Squire) are among the most important, though they are far from giving the collector all the information that he requires. None of them definitely label their first editions as such and none of them record what is one of the most important means of distinguishing between different editions, the so-called "plate-number." Two works to which Eitner was greatly indebted, E. L. Gerber's *Historisch-biographisches Lexikon der Tonkünstler* (two volumes, 1791, 92) and the same author's *Neues Lexikon* (four volumes, 1812-1814) are still of value for the bibliography of the earlier classical composers. For the "romantic" composers, from Schubert onwards, who fall outside the scope of Eitner's work, T. Müller-Reuter's little known *Lexikon der deutschen Konzert-Literatur* (1909, Suppt. 1921) may be consulted. It gives the minimum of information, but what it does give is almost always accurate.

The information that the collector gathers from these sources will vary greatly in extent and value. Sometimes he will find merely the place and date of original publication; if he is lucky he will find a detailed description not only of the first edition proper, but of many later impressions of it. But, however full his information is and however reliable it may seem to be, it will be of little use to him unless he is able to check it and to supplement it by his own researches. Even the fullest bibliography is based upon an inspection of a limited quantity of material; if more had been available its conclusions might perhaps have been different. At any moment the collector may light upon some edition whose existence had been over-looked by previous researchers and he will then be thrown upon his own resources. He must, then, given the necessary data, be able to decide for himself what is a first edition and what is not. For this he needs no profound musical equipment, though the sounder his musical scholarship the better. What he does need is a good knowledge of the special characteristics that distinguish music from other kinds of printed matter and the ability to appreciate their bibliographical significance.

As a preliminary step he could not do better than make up his mind what meaning he intends to attach to the term first edition within his particular field. In view of the special conditions under which music is published, some modification of the terminology now generally in use among book collectors is, I think, unavoidable, but there seems no justification for any radical departure from current usage. On the Continent an attempt has recently been made to distinguish between an *Originalausgabe* (a first edition published during the composer's lifetime, generally but not necessarily with his sanction) and an *Erstausgabe* (a first edition published after his death). The sole object of this distinction is to enhance the status of the editions over which the composer may have exercised some supervision and to relegate to an inferior category those with which he cannot possibly have had anything to do. But the superior authority of the former can surely be taken for granted and does not need to be emphasised by any special label, and in any case the words chosen to mark this distinction are very far from bearing their meaning upon their faces—each might, in fact, just as well have been given the meaning that has been assigned to the other. It seems better, therefore, to stick to the old label "first edition" and to use it as meaning exactly what it implies: the earliest edition in point of time, whenever and however published.[9] More technically it may be defined as: all those copies produced by the first printing from the original plates.

It may happen, however, that these copies are not all exactly uniform. At some stage in the process of printing, the publisher may, for example, take it into his head to pull off a few copies with the vignette or some other feature of the title-page in brown instead of in black, or even to make some slight alterations on the plates themselves. Variations of this kind produce different *states* of the edition. As in the case of books, alterations made after part of the first edition has been put upon the market give rise to different *issues* of it. When at some subsequent date the same publisher, or another publisher who has acquired his stock, prints a fresh batch of copies from the old plates these new copies form a *new impression.* He may, in the meantime, have found it necessary to correct the form of his imprint, to alter the price quoted on the title-page, or even to substitute an entirely new title-page for the old one, but if the main body of the text is still printed from the same plates (it may be with some trifling amendments or additions) these alterations do not give rise to a new edition. Strictly speaking, a *new edition* only comes into existence with the preparation of new plates, but there would be some justification for applying the description to impressions from old plates virtually turned into new by a drastic process of correction, especially if substantial alterations or additions have been made in the text. As often as not a new edition is textually the same as the old: it is only in form that it differs. If the text of such a new edition *has* been corrected or rewritten either by the composer or by some other person, it is best to speak of it as a *revised edition.* Unauthorised editions issued before the authentic edition—and in the eighteenth and early nineteenth centuries they are by no means rare—may be described as *pirated editions;* similar editions issued subsequently, as unauthorised reprints, or simply as *reprints,* if care is taken not to employ this term of later impressions issued by the original publisher.

A few examples will serve to make these meanings clearer and also provide convenient material for further comment. I will take a simple case first. I have before me an edition of one of Mozart's sets of pianoforte variations, those on a March from Grétry's *Mariages Samnites* (No. 352 in Köchel's list). A full catalogue description of it would read somewhat as follows:

Ariette/avec Variations/Pour le Clauecin ou Piano Forte par/W. A. Mozart/No [5]/a Vienne chez Artaria Comp./C.P.S.C.M./68.87.88.89.90. 91.92.110.112.341. 40.Xr.

obl. fol. Engraved. 12 pp. Plate-number: 90. After "Ariette" the words "Marches [sic] des mariages Samnite [sic]" have been added in MS. in this copy. The number 5, denoting its position in the series of variations as published by this firm, is also in MS.

This description requires[10] some explanation. The transcription of the title-page is complete and follows the wording line by line until the letters C.P.S.C.M., with which the text proper may be said to end. Then follow a set of "plate-numbers," in this case at the foot of the page, and the price of the work, here given in its usual position in the bottom right-hand corner. These particulars generally stand outside the main body of the title and are usually quoted, in the order in which I have given them, at the end of the description. The mysterious letters C.P.S.C.M. stand for "Cum Privilegio Suae Catholicae Majestatis" and show that the publisher, Artaria, was in possession of a special "privilege" at the time, giving him limited protection from infringement of copyright. As he only held the privilege from 1782-1792 and from 1806-1816 it is clear that the date of the work's publication must fall within one of these two periods. It is, however, possible to fix its date much more precisely than this. Like most music printed from engraved plates these variations bear at the foot of each page of text a *plate-number* (90) indicating their numerical position in the list of Artaria's publications, and it is obvious that if we already know when some other work bearing a plate-number slightly lower or higher than 90 was published, we can fix the date of this particular work at least approximately. Fortunately we do. From a monograph dealing with Haydn's relations with the firm we learn that Artaria's No. 86 was a collection of easy pianoforte pieces by that composer and that it was published in September, 1786. We are justified, then, in assuming that No. 90 made its appearance much about the same time.[11] As a matter of fact it was advertised as published in the *Wiener Zeitung* for August 5th of that year, along with five companion sets of variations, K.353 (plate-number 87), K.359 (plate-number 92), K.360 (plate-number 91), K.398 (plate-number 89) and K.455 (plate-number 88).

Artaria was at this time the chief publisher of Mozart's compositions and there is every reason to think that the edition which he published in 1786 was the first edition of the work.[12] Is then the copy which I have described a copy of this edition? Obviously not. For in addition to the plate-numbers of the other sets of variations advertised as published at the same time, it bears on its title-page the plate-numbers (110, 112, 341) of three works not mentioned in the advertisement, which must clearly have been published later. In fact a further reference to the monograph I have already mentioned shows that Artaria's 341 cannot have been published before 1791. My copy, then, is not a first edition, but a later impression from the original plates. Other copies exist with additional plate-numbers running up to 805. These constitute a still later impression and cannot have been published before 1800. It is clear that the title-pages of all these successive sets of variations were printed from one and the same plate, new plate-numbers being engraved upon it whenever an addition was made to the series. Consequently all impressions of the earlier sets printed after these alterations had been made bore on the title-page the whole series of plate-numbers up to date. Some time after 1800 Artaria re-issued the whole series with new title-pages worded "Variations pour le Clavecin ou Piano Forte."

As I have said, this is a simple case, but the principle which it illustrates is capable of a much wider application. For in nine cases out of ten what betrays a later impression is some apparently insignificant feature that points to a later date than the other evidence would suggest. A slight change in the publisher's address or in the style of the firm (often carried out so carelessly that the original wording is still faintly discernible as a background), an alteration of the price, an advertisement on the title-page or elsewhere of works known to have been published later—all these may suffice to show that whatever else it may be it cannot be a copy of the first edition strictly so called. Sometimes evidence is present which has, as it were, a backward reference. Many of the vocal scores of Handel's oratorios and operas, for example, exhibit in some numbers two or even three distinct paginations, the superfluous sets being survivals from earlier editions of those numbers either as separate publications or as parts of some miscellaneous collection.[13]

But it is not always possible to distinguish later impressions from earlier so easily as this. Of Beethoven's so-called "Hammerclavier" Sonata (Op. 106), for example, which is known to have been first published by Artaria in September, 1819, there exist at least five different impressions from the original plates.

(1) Has the main portion of the title in French,[14] reading: Grande Sonate/pour le/Piano-Forte/Composée et dediée/à Son Altesse Imperiale Monseigneur/L'Archiduc Rodolphe d'Autriche,/Cardinal et Prince Archevèque d'Olmütz &&&./par/Louis van Beethoven./Œuvre 106./Propriété des Editeurs./A Vienne/chez/ Artaria et Compag:/Leipzig bey Peters, Breitkopf & Haertl, und Hoffmeister [followed by a long list of other foreign firms from whom it could be obtained, and ending . . .] und in den übrigen Kunst-und-Buchhandlungen von/Deutschland, Frankreich, England, der Schweitz, Russland und Pohlen. The title-page bears no price and no mention of the plate-number (2588) which is found inside. There are two "states" of this edition. Some copies have at the foot of the first page a special signature "15 B" (= 15 Bogen or quires) which is absent in others. It is found in all copies of (2) to (5).

(2) Has the title-page in German, reading: Grosse Sonate/für das/Hammer-Klavier./Seiner Kais: Königl: Hoheit und Eminenz,/dem Durchlauchtigsten Hochwürdigsten/Herrn—Herrn Erzherzog/ Rodolph von Oesterreich/Cardinal und Erzbischoff von Olmütz &c &c &c . . . gewidmet/von/Ludwig van Beethoven./Op: 106./Eigenthum der Verleger./ Wien, bey Artaria und Comp:/No. 2588. As will be seen the plate-number is now mentioned on the title-page, but there is still no price.

(3) Is the same as (2), but contains bound up with it a four-page "Catalogue des Œuvres de Louis van Beethoven . . ." up to and including Op. 106, bearing the note "Revidirt von Louis v. Beethoven" at the foot.

(4) Differs from (3) only in having the price (3 fl. 12 Kr.) on the title-page.

(5) Is identical with (4) except that the catalogue of Beethoven's works is now extended to Op. 138 and also includes the works published without opus numbers.

Which of these, then, is the first edition? It is obvious that (5) can at once be eliminated as it contains a reference to works not even composed let alone printed when Op. 106 was first published. (4) again may be reasonably assumed to be merely a later issue of (3). It is also natural to suppose that the impressions without the catalogue are earlier than those with it, for there seems no reason why such a valuable addition should have been dropped once it has been included. But what of

(1) and (2)? For many years even the existence of (1) was not suspected, and when in 1877 T. Steingräber first called attention to it he was curtly told by Nottebohm that according to information he had received from the publishers, no edition with a French title-page had ever been issued. Unfortunately for Nottebohm, Steingräber not only possessed a copy of it, but was ultimately able to retort with another statement from the publishers —presumably from a more conscientious member of the staff—to the effect that the French edition was undoubtedly the first published and that the other did not make its appearance until several years later. In the meantime both contestants had brought forward other considerations to support their case. Nottebohm, for example, pointed out that the advertisement in the *Wiener Zeitung* for September 15th, 1819, though vaguely worded, did at any rate speak of the work as a "grosse Sonate." Steingräber replied that it was recorded with a French title in the *Allgemeine Musikalische Zeitung* for March 1st, 1820. Again Nottebohm asserted that a copy found in the library of the Archduke Rudolph, to whom the work was dedicated, bore the German title; whereupon Steingräber pointed out that another copy formerly in the possession of Wilhelm Rust and inherited by him from his uncle Wilhelm Carl Rust, who made a practice of buying all Beethoven's works as soon as they appeared, had the title in French. Who is to decide where doctors disagree? The answer is—the bibliographer, for there still remains the evidence afforded by the music itself, though it is true that in this case there is very little to go upon. But there is, I think, enough. The fact that in the catalogues which form part of (3) to (5) Op. 106 is described as a "Grande Sonate," that is with a French title, is perhaps not worth stressing. But there is one consideration which is, in my opinion, decisive. If (1) is the first edition and (2) to (5) new impressions of it we get a natural sequence: a French title followed by three German, the German title being retained once it had been introduced. But if the latter came first we have to assume that it was temporarily abandoned for a French title and then readopted for subsequent impressions. We may then accept (1) as the edition which Artaria published in September, 1819. When the other impressions appeared is not known with any certainty. Steingräber assigns (2) and (3) to 1823 and (5) to 1829. The collector is likely to find any one of them, except possibly the last, offered to him as a genuine first edition. In 1856 Artaria brought out a new edition, explicitly described as such upon the title-page. It is perhaps worth noting that this, too, bore the German wording.

This sonata is of special interest to English music lovers as an authorised edition of it appeared in this country almost simultaneously with the original edition. Beethoven had, in fact, at first intended to reserve it for an English publisher. But an all-important letter from Ries, his intermediary, went astray, and becoming nervous as to the success of the enterprise, he thought it wiser to open negotiations with Artaria. However, the London edition duly appeared and cannot have been much later than the Viennese. Realising that it might be rather a tough nut for the British public to crack, Beethoven had suggested—*mirabile dictu*—that parts of the sonata might perhaps be omitted in the English edition. This suggestion was not acted upon, but it was thought advisable to bring out the work in two parts. The first, extending as far as the end of the Adagio, (with the Scherzo misplaced at the end, so that the part might finish in the main key of B flat!) bore the misleading title "Grand Sonata for the Piano Forte. Composed by L. Van Beethoven"; the second was entitled "Introduction and Fugue, for the Piano Forte. Composed by L. Van Beethoven." No opus number was given in either case nor was there any indication that the two works were connected. They appeared with the imprint of "The Regent's [better known as The Royal] Harmonic Institution, Lower Saloon, Argyll Rooms" and bore the plate-numbers 290 and 291. (In a later impression the imprint has been changed to "The Royal Harmonic Institution," the opus number is given, and the price has been reduced.) This edition is worth recording for other reasons than its intrinsic interest, as it displays one feature that is often of the highest importance for the musical bibliographer. The paper on which the first impression is printed bears a date (1819) in the watermark, and it is clear that this furnishes us at least with a *terminus a quo* for the work's appearance. [Editor's insert: See **104-113**, esp. **112**, 101] In the present instance this is not quite what we want: we should like to know not that it cannot have appeared earlier than 1819, but that it did not appear later. If, however, we were dealing with a work which was known to have been first published in 1815, let us say, it would show at once that our copy must be a later impression of it, and this is often all that we want to determine. (I may mention here that the later impressions in this case possess no watermark of any kind.) Unfortunately this practice of dating paper, which was for a time enforced by Royal edict in France, seems later to have been confined to our own country and even here was only in common use from about 1798 to 1825. Whether there were any special reasons for its introduction I have not been able to discover.

A much more detailed picture of the numerous forms in which a piece of music may appear even during the composer's lifetime is provided by the history of Schubert's *Erlkönig*, perhaps the most popular Opus I ever published.[15] Its publication was financed by a few friends of the composer, and it appeared over the imprint of the firm of Cappi and Diabelli, who agreed to sell it on a commission basis. As a check upon sales every copy so issued was numbered and signed by Schubert himself. Three issues of the first impression, which was ready on March 31st, 1821, have so far been distinguished. All have the imprint "Wien, in Comission bey Cappi und Diabelli," all are signed by Schubert and all are without publisher's number on the title-page or plate-number in the text. The second issue, however, already bears at the head of the text a metronome mark which is wanting in the first but is found in all subsequent issues, and the third, though still without plate-number in the text, bears the publisher's number (766) on the title-page, and is further distinguished by the addition of expression marks, for which Schubert himself was responsible, in the text. The control-numbers in Schubert's hand run for the first issue from 1 to about 300, for the second from 300 to about 400, and for the third from 400 to about 500. In 1822 or 1823 Cappi and Diabelli themselves took over all responsibility for the publication and issued a new impression bearing the words "Eigenthum der Verleger," and with their number (766) not only on the title page but also at the foot of the text (C. et D. No. 766). The text itself remained unaltered. In 1824 Cappi parted company with Diabelli and shortly afterwards the *Erlkönig* was duly re-issued with the new imprint "Wien, bey A. Diabelli et Comp.," but otherwise unchanged. A year later the title-page was again amended, slight changes being now made in the wording of the title.[16] The following year saw the publication of a real new edition, the chief characteristics of which were that it consisted of twelve pages instead of the former sixteen, and that the title-page bore a vignette showing the father and son of the song with the *Erlkönig* in the background. Of this there are two states, one with the vignette in black, the other with it in brown; in both the opening words of the title are in brown. The old plate-number was retained, but appears now in the form: D. et C. No. 766. About 1835 another new edition was published, this time described as such, with the words of the song in three languages, German, Italian and French. For this a new title-page was designed showing a medallion portrait of Schubert at the head, flanked on each side by two *putti*. The plate-mark is now: D. & C. No. 766. Some years later a new impression of the edition was issued and the title-page was again changed. Schubert's portrait was retained, but it was now given a different surround: two male figures appearing on his left and two female figures and one male figure on his right. The text remained unaltered. A re-issue of this, by C. A. Spina, Diabelli's successor, which still bears the imprint, "Ant. Diabelli et Comp." upon the title-page, may be detected by means of the plate-number which has been corrected to read: C.S. 766. This cannot have appeared before 1855. A still later issue differs only in omitting the information as to the lithographer which was formerly given at the foot of the title-page. Needless to say the pirates were not idle all this time. Soon after Cappi and Diabelli took over the publication of the work it was reprinted by Cranz of Hamburg and Lischke of Berlin and later other publishers followed suit. For the sake of completeness it is worth recording that the first English edition was published by Wessel and Co. about 1838, with words by Sir Walter Scott.

It will be noticed that in all the examples I have quoted, the various editions—to use the word loosely for once—display certain obvious points of difference that enable them to be readily distinguished from one another. Apart altogether from alterations in the text there are changes in imprint,[17] in plate-mark, in price, in the wording and ornamentation of the title-page, all of which enable the collector, if not to affix a precise date to them, at any rate to arrange them in a rough chronological order.[18] Nor is this list by any means exhaustive. I have, for instance, said nothing so far of the printed wrapper with which music is often issued. In the eighteenth and early nineteenth centuries wrappers were often used for the purpose of protecting the title-page but they were generally blank or at most bore a short form of the title of the work. Later, however, not only did their use become more general and their form more elaborate, but they were found to provide an excellent medium for the advertisement of other works published by the same firm. As these advertisements were continually being altered and added to they obviously provide another easy means by which late impressions can be detected.

Often, however, so far as its actual content goes, a later impression may be identical with its predecessors in every respect. For it sometimes happens that the original plates are used for a whole series of impressions without undergoing alteration of any kind. It is clear that in such cases the evidence of plate-mark, imprint, etc., will be positively misleading, for they will be evidence of the date of issue not of the particular copy but only of the original impression. Even here, however, the collector is not entirely without resource. The character and strength of the impression, to say nothing of the quality of the paper, often tell an unmistakable tale. It may be found, for example, that a direct printing from the plates has been replaced by some stereotype process, or, if the plates have still been used, that they have become worn or cracked with age. Both are obvious signs of lateness of issue.

I began this chapter with a reference to the special difficulties of musical bibliography. I have, I hope, now shown not only in what they consist, but how they can best be surmounted. They arise chiefly from the lack or inaccessibility of the requisite information: not only are the works of reference often silent, but the evidence of the music itself is often ambiguous. In the absence of a date recourse must be had to certain other distinguishing features, some if not all of which may be only survivals from some earlier stage of the work's history. Details which are relevant in one case may be irrelevant in another and often no conclusions are possible at all until a mass of material has been brought together and compared. But to the enterprising collector these difficulties are a stimulus rather than a discouragement. If they were removed his task would be easier, but he would be missing half the fun. At its present stage musical bibliography may be one of the most tantalising, but it is also one of the most fascinating of hobbies. Enough is known to make a start possible, but not enough to take away the joy of discovery. And the collector need not fear that his hobby will make undue demands upon his purse. Musical first editions are still ridiculously cheap. Very few cost more than a few pounds and many can still be picked up for a few shillings. But the market is becoming more and more organised–it is no longer possible to find first editions of Handel in the sixpenny tub, which was where I discovered a few years ago the only first editions of Handel that I possess–and before long the speculative buyers will come rushing in and prices will begin to soar. For the collector of moderate means there is no time like the present. If he waits too long he will find that another "new path" has already been closed to him.

NOTES

[1] It is perhaps worth noting that works published on a subscription basis were often dated, and that certain North German firms, *e.g.,* Hartnoch, of Riga, continued to date their music long after the practice had been generally abandoned. The date of copyright, which often appears on modern music, is, for reasons which will appear later, of little value as a guide to the date of publication.

[2] Metal plates and lithographic stones are obviously in themselves in the nature of stereos, and type-set music has been generally printed from stereotype-plates, at any rate since the early years of the nineteenth century. For a full account of the various processes that have been or still are employed for the printing of music I must refer the reader to William Gamble's *Music Engraving and Printing* (London, 1923), and to the other works mentioned at the end of this paper. I must content myself here with the briefest of outlines. The earliest music printing was either from type or from wooden blocks. Copper-plate engraving, in spite of its obvious suitability for the reproduction of music, does not seem to have been used for this purpose until the end of the sixteenth century, but once it came it came to conquer: for a time typographic music printing was almost driven from the field. Its decline was hastened when, at the beginning of the eighteenth century, the use of plates of softer metal–zinc, pewter, or specially softened copper–simplified the process of engraving by making it possible for the heads and tails of the notes to be stamped by means of a punch. In 1756 Breitkopf, of Leipzig, invented an improved system of printing music from movable type that brought typographic music into favour again for a time. But it necessitated the employment of an enormous number of sorts and proved to be too expensive for general use. In 1796 Senefelder, of Munich, discovered the process of lithography and at once saw the possibilities of its application to music printing. It is well known that the young Weber worked for a time with him and himself lithographed some of his earliest compositions. The subsequent history of music printing has been comparatively uneventful. Most modern music is printed by a combination of the processes of engraving and lithography. The music is first stamped and engraved on pewter plates and then transferred by the off-set process either to a stone or to a sheet of zinc and worked off on a lithographic press. Typographic music printing is now used chiefly for musical quotations printed simultaneously with letter-press. It is generally quite easy to tell by what process a particular piece of music has been printed. In type-set music, even after stereotyping, the joins between the units of type can al-

ways be detected. Music engraved direct from metal plates may be distinguished from lithographed music by the greater sharpness of the impression, and from both lithographed and stereotyped music by the deep ridge produced in the paper by the edge of the plate.

[3]The English Copyright Act of 1842 gave protection for a period of forty-two years (or for the life of the composer, plus seven years, whichever period was the longer) in England and the Colonies, but there was no international protection of musical publications until the Berne Convention of 1886. Previously, particular firms had often been granted "privileges," but these were generally for a short period and had no validity in any territory outside the jurisdiction of the power that granted them.

[4]For instance, in 1787 Haydn sent to Forster, his London publisher, six Quartets (Op. 50) which had been commissioned by Artaria and were on the point of being published by him. Artaria knew nothing of the transaction until Forster's edition had actually appeared—some months before his own. Similarly, Beethoven's *Variations on a Waltz by Diabelli* (Op. 120) were offered by him to Peters in Leipzig, Lissner in St. Petersburg and Boosey in London before Diabelli's edition had been published and without his knowledge. In this case it was the English publisher who was disappointed. Peters and Lissner declined Beethoven's offer. Boosey accepted, on the understanding that the work would not be published in Vienna until he had published it in London, but when Beethoven's manuscript finally reached him a copy of the Vienna edition was already in his hands, and the work had also been published in Paris. But it is to be noted that it is only the way in which these particular transactions were conducted that is open to criticism. In general, the composer's title to dispose of his own foreign rights were fully recognised: they were not as a rule covered by the terms of his original contract, and the only way in which he could draw any profit from the sale of his works abroad was by making his own arrangements with foreign firms. I know of no instance of a composer deliberately selling the same work to more than one publisher in the same country.

In fairness to his "original" publisher, but also to guard against the danger of piracy, the composer generally stipulated that the foreign edition should appear at the same time, or generally not earlier, than the home edition. It was not always his fault if something went wrong and the foreigner got in first. Into the thorny question of simultaneous publication, which may have occurred under these conditions, and certainly occurred later (from about 1840 onwards), when the publisher began to replace the composer as bargaining agent for foreign rights and found in simultaneous publication the only way of securing protection abroad without losing it at home, I cannot enter here, except to say that the collector's chief difficulty is to discover whether in any particular case simultaneous publication actually took place. The fact that if it did he ought strictly to recognise the existence of two "first" editions need not worry him. If he feels that he must make a choice between them he will naturally give his preference to the one issued by the firm with whom the composer first entered into negotiations. Thus he will prefer the Breitkopf editions of Beethoven's Op. 76-79 to those issued at the same time by Artaria in Vienna. In the eighteenth century these foreign editions were usually set up afresh from a manuscript provided either by the composer or by the original publisher, though occasionally, as in the case of Longman's edition of Haydn's *Divertimenti* (Op. 31), the sheets of the original edition were imported and issued with a new title page. In the course of the nineteenth century it became customary for the original publisher himself to print a certain number of copies with special title pages for the foreign market. (For the early history of the practice see H. G. Bohn's *The Question of Unreciprocated Copyright in Great Britain,* London, 1851.) More rarely, as for the English edition of the favourite airs from Bellini's *La Somnambula,* published by Boosey in 1831, the original plates were placed at the disposal of the foreign publisher.

[5]Cf. Rosenthal, "The 'music antiquarian'," above; especially pp. 87-88—*Editor.*

[6]Many of the specific thematic catalogues mentioned are now superceded; see the MLA *A check list of thematic catalogues* (1954) and *Supplement* (1966) cited in full below [**145 & 146,** plus **147,** 181.] —*Editor.*

[7]These remarks refer to the 1905 edition of the Köchel catalogue, not to the current sixth edition published in 1964.—*Editor.*

[8]*Mozart-Drucke,* by O. E. Deutsch and C. B. Oldman (*Zeitschrift für Musikwissenschaft,* December, 1931, and April, 1932).

[9]The case of simultaneous publication of the same work by different publishers I have already discussed. Another difficulty arises in the case of large-scale works such as operas, oratorios, symphonies and concertos, where what is essentially the same work may be issued to the public in more than one form, not only in score and in parts, but also in arrangements of various kinds. Here it is often necessary to recognise several first editions of the same work: the first edition of the score, the first edition of the parts, and so on. Whether these various forms are published simultaneously or successively, and, in the latter case, in what order they are published, will depend partly upon the character of the work (operas, for example, are nearly always first published in vocal score and instrumental works in parts), partly upon the popularity of the composer and partly upon the enterprise (or rashness) of the publisher. Thus Beethoven's potboiler, *Wellington's Sieg* ("The Battle of Vittoria"), was published by Steiner & Co. in 1816 in no less than eight different forms—in score and parts, in arrangements for string quartet, piano solo, piano duet, etc.—at least six of which were on sale on the same day. On the other hand, the score of the "Eroica" symphony, the parts of which appeared in 1806, was not published till 1823, [An unauthorized score of the "Eroica" was, however, published in London by Cianchettini and Sperati in 1809.] and not a single one of Mozart's larger works was published in score during his lifetime. In either case the collector finds himself in difficulty. If publication is simultaneous, he must recognise the existence of several editions with equal claims to be considered the first; if publication is successive, he will often be forced to give precedence on grounds of priority of issue to an edition which does not correspond at all closely to the work as the composer wrote it and may even be incomplete. It is clear that in the former case he must either try to acquire all the editions published simultaneously or content himself with the most important. If either the score or the parts are among the editions first published he can safely neglect all the others as simple arrangements from them. If not, he will give his preference to the version that corresponds to them most closely. In the case of successive publication he is

bound, *qua* collector of first editions, to prefer the edition first published: whether he need trouble himself with the editions which succeed it will depend upon the degree of its correspondence with the work as the composer wrote it. Arrangements made by the composer himself fall into a special class: they possess an independent interest and are best regarded as separate works.

[10] Precisely the type of bibliographic description which Deutsch finds inadequate; cf. n. 11, p. 126–*Editor.*

[11] I must plead guilty to a slight simplification of the issue here. For it appears from the same source that Artaria's No. 93 was published in July, 1789, and his No. 101 as early as 1784. As plate numbers were often assigned to forthcoming works long before they actually appeared, any advance or postponement of the projected date of publication was liable to give rise to anomalies of this kind. Plate numbers are, in fact, never a safe guide to the precise order in which a series of works was published. It will not do, for example, to assume that just because the score of a symphony is numbered 50 and the parts 51 that the former must have been published first. This list of Artaria's editions of Haydn contains only 157 entries. A full list of plate numbers for this and other important firms with the corresponding dates of publication would obviously be an invaluable aid to the collector. Some twenty years ago the late Mr. Barclay Squire, in an article in the *Quarterly Magazine* of the International Musical Society, pointed out the importance of such lists, and published some of the results of his own researches, but no one has yet attempted to follow his lead. [Editor's insert: See **100-103,** 101] Squire headed his paper "Publishers' Numbers" [*Sammelbände der Internationalen Musik-Gesellschaft,* XV (1914), 420-427] but this term is best confined to numbers occurring on the title-page, which may or may not be the same as those in the text. When the latter have, in addition to the number, the initials of the publishing firm, they are best described as plate marks. [Editor's insert: Cf. Meyer-Baer, p. 103, paragraph 5]

[12] Köchel, after wrongly citing Jahn as saying that the work was advertised in 1787 (Jahn correctly gives 1786), gives a list of editions only two of which he qualifies as *Ältere Ausgaben,* one published by André, of Offenbach, and the other by Longman and Broderip. Both were certainly reprints of Artaria's edition, which had been pirated soon after its appearance by Schmitt, of Amsterdam.

[13] See on this point the admirable article by William C. Smith, *The Earliest Editions of Handel's Messiah,* in *The Musical Times* for November, 1925.

[14] During the eighteenth century, and a great part of the nineteenth, French and Italian were the languages most favoured by composers and publishers for the titles and title-pages of their works. The collector must beware of assuming that any edition bearing a title-page in a language other than that of the country in which it was issued must necessarily be of foreign origin or a reprint from a foreign edition.

[15] For this I am indebted to Professor O. E. Deutsch's *Die Originalausgaben von Schuberts Goethe-Liedern* and to private information kindly supplied by him.

[16] *E.g.,* "Erstes Werk" appears for "Ites Werk," "nach Göthe" for "von Goethe," and the words "fur eine Singstimme mit Begleitung des Pianoforte" are added. Moreover the price, formerly given in both "Convention" currency and Vienna currency, is now given in the former only.

[17] Changes in imprint often provide the readiest means of dating music, but the collector is at present hampered by the lack of any comprehensive history of music publishing. The valuable work of Frank Kidson on *British Music Publishers, Printers and Engravers* (London, 1900), has so far had no successors. [Editor's insert: See Duckles 2nd ed., 1186-1255.] There are, however, a few monographs on particular firms and useful articles on the most important of them in the *Dictionaries* by Grove and Riemann.

[18] It is obvious that correct order, which can often be determined on purely bibliographical grounds, is of more immediate importance to the collector than precise dating, which must generally wait until he has opportunities for detailed research.

Music Bibliography and Catalogues[1]

by Otto Erich Deutsch

This article, complementary to "Musical first editions," amplifies and updates certain aspects of Oldman's discussion. A landmark in the literature of descriptive music cataloguing, Deutsch here points out some aids for adequately describing and dating musical compositions.

Three considerations encouraged me to accept the Society's kind invitation to address a gathering of experts on a specialized, and not yet fully developed, branch of bibliographical science. First, the growing recognition among leading British librarians that the difference between music and ordinary printed books is so great that special rules are needed for the comprehensive cataloguing of music. Secondly, the Music Library Association of America has sketched a code of rules for cataloguing music; and lastly, having worked on this subject for over twenty years, I feel that the result of my experience may perhaps be of some help to librarians and bibliographers.

In appearance and make-up bound music books resemble any other printed book; they are, however, very different. Bibliographically, they are in many respects more closely allied to maps than to type-set books. In what follows I hope to explain these differences in so far as they are likely to concern cataloguers of music and music catalogues, and to offer some hints for overcoming difficulties which arise from them.

To engrave, punch, or lithograph music is a craft more akin to that of a calligrapher than to that of a compositor. Whereas a compositor need not be an author in order to avoid errors and misinterpretations in setting up his type, only the engraver of music who is also a musician can hope to do so. The ideal engraver of music would be the composer himself. It is known that Sebastian Bach engraved at least the E♭Prelude in the Third Part of his *Clavier-Uebung;* Telemann and Leopold Mozart also were quite expert engravers, and young Weber was an ambitious lithographer.

The materials used in printing music are different from those used in printing books. To give one example of the confusion which may arise from this cause in detecting an edition or impression: it often happens in the course of printing that some of the copper plates become worn or damaged and have to be renewed before another issue of fifty or so copies of a work can be printed. Despite the fact that these new plates are seldom identical with the originals and often bear new mistakes, as well as alterations and corrections, sometimes authorized by the composer himself, the work is in most cases published with the same title-page, although, from a librarian's point of view, it is, in fact, a different issue. For instance: Mozart's Piano Sonatas, op. VI (K.330–2), published by Artaria in Vienna, is known to me in at least four variants with single damaged plates renewed, so that in the latest variant little more is left but the title-page of the first edition. It is easy for the experienced eye to distinguish the work of later engravers, but the inexperienced scholar may inadvertently use the latest variant as his source when compiling a critical edition. You can well imagine how widely this variant may differ from Mozart's original manuscript.

Another tiresome characteristic of printed music, the absence of dates, is due to the practice of the music publisher. While the publisher of books normally dated his publications and did not conceal the issue of a second or subsequent edition, for nearly 250 years the publisher of music intentionally concealed not only the date but also, more often than not, any indication of the edition. John Walsh, senior (d. 1736), is said to have introduced this bad habit into England, probably with paper and books from the Netherlands. It is not correct, however, to credit him with the famous saying, 'Women and Music should never be dated';

SOURCE: Reprinted from O. E. Deutsch, "Music bibliography and catalogues," *The Library,* 23 (March, 1943), 151–170, by permission of The Bibliographical Society.

this sentence originated in Goldsmith's *She Stoops to Conquer* (1773). Burney remarked, in 1789, that the dates of publication in music were 'as carefully concealed as the age of stale virgins'. The earliest reason for omitting dates on music may have been piracy; later, and during the nineteenth century, it was the custom to believe that 'old music was as unsaleable as old almanacks'. French publishers and some German publishers continued to date their music some time after their English colleagues had abandoned the practice. Walsh dropped it round about 1715, but not completely: for besides dating music which was published for the composer, Walsh senior and later his son also published serials and periodicals which are dated as late as 1756. For some unknown reason they even dated the 'Songs in [Handel's] Alexander Balus' with the exact day: 19 April 1748.[2] It is highly satisfactory to be able on occasion to associate a month as well as a year with a publisher's number, as with *The British Musical Miscellany* for March, June, and July 1734, which bears Walsh's numbers 511, 520, and 522. The introduction of such numbers was another of Walsh's innovations, and is now adopted by the whole trade. Unfortunately, we know only about 150 of Walsh's numbers, out of a probable 700, the earliest being number 57–Loeillet of Ghent's 'Six Sonatas of two parts', *c.* 1715–and the latest number 683, used in 1741 for Hasse's 'Six Concertos op. 4' and about 1745 for Howard's *Musical Companion.* Nobody who knows anything about the Walshes would expect to find their publisher's numbers used in strict chronological sequence; nevertheless they are of some use to the bibliographer.

Thus in many cases it is only by using the methods of a detective that the bibliographer or cataloguer can determine the date of a first edition or the differences between subsequent issues or editions. Many of these distinctions are to be found not only on the title-page, which is normally the cataloguer's main source of information, but also in the text. This branch of bibliography is still so young that few reference books have as yet been published to aid the cataloguer.

It is agreed that any catalogue of a general library has to use short titles, even in the difficult case of music; nevertheless, it is dangerous to abbreviate the title, because in many instances the exact wording of the title is in itself a sufficient indication of the edition. In this connexion it should be noted that even W. Barclay Squire in his *B.M. Catalogue of Printed Music published between 1487 and 1800* (a work used as a main source of information in most British libraries) was compelled to give short titles only, even in cases where he knew that another edition had a title differing only in the missing words. The use of this catalogue as an infallible source is, therefore, very dangerous for a cataloguer who is without the bibliographical knowledge of Barclay Squire and lacks the opportunities he had for examining other editions. Hence numerous mistakes in dating music are made in many music catalogues. But even in a bibliography (for example of Handel's first editions) it would usually suffice if the compiler quoted only one, or at most a few, of the many points of difference between the issues; the points quoted must, however, be the essential differences.

If it is impossible in every case to quote the full title in a catalogue entry, it is all the more essential to include the name of the publisher. In support of this statement the many English editions of Handel's 'Messiah', either full or piano scores, all of which were issued with the same or practically the same title may be quoted. General catalogue rules for books in English libraries often require the name of the publisher and printer to be quoted in the case of rarities only, e.g. books printed before 1641. Music publishing did not become general before about 1700, with the result that great rarities are to be found at a much later date among music: the date before which the publisher is to be quoted must, therefore, be advanced.

It is not of much help to the reader to find the date indicated only by the century. If the cataloguer is not permitted to give the full imprint, he should attempt to ascertain the date as accurately as possible. One obvious source of such information is Frank Kidson's *British Music Publishers,* and similar reference books should be consulted. The dated watermark may be of use, especially in some English publications about 1800.

The cataloguer should be permitted to add to his catalogue entry the publisher's number, sometimes given on the title-page, or the plate-number, to be found (since the end of the eighteenth century) at the bottom of the pages of the text. These numbers are very often a help in dating the publication, and the possibilities of identification by this means will be increased as our knowledge of the chronology of the numbers of the various publishers grows.

Furthermore, the prices, commonly given since about 1800, are sometimes of use in distinguishing editions; but these details, like additional paginations or different types of paper, may be left to the bibliographer.

Let us now consider for a moment the question of format and size. It should be remembered that most music was published unbound and bound subsequently by private owners or by libraries, and that indiscriminate cutting in the process of binding has resulted in great variation in the final size (as in the case of incunabula). To quote the size in centimetres or inches is, therefore, of little value. Probably, the best and simplest method of giving the size would be to give the height of the printed matter, measuring from the top line of the first staff to the bottom line of the last on the first full page of music.

Where a work is not adequately described by its title, particularly in the case of the great masters, its nature should be indicated in the catalogue entry by the method adopted in the standard thematic index (the accepted list of the composer's works) or according to the authorized edition of his complete works (e.g. Mozart, Köchel number; Bach, Bach-Gesellschaft number, &c.).

Additional information, for instance the type of score (full score, vocal score, separate parts, &c.), should be noted where the title does not clearly indicate the nature of the work. While the opus number is of no help in the case of Mozart or Haydn, in others it is most useful.

What is then the present state of music catalogues in the great public, private, and university libraries?

Although the rules for general catalogues apply, with certain restrictions and modifications, to music catalogues, the music catalogues are, so far as I know, formed as separate units apart from the general catalogues—in some cases on cards, in others as bound volumes of slips. The great majority are arranged primarily under the composers' names in alphabetical order. While private collectors of music usually arrange the entries under each composer by following the order given in the standard thematic catalogues, that is to say, mainly in chronological order, the general libraries divide the works of a composer into classes or forms (e.g. Operas, Oratorios, other Vocal Music, Orchestral Music, Chamber Music, other Instrumental Music, &c.) and, within each class or form, arrange the entries either in alphabetical, chronological, or opus order—the number of entries, varieties of titles, or numbering of the works suggesting the final method of arrangement for each composer.

It is unfortunate from the point of view of the cataloguer that we do not possess even a complete list of works for many of the great masters (to say nothing of a complete thematic catalogue). For example, more than two hundred and fifty works of Beethoven, several still not published, are missing in Nottebohm's *Thematic Index*[3] as well as in the so-called *Gesamtausgabe.* In the case of Haydn it is much worse: only very incomplete lists of his works exist, many of the works were never published, and some early printed works are not mentioned at all in the Haydn literature.

It is necessary for music scholars and cataloguers to devise means of dealing with this difficulty. One private collector of music of the great masters, specializing in Haydn, has introduced a thematic card-catalogue, in addition to the usual catalogue—this method being the only possible means of identifying certain of his works from a catalogue.[4] In making an index it is sometimes necessary to use a kind of musical alphabet—in the case of the countless dances of Schubert, for example. All the themes are first transposed into the key of C major and then they are arranged in alphabetical order of the notes in the first bars of each dance. This method which, so far as I know, has been used only by certain editors in preparing new editions, is, no doubt, too complicated to be of use to cataloguers. In exceptional cases, e. g. Domenico Scarlatti's many little piano pieces, a simpler system would be to arrange them in groups, first according to the time-signatures, and secondly in the order of their keys. In fact Ricordi's Thematic Index of Scarlatti's 'Sonatas for Clavicembalo' (Milan, 1937) is arranged 'in order of tonality and rhythm'.

Although Barclay Squire, some thirty years ago, published a few short and incomplete lists of English, German, and Dutch publishers' numbers of the eighteenth century, which he had noted during his experience in two London libraries, private collectors of music were the first to recognize their importance and to make a serious study of the subject. As I said in my introductory remarks, they are often of assistance in dating music.[5] I remember my surprise, many years ago, when I encountered such attempts, first in a private collection in Berlin and later in the pocket-book of a Viennese collector. Shortly afterwards I procured two large books and started a collection of Austrian and German publishers' numbers. In these books I entered, in columns, the names and dates of the publishing firms, and any changes of ownership or address. Down the left-hand side of the page I wrote, in order, the years and under each firm the publisher's numbers and dates of publications as I was able to collect them. Of course, the contents of each column vary; little information has been entered under some firms, but for others, as for instance in the column set aside for Artaria & Co., most of the numbers from 1779 to 1856 have been noted and dated, because all the printed and manuscript catalogues of this firm (about fifty in all) were placed at my disposal. Many entries have also been made for the firm of Brietkopf & Härtel and for some of the smaller German and Austrian publishers. Little is known about the publishers of France, Holland, America, and Russia, and in spite of Frank Kidson's very valuable book it is still difficult to find much useful information about English publishers' numbers. A great deal of valuable knowledge on this subject must have been collected in the past forty years by librarians and bibliographers all over the country, and I think the time is ripe for this knowledge to be placed in a common pool and passed on to some scholar who is willing to include it in a new edition of Kidson's *British Music Publishers.* William C. Smith, who is particularly interested in a new edition of Kidson's book, has added to Barclay Squire's collection of eighteenth-century publishers' advertisements in London newspapers. These advertisements have been a source of great importance for the dating of English music. In the meantime, while working on early Handel editions, I have dealt with the publications of Walsh and his successors, from about 1700 to 1785. With the help of about twenty-five publishers' lists, printed as notes on title-pages or tables of contents, or as supplements, I have compiled an almost complete catalogue of Walsh's publications—something that Walsh himself never attempted! From 1794 to about 1829 a dated watermark is to be found in some English music; curiously enough, where we find the watermark the music is usually printed on inferior paper. Such a watermark may be found a little earlier in French music also. This custom, however, has never been explained.[6] Such dates, of course, give only a *terminus post quem;* and since one may find differently dated watermarks in the same volume, or even a dated title-page and a differently dated watermark in the same volume, only the latest date can be considered.

The recording of publishers' numbers in the music catalogues of general libraries is often opposed by those in authority. In the National Library at Vienna the Keeper of the Music Department has included these numbers for the last twenty years although the practice was not officially sanctioned. Georg Schneider, in his *Handbuch der Bibliographie* (3rd edition Leipzig, 1926, American edition New York, 1934), acknowledges the necessity of including the publisher's numbers except where notice of copyright is given, that is to say, during the last sixty years, since this at least indicates the date of the first edition. He rightly demands that the name of the publisher be given in full. In the University Library, Cambridge, the inclusion of the publishers' numbers and the name of the publisher in the Music Catalogue entries was recently authorized, and I am inclined to believe that the Bodleian and the National Library of Scotland are also anxious to adopt similar methods in cataloguing music. The rules of the British Museum have been more liberal in this respect, but here, too, the publishers' numbers are still not introduced.

To make my suggestions appear less revolutionary I would like to discuss the proposed new rules recently drawn up in America. These proposals are set forth in four booklets issued in 1941–2 under the title *Code for Cataloging Music.*[7] Chapter I is reprinted from *A.L.A. Catalog Rules. Preliminary Second American Edition.* Chapters 2, 3, and a supplement called *Code for Cataloging Phonograph Records* have been compiled by a Committee of the Music Library Association—these also are marked 'Preliminary Version'. Chapter 1 deals with Entry and Heading; Chapter 2 with title; Chapter 3 with Imprint, and Chapters 4 and 5, which have not yet reached me, will deal with Collation and Notes. Preceding the rules there is in each book a carefully compiled list of definitions of terms used for musical forms.

In the chapter on Entry, under the heading, 'Vocal Music' and before the definitions, we find a special introduction in which the following question is asked: 'Does the musical interest of the work outweigh its literary interest?' This consideration did in fact decide the fate of some collections of music in the general libraries of Europe at the beginning of the nineteenth century. At that time, for instance, the Vienna Hofbibliothek collected only vocal music because the authorities were not interested in collecting instrumental music, or indeed any type of music. In other words the *texts* were collected, *not* the music. Judging from the small amount of music of that period in the British Museum, e.g. the few English first editions of Chopin, it would seem the appreciation of music was not much higher among British librarians.

But this question is of practical importance even to-day, if one has to decide whether libretti belong to the music department or to the general library. O. G. Sonneck has dealt with this question in masterly fashion in the preface to his *Catalogue of Opera Librettos printed before 1800* (Library of Congress).[8] Again, the method of dealing with certain classes of songs, &c., in the libraries is also open to question. I am thinking more particularly of literary works which have been set to music and only published in that form. Apparently the general library and the music department have an equal claim, and a compromise might be reached by making an entry in both the General and Music Catalogues.

The Committee of the Music Library Association stresses the need 'to establish a Conventional, Filing, or Standard Title' in the catalogue entry between the composer's name and the title proper. In the case of the title proper the proposed rules differentiate between Distinctive, Generic, Indeterminate, and Collective Titles. To give examples: *Il Flauto Magico*, or *Erlking*; Pianoforte Sonata in E♭ minor, op. 21; *Études*; *Œuvres complètes*, or J. S. Bach's *Das musikalische Opfer*.

Peculiarities confined only to music titles are the Opus Number, the Serial Number, and the Key. Opus numbers have been in common use, particularly in Germany and Austria, since the beginning of the nineteenth century. During the time of Mozart and Haydn, however, they were usually assigned by the publishers, and in consequence, more often than not, one finds these numbers duplicated. The term 'Opus' was even used by some firms for their own publications; e.g. by Rellstab of Berlin or Thaddäus Weigl of Vienna. Serial numbers were for the most part allotted after the death of the composer and are seldom in strict chronological order; hence the use of these old numbers, or letters, for the symphonies of Haydn is both deplorable and misleading.[9] Again, serial numbers were often used by publishers for their own series, e.g. Peters Edition No. 000, Volksausgabe Breitkopf & Härtel, No. 000, &c.; these serial numbers are, however, of no great importance. Key indication can only be given for music subsequent to 1700, since earlier music was based on a different system of tonality. As modern music frequently disregards classical tonality, it may well be that the unhappy music cataloguer of the future will find this indication no longer of any assistance in classifying his refractory material.

The title-pages of printed music, which are only rarely set in type, constitute a problem in themselves. There are, of course, instances of engraved title-pages in ordinary printed books, and here also the question arises how they should be transcribed for bibliographical purposes. In cataloguing, it is necessary to decide the correct order in which words and lines are to be read and quoted. I, personally, adopt the procedure of transcribing first all lines lying on the central axis of the page; secondly, the marginalia, in the order left before right. This procedure, however, is possible only in ordinary cases, where the lines of the title run horizontally. To show an extraordinary case, I reproduce an elegant but strange English title from the beginning of the nineteenth century.[10] Indicating the division of lines and imitating the lettering are of little use; indeed, in the case of English music printed about 1700 I have shown that such a procedure may lead to confusion and to mistakes.[11] Failing a facsimile of the title-page, a simple transcription of the full title is desirable. In general library cataloguing it may be necessary to abbreviate the title; the bibliographer, however, should never do so. Separate issues frequently differ only in their title-pages, which may be modified or completely changed. In general the latter occurs only if the original plate has become worn, as also in the case of individual plates of the text. The American rules make particular mention of polyglot title-pages, and of wrappers with titles and advertisements. The latter may also occur on the title-page itself, on a list of contents, on the last page or, lastly, as a special supplement. In parenthesis I would like to say that such advertisements showing lists of works by a given composer or published by a given publisher are of great importance in deciding the bibliographical standing of the copy in hand or of other works. The presence of such lists should be indicated by the bibliographer in the description of the work; and in the case of publishers' lists I would suggest that a note should be kept of them, and perhaps later they should be reproduced photostatically, collected, and exchanged between libraries. Indications of privilege, often dated and usually printed on separate pages, are of similar importance. In eighteenth-century music printed in England these are usually found at the beginning of the book; if printed in France, at the end. Of importance are also: lists of subscribers, which may be lengthened in later issues, or omitted altogether; a frontispiece, the imprint of which may bear a date or show a change in the name and style of the publisher; a list of errata or alternatives,[12] and finally, in recent times, separate pages with a notice of copyright.

The 'distinctive' title may also be used, generally abbreviated and in square brackets, as the conventional title on the catalogue slip. In the case of polyglot titles, the form used by the composer should be chosen for this purpose; otherwise, that used in the first edition. If, however, the conventional title takes the form of a 'generic' title, it should be translated, if possible, into English. English terms should be used both for the form and for the instruments. The generic form of conventional title includes: the medium of performance, the serial number, key and opus number, if these do not occur in the actual title. In the case of pianoforte works, four hands must be specified, whether on one or two pianos. According to the American recommendations, the order in which instruments should be quoted in describing chamber music and orchestral works is as follows: 'In combination with other instruments the stringed instruments are to be named last; e.g. Trio, flute, violin and violoncello.' All other instruments—wind, percussion, plectral, &c. 'are to be named in alphabetical order in one list; e.g. Bassoon, clarinet, harp, oboe, trumpet'. For general libraries this may be useful. Most private libraries adhere to the order given on the title-page, or in a definitive score, or in the standard thematic index, so as to be able to check rapidly whether parts are complete or not. It is necessary to verify serial numbers in the light of the thematic index (if there is one) or of a standard biography; this is particularly necessary where serial numbers have been misused (for instance, in Mozart's *divertimenti*).[13]

The American recommendations do not mention the dedication often found on the title-page. This also may be helpful to the cataloguer in reaching a decision about the first edition of a particular work. Beethoven's Sonatas, op. 2, for example, are dedicated to Haydn: in the first issue the latter is described as 'Maître de Chapelle'; in the second issue, as 'Docteur en Musique'.

The third chapter of the American recommendations concerns the imprint. It is mentioned that since the beginning of this century (strictly, since 1886) the carefully preserved silence concerning the date has been broken by the notice of copyright—which, however, refers only to the first edition. This is often to be found not on the title-page but on the back of this, or at the foot of the first page of the text—where also, nowadays, may be found an indication of the publisher. The Code observes that the same publishers' numbers are usually used again for new editions; in such instances, therefore, they offer no help in dating. The dated acquisition stamp—a heaven-sent invention of English and American libraries—offers yet another possibility of dating the copy; so does the date of the first private owner. According to the recommendations imprints are to be distinguished even when there are changes only in wording, spelling, or abbreviation of christian names. I would like to add that changes in the address of the composer, who in the capacity of publisher of his own works often signs or initials all copies, may be of importance. This is the case with the valuable editions of François Couperin at the beginning of the eighteenth century.[14] Again, change in the address of the publisher, even in the house number, may be of importance, as in the case of Beethoven's Sonata op. 26, first published by Jean Cappi in Vienna. I would mention also the importance of the price indicated; to understand changes in price it is often necessary to have some knowledge of the history of currency. These details may all be of significance also for the investigator bent on textual revision; they may stimulate him to compare the texts of the various issues. It is interesting to note that the Americans have a special sign for date of copyright, a 'c' above the line, in front of the year date (e.g. '^{c}1890'); furthermore they write 'ca.' before approximate dates—not a question mark, as in the Music Catalogue of the British Museum. The question mark is used only in case of doubt. The Committee recommends that publishers' numbers be quoted *in extenso*; if the publisher acquired the plates from a predecessor, the latter's name should be given in square brackets.[15] I would emphasize the necessity for distinguishing between the publisher's number and the plate number, or plate mark, since, as I have pointed out, these are not always identical. To the first publisher's number on the title-page, successive numbers may be added in later issues; in Artaria's editions of Mozart's Piano Variations, for example, the title-page serves as a *passepartout*[16] for the whole series, while the plate number in the individual text remains the same.

This brings me to the subject of the decoration of the title-page, which the Code mentions only in so far as a warning is given about dating from ornamental title-pages, since these may be earlier than the text itself.[17] In another connexion I have shown elsewhere that, between 1697 and 1714, Walsh senior used no less than 16 *passepartouts*, 10 plain, and 6 ornamental.[18] The subject of ornamental title-pages in printed music has scarcely been touched in England;[19] it deserves particular attention—on artistic, as well as bibliographical, grounds. Attention should also be paid to ornamental title-pages in reprints based on a previous edition. As in many book illustrations, the engraver-copyist often reveals himself by transposing left and right. This is especially dangerous in the case of cherubic or human musicians, who are thus compelled to hold the bow of a stringed instrument in their left hand. Longman's reprint of Haydn's Six String quartets, op. 7, affords an example.

I might add at this point that the indication on the title-page of privilege, publishers' rights, or entry at Stationers' Hall, are all at least as important as the more recent notice of copyright, which, however, is dated.

In the case of music published by the composer himself and sold by a trade house, a number may be stamped on the title-page, indicating a subscriber's copy—as with Handel's 'Radamisto'; or it may be a numerical check on the dealer by the composer, sometimes called Control Number. This occurred more frequently in England than on the Continent.[20] Schubert availed himself of this check and made such indications (number and signature, or initials) usually on the last page of his books.[21]

The last chapters of the American recommendations, entitled Collation and Notes, I have not yet seen. In what follows, therefore, I am venturing into uncharted regions.

With respect to the description of contents, music again differs from printed books. First of all the printing technique adopted for the text is to be noted. It is not always the same as that used for the title-page. Usually, however, both are engraved, or, since about 1865, transferred from metal plates to stone, or lithographic paper—a cheaper process, but flatter and more anaemic in effect. Lithographed title-pages may be associated with an engraved text or conversely. Two periods of type-set music printing are recognized, the second with movable type; the latter is often used today for musical illustrations in the text of printed books. In the eighteenth century and at the beginning of the nineteenth century the engraver or lithographer often placed his signature on the title-page or in the text—if the latter, at the end of the work. In the nineteenth century the printer is often named on the title-page. How important the printing technique may be in dating an edition is shown by the example of Mozart's *Œuvres complètes*, published by Breitkopf & Härtel about 1800, first type-set, then engraved, and lastly lithographed; or in the case of numerous first editions of Brahms which appeared first engraved and later lithographed in transfer. Printing directly from engraved plates is used even nowadays on rare occasions; as for example, in most of the complete editions of the classics published by Breitkopf & Härtel.

If now we turn to the consideration of the contents [i.e., collation], in so far as this does not involve textual criticism, we have first to determine whether the text was written or engraved by one hand. Any change in style may indicate replacement of worn-out or faulty plates.[22] In the case of S. Bach's *Zweyter Teil der Clavier-Uebung* the use of new plates for pages 20–22 indicates the improved second issue of the first edition. We have already considered special pages: dedication, list of subscribers, list of contents, notice of privilege, and and advertisements.[23] We should now consider in turn: the plate mark; the sheet signature (a very rare feature to be found in Cluer's editions of Handel, for example); details of the number of sheets comprised by the work (on this the original price depended) to be found at the foot of the first page, where also a short title may appear; next, the caption title, the metronome indication, introduced early in the nineteenth century and often only found in later issues; lastly, the pagination. In music printed in the eighteenth century, particularly in England, and especially if printed by Walsh, pagination is often of bewildering complexity. It is well known that songs published by Walsh may show as many as four or five paginations owing to repeated use of the same plates in printing them as single songs, and as parts of collections of songs and vocal scores. Simple pagination may then indicate the first edition of the song or of the opera to which it belongs. Furthermore, and not only in the case of Walsh's publications, we often meet with twofold pagination if an appendix follows the main body of the work. There are a few very rare cases where the engraver has indicated no pagination at all, for example, the famous 'Parthenia': the twenty-one pieces comprising this work are numbered with roman numerals; and if a piece continues on a second or third page, the same roman numeral is repeated in the top centre of each page. In such cases the book must, of course, be treated as unpaginated. If the cataloguer should examine the last page only, in such a case, in order to determine the number of pages in the work he would be misled and would mislead others. An instance in which the British Museum Music Catalogue is inadequate is that of Tattersall's *Improved Psalmody*, vol. i, *c.* 1794, the second edition of which contains six forgotten settings of English hymns by Haydn. The first edition has 100 pages, of which the last seven are omitted from the second edition; the latter has 350 pages. The two editions would be distinguished more clearly, therefore, by giving the number of pages, rather than by noting the slight differences in the title-pages. The general regulations of the British Museum now insist upon a statement of the number of pages in all catalogue entries. The subject of pagination includes the presence of blanks and the printing on one side only of certain sheets or leaves; in the latter case the blanks must not be counted separately. The original temporary sewing of such works, and the presence of the original wrappers of grey, unprinted paper, may be particularly noted.

In special cases the quality of the paper on which the text is printed should also be mentioned: for example, the unusually large, thick sheets used in the subscribers' copies of Randall's editions of Handel's works in score.[24] Watermarks, whether dated or not, are to be noted, particularly those of the first half of the eighteenth century. In Walsh's publications these are very rare.[25]

The supplementary American *Code for Cataloging Phonograph Records*, 28 pages in length, is as yet without interest for British libraries, and I must unfortunately omit any discussion of its contents. I would like to quote one sentence only: 'The matrix number is analogous to the plate number in published music scores, and may afford a clue to the date of recording.'

I wish now to say something of the technical terms which are used, or which should be used, in cataloguing printed music and in musical bibliography. Since I came to England I have improved my native vocabulary—like the physician and poet, Lichtenberg, who on a business visit to London wrote to a friend in Germany: 'I really came to England in order to learn German!' As a matter of fact I found it necessary to revise German technical terms when it came to translating them.[26] First editions I have subdivided into Composer's First Editions, Posthumous First Editions, and Pirated First Editions; the second volume of Handel's *Suites de Pièces pour le Clavecin*, published by Walsh, being a good example of a pirated first edition. Each of these groups has a first issue, which may be the only one or may be followed by later issues or states: with altered title-page, altered plates of music, or transferred plates. In addition to these first editions and their variants, there are two kinds of later editions: Authorized Reprints and Postcopyright Reprints, that is, reprints subsequent to the expiry of the nationally or internationally recognized period of protected rights. At this point, a word about issues and states. I would like to restrict the term 'State' to cases in which the differences are purely external and superficial, and to restrict the term 'Issue' to cases of essential textual differences. It is useful to know that the number of copies of a given impression varied between 1 and 100 in the case of Schott of Mainz in about 1800. As a result of a lucky accident we have more accurate knowledge of the number of copies in the various states of Schubert's op. 1, the *Erlkönig*. This work had been ordered by 100 subscribers when Cappi and Diabelli published it on a commission basis. The first edition comprised three slightly different states, all signed by Schubert and with his check or control numbers from 1 to about 600. The first state amounted to about 300 copies, the second to about 100, and the third to about 200. It seems that at least the Austrian and German publishers usually decided the size of their impressions strictly according to the demand; since music is usually stereotyped this was quite easy.

In connexion with a discussion recently printed in *The Times Literary Supplement* I endeavoured to find a term suitable for the case of music published in periodicals which appeared before the first edition of the work. A considerable number of short piano works and songs by many of the great composers, from Handel to Wagner, appeared first in almanacs or periodicals. I should like to suggest that such advance publications of music, or literature, appearing in periodicals, in contrast to the separate and definite first edition, be styled 'First Printings'.

Before I close I would like to express my particular approval: first, of the excellent summary of useful information published by Ernest C. Krohn in the *Musical Quarterly* 1919 (vol. v, pp. 231–54) under the title 'The Bibliography of Music'; secondly, but only in time, of the admirable paper by C. B. Oldman: 'Musical First Editions', first published in a symposium in 1934 and later (1937) amplified and published separately. I wish to thank Mr. D. R. Wakeling of the University Library, Cambridge, who has helped me greatly in preparing this paper. He has brought about highly commendable reforms in the Music Room of the University Library; one can find there: an improved Kidson, lists of the plate numbers of some English publishers, lists of the first editions of the classics in the possession of the library, and a complete index to Purcell's works. Thanks to his influence, his assistant is as familiar with dated watermarks and publishers' numbers as if she had known them from infancy.

A last word on the implication of these recommendations. Twenty years ago Max Seiffert expressed the opinion that a complete bibliography of music, that is, a new Eitner, should be undertaken by the individual countries concerned. The ideal future state of affairs would be that national bibliographies should be available to every cataloguer. The cataloguer would then have nothing more to do than identify the work before him and order the title or set of titles from the National Bibliographical Offices and paste them on cards for his catalogue. It would not then be necessary for every cataloguer to be an expert possessing encyclopaedic knowledge.

In the case of this country, I would like to see a national bibliography office established in the British Museum which would deal with all English printed music, so that titles could be supplied to all libraries. Only when this has been done will the British Museum be an indispensable and authoritative source for music cataloguers in other libraries. Until that goal is reached, however, great circumspection and caution must be exercised in the case of works printed, let us say, before 1850. Until then, unfortunately, if the work of the music cataloguer is to be good, it must also be laborious, and he should not be bound unduly by general catalogue rules.

P.S. In a discussion following these remarks, Mr. Wm. C. Smith mentioned the variation in size of later issues dictated by the need for economy in the use of paper during the years following the last and since the beginning of this war. He implies, I presume, not only reduction in the format of paper but also in the size of the plates by photographic reproduction. He also pointed out other possible differences by the addition or alteration of figured bass in later issues, e.g. 'Songs in the Messiah', and I may add, Bickham's 'Musical Entertainer'.

Mr. C. B. Oldman stressed the importance of including, if possible, the date of later issues, for instance in copyright editions. Provision is made for this in the American Rules ('Imprint', Rule 3). In the case of undated music it is seldom possible to fix a date for later issues or editions. But where the date of the first issue or edition is known, all the later impressions should be indicated in brackets as 'after'; e.g. [after 1760]. In the case of dated or copyright music the printed date should be followed by the actual date, if known, thus [or rather]; e.g. 1890 [or rather 1900].

NOTES

[1] Read before the Bibliographical Society on Monday, 15 March 1943.

[2] Likewise the London firm of D'Almaine & Mackinlay, which was probably the first to introduce this practice, dated its music exactly with a changeable blind-stamp embossed on the title-page about the year 1848, the earliest date known to me being 1 May 1847. So did Addison & Hodson about 1850, Hutchings & Romer about 1882, and the Milan firm of G. Ricordi from *ca.* 1898 till at least 1930 (perhaps still to-day). These dates seem to indicate, however, only the time of delivery of the copy in hand. A more curious type of dated blind-stamp is to be found on two song-books by Bernhard Molique (op. 48 and 49), published *ca.* 1855 by G. Scheurmann in London, but printed apparently at Leipsic: the stamp consists of the Saxon coat-of-arms surrounded by the words 'Vertrag vom 18. Mai 1846'. This date, which I cannot explain, is, of course, without other meaning for the date of the music itself than that it was published some time later.

[3] Superseded by Georg Kinsky, *Das Werk Beethovens; thematisch-bibliographisches Verzeichnis* (München-Duisberg: G. Henle, 1955).–*Editor.*

[4] See Catharine Miller, "For music," pp. 183–184.–*Editor.*

[5] See A. Hyatt King, "Recent work in music bibliography," pp. 138–139 [**69,** 74] for descriptive comments on plate numbers and their utility.

[6] See [**112 & 113,** 101].–*Editor.*

[7] The MLA/ALA cataloguing rules were subsequently published: Joint Committee of the Music Library Association and the American Library Association, Division of Cataloging and Classification. *Music Library Association code for cataloging music and phonorecords* (Chicago: American Library Association, 1958).–*Editor.*

[8] Citation: n. 2, p. 134.–*Editor.*

[9] Haydn's symphonies should be numbered only according to E. Mandyczewski's thematic list in the *Gesamtausgabe* (reprinted in Grove's *Dictionary*); his pianoforte sonatas according to K. Päsler's thematic list in the *Gesamtausgabe*; his string quartets, however, can be known by their opus numbers, which are given in their correct chronological sequence. [See also the most recent Haydn thematic information: Anthony van Hoboken, *Joseph Haydn: thematisch-bibliographisches Werkverzeichnis* (Mainz: Schott, 1957–)–*Editor.*]

[10] I venture to put forward the following as specimen entries for this book for (1) a catalogue, and (2) a bibliography:

(1) *Lanza* (Gesualdo) the younger
Rosa Damaschina: The Damask Rose.
A favourite Rondo with Italian and English words.
The Italian words by Sigr. Caravita. The English words by I. B. Orme.
Button & Whitaker, London, [*ca.* 1810].
(2) + 6 pp. fol.

(2) [Engraved title-page, signed: *I. Girton sct. II, Charles Strt. Soho Sqe.*, having in the top half a rose, hand-coloured in red and green, and in the bottom half an outline drawing of a bird with its beak towards the bottom of the page, bearing in its beak a ribbon, which is twisted back to be caught up over its tail. The words of the title are given on the ribbon and on the body and wings of the bird.]
Rosa Damaschina The Damask Rose A Favorite Rondo with Italian and English Words
The Italian Words by Sigr. Caravita. The English Words by I. B. Orme, Esqr. Sung by Miss Griffith Pupil of G. Lanza Jun. The Music Composed by Gesualdo Lanza. Entd. at Stas. Hall. Price 2s.6d. London: Pubd. for G. Lanza, 8, South Crescent, Alfred Place, Bedford Sqe. by Button & Whitaker, 75, St. Pauls Chh. Yd. by W. Power & Co. Westmorland Street Dublin & to be had of all the Music Sellers in the United Kingdom.
Ca. 1810.
Tp + blk + 1–6 pp. fol.
The title-page signed by the London firm in red ink.
The music plates in the usual frame of Button & Whitaker, with a lyre in each corner. The title, in English, repeated at the bottom of each page. Head title on p. 1 in both languages.

[11] 'Music and Bibliographical Practice', *The Music Review*, Cambridge, August 1941, vol. ii, no. 3, pp. 253–6. [Using Day and Murrie's *English song-books, 1651–1702; a bibliography with a first-line index of songs* (London: Bibliographical Society, 1940), Deutsch points out the inadequacy of conventional methods of title-page transcription in music bibliography. He suggests, instead, the use of facsimile reproductions of engraved title-pages to permit bibliographical interpretation of their individual peculiarities.–*Editor.*]

[12] In the case of Beethoven's Mass in C, op. 86, an alternative was given in a note on a special page; this was inserted on p. (2), (108), or (70) respectively in three successive states.

[13] Mozart's *divertimenti*, like his symphonies, should be called only by their Köchel numbers, since the order of the *Gesamtausgabe* is not reliable.

[14] Cf. O. E. Deutsch, 'Zur Bestimmung der Couperin-Auflagen', *Zeitschrift für Musikwissenschaft*, Leipzig [1930], vol. xii, p. 508 f.

[15] Sometimes a slip is pasted on the original imprint, with the name of the publisher's successor or of a dealer.

[16] The term *passepartout* is employed where the same plate is used for the title-pages of various books. The necessary alterations may be made by a second smaller plate or by hand. In the first case a portion of the original plate may be cut out and a smaller plate inserted, or the part to be altered may be covered with a slip of paper, and the new matter added from the smaller plate in a second process. This latter method may be modified and the new matter may be added in by hand instead of being printed from a second plate.

[17] One curious case of dating music titles by an artist is that of Alfred Concanen (d. 1886) whose practice it was to give after his signature a code-mark indicating the date: he used the letters HA-HE for the years '81–'85, the years immediately preceding the introduction of copyright (though of course he did not know this!). Some of these illustrations are said to be found on single songs from Sullivan's operas.

[18] *The Music Review* of 1941 as quoted earlier.

[19] W. E. Imeson's pamphlet, *Illustrated Music-Titles and their Delineators* [London, 1912], deals only with British music from about 1810 to about 1885.

[20] In England also it is the custom of publishers to sign their names on music; at first it was done in manuscript and later with rubber stamps. Manuscript signatures were, however, used in France even earlier in the eighteenth century.

[21] Haydn stamped the copies of *Die Schöpfung*, published in 1800 by himself, with his initials (without Control Numbers). English composers, since the second half of the nineteenth century, used rubber stamps with their signatures. Control numbers, however, are found occasionally on English music; e.g., on Edward Smith Briggs's *Here's a health to those far away* (Robert Birchall, *ca.* 1796 [watermark 1794] and later), signed, with initials, and numbered in more than 2,700 copies.

[22] The sharpness of the impression, cracked or corrected plates should also be noted.

[23] In exceptional cases explanatory notes are given on separate leaves: e.g. Beethoven's instruction on the use of key in the Violoncello part of his Pianoforte Trio in B flat, op. 97.

[24] Sometimes extra copies were printed in a different colour; e.g., two presentation copies of Schubert's op. 19, printed for Goethe (Landesbibliothek, Weimar), or the presentation copies of Beethoven's posthumous op. 136, for the Courts of Europe.

[25] In the case of Handel, Walsh used paper with watermarks only for the *Coronation* and the *Funeral Anthems*, also–with special reason–for the *VI Sonatas à deux Violons* (op. 2).

[26] O. E. Deutsch: 'The First Editions of Brahms', *The Musical Review*, Cambridge, 1940, vol. i, nos. 2–3, especially p. 128.

The Fundamentals of Music Bibliography

by Cecil Hopkinson

Before I arrive at discussing the fundamentals of music bibliography I think we should take a very close look at the word 'bibliography' and make sure that we know what it really means. In countless books and dictionaries I have looked up the definition, and the general consensus of opinion is that it may have two meanings. Firstly, a list of books relating to a given subject or author and, secondly, the careful and accurate description of certain books, either by an author or on a specific subject, with literal transcriptions of the title-pages, sufficient information for identification between one edition or issue and another, size, gatherings, pages, measurements and so forth. This is a fact of which I need not remind a company of librarians, but I want to make a clear distinction between the two forms that a bibliography may have. Personally, I do not care for the first meaning at all and can never stretch my imagination so far as to flatter a mere list of books by calling it a bibliography. It is not a bibliography at all, it is a check-list, a simple list of books for guidance to the reader wanting to refer to other books on the same subject, or alternatively, by the same author. In Mr. Arundell Esdaile's *A Student's Manual of Bibliography* (Allen & Unwin, 1931), all such are called "List of Books", and this, I maintain, is the correct heading. A bibliography is something far larger, more involved, intricate and detailed. The new Grove uses the work 'bibliography' for a list of books about a composer, and a list of works composed by the composer is designated 'Catalogue of Works'.

To the word 'bibliography' I now want to add another–'music'–and discuss music-bibliography.

Such a thing would appear to be non-existent and of neither importance nor interest, if one can judge by the text-books of musical literature. In the year 1954 there has been published the much-heralded new Grove, almost doubled in size (and almost quadrupled in price), and in attaining to its fifth edition after nearly 75 years, it even yet cannot find space to devote one single line to music bibliography, even if it has spared some 17 pages to Film Music! Whatever one thinks of editor and publisher for such an omission, one can at least say that here was a golden opportunity lost of showing the world how far advanced this country is in its musical research work. Even in the allied subjects only 10 columns are devoted to the enormous subject of music printing and for publishing there is nothing save a few entries under certain publishers.

The pioneer work in Great Britain, unfortunately limited to twenty-five small pages, was the little book, *Musical First Editions*, by Mr. C. B. Oldman (Constable, 1934), which positively cries out for a second and greatly enlarged edition. Nine years later this was followed in March 1943 by the paper on *Music Bibliographies and Catalogues* by Mr. O. E. Deutsch, which was read before the Bibliographical Society and printed in *The Library*.[1] And with this we come to a dead stop; for, search as I may, not a written word can I discover in dictionaries or lexicon on this greatly neglected art, or science, if you prefer it.

What is *the* (as distinct from *a*) bibliography of music, and is it the same as that of books? I cannot see that it differs greatly; for it is the science of determining certain problems; firstly, which is the first edition of a given piece of music (the place of publication follows on with the name of the publisher); secondly, in what year was it published; thirdly, the relation to it of other editions, issues, impressions, variants, etc. with the deter-

SOURCE: Reprinted from Cecil Hopkinson, "The fundamentals of music bibliography," *Fontes artis musicae*, 2 (1955), 122-131, by permission of the International Association of Music Libraries. Also published in the *Journal of Documentation*, 11 (September, 1955), 119-129.

mination of their dates; and fourthly, the noting of any differences either with the manuscript or between the different editions. But what facts should one expect to find in a music bibliography? Surely, sufficient information to be able to identify an edition that one may be holding in one's hand with those described in the bibliographical work one is consulting. There should be a complete and accurate transcription of the title-page with a description of any frontispiece or illustration or vignette on the title as these may quite possibly vary from one edition to another. There should be a full collation of the make-up and it should be stated whether the work is upright or oblong with measurements though this is not as important with music as books for it is the exception to find old music that has not been bound up with trimmed edges at some time. Signatures are a matter of concern only up to about the close of the seventeenth century. There should be descriptions of Privilege and dedicatory leaves and Prefaces and Lists of Subscribers should also be noted for these may also vary in different successive printings. Finally, in the case of instrumental music the number of separate parts should invariably be given with a list of the instruments for which they were printed—highly important in the case of eighteenth century music with a publisher like Walsh who varied the number of parts and who sometimes gave misleading information on the title as to the number one might expect to find.

I maintain that all these points should be contained in a bibliography but at present my ideal state is far from being put into practice and there is far more looseness observed in the use of the word when applied to music than there is when applied to books. In a review of the late Alfred Loewenberg's *Annals of Opera* I have seen it referred to as a "bibliographical triumph" when—may be I am splitting hairs, but in science one splits the atom—it would be more accurately described as a "triumph of cataloguing" for no bibliographical details were given. Sonneck's work on the same subject was correctly described as "A Catalogue."[2] We know that a dictionary is not a bibliography, though maybe it contains much bibliographical information, in which line of research the names of Fétis and Eitner immediately come to mind. A catalogue also may be in the same category, and by far the greatest proportion of Library Catalogues contain no bibliographical information whatsoever, though the Catalogue of the Barcelona Library by Felip Pedrell, published in two volumes in 1908 and 1909, was a full dress bibliography. The same applies to that of the Upsala Royal University, compiled by Rafael Mitjana and Åke Davidsson, in three volumes, dated 1911, 1951 and 1951. Such catalogues as the two I have mentioned are rarities, and some that do not even mention the publisher's name or place of publication are not worth the appellation of catalogue. Here I have in mind the Andrew Deakin Catalogue of Musical Works of a historical, theoretical nature, published in Birmingham in 1892, whose half-title and running headline are flattered with the words "Musical Bibliography"!

Of catalogues in the hands of private collectors, the Stainer Song-Book Collection, privately printed in 1891 calls itself a catalogue, which it is, no more nor less; but the 4-volume Hirsch catalogue contains an enormous amount of bibliographical information, while the first volume (the only one published) of the Alfred Cortot collection is a full-dress bibliography.

When we pass to works that actually call themselves bibliographies, we are faced with a variety of conflicting ideas as to the meaning of the word and the interpretations placed on it by various authors are widely divergent. Michael Brenet's *Bibliographie des Bibliographies Musicales* published in Paris in 1914 turns out to be no more than a check-list, as is J. B. Coover's *Bibliography of Music Dictionaries* published at Denver, Colorado, in 1951, and the Gleason and White *Bibliography of Books on Music* published, apparently both in Rochester and Iowa, in 1948. A similar work on thematic catalogues published last year by the New York Public Library calls itself accurately a "check-list." The new edition, published in 1945, of Sonneck's *Bibliography of Early Secular American Music* gives no strict transcriptions of titles, and the *Bibliography of John Walsh* by William C. Smith, published in 1948, lacks not only this but all collations, and numbers of separate parts. The *Bibliographie des Chansons* of Méray, published at Paris in 1859, turns out to be no more than a mere catalogue of a private collection formed by Viollet-Leduc.

Rimbault's *Bibliotheca Madrigaliana* of 1847 is a remarkable work, especially when one takes into consideration the early date of its production. A true bibliography of course is Eitner's *Bibliographie der Musik-Sammelwerke*, published at Berlin in 1877, and what I do not hesitate to describe as the ideal one is the Day & Murrie *English Song Books*, published by the Bibliographical Society in 1940.

We come now to the matter of Thematic Catalogues, for which obviously there is no counterpart in the bibliography of books. It is here that we begin to touch upon the basis of a Composer-Bibliography; for amongst these will be found a certain amount of information about the presumed first editions and, in some instances, lists of other editions, as in Beethoven-Nottebohm, Schubert-Nottebohm, Bach-Schmieder, Weber-Jähns, Mozart-Köchel-Einstein, while those of Chopin, Mendelssohn, Brahms, Dvořák, Tchaikowsky, Liszt, Saint-Saëns, and so forth state, sometimes accurately, sometimes not so accurately, who were the publishers of the first editions. The Thematic Catalogues prepared by Wotquenne of C. P. E. Bach and Gluck also give the same information with the addition of the most appallingly inaccurate title-transcriptions that have only been excelled by Searle's bibliography of Gilbert and Sullivan, which reached an all time low for all bibliography. The only two Composer-Bibliographies known to me are those by Sonneck of Stephen Foster (1915) and Edward MacDowell (1917), which are models save for the lack of detail on the title-transcriptions. One only regrets that his labours were devoted to such relatively unimportant composers. A full-dress bibliography of Berlioz was attempted in 1951, but I shall have more to say about this later on.

Scattered information is found in booksellers' catalogues, the Altmann catalogues, Müller-Reuter's *Lexikon*, to mention but a couple, and there are endless articles containing a wealth of information on subjects as well as composers in musical journals, newspapers, reviews and periodicals of all descriptions, if one only knows where to find them. These await the gathering together in check-list form by some benefactor to musical mankind who may be in this hall at the moment, but articles such as that of Barclay Squire on Purcell in the *Sammelbände der Internationalen Musik-Gesellschaft* in 1904 should be known to all and not only to the few who chance on it unawares, as I did.

I hope that I have said sufficient to indicate how differently music bibliography is viewed by different people and what latitude is given to its meaning and how nebulous its interpretation is. I trust too that I have established in your minds what my own definitions are, and that I have made myself clear that I am in no doubt myself, rightly or wrongly. It is a comparatively youthful science in musicology, but it is time that the detectives knew exactly where they are heading. Such ambiguity as exists at present should not be permitted to continue. Biographers frequently include at the end of their books a list of works by the composer they are writing about, giving dates against each. Before I became more wary, I took these to be the dates of publication, as they would be, if the work was about an author. But how wrong I was; for far more often they are the dates of composition, and I suggest that compilers of these lists should always state exactly what their dates represent. Or am I stating the obvious?

At this stage I would like to interpolate a few remarks apropos of a study of Grove V during the last few days. The "Catalogues of Works" throughout this book bear no relation to each other in regard to system and it appears to have been left to the discretion or whim of each individual compiler to put in exactly what he felt proper so that each such catalogue has been dealt with on an entirely different basis. Factual or conjectural dates of composition have invariably been given but dates of publication and names of original publishers are remarkable by their absence. On only rare occasions, when a compiler was sufficiently bibliographically minded, have these been vouchsafed to the enquirer with a thirst for knowledge and Librarians should be under a considerable debt of gratitude to a compiler of Mr. Humphrey Searle's generosity. In many cases I have noted that it is not even stated whether a particular work has ever been published, so little is Grove V interested in all matters relating to publishing, with the exception of the so-called "bibliographies," and occasionally one comes up all of a sudden smack, quite irrelevantly it seems, against the name of a publisher. But Grove V has given birth to one idea that is completely novel to me for I have discovered under Handel (vol. IV, p. 54) a column headed "Composed," and then in brackets "Published" so that we find below two sets of dates, completely unrelated to each other, in one column. A footnote, four pages away, explains—"the year of composition is given, without brackets, and whenever necessary" (my underlining—whenever necessary) "the year of first publication in brackets." I pass this by without further comment other than to make a statement that of the 26 items listed in this column only three are given dates of publication!

I come at last to the root and purpose of my talk—the Fundamentals of Music Bibliography. Without doubt, first and foremost, the basic fundamental is accuracy in the bibliographer, accuracy, first and always. His principle task is the determination of the date of the first printing of any given piece of music. How, when faced with several editions of a work, whether all published in one country or in several, can he establish the respective dates and so determine which has priority? In the middle part of the nineteenth century, when music publishing seems to have been at its zenith and most prolific, works of composers such as Bellini, Rossini, Donizetti, Chopin, Liszt, Mendelssohn, Field, and so on, were being published in many countries of Europe, according to their popularity, and it is the fixing of their dates and their relation to each other that must be the primary problem of the detective in music bibliography. Liszt's compositions, as we know from Mr. Humphrey Searle's list, were widely printed in Italy, Germany and France; Rossini's in Austria, Italy, Germany and France; Mendelssohn's in Germany and England; and John Field's in England, France, Russia and Germany to the extent of no less than nine more or less contemporary editions of one work by different publishers in the latter country. In the case of Chopin we know, from the tabulated appendix in Niecks's biography, that simultaneous publication was aimed at in France and Germany while he mentions Polish editions of a few, but I have also encountered contemporary printings in Belgium, Italy, Russia and England in wide profusion. This highly complicated problem of dating can only, generally speaking, be solved by the combination of several facts, so let us examine a variety of possible lines of evidence and see where clues may be picked up:–

1. The publisher's name and style. When was he called plain Henry Smith and when did he take in a partner and become Smith & Williams? When did the firm of Dupont become La Veuve Dupont?
2. The publisher's address. When was Jones at 130 Regent Street and when at 64, and when did he move to Fenchurch Street in the City?
3. The price printed on the title. If it is in neugroschen, between what years was this currency in force? When did francs supercede Livres Tournoises?
4. Dedication on the title or special leaf. Between what years did the dedicatee live? When did the Prince become King?
5. Royal Privilege or Licences. When did these cease to be granted, in France, or in England or Germany?
6. Plate numbers. Have we any serial lists to approximate with a date? (Tread warily here!)
7. Watermarks. If these are dated, we know that the piece could not have been published before that date.
8. Dépôt Légal and Tax Stamps in France and Belgium. When were these in force?
9. Library reception date-stamps, or, in the case of the British Museum, copyright date-stamps.
10. Publisher's or Composer's signature on the title, or a presentation inscription. When did he die?
11. Is it printed from type, or from engraved plates, or is it lithographed? What do we know about these methods?
12. Other works advertised on the title, on a separate leaf or on the wrappers. What can we learn from these?

These are but a few of the questions one has to enquire into, but there are possibly amongst these (and there will never be a combination of more than two or three in any one case) the clues on which to work. Leaving the internal evidence, we proceed to the externals for proofs to substantiate the very bare evidence. Did the composer mention anything about the publication of the work in his correspondence, maybe with the publisher, or to his friends? In what year did it appear in the Hofmeister catalogues? When and where was it reviewed?

Do there exist any advertisements for the work in publisher's announcements in contemporary periodicals? What library catalogue is it in? What do dictionaries of publishers tell us? (Humphries & Smith for Great Britain, Dichter & Shapiro for the United States, and Hopkinson for France). What do the plate-numbers signify? (Deutsch for Germany). Do Eitner, Fétis or Grove mention the work? Does it appear in any contemporary publisher's catalogue? And so on and so forth until at last, maybe we are happy to be able to give it a date, if lucky, without the prefix of *circa*. Yes, we may have a date for it but there still remains the question–is it the first edition and if it is not, what edition precedes it? We take our copy to the British Museum and find perhaps that there is no similar edition here but that they have a copy of another edition which they date *circa* against our definite date as proved by an advertisement. So now our task starts over again, and we have to try to discover if we cannot date the B. M. copy more precisely. In another instance we compare our copy with the B. M.'s and we find a difference in the publisher's style or address? Maybe the price has been raised or lowered? Which is the earlier? Were they printed from the same plates, is an early question to ask ourselves? Again we compare two copies throughout and find that one page is different, a few bars have been re-engraved. Which is the earlier? We may find the whole work is exactly the same, having been printed from the same plates, but the title has been re-engraved, just a few tiny alterations made—a couple of capitals substituted for lower case, and so on. These are the minutiae of bibliographical detective work, as much a science as that concerned with crime!

But worst of all we may have two editions of the same work, printed from the same plates, with the same plate number bearing the imprint of Sieber on one and Pleyel on another. Which was the original publisher, if one took over the plates of the other, or were they published simultaneously? Again I have seen a similar case to this but with different plate numbers, and in the case of one of these publishers, I have seen him publish the same work from the same plates with different numbers, very close to each other too!

Having talked broadly of editions we have now arrived at the problem of different impressions, printings, issues, states, or shall I say variants? In my bibliography of Berlioz I discussed this question at some length in the Introduction. I put forward a hypothetical case and invited comments from my reader, at the same time making an appeal for "the laying down of certain rules by an international committee of librarians and bibliographers, so as to get rid of the lack of existing uniformity" in the terminology and definition of the words original edition, first edition, second edition and so on, impression, issue, state, printing, variants, etc., etc. This is all too involved, and to speak of "three issues of an impression of an edition," as one scholar does, surely shows the need for drastic simplification. Are we surely not the very body to deal with this problem?

What do I mean by different issues or variants? It is possible that some half-dozen or so copies of a particular work exist in practically identical form until detailed examination and comparison reveals minute differences. Two copies have different prices on the title but otherwise are identical. A third has a different address for the publisher, and perhaps the price agrees with that of one of the other two copies, possibly it does not. A fourth has a different publisher's name but is again otherwise identical with any one of the other three. A fifth is no longer printed from the same plates but lithographed. A sixth has a different plate number, and a seventh—but no matter. One could easily run into a dozen variants of such instances; for I have not mentioned alterations made in the music by the composer with consequent re-engraving of the plates, or the endless changes of street-numberings that have taken place in music emanating from Paris during the last 150 years. The reason for these endless variants we know to be as follows:—A publisher, say in 1830, prints 600 copies of a work but only 100 title-pages, as he feels that in the immediate future he can dispose of only 100 copies at the most. In fact the work turns out to be a slow seller, and in five years he finds he has sold a mere 50 copies; so he erases the price from the title and writes one in in ink. Another five years elapse, when he is confronted with a sudden demand for the work and he prints off another 100 titles with a newly engraved price. Ten years pass by, and as he has by now changed his address, he prints off a further 200 new titles. Five years later he dies, and the business is taken over by another publisher, who finds he has acquired 200 sets of sheets. He erases the imprint from the plates, substitutes his own, and prints off 100 new titles. Another five years pass by, and as he still has 100 sets of sheets on his hands, he scraps the original title and prints an entirely new one full of alterations. We have now reached the year 1860, and the first edition—is it so?—is still in print. By 1865 the work is sold out, and, still having the original plates in his possession, he decides to lithograph a new edition. From all the plates he deletes the original publisher's plate number, which had persisted up till then, substitutes his own and prints off another new title maybe.

This may sound exceedingly complicated and somewhat far fetched, but I can assure you that I personally have often encountered such cases in French 19th-century publications and with still more permutations than I have mentioned. (Recently I have been informed of a song by Arthur Sullivan that is still in print after some seventy years, where the owner has some fifteen variants of one sort and another but mostly complicated by the fact that the last page, which bears advertisements of other songs, has been constantly changed with each new printing).

At this stage the question must be posed—as the

example I have been citing is still being printed from the original plates—is it still a first edition? If it is not, then what edition is it? Is it a new impression, and if so should it be given a definite number called, say, the 5th impression. This might be thought too arbitrary; for other variants may throughout the years turn up and change it into the 8th. Is it better to call it an issue? Or a variant of the first edition? Or what? Take the case of Novello, who in the middle of last century got hold of some original Walsh and Randall plates. Walsh had printed in 1747 the first edition of Handel's *Judas Macchabaeus* and about 1770 Randall published the first complete edition with the choruses. What did Novello do but print off from the Randall edition, wed it to the Walsh title, and at no point add his own name? The paper on which it is printed, however, gives the game away, but to the uninitiated it appears as if Walsh printed the first complete edition before Randall! How does one describe this sort of an edition?

However, to return, what we surely have to determine is when a variant becomes a new or a second edition and at what stage in printings, such as I mentioned just now, we cease to designate small changes on the title as another issue? Do we call the printings issues right through the various changes of price and address until we get to the change of publisher and then boldly call it the second edition? Or do we pass through that until we reach the variant that was lithographed? Alternatively, as we are still printing from the original plates, do we go on calling it the first edition until there is a change of plate number? Do alterations in the music constitute sufficient evidence to warrant the work's being called a new or second or third edition? If they do, then how much alteration justifies such an appellation? A mere bar or two? A page or two? Suppose a new ending to a symphony or an opera has been composed and printed, does this make it a new edition? After the first nights of *Madame Butterfly*, *Manon* and *Louise*, Puccini, Massenet and Charpentier altered the ending to the extent of reprinting the last page so that only a few copies of the first version got out. Are these correctly called first edition, advance edition, original edition, first issue of the first edition, earliest printing of the first version, or what? Quite reasonably all of these terms could be, and are in fact, used according to the personal whims of the poor cataloguer. Surely it is time that we had this matter settled and uniformity adopted throughout this country, even if it is not entirely acceptable to other countries in the musical world?

Most of these questions were asked by me in the Introduction to my Bibliography of Berlioz, and I invited comment which I received, very gladly I might say, as well as certain very fair criticism both destructive and constructive at the same time from the pungent pen of that eminent critic, Mr. Richard S. Hill, in his review in the *Journal of the American Musicological Society* (Vol. VI Spring Number, 1953). I certainly advise everyone to read the fifteen columns of this, as it almost amounts to a highly admirable treatise on music bibliography, whether one agrees with it or not.

The distinguished bibliographer, Mr. John Carter, in a paper read recently before the Bibliographical Society of America referred to my work on Berlioz as "a frontal attack on a sector of what is bibliographically a veritable *bocage*" and Mr. Hill opened his critique by calling it "unique," ending up with the same description to which he pleasantly added a fervent hope that it would remain so, as "another example was not needed to underline the basic faults in its conception." In between Mr. Hill asserts that I am mistaken in the purpose of music bibliography and that I am not the right lines, as my work is too bookish and too much of a collector's bibliography. First edition hunting can be quite ridiculous, he maintains, but this is a criticism that strikes across all concepts of collecting and is far too large a subject for me to embark on at this late stage. Mr. Hill claims quite rightly that music is the most important element and that variants should be concerned only with music and not with make up, but he almost ignores the fact that I have noted such changes, alterations of key, and so forth wherever I have been able to discover them, and in the case of *Les Troyens* devoted no less than 14 pages to a minute description of the agonising tortures to which this work has been subjected by publishers and editors with the passage of time. Would Mr. Hill describe as ridiculous the minutiae of bibliography where the late Paul Hirsch discovered two issues of the separate parts of Beethoven's 6th Symphony and spent three printed pages in discussing the differences between, in one instance, a pause on the second of two tied minims and, in the other, a pause over a single minim? This is a highly important trifle, but Mr. Hill jibes at the book collector who paid a fabulous sum for a Wordsworth poem which possessed a typographical error. The omission or insertion of a comma can make a world of difference, as the law has realised.

However, Mr. Hill, with whom I have a tremendous amount in common, proceeds to lay down his ideas, and to these I cannot over much draw the attention of my listeners or readers when this paper is printed. He defines three types of bibliography and their purposes as follows:—

Firstly, the Collector's Bibliography, which is a documented list for collectors to determine the first edition.

Secondly, the Musician's Bibliography, very similar to the Collector's but devoted more to change of music than imprint.

Thirdly, the Historian's Bibliography, in which there is no emphasis placed on first editions. Its purpose should be historical or sociological, and through the listing of *all* editions would indicate how the composer's music became popular in his own country and later spread to others.

I must confess that at the back of my mind in my Berlioz work the date fixing of editions was of paramount importance and consequently the book was intended as both a Collector's and Musician's Bibliography. But why should collectors be scoffed at? Why should a private collector be despised? Who are the greatest collectors in the world, now that the change of time and the redistribution of wealth have almost eliminated the really great and affluent private collector? The greatest collections have now practically all passed to the largest libraries in the world, who are continually adding to them. And what are the Libraries if they are not collectors? I hesitate in this country to say that they are not interested in knowing whether or not they possess the first edition of certain works, partly because of their rarity, and having all their editions defined and dated for them by the use of a Collector's Bibliography. On the other hand there are many libraries, suburban and provincial, which are essentially "players" libraries for practising musicians and readers who, quite understandably are not interested in what edition they possess so long as it is accurate, clear and legible. Mr. Hill's third type of bibliography I am engaged on at present in an attempt to combine it not only with the first two but with a thematic catalogue, so that I shall hope to provide not only for Mr. Hill but for all worlds. This work deals with the compositions of John Field and, from the historical and sociological angle, will demonstrate how tremendously popular his works were on the continent and at the same time how little they were appreciated both in the country of his birth and our own—a reversal of Mr. Hill's suggestion.

As I draw to a close, I cannot refrain from mentioning a somewhat amusing personal experience. One day I was troubling one of our own most important librarians—he is not one hundred miles distant from me at this moment—with some questions, petty and pedantic, bibliographical *peccadillos* (you all know the sort of thing), when at last he could endure it no longer and turned on me rather peevishly—"it is time you realised," he said, "that I am a librarian and *not* a bibliographer," which made me think that I was nothing more than a fussy old man concerned only with mere trivialities. I cannot refrain from commenting on this remark, as I ventured to be so bold as to tell him he was talking nonsense. How on this very earth a librarian is not at the same time a bibliographer is quite beyond my comprehension, and if he is not a bibliographer, then he has no right to be a librarian. The reverse does not hold good, as is proved by your speaker, who is no librarian. That I consider I have won the day in this academic point is borne out by the fact that my views are corroborated by no less an authority than the reborn Grove in which my friend the librarian, has a word slipped in *before* (mark you, first and foremost) his definition as librarian, and that is—bibliographer. However, he made ample amends to me last Christmastide by sending me as a gift, a book written by himself, with not only an inscription, but a whole page "bibliographical note" in his own hand on the various transformations through which the book had passed.

On a couple of occasions on which it was announced that I should give this talk, or rather open a discussion—for it is not intended as a lecture—Mr. Hyatt King very kindly said that he thought it would prove stimulating and provocative. I hope that I have proved to be both, otherwise discussion is apt to be limited and jaded. I have asked a great many questions to which I, myself, have never yet found the answers, and I sincerely hope that tonight some will be received, or an impetus may be imparted, as I suggested earlier on, to the search for solutions of problems in the field of music bibliography that await decisions which will be adopted universally.

NOTES

[1] Both Oldman and Deutsch are reprinted above, pp. 107–126.–*Editor.*

[2] U.S. Library of Congress. Music Division. *Catalogue of opera librettos printed before 1800,* prepared by O. G. T. Sonneck. Washington, D. C.: Gov't Printing Office, 1914. 2v.
See annotation in Duckles 2nd, 1120.–*Editor.*

Towards A Definition of Certain Terms in Musical Bibliography

These resolutions culminated a two days discussion at the Fifth Congress of IAML held at King's College, Cambridge, July 1 and 2, 1959. The Chairman's report of the entire discussion prior to the presentation of resolutions is published in Music, libraries and instruments, *Hinrichsen's Eleventh Music Book, pp. 147–155 (London: Hinrichsen Edition, 1961). The summary is very interesting reading, especially for the philosophical disagreements among bibliographers who had–at that point in time–divided themselves into two almost mutually exclusive groups: collectors and librarians.*

RESOLUTIONS

1. Proposed by Mr. L. A. Hyman, seconded by Dr. R. S. Hill and carried unanimously that "A small International Corresponding Committee be formed to consider and report on standard definitions of terms in Musical Bibliography with particular reference to those employed in identifying priorities and variations in editions."
2. On suggestions in the paper read by Mr. A. Rosenthal it was proposed by Mr. Jeremy Noble, seconded by Mr. O. W. Neighbour and carried with only one dissentient (see No. 3 below), and resolved that

   "The use of the term 'edition' might be limited to two events, (A) a publication in which the music and related subject is newly printed, newly engraved, or otherwise newly produced (B) cases, in which either the composer himself, or an editor, or a publisher, have made intentional alterations, emendations, improvements, etc. in the musical matter and perhaps other subject matter, such as song texts, prefaces, or the like."
3. Proposed by Dr. C. B. Oldman (the dissentient in No. 2), seconded by Dr. Edith Schnapper and carried unanimously that

   "When the summary of our discussions was ready it should be circulated to all the Branches of the Association with a statement to the effect that an English Committee, already set up, was going to study the question of musical bibliographical terminology, accompanied by a request that Branches in other countries should form their own committees to do the same."

He further suggested that no final decisions as to terminology should be taken until the next International Congress in 1962.

SUGGESTION

By Mr. J. H. Davies (not put as a resolution to the Meeting) that

"Representations be made by I.A.M.L. to all music publishers for adequate bibliographical information to be printed from now on on the versi of the title pages of all their publications."

Cecil Hopkinson, Chairman

SOURCE: Reprinted from *Fontes artis musicae*, 6 (1959/2), 48–49, by permission of the International Association of Music Libraries.

Some Trials of a Music Librarian

by Donald R. Wakeling

When Fritz Kreisler in 1935 revealed the facts of his amazing and lengthy leg-pulling of the musical world I am sure there was nobody who did not envy him the hearty silent laughter he must have enjoyed over a long period; nobody, too, begrudged Paul Klenovsky his flying visit to (or for that matter, regretted his equally hurried departure from) the realms of Apollo. This otherwise sombre generation of ours (and it has been through enough to make it sombre) likes nothing better than a good joke, and if the joke is on us we like it none the less for that. Probably the greatest victims of these practical jokers are the music librarians whose carefully prepared catalogues are not printed without an infinite amount of verification and patient research in order to ensure that each item included shall appear under its authentic composer and title. How much time and trouble, I wonder, has been spent by these worthies searching through the works of Couperin, Francoeur, Martini and others for mythological works, or through innumerable biographical dictionaries for elusive Russian composers. Is it realized how many entries have had to be cancelled and reprinted, how many cross-references have had to be added, and what this means in the way of money and lost man-hours, to say nothing of grey hairs and loss of sleep? That, however, is a cheap price to pay for anything intended to brighten this dull world, even if the number of people enjoying the fun is limited to the perpetrators of these pranks.

These practical jokers are but some of the thorns in the side of the music librarian. There is the obscurantist who collects and arranges forgotten and often unknown works of the Masters, many of which delight and intrigue us. The intriguing, however, is usually caused by the arranger forgetting, intentionally or unintentionally, to give us any indication of the source of his arrangement. I wonder why. Is it done to create an aura of mystery around the works or to infuse some additional interest? Maybe it is some new and fashionable form of puzzle game. On the other hand, is it done intentionally to exasperate the musicologists into compiling complete thematic catalogues of all composers so that they can with ease and speed solve these puzzles? If this last be the reason then by all means give the obscurantist every encouragement, in fact spur him on to greater efforts; apart from rescuing a few gems from oblivion, if his curious method of persuasion succeeds with the musicologists, he will have performed a great service to music and music librarians.

Whatever may be the modern intention of this habit, the habit itself is not new. The great Masters themselves were guilty, as is shown by the classic example of the *Sehnsuchtswalzer–Trauerwalzer*–or whatever your personal choice prefers to call this haunting melody. It is evident, too, that publishers or editors had a hand in these deceptions, for it is hard to believe that Schubert claimed the Guitar Quartet in G as an original composition. Why should he wish to steal the thunder of the poor Bohemian guitar player Matiegka?

To call a crow a nightingale does not make it sing more sweetly. To call a Voluntary a March makes little difference; whether the trumpet was Purcell's or Clarke's the familiar clarion call will sound the same wherever or whenever it is performed, and the score will remain unaltered. Not so in our music catalogues. Here are the mighty fallen; the famous Purcell must retire and give pride of place to his less famous contemporary, involving in the process the usual cancellations and cross-references. Is this, I wonder, some compensation to poor Jeremiah Clarke for the loss of his lady love which led with such disastrous results to

SOURCE: Reprinted from Donald R. Wakeling, "Some trials of a music librarian," *The Music Review,* 6 (1945), 13–16, by permission of the publisher, W. Heffer & Sons Ltd., Cambridge, England.

his death by a screw pistol? If so, we will look upon the extra work he has given us as a reverent obligation and not as a disagreeable duty.

It is more usual, and more understandable, to find works by greater artists ascribed to lesser artists—usually by the lesser artists themselves—than the works of lesser artists ascribed to greater, and exceptions to this order are looked upon with suspicion. When, therefore, some years ago the late Sir Arthur Somervell arranged two songs from Calphurnia (*No, oh Dio* and *Un ombra di pace*), attributed them to Handel and died without telling us why, we were a little diffident about cataloguing them under Bononcini. Handel, we know, was an inveterate borrower, but from his rival—Never! Despite the fact that

> "Some say compared to Bononcini
> That Mynheer Handel's but a ninny."

Nevertheless, since the two songs were published under the name of Handel they presented yet another test of the cataloguer's ingenuity.

It does not come within the sphere of duties of a music cataloguer to criticize or condemn composers for plagiarism, but it is a valuable asset if he or she is able to identify at a glance a great number of musical compositions—the greater the better. This asset, however, becomes a little disconcerting and riling at times when one recognizes, shall we say, a Romance of Schumann's and has to catalogue it under the name of some almost unknown plagiarist.

I might add that in order to satisfy the demands of the many casual enquirers who come along with "Do you happen to possess a copy of this?"—then proceed to make strange sounds accompanied by the words "Tum-te-te-tum-tum," which they assure you are the first bars of the work they seek, it is an additional advantage to be able to recognize by sound as well as by sight not only a large number, but also a wide variety of works ranging from "Sumer is icumen in" to "Lily Marlene," from the most primitive melody to Shostakovich's *Leningrad* Symphony.

In the appalling cases of jazzed classics I feel that cataloguers are perfectly justified, nay, in duty bound to omit all reference to the already injured Master, and make the jazzist solely responsible for the unholy cacophony usually resulting from such sacrilege. Fear of the Law of libel forbids me to particularize or expand my observations on the subjects of plagiarism and jazzed classics, and since they do not affect cataloguing, unless the composition to be treated is stolen *in toto,* we will leave these unsavoury topics to their own devotees.

How valuable an asset to the music cataloguer is the ability to recognize at sight the greatest possible number of musical compositions, may be judged when it is realized how vast is the amount of arranged music that passes through his hands christened with titles never dreamed of by the original composers. Vocal music arranged for instruments and instrumental music arranged for voices, the arrangers of which, like our old friends the other obscurantists, seldom give a clue to the original source. Let me give a few examples, but, be it remembered, there are hundreds of others not so familiar, and even the best music librarian can hardly be expected to recognize every work of even the great Masters, still less all the movements of a work, and it would be considered a miracle if he recognized all the music that has been arranged and re-arranged. The lack of adequate reliable and complete thematic catalogues—the surest and quickest medium for tracing the source—is only too well known.

Golden light: Agnus Dei, pour contralto ou baryton, violon solo ou violoncelle, piano ou harpe, harmonium ou orgue, as a title very effectively camouflages Bizet's *Arlésienne Suite, '2, Intermezzo.*

From the title *Sleep, my little dove. Christmas carol for mixed voices with soprano solo (or junior choir). From an old Alsatian carol,* Gluck himself would never have recognized the chorus *Non sdegnare, o bella Venere* and aria *Come consuma l'avida fiamma* from his opera—*Paride ed Elena.*

Chopin's 12 *Grandes Etudes, Op.* 10, *No.* 3, has received considerable attention and appears under various titles: *Tristesse—So deep is the night—Reviens mon amour,* etc.

Liszt's *Liebesträume. Notturno* 3, too, has many aliases: *Vesper bells—Woodland dreaming—O, kindly light,* etc., etc.

But Handel's *Ombra mai fù* from *Xerxes* must surely head the list with almost every title under the sun except *Pop goes the weasel.*

". . . Newly discovered MSS. never before published," especially when alleged to be by one of the great Masters, are bound to cause some sensation in the musical world and some new entries in the music catalogues. Music librarians, in consequence of their bitter experiences, are suspicious creatures and do not accept such statements as gospel truth. The vast store of material for reference and verification, usually to be found in the larger libraries, will sometimes prove the statement, so proudly displayed on the title-page, somewhat exaggerated, and, if his luck still holds good, the librarian might also recognize a MS., say, in the handwriting of Beethoven or Mozart, to be a composition by Kozeluch, thus blowing sky-high a long-standing attribution by some very learned musicologists—not by his superior knowledge or deeper research, but simply because he happened to know and recognize at sight Kozeluch's composition. But I am beginning to spoil an interesting story which, it is hoped, will be published by an eminent scholar in the near future, and it is best told in his own words.[1]

Another ingenious trap which our cataloguer must be prepared to meet if he wishes to bring all the compositions of a man together is the queer method used by some composers of adopting as many different names as there were colours in Joseph's coat. Alfred W. Rawlings, for example, who died in 1917, according to A. E. Wier, is known to have published works under the following names:—Charles Arthur Rawlings, Theodore Bonheur, Denis Dupré, Florence Fare, Frederic Mullen and Gustav Krenkel, and for all we know he may have used a dozen others besides. Frequently one finds a composer who has used two or three pseudonyms; even Johannes Brahms, in his youth, wrote some pot-boilers under the name G. W. Marks.

It will be observed that all these little things sent to try us were perpetrated in fairly recent times, but for sheer diabolical awkwardness, obscurantism and deception the snares laid by the earlier music publishers in general, and by John Walsh in particular, make these trials seem mere child's play. It is not intended here to enlarge upon their methods, but if the reader is interested to learn more of the serious pitfalls that beset the music librarian together with some suggestions for avoiding and overcoming these difficulties (and I have only playfully touched upon the fringes of the subject) he would do well to glance through a very enlightening paper read before the Bibliographical Society on 15th March, 1943, by Professor O. E. Deutsch printed in *The Library N.S.*, XXIII, No. 4.

NOTE

[1] O. E. Deutsch, "Kozeluch ritrovato," *Music & Letters,* 26 (January, 1945), 47–50.

B. Cataloguing and Classification

SELECTED BIBLIOGRAPHY

115. Spivacke, Harold. "Exchange cataloging," *Notes,* 1st series, no. 5 (November, 1937), 30–34.
A proposal for the informal exchange, among the membership of MLA, of sets of catalogue cards which analyze *Gesamtausgaben.*

116. Cunningham, Virginia. "Heart of the library," *Music Journal,* 4 (May–June, 1946), 11, 52–55.
A layman's guide to music catalogues and cataloguing. Too elementary, perhaps, for librarians, but fine for students and library patrons.

117. Heyer, Anna Harriet. "Policies of cataloging and classification in self-contained music libraries." Master's thesis, Faculty of Library Service, Columbia University, 1939.

118. Elmer, Minnie Agnes. "Music cataloging; with an annotated bibliography of useful references and sources." Master's thesis, Faculty of Library Service, Columbia University, 1946.
"Appendix A: Annotated bibliography of reference books useful in cataloging music": *ll.* 52–105. "Appendix B: List of sources": *ll.* 106–113.

119. Look, Wallace C. "The classification and cataloging of music scores in libraries." M. A. thesis, University of Chicago, 1951.
Includes a brief description of American cataloguing codes and classification schemes in use in 1951.

120. Elmer, Minnie. "The music catalog as a reference tool," *Library Trends,* 8 (April, 1960), 529–538.

121. Foster, Donald Leroy. *Notes used on music and phonorecord catalog cards.* Occasional papers, no. 66. Urbana: University of Illinois Graduate School of Library Science, 1962.
See annotation in the MLA *Manual,* p. 52.

122. Cunningham, Virginia. "Inside LC's Music Section," *Notes,* 25 (December, 1968), 205–208.

* * * * *

CATALOGUING CODES FOR MUSIC (complementary to Hill's bibliographical essay below, pp. 156–162):

123. Bishop, William W. "Report of the [ALA] Committee on catalog rules: Rules for cataloging musical scores," *ALA Bulletin,* 14 (1920), 295–296.
Prints the rules for cataloguing music which the Committee submitted to the ALA for comment.

124. Joint Committee of the Music Library Association and the American Library Association, Di-

vision of Cataloging and Classification. *Music Library Association code for cataloging music and phonorecords.* Chicago: American Library Association, 1958.

125. International Association of Music Libraries, International Cataloging Code Commission. *Code international de catalogage de la musique.* Frankfurt: C. F. Peters, 1957–

v. 1. Grasberger, Franz. *Der Autoren-Katalog der Musikdrucke. The author catalog of published music,* translation by Virginia Cunningham. 1957.

v. 2. *Code restreint.* Rédigé par Yvette Fédoroff. *Limited code. . .* translation by Virginia Cunningham. *Kurzgefasste Anleitung. . .* Übersetzung von Simone Wallon. 1961.

v. 3. *Rules for full cataloging.* Compiled by Virginia Cunningham. *Règles de catalogage détaillé. . .* Traduction de Yvette Fédoroff. *Regeln für die vollständige Titelaufnahme. . .* Übersetzung von Kurt Dorfmüller. 1971.

126. Cunningham, Virginia. "The International Code for Cataloging Music," *Notes,* 18 (September, 1961), 559–562.

Summary of the meeting on the international cataloging code held as part of the "Institute of International Music Library Problems, sponsored by The Music Library Association and The International Association of Music Libraries, American branch, September, 13–15, 1961." See also the annotation for the Code in the MLA *Manual,* p. 53.

127. ———. "From Schmidt-Phiseldeck to Zanetti," *Notes,* 23 (March, 1967), 449–452.

A history and description of the work of the International Cataloguing Code Commission of the International Association of Music Libraries.

128. *Anglo-American cataloging rules,* prepared by the American Library Association, the Library of Congress, the Library Association, and the Canadian Library Association. North American text. General editor: C. Sumner Spalding. Chicago: American Library Association, 1967.

129. ———. North American text, with Supplement of additions and changes. Chicago: American Library Association, 1970.

130. *Rules for the brief cataloging of music in the Library of Congress; exceptions to the Anglo-American cataloging rules.* Ann Arbor, Michigan: Music Library Association, 1970.

131. *Music cataloging bulletin,* v. 1, January 1970–Ann Arbor, Michigan: Music Library Association, 1970–

* * * * *

CLASSIFICATION SCHEMES FOR MUSIC:

132. Pethes, Iván, comp. "The classification of music and literature on music," *Fontes artis musicae,* 15 (1968/2-3), 83–102.

"Bibliography" of classification schemes and literature: pp. 99–102, with the following Addenda:

133. Ayer, Clarence W. "Shelf classification of music," *Library Journal,* 27 (January, 1902), 5–11.

Includes an outline of the Harvard classification for music and music literature.

134. Cutter, C. A. "Shelf classification of music," *Library Journal,* 27 (February, 1902), 68–72.

Includes an outline of the music class of Cutter's *Expansive classification.*

135. Allen, Jay. "Proposed alternate scheme for Dewey M780: Preliminary edition–1951," *Notes: Supplement for Members,* No. 17 (December, 1951).

136. Peck, John Grove, Jr. "The music schedules of the *Decimal Classification,* a historical and critical study." M.S.L.S. thesis, University of North Carolina, 1956.

137. [Cunningham, Virginia] "Music classification" [condensed LC classification, class M–Music] *Notes: Supplement for Members,* No. 15 (June, 1951), 9–15.

A proposal; see next item.

138. Rovelstad, Betsy. "Condensation of the Library of Congress M classification schedule," *Notes: Supplement for Members,* No. 34 (June, 1963).

139. Line, Maurice B. "A classification for music scores on historical principles," *Libri,* 12 (1963), 352–363.

A synopsis of Line's classification scheme is printed, pp. 359–363. The classification is notated similarly to the LC classification so that it can be substituted as Class M.

140. Langridge, D. W. "Classifying the literature of jazz," *Brio,* 4 (Spring, 1967), 2–6.

141. Bradley, Carol June. *The Dickinson classification; a cataloguing & classification manual for music.* Including a reprint of the George Sherman Dickinson *Classification of musical compositions.* Carlisle, Pa.: Carlisle Books, 1968.

142. Whiting, Bernard C. *A classification for baroque music.* Occasional paper no. 3. Liverpool: Liverpool School of Librarianship, 1969.

* * * * *

MUSIC SUBJECT HEADINGS (exclusive of those lists cited in the MLA *Manual,* pp. 49-57):

143. O'Meara, Eva Judd. "Music subject headings," *Notes,* 1st series, no. 3 (April, 1935), 16-17.
Background of the first list of music subject headings–largely extracted from the general LC list–prepared by members of the MLA.

144. Waters, Edward N. "Subject headings," *Notes,* 1 (June, 1944), 51-52.

Cataloguing of Music

by James Duff Brown

James Duff Brown, 1862–1914, was an English librarian of sufficient stature among musical scholars to merit entry in the second edition of Grove's Dictionary *(1904). A bibliography of his writings includes:*

Biographical dictionary of musicians, with bibliography. *Paisley, 1886.*
"Subject lists: I.–Music," The Library, *series 1 (1891), 147–151, which is a bibliography of "the books no public library should be without."*
A guide to the formation of a music library. *Library Association Series. London: Simpkin, Marshall, Hamilton, Kent & Co., 1893; a list of recommended titles and editions for public libraries.*
Manual of library economy. *London: Scott, Greenwood & Co., 1903.*
Subject classification, with tables, indexes, etc., for the subdivision of subjects. *London: Library Supply Co., 1906; which enjoyed a measure of success in British public libraries.*

As Librarian of the Clerkenwell Public Library, Brown wrote the following guidelines for cataloguing music which I believe to be the first English-language, published, consideration of the problems of entering music in library catalogues.

CATALOGUING OF MUSIC

Mr. Brown of Clerkenwell writes:–I submit with considerable diffidence the following notes on this matter, which seems to have come to the front somewhat prominently since the "Guide to the Formation of a Music Library" was issued in 1893 by the Library Association. This "Guide" does not enter into the question of cataloguing, and as the ordinary rules do not apply very well, the following suggestions are made in the hope that they may be of service. Music is such a concrete subject that there is little, if any, advantage in distributing its component parts throughout an alphabetical catalogue under subject heads like Harmony, Singing, Pianoforte; or *form* heads like Operas, Oratorios, Songs, &c. Especially is this method futile when only a few general works are entered under Music, without cross-references to specific sub-heads. For dictionary catalogues I accordingly recommend that ordinary author entries under the names of composers be arranged in the general alphabet of the catalogue. For every purpose of utility the composers' names will usually serve, but if, in the case of operas or oratorios, &c., it is felt that the poets or librettists should be noticed, then brief entries can also be made at their names. Doubtless, when the poet happens to be Shakespeare, Scott, Scribe, W. S. Gilbert, Goethe, or someone of literary importance, there is an advantage in having a reference at any rate, if not an entry. But the Oxenfords, Weatherlys, and Bunns must be dealt with at discretion. Translators and editors might, I think, be ignored, as very few persons will care to know how many operatic or other libretti adapters, like Ball, Farnie, Troutbeck, &c., have tinkered. These remarks apply mainly to operas, oratorios, and similar works. As regards musical editors of instrumental works, although there may be some little advantage in stating that Beethoven's sonatas are edited by Halle, Pauer, Zimmermann, or others, there seems no particular advantage in making references from such names. Editors of

SOURCE: Reprinted from [James Duff] Brown, "Cataloguing of music," *The Library*, series 1 (1897), 82–84. This article is variantly titled in some bibliographical sources "Classification scheme for music libraries."

collections of national music, &c., should be treated as authors. As a rule, such collections are known by their editorships, as Wood's "Songs of Scotland," Richards' "Songs of Wales," Stanford's "Songs of Old Ireland," and so on. This applies generally to all collected works, save those of individual composers, as already stated.

Under the main subject-heading "MUSIC," I recommend an entry of every musical work in the library, arranged according to the scheme set out below. Cross-references can be made from the body of the catalogue to each specific head. It will facilitate finding if arbitrary numbers are applied to the different sections.

Music

1. *General.*—Criticism, &c.
2. *History.*—
3. *Theory.*—General (Nomenclature, Sound, &c.)
4. *Theory.*—Elements of Music.
5. *Theory.*—Harmony.
6. *Theory.*—Counterpoint and Fugue.
7. *Theory.*—Composition and Form.
8. *Practice, Instrumental.*—Orchestra, Instruments and Instrumentation, works on generally.
9. Orchestra: Symphonies, Overtures, Quartets, and other concerted music. (Full scores and parts to be discriminated, with references to pianoforte and other arrangements.)
10. American Organ. (*a*) Instruction or History. (*b*) Music for.
11. Banjo. (*a*) Instruction or History. (*b*) Music for.
12. Bassoon. (*a*) Instruction or History. (*b*) Music for.
13. Clarinet. (*a*) Instruction or History. (*b*) Music for.
14. Concertina. (*a*) Instruction or History. (*b*) Music for.
15. Cornet. (*a*) Instruction or History. (*b*) Music for.
16. Double Bass. (*a*) Instruction or History. (*b*) Music for.
17. Drum. (*a*) Instruction or History. (*b*) Music for.
18. Flute. (*a*) Instruction or History. (*b*) Music for.
19. Guitar. (*a*) Instruction or History. (*b*) Music for.
20. Harmonium. (*a*) Instruction or History. (*b*) Music for.
21. Harp. (*a*) Instruction or History. (*b*) Music for.
22. Horn. (*a*) Instruction or History. (*b*) Music for.
23. Oboe. (*a*) Instruction or History. (*b*) Music for.
24. Organ. (*a*) Instruction or History. (*b*) Music for.
25. Pianoforte. (*a*) Instruction or History. (*b*) Music for.
26. Trombone. (*a*) Instruction or History. (*b*) Music for.
27. Viola. (*a*) Instruction or History. (*b*) Music for.
28. Violin. (*a*) Instruction or History. (*b*) Music for.
29. Violoncello. (*a*) Instruction or History. (*b*) Music for.

Practice, Vocal.

30. Voice and Singing.
31. Choir-Training.
32. Operas, Masques, &c.
33. Oratorios.
34. Cantatas, Services of Song.
35. Church Services, Masses. (*a*) Collections. (*b*) Individual composers.
36. Anthems, Motets. (*a*) Collections. (*b*) Individual composers.
37. Psalms and Chants. (*a*) Collections. (*b*) Individual composers.
38. Hymns and Carols. (*a*) Collections. (*b*) Individual composers.
39. Part-Songs. (*a*) Collections. (*b*) Individual composers.
40. Glees, Madrigals, &c. (*a*) Collections. (*b*) Individual composers.
41. Trios, Duets, &c. (*a*) Collections. (*b*) Individual composers.
42. Songs, Ballads, Nursery Music. (*a*) Collections. (*b*) Individual composers.

In small collections, 33–34, 35–38, 39–41, can be grouped together under such words as "Oratorios, Cantatas, &c."; "Church Music"; "Concerted Vocal Music," or other appropriate heads. Headings like "Dance Music," "Comic Songs," &c., have no great value, as the selection of works of this class depends very much on the instrument possessed by the borrower. Thus, the owner of a pianoforte would not want to take out a volume of dances, or other popular melodies, arranged for the flute. It is very important that each entry should show clearly how a particular work is arranged. A pianoforte score of an opera or overture is a very different thing from a full score, which in its turn is quite another thing from the separate parts for each instrument. The nature of each work should therefore be clearly described. Many collections of songs have no accompaniments of any kind, while others have simple or elaborate accompaniments for the pianoforte alone, or in combination with other instruments. Librarians who pin their faith on the alphabet can arrange the topics in the above subject-heading alphabetically. Of course the other alternative exists of arranging the works by authors and composers alphabetically under "Music," with a brief subject-index at the end, and cross references from all over the catalogue.

Title-entries if thought necessary can be inserted in alphabetical order throughout the catalogue, or may be added to the subject-heading "Music" as an appendix, whichever seems convenient. In Class Lists the Index will of course meet every demand.

Biography has been omitted from the "Music" heading. In dictionary catalogues collective musical biography would be put under "Musicians" or at "Biography"; individual biographies being dealt with in the usual way. I shall be glad to correspond with any librarian on this subject, as there may be points which I have not touched upon. It is difficult to notice every detail in such a small space.

Cataloging Special Publications: Music

by O. G. Sonneck

In the fourth edition of his Rules for a dictionary catalog *(1904), Charles A. Cutter, Librarian of the Forbes Library, Northampton, Mass., included some recommendations for cataloguing music prepared by Oscar Sonneck, Chief of the Music Division of the Library of Congress. Reprinted here without comment, they appear merely quaint at first glance, but closer examination reveals them to be the basic cornerstones on which music cataloguers have built since 1904.*

It is no accident that Oscar Sonneck prepared the way for music cataloguers. He was a musicologist by training and a music librarian by instinct. See also the introductory comments to his pioneer essay "Music in our libraries," p. 5.

Music cataloging and book cataloging are essentially the same. The differences between the two are few and do not really affect the principles of bibliographical description. They either find their explanation in musical terminology or in traditional peculiarities of composers and publishers.

AUTHOR

Enter musical works under composer, with added entry for the author of words in case of operas, oratorios, cantatas, etc. Librettos enter under librettist with added entry for composer.

TITLE

Music issued in book form generally has a regular title page. If published in sheets, however, it often has what may be termed a collective title page, i.e., the page is filled above the imprint with several titles by different composers, or with several titles by one composer. The publisher, in order to identify the particular piece, underscores its title on this page. Such titles, as a rule, are too short for cataloging purposes. Instead, either the cover title or the caption title should be used, with a note to that effect.

IMPRINT

Music publishers, with very few exceptions, do not give the date of publication in the imprint. This practice may be due to some strong commercial consideration, but it certainly is very annoying to those who have to pay bibliographical attention to music, and often more than it is worth. As the finding of the date of publication has its many and tiresome difficulties it is generally either omitted by bibliographers, or given with the wide margin of centuries; f.i. [18–?].

In recent years publishers, though not compelled by law to do so, add the date of U. S. copyright. This is obviously the next best to the real date of publication and should be used without hesitation, perhaps in this form, ^{c}1903, or in brackets if required. Other means for accurately or approximately fixing the imprint date depend upon the bibliographical resources of the cataloger.

By consulting Hofmeister's Handbuch the dates of the majority of European compositions published during the last sixty years may be ascertained within a decade, and [187-?] looks decidedly less awkward than [18–?].

By using thematic catalogs, etc., and by referring to back numbers of musical periodicals a cataloger may even succeed in finding the exact dates.

If the composition be an opera, oratorio, or the like, the year of first performance, which is easily

SOURCE: Reprinted from Charles Ammi Cutter *Rules for a dictionary catalog*. 4th ed., rewritten, pp. 138–140: "Music," prepared by O. G. Sonneck. Washington, D. C.: U. S. Government Printing Office, 1904.

ascertained, may be added to some advantage, if a closer date is not obtainable. Perhaps in this manner: [p1866].

An indirect method of fixing the date of publication takes the publisher's (plate) number as a starting point. (It is usually to be found at the bottom of the pages. It should be kept in mind, however, that this number does not always coincide with the edition number given by the publisher in his catalog. Beer-Walbrunn, Deutsche Suite, has "Edition Peters 8718" at the bottom of the pages, whereas the title page and the catalog give it as "Edition Peters No. 2037.") By comparing the different dated issues of the publisher's catalog, the latest or earliest possible date of publication of certain compositions may be found. It will, for example, appear that nos. 1-3000 were published before 1879, nos. 5000-7000 after 1889. Consequently nos. 3001-4999 must have been published between 1880 and 1889.

This method will prove to be of particular value in cataloging full scores of modern operas. In fact, it will frequently be the only means of approximately fixing their date of publication, as many of them are neither on the open market, nor advertised for sale, nor otherwise recorded.

NOTES

As far as the cataloger's notes deal with pagination, contents, size, etc., music hardly calls for special rules, but it is advisable to state whether the cover or caption title were used, and to distinguish sheet music with an s. For purposes of identification the publisher's number should always be entered, and also the kind of voice for which the composition was written or the key in which the composition stands. The latter rule applies especially to song literature. Care should also be taken to distinguish clearly between the different kinds of scores and parts, if the title lacks sufficient information of this character, which is often the case. The term *score* may be used with safety for chamber music, whereas for orchestral and dramatic music, for concertos, etc., *full score* is to be preferred. *Orchestral score* is too narrow for a certain class of literature, as is *Vocal score* for such arrangements as really are *vocal scores with pianoforte accompaniment. Pianoforte score* designates an arrangement of the entire score for pianoforte, and should retain this meaning; but it seems hopeless to suggest a fixed terminology in these confused matters.

Chamber music for pianoforte and other instruments is published almost exclusively in parts, but the pianoforte part is nowadays invariably—and this for good reasons—printed to resemble a score. However, to remark in a note, as generally is done, "Score and parts," is obviously incorrect and misleading. Either one will have to say simply *Parts,* or *Piano, violin, and violoncello parts.* He who knows needs not to be instructed that the pianoforte part offers advantages similar to the real score, and he who does not know very probably will never disturb the tranquillity of his mind by pondering over the difference between scores and parts.

Examples

Chadwick, G[eorge] W[hitfield] 1854–
. . . Quintett für pianoforte, 2 violinen, viola & violoncell, von G. W. Chadwick . . . Boston & Leipzig, A. P. Schmidt [^{c}1890]
69, 11, 11, 11, 11 p. 35 × 26½^{cm}.
Publisher's no., A. P. S. 2569-2569 D
Parts.

Gaynor, *Mrs.* Jessie L[ove (Smith)]
Cradle song. Words by T. B. Aldrich. Music by Jessie L. Gaynor. [Chicago, C. F. Summy, ^{c}1903]
Caption title, 2-3 p. 34½ × 26^{cm}. s.
Publisher's no. C. F. S. Co. 182 d.
Mez. sop. (Violin or cello obligato ad lib.)

Götz, Hermann, 1840-1876.
Der widerspänstigen zähmung. Komische oper in 4 akten nach Shakespeare's gleichnamigem lustspiel frei bearbeitet von Joseph Viktor Widmann.
Musik von Hermann Goetz . . . Leipzig, F. Kistner [187-?]
1 p. l. 238 p. 36½ × 28^{cm}.
Publisher's no. 4520 (Overture, 4520, 4569)
Full score.

MacDowell, Edward [Alexander] 1861–
Six idyls after Goethe, composed for the pianoforte by Edward MacDowell . . . Opus 28. Newly revised and augmented edition. Boston, New York. A. P. Schmidt, ^{c}1901.
19 p. 31 × 24^{cm}. (Edition Schmidt, no. 57)
Publisher's nos., 5639^{a}-17–5639^{f}-17.
Contents.—In the woods.—Siesta.—To the moonlight.—Silver clouds.—Flute idyl.—The bluebell.

Classification, Cataloging, Indexing

by Minnie Elmer

Minnie Elmer, a distinguished American music cataloguer, died on April 25, 1965 [see a short Memorial by Virginia Cunningham in Fontes artis musicae, *13 (1966/2-3), 154]. Miss Elmer's thesis [***118,** *139] remains an extraordinarily valuable tool for beginning music cataloguers. The following paper is concerned with the purpose and philosophy of music processing and patterns of administration in American music libraries.*

Whether or not we initially have any intention of specializing in processing, we are all concerned with it in one way or another as soon as we begin our library careers. If we are not busy constructing a catalog, we are called upon to interpret one, and to supplement it by our special knowledge and by special indexing projects. One of our greatest assets as librarians in any part of the field is a thorough understanding of cataloging principles, and an intimate acquaintance with the particular catalog or catalogs with which we work daily.

Let us consider for a moment the purposes which are served by our processing activities. When our materials have been bound or otherwise prepared for use and shelved, we need first a finding list or index which will tell us what is in the library and where it is located. We choose as entry word in our list the one that best expresses what we think of as the basic approach to the material. We designate by a call number or other symbol the shelf location of the individual work, and according to the classification system we have chosen, of related works. When we have thus arranged and indexed our materials, we have performed the basic processing activities, and can begin to function as a library. Long ago we decided to add to the index functions of our catalog those of bibliographical description and subject bibliography. When we arrange our unit cards under a personal name we are creating an author bibliography; when we arrange them under a subject heading, a subject bibliography.

All of this is simple and clear cut. However, as soon as we begin indexing, classifying, and so forth, we come to the problem of the unit to be indexed. Is it the physical object: the volume, the set of volumes, the score, the monumental edition, the phono-disc, the album of records, the microfilm? Or is the unit of measurement the individual writing of an author, or the work of art, regardless of the form in which it occurs, as an entity or part of a larger whole? I think we would all agree that ideally, the unit of measurement should be the latter. We would like our catalog to list under Beethoven's name in a logical order of some sort each individual work of Beethoven that the library contains. We would like to have gathered together under a given subject all the material the library contains on that particular subject. Here we have compromised. We have made the unit of measurement the physical object, and have presented content by means of what we call analytical entry. As our collections have grown larger and larger, the amount of analysis has grown smaller and smaller.[1] If we were to need for some hypothetical purpose every possible version of a single song, printed, manuscript, or recorded, contained in a library, we could not find these listed together in one place in the average catalog. We would need to look through the contents of complete or miscellaneous collections of works by the composer, through miscellaneous song collections, and through special song indexes, printed, like Sears' index,[2] or a card index of songs like the one maintained by the New York Public Library. Here, then, is an example of supplementary cataloging carried out in addition to, and usually apart from, the main work of a catalog department.

SOURCE: Reprinted from Minnie Elmer, "Classification, cataloging, indexing," *Notes: Supplement for Members,* No. 25 (December, 1957), 23-28, by permission of the Music Library Association.

A few years ago scores and records were considered specialized material, too unusual to be handled satisfactorily in a catalog department whose primary responsibility was for books and book-like material. Many of our older music libraries created their own catalogs, evolving special rules and practices according to their individual needs. There has been a trend in recent years toward centralized cataloging of all library materials, and cataloging responsibilities have been in some cases shifted to the general cataloging department. Sometimes there is a division of responsibility, descriptive cataloging and classification, perhaps, being assigned to the central department, subject cataloging and catalog maintenance of the separate branch catalog, together with supplementary indexing, being retained in the music department. Or the division may be along the lines of material cataloged, record cataloging remaining the only branch responsibility.

The shift toward centralized cataloging of special materials has been made possible in large part through the development of special codes, which, theoretically at least, can be applied satisfactorily by catalogers with little music training. As long ago as 1915, the American Library Association appointed a music cataloging committee whose recommendations were largely embodied in Ruth Wallace's *Care and Treatment of Music in a Library,* published in 1927. Our own association prepared an elaborate *Code for Cataloging Music* in 1941-42. This, in turn, became the basis for the music section of the Library of Congress *Rules for Descriptive Cataloging* which appeared in preliminary edition in 1947, and was adopted by both the American Library Association and the Music Library Association in its final form in 1949. The same year saw the publication of the revised ALA cataloging rules for author and title entries, similarly approved by both associations. In 1953 came the Library of Congress supplementary rules for phonorecords. At present we have available not only a proportion of Library of Congress cards for scores and records as well as for books, but a printed Library of Congress catalog for materials in our field. The new version of the MLA code, which is nearing the point of publication, will give us the ALA rules for entry, the descriptive cataloging code of the Library of Congress for scores and phonorecords, and a set of alternative rules for simplified cataloging.[3]

In the matter of classification we are farther from a uniform solution than in cataloging. The Library of Congress schedules for music have not been revised since 1917. The standard edition of Dewey, 1951, incorporated only minor changes in the music schedules. Several alternatives to Dewey are available. McColvin and Reeves in their book on music libraries, 1937-38, presented alternative schedules within the Dewey framework. The Music Library Association Supplement for Members, in December 1951, contained another alternative[4] based partially on the Dickinson system. There remains the Dickinson classification itself, a practical and highly adaptable set of schedules for music.[5] However, most of us are obliged by our general cataloging policies to follow either Library of Congress or Dewey.

As to subject headings, our only practical tool is the Library of Congress list of *Music Subject Headings used on Printed Catalog Cards of the Library of Congress.*[6] Some of us may have on our library shelves the two lists mimeographed by the Music Library Association in 1933 and 1935, one for music literature drawn from the general Library of Congress subject headings, and one for music itself, representing headings formerly used in the Music Division catalog at that library. Headings for music appear, of course, in the ALA list of subject headings, and in the Sears list of subject headings for small libraries. These are designed for use in a general dictionary catalog, whereas the Library of Congress list is applicable either to a general dictionary catalog, or, with a few modifications, to a separate departmental catalog.

With this brief survey of present tools, we have looked at the materials with which the cataloger will work. Now let us turn to the place where he will work and the kinds of opportunities open to him. In the small library, where there is not enough work to support a full-time music cataloger, there are two possible patterns of organization. Either the cataloger will spend part of his time working with music, and part working with general materials of some sort; or he will devote all of his time to music, and divide it between cataloging activities and service to the public in his special field. From many points of view the latter is preferable. The cataloger who works with the public has the advantage of seeing at first hand the values and shortcomings of his work. Since he knows the collection and the catalog both, he can be of inestimable value to the library's public. He will be able to balance departmental needs against cataloging economies, and to make wise and well-founded recommendations on catalog content and the relative values of different kinds of approach to the materials of the collection.

In the large library, on the other hand, there will be ample work for one or more special catalogers. The likelihood of departmental interchange decreases with the size of the organization. The larger the catalog department, the more involved the techniques, the greater the emphasis on procedures and routines, and the smaller, usually, the opportunity of the cataloging specialist to work part of his day in the departmental library. In the extremely large library there may even be, as at Library of Congress, a division according to process: descriptive cataloging as against subject cataloging and classification; or at the University of California, a division by material, scores being handled by one cataloger, recordings by another.

The forms that were distributed at the business meeting illustrate a wide variety of patterns of organization. I have selected as typical six public and six university library music departments. Of the public libraries, four among the six represent departments in which music is combined with art or drama. The largest has seven professional positions in the music and drama department as against two full time music positions in the catalog department; the smallest, one full time position in each department. In three, all of the materials intended for the music library are cataloged, classified, and assigned subject headings in the catalog department. In one of these three, catalog maintenance is the responsibility of the catalog department; in the other two, a shared responsibility. Two of the remaining music departments catalog and assign subject headings for phonograph records. In these two catalog maintenance is the responsibility of the music library staff. The sixth music department catalogs its own scores as well as the recordings. In the largest library, cards for all materials appear in the general catalog as well as in the departmental catalog; in two, cards for books and scores are duplicated, and in the other three, cards for books on music only. In one library the music catalogers work at the music library desk on Sundays, and in one other plans are being worked out for exchange of personnel.

The six university libraries vary more widely in pattern of organization. The largest has four full-time professional positions in the music department; the smallest, one professional librarian who divides her time between cataloging and public service activities. In two libraries, all processing for the department is done by the music library staff. In both of these, cards for books on music are filed in the general catalog of the university, while those for scores and recordings appear only in the departmental catalog. In a third, all materials are handled by a member of the catalog department, who, however, spends one day per week in the music library working with phonograph records. The fourth conforms to one of the public library patterns, with all materials except records handled in the catalog department. Here, cards for all material other than records are duplicated for the general catalog. In the last two, books on music are processed in the catalog department, all other materials in the music library. In all but one, books are the only departmental material represented in the general catalog. Obviously, where the music library staff does a large proportion of the cataloging, it also assumes responsibility for catalog maintenance.

Generalizing from these few examples, it would seem that in public libraries the catalog department tends to do most of the processing, and that in the university library the music department is apt to take on more cataloging responsibility. One of the reasons for this may be the location of the music reference collection. Since the university music library is often housed in a building apart from the main collection, it may be more convenient to do cataloging research in the music library itself. Another explanation might lie in the original status of the music collection. The tendency might be for cataloging to continue to be done in the general catalog department if the music library has recently been withdrawn from the main collection. It seems surprising that scores and records, which are basically two forms of the same material, are so often cataloged by different agencies.

Our statistics are too limited to indicate very much as to standardization of practices. Five of the six public libraries use Dewey classification for books, and Dewey or modified Dewey for scores. Most of us arrange our records by accession number. Of the university libraries, two use the Library of Congress classification for both books and scores; four, Dewey or modified Dewey for scores, and one the Dickinson classification for scores. We are consistent in using the LC cataloging code for books on music, with only one of fourteen libraries reporting use of another set of rules. There seems to be a little more variation in score cataloging; eight of fourteen libraries follow the LC code, with or without modification, for scores. The same proportions hold true as to use of LC subject headings for books and scores; only six libraries follow them for records. Seventeen libraries reported on their use of LC cards; of these, sixteen order them for books, fourteen for scores, seven for recordings.

In addition to cataloging proper, many libraries engage in a good deal of supplementary indexing. Specific examples have been mentioned in previous meetings, and the need for cooperative efforts pointed out.

We have examined some of our cataloging tools, and outlined some of the kinds of position available to the person who wishes to specialize in music cataloging. A question remains as to what will be his contribution to the field. Have we completed the era of experimentation? Is it time for us to work for standardization and conformity, or is there still room for individual variation in libraries of different types?

NOTES

[1] Analysis of *Denkmäler* (Monuments) and *Gesamtausgaben* (Complete Editions) is especially difficult to achieve. Quite a few *Denkmäler* were analyzed by cooperating music libraries in the 1930's and that copy circulated on Library of Congress cards. It is dismaying to report that 1) those cards were out-of-print for quite a while, and 2) now that LC will reprint them on request, it truncates them by deleting the contents notes and tracings with which to analyze a volume of thirty compositions by twenty different composers. For instance, the first two cards below were purchased from LC in the 1930's; the latter two, with the same LC card number, were purchased in October, 1971.

Newe deudsche geistliche gesenge für die gemeinen schulen. Gedrückt zu Wittemberg/durch Georgen Rhau, 1544. Herausgegeben von Johannes Wolf. Leipzig, Breitkopf & Härtel, 1908.

xviii, [6], 196 p. incl. port., facsims. pl. 35½cm. (*Added t.-p.:* Denkmäler deutscher tonkunst. 1. folge ... bd. 34)

With facsimile of original t.-p., preface, etc.

Lutheran church music, 123 compositions to 70 texts—hymns, rhymed paraphrases of psalms, liturgical texts (prose or rhymed) German words, by Luther and others; many translations from Latin.

For 4 or 5 voices (a few for 3 or 6); unaccompanied. Open score.

Composers: Martinus Agricola; Anonymous (Georg Rhaw?); Huldricus Bretel; Arnoldus de Bruck; Sixtus Dieterich; Benedictus Ducis; Georg Förster; Vergilius Hauck; Wolff Heintz; Lupus Hellingk; Stephanus Mahu; Nicolaus P. [*i. e.* Piltz?]; Baltasar Resinarius; Ludovicus

(Continued on next card)

A C 34–3187 Revised

[r35g2]

2

Newe deudsche geistliche gesenge für die gemeinen schulen ... 1908. (Card 2)

Senffel; Johannes Stahl; Thomas Stoltzer; Georgius Vogelhuber; Johannes Weinmann.

1. Hymns, German. [1. Hymn collections: German] 2. Choral music, German [2. Part-songs: Early: Sacred] I. Rhaw, Georg, 1488–1548. II. Wolf, Johannes, 1869– ed. III. Luther, Martin, 1483–1546. IV. Agricola, Martin, 1486–1556. V. Brätel, Ulrich, d. 1544 or 5. VI. Arnold von Bruck, d. 1544. VII. Dietrich, Sixtus, 1490 (ca.)–1548. VIII. Ducis, Benedictus, fl. 1532. IX. Forster, Georg, 1514 (ca.)–1568. X. Hauck, Virgil, fl. 1540. XI. Heintz, Wolffgang, fl. 1543. XII. Hellinck, Johannes Lupus, d. 1541. XIII. Mahu, Stephan, 16th cent. XIV. Piltz, Nicolaus, 16th cent., supposed author. XV. Resinarius, Balthasar, fl. 1543. XVI. Senfl, Ludwig, 1492 (ca.)–1555. XVII. Stahl, Johannes. XVIII. Stoltzer, Thomas, d. 1526? XIX. Vogelhuber, Georg, 16th cent. XX. Weinmann, Johann, d. 1542.

A C 34–3187 Revised

Title from Yale Univ. Library of Congress

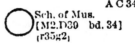

Sch. of Mus. [M2.D30 bd. 34]

[r35g2]

Newe deudsche geistliche Gesenge für die gemeinen Schulen. Gedrückt zu Wittemberg durch Georgen Rhau, 1544. Hrsg. von Johannes Wolf. Leipzig, Breitkopf & Härtel, 1908.

xviii p., score (196 p.) port., facsims. 36 cm. (Denkmäler deutscher Tonkunst. 1. Folge, Bd. 34)

Lutheran church music, 123 compositions to 70 texts — hymns, rhymed paraphrases of psalms, liturgical texts (prose or rhymed) German words, by Luther and others; many translations from Latin. For 3–6 voices.

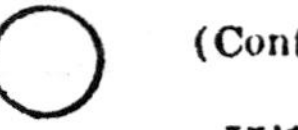

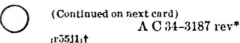

(Continued on next card)

A C 34–3187 rev*

[r55j1]†

Newe deudsche geistliche Gesenge für die gemeinen Schulen. 1908. (Card 2)

Contains works by Martinus Agricola, Anonymous (Georg Rhaw?), Huldricus Bretel, Arnoldus de Bruck, Sixtus Dieterich, Benedictus Ducis, Georg Förster, Vergilius Hauck, Wolff Heintz, Lupus Hellingk, Stephanus Mahu, Nicolaus P. (Piltz?), Baltasar Resinarius, Ludovicus Senffel, Johannes Stahl, Thomas Stoltzer, Georgius Vogelhuber, and Johannes Weinmann.

1. Hymns, German. 2. Part-songs, Sacred—To 1800. I. Wolf, Johannes, 1869–1947, ed. (Series)

M2.D39 Bd. 34 A C 34–3187 rev*

Yale Univ. School of Music. Library for Library of Congress [r55j1]†

Gone is the information for which a cataloguer orders LC cards! It's no trick to transcribe a title-page, but to prepare and type a complete contents note and establish and trace twenty composer analytics can be more than a day's work. In the example below, the contents and medium notes have been deleted.

Tunder, Franz, 1614–1667.

Franz Tunders gesangswerke; solocantaten und chorwerke mit instrumentalbegleitung. Herausgegeben von Max Seiffert. Leipzig, Breitkopf & Härtel, 1900.

xi, [1], 159 p. $35\frac{1}{2}$cm. (*Added t.-p.: Denkmäler deutscher tonkunst* [1. folge] ... 3. bd.)

Sacred music for from 1 to 5 voices, with accompaniment of from 1 to 6 string instruments and bass (figured or unfigured) for organ or harpsichord. 18 compositions.

Latin or German words.

CONTENTS.—1. Salve Cœlestis Pater, basso solo con violino.—2. O Jesu dulcissime, basso solo con 2 violini.—3. Salve mi Jesu, contra alto solo con 5 viole.—4. Da mihi Domine, basso solo con 5 viole.—5. Herr, nun lässest du deien diener, 2 bassi con 5 viole.—6. Nisi Dominus aedificaverit, dialogo o concerto a 2 canti, basso con 2 violini.—7. Dominus

(Continued on next card)

A C 34–3161

[2]

Tunder, Franz, 1614–1667. Franz Tunders gesangswerke ... 1900. (Card 2)

CONTENTS—Continued.

Illuminatio mea, 5 voci con 2 violini.—8. Nisi Dominus aedificaverit, 5 voci con 5 viole.—9. Hosianna dem Sohne David, in adventu. Jubilate et exultate, vivat rex Carolus, 5 voci con 5 stromenti.—10. Aria, Ein kleines kindelein, soprano solo con 5 stromenti.—11. Ach Herr, lass deine lieben engelein, soprano solo con 4 viole.—12. Wachet auf! ruft uns die stimme, canto solo con 3 viole.—13. An wasserflüssen Babylon, canto solo con 5 viole.—14. Aria, Streuet mit palmen, 5 voci con 5 stromenti.—15. Helft mir Gott's güte preisen, 5 voci con 5 viole.—16. Wend' ab deinen zorn, lieber Herr, mit gnaden, 6 voci con 6 stromenti.—17. Ein' feste burg ist unser Gott, 4 voci con 2 violini e 4 viole.—Anhang: Sinfonia à 7 viole. Diese sinfonia ist gesetzt für ein muttedt, Da pacem Domine.

1. Songs, German. [1. Songs: Early: Sacred] 2. Choral music, German. [2. Choral music: Early: Sacred] I. Seiffert, Max, 1868– ed. [2]

Title from Yale Univ. Sch. of Mus. A C 34-3161
Library of Congress [M2.D39 bd. 3]

Tunder, Franz, 1614–1667.
[Works, vocal. Selections]

Gesangswerke; Solocantaten und Chorwerke mit Instrumentalbegleitung. Hrsg. von Max Seiffert. Leipzig, Breitkopf & Härtel, 1900.

xi p., score (159 p.) 36 cm. (Denkmäler deutscher Tonkunst, 1. Folge, Bd. 3)

Sacred music for 1–5 voices with 1–6 string instruments and organ.

Latin or German words.

1. Solo cantatas, Sacred—To 1800—Scores. 2. Choruses, Sacred (Mixed voices) with various accompaniment—To 1800—Scores. I. Seiffert, Max, 1868–1948, ed. (Series)

M2.D39 Bd. 3 A C 34-3161

Yale Univ. School of Music. Library
for Library of Congress [r70c2] rev M

A justification for less analysis in the card catalogue is the existence of Anna Harriet Heyer *Historical sets, collected editions, and monuments of music; a guide to their contents.* Second edition (Chicago: American Library Association, 1969). However, that second edition has a cut-off date of Spring, 1966; further, the physical format of the publication allows no room for recording a library's call numbers, holdings, or additions. As an auxiliary to the card catalogue,

Heyer should be published in a library edition: in a loose-leaf binder, printed on one side of the paper only, with generous margins to permit writing in library call numbers, and to be interleaved with typewritten entries for new series.

Although the existence of a tool such as Heyer is of inestimable value to music librarians and knowledgable music scholars, many students leave the library without finding it; or, if they do know of it, they are loathe to go through the four or five steps required to proceed from Heyer's "Index" to the appropriate volume on the library shelf. Or, the music needed by the student has been published since 1966, Heyer's cut-off date. If that volume of music has not been analyzed in the library's card catalogue, it is indeed lost to many library patrons until the next edition of Heyer is published.

The ideal solution would be to analyze *Denkmäler* in the card catalogue, to record new volumes of *Gesamtausgaben* in their appropriate thematic catalogues, to have a library edition of Heyer for use within the library until catalogue copy is available for the card catalogue, and a paper-bound edition of Heyer for students' and scholars' home use.–*Editor.*

[2]and Desiree De Charms and Paul F. Breed *Songs in collections, an index* (Detroit: Information Service, Inc., 1966).–*Editor.*

[3]Subsequently published [**124,** 139].–*Editor.*

[4]Item **135,** p. 140.–*Editor.*

[5]See also [**141,** 141].–*Editor.*

[6]and those of The New York Public Library. Reference Department. *Music subject headings, authorized for use in the catalogs of the Music Division* (Boston: G. K. Hall, 1959).–*Editor.*

Some Pros and Cons Regarding an International Code for Cataloging Practical Music

by Richard S. Hill

There is no way to introduce Richard S. Hill in a few sentences or paragraphs; an extended biography of his professional life would be more appropriate. Just a list of his professional affiliations and accomplishments becomes a sterile image in which nothing warm and living is reflected. Better to see the thoughtful man, dedicated to the growth and refinement of his profession, in the mirror of his work for the Music Library Association, most particularly his seventeen-year editorship of Notes. *[As introduction to those years, see Donald W. Krummel, "Twenty years of* Notes*–A retrospect,"* Notes, *21 (Winter-Spring, 1963-64), 56-82.]*

Two memorial essays written shortly after Hill's death on February 7, 1961, are the best published appraisals of his activities as music librarian-bibliographer-researcher-scholar.

Duckles, Vincent. "Richard S. Hill, 1901-1961," Notes, *18 (March, 1961), 193-196.*
Fox, Charles Warren. "Richard S. Hill: A reminiscence," Notes, *18 (June, 1961), 369-374. With a list of Mr. Hill's published writings compiled by Carroll D. Wade and Frank C. Campbell, pp. 375-380.*

In the following paper, written to convince IAML of the need for an international code for cataloguing music, Mr. Hill reviewed existing codes for cataloguing music. The Association heeded his persuasions and to date, three volumes of the Code *have been published [***125***, 140].*

This paper has one and only one purpose–to present for your consideration the proposition that this Association appoint a committee for drawing up an international code for cataloging music. It probably should go without saying that my colleagues entrusted this assignment to me in the hopes that somehow I would find a way of making the proposition as enticing as possible. At first, this element of enticement made it seem as if I might talk to you about practically anything in the world except cataloging codes. For what, after all, is a cataloging code except a set of rules determining procedures, stating in the simplest and most obvious manner exactly how the cataloger shall make the entry for as many different kinds of entries and under as many different circumstances as a long line of extremely astute catalogers have been able to devise, and then proceeding on to the consideration of added entries, methods of transcribing the title-page, the proper method of recording–or of *not* recording–the imprint, the collation, series title (if any), and notes. I doubt if there is anyone capable of making such matters enticing to a group with such variegated interests as those of the present company, and certainly I know that it is far beyond my spellbinding powers. As a consequence, my only alternative is to eschew as completely as pos-

SOURCE: Reprinted from Richard S. Hill, "Some pros and cons regarding an International Code for cataloging Practical Music," in International Association of Music Libraries. 3e congrès international des bibliothèques musicales, Paris, 22-25 juillet 1951. *Actes du congrès . . .*, pp. 37-45. Kassel: Bärenreiter, 1953, by permission of Bärenreiter-Verlag.

sible all mention of specific cataloging rules as such.

In doing so, however, I would not for a moment have you suppose that I look down upon cataloging codes or the rules of which they are comprised. Actually, there is something almost beautiful about a properly constructed cataloging code. Although they have other attractions in addition, the thing that has fascinated me most in looking through an extensive series of codes these past few months is their form. It may sound absurd to say so, but a good code has the clarity of outline and the articulation of structure of a classical sonata. It is true enough that at times this form takes on a certain aspect of unreality. Who was it that said: "The art of cataloging is the art of compromise"? But even if there is an element of truth in this, there can be no gainsaying that the close study of cataloging problems and the careful adjustment of the different elements involved, with the end in view of making the description of the composition immediately and easily comprehensible, is a discipline entirely worthy of the music librarian. Indeed, it falls well within the meaning of several of the paragraphs describing the purposes of this Association in our new Constitution, but none more than the fifth Purpose which states that we shall stimulate and further by every means the inventory of all music collections, *so that they may be made available to researchers*. Making our holdings available quickly and easily to all visitors to our libraries should, after all, be our primary duty, and if a standard, widely accepted code for cataloging music will facilitate the formation of larger, more complete, and better organized catalogs, we would seem to have relatively little choice in the matter.

If this is true, one only wonders how the world managed to survive for so many years with so few and such inadequate cataloging codes. That it most obviously did so is probably due in part to a variety of conditions, some of which are apparently changing at a constantly increasing rate. For one thing, there were far fewer music libraries, even as recently as the last century. And the few libraries that there were had many less readers. What is more, restrictions on readers were sufficiently strict to limit the use of libraries to regular *habitués*, who knew the collection of the library quite as intimately as the librarian himself, and consequently there was less need for a catalog. Today, in many countries, both the number of music libraries and the number of readers in each library are on the increase. There are not only more musicologists and well-equipped scholars, but there are more practical musicians and amateurs using the music libraries regularly. Far worse still for the music librarian, there is infinitely more music coming from the presses, and it is obviously essential to discover some means by which this flood can be rapidly put under control and worked into our collections in ways which will get the utmost use from it.

I suspect that in the phrase—"the utmost use"—lies hidden the chief reason for the growing interest in codes for cataloging music. So long as our public consisted largely of scholars who knew exactly what they wanted, it made relatively little difference how any particular piece was cataloged. A simple composer entry, a few identifying words from the title, possibly the last name of the publisher, and the cataloging was completed. Actually, I have recently seen a catalog in actual use in one of the most musical cities of Europe where the composer's name was entered only once at the top of a large, commodious card, and below it a confusing series of titles and editions entered in the order in which the material was acquired. The method unquestionably saved time for the librarian, but every reader lost many minutes seeking each piece he wanted, and when he did not find it, he could never be quite sure he had not simply overlooked it in the confused mass of information presented to him.

If this state of affairs is rather worse than the norm, something not too dissimilar is undoubtedly within the experience of most of us. And certainly no one can be unfamiliar with the practice of many large libraries which are tied, for better or worse, to the book catalog system with a single entry for each publication in the collection. Obviously, for the preparation of such catalogs a fairly rudimentary code suffices. In fact,—and here comes, I'm afraid, the crux of the whole problem—it is largely only when one reaches the stage of cataloging each piece on a multiple series of cards to bring out and codify its various aspects that an elaborate code becomes practically essential. The Prussian *Instruktionen*, the Vatican's remarkable *Norme*, and the British Museum's *Rules* are all entirely adequate for the preparation of entries for a book catalog, even if none of them devote more than a page or two to the special rules for cataloging music, and regardless of the fact that these rules are largely limited to how the main entry should be given. They would be far from adequate, however, for the preparation of a multiple series of cards, where one card was to be filed under the original composer and other cards under a whole string of added entries (arranger, editor, author of text, etc.), and still more cards for the title, the plate number file, various subject headings based on musical forms, instrumentation, and the like. And yet it is only this sort of cataloging that can possibly get "the utmost use" from the material in a collection. I do not exaggerate in regard to this question of multiple entries—and what is more, I am not simply offering you an American pipe-dream. It is a system which is in use in several European libraries as well. For example, M. Fédorov, in describing the cataloging practices in the relatively new Music Division of the Bibliothèque Nationale, wrote that in addition to the general, main alphabetical catalog, they had thirteen special catalogs. Some of these would not be formed automatically from the catalog cards for music, since the thirteen include a separate libretto catalog, a periodical catalog, an index to periodicals, and so on. But the list did include catalogs for titles and first lines, authors of words, illustrators, musical incipits, and subjects.

Needless to say, the old argument of card catalog versus book catalog is not one which can be settled simply as a by-product of our present problem. But it does seem to me that we must look that problem squarely in the eye, since it is manifestly a decision that must be made before we can decide what sort of a code, if any, we are to make. No code is an end in itself. It is merely a means to an end, and consequently we must first determine what the end is to be before we can tell whether a code is required.

To get the utmost out of a collection of music we must bring out and record more than simply the name of the composer. A catalog is not simply a tool for locating on the shelf the works of a given composer. It can just as well bring out and organize information on any number of other aspects of the collection. I have yet to see the book catalog that is as versatile and can so easily be adapted to so many purposes as a card catalog. And yet, unfortunately, there is no way of getting around the fact that many of the world's largest and best music libraries are indissolubly wedded to the book type catalog—and some of them seem very happily married indeed. Usually where this is true the collection goes back many decades and sometimes even centuries. The cataloging practices were established when less was expected of a librarian, and now that tons of music have been cataloged in the one form, it would be impractical, if not impossible, to change. As far as this Association is concerned, however, the question is not entirely one of practicality. New music libraries are being established periodically, and old ones are occasionally changing over to card catalogs, at least for new acquisitions. It thus becomes a question of whether our Association wishes to throw its weight on one side or the other in this long struggle, since the type of code we are to make (ignoring for the moment the question of whether we are to make any code at all) obviously depends upon the type of catalog we choose to sponsor.

Perhaps a survey of previous cataloging codes may help us to an answer. The earliest codes, like the ones mentioned above, were primarily codes for cataloging books, and treated music similarly. The British Museum's *Rules*[1] were issued again in a revised edition as recently as 1936, and by itself this would seem to indicate that the British Museum still finds them adequate for its purpose. Mr. A. Hyatt King writes that certain modifications are necessary because of the special and peculiar nature of music, and that he has often felt that a written set of rules, embodying these modifications, would be most desirable. In mentioning the various points to be covered, however, he says that the list he would like to make would be in substantial agreement with the list of elements which were to be considered for inclusion in each entry in the British *Union Catalogue of Music.* This list was given by Dr. Vincent Duckles in his recent article on the Union Catalogue in the March 1951 issue of NOTES,[2] and I believe that if you will examine it you will find it well removed from the sort of code under discussion here. In the hands of a practised and intelligent cataloger, the list would undoubtedly give counsel and ample aid, but it prescribes very little and leaves almost everything to the decision of the cataloger. It comes closer to the list of rules (Vorschriften) which the Deutsche Bücherei supplies to publishers to indicate the form in which it wishes entries to be submitted for its catalogs, except that the latter in some regards is more specific.[3]

As might be expected, most of the early efforts to deal specifically with the problem of cataloging music are relatively brief, but I find it significant that the earliest one found—an article on "Cataloguing of Music," published in *The Library* in 1897[4]—is concerned with cards for music as part of a general catalog. Next, the section on music cataloging furnished by Oscar Sonneck for Cutter's *Rules for a Dictionary Catalog*,[5] again provides rules for making cards, and includes a remarkably interesting discussion, particularly considering the date, of the importance of publisher's plate numbers in establishing the imprint. There is a short and curious section on music in a volume published in Madrid in 1910 for the guidance of public libraries,[6] which requires that the title of a composition be used as the main entry, with a cross-reference only to its composer. The August 1915 issue of the *Library Journal* was devoted entirely to music, and the procedures of cataloging in a rapidly growing public library were discussed.[7] Five years later, a report on rules for music cataloging appeared in the American Library Association *Bulletin*.[8] These rules, prepared by a special committee, were concise, but they were the first set of rules to take on some semblance of the basic structure of more modern codes, and in somewhat expanded form they were used as the basis for the chapter on cataloging in Ruth Wallace's *Care and Treatment of Music in a Library*.[9] Meanwhile, the first major European attempt to cope with the problem—Kay Schmidt-Phiseldeck's *Musikalien-Katalogisierung*[10]—had appeared in a separate volume.

Except for the *Rules*[11] issued by the University Library in Cambridge, England, and a few short, if sometimes excellent, sections in general works on cataloging,[12] the topic was allowed to lie fallow for a full decade. But then it came suddenly to life once more. The discussion of music cataloging in the revision of McColvin and Reeve's *Music Libraries* advances the subject materially, particularly in regard to the problem of title-pages, and a Russian code, compiled by Elena Andreevna Novikova, was published the same year in Moscow.[13] In mentioning this Russian code, it may be as well to say now that Novikova revised her code extensively in 1939 in a volume which unfortunately has not been available during the preparation of this paper. A certain amount of information about it, however, may be deduced from another of her publications, issued in Moscow in 1948,[14] in which she gives a careful and extended philosophical discussion of much of the literature on the subject. Any future study of the subject will surely have to consider this publication most carefully. To return to our chronological course, the following year, 1938, saw the publication of E. Weiss-Reyscher's *Anweisung zur Titelaufnahme von Musikalien*,[15] prepared in the Berlin Bibliotheksschule, as well as J. F. Russel's article, "Cataloguing of music," published in the June number of the *Library Association Record*. The latter presented the code of rules used at the Henry Watson Music Library in Manchester, England.[16]

In 1941, or more properly in 1942 (regardless of the date of the imprint), the preliminary version of the code issued by the Music Library Association appeared in a series of chapters.[17] It was carefully analysed by Professor Otto Erich Deutsch in his study, "Music bibliography and catalogues,"[18] and has been undergoing revision almost constantly ever since at the hands of a special joint committee of the Music Library Association and the American Library Association. During this period, the whole subject of Descriptive Cataloging had come under close scrutiny at the Library of Congress, and a preliminary survey, entitled *Studies of Descriptive Cataloging*[19] was published by the Library in 1946. The studying was continued, with the Library planning to issue a complete code covering all special fields. Thus, although the revised MLA-ALA code was ready early in 1949, it was decided to hold up publication until a special committee could go over it carefully with the view of bringing it into line with the new Library of Congress code. By the time this had been accomplished, the MLA-ALA committee had completed the revision of the chapter on the cataloging of phonograph records, and for a time it was thought that the complete MLA code might be published during the winter of 1950-51. Again, however, it seemed best to hold back on it once more to wait for the Library of Congress to finish its record code so that the two might be brought into agreement. This general process, unfortunate as it may seem at first, is actually to the benefit of everyone concerned, since agreement down to the last comma is essential in the United States. The Library of Congress supplies printed cards for a large proportion of the country's libraries. In addition, many libraries also do a certain amount of their own cataloging. Since some of these institutions might conceivably wish to use the MLA-ALA code in producing their own cards, the two underlying systems must correspond closely enough to permit the interfiling of both types of cards. The combined record code is now in its last stages of preparation, and once it is finished, it is hoped that there will be no further delays in bringing out the complete MLA-ALA code, since it will undoubtedly be convenient to have a complete code for cataloging music in a separate volume.[20] In the meantime, the rules for all of the chapters except the record code may be found in two general codes. The rules governing the main entry are in the *A. L. A. Cataloging Rules for Author and Title Entries*,[21] and the remainder in *Rules for Descriptive Cataloging in the Library of Congress*.[22]

Once again, the discussion of various editions of a code has put us rather ahead of ourselves, and we must back up to mention an interesting study published in 1945 by the Schweizerische Landesbibliothek in Bern—a joint work in which Dr. Paul Sieber discusses some fundamental problems in running music libraries, including the cataloging of music, and Dr. Hans Zehntner (our colleague on the Preparatory Commission of this Association) reports on the Music Division of the University Library in Basel.[23] Dr. Sieber discusses cataloging philosophically and presents alternate solutions for most of the problems, rather than a series of undeviating rules, and as a consequence it has turned out to be a little difficult to abstract his recommendations. The recommendations have nonetheless been carefully thought out, and will certainly have to be studied whenever anyone contemplates the compilation of a new code.

Next in the series I might mention a very special solution to the problem. In 1946, the Copyright Office in Washington undertook to prepare catalog cards for the Library of Congress of all items registered for copyright in Washington, and a special division was set up for that purpose. The volume of material that had to be handled—some 12,000 printed compositions and approximately 45,000 unpublished compositions—made it absolutely essential to devise a set of rules that would allow the material to be processed with dispatch, and consequently a mimeographed set of *Rules for Brief Cataloging of Published Music* was prepared, strictly for intramural use. Except for certain prescribed omissions to be used in preparing simpler entries for certain types of unpublished material, the *Rules* are not too dissimilar to the regular rules of the Library of Congress, and for us they are probably of less interest in themselves than in what they produce—the semi-annual catalogs of *Published Music* deposited for copyright. The new cataloging division has made so many improvements over the previous copyright catalogs that these volumes have taken on much of the significance of the pre-war Hofmeister *Verzeichnisse.* In some ways, they surpass those volumes, since they are not limited to the publications of any one country, but include almost as many entries for European publications as for those issued in the United States, and thus come closer to an international catalog of current music than any other catalog being published to-day.

And finally we come to what is probably the latest contribution to the subject of music cataloging. It was issued in 1949 by the Département de la Musique of the Bibliothèque Nationale, and is entitled *Règles adoptées pour la rédaction des catalogues du département.* It is cast in quite a different form than most of the codes discussed previously. Instead of first discussing the entry, and then following through with the various subsidiary sections of the description, all of the usual terms are arranged alphabetically, starting with "Abréviation," and following through with "Adjonction," "Adresse," and so forth to "Tonalité," "Traduction," and "Transcription." The definitions, however, supply all of the information found in a regular code, and the new arrangement has several things to recommend it. Apparently in practical use, however, the advantages are outweighed by disadvantages, and the material is to be re-worked into the conventional form of presentation.

If there is anything to be learned from this very hasty survey,[24] probably it is that the rise and development of elaborate codes for cataloging music is closely tied to the spread of the card catalog. Indeed, one might almost say that the type of code needed for preparing music entries for a book catalog is so simple that it scarcely calls for separate publication. The necessary specifications can easily be given on a page or two at the end of a library's rules for cataloging books, and adequate codes for this purpose already exist. In this one respect, our problem is considerably simplified, since now we need only decide whether we shall or shall not make a code for producing a card catalog.

True, even if the answer is in the affirmative, our course is not as simple as it might be. Where so much has been written on a subject, it would manifestly be very foolish to expect anything like complete agreement in regard to the solutions found. There is even a grave doubt in my mind as to whether it will ever be possible to persuade all of our various lions and lambs to lie down in amical agreement. We all have certain established traditions to follow and our cataloging methods have been designed to gain certain ends. Cataloging is not yet an absolutely pure art, existing for and of itself. Any set of rules must take into consideration the purpose of the catalog which they are designed to create, and as those purposes differ, so will at least some of the rules. A scholarly library with a relatively small collection of immensely valuable publications may be able to afford a detailed type of description which would be completely nonsensical if applied to a public library with nothing but cheap, contemporary editions in its collection. Furthermore, rules are bound to be conditioned to some extent by purely monetary considerations, particularly in respect to the amount of money available for paying the cataloging staff. If two individuals must do the work of ten, the rules must be reduced to the uttermost simplicity, and no amount of persuasion will convince the gentlemen in charge of the purse-strings that more elaborate rules are justifiable.

Or would it? There is certainly no sense in allowing a good idea to be killed off by mere pessimism. Is it not possible that if the International Association of Music Libraries were to perfect a workable code for cataloging music—a code which took into consideration all of the experimentation and study of the past half century, and ended as being demonstrably the best code that could be devised under the circumstances—the Association would be putting a powerful lever into the hands of its members? Armed with such a code and with certain statistics derived from his own cataloging department, a music librarian might be able to persuade his chief that a larger staff was absolutely essential if the library was to hold its position in the field. One rarely gets anything worth having without asking for it, and the more pressure one can apply at crucial points, the better are the chances of getting what one needs. If this Association is to stimulate the activities of its member libraries, as the second Purpose of our Constitution prescribes, then we must manifestly forge the tools needed for raising our profession to higher levels of achievement.

Actually, we are not faced with the necessity of achieving complete agreement, and perhaps it would be just as well if we did not attempt it. The missionary work of the Association will be accomplished if we merely *improve* cataloging practices by suggesting better procedures, leaving each institution to decide to what extent it is currently able to put those procedures into practice. Considered in such terms, our chief problem will be to agree among ourselves as to what the best procedures are. And if at first this seems to be a large enough task by itself, an examination of the literature permits one to hope for its eventual solution. As a matter of fact, there is a fairly large area of agreement already among many of the published codes. Miss Minnie Elmer of the Copyright Cataloging Division of the Library of Congress has been kind enough to draw up a chart. It was obviously out of the question to abstract completely even as many as seven different codes on a sheet of reasonable size, and Miss Elmer has to satisfy herself with selecting certain typical points to illustrate some of the topics on which there is substantial agreement, and other striking points of emphatic disagreement. Examination of the chart seems to indicate that the points of agreement far outnumber the points of disagreement. Furthermore, these latter points often have an air of chance or happenstance about them, and in some instances the conflict can doubtless be resolved without a struggle. Perhaps, if further study of the chart leads to the conclusion that an International Code for Cataloging Practical Music is as reasonable an idea as it seems to be, someone among you will rise to make the necessary motion to start it on its way towards ultimate realization.

NOTES

[1] British Museum, *Department of Printed Books:* Rules for compiling the catalogues of printed books, maps and music . . . London, 1936.

[2] *Notes,* Vol. VIII, no. 2, March, 1951, p. 281.

[3] I am indebted to Dr. Martin Cremer of Marburg for a transcription of these rules.

[4] J. D. Brown: "Cataloguing of music", in *The Library*, vol. 9, 1897, p. 82-84. [Reprinted above, pp. 143–145]

[5] O. G. T. Sonneck: "Music", in C. A. Cutter's *Rules for a dictionary catalog*, Washington, D. C., U. S. Government Printing Office, 4th ed., 1904, p. 138-40. [Reprinted above, pp. 146–147]

[6] Spain. *Junta facultativa de archivos, bibliotecas y museos: Instrucciones para la catalogación de manuscritos, estampas, dibujos originales, fotografías y piezas de música, de las Bibliotecas Públicas, redactadas por la Junta Facultativa del Ramo*, Madrid, Imp. de la "Revista de Archivos", Olózaga, núm. I, 1910. (Música, p. 75-82).

[7] Music number, a symposium on music and music records in American libraries, *Library Journal*, vol. 40, August 1915, p. 561-94.

[8] American Library Association, Committee on Catalog Rules: Report . . . "Rules for cataloging musical scores", in *A. L. A. Bulletin*, Vol. 14, July 1920, p. 295-96.

[9] Ruth Wallace: "Cataloging rules", p. 15-31 in her *Care and Treatment of Music in a Library*, Chicago, American Library Association, 1927.

[10] Kay Schmidt-Phiseldeck: *Musikalien-Katalogisierung; Ein Beitrag zur Lösung ihrer Probleme*, Leipzig, Breitkopf & Härtel, 1926. (44 p.)

[11] Cambridge, University Library: *Rules for the catalogues of printed books, maps & music*, Cambridge, The University Press, 1927.

[12] Fritz Milkau: *Handbuch der Bibliothekswissenschaft,* Leipzig, O. Harrassowitz, vol. 2, 1933: see especially "Die Musikabteilung", by Johannes Wolf; *Lexikon des gesamten Buchwesens,* hrsg. von Karl Löffler und Joachim Kirchner unter Mitwirkung von Wilhelm Olbrich, Leipzig, K. W. Hiersemann, 1935-37: see especially articles on "Musikalienkatalogisierung", "Musikbibliographie", and "Musikbibliotheken" by Constantin Schneider; H. A. Sharp: *Cataloguing, a textbook for use in libraries,* London, Grafton, 1937: see section on "Music", p. 300-307.

[13] Novikova, Elena Andreevna: *Rukovodstvo po katalogizacii muzykal'nykh proizvedenij . . .*, Moskva, 1937.

[14] Novikova, Elena Andreevna: *Bibliografičeskoe opisanie i organizacija kataloga notnykh izdanij,* Moskva, 1948.

[15] E. Weiss-Reyscher: *Anweisung zur Titelaufnahme von Musikalien.* (Veröffentlichungen der Berliner Bibliotheksschule, herausgegeben von Wilhelm Schuster und Wilhelm Krabbe.) Leipzig, Einkaufshaus für Büchereien, 1938.

[16] *Library Association Record*, 40 (June, 1938), 247-250.–*Editor.*

[17] Music Library Association: *Code for cataloging music; compiled by a committee of the Music Library Association. Preliminary version issued by chapters . . .* [Washington], 1941-42.

[18] O. E. Deutsch: "Music bibliography and catalogues", in *The Library*, ser. 4, vol. 23, March 1943, p. 151-70. [Reprinted above, pp. 117-126]

[19] *Studies of Descriptive Cataloging.* A report to the Librarian of Congress by the Director of the Processing Department. Washington, U. S. Government Printing Office, 1946.

[20] Published in 1958; see [**124,** 139].–*Editor.*

[21] *A. L. A. Cataloging Rules for Author and Title Entries.* Prepared by the Division of Cataloging and Classification of the American Library Association. Second Edition. Edited by Clara Beetle. Chicago, American Library Association, 1949, p. 28-35.

[22] *Rules for Descriptive Cataloging in the Library of Congress.* (Adopted by the American Library Association.) Washington, D. C., The Library of Congress, Descriptive Cataloging Division, 1949, p. 75-95.

[23] Paul Sieber: *Grundsätzliche Fragen zum Sammeln, zur Katalogisierung, Aufstellung und Ausleihe von Musikalien an Schweizerischen Bibliotheken, nebst einer Wegleitung zur Titelaufnahme von Musikalien*; Hans Zehntner: *Die Musikabteilung der Basler Universitätsbibliothek.* Selbstverlag der Vereinigung Schweizerischer Bibliothekare. Bern, 1945.

[24] This survey of cataloguing codes is brought up-to-date for English-language codes by appending items [**124, 125, 128-130,** 139-140].–*Editor.*

The International Code for Cataloguing Music

by Isabelle Cazeaux

In her review of the first two volumes of the Code, *Dr. Cazeaux has actually provided a fine philosophical essay on the knotty problems of music cataloguing; especially valuable is her lengthy discussion of the merits of conventional or filing titles. It is extremely important for the reader to remember that this review, originally published in 1963, applies to only the first two volumes of the* Code; *although the third volume bears a 1971 imprint, it has neither been reviewed elsewhere yet, nor is it reviewed here [December, 1971].*

The International Association of Music Libraries has undertaken the enormous task of compiling an international code for cataloguing music, in five volumes, the first two of which have already appeared.[1] Forthcoming volumes will include: *Code for full cataloguing, Code de catalogage des manuscrits,* and *Code de catalogage des enregistrements sonores.*

In view of the wide divergences which exist in the cataloguing theory and practice of various libraries of the world—not to speak of individual librarians, it is quasi-miraculous that a committee could be formed to draw up an international cataloguing code and that individual members could give up certain pet theories for the good of the whole. The two persons responsible for volumes 1 and 2 cannot be praised too highly for their clear and detailed writing. Much credit is also deserved by the translators, who successfully rendered the spirit, and most of the time the letter, of the difficult technical material. It is extremely useful to have the three versions—French, German and English—side by side; in the event of doubt, one can always compare the original and the translations.

The code states the aim of the commission: to establish, on the basis of existing systems, a code which all libraries could use and from which each could derive some advantage, according to circumstances, owing to the experiences which the code would resume, and owing to the historical and comparative introduction.

Volume 1 is a comparative study of music cataloguing for the author catalogue—chiefly problems of main heading, descriptive cataloguing and filing arrangements. Accounts are given of actual cataloguing procedures used by several libraries or recommended by individual writers on cataloguing. Illustrations by means of sample cards from various institutions which have catalogued identical works, together with the title-pages of the pieces in question, serve to complete the picture. A brief survey is made of problems encountered in cataloguing music literature in general, libretti, program notes, music publications, manuscripts, phonograph records, tape recordings, pictorial representations, photocopies and microfilms. Tables of concordance of practices prevalent in several American libraries have been compiled by Minnie Elmer.

Volume 2 is a limited code for cataloguing music according to the decisions made at the meetings of the Committee on the Cataloguing Code from 1952 to 1955. It is designed primarily for the newly established music library, for the music section of a library or for libraries having a basic music collection which is uncatalogued, or superficially catalogued. The code allows for the adaptation of rules by a trained book cataloguer to the usage of his library. Included are a concise discussion of the problems of conservation of publications (binding and shelf classification) and a main section on the preparation of cards (i.e., the cataloguing aspects of the question and not the mechanical ones, such as reproduction and distribution of cards). This section deals with the catalogue of authors and anonymous works: main heading, descriptive cataloguing, and secondary

SOURCE: Reprinted from Isabelle Cazeaux, "The International Code for Cataloguing Music," *Fontes artis musicae,* 10 (1963), 20–29, by permission of the International Association of Music Libraries.

cards within the author catalogue. Secondary catalogues for authors of words, subjects, titles and incipits are considered, as well as filing arrangements for a given author's works. Appendices consist of manuscript cataloguing rules, principles for establishing conventional titles, and a classified arrangement of a subject catalogue according to a simplified version of the scheme used in Hofmeister's *Jahresverzeichnis.*

Upon reading that the code proposes to be useful to all libraries according to circumstances, one is reminded of the four musical pieces published as a supplement to Ronsard's *Amours* in 1552. The tunes were to serve for singing all sonnets. Is such a broad goal realistic? A thorough examination of the code reveals that, although it cannot provide one magic cure for all evils, it is sufficiently flexible in scope and treatment to benefit most libraries in some way. The older established ones can re-examine their policies in the light of present practices of other institutions and of principles presumably accepted by a representative number of librarians. Newer libraries, or those yet to be formed, can profit by the comparative historical study as a background and can take or leave any of the many alternate procedures shown.

The number of libraries used for purposes of the comparative study is limited and selective. Only some thirty relatively large institutions were chosen, and they include public, conservatory, and college libraries. We understand that the committee had good reasons to be selective. One of them could be that many institutions may not have been able to co-operate with the project. It seems regrettable, however, that more types of libraries (e. g. specialized ones such as those of radio stations) could not be represented, or that the number of libraries using a given procedure could not be mentioned (except, in the case of American libraries). It would have then been possible to know how representative the examples were.

We shall now examine some of the details of the code. In the discussion of the systematic versus the alphabetical subject catalogue, volume 1 states that the latter system is satisfactory in Anglo-American libraries, *"as there are always cross-references between related subject headings."* The description fits the situation in some libraries, to be sure, and refers to an ideal in others; the word *always* (in the English version) is perhaps a kindness on the part of the translator.

Mention is made of the unavoidable need for indexing musicological periodicals in the larger libraries. A statement such as this could lead to the establishment of better standards, in this respect, in music libraries, and the insistence on having the necessary personnel to do the work. We appreciate that the code took this stand. We might add that if a periodical is not included in printed indexes and is to be analyzed, then all articles comprising it should be considered, and not merely those which interest the particular librarian making the choice. Limited indexing of a given work is sometimes done for economic reasons, but the soundness of such a policy may be questioned in the light of future needs.

In the discussion of libretto cataloguing in various countries, and the various possible main headings, under author of literary text, composer, or title, the first volume considers the title as a searching element *"properly a natural condition."* That it may not be perfectly natural to everyone is shown by the variants in libretto cataloguing practices throughout the world. Whether or not *"operas are primarily known under title"* is also open to question.

Exception could be taken to the categorical statement that a libretto has no independent character as a literary work because music and text form a unit. Certain dramatic texts were published independently before they were set to music. The fact that they later came to be used and published as libretti does not seem to alter their essential character as printed literary works, or make them less useful to persons wishing to study them as literature. (We should note, however, that the American Library Association *Cataloging Rules,* among others support Dr. Grasberger's position. They make a serious distinction between works published as libretti and as independent dramatic works, although no music is present in either.) The *Limited code* wisely suggests entry under either the author of the literary text or under the title, in view of the fact that in the eighteenth century especially, a given libretto may have served for several composers.

In using volume 1 of the code, we must bear in mind that, since its publication, some of the procedures described may no longer be in force. Information on Library of Congress practice was undoubtedly accurate when the volume was written and holds true for the bulk of the existing collection. The selection of the form of personal name for entries, in some of the more recent acquisitions, however, has been according to the form used by the author in the work in hand, unless it conflicts with a form already established in the authority files. The name is not necessarily established according to the fullest form used on published works. The surveys were based on sample cards received from various libraries; even at the time of publication, the compilers of the code quite rightly disclaimed responsibility for discrepancies between the cards and actual practice of the institutions involved. Without blaming anyone, we would like to note a slight error of omission. Nothing was mentioned to the effect that many of the procedures ascribed to the New York Public Library are characteristic of its Reference Department only. (The Washington practices were more accurately described by differentiating between those of the Library of Congress [Music Division] and those of the Library of Congress Copyright Office.) The New York Public Library's Reference Department catalogues for its internationally known music research collection, to be consulted within the central building, but it does not deal with the total of the library's music. There is also a Circulation Department, in charge of more than eighty branches throughout the city, where readers may borrow items for home use. Music and phonorecords form no small part of this material, which is catalogued independently, according to somewhat different principles from those of the Reference Department. The sample cards shown obviously came from the Reference Department; so did one of the distinguished delegates, Miss Inger Christensen, who compiled its music cataloguing rules. Under the circumstances, it is certainly forgivable that the committee assumed cards and rules to be representative of the New York Public Library as a whole.

Various possible filing arrangements for a given composer's work are impartially presented—i.e., filing alphabetically by title, or systematically by instrumentation or opus number. Two American systems of conventional titles (also known as standard or filing titles) for an author's works are explained briefly—those in use at the Library of Congress and at the Reference Department of the New York Public Library.

The first volume wisely concludes that *"the author catalog of published music requires particular care and thorough theoretical consideration."*

The *Limited* code has to its credit a very clear organization and style. It cannot answer every question that may arise, but it considers in some way, however briefly, the important areas of cataloguing—author and title headings, descriptive cataloguing, subject cataloguing, cross-references, shelf arrangement and filing. The headings, descriptive cataloguing and filing are treated more fully than the other problems. A definite position is taken on certain questions, as to what is considered the best practice (by the committee); on other topics, enough margin is allowed for the cataloguer to make his own decision, with the help of the historical volume, and by using his judgment as to what best fits the particular situation.

The reader may be amused to discover that the American spellings *catalog* and *cataloging,* which were used in the English version of the first volume, have been altered to the more conservative *catalogue* and *cataloguing* in the second. We believe the change was made by deliberate choice and not by accident, because a given form is used consistently within a volume.

The code accepts the composer of the music as main heading (even in vocal compositions, in preference to the author of the literary text). This principle is presented as practically self-evident. We might recall that before it was accepted in America, long discussions on the pros and cons took place among librarians.

For a work written in collaboration by several composers (the maximum number to be determined by the practice of the cataloguer's library) each of the authors receives an identical card; the heading alone is changed. The first author's name does not appear as a heading in the example shown; it is replaced by the second author. Here, we see that the question of main and added entries on multigraphed cards is neatly avoided. The same importance is given to each of the collaborators, and each card looks like an American main entry. (If joint authors had been given added entries, the name of each would have been typed or written as the first line of a unit card, over the name of the first author.) It is logical to give equal treatment to joint authors, rather than to make one appear subsidiary by virtue of his position on the card. Some of this logic has to be sacrificed if the advantages of unit cards are to be enjoyed.

For works whose author or editor cannot be identified, a heading is prepared from the first few words of the title, in capitals, followed by ellipses. Then the full title is given in the transcription of the title-page. One wonders whether the American title entry, with no preambulum would not save time and space. The repetition of the title incipit seems somewhat redundant. However, the reason may be that, for the sake of uniformity and legibility, headings should all be in capitals, as shown in the examples. If nothing except the title-page were given, but with the incipit capitalized, this would result in a misleading transcription.

The possibility of using corporate authorship is recognized, provided that the library has already adopted it for its non-musical collection. Otherwise, it is not considered essential for music. If such an entry is used, adequate cross-references must be made from personal author and title. The examples given make it clear that the composition of a corporate heading acceptable to every library is no small matter. Only one attempt was made to translate a French model (into German). The other examples are entirely new in the various languages.

Cadenzas are entered under their true composer, rather than the composer of the corresponding concerto; the latter is nevertheless the object of a cross-reference. This very sensible practice is presented as if it were generally accepted. The opposite alternative—using the composer of the concerto as main heading—is not mentioned as a possibility, although it is advocated by the rules of the American Library Association. That one may not agree with such a rule is understandable. The fact remains that it is used in several important institutions, and perhaps some mention could have been made of it.

We are not told about authority files or how to determine the form of personal or corporate name to be used, and whether dates of birth and death should be added when possible. However, the historical volume explains the practice of enough libraries on that matter, so that a choice could be made.

The section on transcription of the title offers two excellent principles: the order of elements must not be inverted, and omissions are to be shown by ellipses. Besides simplifying the work of the cataloguer (he does not have to decide how and when to transpose elements) the application of these rules results in an accurate, though not necessarily full transcription, which a reader could use, in an emergency, for a bibliographic citation. He could use it also as a means of differentiating one edition from another. This he can hardly do if parts of the title are not in their original position. The required information as to editor, title, etc., is then present, to be sure, but it might almost be better to give these items in the form of answers to a questionnaire. Then the reader would not suppose that he is looking at a true title-page transcription. (It should be noted that present Library of Congress practice reflects the opposite point of view. The use of a catalogue in lieu of a bibliography, even in emergency, is probably frowned upon, and it may be considered simpler for the reader to see the various elements in a standardized position than for him to have to hunt for them in their original arrangement, which may be complex.) The procedure suggested by the code for transcribing title-pages in several languages precludes the inversion of elements. The title proper is transcribed in all the languages and any additional information appearing on the title-page is copied in the original language of the publication only. Ample use is made of the three dots of omission. Pertinent information may be added in brackets, at the end of the title, if possible, so as to preserve its original aspect. By putting these appendages in the main body of the card, space is saved which would otherwise be allotted to drop notes.

Special treatment is properly advocated for sixteenth century prints—i.e., the inclusion on the card of the paging of individual part-books forming a set. A limited but useful bibliography is given to help date publications.

Conventional methods of determining an item's format are explained. Since sizes of identical editions may vary according to the amount of cutting which took place at the time of binding, O. E. Deutsch had suggested that it might be more accurate to *"give the height of the printed matter measuring from the top line of the first staff to the bottom line of the last on the first full page of music."*[2] Librarians not committed to follow past practices might consider this method, although it is not mentioned in the code.

A small note on minor typographical errors: page 26, item 25, English version, reference to item 29 should be 31; page 27 (V: 29) caption should be "Contents."

We read, in the section on secondary cards, that the term refers to cross-references; however, the first example given (Delécluse) appears to be an added entry; or is it a cross-reference with the word *"see"* omitted? If one has multigraphed cards, an added entry can frequently be used in the place of a cross-reference. Perhaps the example deals with such an instance. The code may be using the term *"cross-reference"* in a broad sense.

In addition to the main author catalogue, others of secondary importance are possible—for authors of words, subjects, titles and incipits. These cards may be filed separately, so as to form a divided catalogue, or they may be interfiled in the main catalogue, according to the *"dictionary catalogue"* principle prevalent in America. Dissertations could be written on subject cataloguing for music. The code can only give the briefest of suggestions. A list of main designations of musical types amounts to twenty one in French and German, and eighteen in English. They can be subdivided, of course. We do not know whether the catalogue of titles (and eventually incipits) refers to musical as well as textual incipits. Only a literary incipit is shown. Perhaps experiments in filing by musical incipits are not yet considered in the domain of limited cataloguing. This may be why Mme. Fédoroff did not choose to give such examples. Had she wished to do so, there is no doubt that she, as a librarian at the Bibliothèque nationale, Paris, would have known better than anyone else where to find them.[3]

The third section, on the filing of the author catalogue, explains, with the help of examples, simplified versions of both alphabetical and systematic arrangements, without favoring either method over the other. A very significant statement is made, which should be memorized by all persons responsible for a catalogue: *"It is not possible to give a unique model of arrangement applicable to all composers."* Indeed, countless difficulties could be prevented by not trying to force every item into a pre-conceived mold for which it was not made. The simplified rules for establishing conventional titles state that if the original title cannot be found, then the best-known title may be used. Can the title be a nickname? The "best-known" title may serve the purpose of bringing together different editions of the same work in one place in the catalogue, but not necessarily under the original title; it seems paradoxical to find the suggestion in the *Limited code,* whereas the comparative study took a firm stand against the use of popular names as titles in the main catalogue. (Of course, the *Limited code* does not say that nicknames may be used; on the other hand, we do not know to which category of readers the title should be best-known.) Many points are left unanswered. For example, it is not clear whether form-titles preceded or followed by adjectives or adjectival phrases are to be considered distinctive or generic, and exactly what the punctuation should be in a sufficient number of instances. In Section 6 (p. 46) punctuation for the same example varies from the original French in the two translations. How does one assign a collective title to a publication consisting of several works by a given composer? Perhaps the compiler assumes that the cataloguer is already familiar with more extensive rules, such as those of the Library of Congress. If he is not, he will have to devise his own rules for individual problems as they arise. One cannot avoid help wondering whether two persons cataloguing the same item with the help of the code would come to the same conclusion in matters of standard title. But surely these rules are meant as a guide rather than a substitute for using one's intelligence. And herein lies their strength. They would probably be most useful in places where a single person is responsible for assigning filing titles. In some large institutions, where several cataloguers are doing the same type of work, but are not all located in the same building, more or less uniform reactions are expected of them. In order to lessen the margin of variance, detailed rules must be devised.

We are pleased to see that provision is made for cataloguing with and without the standard title. Many American libraries find it satisfactory and have been using it long enough so that it would be impractical to change to another system. At the same time, many libraries throughout the world have lived happily without conventional titles and continue to do so. For the sake of librarians who, in spite of the time and cost, are considering the possibility of using filing titles, because they have sometimes been presented as the only workable solution to catalogue searching, it is good that the code presents other simpler systems as equally acceptable. The resolution to catalogue with or without a standard title cannot be reached lightly; it is significant to the economy of a cataloguing department. Once the procedure has been made part of the descriptive cataloguing, it cannot be abandoned without creating havoc in the filing scheme. The importance of the decision to be made by newer libraries, we believe, justifies an amplification of the discussion of complex conventional titles treated in volume 1 and the simpler rules formulated in volume 2 of the code.

The comparative history finds that *"cataloguing by title makes it easier to search a certain work than does systematic cataloguing according to instrumentation. The latter, however, makes it easier to make the search from the musical point of view."* At the last congress of the International Association of Music Libraries, in Washington, Mme. Fédoroff apparently caused many ears to perk when she mentioned that she did not consider the standard title to be a cataloguing problem, but a filing matter. Why so much complication on a card, when the question can be settled at the time of filing, with the help of guide cards—presumably in a systematic arrangement? And Mme. Fédoroff was absolutely right in the light of a system such as the one used at the Bibliothèque nationale, for example. There, the filing is done by the cataloguer, or a person with enough musical knowledge to understand the nature of the material he is filing and be able to make meaningful guide cards. In some American libraries, however, the situation is different. The American Library Association and individual institutions which accept its standards classify certain library duties as professional and others as non-professional[4] (or whatever equivalent designations may be used). The first category, theoretically, is to be performed by persons who have a degree in librarianship, and the second, by persons who do not; yet in practice, there is often overlapping, depending on the staff resources at hand. In large institutions, filing, in principle, is done by "non-professional" employees, subject, in some, but not all libraries, to revision by a "professional." Since filers are not paid as much as full-fledged librarians, they can hardly be expected to be great music specialists. (The fact that several "non-professionals" have that quality should be considered a bonus by the institution employing them, but cannot be taken for granted.) Everyone agrees that music presents more filing problems than general printed works, primarily to a non-specialist. It is to help these persons that filing titles are probably necessary in many established American libraries. Before deciding whether or not to accept standard titles, a new library would do well to consider, among other things, its administrative policy as to position classification. Will it be worth the amount of money saved by hiring a non-specialist to file if the burden of facilitating the task for him falls to the better paid specialist at the time of cataloguing? Or should the filing be done by a specialist? By not establishing a conventional title, the cataloguer would not necessarily save time normally spent on research. He most likely would want to give the information usually shown in filing titles somewhere on the card, for the benefit of the reader, or at least, he would need to have that information himself, in order to place the card under the proper guide card in the catalogue. But this information would not have to be given in a standardized form, which takes a significant amount of time if done properly. Even after the cataloguer has found the pertinent information, he has to consider, depending on which rules he follows, how to arrange the elements, which language to select for certain distinctive titles—if the original title is not in one of the seven *"most commonly read"* in the country, according to Library of Congress rules, etc. (It is not always immediately obvious, for example, whether a given work is better known in the United States in its original Czech title or in English—and if in English, under which of several possible versions.) Many of the standard title rules of the Library of Congress and the New York Public Library Reference Department are complex. Detailed as they are, they do not furnish an automatic solution to every problem that arises, and are frequently subject to the interpretation of the cataloguer. This is as it should be, because very few cataloguers would be happy if they did not have to use some judgment based upon their knowledge of the subject field. Often a decision on a filing title has to be influenced by past practice, and the only way to ascertain what this practice has been is by leaving one's desk and examining the catalogue (or whatever official file gives the information). Without a standard title, this part of the work could be done by a specialist at the moment of filing.

New libraries might also consider whether standard titles on cards will invariably help the non-librarian who consults the catalogue. After all, a major goal of the catalogue is to help the reader find what he wants. Does a conventional title always facilitate the search for him, or does he need the help of a specialist to consult the files? Harry Dewey has undoubtedly expressed the feelings of many library users when he objected to the use of the original distinctive title rather than the English version in the standard title of certain works, because the practice violates the principle of probable association—i.e. filing where a reader is most likely to look.[5] Although we would agree that filing titles are sometimes difficult to use, it is not on those grounds that we would find fault with them. Readers are of varying backgrounds, and it is not always easy to predict where they will look first. Popular titles sometimes change for a given work, whereas the original title has the merit of remaining constant. If adequate cross-references are made, no great harm is done. What seems to be more confusing, as has been pointed out by several librarians, is the use of both alphabetical and classed arrangements for the same category of works, although the use of standard titles presumably should facilitate an alphabetical search by original title. How is an innocent reader to know, for example, that under Library of Congress rules, Verdi's *Aida,* published together with two other of his operas, will be found under his *"Operas. Selections"* (a classed arrangement) whereas the same opera published separately will be located alphabetically under the *a*'s in the Verdi file? Then, is it not possible for a novice to miss some of a given author's sonatas, which may not necessarily be filed under "*Sonatas*"? If the original title was "*Grand sonata*," the standard title will begin with the word "*Sonata*"; the initial adjective will be omitted because it is laudatory and not considered an integral part of the title. On the other hand, if a work was first published as *"Little sonata,"* the adjective, by virtue of its modesty, no doubt, would be retained, and the card filed under the *l's,* where it may well be lost to the uninitiated. Not only an amateur but even a musical scholar would be excusable for not knowing the original title of certain composers' sonatas unless he had made a special study of them. And he cannot always be blamed if he was not born with an inherent understanding of all the peculiarities of the filing scheme.

One must consider the possibility that the cataloguer, however competent he may be, will not always be able to find the original title of a work, after a reasonable amount of searching. The library does not always have all the necessary books required to find the information. The composer may be relatively unknown; little or nothing may have been written about him; or his output may be of such mediocre quality that it would not warrant an undue amount of searching time on the part of the cataloguer. In such instances, the only possibilities are to compose a standard title without being certain of the original title, or not add a conventional title at all. If the second alternative is chosen, it may become difficult to interfile the card with those having filing titles. In order to keep the strict alphabetical order, the logical sequence is often interrupted, or vice versa.

Whether non-specialized filers themselves are grateful for standard titles is an open question. Detailed titles require complex rules for filing and sub-filing, which sometimes prove to be exacting to specialists themselves. Some persons who order and receive printed catalogue cards containing standard titles have been known to disregard these titles when filing the cards.

Standard titles may be a mixed blessing, but for all their inconveniences, they are probably the best of several solutions (none of which are perfect) for large American-type libraries, whose public has been conditioned, over the years, to work with an alphabetical arrangement. There can be no question of discontinuing the use of filing titles in libraries which have had them for several years. It is therefore entirely fitting that the international code make provision for them without recommending them as necessarily the best solution for all. If, at some future date, international catalogue cards come to be printed, we hope that they will have enough space between the heading and the title-page transcription so as to allow for the insertion of a standard title, if desired. This will benefit those who want it and at the same time will not hinder anyone else.

Was the new code essential and does it live up to the aims set up for it by the responsible committee and by others? Before the code was established, R. S. Hill raised the question of whether there existed the necessity for one on an international scale, and assuming there was such a need, what the aims of a good code should be. He believed that rudimentary book catalogues were no longer adequate for expanding libraries; as more and more aspects of a given item must be brought out, for the benefit of readers, multiple cards, he judged, were a better solution. The more cards used, the more complicated the code should be. Most existing rules are sufficient for a book catalogue but not for one on cards. Mr. Hill considered that a workable code should take into account past experiments and studies, and should represent agreement on what the best procedures are, in order to improve cataloguing standards; individual institutions can then decide to what point they may apply them in specific instances.[6]

In the foreword to the first volume of the code, A. Hyatt King expresses the hope that as a result of the committee's work, older libraries may eventually achieve some measure of uniformity, which would facilitate the consultation of their catalogues, and that newer libraries may find a good point of departure for their work.

The Library of Congress supplies catalogue cards to those who wish to buy them. Would it be too optimistic to hope that if enough agreement could be reached in the principles of cataloguing, a central international agency could be formed to print cards and distribute them to various libraries of the world? The cards could then be adapted to the use of each library.

That the international code was a necessity can safely be asserted. No comparative study of such large scope had been made previously. Cataloguers everywhere needed to broaden their horizons by learning about other practices besides their own; the code affords an opportunity of doing this painlessly. Although much information had to be summarized, the salient features of several systems are given. The reader can then consult more detailed sources on whatever practice he believes he could use profitably.

The code does not reflect general agreement on all points. But concurrence may not have been a valid goal in the first place. Uniformity as an end in itself can be rather pointless; as a means of achieving more useful cataloguing, it is another matter. Some consistency will have to be achieved by each library within its own system after it has chosen among the various possibilities offered by the code. There is agreement to the extent that the catalogue must give certain basic information about a given work to the reader. How this information will be shown—by means of descriptive cataloguing, tracings, cross-references, or extra files can be decided by individuals. It was not up to the code to dictate the one perfect solution. In this respect, it is less precise, but much more flexible than cataloguing manuals of individual libraries or national codes. (It avoids the complacent attitude implied by numerous writings on cataloguing—i.e., this is what we do at such and such a place; we are happy with the system and believe you will be, too.)

Librarians may reconsider and modify some of their practices in view of the elements they like in the international code, or even those they do not like. Often one blandly accepts certain principles because they have been perpetuated for many years. When one sees them described in print, however, alongside of other systems, possible shortcomings become apparent. At any rate, the code offers a challenge to anyone who reads it. He is forced to think constructively about his own work, and that is always beneficial.

Mr. Hill did not think that detailed codes were necessary if book catalogues were to be used. Nevertheless, since the code now exists for card catalogues, there is nothing to prevent one from using it to make better and more detailed book catalogues. With sufficient indexes and forms of approach, a book catalogue, under certain circumstances, could serve the same purpose as one on cards. Besides, it could help to identify holdings at a distance.

Whether it will ever be possible to have centralized cataloguing on an international scale, as a result of the code is unpredictable at this time. The main impediment would be the present divergences in the form of personal and especially corporate names used as headings. The code shows various possibilities, but does not attempt any solution of that particular problem. At any rate, it was not the compilers of the code who suggested centralized cataloguing as one of its aims.

Because the code avoids making too many specific pronouncements, it is difficult to determine how effectively it could be used to set minimum standards in music cataloguing (in organizations requiring hard facts and figures). But when one observes the examples which the code gives, even more than what it preaches, it becomes apparent that many details about a work must be shown in the cataloguing. In relation to this point, even the *Limited code* could put many an existing catalogue to shame. By showing the examples to an administrator, it might be possible to insist on sufficient staff to do work of the same caliber. One glance at the code should convince said administrator that he needs specialists to catalogue music.

Classes in cataloguing and music librarianship in library schools will surely need to include the code among the required list of books. In addition to the code's other qualities, students and teachers will appreciate sample cards.

The aims expressed in the code itself are not overly utopian. As the committee realized, the main value of the code should be for relatively new libraries, rather than older, well-established ones, who can hardly be expected to change existing practices to any great extent without a good reason to justify cost and work. Newer establishments would have more freedom to try something different without being burdened by past errors in judgment. It seems, therefore, that a golden opportunity may have been missed by the comparative study to show what drawbacks exist in present practices of the various libraries. Surely none are perfect. The librarians using a given system must be aware more than anyone else of its strong and weak points, as shown by everyday use. These persons would have been in a position to evaluate the practices in force in their own library and could have saved prospective imitators from taking over their less successful elements. But perhaps librarians were reluctant to discuss particular problems of specific institutions to which they belong. *On lave son linge sale en famille.* Again, for the sake of the newer libraries, it might have been profitable to show, in addition to existing systems, some theoretical ones which could be considered by libraries willing to experiment. Devices used by private collectors might also have been investigated.

But the code was not meant to be an encyclopedia. It needs no apology to be accepted on its own terms. In all humility, one can appreciate the extraordinary amount of time, patience and serious thought that went into its preparation. In view of its successful accomplishment thus far of the goals it had set for itself, one certainly looks forward to the forthcoming volumes with great eagerness.

NOTES

[1]Three volumes have appeared; see [**125,** 140]. This review applied to the first two volumes only.

[2]Otto Erich Deutsch, *Music bibliography and catalogues,* in: *The Library,* ser. 4, v. 23, no. 4 (Mar. 1943), p. 155. [Reprinted above, pp. 117–126]

[3]Nanie Bridgman has given a very clear account of the system she uses at the Bibliothèque nationale in her article *Nouvelle visite aux incipits musicaux,* in: *Acta musicologica,* v. 23, fasc. II–IV (1961) p. 193–196.

[4]See: American Library Association. Board of personnel administration. Subcommittee on analysis of libraries. *Descriptive list of professional and nonprofessional duties in libraries. Preliminary draft,* Chicago, American Library Association, 1948, 75 p.

[5]Harry Dewey, *Music and phonorecord code criticized,* in: *Library Journal,* v. 83 (1 June 1958), p. 1665–1668.

[6]Richard S. Hill, *Some pros and cons regarding an international code for cataloging practical music,* in: *Association internationale des bibliothèques musicales. 3e Congrès (22–25 juillet 1951). Actes,* Kassel, Bärenreiter (1953), p. 37–45. [Reprinted above, pp. 156–162]

Classifications in American Music Libraries

by Kathi Meyer-Baer

There are some few methods of classification for music libraries. Of these the most popular in the United States are the Decimal–or Dewey–system, the Library of Congress system, and a group of systems that are formed more or less on the European pattern.[1]

The Decimal system is used in most of the average public libraries of which every town has one, and also in many of the older college libraries. The Library of Congress system is used, of course, in the Library of Congress and in college libraries formed more recently, that is in the last 25 years. The European system is used in some of the college libraries and in the New York Public Library in the 42nd Street division.

With the rich development of modern music as well as of music research in the last 70 years the use of the Decimal system has lead to such confusion that it seems proper to discuss its inconsistencies. The method of the Library of Congress has been elaborated in the music section by the excellent Oscar Sonneck, and its shortcomings are by far smaller; but they also will be felt soon.

During the years when I had the luck to work in the Paul Hirsch Library, I could elaborate a method which was used and operated easily, and which I also found practical in the reorganization of some American college libraries. With this system it was easy to allot any book to one of its classes, and it proved also practical in putting books of similar sizes together, and thus save room, which is, as every librarian knows, an important advantage.

This classification has four great classes and requires all in all 30 subdivisions for an average collection. The classes are:

MG (general)

- 1 Periodicals.
- 2 Reference books–Bibliographies, Dictionaries, *etc.*
- 3 Rare books, *curiosa.*

MH (history)

- 1 General histories of music.
- 2 History of special periods (arranged by authors).
- 3 Local histories (arranged by localities, countries, cities, institutions, *etc.*).
- 4 Biographies and criticism (arranged by composers).
- 4a Collected biographies (arranged by authors or editors).

History of special forms.

- 5 History of Church Music.
- 6 History of the Opera.
- 7 History of the Dance.
- 8 History of other forms (songs, instrumental forms; this class might be subdivided).
- 9 Instruments, history and structure.
- 10 History of notation, paleography.

MT (theory)

Aesthetics.

- 1 Philosophy and general.
- 1a Physiology.
- 2 Applied Psychology, appreciation, analyses.

Education.

- 3 Textbooks for schools, and concerning performance.
- 4 Textbooks on composing: harmony, counterpoint, *etc.,* including acoustics.

M (music)

- 1 Complete works and sets (the complete works arranged by composers, the sets as *e.g.* Fellowes' *Madrigal School* by editors or by titles).

SOURCE: Reprinted from Kathi Meyer-Baer, "Classifications in American music libraries," *The Music Review,* 12 (February, 1951), 76–82, by permission of the publisher, W. Heffer & Sons Ltd., Cambridge, England.

2 Monuments (editions of mediaeval manuscripts, facsimile editions, *etc.*).
3 Opera (might be divided into scores and piano scores).
3a Incidental music.
3b *Libretti.*

Vocal Music.
4 Voices and orchestra, secular (Haydn's *Creation*), also arrangements.
5 Voices and orchestra, sacred (Masses, Requiems).
6a *A cappella*, part songs with sacred or secular text.
6b Sacred hymns, for solo or several parts.
7a Art songs and folksongs (songs for solo voice and piano, also songs from operas; folksongs, for solo or several parts).
7b Songs for voice and several instruments (solo voice with quartet, solo voice with orchestra).
7c Singing exercises.

Instrumental music.
8 Orchestra (symphonies, suites, variations, concerti grossi, also separate overtures).
  a Scores.
  b Miniature scores.
  c Parts.
9 Orchestra and solo instrument.
  a Piano.
  b Violin.
  c Violoncello.
  d Other instruments.
  e For more than one instrument.
10 Chamber music.
  a Scores.
  b Solo and duos, also arrangements for violin and piano.
  c Trios and trio sonatas.
  d Quartets.
  e Quintets.
  f Six and more instruments.
11 Music for band.
12 Piano music.
  a Solo, also arrangements for piano solo.
  b For four hands.
  c For four hands and two pianos.
  d For eight hands.
13 Music for organ, including monuments.
14 Studies–Études, Exercises.
  a Piano.
  b String instruments.
  c Wind instruments.
  d Other instruments.
15 Dance, including folk dance, rhythmical studies.

THE DECIMAL SYSTEM

The Decimal or Dewey system, named after its inventor Melvil Dewey, is planned for every possible section of literature and knowledge, and uses numbers for the marks. Before we reach the music section, which alone shall be discussed here, 780 categories have been segregated. The system was elaborated 70 years ago and made for the standard of its period, without imagining the great developments that have taken place since.

The music section accounts for the numbers 780-789; the headings follow:

780 General.
781 Theory and technical.
782 Dramatic music. Theatre music.
783 Church music.
784 Vocal music.
785 Instrumental music.
786 Keyboard music.
787 Stringed instruments.
788 Wind instruments.
789 Percussion and mechanical instruments.

The numbers are supposed to give by their decimal order a picture of the importance of their section. By adding further decimals the sections are subdivided, to the effect that most of the music books are marked with nine numbers.

Our first objection is that the order of the numbers does not correspond to the importance of the classes. Already a first look at the nine sections tells us that the divisions are not logical. If there is a section for instrumental music, the classes for the different instruments should be subdivisions, and the keyboard and percussion instruments should not have classes for themselves. Also, the section "theory and technical" does not correspond in importance to divisions such as "church, vocal, *etc.*, music" which should be subdivisions of "music."

Our second objection is that the divisions are not clear. I want to give some examples of the ensuing muddle. The class 780–General–lists books of the first three groups of our system: dictionaries and yearbooks–780.3; 780.58–our MG; history of other general treatments [*sic*] –

780.9 and biography–780.92–our MH; instrumental and other types distinctly suited for sight-reading–780.77–our MT.

In the second class 781–theory and technical–we have some sections concerned with thorough-bass, *etc.*; but we have here also history of notation, neumes and tablatures; we have also different kinds of music such as *Allegro, Andantino, Minuets, Finale [sic]*. Incidentally, we have here class marks with nine numbers; minuets sonata has 781.508.223 [*sic.*]. Then follows a section Overtures, *Entr' actes,* Interludes, with the added note "Compositions and executing of a special kind of music is classified with that kind," and beside we have a section "Composition in general" [*sic*], corresponding apparently to the "miscellaneous" of office files. Then we come again to some sections for theory proper, to jump right back to history of music. Here we have a class–theories and forms: racial, national, *etc.*–with cross-references to the small group of outspoken headings of history in the class 780. In this racial section we have the following groups: Primitive and savage people–People not otherwise provided for [*sic*], Gipsies–Ancient music, theories, modes and forms–Various questions. Then we jump back again to books of our class "general–MG" and listing: "Museums and collections, Music bibliographies, catalogues," with the note "bibliography of writings see 0.16.78 (that is a section completely different from music) . . . then "catalogues," *etc.*

The third reason for difficulties in working with the Decimal system is that some sections are too small and others too big. The classes for the books on history of music are too small; the class 789, percussion instruments is too big; the third class 782, Dramatic music is too big, too much divided and outdated. It starts with: Polygraphy–and lists works which we would allot to either MG (general) or MH (history), works which are of book size. Then are listed: Grand Opera, Epic Wagneriana [*sic*], Other German Grand Opera, French Grand Opera, Italian Grand Opera, Comic and satiric [*sic*] opera, *Opera bouffa,* Operettas, Parodies, Pantomimes and Masks–these are all separate sections. No word is said whether we have here music or books on music, neither whether we have scores, piano scores or parts. Further, we would expect in such a detailed paragraphing a section "Lyric opera" or Singspiel"; besides, who to-day knows the difference between Grand opera and Lyric opera?

With all these divisions the allotment of odd works is not easy. Where should we put Mendelssohn's *Midsummer Night's Dream* music? There is no place for it in the class Dramatic Music 782; perhaps we should list it in 781.6 "Overtures, *Entr' actes,* Interludes"; but no, it comes under 785.22 "Dramatic, illustrative, descriptive, programme, imitative [*sic*]," a part of the section "Instrumental *ensemble*." "As for the music section of Dewey's scheme with its haphazard overclassification and the confusion of music literature and music, it must provoke nightmare in any one," writes McColvin.

To summarize: the three faults with the Decimal system are that the numbers do *not* correspond to the importance of the section; that the sections overlap and that the headings are partly outdated (Epic Wagneriana) and that important headings (Gesamtausgaben) are lacking.

It has been thought that this system eases the work of a librarian who is not familiar with the content of the books which he has to handle. Concerning this point I have to tell of a contrary experience which I had in the very good small library in the suburb of New York where I live. I wanted to look up some facts in the two similar books *The World History of Dance* and Paul Nettl's *History of Dance Music.* The music division in our library is small and has perhaps about 200 items. I found the two mentioned books in two different rooms, one in the class 781, a music section, the other book under 793, under: Dance–Entertainment [*sic*].

THE LIBRARY OF CONGRESS SYSTEM

This system was elaborated in 1902, put into force in 1904, and revised in 1917, by Oscar Sonneck. It has three great classes: M Music–ML Literature of music–MT Musical instruction and study. It has *c.* 15,000 divisions, but the number alone should not deter one from using it; because it is not necessary to use the whole numbers, and it can be simplified. The headings are not so awkward as in the Decimal system, and most headings which we would expect in a music classification are listed. What we object to is that the three great divisions, and sometimes the subdivisions, are not clear but overlap.

To give some examples: Dictionaries–ML 100-110–can contain historical (ML) and theoretical (MT) information (Riemann). In the class ML the bibliography–ML 111-158–is listed separately from History–ML 159-3790; some books, such as Eitner, might belong to both of these classes. It is especially the whole group ML 3800-3920, called "Philosophy and physics" which is so closely related to the theory of music that these sections should be listed under MT; or the whole class MT should go into "Literature of music–ML."

The term Literature of music seems to me too general and too vague and makes the class ML too large to give help. The four sections which we used in the Paul Hirsch Library make the finding of a book easier. The classification of the Library of Congress means little more than a division into music, and not music proper. Besides, the divisions are not clear. The books on theory of music, allotted in the Congress system to the section "Musical instruction and studies" are none the less books on music and thus belong to Literature of music.

CONCLUSION

The discarding of the Decimal system and its replacement by a reasonable classification is quite a financial problem. The reorganization of the music divisions in the many public and college libraries, small though they may be, would need time and money. But the sooner it is done the better. The system of the Library of Congress has fewer inconsistencies than the Dewey system, but perhaps its use is thus more dangerous, because the damage will be felt more slowly.

In conclusion I will try to outline the points that seem most important in organizing a music division.

A library is a living institution, and not a dead thing. It develops according to our general knowledge and to the general trend. A rigid classification, fixed once and for all, cannot follow this development. Therefore a method of classification should be flexible and should define some few basic classes only.

The classes should be clear and not overlapping. For reference books, which often include chapters from different sections, an extra class–our General–should be formed.

We shall obtain clear headings only if we base them on the different powers which the reader activates while using a book. In our field of music the reader will approach a book in these different ways.

(1) The reader may look for music which he wants to play and/or read; all books of this kind would go to the class M–Music; or
(2) he wants to deepen his understanding of a piece of music. This he can do again in two ways. He can study the structure of a piece, or he may want to discover its meaning and to evaluate it. Books which the reader reads for these purposes should all be put into the one class MT–Theory of music. The subdivisions of this class would be theory proper for the first and music appreciation, criticism or aesthetics for the second one. It is confusing to separate these two kinds as the method of the Library of Congress does.
(3) There is one other approach, that is the historical method where a student tries to define the style of a piece, to determine its period, its author, *etc*. Books giving information in this manner should be put into the class MH–History of music.

Classes should be neither too big, nor too small, the classes themselves as well as the subdivisions. Classes that are too large run the risk of becoming vague, as is the case with the "Literature of music" in the Congress scheme. Too small divisions confuse and force the reader to start the alphabet anew after a couple of books, see the division into biographies of composers, of pianists, of violinists, *etc.,* in the Decimal system.

Whether a class has to be large, or whether it has to be divided into more or fewer subdivisions depends upon the individual collection. In every library these sections develop from the material as well as from the needs of the readers. In the Paul Hirsch Library the collection of first editions formed a special group, in the New York Public Library the Popular Songs are such a special collection. The special classes will need also specialised handling, bibliographically and in cataloguing; but this problem is not in the scope of our article.

As the material is continuously changing it would be extremely useful to have one centre where information could be obtained from one specialist or from a staff of specialists. Such information cannot be laid down in printed books. The requirements of the questioners vary greatly. The centre of information should give advice to the librarian who is not well versed in music as to what books he has to add to his collection from the current publications as well as rare books; and if the librarian is in doubt, it should tell him the class to which to assign a book.

NOTES

[1] For European schemes see: Lionel Roy McColvin, *Music in Public Libraries,* 1936; for the early attempts see James Brown: "Guide to the formation of a Music Library." *The Library Association Series,* No. 4–1893.

The Library of Congress Classed Catalog for Music

by Virginia Cunningham

The Music Division in the Library of Congress has the only classed catalog devoted to music in the United States. While not a perfect instrument, it does provide adequate subject analysis of the collections, and improvements in it are continuously being made.

In 1943 the subject catalog for music was converted to a classed catalog. Without any change being made on the cards, the entries were re-filed by class number. They could not, as is customary in other classed catalogs, be filed by full call number because many classes in the M schedule are not Cuttered. The call number, in these classes, consists of the class number and the filing initial; e.g. M25 .R for Wallingford Riegger's *Toccata for Piano*. Thus the filing elements are class number, heading (name or title), title, and date.

The organization of the M classification schedule is, in general, based on medium of performance. This means that the first approach in the classed catalog is by medium. For each musical work processed, a card is filed under the class number. The numbers in the classification schedule are also used as reference numbers, serving as an approach for alternative medium of performance. For example, a work for violin or flute and piano is classified in M219 (violin and piano) with the reference number M242 (flute and piano). The regular numbers also provide an approach by topic or subject. Thus Roy Harris' *Abraham Lincoln Walks at Midnight* is classified in M1613.3 (a work for solo voice and small instrumental ensemble) and has as a reference number M1659.L5 (songs about Lincoln).

But a further approach by musical form, not provided by the classification schedule, is also needed. Beethoven's *Fuge,* op. 137, for example, is classed in M552 because the medium of performance is 2 violins, 2 violas, and violoncello. A card is filed under M552 in the classed catalog, but the approach to the work as a fugue is not provided. To solve this problem, the late C. J. Mazney, at that time on the staff of the Subject Cataloging Division, developed a scheme of reference numbers, "imaginary numbers" in that they are not used for shelving material.

As a part of the scheme, a pattern of decimal numbers was set up. These numbers are added to class numbers as reference numbers wherever such subdivision is not included in the schedule.

.1 Sonatas
.2 Suites
.3 Variations
.4 Fugues
.5 Marches
.6 Dances
.62 Duple time
.63 Triple time
.7 Potpourris
.8 Orchestral and band music
.81 Symphonies
.82 Symphonic poems
.84 Overtures, entr'actes
.85 Concertos
.86 Operas, ballets, oratorios, cantatas
.87 Songs, part-songs, chamber music

For the Beethoven work previously cited, a card is filed in the classed catalog under M552.4, providing the necessary approach to the work as a fugue.

Helen E. Bush of the Descriptive Cataloging Division has continued to expand the list of reference numbers as need arises. M1105 is a case in point. Separate numbers for solo instruments with string orchestra are not provided in the M1100's as they are in M1005-M1041. These compositions continue to be classified in

SOURCE: Reprinted from Virginia Cunningham, "The Library of Congress classed catalog for music," *Library Resources & Technical Services,* 8 (Summer, 1964), 285–288, by permission of the American Library Association.

M1105, but they are also assigned appropriate reference numbers in M1108–M1141. Reference numbers have been established in the M5000's when they could not logically be fitted into the printed schedule. M5100, for example, represents instrumental settings of carols; M5700, funeral music.

When the subject catalog was converted, many cards were filed without the reference numbers being written on them. This was an expedient that had to be resorted to because of pressure of time and lack of personnel. Since that time, large quantities of these cards have been identified and the numbers added. For all current cataloging, both the classification numbers and the appropriate reference numbers are assigned by the cataloger. When the cards are prepared for the classed catalog, the reference number is written in red pencil above the classification number. Cards with reference numbers and those with class numbers only are interfiled.

The ML class provides primarily for the literature of music, but certain classes for music of musicological rather than musical interest are included: ML96 and ML96.5 (holographs and facsimiles), and, in part, ML29–ML31 (foundations in the Library of Congress). Cards are filed in the classed catalog for the music classified in each of these classes. In the near future, cards in the libretto classes (ML48–ML54) will be added; this is logical since entry for librettos is made under the name of the composer.

The classed catalog, like the other Music Division catalogs, contains a variety of cards: typed entries prepared in the Music Division from about 1900–1943; printed cards prepared in the Processing Department from about 1900–date; multilithed cards with heading under composer, prepared in the Copyright Office from 1947–1957; multilithed cards prepared in the Descriptive Cataloging Division, 1957–date; multilithed cards with entry under title, prepared in the Copyright Office, 1957–date. These last-named cards are used for the music which is classified for shelving but is not cataloged.

The index. An index to the classed catalog was prepared at the time of the conversion, but even then it was known to be inadequate. A new index, developed by Dr. Bush on a systematic basis, was sent to the Music Division in 1962. It contained approximately 7,000 entries; new entries are being added at the rate of about 250 a year.

Library of Congress subject headings are used as index entries when they provide the most direct approach to the material; e.g. Folk-music, Swedish; Violin and piano music. Cross-references are not used. They are replaced by index entries in uninverted form (Swedish folk-music) or in reverse form (Piano and violin music).

Subject headings with a subheading do not provide the most direct approach. In such cases, commonly-used phrases are used as index entries. Examples are Jewish religious music, instead of Jews. Liturgy and ritual, and Safety songs, instead of Topical songs (Safety). A special problem arises when one number in the M schedule encompasses both collections and separate works, or original works and arrangements. A form card has been devised to cover these cases. The text of the form card appears in one of the examples below.

For each class number in the M schedule, for each sub-class or subject Cuttering, and for each reference number, at least one entry is provided in the index. Typical entries are shown below.

The foregoing description shows that the classed catalog analyzes the music collections by medium of performance, subject, and musical form. This analysis parallels that provided by Library of Congress subject headings. The catalog has a good index, permitting effective use by librarian and public alike. Moreover, for those persons familiar with the M classification scheme, use of the index is not necessary—they can go directly to the proper class number in the catalog. Subject catalogers, and not only those in the field of music, will find an inspection of this classed catalog profitable.

Bird songs

M1977.B5; M1978.B5

Mixed voices, Music for

Sacred
Unaccompanied: M2082; M2092
With orchestral acc.: M2020-2028
With piano or organ: M2062; M2072

Secular

Unaccompanied: M1579-M1582-88
With orchestral acc.: M130-37
With piano or organ: M1549; M1552-58

Oboe and harpsichord music
M245-7

Collections and separate compositions, both original works and arrangements, are included in the above numbers.

C. Thematic Indices

SELECTED BIBLIOGRAPHY

145. Music Library Association. Committee on Thematic Indexes. *A check-list of thematic catalogues,* prepared by a Committee of the Music Library Association. New York: The New York Public Library, 1954. Preface signed: Helen Joy Sleeper.

146. *Queens College supplement (1966) to the Music Library Association's Check-list of thematic catalogues (1954).* Flushing, New York: Queens College, 1966. Introduction signed: Barry S. Brook. "Literature about thematic catalogues": pp. 27–34.

147. *Thematic catalogues in music; an annotated bibliography.* Hillsdale, New York: Pendragon Press, 1971. "Introduction by Barry S. Brook."

Pictures Invade the Catalog; Two Examples of Illustrated Cards: For Music

by Catharine Keyes Miller

It has been found useful in the Music Division of The New York Public Library at 42nd Street and Fifth Avenue[1] to place thematic incipits, such as that in the accompanying illustration, on the main catalog cards of individual works of certain of the great and voluminous composers for the purpose of identification. In some cases–Palestrina, Bach and Schumann–the idea has been carried throughout the entire composer file on the cards analyzing their Complete Works. It is probable that such thoroughgoing treatment is unnecessary for the average library, and especially so for those already owning the standard thematic indexes in book form; but a limited application of the idea, as practiced in the Oberlin Conservatory Library, for example, can be a time-saver for the reference or circulation worker that will quickly repay the few minutes it takes to sketch in the incipit by hand.

The reasons that music is often hard to identify are numerous. Sometimes a work has been published under more than one title and/or number. Some of Bach's *Preludes and Fugues* for organ, for example, have been published as *Fantasias and Fugues* or *Toccatas and Fugues,* and vice versa; and various numberings have been adopted by the various publishers. Sometimes a composer has written more than one work in a given key with the same generic title, e.g. Mozart's or Haydn's piano sonatas. Sometimes the library user knows the opening notes of the work, but has only a hazy notion of the original title or key. And so it goes. If conventional titles are used together with incipits, the problem of identification can usually be solved at the catalog without resorting to the shelves. It might be argued that opus numbers, editor's numbers (e.g. Köchel for Mozart) and such should settle

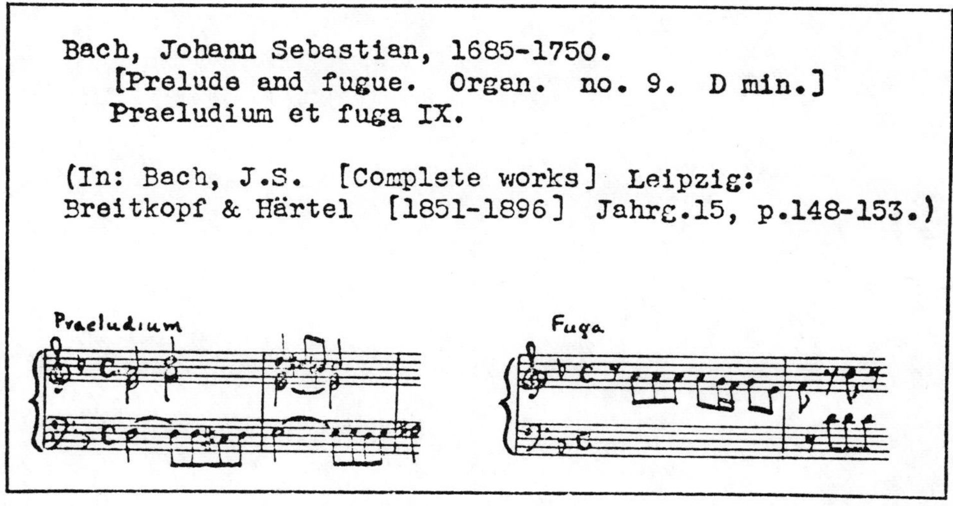
Bach, Johann Sebastian, 1685-1750.
[Prelude and fugue. Organ. no. 9. D min.]
Praeludium et fuga IX.

(In: Bach, J.S. [Complete works] Leipzig: Breitkopf & Härtel [1851-1896] Jahrg.15, p.148-153.)

SOURCE: Reprinted from *Library Journal,* June 1, 1946. Published by R. R. Bowker (a Xerox Company). Copyright c1946, R. R. Bowker Company.

the matter, but that is true only for those who have memorized their meaning.

Works with titles that may be met with more than once in a composer's output are certainly in line for such treatment. The Bach *Preludes and Fugues* for organ are a case in point. For example, no. 9 in D minor (so numbered in the Bach-gesellschaft edition) is thus at once identifiable and not to be confused with no. 8 (the "Dorian") or the big *Toccata and Fugue* in the same key. At Oberlin, incipits are sketched in on cards for all three works. It is, of course, necessary to do so on one card only for each title, because all separate editions of each of these three file together, as provided by the rules for conventional titles. Other examples are the two Schubert songs entitled *Wiegenlied* (Op. 98, no. 2 and Op. 105, no. 2) or the three entitled *Sehnsucht* (Op. 8, no. 2; Op. 39 and Op. 105, no. 4).

Thematic incipits, then, may be adopted sparingly at the points where doubt as to identification may arise, or more generously as a matter of policy. In either case, they will prove their worth.

NOTES

[1] Now part of the Library and Museum for the Performing Arts, Lincoln Center, 111 Amsterdam Avenue, New York, New York.–*Editor.*

The Historical Development of the Thematic Catalogue

by Lenore Coral

HISTORY

The growth and development of the thematic catalogue can be closely tied to the uses to which this tool has been put. Since the first such printed index appeared in 1762[1] it has variously served as advertising matter, as an aid to the layman wishing to learn the name of a theme, and to the scholar seeking bibliographic information on a composer's work. Of the 362 items listed in the Music Library Association's *A Checklist of Thematic Catalogues*,[2] 129 are catalogues of the works of individual composers. The remaining indexes are divided among collections of anonymous works or of works by more than one composer, library catalogues, and catalogues of publishers—the last having the fewest examples.

Each of these types of catalogues serves a specific purpose. Thematic catalogues of collections generally act as indexes to the works included in a publication, although in some cases such indexes may be the only thematic catalogues for the works of a composer. Thematic incipits in printed library catalogues are very unusual. Few libraries can afford the added expense of including them in a printed catalogue. In fact, it is really unnecessary to do so for the music in the standard repertory which forms the basic collection of a music library, but where feasible the inclusion of incipits for works of little known composers (e.g., eighteenth-century symphonists or unique works of anonymous composers in renaissance manuscripts) could prove invaluable to the scholar. In fact, it was quite common to find incipits added by hand to library catalogue cards in the United States in the early part of the twentieth century for those works for which no distinctive title or number was yet available. Publishers' catalogues are particularly interesting because they represent the earliest form of printed thematic catalogue and were the first to include notice of the thematic material in their titles. Their publication diminished as the cost of music decreased and as the number of catalogues of the works of individual composers with identifying numbers assigned to the pieces increased. This last is the most numerous kind of catalogue and greatest attention will be paid to it here.

This study will consist of two sections: the first is an attempt to trace briefly the history of printed thematic catalogues by type; the second is a discussion of the many recent developments which have been brought about by technological advancements and by the need to maintain bibliographic control over musical works which do not have distinctive titles.

The earliest known printed thematic catalogue[3] is that of the publishing house of Johann Gottlob Immanuel Breitkopf of Leipzig, issued in 1762.[4] The purpose of this catalogue, described by Burney as "an index in notes, containing the subjects, or two or three first bars, of the several pieces in each musical work,"[5] was to help a prospective buyer ascertain whether he already owned the advertised musical item. The Breitkopf catalogue was issued in six parts and sixteen supplements and by the year 1787 had covered every class of musical composition. It is interesting to note that the same firm is credited with the invention of a process of typesetting for music which greatly reduced the cost of printing[6] and thus made feasible the inexpensive printing of thematic incipits in their catalogs. In addition, Breitkopf began the extensive printing of piano reductions of operas and other music suitable for use in the home and was one of the first firms to keep a stock of printed scores. Since the eighteenth century was the period in which music became a pastime of the middle class and not only the pleasure of the nobil-

SOURCE: Especially prepared for this *Reader*.

ity, this catalogue represented just one manifestation of the social changes which moved music from an activity of the court and church into the home.

The next thematic catalogue to be issued[7] and the first one to bear an indication of its contents in its title was a catalogue of the firm of J. J. and B. Hummel of Amsterdam.[8] The dates given are variously 1788[9] and 1768-1770.[10] This index was entitled *Catalogue thématique ou commencement de touttes les oeuvres de musique qui sont du propre fond de J. J. et B. Hummel* and was intended to aid the amateur in determining whether a work presented to him as new had already been printed. This and the Breitkopf catalogues were the work of business firms desiring to sell their wares, yet concerned lest the lack of readily identifiable titles should tempt the amateur into purchasing an item he already possessed.

The fact that Hummel found it necessary to define the term "catalogue thématique" in his title indicates not only that it was a new term but also that it was capable of two related but not identical meanings. A digression from the historical survey may be in order here to discuss what it is that constitutes a theme. Although the amount of literature on the subject of thematic indices is small, much of it has been devoted to this problem. "Theme" has been defined both as the "principal melodic feature in a composition, differing from a subject by greater length and more self-contained completeness"[11] and as "the introductory bars of a musical piece."[12] The use of this term in connection with the catalogues which are the subject of this study is almost exclusively the second meaning, that of the incipit or beginning motive of a piece of music. Such incipits usually comprise three or four measures of the leading voice and ideally include the clef, key signature, meter, any written indications of style or tempo, and where relevant the instrument on which the piece is played. Thus the use of the term "thematic" in the title of an index, while it does not necessarily imply the first of these definitions does unequivocally indicate the use of musical quotations within the catalogue.

There are three other eighteenth-century publishers' catalogues which contain musical themes:[13] those of Christian Ulrich Ringmacher of 1773,[14] Christian Gottfried Thomas, 1779,[15] and J. Bland, 1790.[16] Since these catalogues were intended to aid the musician in deciding what music he wished to buy, they were arranged by composer and generally also by form of composition.

The eighteenth-century publishers' catalogues which are extant today—such catalogues were probably issued by a number of publishing houses, but few have been preserved—aid the musicologist as guides to musical taste of an era. They also serve as records of the compositions of some composers (five Vivaldi *sinfonie* are known only through the incipits appearing in the 1762 Breitkopf catalogue and Hoboken has used such catalogues in dating Haydn manuscripts), and as secondary tools in determining the authenticity of a work. Deutsch says in his preface to the thematic catalogue of the works of Schubert, "apparently . . . the early thematic catalogues were partly destined for music dealers whose reference books were still insufficient. The information given for libraries and collectors was not very reliable."[17]

These catalogues illustrate one type of thematic index—that of the music publisher. More important are the thematic catalogues of the works of specific composers. Such catalogues are generally organized chronologically, though some use other principles of organization. The first of these is illustrated by the Köchel catalogue of the works of Mozart,[18] the Schmieder catalogue of the works of J. S. Bach,[19] or the Hoboken catalogue of the works of Haydn,[20] all catalogues which list the works in chronological order. Since in some cases this is impossible, others, like Zimmerman's catalogue of the works of Purcell,[21] use some other principle of organization such as form (sonatas, concertos, etc.), instrumentation or key. These catalogues are useful to the librarian who has the music before him and who wishes to verify information in establishing the uniform title, or to the scholar seeking bibliographic information. The user who knows only the tune will not find a chronological catalogue a very efficient aid. In order to help him catalogues such as May deForest McAll's *Melodic Index to the Works of Johann Sebastian Bach*[22] have been devised. Here, by a clever system of shaped pitch graphs, a listener can find the title of the theme without knowing more about the piece than that it was composed by J. S. Bach. This index will be discussed in greater detail later.

Among the earliest catalogues of the works of an individual composer was the manuscript diary-thematic catalogue of his works kept by W. A. Mozart from February 9, 1784, until November 15, 1791 less than one month before his death. The chronological scheme of organization employed by Mozart in his catalogue, which was published in 1805,[23] became the model for most of the early published thematic catalogues of the works of composers.

The basic idea of chronological organization of thematic catalogues can be seen as another manifestation of historical awareness which developed in the age of romanticism. And the growth of the artist's newly awakened consciousness of his own historical role is reflected, for example, in the fact that Beethoven was the first composer to assign systematic opus numbers to his works.[24]

After the turn of the nineteenth century many catalogues of the works of individual composers appeared. A number of these were published by Breitkopf and Härtel, who were responsible for the publication of early editions of the complete works of many composers. From this time on such thematic catalogues became the rule.

Probably the earliest published thematic catalogue of the works of a single composer[25] is a guide to the works of Pleyel published by his Viennese publisher Artaria as an extra page in that publisher's edition of Pleyel's Eighth Quintet in 1789.[26] The next such list is that of Hoffmeister who published a thematic list of all his own works for the flute in 1800.[27] J. A. André published a lithographed edition of Mozart's own manuscript catalogue in 1805;[28] it may be remembered that this is the same André who was so helpful to Alois Senefelder in getting the lithograph process accepted as a printing method.[29] In 1819 a catalogue of Beethoven's works through Opus 102 was published;[30] and then for the next thirty years there was a succession of catalogues of the works of individual composers most of whose works are disregarded by scholars and audiences alike today but which reflect the taste of the period. This list includes such names as Moscheles,[31] Gelinek,[32] and Fesca.[33]

The publication of complete editions of composers' works was begun about 1850, and from this time on there is a distinct correlation between thematic catalogues and the publication of collected works. The development of scholarly study in music is of German origin—the first chair of musicology in an institution of higher learning was at the University of Berlin in 1826.[34] The early German musicologists undertook the editing of the *Gesamtausgaben* and produced the first comprehensive thematic catalogues. The Köchel catalogue of the works of Mozart,[35] which was published in 1862 by Breitkopf and Härtel, set such high standards of comprehensiveness that few other catalogues issued in the next forty years were able to match them. This catalogue included with each theme the location of its autograph, details of first editions, and bibliographies of literature on the works. Köchel attempted to arrange the catalogue in chronological order and based his work partly on a manuscript listing of Mozart's works in classified order which had been compiled by Aloys Fuchs as early as 1837, but which has never been published.[36] Köchel assigned to each of Mozart's works the identifying number which is today familiar to any musician or concertgoer. However, Alfred Einstein in his 1937 revision of the catalogue,[37] did not maintain the integrity of the originally assigned numbers, as he rearranged the order of the works to conform to the latest research. Consequently many of Mozart's works are armed with two identifying numbers which add little but confusion to the situation.

The next publication to add anything new to the apparatus of the thematic catalogue was F. W. Jähns, *Karl Maria von Weber, chronologisch-thematisches Verzeichniss seiner sämmtlichen Compositionen* (1871)[38] which, while not so detailed bibliographically as the Köchel-Mozart catalogue, contained details regarding performance which make it useful as a source book as well as a thematic catalogue.

In the late nineteenth century catalogues of the works of Bach,[39] Beethoven,[40] Chaikovsky,[41] Chopin,[42] Glinka,[43] and Schubert[44] appeared. All strove to match in completeness and detail the work of Köchel. However, for most of these composers it was not until the mid-twentieth century that this goal was reached.

All the thematic catalogues of the twentieth century have more or less followed the precedent set by the Köchel-Mozart catalogue in their organization and contents. The first volume of the long-awaited Hoboken catalogue of the works of Haydn (1957)[45] varied the procedure slightly, ordering the works first by form and then by chronology as much as was possible. Hoboken in describing his work says that he relied heavily on early advertisements for the dating of works.[46] Georg Kinsky in arranging the thematic catalogue of Beethoven's works published in 1955[47] made no changes in the traditional opus numbers, correcting chronological errors with notes and placing the unnumbered works in a separate section at the end. Kinsky's index is further distinguished by the inclusion of thematic quotations, "each one of them . . . as long as it has to be in order to make musical sense. That is, both melody and harmony are unequivocal."[48] This is in contrast to many of the catalogues where the cursory quotations barely identify the work.

Though the catalogues which are discussed above are useful tools for the scholar and the librarian, they certainly are not adequately arranged to provide information in all situations. Often it is the case that a work must be identified when little is known but the composer or even a theme without the name of its composer. Several catalogues attempting to solve this problem have been published. These fall into two categories: those devoted to a single composer and those devoted to a collection of themes by many composers. Of the first type there is one outstanding example, the McAll *Melodic Index to the Works of Johann Sebastian Bach*[49] mentioned briefly above. In this index the works are grouped by melodic pitch patterns with rhythm and actual pitch disregarded. Thus a user knowing the theme (its direction, relative intervals, and the degree of the scale on which it starts) can find a list of all Bach works which begin in this way, and then by examining thematic quotations of each of these pieces he can determine which of them is the work he wishes to identify. There is an index to the works of Beethoven which is basically the same.[50]

The arrangement just described is useful in the case of a composer whose themes tend to vary enough to produce a fairly broad spectrum of melodic graphs. However, if one considers the works of a composer such as Vivaldi, whose opening melodies tend, with amazing regularity, to one of a very small number of designs and whose output is large, the absence of rhythmic patterns would render such an index of little use.

The second kind of index, containing works of many composers, is exemplified by the Barlow and Morgenstern *A Dictionary of Musical Themes.*[51] This work, which contains 10,000 themes four- to eight-measures long (here the definition of theme must be the broad one, for this guide includes not only incipits but themes in the sense of principal melodic ideas), is arranged in three sections: alphabetically by composer and title, alphabetically by letters corresponding to the pitches of the themes if transposed into C major or A minor,[52] and lastly an index by title.

Among the limitations of this index is the fact that it includes only themes of very well known works rather than the more obscure ones which are consequently more difficult to identify. Also, transposition of all themes into a standard key can add considerable confusion to the problem of identifying a work. As an example, in the works of Vivaldi about one-fifth of his compositions begin with an ascending tonic triad (incidentally, it is to be noted that Barlow and Morgenstern do *not* indicate the direction of motion from one pitch to the next in their melodic index). If all of these themes by Vivaldi were transposed into the key of C major, one would be forced to hunt through approximately 100 themes to identify the one in hand.

Both McAll and Barlow and Morgenstern serve useful purposes but, as the reader can see, they are only beginnings to the solution of the problem of access to material which is lacking in sufficient external identification.

THE DEVELOPMENT OF NON-MUSICAL SYSTEMS

Since the turn of this century and particularly since the end of World War II many schemes have been devised to order music by its musical incipit. Most of these have been intended for works which lack identifying titles or numbers and in almost every case the scheme has been highly specialized. This section will be devoted to describing these schemes which do not use traditional music notation and which recently have begun to incorporate the resources of the information sciences in their designs.

The idea of using symbols other than those of traditional music notation, which is both expensive and space consuming to reproduce in a catalogue, did not receive systematic discussion until 1902, and for the next forty years was related only to the problems besetting those who wished to study the melodies of folksongs. Although such songs usually have texts, these texts may vary greatly and often the same tune appears in several places with quite different words. Thus if a scholar wishes to study a single tune, a method of melodic indexing must be designed which will allow him access to all similar melodies regardless of their texts. Folk melodies have certain characteristics which are basic to the schemes which were devised to index them and which limit the usefulness these schemes have when applied to indexing other forms of music. Folk tunes are generally short. They can be distinguished by their melodic shape without reference to rhythm and they can still be distinguished from each other even after being transcribed into a common key.

The earliest scheme for indexing folk melodies using non-traditional symbols was devised by Oswald Koller in 1902.[53] He transposed all the tunes into a single key and assigned numbers to represent the interval from the tonic, an Arabic numeral if the note was above middle C and a Roman numeral for a note below, middle C was represented by zero. The author of this scheme was not concerned with accidentals, ornamental figures (such as trills and grace notes), or rhythm. He did include at the end of each quotation the key or mode of the original piece.

This scheme was challenged almost immediately by another proposed by Ilmari Krohn[54] which, in addition to the items selected by Koller, included references to the harmonic structure of the cadences.

The next major contribution to the problem of indexing was made by Sigurd Hustvedt,[55] whose particular effort was directed towards a melodic index to the tunes of the Child ballads. In his scheme the first musical phrase is represented by the actual letter names of the notes including accidentals and a crude rhythmic outline. However, no allowance is made for the inclusion of melodic ornaments which are essential for distinguishing folk melodies. All of these schemes have built into their systems a means of telling the exact pitch of a note and its relationship to middle C. Each was designed to index a repertory of folk tunes for inclusion in a printed index.

The next major scheme to be devised was intended for use on catalogue cards to identify and group together like works in a library's collection. The project, at the Bibliothèque nationale in Paris, is under the guidance of Nanie Bridgman.[56] Originally these thematic incipits for catalogue cards were intended to cover all periods of western music in the Bibliothèque nationale's collection. However, this plan was soon narrowed to include only works up to 1800 and more recently it has become clear that the scheme that has been adopted will only suffice for certain types of works through the sixteenth century.[57] Subsequently, other union thematic catalogues of eighteenth-century symphonies[58] and sonatas of the eighteenth century[59] have been started.

Madame Bridgman describes the system which she employed as being very close to that of Koller with modifications to account for the fact that in different sources for the same piece of music in the fifteenth and sixteenth century it is often the case that one long note may be replaced by several repeated shorter notes—consequently repeated notes have been omitted. More important, since in such a catalogue (and particularly for the period covered here) all known editions of a work should be brought together regardless of what transposition may have occurred from one source to another, Madame Bridgman uses numbers alone to represent half-step intervals. No rhythm per se is shown, but numeric values have been assigned to each of the commonly used note types of the period. These values are applied to the first five notes and the sum is entered on the card. Only the top voice of a piece is used regardless of whether or not this voice contains the melody.

Such a scheme as the one just described is very limited in its applications. It does not lend itself to the indexing of music from more recent periods. Consider the problems of constructing a scheme for indexing themes to eighteenth-century symphonies. Unlike medieval and renaissance music which may be recognizable when both rhythm and repeated notes have been ignored, the themes of eighteenth-century music are not intelligible without these elements. Since transposition of pieces was no longer a common phenomenon and since transposition of the incipits into a common key would make such an index extremely cumbersome, it is not desirable to adopt such a scheme.

Jan LaRue, in founding the *Union Thematic Catalogue of 18th-Century Symphonies*, chose to ignore rhythm in his initial catalogue although he did divide the works by meter before ordering them by pitch. Only three years later, he proposed a new system of incipits for thematic catalogues.[60] This scheme is the first printed attempt to provide a system which would serve all periods of western music. This is highly desirable, because the necessity of learning a new system for every catalogue to be consulted is a deterrent to the user. And since many potential users are hostile to the idea of notating music in any but conventional music notation, it is necessary that such a scheme be adaptable and yet not too complicated to learn.

With this in mind let us examine the second LaRue scheme and two other schemes which have been proposed subsequently. LaRue had the idea that it would prove very useful to be able to include incipits on regular library catalogue cards. Not only would they serve as identifying elements but they could be used as added entries and would thus form a thematic index within the card catalogue. In order to facilitate this LaRue devised a scheme based solely on typewriter symbols. His system assigns numbers to pitches (but not to each half-step) so that the pitches of the middle octave are represented by the numbers 1-7 and other octaves are shown by placing an appropriate number of apostrophes or commas before the numeral. Unfortunately, numbering only the diatonic scale and not the chromatic scale means that much space must be wasted including accidentals which could have been eliminated by identifying each chromatic tone. Where LaRue's system is weakest however, is in the indication of rhythm. As constituted it shows the number of notes within a given beat but not the specific values so that , , and all appear as identical three-note groups. Aside from this he uses the dot to denote a pitch carried over to a succeeding beat "recalling the dot in musical notation."[61] However, the dot in musical notation has a very specific meaning, i.e., it represents a duration exactly one-half the length of the note it follows. In LaRue's scheme it may represent a duration twice as long, equal to, or one-half as long as the original note. The broad use of a symbol which normally has a very specific meaning tends to confuse rather than help the user of the catalogue in visualizing the music which is being represented.

Of the two most recent contributions one, proposed by Lawrence Bernstein,[62] is merely an adaptation of Mme. Bridgman's scheme for keypunch machinery. Its only additional contribution is that it cross-indexes all the voices of the chansons with which Bernstein is concerned. Again the scheme does not include rhythmic patterns and consequently is not generally adaptable.

The latest and by far the most comprehensive scheme has recently been set forth by Barry Brook under the title, *Notating Music with Ordinary Typewriter Characters.*[63] In his introduction Mr. Brook states the following conditions as determining the effectiveness of any such scheme:

1. It must be speedy, simple, absolutely accurate as to pitch and rhythm. It should be as closely related mnemonically to musical notation as possible, so that it appears natural and right, avoiding arbitrary symbols. It should require only a single line of typewriter characters without the need for back-spacing or for a second pass over the line. It should be usable by non-musicians with only a few minutes of instruction. It must be easily recognizable as music from the symbols alone and immediately retranslateable, without loss, into conventional notation.
2. It must be applicable to all western music from Gregorian chant to serial music.
3. It must be universally understandable and internationally acceptable.
4. It must be so devised as to be readily transferable to electronic data-processing equipment for key transposition, fact-finding, tabulating and other research purposes.[64]

The Brook system provides for a very detailed notation of a musical incipit in a single line and employs only standard typewriter symbols. It is so constructed as to be easily transferred to high speed data processing equipment but unfortunately this kind of equipment is not readily available to every library and scholar wishing to employ such a scheme today. In addition, as has been amply pointed out in the critical commentaries[65] which followed this scheme's publication, it does not in its typewritten form make it possible to collect the various transpositions of a piece in one place.

These are not the only drawbacks of the Brook system. It is so designed that the designation of the octave of a given pitch is based on the pitch preceding it so that it is not possible for a user to discern immediately the shape of a melody. Again, this might be of little consequence if computers were available to all users. However, the expense of operating a computer is not justified for many projects involving the use of a thematic catalogue which are merely a matter of one-to-one comparisons and could readily be done manually. It should not be necessary to require the costly operations of encoding, running through a computer, and decoding for relatively simple operations.

If machinery is to be used for such basic operations it is very possible that a more efficient machine code could be designed. For instance, if the card catalogue were to become a machine catalogue and the user's information would be translated as it was fed out, it might be more efficient to assign an individual symbol to each pitch in the entire range of pitches of which there are just under 100 from the lowest note of the contrabassoon to the highest note on the piccolo. A table of transposition equivalences could then be set up and both of the outstanding problems of this scheme would be solved. However, it seems unwise to propose another detailed system until it is clear that the Brook system will not with some adjustments be adequate to the tasks it must perform.

It must never be forgotten that the value of thematic catalogues lies in the help they give the user in identifying musical compositions, although their format also makes them an ideal way of presenting an overview of a composer's works.

NOTES

[1]Alexander Hyatt King, "The past, present and future of the thematic catalogue," *The Monthly Musical Record*, 84 (January, 1954), 11.

[2]Music Library Association, *A Checklist of Thematic Catalogues*, prepared by the Committee on Thematic Indexes (New York: The New York Public Library, 1954). A *Queens College Supplement (1966)*, increased the number of known catalogues by an additional 230.

[3]Probably the first thematic catalogues were the manuscript tonaries of the eighth and ninth centuries which listed Gregorian chants arranged according to their modes.

[4]Johann G. I. Breitkopf, *Catalogo delle sinfonie, partite, overture, soli, duetti, trii, quattori e concerti per il violino, flauto traverso, cembalo ed altri stromenti, che si trovano in manuscritto nella Officiantt musica di Giovanni Gottlob Breitkopf in Lipsia* (6 parts and 16 supplements; Leipzig: J. Breitkopf, 1762–1787). A modern reprint has been published by Dover Publications, (New York: 1966).

[5]Charles Burney, *The Present State of Music in Germany, the Netherlands, and United Provinces* (London: T. Becket, 1775), II, 74.

[6]Alexander Hyatt King, *Four Hundred Years of Music Printing* (London: The British Museum, 1964), p. 23.

[7]King, "Thematic catalogue," p. 11.

[8]J. J. and B. Hummel, *Catalogue thématique ou commencement de touttes les oeuvres de musique qui sont du propre fond de J. J. et B. Hummel* (Amsterdam: J. J. et B. Hummel, 1778 [?]).

[9]Music Library Association, *Checklist*, p. 27.

[10]Otto Erich Deutsch, "Theme and Variations with Bibliographic Notes on Pleyel's Haydn Editions," *The Music Review*, 12 (1951), 69.

[11]Eric Blom, *Everyman's Dictionary of Music* (New York: Dutton, 1958), p. 619.

[12]Deutsch, "Theme and Variations," p. 68.

[13]Both the Ringmacher and Thomas catalogs are listed in the MLA *Checklist*, p. 28. Neither contains indications in the title which shows music to be included. As I have been unable to examine copies of these catalogs I will assume that they do contain thematic material. The Bland catalog specifically mentions the inclusion of musical incipits in its title.

[14]Christian Ulrich Ringmacher, *Catalogo de' soli, duetti, trii, quadri, quintetti, partito, de' concerti e delle sinfonie per il cembalo, violino, flauto traverso ed altri stromenti che si trovano in manoscritto nella officina musica di Christiano Ulrico Ringmacher libraio in Berelino* (Berlin: C. Ringmacher, 1773).

[15]Christian Gottfried Thomas, *Des musikalischen summarischen Verzeichnisses erster Nachtrag von Sinfonien, Partien, Concerten, Divertimenten, Quintetten, Quartetten, Trios, Duetten, und Solos auf allen Arten Instrumenten, etc., die zu bekommen sind bey Christ. Gottfr. Thomas* (Leipzig: C. Thomas, 1779).

[16]John Bland, *Catalogue of Subject or Beginnings of the Several Works, for the Harpsichord, Piano Forte, and Organ, Which are Printed and Sold by J. Bland* (London: J. Bland, 1790).

[17]Otto Erich Deutsch, *Schubert, Thematic Catalogue of All His Works* (London: J. M. Dent, 1951), p. ix.

[18]Ludwig Ritter von Köchel, *Chronologisch-thematisches Verzeichniss sämmtlicher Tonwerke W. A. Mozart* (Leipzig: Breitkopf und Härtel, 1862).

[19]Wolfgang Schmieder, *J. S. Bach. Thematisch-systematisches Verzeichnis der musikalischen Werke* (Leipzig: Breitkopf und Härtel, 1950).

[20]Anthony van Hoboken, *Joseph Haydn, Thematisch-bibliographisches Werkverzeichnis* (Mainz: B. Schott's Söhne, 1957–).

[21]Franklin P. Zimmerman, *Henry Purcell, 1659–1695, An Analytical Catalogue of his Music* (London: Macmillan and Co., 1963).

[22]May deForest McAll, *Melodic Index to the Works of Johann Sebastian Bach* (New York: C. F. Peters, 1962).

[23]Wolfgang A. Mozart, *Thematisches Verzeichniss sämmtlicher Kompositionen* (Offenbach: A. André, 1805).

[24]See the article "Opus" in the *International Cyclopedia of Music and Musicians*, 9th ed. (New York: Dodd, Mead and Co., 1964), p. 1518.

[25]Music Library Association, *Checklist*, p. 17.

[26]Ignaz Pleyel, *Catalogue thématique ou commencement de chaque quatuor, quintet, trios et duo compose par I. Pleyel* (in his *Quintetto per due violini, due viole, e violoncello . . . no. 8*, 2 pages preceding p. 1 of the second violin part) (Vienna: Artaria, [1789?]). Deutsch in his Schubert catalog says that there was no list of works devoted to a single composer until Pleyel published his thematic catalog of the quartets of Joseph Haydn in 1802. Deutsch, *Schubert*, p. ix.

[27]Franz Anton Hoffmeister, *Catalogue thématique de tous les oeuvres pour la flûte traversière composés par F. A. Hoffmeister* (Vienna: F. A. Hoffmeister, 1800). Cited in King, "Thematic catalogue," p. 12.

[28]Mozart, *Thematisches Verzeichniss.*

[29]King, *Printing*, p. 27.

[30]Ludwig van Beethoven, *Thematisches Verzeichniss der Compositionen für Instrumentalmusik welche von den berühmtesten Tonsetzern unsersers* [*sic*] *Zeitalters erschienen sind* (Leipzig: F. A. Hoffmeister, 1819).

[31]Ignaz Moscheles, *Catalogue thématique des oeuvres de J. Moscheles revu par lui-même* (Leipzig: Probst, 1825).

[32]Josef Gelinek, *Thematisches Verzeichniss der Variationen des Abbé Gelinek für das Pianoforte von No. 1 bis 100* (Offenbach: A. André, [1820?]).

[33]Friedrich Ernst Fesca, *Catalogue thématique des ouvrages contenus dans la Collection de quintetti et quatuors de F. E. Fesca* (Paris: S. Richault, [182–?]), in the 1st violin part, p. 1.

[34]For further information on the development of the field of musicology see: Paul Henry Lang, *Music in Western Civilization* (New York: W. W. Norton and Co., 1941), pp. 985–89, and Frank Ll. Harrison, Mantle Hood and Claude V. Palisca, *Musicology* (Englewood Cliffs, N.J.: Prentice-Hall, 1963).

[35]Köchel, *Chronologisch-thematisches Verzeichniss.*

[36]King, "Thematic catalogue," p. 40.

[37]Ludwig Ritter von Köchel, *Mozart, Thematisches Verzeichniss*, ed. Alfred Einstein, 3d ed. (Leipzig: Breitkopf und Härtel, 1937).

[38]F. W. Jähns, *Karl Maria von Weber, chronologisch-thematisches Verzeichniss seiner sämmtlichen Compositionen* (Berlin: Schlessinger, 1871).

[39]"Die Gesangeswerke Bach's . . . , Die Instrumentalwerke Bach's. Thematisches Verzeichniss." In his *Werke*, ed. Bach-Gesellschaft (Leipzig: Breitkopf und Härtel, 1851–1926), Jahrg. XXVII, p. ii; Jahrg. XLVI.

[40]*Thematisches Verzeichniss der im Druck erschienenen Werke von L.v. Beethoven* (Leipzig: Breitkopf und Härtel, 1851).

[41]B. Jurgenson, *Catalogue thématique des oeuvres de P. Tschaikowsky* (Moscow: Jurgenson, 1897).

[42]*Thematisches Verzeichniss der im Druck erschienen Compositionen von Friedrich Chopin* (Leipzig: Breitkopf und Härtel, 1852).

[43]K. Albrecht, *Thematic List of Romances, Songs and Operas of M. I. Glinka* (Moscow: Jurgenson, 1891).

[44]*Thematisches Verzeichnis im Druck erschienenen Compositionen von F. Schubert* (Vienna: Diabelli, 1852).

[45]Hoboken, *Joseph Haydn.*

[46]Anthony von Hoboken, "The First Thematic Catalogue of Haydn's Works," *Notes*, 9 (March, 1952), 226. See also *ibid.*, 28 (December, 1971), 209–211.

[47]Georg Kinsky, *Das Werk Beethoven; thematisch-bibliographisches Verzeichnis seiner samtlichen vollendeten Kompositionen* (Munich: G. Henle, 1955).

[48]Paul Henry Lang, Review of *Das Werk Beethovens; thematisch-bibliographisches Verzeichnis* . . . by Georg Kinsky, *The Musical Quarterly*, 44 (April, 1958), 257.

[49]McAll, *Melodic index.*

[50]This index is described in King, "Thematic Catalogues," p. 40, where he misattributes its authorship to Wilhelm Hess. It should read Wilhelm Haas, *Systematische Ordnung Beethovenscher Melodien.* Veröffentlichungen der Beethovenhauses Bonn, 7–8. (Leipzig: Quelle & Meyer, 1932). There is also a Mozart index by George R. Hill and Murray Gould, *A thematic locator for Mozart's works as listed in Köchel's Chronologisch-thematisches Verzeichnis, sixth edition* (Hackensack, N.J.: J. Boonin, 1970) *Music Indexes and Bibliographies* 1.

[51]Harold Barlow and Sam Morgenstern, *A Dictionary of Musical Themes* (New York: Crown Publishers, 1948).

[52]An example *ibid.* (p. 527): AAAAAB, AAAAAG, AAAABA.

[53]Oswald Koller, "Die Beste Methode, Volks- und volksmässige Lieder nach ihren melodischen Beschaffenheit lexikalisch zu ordnen," *Sammelbände der Internationalen Musikgesellschaft*, 4 (1902), 1–15.

[54]Ilmari Krohn, "Welche ist die beste Methode, um Volks- und volksmässige Lieder nach ihrer melodischen (nicht textlichen) Beschaffenheit lexikalisch zu ordnen?" *Sammelbände der Internationalen Musikgesellschaft*, 4 (1903), 643–60.

[55]Sigurd Hustvedt, "A melodic index of Child's ballad tunes," *Publications of the University of California at Los Angeles in Languages and Literature*, 1, No. 2 (1936), 51–78.

[56]Nanie Bridgman, "L'Etablissement d'un catalogue par incipit musicaux," *Musica Disciplina*, 4 (1950), 65–68.

[57]Nanie Bridgman, "Nouvelle visite aux incipit musicaux," *Acta Musicologica*, 33 (1961), 193–96.

[58]Jan LaRue, "A Union Thematic Catalogue of 18th-Century Symphonies," *Fontes artis musicae*, 6 (1959), 18–20.

[59]A Zimmerman catalog is described in Nanie Bridgman, "Le Classement par incipit musicaux," *Bulletin des Bibliothèques de France*, 4 (1959), 305.

[60]Jan LaRue and Mary Rasmussen, "Numerical Incipits for Thematic Catalogues," *Fontes artis musicae*, 9 (1962), 72–75.

[61]*Ibid.*, p. 73.

[62]Lawrence Bernstein, "Data Processing and the Thematic Index," *Fontes artis musicae*, 11 (1964), 159–65.

[63]Barry Brook and Murray Gould, "Notating Music with Ordinary Typewriter Characters," *Fontes artis musicae*, 11 (1964), 142–55.

[64]*Ibid.*, pp. 142–43.

[65]"Commentaries," *Fontis artis musicae*, 11 (1964), 155–59.

D. Application of Data Processing Techniques

The duplication and manipulation of thematic incipits is a natural bridge from discussion of the traditionally-prepared single entry description and identification of music to the automated preparation of detailed, multi-faceted indexes from a single encoding of information. LaRue and Rasmussen [p. 192, n. 60] summarized musicologists attempts to 1962 to notate musical incipits in some non-musical symbols so that they could be compared with each other for the purposes of musicological research. In 1964, Professor Barry Brook and Murray Gould published the results of their experimentation in the notation of music with ordinary typewriters [**149**, 194]. In 1965, Prof. Brook proposed before the International Association of Music Libraries that the "Plaine and easie code" be adopted as the international scheme for notating music in non-musical symbols and that thus encoded thematic incipits be added to the RISM catalogue entries for printed music [**150** below].

This subdivision is specifically devoted to the automated manipulation of music-related materials. Prof. Brook's article discusses the use of automation in music libraries, and particularizes it in his proposal for a computer-produced and indexed bibliography of scholarly musical literature. The *Selected Bibliography,* the extensive bibliography in item **148**, and the bibliographical references in Brook's article record the progress of automation in music libraries to 1971. Unfortunately, many of the programs described—including RILM itself—are in financial difficulty and many have been discontinued altogether. It is probably too true that, except for the accomplishments of RILM, musical scholarship and music libraries have not yet realized the potential of automation.

SELECTED BIBLIOGRAPHY

148. *Musicology and the computer; Musicology 1966–2000: A practical program.* Three Symposia. Barry S. Brook, ed. New York: Greater New York Chapter, American Musicological Society and CUNY Press, 1970. "Bibliography" current to 1970: pp. 231–270.

The bibliography supersedes Gary Berlind's compilations, "Writings on the use of computers in music" [New York: New York University, Institute for Computer Research in the Humanities, 1965; and *College Music Symposium,* 6 (1966), 143–157].

* * * * *

149. Brook, Barry S. and Gould, Murray. "Notating music with ordinary typewriter characters: (A plaine and easie code system for musicke)," *Fontes artis musicae,* 11 (1964/3), 142–155. Also: Flushing, New York: Queens College of the CUNY, 1964.

150. Brook, Barry S. "The simplified 'Plaine and easie code system' for notating music: A proposal for international adoption," *Fontes artis musicae,* 12 (1965/2-3), 156–160.

151. LaRue, Jan and Logemann, George W. "EDP [electronic data processing] for thematic catalogues," *Notes,* 22 (June, 1966), 1179–1186.

152. Bengtsson, Ingmar. "Numericode: a code system for thematic incipits," *Svensk tidskrift för musikforskning,* 49 (1967), 5–40.

Full description and explanation of a code system for thematic incipits.

153. LaRue, Jan. "Two options for input of thematic incipits," *ICRH Newsletter,* 4 (November, 1968), 3–6.

154. Lincoln, Harry B. *Development of computerized techniques in music research with emphasis on the thematic index.* Washington, D.C.: U.S. Office of Education, Bureau of Research, 1968.

* * * * *

155. *ICRH Newsletter,* v. 1, 1966–v. 4, 1969. New York: New York University, Institute for Computer Research in the Humanities, 1966–1969.

Articles and information notes of computer-assisted projects in the humanities.

156. *Computers and the Humanities: A Newsletter,* v. 1, September, 1966– New York: Queens College of the CUNY, 1966–

The September issue is usually an "Annual survey of recent developments," one chapter of which is devoted to music. The 1971 music survey is:

157. Kostka, Stefan M. "Recent developments in computer-assisted musical scholarship," *Computers and the Humanities,* 6 (September, 1971), 15–21.

Bibliographical notes.

158. Coover, James B. "Computers, cataloguing, and co-operation," *Notes,* 25 (March, 1969), 437–446.

159. Tanno, John W.; Lynn, Alfred G.; and Roberson, Robert E. "An automated music library catalog for scores and phonorecords." In *The computer and music,* edited by Harry B. Lincoln, pp. 328–346. Ithaca: Cornell University Press, 1970.

Written—in three sections—from the viewpoints of 1) the music librarian, 2) the systems analyst, and 3) the manager of the data processing center.

160. "[Preliminary draft of the MARC format for sound recordings, meeting of the New York Chapter, Music Library Association]" *Music Cataloging Bulletin,* 2 (June, 1971), 3–4.

Quotes the serious reservations about the adequacy of the draft which were read by music librarians at the meeting.

* * * * *

161. *RILM abstracts of music literature,* I, January/April, 1967– Flushing, New York: International Repertory of Musical Literature, 1967–

162. Samuel, Harold. "Notes for *Notes: RILM: Abstracts of Music Literature,*" *Notes,* 24 (December, 1967), 251–252.

163. Brook, Barry S. "RILM Inaugural report: January, 1967," *Notes,* 23 (March, 1967), 462–467.

164. ——. "RILM: Report No. 2, September 1967," *Fontes artis musicae,* 15 (1968/1), 2–9. Also: *Notes,* 24 (March, 1968), 457–466.

165. ——. "RILM: Report No. 3: September 1968," *Fontes artis musicae,* 16 (1969/1-2), 24–27.

166. ——. "RILM Report No. 4, Amsterdam, August 1969," *Fontes artis musicae,* 17 (1970/1-2), 41–44.

167. ——. "Music literature and modern communication; revolutionary potentials of the ACLS/-CUNY/RILM Project," *College Music Symposium,* 9 (1969), 48–59.

The history, scope and preparation of *RILM Abstracts.*

Utilization of Data Processing Techniques in Music Documentation

by Barry S. Brook

THE PRINCIPAL REPORT

Documentation as a general term has been defined as "the group of techniques necessary for the ordered presentation, organization and communication of recorded specialized knowledge, in order to give maximum accessibility and utility to the information contained."[1]

There is at present a serious crisis in documentation in virtually all disciplines. It will grow worse. Every one of you, I'm sure, has seen it in his own work. It has been demonstrated that the number of scholarly periodicals doubles roughly every fifteen years and increases tenfold every fifty years. Derek de Solla Price has shown that "80 to 90 per cent of all scientists that have ever been alive are alive today."

Furthermore, to quote Eric Boehm, "a given subject with a dozen qualified scholars today, may have hundreds in a decade and thousands in 50 years."[2] Unless something is done about it, keeping abreast of one's discipline, even one's little corner in the discipline, will become an increasingly frustrating and impossible occupation: search time and search fatigue with resultant inefficiency will multiply exponentially.

This challenge is being met head-on with the aid of the computer in many branches of science, in business and in government. The humanities, with some exceptions to be mentioned later, seem to be sinking rather than swimming in their uncharted sea of documentation.

It must be made very clear that automation offers no immediate pie in the bibliographical sky. Every forward step in the field of information storage and retrieval has been hard fought and extremely costly of time and funds.

However, there have been many impressive steps in a very few years; to mention just a few: some of you may be familiar with the *Index Medicus* of the National Library of Medicine which aims for total bibliographical control of current medical literature. In a field where international information exchange can effect the savings of lives all over the world, the automated *Index Medicus* is bringing considerable order out of potential chaos in information dissemination.

Another example from the field of medicine is the joint medical library project of Yale, Harvard and Columbia Universities, a brilliant example of the effectiveness of a cooperative computer-oriented library operation. In chemistry, biology, geography, engineering, etc., hundreds of thousands of articles and reports are abstracted annually and automatically indexed in depth by data processing equipment.

In the legal profession, full control of all U.S. decisional law, both state and federal, is well on its way. In New York State, for example, Law Research Service, Inc., a commercial firm, provides its lawyer clients with "legal research by computer." For a modest fee, it will search its computer-indexed and stored legal library in answer to specific questions. Within forty-eight hours the client is provided with complete xeroxed copies of all pertinent decisions that might serve as precedents in preparing his brief. Examples from many other disciplines could be cited to amplify this picture.

Present experimentation with optical scanners, microphotography, photon print-out, and consoles with screens communicating with central computer memories provide tantalizing promise of future conveniences. We may even dream of that famous little black box in which the entire contents of the Library of Congress or of the Bibliothèque Nationale, or both, is stored in immediately recallable form. The scholar-librarian in this

SOURCE: Reprinted from Barry S. Brook, "Utilization of data processing techniques in music documentation," *Fontes artis musicae*, 12 (1965), 112–122, by permission of the International Association of Music Libraries.

brave new computerized world sits in front of a screen in his office or in his study at home pushing buttons with one hand and holding a vermouth with the other. His special typewriter enables him to hold "conversations" with a computer many miles away. Notetaking is hardly necessary since any page passing before him on the screen can immediately be reproduced in paper form or be recalled at will later.

Whatever the future may hold—and let us be wary of naive speculation—the *present* already contains many valuable techniques that we must learn to utilize. This paper is primarily concerned with outlining some answers to the following questions: What is the documentation situation in music and the humanities? What data processing techniques are applicable today in the music library and in musical documentation in general? What concrete steps can be taken to control the "information explosion" in music documentation?

First, for those attending this Congress who may never have met any data processing equipment face to face, a few brief words about the principal data processing machine called the "computer" or "ordinateur" or "elektronische Datenverarbeitung." The modern electronic digital computer is a machine, or rather a group of machines, created by the human brain to meet the inescapable necessities of our time. It is a tool that can add, subtract, multiply and divide; it is a tool that can store information given to it in the form of numbers, letters or other symbols; it is a tool that can make logical comparisons; it can move data around within itself and thus can operate upon and organize and reorganize its stored information in a multitude of ways; it is a tool that is tireless and performs at incredible speeds. A computer's minute of time is like an eternity; its operations are measured in microseconds; a microsecond equals one thousandth of a millisecond which is one thousandth of a second. To put it another way, a microsecond is to a second as a second is to a week and a day. And in half a second the modern computer can execute around 100,000 instructions! A computer driven satellite printer of recent vintage can print out its results at a relatively slow speed of 1600 lines per minute; this means that at, say, 40 lines per ordinary book page, 40 pages can be printed in one minute and a 400-page volume in ten minutes. (At this point, through the courtesy of the International Business Machines Corporation, a film on Electronic Data Processing was shown.)

But no matter how blinding its speed, the computer remains a dumb machine, a creature of the human intelligence. It requires the most precise set of man-made instructions, called a Program, in order to operate at all. Its data has to be prepared for it and fed into it with infinite care and considerable time and labor by human action. This is not the moment to discuss basic questions of man's relationship to the machine. Clearly, however, automatic rejection of the computer on philosophical grounds makes as much sense as fear and rejection of the typewriter, the adding machine or the telephone.

We may find it appropriate to write out certain letters in longhand rather than to dictate them to a secretary to be typed, but it is good to have a choice. We may decide that it is advisable to visit a specific friend in person rather than telephone him, but in many cases the telephone will save a good deal of time and energy. By the same token, many bibliographical and scholarly investigations in music will probably always be better carried out "by hand" while others will profit immeasurably from electronic assistance. We concur with Lewis Lockwood in his pithy remark, "Having a computer is no substitute for having an idea" and add a corollary in which he would surely concurr "Having an idea need not require having to perform tedious labors that a machine could do much more easily and rapidly."

One cannot speak of the computer in relation to documentation in any field without recognizing the implied dangers. "Information" and "knowledge" are not the same thing. A genuine contribution to knowledge can be made using a limited amount of information but a third rate intelligence is not likely to do much with even an oceanful of computerized information. Yet there is no denying the existence of an "information explosion." It must be faced. Whatever the relationship of this "explosion" to population growth, to literacy, or to knowledge, we see that research libraries are being inundated by it. This situation coupled with the increased scholarly utilisation of extant source materials and literature, demands new techniques for cataloguing, organizing, and rapid search and retrieval of both old and new information. Necessity has to some extent been the mother of professional concern and invention. The library world, especially in the United States, has long been studying the question—the literature on the subject is already enormous.[3]

In our own field a growing interest in automation on the part of music librarians and musicologists is evident from such developments as the establishment of a Committee on Automation in Music Bibliography by the American Music Library Association, the Tagung of the Deutsches Musikgeschichtliches Archiv in Kassel organized by Herr Heckmann, the series of university conferences throughout the United States (Rutgers, Yale, University of California at Los Angeles, Boston, Georgetown, etc.) with titles such as "The Digital Computer as a Servant of Research in the Humanities and Arts," the recent symposium of the Greater New York Chapter of the American Musicological Society entitled "Musicology and the Computer,"[4] the present meeting of IAML in Dijon, and forthcoming national meetings of the American Musicological Society and the Music Library Association which will feature sessions devoted to the computer.

In the humanities in general, computer-aided research is a rather recent development but it has been increasing at an extraordinary rate. To cite a few examples: Analytical indexes and concordances have been prepared by computer for the Dead Sea scrolls, for the writings of St. Thomas Aquinas and for the works of a number of English and Spanish poets. A recent monograph on Milton's influence on Shelley has been considerably aided by the computer's discovery of hundreds of word-group relationships that had previously gone unnoticed by human eye and ear.[5]

In a much celebrated study, two statisticians, working with computer help were able to determine which of two possible authors, Madison or Hamilton, wrote the anonymous portions of the American Federalist Papers, authorship of which had long been in dispute.[6]

In the areas of machine translation and linguistic analysis a great deal of computer-aided research has been in progress for over a dozen years; to cite a single project: in Gallarate, Italy, the *Centro per L'Automazione dell' Analisis Letteraria* has processed and is analyzing fifteen million words in seven languages and in three alphabets (Hebrew, Greek and Latin).[7]

Finally, the inter-disciplinary nature of computer research is emphasized by the establishment, last year, of an "Institute for Computer Research in the Humanities" at New York University.

Turning to musicology, here are some computer applications that have been developed in the United States only during the past two or three years. At Yale, Allan Forte has been investigating "The Structure of Atonal Music" through a computer-oriented research project. At Princeton, Arthur Mendel and Lewis Lockwood have led a group of colleagues and graduate students in a study of the stylistic properties of the Masses of Josquin; thus far (summer, 1965) twenty-two complete masses and mass movements, about 600 pages of the Smijers edition, have been encoded and stored within the computer; "moderate progress" is reported in such areas as the discovery of errors of transcription and typography never reported before, in the expectation that the computer will be of help in the understanding of *musica ficta* problems.

At New York University, a whole series of projects in analysis and bibliography has been underway under the guidance of George Logemann. Lawrence Bernstein, for example, is preparing a thematic index, with computer help, of 15,000 sixteenth-century printed chansons in his study of the influence of borrowing techniques. Jan LaRue is using the computer to assist in a probing style analysis of the symphonies of Joseph Haydn, testing such elements as harmonic rhythm, phrase length, etc. and their correlation.

The author, together with Murray Gould of Queens College, has developed a *Plaine and Easie Code System for Musicke* which is being used, among other purposes, for a computer-oriented thematic index of available symphonic scores in print, in manuscript, in libraries and private hands collated where possible with available disc and tape recordings.

Let us turn now to questions of the application of data processing techniques to library operation. This can often be accomplished with relatively unsophisticated equipment without the need of high speed computers. Virtually every large library in the United States and many in Europe has been investigating the possibility of automating their operations. A substantial number, especially business and scientific libraries, have instituted data processing equipment for all or part of their work. In most cases results have been excellent, even from the point of view of long-run costs. In some instances, however, automated systems have proven to be too costly or inefficient—usually because they were poorly conceived for the specific installation. Recent library automation systems developed by commercial concerns stress the "total system approach" which attempts to integrate all library functions within a unified system. The principle is simple: a single original master form serves as the basis for a whole series of future operations which are carried out and printed out automatically with the least possible amount of repetitious human effort. Take the following typical library operations: most are subject to automation which will reduce search time and remove the need for repeated copying of names, titles, and call numbers. Furthermore, catalogue cards, accession lists, and forms of all kinds, can be printed out automatically and without danger of human copying error.

A. Receive request: establish master form, key-punch available data to be amplified later.
B. Review request
C. Search in catalogue
D. Review search report
E. Assign vendor: from a pre-established dealers' file.
F. Type order forms
G. File forms
H. Receive book
I. Check book and invoice for accuracy
J. Record receipt
K. File invoice
L. Authorize payment: send out approved invoice to accounting department.
M. Send book to cataloguing

At this point, the trained professional cataloguer does his job and completes the final portions of the master form.

N. Catalogue cards can then be automatically printed out, in upper and lower case letters, on 3 × 5 inch cards, and in as many copies as needed.
O. Accession lists and specialized subject lists automatically printed out
P. Notification of book's availability to the person who initiated the request, to others whose interest in the general subject has been previously automatically filed and incorporated in the system.

In a circulating library, additional elements may be incorporated in the total system, e.g. circulation control machines simultaneously recording book cards (automatically printed) and borrowers badges; overdue notices, and bills for lost books, automatically printed, addressed, and sent out at the appropriate time.

Obviously, the music division of a large library could not institute such a system unilaterally; the entire institution would have to be automated. It is essential, however, that the music librarian not wait till automation is imposed from above since his collection has many special problems not shared by other divisions (especially in variety of items: scores, parts, books, tapes, discs, etc.) and this must be carefully planned for.

It hardly needs to be stated that the initial costs of total system data processing equipment in a library are high; on the other hand, the increase in speed and accuracy and effectiveness of operations can be spectacular.

In bibliography giant strides have taken place. Modern automatic indexing and information retrieval techniques are changing the face of the art. We can only touch upon a few aspects of the "retrieval revolution." The essential principle is the same as that of the "total library system," to wit, minimize all human clerical operations by programming the machine to do the job. One need only key-punch individual bibliographical entries and "read" them, in any order, into the computer's "memory" (tape or disc file or bulk storage etc.). These entries are then internally processed according to programmed instructions and are transformed into any desired author, title or subject index. But the computer can do much more than produce conventional indexes and reduce human weariness quotients! For example, it can make possible the creation of subject indexing to a depth humans would not dream of attempting; why not 15 or 20 subject headings for a book, rather than the often utterly inadequate two or three? Furthermore, creative programming has invented new kinds of computer prepared permuted indexes—completely machine inspired—such as KWIC (Key Word in Context), KWOC (Key Word Out of Context) and WADEX (Word & Author inDEX).

When it comes to the preparation of concordances, there are few scholarly techniques which seem more appropriate for computer application. The number and excellence of computer assisted literary concordances produced thus far is extremely impressive. Musical concordances, using basically similar programming procedures, will soon be following suit. Obviously, as in the case of thematic catalogues, musical notation requires coding into machine-usable symbols, such as numbers and letters. A number of workable codes or "input languages" have been developed for this purpose,[8] one of them being described elsewhere in these Proceedings.[9] The use of such codes for music makes possible, for example: the preparation of thematic indexes classified in a multitude of ways, the automatic transposition of all incipits to C major or C minor, the identification of anonymi and the discovery of works of double attribution.

An invaluable device of modern bibliography is the abstract. In the bibliographical control of current literature, there seems to be a Mannheim-type crescendo of abstracting activity, with and without an obbligato of computerized indexes. There are over 2000 professional abstracting organizations in the world today, at least 500 of them in the United States. As yet no such organization exists for the abstracting of musical literature (see RILM proposal below). Computer indexing of man-made abstracts is common. Furthermore, it is now possible, by storing the entire article within the computer, to obtain computer produced automated abstracts. Abstracts are also employed in an effective system of getting the right documents to the right people; commercially this has been called Selective Dissemination of Information (SDI). The key to this system, developed by IBM, is the "user profile." Every user submits a list of his specific scholarly interests, his "user profile," which is stored within the computer. Current literature in his discipline is abstracted and the abstracts are likewise stored within the computer. User profile and abstract key words are compared by computer. When a "match" is discovered, the user is sent a post card containing the entire abstract, and a second post card which he sends back after pushing out one of the following four partially punched out boxes:

Of Interest, Document Requested. __________
Of Interest, Document Not Wanted __________
Of Interest, Have Seen Before . . . __________
Of No Interest. . . . . __________

The returned post card is automatically processed; the document is sent to the user if he has requested it. The computer tabulates post card responses, thus interacting with its users to make the system more efficient.

Brief mention must also be made of several other devices and techniques, already fully developed technologically, which may be of help in music documentation. A valuable device is the "aperture card." This is the name given to a punch card on the right side of which there is a "window" containing a full frame of microfilm ($1\frac{1}{2}''$ by $2''$). The left side of the card is key-punched in the normal fashion. This makes it possible to have a photographic record of a document together with punched out information about it used for identification, sorting, coding, etc. Harry B. Lincoln, of Harpur College, New York, has been using aperture cards most effectively to compile a thematic catalogue of the entire corpus of sixteenth-century Italian *frottole*.

The concept of the aperture card can be combined with that of supermicro-photography to produce the following pleasant fantasy: take an entire score or volume of text, several hundred pages in length; reproduce it photographically (greatly reduced) in a single aperture window; add identifying call numbers and cataloguing data by key-punching information onto the left side of the same card; cards are then sorted and stored automatically; the user, seated before a television type "micro-reader," presses buttons to call for the visual display of the library's computer-prepared catalogues; he then asks for the desired "volume" by dialing its identifying call number; data processing equipment locates the aperture card in seconds, and transmits it automatically to the "micro-reader"; the user never touches the aperture card; he can xerographically reproduce any page he sees by pressing the "print" button.

It should be added that a thousand cards take about as much space as a shoe box! It is true that no "aperture card" library is in existence at the present time. It is also true that no step of this bibliographic Eldorado is at present technologically unfeasible. A rather similar system called "Walnut" also combines photographic miniaturization with data processing document retrieval speed; it has been in operation for several years.

A word about automatic scanning devices that are now capable of "reading" several different type fonts directly into the machine. These devices by-pass the slow, potentially error producing input process of key-punching or of typing on machine readable paper tape.

A "scanner" for musical notation is technologically completely possible. At the present time, it appears that the need for funds alone is holding back its construction. On the other hand, the automatic print-out of music is already a reality. At the University of Illinois, Lejaren A. Hiller has developed the computer driven Musicwriter for this purpose. Music printing by Photon disc and cathode ray tube is also in the offing.

SUMMATION AND CONCLUSION

In discussing the utilization of data processing techniques in general and in music documentation in particular, it is easy to gloss over the problems, the difficulties and the costs. Let there be no mistake about it: electronic data processing is expensive and full of pitfalls. The point, however, is that there is no alternative to automation except inundation. This has already shown itself to be true in the sciences; it is increasingly apparent in the humanities; and it holds for libraries as well.

This means new as well as old and established research libraries.

It is appropriate here to depart from the spoken text and to refer to the important question posed by Madame Elizabeth Lebeau of the Bibliothèque Nationale during the discussion period following the reading of the paper and not adequately answered at that time. Her question may be paraphrased as follows: "These new data processing techniques may be wonderful for small or new libraries, but how can they be applied to the great and centuries-old national libraries whose vast holdings are already fully catalogued and properly shelved? Would it not be necessary to start from scratch, re-examining and re-cataloguing every single volume for electronic data processing purposes?"

The answer, which properly fits into our concluding section, is not simple. It should first be reiterated that at present expansion rates, no "living library" will be able to cope with the information explosion using conventional methods. (A living library may be defined as one that continues to do its job thoroughly in today's world rather than stop its acquisition of current materials to become the repository of sources prior to a specific date.) Secondly, it should be pointed out that major changes in library cataloguing and classifying operations have occurred before, usually as a result of dire necessity; the Bibliothèque Nationale itself still employs a combination of manuscript, book and card catalogues for document retrieval. It follows that it may prove advisable to automate for all acquisitions after a certain date and maintain double cataloguing procedures for many years until the earlier holdings can be incorporated into the electronic system. Ultimately, visual scanners may be perfected to the point of reading existing catalogue cards automatically, whatever the type face, and transmitting the data to the machine. Lastly, Madame Lebeau's question has already been answered by recent surveys and reports of the Library of Congress. For example, in "Automation and the Library of Congress" (see footnote 3 above) the necessity, the feasibility and the promise of automation are dramatically demonstrated. Furthermore, automation's promise goes far beyond the mechanization of current functions; it includes revolutionary methods of document and information storage, retrieval and display, of high-speed processing of vast quantities of materials, of output printing of union catalogues and specialized bibliographies, all designed to make the library an infinitely more active and effective organism to assist the scholar in his research activity.

Fortunately, the inter-disciplinary nature of automation makes it possible to profit from the advances in other fields of computer research to solve the problems of music documentation. However, music has at least two characteristics peculiar to it alone, that must be borne in mind and planned for. First its notation is not an alphanumeric language and thus needs special coding for the data processing of thematic indexes, etc. Secondly, its very documents differ physically in many instances from those of other disciplines, e.g. scores, parts, discs and tapes.

In conclusion, we offer a concrete proposal, designated as RILM, that will take advantage of the potential of data processing to meet a pressing need in music documentation. This proposal is presented here in the amplified form in which it was submitted to and later approved by the executive boards of the International Musicological Society and the International Association of Music Libraries. Recently, the author received a Grant-in-Aid from the American Council of Learned Societies to make a study of the "policies, procedures and techniques best suited for the organization and operation of RILM." He would be most grateful to receive comments, suggestions and assistance.[10]

RILM

Répertoire International de la Littérature Musicale
(RILM)
International Repertory of Music Literature
(IRML)
Internationales Repertorium der Musikliteratur
(IRML)

Introduction

RILM is an abstracted, computer-indexed bibliography of scholarly literature on music jointly sponsored by the International Musicological Society and the International Association of Music Libraries. It has been conceived as the counterpart in music literature of the similarly sponsored twelve-year old, International Inventory of Musical Sources (RISM). Like RISM, it would be governed by an international commission. Unlike RISM which is based in Europe where most of the earlier musical sources are to be found, RILM would have its international center in the United States where both the literature and the computers are available. (Several computer centers in the United States, including the Institute for Computer Research in the Humanities of New York University, have indicated their willingness to participate in the project.)

RILM would have two principal publication series, one of current literature and the other for retroactive material. It would publish current abstracts and indexes every three months and ultimately publish a series of volumes devoted to retroactive bibliographical work. Automatic indexing by computer will make possible very extensive cross indexing and effective retrieval of information. Cumulative indexes, automatically produced and printed, will be published regularly. Specialized bibliographies of all kinds with and without abstracts will be published individually. Scholars working on specific research projects will eventually be able to request a bibliographic search by the computer of its stored information and to receive an automatically printed out reply. Ultimately RILM should be self-supporting from the proceeds of its publications, and from the fees from institutions and individuals requesting specialized information retrieval.

General Problem

It is hardly necessary to emphasize that the crisis in musical documentation is extremely serious and rapidly growing worse. The number of books and dissertations appearing yearly increases rapidly and a new scholarly periodical seems to be born every month. Existing bibliographies of current literature, such as the Bibliographie des Musikschrifttums and the Music Index, are years behind now and get further behind as each day passes. Although RILM's mythical goal: total bibliographical control of all scholarly information about music, past and present, may be only partially approachable; and although RILM's potential hurdles: international cooperation, financial support, multiplicity of languages, may be frightening to contemplate; it is clear that the time has come for action and it is increasingly obvious that electronic data processing plus international cooperation is the answer.

The need for an international solution to the documentation problem in music has not wanted for recognition. Vladimir Fédorov was concerned about it at the Lüneburg congress in 1950 (*Entente et organisation internationales pour le dépouillement des périodiques musicaux,* in: 2. *Weltkongress der Musikbibliotheken, Lüneburg, 1950, Kongressbericht,* pp. 49–52). Alexander Hyatt King amplified the discussion to include abstracts in the Paris congress in 1951 (*International scheme for publishing summaries of articles in musical periodicals,* in: *Troisième congrès international des bibliothèques musicales,* Paris, 1951). In 1955 *Fontes Artis Musicae* published a Communiqué du Secrétariat entitled *Musicological Index* (*Fontes* 1955 No. 2., 97–103). There the promising plan was dropped; several of its features will be found incorporated in the present outline. It should also be pointed out that a quarter of a century ago the American Council of Learned Societies sponsored the publication of a series of musicological abstracts entitled "A Bibliography of Periodical Literature in Musicology and Allied Fields assembled for the Committee on Musicology of the ACLS by D. H. Daugherty, Leonard Ellinwood, and Richard S. Hill." Only two volumes appeared: 1938–39 and 1939–40. In the second volume for example, 57 contributors examined 245 journals, including non-musical ones, in many languages. The roster of contributors of abstracts includes such names as: Otto E. Albrecht, Willi Apel, J. Murray Barbour, Hans T. David, Leonard Ellinwood, Glen Haydon, George Herzog, Ernst Krenek, Ernst C. Krohn, Arthur Mendel, and Leo Schrade. These volumes mark an admirable but isolated attempt.

Today the need for a solution is twice as pressing; the major difference is the potential of data processing assistance. It is comforting to realize that the literature on music is far less voluminous than that of other disciplines and many of the latter have already made substantial progress in the directions suggested herein (*Index Medicus, Historical Abstracts, Chemical Abstracts, Folklore Abstracts,* etc.).

Immediate Goals and Procedures

RILM's immediate and specific goal is to control current periodical literature; subsequently theses, books, Festschriften, annuals, etc., will be included. Every effort should be made to work in closest cooperation with existing bibliographical agencies such as the *Music Index* and the *Bibliographie des Musikschrifttums* in order to avoid duplication of effort and perhaps even to effectuate ultimate amalgamation. (I have been in contact with Florence Kretzschmar, publisher of the Music Index, who has agreed to work toward the greatest possible cooperation. I shall, of course, also communicate with Herr Dr. Schmieder.)

Abstracting

All abstracts will be signed. Abstracting of periodical articles etc. should begin as soon as possible, preferably with all material dated after January 1, 1966. The longer the delay, the more difficult the job becomes. Computer storage and indexing of the data will take a good deal of time to be put into operation. Once set into motion, however, the process could move rapidly and it would have a body of previously prepared abstracts to work with. A list of suggestions regarding bibliographic format and abstracting procedures is now being prepared.

On the question of who will do the abstracting, different approaches may be necessary depending on the country and subject matter.

(1) *Journal Abstracts:* We might follow the example of the sciences and invite all musical journals to publish or otherwise provide abstracts of their articles. Several journal editors have already indicated their willingness to supervise such abstracting and to recruit the abstractors. The abstract need not necessarily be published with its article but may be submitted separately to RILM.

(2) *Author Abstracts:* Journal editors will be asked to invite all authors to provide their own abstracts. In many instances, especially after RILM becomes widely accepted, authors may themselves wish to provide abstracts of books, theses, etc.

(3) *Library Abstracts:* In some countries, the chief of the music division of the national library may be the natural person to serve as the clearinghouse for the abstracting process.

(4) *Abstracting by Graduate Students:* Librarians and professors of musicology who conduct graduate classes in music bibliography, would supervise the abstracting of specific works or journals by their advanced students. (A number of leading librarians and professors already have indicated their willingness to participate.)

It is also possible, and on occasion advantageous, to have two abstracts: one by the author, and one by a more impartial person.

It is helpful to note that data processing equipment can admit of great flexibility. For example, it is perfectly possible to combine, for automatic indexing purposes, different kinds of entries: abstracts made up of several extended paragraphs, others which employ only a series of key words or subject headings, other which have *both* resumés and subject headings, and still others in which the title alone is deemed sufficient.

Language and Subject Headings

We must agree with Eric Boehm, Editor, *Historical Abstracts,* when he says, "Languages are a much more serious barrier to research than is commonly assumed and parochialism in research is much more pronounced than we permit ourselves to believe." Here the computer may be of great assistance. A list of subject headings (Schlagwörter, mots clefs) in three languages (English, French, German) will be in perpetual development and regularly published in cumulative form. Ultimately it will be possible to store the entire contents of the forthcoming *Polyglot Dictionary* within the computer; questions could then be asked using subject headings in any one language and the machine would search its stored data under corresponding terms in all languages. Ultimately machine translation into any of the stored languages may very well be possible.

Conclusion

A great value of automatic data processing is that once the data is stored a variety of indexing techniques and automatic print-outs are possible. The entire system must be designed to be flexible and open-ended. It should anticipate the ultimate application of automatic abstracting by visual scanners now being experimented with.

RILM represents an attempt to solve a grave problem. Certainly some solution must be found if we wish to remain alive to developments in our discipline or even in a corner of our discipline. We are already faced with an "uncharted sea of information" and a breakdown in present indexing methods. Furthermore, the quantity of scientific information in all fields is said to double every fifteen years!

NOTES

[1] James D. Mack and Robert S. Taylor, quoted in *Information Storage and Retrieval* by Joseph Becker and Robert M. Hayes, New York, John Wiley & Sons, 1963, p. 44.

[2] Eric H. Boehm, *Dissemination of Knowledge in the Humanities and the Social Sciences,* in: *American Council of Learned Societies Bulletin,* XIV/5 (May 1963) 4.

[3] Apart from the vast and important periodical and "report" literature, mention may be made of the following major books: Barbara Evans Markuson, ed. *Libraries and Automation:* Proceedings of the Conference on Libraries and Automation held at Airlie Foundation, Warrentown, Virginia, May 26–30, 1963, under sponsorship of the Library of Congress, National Science Foundation, Council on Library Resources, Inc. Washington, D. C., Library of Congress, 1964. *Automation and the Library of Congress:* A survey sponsored by The Council on Library Resources, Inc. Submitted by: Gilbert W. King, Chairman, Harold P. Edmundson, Merrill M. Flood, Manfred Kochen, Richard L. Libby, Don R. Swanson, and Alexander Wylly. Washington, D. C., Library of Congress, 1963. J. C. R. Licklider, *Libraries of the Future,* Cambridge, Massachusetts Institute of Technology Press, 1965. Joseph Becker and Robert M. Hayes, *Information Storage and Retrieval: Tools, Elements, Theories,* New York, John Wiley & Sons, Inc., 1963. Charles P. Bourne, *Methods of Information Handling,* New York, John Wiley & Sons, Inc., 1963.

[4] The published proceedings of this symposium, scheduled to appear in the spring of 1966, will include an extensive bibliography of *Writings on the Use of Computers in Music* [see **148,** p. 193 above].

[5] Joseph Raben, *A Computer-Aided Investigation of Literary Influence: Milton to Shelley,* in: *Literary Data Processing Conference Proceedings,* IBM Corporation, 1964, 230–274.

[6] Frederick Mosteller and David Wallace, *Inference in an Authorship Problem,* in: *Journal of the American Statistical Association,* LVIII (1963), 275–309.

[7] Roberto Busa S. J., *An Inventory of Fifteen Million Words,* in: *Literary Data Processing Conference Proceedings,* IBM Corporation, 1964, 64–78.

[8] A conference devoted specifically to *Computer Input Languages for Music,* jointly sponsored by the Music Library Association Committee on Automation, the American Musicological Society Greater New York Chapter, and the IBM Corporation, was held in New York on May 15, 1965.

[9] Item **149** above, p. 194.–*Editor.*

[10] See items **163–166** above, p. 194.–*Editor.*

E. Copyright and Music

SELECTED BIBLIOGRAPHY

Compiled by Harry Kownatsky

LAW DIGESTS AND MANUALS:

168. *Copyright law of the United States of America.* Bulletin 14. Washington, D.C.: Copyright Office, Library of Congress, 1969.

Title 17 of the United States Code. Revised editions are issued as necessary. Edition quoted above includes the Regulations of the Copyright Office and the text of the Universal Copyright Convention.

169. Mertz, Henriette. *Copyright bibliography.* Washington, D.C.: Copyright Office, Library of Congress, 1950.

A bibliography of English and foreign titles.

170. *Copyright Law Revision Studies.* Washington, D.C.: Copyright Office, Library of Congress, 1960–1961. [Available from the Register of Copyrights, Library of Congress, Washington, D.C. 20540; $4.35 per set, including Index.]

Studies 1–4:

1. Goldman, A. A. *The history of U.S.A. Copyright Law revision from 1901 to 1954.*
2. Blaisdell, William M. *Size of the copyright industries.*
3. The staff of the NYU *Law Review* under the guidance of Prof. Walter J. Derenberg. *The meaning of "writings" in the Copyright Clause of the Constitution.*
4. Strauss, William S. *The moral right of the author.*

Studies 5–6:

5. Henn, Harry G. *The compulsory license provisions of the U.S. Copyright Law.*
6. Blaisdell, William M. *The economic aspects of the compulsory license.*

Studies 7–10:

7. Doyle, Vincent A.; Cary, George D.; McCannon, Marjorie; and Ringer, Barbara A. *Notice of copyright.*
8. Blaisdell, William M. *Commercial use of the copyright notice.*
9. Rogers, Joseph W. *Use of the copyright notice by libraries.*
10. Berger, Caruthers. *False use of the copyright notice.*

Studies 11–13:

11. Kaminstein, Abraham L. with supplements by Lorna G. Margolis and Arpad Bogsch. *Divisibility of copyrights.*

12. Cary, George D. *Joint ownership of copyrights.*
13. Varmer, Borge. *Works made for hire and on commission.*
Studies 14–16:
14. Latman, Alan. *Fair use of copyrighted works.*
15. Varmer, Borge. *Photoduplication of copyrighted material by libraries.*
16. ——. *Limitations on performing rights.*
Studies 17–19:
17. Kaplan, Benjamin. *The registration of copyright.*
18. Berger, Caruthers. *Authority of the Register of Copyrights to reject applications for registration.*
19. Latman, Alan, assisted by Lorna G. Margolis and Marcia Kaplan. *The recordation of copyright assignments and licenses.*
Studies 20–21:
20. Dunne, Elizabeth K. *Deposit of copyrighted works.*
21. Dunne, Elizabeth K. and Rogers, Joseph W. *The Catalog of Copyright Entries.*
Studies 22–25:
22. Strauss, William S. *The damage provisions of the Copyright Law.*
23. Brown, Ralph S., Jr., with the assistance of William A. O'Brien and Herbert Turkington. *The operation of the damage provisions of the Copyright Law: An exploratory study.*
24. Strauss, William S. *Remedies other than damages for copyright infringement.*
25. Latman, Alan and Tager, William S. *Liability of innocent infringers of copyright.*
Studies 26–28:
26. Ringer, Barbara A. *The unauthorized duplication of sound recordings.*
27. Strauss, William S. *Copyright in architectural works.*
28. Varmer, Borge. *Copyright in choreographic works.*
Studies 29–31:
29. Strauss, William S. *Protection of unpublished works.*
30. Guinan, James J. *Duration of copyright.*
31. Ringer, Barbara A. *Renewal of copyright.*
Studies 32–34:
32. Bogsch, Arpad. *Protection of works of foreign origin.*
33. Berger, Caruthers. *Copyright in government publications.*
34. Varmer, Borge. *Copyright in territories and possessions of the United States.*
Subject Index to Studies 1–34.

171. Bogsch, Arpad. *The law of copyright under the Universal Convention.* Leyden: A. W. Sythoff; New York: R. R. Bowker, 1964.

172. Pilpel, Harriet F. and Goldberg, Morton D. *Copyright Guide.* 4th ed. New York: Bowker, 1969.
A general background information booklet in question and answer form.

173. Nicholson, Margaret. *A manual of copyright practice for writers, publishers, and agents.* Second edition: With a new Preface, 1970. New York: Oxford University Press, 1970.

174. *Martindale-Hubbell Law Directory in five volumes.* One hundred and third annual edition, 1971. Volume V. Summit, N.J.: Martindale-Hubbell, Inc., 1970.
Comprehensive digests of the laws, including copyright, of the United States and its territories as well as foreign countries.

CURRENT STATUS AND GENERAL DISCUSSIONS OF COPYRIGHT:

175. Heilprin, Laurence B. "Technology and the future of the copyright principle," *Phi Delta Kappan,* 48 (January, 1967), 220–225.

176. Mount, Douglas N. "Copyright: The situation now," *Publishers' Weekly,* 200 (July 5, 1971), 24–27; (July 12, 1971), 46–48.
Report of the Association of American Publishers' copyright seminar-workshop, NYC, June 2–3, 1971.

177. Ringer, Barbara A. "International copyright turns another corner," *Publishers' Weekly,* 200 (November 8, 1971), 22–25.

178. Lacy, Dan. "The © Quagmire," *Saturday Review,* 49 (November 27, 1971), 24–28.

COPYRIGHT AND LIBRARIES:

179. Smith, Louis Charles. "The copying of literary property in library collections," *Law Library Journal,* 46 (August, 1953), 197-206; 47 (August, 1954), 204-208.

180. Varmer, Borge. *Photoduplication of copyrighted material in libraries.* General revision of the copyright law, study no. 19. Washington, D.C.: Copyright Office, Library of Congress, 1959.

181. Price, Miles O. "Photocopying by libraries and copyright," *Library Trends,* 8 (January, 1960), 432-447.

Includes an extensive bibliography.

182. Joint Libraries Committee on Fair Use in Photocopying. "Report on single copies," *Special Libraries,* 52 (May-June, 1961), 251-255; *Bulletin of the Copyright Society of America,* 9 (October, 1966), 79-84.

183. Freehafer, Edward G. "Summary statement of policy of the Joint Libraries Committee on Fair Use in Photocopying," *Special Libraries,* 55 (February, 1964), 104-106.

184. Lazowska, Mrs. Edward S. "Photocopying, copyright, and the librarian," *American Documentation,* 19 (April, 1968), 123-130, 206-207.

185. Clapp, Verner W. "Copyright—A librarian's view." In *Libraries at Large,* edited by Douglas M. Knight and E. Shepley Nourse, pp. 242-263. New York: R. R. Bowker, 1969.

Prepared for the National Advisory Commission on Libraries. The most comprehensive statement of copyright practices and libraries written to date. Includes bibliographic notes, almost all of which are omitted from this *Selected Bibliography*—both to save space and because *Libraries at Large* is generally available.

COPYRIGHT AND MUSIC:

186. Kramer, A. Walter. "Observe the copyright law," *Music Journal,* 4 (July-August, 1946), 50-51.

A list of some common copyright infringements with which library materials may be involved.

187. DeWolf, Richard C. "Copyright in music," *Notes,* 1 (December, 1943), 3-13.

188. Kownatsky, Harry. "Copyright law revision: The zero hour approaches," *Notes,* 18 (March, 1961), 197-208.

189. Seeger, Charles. "Who owns folklore—A rejoinder," *Western Folklore,* 21 (April 2, 1962), 93-101.

190. Music Publishers' Association and Music Publishers' Protective Association. *Clearance of rights to musical compositions; a guide and directory.* New York: Music Publishers' Assoc., 609 Fifth Ave., 10017.

See annotation in *Notes,* 22 (June, 1966), 1205.

191. "Report of the Committee on Out-of-Print Copyrighted Music," *Notes,* 25 (December, 1968), 211-212.

Background statement and reproduction of the form on which to request permission to copy out-of-print copyrighted music for library use.

192. Berk, Lee Eliot. *Legal protection for the creative musician.* n.p.: Berklee Press, 1970.

Copyright: An Introduction

by Harry Kownatsky

"The Congress shall have Power . . . To promote the Progress of Science and useful Arts, by securing for limited Times to Authors and Inventors the exclusive Right to their respective Writings and Discoveries."–U.S. Constitution, Article I, § 8

Copyright in the United States has existed since colonial times and, quite naturally, has its roots in English Law. In England, a monopoly in the form of a privilege or grant was given to printers as early as the 15th and 16th centuries. Not until the Statute of Anne, 1709, was the author deemed to have some right in his writing; it was then that he first received some protection under the law.

Two centuries later, in 1909, the present copyright law of the United States was enacted at the insistence of President Theodore Roosevelt. In 1905, Roosevelt had stated in a message to Congress that the existing laws were ". . . imperfect in definition, confused and inconsistent in expression, . . . difficult for the courts to interpret and impossible for the Copyright Office to administer with satisfaction to the public. . . ."

The 1909 law marked definite advances, but three quarters of a century later it remains–except for amendments–essentially the same despite tremendous advances in technology and mass communication. President Roosevelt's message could well have been delivered to Congress in the middle of the 20th century when an effort at a complete revision of the law was begun.

The Copyright Law of the United States gives to the copyright owner certain rights providing certain conditions are met. Under the law the copyright proprietor has the exclusive right "to print, reprint, publish, copy and vend the copyrighted work. . . ." It includes also the right to translate or make another version of a literary work, to adapt or arrange music, to publicly perform a drama, etc. For music, lectures and the like, the law specifically mentions public performance *for profit.* For music a so-called "juke box" clause provides that once authorization is given to record a work for mechanical reproduction, others may make similar use of the work if the copyright owner is paid a royalty of 2¢ per copy.

For the other important sections too extensive for discussion here, consult [**168**, 205 or **173**, 206].

Librarians should be aware that except for the "juke box" clause noted above, nothing in the law can be construed as allowing others *any* of the rights of the copyright proprietor.

The duration of statutory copyright protection is 28 years with the privilege of renewal for another 28 year term. Renewal must be applied for within the year prior to the expiration of the original term. The law specifies that registration of the copyright may be made with the Copyright Office; however, registration is not compulsory since copyright is obtained by the act of publication with proper notices. On the other hand, the law does not permit the Copyright Office to issue a renewal, nor will courts of law entertain litigation in case of infringement unless registration has been filed sometime within the first term. Upon expiration of copyright protection, the work falls into public domain.

The law is rather stringent about the copyright notices which must appear in a proscribed form in a specified place; there have been cases of forfeiture of copyright, sometimes inadvertently, because of improper notices or omission of notices. While the courts recognize the possibility of error, they assume that the error will be corrected without delay and that only a few copies will be distributed to the public before the correction is made. Lack of notice in a particular copy is not necessarily an indication of lack of copyright.

Publishers are very much aware of their responsibility and comply with all the requirements to make certain that maximum protection is secured in the United States and abroad.

SOURCE: Written especially for this *Reader.*

The copyright law does not permit any copying or extensive quotation of copyrighted material. However, over the years, the courts have recognized a "fair use" concept to satisfy the needs of scholars, researchers, and others (critics and reviewers) to use existing material as a "springboard" for creativity and to quote from the original as part of their comments and criticism. "Fair use" has never become part of the law and how much copying or quotation may be permitted before it constitutes infringement is somewhat vague. The applicable measure is "reasonable" use: how much is copied and for what purpose are the factors involved. If the use were extensive enough or in such a form as to result in loss of revenue to the copyright owner, the courts would undoubtedly favor the owner in an infringement suit.

With the proliferation of do-it-yourself copying devices available to the public and the practice of making multiple copies for classroom use, etc., publishers have become greatly concerned. The excuses for this practice may have some validity but the publisher does lose thereby.

In the past, no public library has been sued for infringement—which is not to say that it cannot or will not happen. The Williams and Wilkins Company has sued the United States for infringement, alleging that the Department of Health, Education and Welfare—through its agencies, the National Institutes of Health Libraries and the National Library of Medicine—has infringed its copyright by supplying to its patrons and others unauthorized photocopies of articles in medical journals published by Williams and Wilkins. A United States Commissioner filed a report to the United States Court of Claims upholding the publisher's claim of infringement. The defense of "non-infringement, fair use and license to copy" was rejected, despite the fact that multiple copying had not taken place.

Many libraries will not make copies of copyrighted material although they may have copying machines available in various areas of their buildings for the convenience of their patrons. The reasoning is apparently that the responsibility for the ultimate use remains with the patron. Warning notices placed on the machines inform the patron of the necessity of restricting his use to study and research.

* * * * *

There is no automatic international copyright. Protection in particular countries depends on national laws, existing treaties, and conventions among nations. Authors in the United States who wish to obtain foreign copyrights must determine those requirements before they publish anywhere because publication may effect the copyright procedure.

The Universal Copyright Convention (UCC) [**171**, 206] was ratified by the United States in 1954 and went into effect on September 16, 1955. Participating countries offer the works of foreign authors the same protection as domestic material without formalities when the work is published in a UCC country. International copyright protection is, however, predicated on observance of the copyright regulations of the author's nation.

Under UCC, the copyright notice must include the symbol © (the letter c in a circle). Previously, United States notices needed only the word "Copyright" or its abbreviation "Copyr.," the year date of first publication, and the name of the copyright owner. Now some sources suggest that the notice be a combination: i.e.,

Copyright © 1972, John Doe

combining all the essentials of word, symbol, year date, and name of the proprietor. Since the symbol © affords protection in all UCC nations it would seem of prime importance to make certain that this is included in the notice.

The United States, along with a number of Latin-American countries, is a signatory also to the Pan-American Convention of Buenos Aires (1910). Authors securing copyright in their own countries enjoy the rights accorded in each of the other countries when the published work bears a statement indicating the reservation of property rights, i.e., "All rights reserved."

The Berne Convention (The International Union for the Protection of Literary and Artistic Works) is the copyright convention to which most of the large countries of the world belong. The United States is *not* a signatory to this convention. After World War I, several bills were introduced in Congress in an effort to effect this country's entrance but no action was taken on any of them.

Under the Berne Convention, a citizen of any country receives protection upon first or simultaneous publication in any member country. United States authors and publishers are thus able to take advantage of this despite the fact that the United States is not a member. Conditions are very liberal since it is publication which is significant. Formalities such as notice, registration, etc., are not required.

Publishers in the United States will add the words "International Copyright Secured" to indicate in the notice that the necessary steps have been taken to secure copyright under all of the conventions. It is not unusual in music to see all three notices printed in their proper places. European publications may have only the notice now used in the United States in order to have the necessary requirement fulfilled.

In 1955, at the behest of Congress, the Copyright Office began a series of studies of the copyright law and practices [**170**, 205]. Over a period of several years eleven committee prints, covering more than thirty aspects of copyright, were completed. Perhaps the most important to librarians were those on duration, notice, photoduplication, and fair use. These studies culminated in positive recommendations for a general and complete revision of the 1909 law; such a bill was finally prepared and presented to Congress. Numerous hearings have been held over the years and, in some areas, still continue. Conflicting interests, including libraries, have been responsible for some revision of the bill as originally presented. These interests have also been responsible for delay upon delay. Meanwhile, during this interim period many works were scheduled to fall into public domain because of copyright expiration. To avoid this, Congress has passed, each year, a law extending for another year the copyright protection of works in their second term. This does not apply to works in their original term for which renewals may be obtained. Presumably, Congress will continue to pass these extensions until such time as a new law goes into effect.

One of the most significant changes for which publishers have been pressing is to lengthen the duration of copyright to life of the author plus fifty years. This is the duration of copyright in most of the major countries of the world and would place the United States in conformity with these nations. (It is interesting to note that Germany, in 1965, extended its term to life of the author plus seventy years [**174**, 206]. Renewal would no longer be a concern and notices would not require dating. Librarians would need, however, to be able to check death dates easily and quickly.

From the amount of literature published so far it appears that photocopying [**179–184**, 207] is the main concern of libraries. The revision of the law has been written so as to provide for reproduction of no more than one copy of a work or phonorecord—if reproduction or distribution is made without any purpose of direct or indirect commercial advantages, i.e., for archival or scholarly use. A paragraph on fair use immediately precedes this section and, although it does not spell out exactly what constitutes fair use, it does describe the criteria for making a determination. Emphasis is on single copies and the final clause of this section is formulated to guard against repeated requests for the same work which might result in distribution of multiple copies.

On October 15, 1971, President Nixon signed into law an "antipiracy" bill to protect recordings from unauthorized duplication. This bill will remain in force until January 1, 1975, apparently on the assumption that by then the United States will have a new copyright law.

Passage of a completely revised bill has been difficult because there are so many divergent views. Authors, publishers, librarians, Cable Antenna TeleVision and the recording industries, as well as many others, have been examining the problem in all its facets. Undoubtedly, the work which the Copyright Office has done would solve many existing problems. Hopefully, a new law will minimize those problems now and for the foreseeable future.

Copyright Law Revision and Music Librarians

by Abe A. Goldman

Everyone who deals professionally with music has a stake in the revision of the copyright law. In the forefront are composers, authors, publishers, record producers, and various groups of users of music, and they have made their voices heard in the discussions of revision proposals which have gone on over the past several years. Among others who have expressed their interest in some of the issues are music librarians, as well as librarians in general.

The copyright revision program was started nearly ten years ago[1] with a series of studies. It has gone through innumerable proposals, meetings, conferences, discussions, and comments. The important fact now is that it has reached the stage where a bill for a complete new copyright law is pending in Congress. The general revision bill was first introduced in Congress last July 20 (S. 3008 and H.R. 11947 in the 88th Congress), and with some modifications, a substantially similar bill (S. 1006 and H.R. 4347) was introduced in the 89th Congress in February. Congressional hearings are likely to start in this session.

I have tried to select, from the many issues covered by the comprehensive bill, those that I think will be of greatest interest to music librarians. But I urge your study of the entire bill, and I believe many of you will find other points of interest.

1. FAIR USE

Librarians in general have shown great concern about the reproduction of excerpts from copyrighted materials for the use of their patrons in research. Music librarians, I assume, receive requests for short excerpts of both musical scores and textual matter. This is not a new problem, of course, nor is it confined to librarians. I think it is fair to say that almost everyone who uses copyrighted materials to any great extent finds the need at times to copy short passages. Authors and publishers themselves commonly use brief quotations from the works of others.

The present copyright statute gives the copyright owner the exclusive right to copy his work, and this right is stated in absolute terms without qualification. Nevertheless, the courts have recognized the practical necessity for some limited copying and have developed the doctrine of "fair use." Since the use of excerpts may occur in so many different situations, the concept of "fair use" is necessarily vague and flexible. How much may properly be copied may depend upon the length of the work and the relative length and importance of the excerpt; it may differ as between a book of text, a musical score, a map, a photograph, and an art work. "Fair use" cannot be reduced to a precise formula any more than, say, "due care" or "good faith" or "honest dealing." In essence, it is aimed at permitting the use of a relatively small portion of a work for a legitimate purpose, where that portion is not the substance of the work and the use made of it will not undercut the potential demand for the work.

Perhaps it is worth mentioning that the court decisions which have fashioned the doctrine of fair use have dealt mainly with quotations from one work in another. The courts have not ruled specifically on cases involving the reproduction of copies for purposes of research or teaching. But the general criteria on which the courts have based their decisions would seem to make the doctrine applicable to limited reproduction for such purposes.

The bill introduced last July[2] included, in section 6, a specific provision designed to give statu-

SOURCE: Reprinted from *Library Journal,* March 15, 1965. Published by R. R. Bowker (a Xerox Company).

tory recognition to the doctrine of fair use. Because of the inherent nature of the doctrine, as already indicated, the statutory provision was couched in general terms. It was intended to affirm the doctrine as developed by the courts, and to maintain the general criteria on which the judicial decisions have been based, but to avoid freezing the doctrine or preventing its further evolution.

The fair use provision in the 1964 bill was attacked by some on the ground that, because of its generality, it might be construed and applied too broadly, and by others who expressed the fear that its general terms might be construed too narrowly. The 1965 bill retains a provision specifically recognizing the doctrine of fair use, but without any attempt to indicate the application or define the scope of the doctrine.

Photocopying by Libraries

I should mention in passing that at an earlier stage of the revision program, the Copyright Office presented a proposal specifying the conditions under which libraries could make single copies of copyrighted materials for their patrons. The proposal was strenuously opposed by authors and publishers as being so broad as to pose a potential threat to their market for copies. It was also opposed by library groups as being unduly restrictive. Both sides urged, though for opposite reasons, that no special provision on photocopying be included in the statute. The present bill contains no such provision but allows the question to rest, as it does now, on the doctrine of fair use.

2. DURATION

A feature of the revision of the law that seems to interest almost everyone is the proposal as to the duration of copyright. Closely connected with this is the matter of the protection given to unpublished works.

At present, unpublished works are protected under the common law, and this protection continues with no time limit as long as the work remains unpublished. There is an exception to this, since some unpublished works, including music, can now get copyright protection under the statute by a voluntary registration; but we need not go into that here. The important point is that works which have neither been published nor registered are now protected without any time limit.

When a work is published, common law protection ceases and statutory copyright becomes available. The copyright endures for 28 years from publication, and is renewable for a second term of 28 years, or a total of 56 years.

The bill provides for a term of copyright that would apply to all works whether published or unpublished. The basic term would be the life of the author and 50 years after his death. A different term would be necessary for anonymous works and for works made for hire: the term for these works would be 75 years from their publication or 100 years from their creation, whichever is shorter.

One of the principal reasons for adopting the basic term of life-plus-50 years is to have the term in the United States correspond with that in most foreign countries. The international use of copyright materials—and music is a prime example—is extensive and growing. In almost all other countries having copyright laws the term is based on the author's life; and the most prevalent term, particularly in the countries of major importance, runs for 50 years after the death of the author.

The author groups seem to feel that adoption of the term of life-plus-50 years is the most important feature of the entire revision bill. The opposition has been scattered and rather mild.

There is at least one difficulty, however, with a term measured from the death of the author: it may often be hard or impossible to find out when an obscure author died. The bill tries to ameliorate this difficulty by providing for a record of death dates, and a presumption as to the time of death when there is no record.

Manuscripts

For those who are interested in manuscripts of unpublished works, it may be worth repeating that while they now remain under common law protection indefinitely, the bill (Section 21) would ultimately put them in the public domain. In most cases this would happen when the author has been dead for 50 years or when the manuscript is 100 years old. But for existing manuscripts, protection would be continued for at least 25 years from the effective date of the new law.

It might be added that even when the content of a manuscript had gone into the public domain, a depository library might still withhold the manuscript from public access if the donor imposed such a restriction.

3. NOTICE

The requirement of the present law that the published copies of a work must bear a copyright notice in order to have protection has long been attacked by some of the copyright interests. Most foreign countries have no such requirement except for special kinds of works.

The main objection to the notice requirement is that inadvertent omissions or errors frequently cause the forfeiture of copyright. The bill (Sections 24–28) would continue to require the notice in published copies; but it would preserve the copyright in the case of its omission if the copyright is registered, and would permit the correction of errors. At the same time, anyone who is misled by the omission or error would be shielded from liability for acting in reliance on the absence of notice or on the erroneous notice.

Some of the author groups are still opposed to any notice requirement, even with the provisions in the bill to avoid forfeiture for omission or error. They have suggested that the use of a notice might be encouraged, by limiting the copyright owner's recovery against an innocent infringer who is misled by its absence, but should not be a requirement in any case. They have also objected to requiring the year date of publication as part of the notice, inasmuch as the copyright term would generally be based on the author's life.

On the other side, some of the user groups, including library organizations, have strongly urged that the notice provides useful information and should continue to be required. Librarians have made special mention of the value of the year date.

4. MANUFACTURING AND IMPORT RESTRICTIONS

The present requirement that the manufacturing of copies of certain textual and pictorial works be performed in the United States, and the attendant limit of importation to 1500 copies of foreign editions, have been the subject of sharp controversy between copyright interests and the printing industries. The bill has sought to propose a practical compromise that would loosen the present restrictions without denying the protection that the printers insist they need against foreign competition.

The manufacturing and import provisions do not apply to musical compositions. They do now and would continue to apply to books of text about music if they are in the English language and by American authors. One of the proposed changes is to raise the import limit from 1500 to 3500 copies.

Of special interest to libraries is the fact that the bill would continue to permit them to import copies of foreign editions for their collections.

The topics I have discussed here are probably not the only features of the revision bill that may hold some interest for librarians. And my brief review has necessarily been an oversimplification. Mr. Harry Kownatsky and his committee of the Music Library Association have done a commendable job in following the revision proposals preceding the introduction of the bill. So have committees of other library associations. I hope that the several library groups will give their attention to the bill as it advances through the legislative process, and will help in getting a new copyright law enacted that will be fair to all concerned.

NOTES

[1]Written in 1965.–*Editor.*
[2]July, 1964.–*Editor.*

F. Exhibitions

SELECTED BIBLIOGRAPHY

193. Shepard, Brooks, Jr. "Museum aspects of the music library." In MLA *Manual*, pp. 129-136. "Selected bibliography": p. 136.

194. "Talking about exhibitions: Hector Fernandez talks to Ruzena Wood," *Brio*, 7 (Spring, 1970), 4-8.

195. "Music on display: Hector Fernandez talks to Ruzena Wood," *Brio*, 8 (Autumn, 1971), 6-11.

* * * * *

The following three catalogues of strictly musical exhibitions are exemplary of the techniques of musical exhibition explained in Barksdale's article reprinted below:

196. Littleton, Alfred Henry. *A catalogue of one hundred works illustrating the history of music printing from the fifteenth to the end of the seventeenth century, in the library of Alfred Henry Littleton.* London: Novello, 1911.

Most of the notes and illustrations were originally prepared for an Illustrated Catalogue of an Exhibition held at Fishmongers' Hall in 1904.

197. Grolier Club, New York. *An exhibition of printed music held at the Grolier Club, New York City, December 17, 1937–January 16, 1938.* The New York Public Library, 1937 (microfilm).

198. Toledo. Museum of Art. *The printed note; 500 years of music printing and engraving.* [An exhibition] January 14–February 24, 1957. Toledo, 1957. "Bibliography": pp. 141-144. List "of works consulted in the preparation of the catalogue": p. 8.

199. Barksdale, Mildred K. "History of music printing illustrated by Toledo Museum," *Musical America*, 77 (January 15, 1957), 16, 21.

Illustrated description of the exhibit, "The Printed Note," January 14–February 24, 1957, at the Toledo Museum of Art.

On the Planning and Arranging of Music Exhibitions

by A. Beverly Barksdale

The exhibition, *Medieval and Renaissance Music Manuscripts,* which was held at the Toledo Museum of Art during January and February, 1953, represented the first important showing of such materials in this country for their musical interest. It is logical that such an exhibition should have originated in Toledo, since the Museum has pioneered in the music field, being the first museum to offer courses in music, to build splendid facilities for concerts, and to assemble a comprehensive collection of phonograph records.

After the luncheon at the Cincinnati meeting of the Music Library Association on February 27, 1953, the writer described that exhibit, illustrating his talk with colored slides to show the different ways in which the manuscripts had been displayed. Although the techniques used in the exhibit were derived to some extent from standard museum procedures, it developed during the discussion which followed the talk that several of the techniques might be put to wider use in planning exhibits in music libraries. Certainly, the basic ideas may easily be adapted to serve with types of objects other than early manuscripts, and it was therefore thought that an article dealing with the general planning and arranging of an exhibition might prove useful. It will be simpler, however, to proceed from the specific to the general, and thus much of what follows will be presented in terms of how the manuscript exhibit in Toledo was organized.

An exhibition of any scope involves four stages which I call the four P's: Planning, Procuring, Presenting, and Promoting. There is considerable overlapping of these categories, as will develop later, but they do indicate some sort of chronological order.

The first step in the planning stage consists of arriving at a central theme for the exhibition. What basic idea is to be established through this exhibition? What is it intended to accomplish? The answers to these questions should result in a kind of blue print for the exhibition. This will, of course, be subject to later modification, depending on the availability of the desired materials and on budget limitations. It is usually better to start the planning on a fairly grand scale, however, even if this means considerable reduction when the estimated costs are added up and the availability of materials has been explored.

In the first music exhibition at the Toledo Museum, held in 1952, we presented *Musical Instruments through the Ages.* It was a beautiful show and attracted considerable attention, although there was nothing particularly original about it except, perhaps, in the manner of installation. It was done on a modest budget with the items borrowed from nearby collections.

Unless an exhibition is especially planned for a particular group or for an important occasion, it should be designed to appeal to the average visitor. In the instrument show we attempted to represent not only a portion of music history in terms of the instruments for which the music was written, but we sought to appeal to a wider group to whom the objects would be beautiful to look at and interesting to see. There was even a distinct fascination for the non-musical or art-minded among the visitors in the mechanical aspects and workmanship of the instruments.

The success of this initial exhibition encouraged us to begin immediately to lay plans for a larger and more important one. Our first idea was to assemble a comprehensive exhibit of music manuscripts from Medieval times to the present, but soon after we began searching for materials, we discovered that there was much too much of it available in American collections for any one exhi-

SOURCE: Reprinted from A. Beverly Barksdale, "On the planning and arranging of music exhibitions," *Notes*, 10 (September, 1953), 565-569, by permission of the Music Library Association.

bition. It was decided to limit the period of our first exhibit to Medieval and Renaissance music manuscripts, leaving the composer manuscripts from then to the present day to serve as the subject of a future exhibition.

The superabundance of items was not the sole factor in this decision. We found that in most American collections the various aspects of the Medieval manuscripts containing music had rarely been taken into consideration simultaneously. Some magnificent examples were located in museums that had purchased them solely for their illuminations with little or no attention paid to the music they contained. Examples of almost every type of early notation were found, but seldom had the type been identified. On the other hand, some very important manuscripts had been acquired by music institutions, and here the decorative features were usually disregarded. In only a few instances did we find a manuscript regarded as a whole.

On the positive side, I should like to cite one essay that approaches the ideal in describing a music manuscript. It is the essay on "The Laborde *Chansonnier*" by Helen E. Bush published in the *Papers of the American Musicological Society* for 1940. To be sure, Dr. Bush's interest is primarily concerned with the compositions represented in this wonderful little manuscript, but she touches on almost every other aspect of it: its history (so far as the history is known), a description of the volume itself, an analysis of the contents, the illumination, handwriting, and so forth, and even suggestions for performance of the music. From the art field another example comes to mind: *The Exultet Rolls of South Italy*, by Myrtilla Avery (Princeton University Press, 1936). In addition to the complete and scholarly description of all visual aspects of these rolls, Dom Gabriel Beyssac has contributed a precise paragraph on the music and the notation in each roll. With examples such as these to serve as a guide, we sought to include in the catalog[1] published for our exhibition—naturally within the limits of its size—at least a mention of each important aspect of the manuscripts. Since so little material on early notation is available in English, we felt that the catalog should contain a brief description of all the recognized types represented in the exhibit.

Procuring examples for the exhibition involved extensive correspondence with many institutions and a certain amount of travelling. As a starting point, we had the De Ricci and Wilson *Census of Medieval and Renaissance Manuscripts in the United States and Canada* and a number of exhibition catalogs of various sorts where manuscripts had been included. But for the most part, it was a matter of inquiring. As people became interested in what we were doing, they steered us to other collections. I have no doubt that there are many treasures we did not hear about, and others were overlooked for the lack of adequate descriptions, but almost everybody we approached helped in some fashion and we had very few refusals to requests for loans.

The manner of presenting an exhibition is perhaps the phase which requires fullest discussion. First of all, a catalog of some sort should be prepared. This may be a simple mimeographed checklist that merely gives titles and briefly identifies each object, or it may range up to a full catalog furnishing a virtual textbook on the subject. The limits can only be set in terms of the time available for its preparation and the funds allotted for its publication.

In an exhibition, the visual presentation of the items—or to use a museum term, their installation—is naturally of the greatest importance. Ideally, cases should be constructed that correspond to the nature of the objects to be shown and highlight their inherent characteristics. Except for important permanent installations, this is normally impractical, and most of us must make the best of whatever equipment we may have. Under such realistic limitations, imagination must be brought fully into play to imbue the available exhibition space and equipment with all the freshness and originality possible. A few principles may prove helpful guides:

1. Although subject continuity is to be desired, the distribution of the cases, stands, and other furniture in every room or gallery used for an exhibition should be designed to create an harmonious whole. In the different rooms, the problems of distribution may be solved in very different manners, but within any room the objects should all be placed to their best advantage.

2. There ought to be contrast within the gallery as to type of installation. Many institutions own standing, wall, and table cases. Each type offers different problems and opportunities for contrast of installation. Further contrast may be secured by using wall frames for flat pieces, or single leaves or sheets of music may be mounted on the wall under a pane of glass securely fastened all around.

3. Within the cases, the objects should be arranged so that they have breathing space between

them, since there is nothing that kills appearance of an exhibition more than crowding. Each case should be regarded as a unit, and its contents placed in a manner that will create an artistic and pleasing impression. While catalog or chronological sequence is important, only objects that complement each other visually should be shown together.

4. Use related materials in the background to set off the principal objects. Pictures, tapestries, prints, decorative objects, and so forth may be used to good advantage and will enhance the objects on exhibition, provided such materials are kept in the background and not allowed to take precedence over the main objects.

5. Provide background within the cases from such materials as are available. Fabrics may be thumbtacked over beaverboard panels and will provide colorful backing for a case. Beaverboard can be painted quickly and cheaply with water-soluble paint. The colors should be chosen to enhance the objects shown. Also, we have found it best to tie volumes open with strips of cellophane. Since cellophane is transparent, the strips may be broader than is practical when strings or ribbons are used, and the increased breadth distributes the pressure more gently over a wider surface of the page.

6. The standard exhibit case inevitably erects a barrier between the object exhibited and the visitors to the exhibit. To encourage the establishment of a more direct relationship, some objects may be shown in the open. Naturally, this can only be done with the permission of the owners of the objects, and even then should only be attempted with objects that cannot easily be damaged. Such objects should be protected with heavy cellophane or transparent sheets of plastic, and either mounted out of the reach of visitors or displayed on open pedestals or stands. In the present show, three large choir books were shown on stands where the visitors could come up and examine them closely.

7. Most cases and other installations can use all the light you can get on them. At any rate, the intensity of the light within the case ought to be greater than that outside it. Whatever is done, never show manuscripts lit with incandescent bulbs within the case. Such lights generate sufficient heat to dry out the manuscripts and in time will seriously damage them. Today, nearly all institutions employ cold, fluorescent lighting. The fluorescent tubes can be installed directly in the case or placed in a housing on top of the case with the light shining down through the glass. Furthermore, fluorescent light more nearly approximates good daylight and colors can be seen with greater fidelity. Whenever possible, objects outside cases should be spotlighted.

Work on the last of the four P's—the promoting of an exhibition—must be started long before the show opens. If the exhibit is an important one, there should be advance publicity in the newspapers and in all specialized journals conceivably interested in the subjects to be covered in the exhibit. A release might be prepared in the form of a letter in which the four W's would be given: who, what, when, and where; also, the purpose or central theme of the show should be described, together with something of its scope and mention of unusual items or features.

This should be followed up with more detailed opening publicity. Here all the resources of modern promotion should be brought into play: newspapers, radio, television, posters for windows and bulletin boards, and announcements mailed directly through your usual publicity channels. A large sign placed outside the building or somewhere inside the entrance is usually helpful. There should be continuous publicity in the newspapers, including all kinds of little items and human interest features, as well as longer articles on special aspects of the show. Most radio and television stations are willing to use spot announcements if copy lasting thirty seconds to one minute is provided. If television programs can be arranged, use a few objects from the exhibition, selecting only those which are not too fragile or valuable to be transported to the station. Care should be taken to choose objects which will show up well on TV screens.

Plan lectures and guided tours of your exhibition. Get announcements out on this service to all schools nearby and to club groups. Many of the latter welcome an interesting and instructive talk of this sort. If you notify them before the beginning of the season, they can often include a listing in their yearbooks. During the seven weeks of our exhibition, we talked to over 3,000 children and adults, in groups ranging from ten to ninety.

Wherever possible, bring a music exhibition to life through recordings and concerts, where music seen can also be heard. We arranged for three large public lectures with full musical illustrations: Gregorian Chant, Guillaume de Machaut, and Vocal Music of the Renaissance. We set aside recordings of music in the exhibition on a special shelf in our record library, and even arranged to have new LP's of this music sold at the sales desk. An extra display of books relating to the exhibition was set up. These and many other devices can be used to stimulate interest in the exhibition and to maintain that interest throughout the duration of its showing.

NOTES

[1] *Medieval and Renaissance Music Manuscripts*, [Toledo, Ohio], The Toledo Museum of Art, 1953. [xv, 40 p., 12 plates, 8vo]

IV

MECHANICAL PROCESSES OF A MUSIC LIBRARY

A. Acquisitions

SELECTED BIBLIOGRAPHY

200. Dart, Thurston; Emery, Walter; and Morris, Christopher. *Editing early music.* Novello, Oxford University Press, Stainer & Bell, 1963.

Sets out minimum scholarly standards for performing editions.

201. Samuel, Harold. "Notes for *Notes:* Improperly edited performing editions," *Notes,* 25 (March, 1969), 468-470.

* * * * *

202. Finney, Theodore M. "Not in the B. U. C. [British Union Catalogue], or, Lost in a binder's collection," *Notes,* 21 (Summer, 1964), 335-337.

An explanation of the term, "not in the B. U. C." and its use in dealers' catalogues.

203. "Antiquarian music dealers," *Notes,* 23 (September, 1966), 5-33.

"A librarian speaks": Donald W. Krummel, "Observations on library acquisitions of music," reprinted below, pp. 225-231.

"A European dealer speaks": Richard Macnutt, "Music-dealing from Europe," pp. 17-22.

"An American dealer speaks": Gordon B. Wright, "Musical literature and its dealers," pp. 23-27.

"Survey of dealers specializing in antiquarian music and musical literature": pp. 28-33.

* * * * *

204. Myers, Kurtz. "Music book publishing," *Library Trends,* 7 (July, 1958), 169-180.

205. Greener, Barbara R. "Comments on music reprinting," *Reprint Bulletin,* 12 (March, 1967), 3-9.

Includes a list of music reprints (ca. 1967) and "Partial directory of music reprint publishers."

NB—*Reprint Bulletin* was formerly *Reprint Expediting Service Bulletin.*

206. Samuel, Harold E. "Notes for *Notes:* Reprints," *Notes,* 24 (March, 1968), 467-469.

Some pros and cons of the proliferation of reprint editions.

207. Freedman, Frederick. "Perspective: Music reprint industry [and] Music reprinters," *Choice,* 6 (October, 1969), 977-985.

208. Gerboth, Walter. "Criteria for quality in reprint publications," *Notes,* 26 (June, 1970), 718-719.

209. Blum, Fred, comp. "Music serials in microfilm and reprint editions," *Notes,* 24 (June, 1968), 670-679.

* * * * *

210. Van Patten, Nathan. "A few observations concerning the acquisition of musical manuscripts," *Notes: Supplement for Members,* No. 16 (October, 1951), 16-19.

211. Lenneberg, Hans. "Problems in the international exchange of microfilm," *Fontes artis musicae,* 15 (1968/2-3), 75-78.

Comments by Lesure, pp. 80-81 and Rita Benton, pp. 81-82, follow.

212. Spivacke, Harold. "The collection of musical material of local interest," *Notes,* 1st series, no. 8 (August, 1940), 49-54.

213. Epstein, Dena J. "On collecting materials for local music histories," *Notes,* 24 (September, 1967), 18-21.

Observations on Library Acquisitions of Music

by Donald W. Krummel

Music dealers have often expressed puzzlement at the way in which most libraries buy music. Indeed, if all dealers were somehow to get together and compare the orders they had received in a given period, hoping to learn the policies and practices of their customers, they would be quite shocked at the lack of planning. If the matter were not without serious overtones to all parties concerned, they could enjoy a good round of laughter. More specific evidence of the deficiencies involved can be found in the subscriber lists for major series, in the erratic patterns reflected in union lists, and in impressionistic scannings of library shelves and card catalogues—and it leaves one to conclude regretfully that in most libraries the music acquisitions program is sketchily developed and inconsistently managed. This article, by way of contributing a librarian's viewpoint on the subject, explains a few of the weaknesses and shortcomings rather than apologizing for them or offering immediate solutions. Actually, of course, changes are now taking place which should greatly improve matters; and while many major points of this article have already long been taken for granted in more progressive institutions, these points bear repeating as the basis for several future suggested developments.

Our basic and most obvious problem is a lack of money. Given adequate funds, music librarians could all build better collections. However apparent such a truth may be, it is also a sad fact that wealth usually poses more serious problems than poverty.[1] Close on the heels of any increase in funds will, or at least should, follow many nebulous, complicated, and changing problems which will commit a conscientious librarian to a geometrically increasing total of the working hours of the day. Affluence also brings with it two unenviable assignments: maintaining a thoroughness of coverage which can dependably be achieved by nothing less than a complex network of citation sources; and producing the type of impressive and conspicuous reservoirs which top administrators feel are needed to supplement the "think tanks" of today—building "instant British Museums," in a sense—accomplishing in five years what few of the finest libraries have ever done in less than twenty-five, and then under more advantageous market conditions.

As an excuse for a lack of direction in his acquisitions program the music librarian has often shifted the blame to his faculty, or to the musicians and scholars who advise him. There is justification for this, especially when final authority for building the collection rests with such parties (who will hereinafter be referred to as "users" of the library). For several reasons, the trend appears to be shifting away from user-built collections to librarian-built collections. Specialists in research or performance are likely to be staunch partisans in the political arenas of our cultural world. They usually have strong and highly personal views on the virtues and shortcomings of particular composers, editors, authors, subjects, even national traditions and historical periods. A good library must be more catholic, seeking a comprehensive coverage within its defined objectives of collecting. Above all—and this point is one which will recur throughout this report—building a good collection requires time of the most painstaking slowness, the likes of which few library users can afford. Finally, ambitious scholars and performers often move on to greener pastures after a few years, leaving behind them the beginnings of a specialized research collection which may or may not interest their successors.

The special interests of today's users of the music library most often lie within the areas of Renaissance and contemporary music. In the

SOURCE: Reprinted from Donald W. Krummel, "Observations on library acquisitions of music," *Notes,* 23 (September, 1966), 5–16, by permission of the Music Library Association.

former area, almost all of the source materials are long removed from the market, and now many of the secondary works—recent historical sets and German doctoral dissertations, for instance—sell at higher prices for battered and crumbling originals than one would pay for full-size photocopies on good paper. The area of contemporary music suffers from unstable publishing conditions and poor bibliographical control. It is an unfortunate fact that composers and music librarians, for all of their genuine and enthusiastic respect for one another, have not been able to be of much help to each other in formal and tangible ways.

The various other areas, which are of little interest to scholars and performers today, would appear to be bargain-hunting grounds for collection builders. Users are understandably of little help in determining which of these always will be intrinsically dull, and which are only momentarily out of fashion. Specialists are committed by standards of taste and by well-trained critical faculties. Their study, being largely independent and creative, must result from a deep personal motivation in which the conditioned musical experience plays a major role. They should hardly be called on to champion music which they know to be inferior.

In their attempts to collect source materials for posterity, librarians are perhaps being naïve in setting a goal of keeping one step ahead of research. After Haydn, scholars and performers may indeed descend to Johann Nepomuk Hummel—or they may just as well choose to abandon the music library entirely, turning in desperation to fields like epistomology. The music librarian who plays the horses of scholarship frequently turns up a few thesis topics. The gods are more sparing in releasing the funds, timing, and insight which stand behind the great research collections—and even the most fortunate of these institutions are now finding the main tangible effect of their holdings to be microfilm orders. For some strange reason, scholars prefer to spend their busmen's holidays visiting the original locality of their research or discussing their work with stimulating and sympathetic colleagues—not in running down remotely located copies of their sources. An element of geography having been introduced, it is now appropriate that a major suggestion be made. Instead of scrambling for the remaining treasures of the past, a music librarian seeking to build an archive for future scholarship should look for materials needed in the study of locally significant music. Such an objective need not be foolish in either extreme of ridicule or chauvinistic praise; when such is the case, the resulting archive will be uniquely appropriate to the cultural needs of the community and invaluable to the cause of the music library's role in that culture.[2] And yet, how many libraries have all the programs of important local musical events? How many of our university collections can claim the manuscripts, sketches, and correspondence of their own composers-in-residence? And where would one go to learn how those first efforts of a major musical talent of today—written probably in the Walter Pistonesque idiom of a G.I.-Bill composition class in the late 1940's—will have differed from the equally Walter Pistonesque efforts of his less successful classmates?

Poor implementation of an acquisitions program is another matter again. For this the music librarian has usually passed the blame to a centralized acquisitions department serving the entire library complex (hereinafter referred to, with all due misgivings, as the "acquirers"). Most such departments today have at best a heavy and snugly scheduled workload; more often, their staff members' very existence is sustained by that homely motto "Keep Smiling," in the face of overwhelming backlogs and arbitrary priorities among the calculated risks and arrearages. Such departments are understandably least unhappy when they can work with as few dealers, advisors, invoices, and problems as possible.

One of the greatest pitfalls in music acquisitions work, incidentally, grows out of nothing less noble than that master achievement of music librarianship—conventional titles. However much music cataloguers love them, they are a menace to acquisitions work for a simple reason: they require searchers, and others working from a citation only, in effect to establish, the contents of an edition without having seen the edition; a searcher must imagine a conventional title before he can determine the presence or absence of the edition in the card catalogue. The problem is usually a minor inconvenience, once the searcher has been trained—converting "Erste Sinfonie" into "Symphony No. 1," for instance. In working with prolific composers with complex conventional-title practices (among them Mozart, Vivaldi, or Clementi), a searcher is really not sure that an edition is lacking until upwards of a dozen, sometimes several hundred, cards have been filed through one by one.

A digression is appropriate at this point for purposes of suggesting several ways in which music dealers can be of greater service to libraries.

Many dealers' practices still recall days when most buyers of books were collectors. Selling books was like fishing: an appealing but honest lure was needed, placed just right to catch the customer's eye. Today's librarian, however, is buying books as if, in the words of one lady on our acquisitions staff, "they were going out of style" (and perhaps, alas, they are: but this is another matter). And today's dealer resembles the fisherman who wishes he had six extra lines—or, to come to the basic point, who often wishes he were fishing with nets instead of hooks. Books of great value, of course, will always deserve to be part of the world of the quest, with all of the excitement involved. The vast majority of the music titles one sees listed today, however, is not rare. All but a very few of the items one sees in music antiquarian catalogues today should be finding their way into the general rather than the restricted collections of a library.

The library book selector—the specialist who used to stay up nights scanning lists and marking items for tomorrow's searching—is today a busy man who looks for the chance to tell his searchers, "I'm sorry, but this catalogue is too good to pass up. Search the whole thing." He knows that his own mind is fallible, and that his library is so large that he can't possibly remember all of what is in it. He would really prefer to slash through the titles he has actually handled recently, leaving the rest for searchers either to eliminate or to order. The dealers' catalogues which will receive such favorable handling will be those in which the selector finds three factors to be present.

First, out of consideration for his searchers, he will look for an alphabetical arrangement by established main entries—author or composer in most instances, *not* subject, date, *Festschrift,* or librettist, though such elements may usefully be brought out through indexes and cross references. Searchers work much faster and more accommodatingly when they can begin with "A" and end with "Z." Since most searchers now undertake some minimum verification of entry in the Library of Congress catalogues, a dealer can expect fewer books returned to him as duplicates when his entries conform to A.L.A. rules. In matters of accuracy and completeness, dealers can not place too much emphasis on the main entry—H. Reimann and H. Riemann being perhaps a hundred cards apart in a library catalogue today—the unfailing mention of series notes being a close second in importance.[3]

Second, the selector will learn to favor quality. Just as he avoids the dealers who send him "cripples" and "dogs," so he will ignore catalogues filled with Jadassohn, LaMara, and the *Victrola Book of the Opera.* There is, however, another type of quality which he will come to respect and favor: a dealer's catalogue thoughtfully conceived around a single topic. One sees many general music lists and a number in broad categories (opera scores, books about music, chamber music parts, etc.), but few devoted to smaller topics such as Renaissance music, biography, theory, or bibliography. Lists even more narrowly defined would appear to stand especially good chances of receiving cover-to-cover searching. Such lists, for instance, might be made up of editions, in- and out-of-print, of Bach, Beethoven, Mozart, and other standard composers—editions that will not be superseded by presently conceived *Gesamtausgaben* (the entries here preferably with conventional titles). Titles from standard bibliographies—such as those of Allen on music history books, Dean-Smith on English folksong collections, the Music Library Association's checklist of thematic catalogues, or Sears and now De Charms on song anthologies—would also complement nicely a library's program for marking copies of such lists for reference purposes.

Third, the selector's decision will be affected by the likelihood that the books he orders are actually available. Reports of books being already sold are doubly discouraging to the librarian, not only because the books are needed, but also because expensive searching time has already been spent before this fact is determined. By way of a visionary suggestion, is it not possible for a dealer, working in conjunction with a photocopier and perhaps a bindery, to offer to have copies made? There are many mechanical problems to any such arrangement, but these would probably be offset by more library orders.

Such remarks obviously apply to out-of-print books; and of course the dealer who has good books to offer may for the present do much as he pleases. Our seller's market has sent prices skyward with no end in immediate sight. In the more competitive areas of current "in-print" books, a dealer stands to flourish because he provides other special services to libraries. The library, for instance, usually spends three dollars to buy a book and three or four dollars more to give it a permanent binding. This is hard enough to justify on the average trade book, which now costs about seven dollars; it is even more difficult to justify spending on musical materials, which probably cost on the average less than half of that amount. The dealer who can help a library reduce its music processing costs should thus find many grateful customers. It is a mystery to me why no dealers now offer sets of Library of Congress cards (or at least cataloguer's copy) with the music they sell to libraries. More complicated problems are involved in providing a similar service in library bindings.

Returning to the main thesis of this paper, it should be noted that the aforementioned acquisitions problems exemplify a rather common breakdown of a time-honored administrative situation. Call it Parkinson's Law or call it institutional sophistication in an expanding intellectual universe, a two-party, user-plus-acquirer arrangement can no longer sustain a music acquisitions program of any importance. Such a relationship may have worked in the days when the music collection consisted of course reading assignments plus a handful of reference books. Today things are different: libraries are developed for purposes of providing varied specialists and non-specialists alike with a consistent quality and quantity of coverage of all areas of music committed to the written record. The music librarian must necessarily become the third party in such a picture. His role involves two types of special assignments: those negative activites which grow out of his concern for the shortcomings just described, and those positive activities which are central to the needs and objectives of music librarianship.

The one side of this activity should be characterized as negative for several reasons: it is political, perhaps even "Machiavellian" in the current sense; it consumes endless amounts of time and energy; and its final result seldom leads directly to a feeling of certainty. It requires that the music librarian establish a position of strength and respect midway between his users and his acquirers, at the same time depending on each for an intensive level of cooperation. He must make full use of the abilities of musicians, scholars, and faculty to enhance the reputation and holdings of the music library. He must also recognize the arbitrary power that a library acquisitions department has to weaken a music program through indifference and neglect. In such tasks the successful music librarian must become something of a master strategist. Since the breakdown of the two-party relationship is largely a matter of more complicated functions having become a part of the picture, he must also be prepared to spend the large quantities of time involved in these functions. Computers nowadays are even better than humans, we are told, when it comes to making arbitrary decisions. Decisions on which *Urtext* edition to buy must be made in the light of a particular type of relevant evidence, requiring pleasant and informative, but frightfully time-consuming, assignments, such as digging up bibliographical history and uncovering bibliographical points, scanning reviews, and appraising the names and reputations of editors. The excellence of a music library's holdings further depends on filling gaps in serial holdings, working with dealers on a personal basis, and locating the out-of-the-way item which will appear in the *next* edition of a standard bibliography. Finally, the music librarian must realize that he lives in a highly imperfect world. His users, if they are worth serving, will demand an unbalanced collection favoring their areas of study. His acquirers will continue to work under varying pressures and fluctuating workloads, in terms of "use it or lose it" funds, and with limited capacities for taking the pains needed to do their work as it should be done. The consolation for the music librarian may well be the collection he builds and the respect he gains from the two parties he deals with. It should also be viewed as a privilege he has gained for dealing with several of the positive aspects of music librarianship, to which we now turn.

Foremost among these professional assignments is the pleasure of knowing the books and musical editions in question. The musicologist is motivated by a love of music and history; on the same basis, the music librarian should be motivated by a love of music and books.[4] Music librarianship would appear to have yet to learn what rare-book librarianship has long presumed: the value of experience in the commercial world of books. Any institution seeking to assign the major or exclusive task of building a collection would be well advised to recruit a person neither from the world of scholarship nor the world of librarianship but from the antiquarian music trade. A dealer is obviously in the best position to know which of his former collegues is likely to turn up an item on a desiderata list. He will probably have seen in one year more music books than the average music librarian sees in his own single library in a lifetime. He will quickly learn which eighteenth-century books are still common, and which from 1962 are already scarce. He will know better than most librarians when to refer a hurried reader to an inter-library-loan copy and wait one to five years for one on the market, as opposed to situations where microfilms or other photocopies should be acquired at once and permanently.

Second, music librarians should undertake to come up with statistical evidence on the cost of musical materials. Much needed is a "musical editions" counterpart to the Cost of Library Materials Index (possibly also one for phonorecords). More speculative is the question, "How much does a good music library cost?" If anyone should be so foolish as to want to buy one copy of every book on music and musical edition now in print, he could probably spend about $100,000. If he were to buy judiciously but extensively on the antiquarian market, he could probably spend an additional $300,000 to good advantage. Beyond this point he would find himself confronted largely with items specially priced for his benefit alone; and even *at* this point, he would probably find his entire library still somewhat less significant, in quality and quantity, than a dozen or so American institutions. Such fantasies may be pleasant. More relevant to this discussion is a question often asked by library administrators: "How much money do you need annually to buy the publications appropriate to our collections?" A sum of $10,000 would probably cover a year's output of the world's musical materials within the purview of the "canons" to be formulated below;[5] but here again it would be much better for a music library committee to undertake a more reliable statistical approach to this question.

It is unfortunate, incidentally, that music librarians have generally not reconciled themselves to the prevailing library philosophy of acquiring current books first, with lower priority for those from earlier periods. The demands of musicologists for antiquarian materials, the failure of music librarians to define their standards for selection in the face of much apparently ephemeral material, the relatively recent interest in music in American libraries, and the glaring gaps in even the best of our collections—such matters have encouraged the music librarian to "fight 'em rather than join 'em." Three arguments support the current-materials-first approach. First, the price for in-print items is as low now as it will ever be. Second, the ordering of in-print items can generally be handled on a scheduled basis, rather than the more expensive demand basis needed to get good items from antiquarian catalogues. Finally, the cataloguing of current titles is usually less expensive, and can be made even less so if enough libraries can be persuaded to enhance the music coverage within the framework of our National Union Catalogue.

The third matter—development of an acquisitions policy—goes hand in hand with such budgetary considerations. The music librarian's request for funds is usually and understandably countered by his administrator's question, "What do you want to get?" How many music libraries have formulated policies for selection? In most institutions, the acquisitions rationale could probably be reduced to five emotional attitudes. First, there is the trade-book type of publication, including periodicals, historical sets, and other types of bound materials: these we buy willingly, presuming comprehensiveness within our collecting areas and budgetary limitations. Second are the performing editions, popularized books on music, and pedagogical materials, requested or presumably needed by the clientele of the library for avocational enjoyment: these we buy dutifully and with relative indifference. Third come the editions of particular composers we respect and editions representative of areas in which we wish to promote a greater interest: these we buy righteously, but more erratically than we would ever care to admit. Fourth come the research materials from earlier historical periods: these we buy joyously and impulsively as funds are available. Finally come the research materials of regional significance—works by and about local composers or musical life and works accumulated as part of a regional repository: these we buy grudgingly, preferring invariably that the material come in as painlessly as possible (which may or may not mean as a gift). If this personal appraisal of the typical situation is indeed correct, any acquisitions policy would be obviously difficult to rationalize.

The following eleven "canons," in the author's opinion, should constitute the minimum acquisition objectives of any major music library:

1. Acquisition of all serious new books about music and all substantially new editions of them, covering serious as well as popular music, including periodicals, excluding only material in designated foreign languages, perhaps on a qualitative basis, and material of a regional interest in distant areas
2. Acquisition of all practical editions, known or likely to be definitive, of music now or likely someday to be a part of the "standard repertory of serious music" (itself, of course, in need of definition), excepting

only performance parts of large-scale works when scores are available

3. Acquisition of all scholarly editions of early music
4. Acquisition of pedagogical materials, editions of popular music, and popularized books about music to meet identified needs of users of the library
5. Acquisition of research material from earlier periods in original editions and in photocopy, with the advice and encouragement of specific users of the library
6. Acquisition of research material for purposes of documenting local musical developments–arranged by the music librarian himself, possibly with the help of a special local committee appointed to offer guidance and support
7. Acquisition of materials beyond the purview of any of the above, especially current publications of defined geographical areas, for purposes of providing a regional research repository on the basis of co-operative agreements between several libraries
8. Acquisition of materials in any of the above categories *regardless of the size of the publication* (e.g., two-page art songs, programs, and other materials of permanent interest above and beyond the ephemera assigned to a vertical file)
9. Provision for the removal of superseded editions from the library, especially that acquired under *1* through *4* above
10. Formal designation of selected reviewing media to serve as the basis for qualitative decisions on new current publications, especially as needed in *1* through *3* above; also, continuing efforts to encourage the cause of these reviewing media, particularly those which cover new musical editions[6]
11. Establishment of a network of citation sources–national bibliographies, prospectuses, dealers' announcements, *Notes* lists, and the like–for current publications, covering *1* through *4* and *7* above, where qualitative considerations may not be relevant or where immediate acquisition is desired

Such, in a relatively unpolished state, are the pious truths which we should all wish to profess,[7] with refinements and modifications from the readers of this Journal, on grounds of doctrine or human expediency, as the author hopes may be forthcoming. Yet, of those music librarians who would claim to follow some or all of the above "canons," how many placed a subscription to the excellent Italian journal *L'Organo (cf.* canon *1)?* How many know for a fact that they have the best performing editions of the Mozart sonatas for piano-four-hands or the J.S. Bach 'cello suites *(cf. 2)?* Who has all of the old Dessoff choral series and the *Mitteldeutsches Musikarchiv (cf. 3),* or all of the shorter choral works and art songs of Charles Ives, Henry Cowell, and Virgil Thomsom *(cf. 8),* or any of the handsomely designed educational materials issued over the past ten years in Poland and Scandinavia *(cf. 4 and 7)?*

Once having arrived at such guidelines, there is no reason why most of the subsequent acquisitions steps could not be turned over to dealers. The library would probably end up just as complete, and any higher cost of the materials would more than be compensated for by lower costs in staff time. I personally would be reluctant to do this, however. The direct exposure to the materials themselves, as part of the acquisitions process, provides a useful outlook on the present bibliographical state of the music world. Acquisitions work may be distinguished from that of the cataloguer, who seeks to place a work in the context of a system for encompassing the totality of knowledge, or that of the reference librarian, who seeks to place the item in a context relevant to the needs of users. The acquisitions process involves locating citations and then locating copies, between which comes a moment of truth, a yes-no decision based on an anticipation of the publication filling a unique and important function in the contexts of cataloguers and reference librarians (from another viewpoint, this should be synonymous with saying that a work is appropriate to the library's selection "canons"). Delegating the whole job to a dealer–asking him to locate the citations, apply the "canons," find a copy, send a bill, soon perhaps even to bind and catalogue the item–is the kind of efficiency that today's libraries greatly need, but that would probably leave a library staff much the poorer in many unnoticeable ways for not having done the tasks itself.

Fourth and finally among the areas of professional planning are those in which co-operative programs between institutions are desirable. A musical "Farmington Plan" for less-well-known works from remote areas has often been proposed.[8] At last winter's MLA meetings, Mr. Paul Fromm suggested a program involving a new type of outlet for the works of our contemporary composers through the music library. There is no reason why the entire contents of R.I.S.M. should not be published in microform, and perhaps our country may someday develop a counterpart to the Deutsches Musikgeschichtliches Archiv in Kassel. A different and more difficult project grows out of the eighth of the above "canons" (its heroic outcry heightened by italics) and the conviction that a commitment to acquisitions ought to be also a commitment to cataloguing and preservation. Our present rules and procedures, conceived mainly for purposes of handling trade books and scholarly journals, are neither well suited bibliographically to performing editions and sheet music nor economically justified in relation to the purchase price. Many more such ideas could be suggested here; proposing them is easy, pleasant, and inspiring but less needed than the hard work of developing productive programs.

It is an obvious truth that the strength of a music library, like the strength of its cataloguing and reference services, depends on its specialized personnel. More paradoxical and problematical are the two main predications of this article: that the effectiveness of the music librarian in the acquisitions process depends on his ability to call on the support of his users and his acquirers, while at the same time taking away from them some of their duties; and that the tediousness, unimportance, and uncertainty once associated with these duties are actually the very factors which today contribute dignity and excitement to music librarianship.

NOTES

[1]"The [inadequacy of academic libraries] is not confined to those institutions with the smallest libraries and the most rapidly expanding budgets. Harvard, with the largest university library in the world, has recently reported that it is more frequently made aware of its deficiencies now than 20 years ago when it was only half as large."—Gordon Williams, in "Academic Librarianship: The State of the Art," *Library Journal*, XCI (1966), 2413.

[2]cf. Goethe, "Wer den Dichter . . ."

[3]As stated here, the point applies to American libraries. The needs of the foreign librarian, book collector, and performer are different, and it is probably best that they should remain so. No less useful a tool than *American Book Prices Current* disregards library entry rules in favor of citations under titles, editors, private presses, or illustrators; and librarians have often found that Mr. Lazare's "wrong" entries have sent them to copies recorded in their own catalogues, as entered by cataloguers who followed either their instincts or an older set of rules. This situation does not alter the basic point that dealers can do much in adapting their catalogues to the needs of their American library customers.

[4]The terms of this comparison grow out of Arthur Mendel's provocative remarks on "Evidence and Explanation" (International Musicological Society, *Report of the Eighth Congress, New York, 1961, Volume 2: Reports,* edited by Jan LaRue [Kassel, etc.: Bärenreiter, 1962], p. 16. I regret having to leave this observation in such an epigrammatic state. A greater elaboration, however, would quickly become a cumbersome apologia for all of music librarianship. Mr. Mendel's remarks are essentially concerned with the basic responsibilities of scholarship to the documentary evidence of the past. In a way, the librarian starts at the other end of a communications process, with basic responsibilities to the cultural community, which he fulfills through the institution of the library and with the help of its bibliographical resources.

[5]It is curious that the editor of this journal has quite independently arrived at exactly the same total, also the same estimated cost of musical materials suggested earlier. See *Notes,* XXII (1966), 1202f.

[6]See the author's "Bibliography's Step-Child: The Printed Note," *Library Journal,* XC (1965), 1252–53. [Reprinted above, pp. 77–80].

[7]Smaller institutions should be able to adapt these "canons" to meet their needs through modifying phrases, especially the first four. The expression "on a qualitative basis," however, is to be recommended in preference to hard and fast categorizations. Numbers five and seven may justifiably be eliminated altogether by a small library, but six and the last four are essential under any circumstances..

[8]To my knowledge, such a program was first proposed by Lester E. Asheim, *The Humanities and the Library* (Chicago: American Library Association, 1957).

The Ordering and Supply of Sheet Music

by H. P. Dawson and B. R. Marks

A fine set of definitions of the various forms in which music is published and can be purchased from dealers. Written by two music dealers for the non-specialist (or new music librarian) obliged to order musical items, it carefully points out the information required by the dealer before he can supply the version, edition, or arrangement the library needs.

The importance of the role played by the music supplier to the music librarian need not be stressed, yet very little has been said on the subject. It is hoped that the following notes, written from the point of view of the supplier will give librarians a better understanding of some of the day-to-day problems confronting those who serve them.

First, a few general notes concerning the music trade. Until recent years nearly all the larger music publishers and agents for foreign editions were situated in the West End of London. This concentration of the trade in one area greatly facilitated the work of the supplier, as the close proximity of the firms made the collection of music an easy matter, resulting in swift dispatch to the library. In the last few years, however, the trend has been for music publishers to leave the expensive central London area, with a resulting delay (sometimes as long as a week) in obtaining certain publications. The trade departments of well-known firms such as Augener, Boosey and Hawkes, Eulenberg, Lengnick, Novello, Oxford University Press, Schott, Stainer and Bell, etc., are now situated in Greater London or the provinces, which all adds to the difficulties of supply.

Library suppliers naturally hold extensive and varied stocks of all publishers, but it is impossible to cover everything (*e.g.*, sets of part-songs, choral works and orchestral material). In consequence there is always a large amount of music to be ordered. Generally speaking, (there are exceptions, of course) the music trade is a long way behind the book trade in modern production techniques and publicity. Scores are frequently published without any notification being given to the trade which makes the work of the supplier all the more difficult.

Where the relationship between music librarian and music supplier is concerned one of the most important keys to a smooth and efficient service lies in knowledgeable ordering on the part of the librarian. The use of wrong terms, or the omission of vital information frequently leads to delays or incorrect scores being received. One of the most frequent errors found in library orders is the use of the term full score, when a vocal score is required.

The following notes on this subject, therefore, are not intended for the fully experienced music librarian who knows the importance of correct ordering but are given as a guide to the non-specialist assistant who has to deal with music requests.

Judging from the number of orders received by suppliers which merely give the composer and title of the work required, without any further details of edition or arrangement, it is apparent that the necessity of providing more information is not generally appreciated. A large number of works are published in at least two forms—usually a score (for conducting or following a performance) and a performing edition. For example, Beethoven's Piano Concerto No. 5 is available as (1) Full orchestral score; (2) Miniature score; (3) Two-piano arrangement; (4) Piano solo arrangement. The main problem for the supplier is to decide which of the four editions is most likely to be required, when the information is not stated on the order.

There are, of course, many other difficulties which arise, a common error being the misuse of the word score (which is vaguely defined in the dictionary as "an arrangement of music on a number of staves . . ."). It is essential that the word

SOURCE: Reprinted from H. P. Dawson and B. R. Marks, "The ordering and supply of sheet music," *Brio*, 2 (Spring, 1965), 8–10, by permission of the authors.

'score' has a qualifying word with it *e.g.*, full score, miniature score, vocal score, piano score, etc. These can be defined as follows:–

1. Full Score
   Indicates the complete orchestration, instrument by instrument, of a work set out in large format for use by a conductor.
2. Miniature Score
   Identical with the above, but published in a small size intended for study or to follow a performance of a work. These smaller scores are also known as study scores.
3. Vocal Score
   A reduction of a vocal work (opera, cantata, etc.) for voice and piano.
4. Piano Score
   An arrangement of a work for piano solo. This is sometimes referred to as a piano reduction.

Before turning to other points, it may be helpful to enlarge on the term piano reduction, in relation to concertos. Piano concertos are published in arrangements for two players, with the solo piano part printed above the second piano (which is a piano reduction of the orchestral part).

Concertos other than piano (*i.e.*, violin, clarinet, etc.) are published in an arrangement with the solo part printed above the piano reduction and with a separate part for the soloist. This separate solo part is usually only sold complete with the piano part.

The following is a miscellaneous list of problems which often arise in music ordering:–

1. Vocal Works for Solo Voice
   These are often published in more than one key. Preference for original key, or low, medium or high voice should be stated.
2. Classical Works
   It is preferable to state which edition (*i.e.*, publisher or editor) is required. For example, Beethoven Piano Sonatas are available in at least six different editions.
3. Works for Two Pianos
   Owing to the fact that some of these have two copies included under one cover, and others only one, it is advisable to state "copies for two players" if the work is needed for performance on two pianos.
4. Librettos
   The language required should be stated, as some are available in three forms: Original text, English translation, or both combined.
5. Orchestral Parts
   Here again publishers issue parts in two ways.
   1. As a full orchestra–one of each orchestra part under one cover, at an inclusive price.

   or

   2. Each part individually. In addition, some publishers only sell the wind parts complete as a set, and not separately.

   The most satisfactory method of ordering, therefore, is as follows:–

   Full score and parts: 6, 6, 4, 4, 2, set of Wind, Brass, Percussion (as available). In full detail this means one full orchestral score, six first violins, six second violins, four violas, four cellos, two basses, one each of all other parts published.
6. Miniature Scores
   These tend to vary a great deal in size, especially scores of modern works. Sometimes there is little difference between full and miniature size, *e.g.*, the Vaughan Williams Symphonies of Oxford University Press which state 'full score' on the title page, but are intended for use as study scores as well.
7. Mozart
   It is advisable to state the Köchel catalogue number after the title, as this is the most satisfactory method of identifying a work.
8. Foreign Publishers
   Many of these now have English agents, but often the works are only to order from abroad. It is helpful to indicate if there is a time limit involved when ordering.
9. Part Songs
   Always state full details of voices required, such as S.A.T.B. (soprano, alto, tenor, bass). Often the same work is published in three or four different editions, *e.g.*, unison, two-part, three-part, four-part male and mixed voices.

The qualified music librarian may question the need to restate such obvious facts concerning music ordering as given above, but a perusal of the day-to-day orders received by suppliers would soon dispel any doubts on this point. As stated earlier, the greater part of this information is given for the benefit of those librarians who are faced with the task of ordering music but have had little experience in handling it. Should these notes help to solve any problems (or perhaps create any doubts!) the contributors would be pleased to hear from librarians in either case.

Book-Buying in a University Music Library

by Vincent H. Duckles

A number of influences play their part in the determination of the collecting policy for any large university music library. A few of the more significant are listed below.

1. *The over-all selection policy of the library.* The University of California Library has assumed certain regional responsibilities in book selection, determined in part by its location and by cooperative arrangements with other libraries. It is not necessary to describe the policy in detail here; suffice it to say that there is a concentration of interest in material of the Pacific area. Large over-all policies seldom have any direct bearing on the selection of books in the music field, particularly since our efforts at the present time are directed towards securing the minimum essentials of a research collection. However, the general library policy cannot be ignored in giving a complete picture of the selection process in one of its branches.

2. *The character and emphasis of the Music Department.* In any library which implements a teaching program, this must be the most important consideration. The kind of teaching carried on in the department will determine the kind of collection maintained.

3. *The activities of particular scholars within the department or in the university at large.* The work of certain faculty members here at the University of California has stimulated the collection of research materials in the field of 15th century music. A doctoral project in American Indian music has caused us to check our resources in primitive music as a whole. The activities of the Griller Quartet, now in residence on the campus, has brought the weaknesses of our chamber music collection into the open. Such influences often extend beyond the range of the department itself. For years the acquisition of materials on ballads and folk-songs has been stimulated by a professor in the English Department. Collections of theatre music and dance music have also received their impetus from the outside.

4. *The strength or weakness of the existing collection.* Any collection tends to perpetuate the features that have been developed over a long period of time. The fact that we already have a good representation of early music theory works encourages further buying along this line. On the other hand, we have deliberately chosen to minimize early American sheet-music. Rarity items, such as first editions, original manuscripts, etc. are not sought unless they have primary research value.

The materials in the university music collection can serve any or all of four purposes:

a. Research material, primary and secondary sources: These may be in the form of books, manuscripts, scores, or microfilm.
b. Performance material: Scores; sets of band or orchestra parts; practical editions of vocal and chamber works.
c. Instructional material: Chiefly recordings, whether on discs, tape, or wire; slides and film-strips might also be included here.
d. Music education material: Books, scores, manuals, courses of study, and other materials related to teacher training.

Here again, the question of the department's objectives comes to the fore. Is it a department of musicology, with emphasis on graduate studies? Is it a "school of music" of the conservatory type, with emphasis on the preparation of performing musicians? Or is it a teacher-training institution where the development of public school teachers is stressed? The answers to these questions will determine the character of the music library and the way in which book funds will be spent. Rarely do we find an institution where one of these purposes is isolated and pursued to the exclusion of

SOURCE: Reprinted from Vincent Duckles, "Book-buying in a university music library," *Notes: Supplement for Members*, No. 8 (1949), 14-17, by permission of the Music Library Association.

the others. In a large state university, such as the University of California, these purposes tend to be combined, not to say confused. All play their part in the budget planning for this music library, with the weight of emphasis decreasing in the order in which they were listed; that is to say, *research material* takes the largest slice of the budget, *music education material*, the smallest.

The financial support of the music-buying program depends upon a number of sources, which in this library total approximately $5000.00 per year. This figure in itself is not very meaningful since the program has not become stabilized as yet. In the last two years the transition from a small departmental library to a *branch* of the general library has been accomplished, a change which involved a great many changes in budget arrangements. At present there are five principal sources of funds:

1. *Departmental book and music fund*: The department supports the buying of most of the recordings, as well as a large part of the performance material. Sets of parts for band and orchestra, and multiple copies of vocal scores for the University Chorus are purchased largely on departmental funds.

2. *The library music allotment*: Most of the research material, old and new books on music, study scores, and about one-third of the recordings are accounted for in the library's music allotment. This allotment is not a precisely defined sum but a "control figure" indicating approximately what the branch is expected to spend for library materials.

3. *Special allotments*: Such allotments are designed to provide for special non-recurring needs, such as the development of a new course or activity in the department, opportunity to purchase a valuable collection, or unusual research requirements on the part of a particular scholar. For example, in anticipation of the activity of the Griller Quartet, appointed quartet in residence for the Spring of 1949, the Library Committee authorized a special allotment of $500.00 to build up the chamber-music collection.

4. *General allotments*: The Music Branch can participate in the use of several funds set up to meet general library needs: (a) General Interest fund, for materials of general or inter-departmental value; (b) Current Serials fund, for periodicals and continuations; (c) Librarian's fund, for general reference books, and rare items when they can be justified in terms of research importance.

5. *Gifts and endowments*: It is recognized by the library administration that the funds required to maintain the collection will not, at the same time, build it up to full strength as a research tool. Musical scholarship is still too young in America to have the support of fully developed research collections such as are found in other areas of the humanities. Plans are under consideration which will provide additional endowment funds for the purchase of music library material for the next ten years.

In our present stage of growth in the University of California Music Library, funds are apportioned according to the following schedule. The figures are approximations. For research materials: about 40%, chiefly from the Library allotment; for performance material: about 35%, chiefly from the departmental allotment; for instructional material: about 22%, from both library and department funds; for music education material: about 3%.

Selection Policies for a University Music Library

by James B. Coover

Looking through the literature of music librarianship, one is struck by the curious fact that what is considered by music librarians to be their most profound and sacred professional trust—the intellectual activity of selecting materials with which to build a strong collection—has received relatively little attention. Few articles beyond those which touch in the most general way upon what a music library ought to contain (e.g., the articles cited and reprinted in Subdivision II above) deal with the problem of selection policies in any detail. Here and there writers admonish us to acquire the "standard materials," the "valuable books," the "best editions," the "definitive editions of standard repertory," and the "materials of permanent interest." These are fine-sounding criteria of limited practical utility. We are also told by a number of writers how to conduct the mechanical phase of acquisitions, the actual ordering procedures. But to date, no one has published detailed statements of policy about which scores, books and recordings to select—policies against which each of us may measure and compare our own, or on which the librarians of emerging libraries may pattern theirs.

We have been left to our own devices. Nor is it sufficient to say that each library's selection policy is unique, arising out of the needs of each library's users. Such a truism begs the issue. A library basing a selection policy strictly on the needs of its users soon discovers that those needs are day-to-day, title-by-title, immediate, modish and sometimes exaggerated in the sweep of history. That a music library in a university must and will prepare for the Music Department's newly-established program in ethnomusicology is hardly to be argued, but any new interest in acquiring materials to support such a program must be in extension of, or adjunct to, an already-existing, carefully-drawn selection profile. Library collections are built for all time, presumably, and should grow deliberately, not whimsically in panicky responses to day-to-day or year-to-year needs.

That may seem to state the obvious, but because of the dearth of writings on the subject of selection policies for music libraries, one wonders if indeed it is. A host of questions come to mind: What are the criteria most music libraries follow with regard to the purchase of autobiographies of composers, conductors, performers, and writers on music? Are they bought only in English, in certain languages, in all languages? Although most music libraries attempt to correlate their purchase of scores with their purchase of recordings, how do they accomplish this? What are music libraries' policies respecting the purchase of pianoforte reductions of operas, ballets, works for voice and orchestra, works for voice and chamber ensemble? How many libraries have policies which specify the physical size of score and the type of binding? What guidelines have librarians established to use when deciding whether or not to enter standing orders for new monographic series, for new *Denkmäler* and new *Gesamtausgaben*? What is the rôle of the language of the text?

A number of libraries in recent years have been forced to confront and resolve such problems, and from their answers to construct selection profiles. For reasons of speed, economy and convenience, many of them have entered into the "blanket approval" order plans, as have the larger library systems of which they are a part. Able's ELAP (English Language Approval Plan) and Stechert-Hafner's LACAP (Latin American Cooperative Acquisitions Project) are two of these for book materials. Approval plans for music scores have been devised and put into operation by dealers such as Alexander Broude, Joseph Boonin, Inc. and Otto Harrassowitz (the last uses a plan based on a profile constructed by the Music Library at the State University of New York at Buffalo in January of 1968, reprinted below).

That such plans can work is not in question.

SOURCE: Written especially for this *Reader*.

They do save clerical time by avoiding the preparation of title-by-title orders. They do tend to assure comprehensive coverage of the desired subject areas and subdivisions–if the profiles are wisely drawn! They do tend to enhance discount rates, because all orders are placed with one dealer. They often save time from the selection process, since items pre-selected by the dealer are finally evaluated by the librarian with the items in hand rather than from painstakingly sought-out reviews. They do, in some cases, offer a more dependable projection of expenditures for the fiscal year. And they can speed up the library's receipt of current and newly-published materials.

The disadvantages seem slight. The most frequently heard criticism is that such plans require the librarian to delegate his most sacred duty–selection–to a dealer. This is not a valid demurrer, however, for approval plans affect only the mechanical order processes, not the intellectual activity of selection. The librarian draws the detailed, workable profiles which dealers then use to evaluate the materials they may supply. The librarian remains firmly in charge of selection. He also has the duty to approve or reject the materials ultimately sent him by the dealers. And finally, since music is a humanistic discipline which depends heavily upon antiquarian items–current and new materials represent only a portion of those which are acquired in each budget year–the librarian is continually active in selecting from the antiquarian and o.p. market offerings.

Whether involved in approval plans or not (and it is probably safe to predict that more and more libraries will be), each music library should have detailed policies for the selection of books, scores and recordings. They ought to be in writing, subject to occasional review, and sufficiently flexible to accomodate new areas of interest. The reasons are numerous and obvious.

Nothing facilitates the formulation of such policies better than the opportunity to compare one's own policies point by point (written or unwritten) with those of another institution. The following are offered, therefore, not because they are perfect or because they are usable in any library except the one for which they were devised at a particular stage of its development, but because they may be provocative and provide models against which other libraries can measure their own decisions. They are "food for thought."

They deal, for the most part, with what I have elsewhere [MLA *Manual,* pp. 1-6] called the "meat and potatoes" of a music library's collections, not the "condiments"–the microforms, archival materials, letters, manuscripts, programs, musical instruments, and the like, for each of which more individualized policies are necessary. With few exceptions, they are policies which can be applied or easily adapted for out-of-print as well as current materials.

While they were designed for an "accelerated growth" music library in a rapidly-expanding university, they may, with minor alterations, also serve as basic guidelines for certain smaller institutions. At the very least, they ought to provoke librarians into answering some profound questions and arriving at some decisions which will make their selection activities both easier and more productive.

SELECTION POLICIES
MUSIC LIBRARY
STATE UNIVERSITY OF NEW YORK AT BUFFALO

Books

General Instructions

A. These guidelines apply only to books printed in the Latin alphabet. Works in Cyrillic, Urdu, Hebrew and other such alphabets shall be individually judged.
B. "Worthwhile," "important," "useful," and "good" in the following shall be determined by concensus of reviews of the works in question or by assumption based on the author's or the publisher's reputation or, finally, upon the degree of need for material in that specific subject.

Policies (by LC class)

1. Periodicals. We will subscribe to all periodicals (including house organs) in English, French, German and Italian which treat of music history, music theory, organology, opera, composition (es-

pecially contemporary), church music, musical acoustics, ethnomusicology, musical esthetics, and music bibliography and librarianship.

We will subscribe to all periodicals (including house organs) in English which treat of music education. Those in other languages will be individually evaluated.

We will subscribe to periodicals in languages other than English, French, German and Italian only if they are of significant musicological content (e.g., *Dansk Aagbog for Musikforskning*).

We will subscribe, selectively, to English language periodicals dealing with audio and high-fidelity recorded sound attempting to complement, rather than duplicate, the holdings of the public library in the city.

We will not subscribe to *Billboard, Variety,* and the like so long as the public library maintains files of these.

2. We will purchase reports of conferences in the areas noted in Policy Guideline 1 (above), first paragraph.
3. We will purchase *Festschriften* in honor of musicologists in all Latin alphabet languages, those celebrating other musicians primarily in English, French, Italian and German.
4. Essays, papers and addresses of one author will, in general, be purchased in the four main languages.
5. Collections of portraits of musicians or pictorial works related to music will, in general, be secured regardless of language of text.
6. Biographical dictionaries, encyclopedias and terminological dictionaries similar in scope and authoritativeness to those in Duckles will be secured, whatever the language (in this case, including Cyrillic).
7. In general, any bibliography or catalog published in the Latin alphabet will be purchased. Those in Cyrillic will be selectively purchased.

   In this same general class, all works on music printing and music librarianship in the Latin alphabet will be secured. Again, those in Cyrillic will be individually evaluated.
8. Any history, in the Latin alphabet, whether general or special, which presents new information or is a valuable recast of previously existing information will be purchased. This covers all periods, all nationalities and geographical areas, as well as special topics such as Troubadours and the history of music theory. Special attention will be paid to the history of American music, serious and popular, including folk, jazz and rock.
9. Collected biographies will be purchased when the biographies are unusual, i.e., when full-scale books do not exist for a significant number of the biographees. Collections of biographies of standard composers for whom full-scale studies exist in quantity—e.g., Bach, Mozart, Haydn—will not be secured unless the author is a significant figure.
10. All individual biographies noted in bibliographies at the end of entries in such works as *Baker's Biographical Dictionary, MGG* and others will be secured, plus any new biographies which offer significant new information or a new point of view, written in the Latin alphabet. Cyrillic texts will be selectively purchased.

    Preference will be given to English translations, when they exist.

    Studies and analyses of individual works or groups of works by the master composers will be purchased based, primarily, on an evaluation of the author of those texts, the particular need for such a study, and what is already in the collection.

    All collections of letters of major composers—in original language *and* in translation—will be secured as available.

    Biographical works on Wagner will be evaluated individually.

    All autobiographies of composers—in the original language and translation—will be purchased. Likewise, those of *important* conductors and performers.
11. Organological works (catalogs, histories, theory and repair) will be individually evaluated, but those which are in some way a contribution to an understanding of performance practice should be purchased regardless of instrument, period or geographic area discussed.
12. Likewise with texts dealing with chamber, orchestral, vocal and choral music, with special attention given to works on the medieval and renaissance literature, song literature, church music and opera.

13. In general, all works dealing with ethnomusicology, particularly those on tribal musics (as contrasted with folk music) will be secured. Works on folk music will be more painstakingly appraised before purchase. For tribal music studies, the area covered is the main criterion; for folk music studies, the area covered and the author's reputation or reviewer's evaluations are all equally important criteria.
14. Works on acoustics will be individually evaluated but in general, all works which deal with electronic music and *musique concrète* will be automatically purchased.

    The standard texts on the esthetics of music as well as any significant new works will be secured. In general, all those dealing with the "new" music will be secured.
15. All reprints of early works on music theory—in book- or micro-form—will be purchased as available. All translations of early works on music theory will be purchased.

    New didactic works will be evaluated as they appear, but in general, most with English language text will be purchased—whenever possible with the teacher's manual.

    Works devised for teaching theory at the elementary level will be purchased when they offer a novel approach worth the perusal of music education students.
16. Works on music education (the theory and history of and psychological studies in) will be purchased almost automatically if in English. Special attention will be paid to monographic series issued by institutions, and to doctoral dissertations on microfilm. Works in foreign languages will be carefully evaluated before purchase.

    Juvenile literature will not be purchased nor will series of school songsters.

    Works on the teaching of instrumental or vocal techniques will be carefully evaluated before purchase, and the library will make no attempt to have a complete—or even comprehensive—collection of "methods" for various instruments or the voice, save those which are historically significant (e.g., Quantz, C. P. E. Bach).

GUIDELINES FOR BLANKET ORDER FOR MUSIC SCORES*

[General instructions:

A. Furnish works 1) which fit these guidelines, 2) which bear the current year's imprint, and 3) which emanate from any of the publishers on appended List I.
B. Furnish works by all major composers before 1900 and by those composers after 1900 whose names are on appended List II.]

1. The order is not to include: *Denkmäler, Gesamtausgaben* [see Addenda, 1971, below], Periodicals, or Monographic series. (These will be ordered separately.) It is not to include popular or salon music. It is not to include any arranged works; we want compositions only in the original medium. In a few media, as set out in detail below, we will accept scores for works where the accompaniment has been arranged for keyboard.

   We will accept the infrequent preprint of portions of *Denkmäler* or *Gesamtausgaben* (vide Mendelssohn recently), but we do not wish to be supplied automatically with separate scores and sets of parts for portions of *Denkmäler* and *Gesamtausgaben* (vide Telemann concerti).
2. We want, with the qualifications to follow this paragraph, works in these general media: [Precedence according to the Dickinson Classification for music]

   KEYBOARD (piano, clavichord, harpsichord)

   ORGAN

   INSTRUMENTAL MUSIC, solo and with accompaniment, for string, woodwind, brass, and percussion instruments

   CHAMBER MUSIC, whatever the ensemble

   ORCHESTRAL MUSIC (which is taken to include concerti with orchestra, small and chamber orchestra, and string orchestra)

   VOCAL SOLOS (with and without accompaniment)

VOCAL ENSEMBLES AND CHORUSES for mixed, men's, women's and youth choral groups, with and without accompaniment, both sacred and secular

OPERAS, BALLETS, and INCIDENTAL MUSIC

3. We want all facsimiles of composers Mss, as well as items in facsimile such as, e.g., the *Leisentrit* and *Babtsches Gesangbuch,* unless the publication is part of a series (e.g., *Documenta Musicologica*).
4. We want the largest score size available when there is a choice. We prefer folio, quarto, or octavo conductor's score to miniature always.
5. Send parts, when available, for all works for ensembles requiring up to and including ten instrumentalists for performance. Send scores only of works which require eleven or more.
6. Send two copies of works originally for 2-pianos, 4-hands. [However, if only playing scores are published for certain chamber ensembles instead of the normal parts (e.g., Berio *Sincronie*) send one copy (score only) unless otherwise instructed.]
7. Send graphic scores and scores for all avant-garde works even if medium is indeterminate.
8. Send both full and piano-vocal scores of operas when available, except when the underlaid text does NOT include the original language. Do not, therefore, send *Traviata* score with the text only in German.
9. Send no separate items of folk music, but do send collections of folk music when the collection has significant scholarly merit (e.g., Lilliencron, Thibaut, Jeanroy, etc.).
10. Do not send single issues of, e.g., songs, choruses, piano pieces, which are contained in and are extracted from albums or collections or larger works. Do not send, therefore: separate arias from operas, oratorios, cantatas; one song from a cycle; one prelude and fugue from a total of 24, as in the case of Shostakovich.
11. We will accept collections of songs with piano accompaniment for both high and low tessitura, provided one of the versions supplied is the original.
12. Avoid sending 8° copies of small choral works, especially those which are arrangements and those which are merely extracted from scholarly collections of a composer's works (e.g., extracts from the *Gesamtausgaben* of Lechner, Senfl, Beethoven, etc.).
13. In general, do not send issues which are part of a publisher's numbered series (e.g., Nagel-Archiv). DO send parts of a publisher's unnumbered series, but only after checking with the University to determine whether or not they are already on order.
14. If there is a choice of binding, always send the best available. We prefer cloth to wrappers, linen to cloth, half-leather to linen, etc.
15. Notify us about didactic material ("*Schulen*") before sending; we wish to select.
16. Notify us before sending works which come "off hire" and bear copyright or publication dates earlier than the year in which the works become commercially available for purchase.
17. To clarify line 5 [ORCHESTRAL MUSIC] of paragraph 2 and paragraph 8: We will accept scores for concerti, operas (and large choral works, too) where accompaniment is arranged for keyboard. We do not wish to accept these *in lieu of* the full score, if that is also available for purchase. We will accept both if both are available.

[Addenda, 1971:

18. We will enter standing orders for all new *Gesamtausgaben* as issued and attempt to secure (in the original or reprint) all of those listed in J. Coover's *Gesamtausgaben: A Checklist* 1970 [**63**, 73].
19. We will subscribe to all *Denkmäler,* regardless of language of editorial apparatus or country of origin, which provide coverage of periods, areas, schools or individuals of historical significance. We will also subscribe to all well-edited series of important works for performance, such as *Diletto Musicale, Hortus Musicus,* and *Corona.* The only series—of either type—to be excluded are those which are poorly edited, shabbily printed or which duplicate materials already owned in acceptable editions.
20. We will purchase all anthologies designed to illustrate by example the history of music (Schering and *Das Musikwerk,* for example) or any of its periods (Parrish, Gleason, Jander).]

List I: Firms whose Scores will be Supplied by Harrassowitz under Agreement of January, 1968

Ahn & Simrock
Alkor
Artia
Bärenreiter
Belaieff
Benjamin/Simrock
Billaudot
Boosey & Hawkes
Bosse
Bote & Bock
Bruzzichelli
CeBeDem
Choudens
Curci
Deutscher Verlag für Musik
Dilia Verlag (Prag)
Doblinger
Donemus
Durand
Editio Musica
Eschig
Eulenberg
Faber
Gerig
Hansen
Heinrichshofen
Ed. Henn
Heugel
Hinrichsen
Hofmeister
Hug & Co.
Leduc
Leuckart
Merseburger
Ed. Modern/Hans Wewerka
Moeck
Moeseler
Musik-verlag zum Pelikan
Musikwissenschaftlicher Verlag (Wien)
Nagel
Novello
Panton (Prag)
Peters
Polskie Wydawnictwo Muzyczne
Ricordi
Russischer Staatsverlag
Salabert
Schott
Sikorski
Statni Hudebni Vydavatelstvi (Prag)
Ed. Tonos
Ed. Musicales Transatlantiques
Verlag Neue Musik
Zanibon
Zenemükiado
Zerboni
Zimmermann

List II: Composers whose Works are Purchased automatically as Issued

Amy
Austin
Bacewicz
Baird, T.
Barber
Barraqué
Bartók
Beeson
Ben-Haim
Bentzon
Berg
Berio
Blitzstein
Bloch, E.
Blomdahl
Boulez
Britten
Bussotti
Cardew
Carter
Chanler
Copland
Crawford (Seeger)
Dahl
Dallapiccola
Davies
Evangelisti
Fine, I.
Foss
Gershwin
Ginastera
Górecki
Griffes
Hába
Hartmann
Haubenstock-Ramati
Hauer
Hiller
Hindemith
Honegger
Ives
Jelinek
Kagel
Kirchner
Kodály
Koechlin
Layton
Ligeti
Loeffler
Logothetis
Lutoslawski
Lutyens
Maderna
Martin
Martinu
Messiaen
Moevs
Nielsen
Nilsson
Partos
Penderecki
Piston
Poulenc
Pousseur
Prokofiev
Riisager
Riley
Rorem
Ruggles
Sauget
Schäffer
Schmitt
Schönberg
Serocki
Shostakovich
Still
Stockhausen
Stravinsky
Tippett
Varèse
Vaughan-Williams
Webern
Weill
Wolpe
Xenakis
Yun

List III: Composers whose Works are Evaluated individually as Issued

Amram	Egk	Kadosa	Schafer
Anhalt	Einem	Kelemen	Schoeck
Antheil	Elgar	Khachaturian	Schuller
Archer	Enesco	Klebe	Schwartz, E.
Babbitt	Erb	Kupferman	Sessions
Bacon	Etler	Kurka	Shapero
Badings	Falla	Laderman	Shapey
Bassett	Farberman	Lees	Siegmeister
Beckwith	Feldman	Lessard	Skalkottas
Berger, A.	Fine, V.	Malipiero	Somers
Bergsma	Finney	Martino	Stenhammer
Bernstein	Fortner	Mennin	Subotnick
Blacher	Francaix	Menotti	Talma
Blackwood	Fricker	Moore	Thompson
Bowles	Gaburo	Mortensen	Thomson
Brant	Ghedini	Nabokov	Toch
Brown, E.	Gideon	Nono	Tomasi
Cage	Goeb	Nowak	Trimble
Casella	Hanson	Oliveros	Villa-Lobos
Childs	Harris	Orff	Vlad
Colgrass	Harrison	Pentland	Walton
Cowell	Henze	Persichetti	Ward
Creston	Hoiby	Petrassi	Weber
Crumb	Hovaness	Pizzetti	Weinzweig
Davidovsky	Husa	Porter	Wellesz
Dello Joio	Ibert	Rawsthorne	Wuorinen
Diamond	Imbrie	Rochberg	Zimmermann
Donavan	Jolivet	Rosenberg	
Druckman	Kabalevsky	Roussel	

SELECTION POLICIES
MUSIC LIBRARY
STATE UNIVERSITY OF NEW YORK AT BUFFALO

Recordings

1. All anthologies of chant, of medieval, and of renaissance music will, as a rule, be purchased automatically as they appear.
2. Anthologies of performances by famous performers of the past (e.g., Rosenthal, Cortot, Nordica, Plancon) will be evaluated individually and an attempt will be made to secure only a representative sampling of their artistry.
3. We will buy all anthologies (including those in series) of contemporary works of composers in various countries (e.g., *New Music of Spain, Modern Czech Music, South African Music, Avant-Garde*).
4. We will attempt to purchase at least one version of all works by the master composers before 1900—Boccherini and Franck, as well as Bach, Beethoven, and Mozart—and several different performed versions of their more important works (e.g., Bach masses and passions, Beethoven symphonies and sonatas, Mozart concerti).

5. We will attempt to purchase all recordings available of works by those composers since 1900 included in List II appended to our policy for score selection (e.g., Berio, Rorem and Tippett as well as Bartók, Stravinsky and Webern) and several different performances of the more important large works (e.g., Stravinsky ballets, Hindemith orchestral works, Britten operas).
6. We will attempt to have at least one version of every complete opera recorded on either domestic or foreign labels, and for those in the standard repertoire—Mozart, Verdi and the like—as many versions as budget will permit.
7. We will purchase all recordings, foreign and domestic, of contemporary compositions involving tape or electronically produced sounds.
8. We will purchase all recordings of tribal musics (as contrasted with folk music—e.g., Joan Baez) leaving the purchase of folk music recordings to the public library.

   We will purchase representative samples of classical Eastern and Indian music (Chinese opera, South Indian ragas, etc.). The State University College will attempt to have a complete collection of this genre.
9. When we have built a basic historical collection of "rock" music from published lists now in hand, we will purchase additional items on request.
10. We will purchase jazz recordings of historical significance (e.g., reissues of early recordings of important jazz musicians) as they appear, and others on request.
11. We will purchase didactic performance discs (e.g., "James Pellerite Plays Flute," which includes many works in arrangements) only on request.
12. We will purchase some organ recordings based solely on the organ used in the performance with little regard for the programming.
13. We will purchase all didactic recordings having to do with ear training (the Rutgers series, e.g.) or orchestration (the Beckett set), temperament or performance practice.
14. Superior, "revelatory," or "transcendent" performances, in the concensus of reviewers, will be purchased automatically with little regard for the program involved or the degree of duplication of titles in the record collection.
15. With similar disregard for the works involved, we will purchase all recordings where the composer conducts or performs his own works.

NOTES

*Written by the Music Library, State University of New York at Buffalo and used by Harrassowitz—beginning in January, 1968—to supply music on approval to the Music Library. Information in square brackets [ ] is original here.

B. Binding

SELECTED BIBLIOGRAPHY

214. Lawton, Dorothy. "Binding problems in music: Methods and costs," *Notes,* 1st series, no. 5 (November, 1937), 24-28.

GENERAL LITERATURE ON LIBRARY BINDING, NONE OF WHICH DISCUSSES THE BINDING OF MUSIC (SCORES AND PARTS):

215. Feipel, L. N. and Browning, E. W. *Library binding manual,* prepared under the direction of the Joint Committee of the ALA and the Library Binding Institute. Chicago: ALA, 1951.

216. *The Bowker Annual of Library and Book Trade Information.* New York: R. R. Bowker, 1955.
Index under: "Binding, standards" and "Bookbinding–Standards"; title varies slightly.

217. Library Binding Institute, Boston. *Standard for library binding.* Boston: The Institute, 1958.

218. ——. *Standard for pre-library bound new books.* Boston: The Institute, 1958.

219. Schick, Frank L. "Bookbinding problems and promises: Steps toward a re-evaluation of standards," *Library Resources & Technical Services,* 4 (Spring, 1960), 131-138.
History of library binding in the United States, with an outline of a proposed study on performance standards for library binding. The study was subsequently made; see items below. Bibliographic notes.

220. American Library Association. Library Technology Project. *Development of performance standards for library binding, Phase I; report of the survey team, April 1961.* Library Technology Project publication no. 2. Chicago: ALA, 1961.

221. ——. *Development of performance standards for binding used in libraries, Phase II; report of a study conducted by the Library Technology Project.* Chicago: ALA, 1966.

222. Library Binding Institute, Boston. *Library binding handbook.* Boston: The Institute, 1963.
"Appendix one: Library Binding Institute standard, fourth edition, revised March 1963": pp. 34-49.
"Appendix two: Historical note": pp. 45-49.

Binding

by Gladys E. Chamberlain

Binding is a problem which has disturbed many a music librarian's sleep and wrecked many a budget. Rising costs in this field have given the general librarian some concern, but the average price of his new volumes is $3.00 to $5.00 with a considerable discount and he doesn't have to consider binding until it has circulated 25 or 30 times.

The music librarian, on the other hand, receives most of his material unbound, gets little or no discount, and must often wait several months and spend several additional dollars before he can give it to the public. A Puccini opera score, for example, costs $9.00 in paper, plus $3.75 for binding,[1] with a delay of two or three months before it is available for circulation, since bindery shipments are not made every week. There are further difficulties connected with chamber music, in which several parts must be kept together as a unit.

Those who are developing or expanding music departments may be interested in some suggestions for handling these problems,[2] especially since the subject is not mentioned in the recent ALA *Binding Manual.*

For heavy standard works that will receive constant use there is no substitute for a regular binding, remembering always that music, in order to lie flat on the rack, must be handsewn through the fold. The popular opera scores, Beethoven Piano Sonatas in two volumes, or collections of Schubert songs, deserve such treatment. For about five years the New York Public Library has bound strong new scores without taking them apart and re-sewing, and while a page occasionally becomes loose, the method is generally satisfactory and saves considerably time and effort, as well as reducing the cost by about $1.25 on each volume.

There are many inexpensive collections of songs and piano music which most libraries find useful, though the paper and the editing may leave something to be desired. These may be adequately protected by Plasti-Kleer Universal covers (Library Service, 59 East Alpine St., Newark 5, N.J.). Two plastic envelopes bound on the three closed sides with acetate fibre tape are slipped over the front and back covers of the music. If the cover of the volume is not stiff enough in itself, it may be strengthened by 2 cardboards slipped into the envelopes. Half-inch nylon, or banding, tape is used to attach the open inside edge to the cover of the music and extends ¼ inch on the body of the book, thus giving the cover a secure hold. The plastic envelopes are joined around the back by wide, colored adhesive tape (Book-Aid tape) which can be lettered. Where the volume has a wide back it is sometimes desirable to use a strip of plastic with tape on each edge to attach the two outside covers, leaving the lettering visible but protected.

For music with only one signature, pamphlet binders offer a convenient solution. They may be purchased from Remington Rand, Gaylord or Demco, though an adequate supply is seldom available and there is usually a delay in delivery.

Pamphlets are made of various materials. The photomount binders are least expensive and very convenient but absorb dirt and stain. For hard usage it is best to buy the pressboard binders which are about 50 per cent more expensive but have a hard surface. Demcoboard has an attractive surface, but like most pamphlets is provided with a back strip too dark for lettering with India ink. Since white ink is more difficult to handle, the library supply firms, which generally use dark green, brown, or black on the fold might well stock binders with bright red, light green or blue, or tan backs for ease in lettering. A spray of Plasti-Lac (Library Service, 59 E. Alpine St., Newark, N.J.) should prevent soiling or rubbing.

SOURCE: Reprinted from *Library Journal,* November 1, 1951. Published by R. R. Bowker (a Xerox Company).

Even without a protective coating India ink will be legible for a long time, especially if the lettering is concentrated at the two ends where it doesn't come under the hand of the person carrying the volume.

Chamber music offers the greatest problem, and libraries have worked out various types of portfolio or folder, or have used manila or red rope envelopes. Some libraries use the Gaylord pamphlet binder with one or two pockets for thin chamber music works. Those made of the lighter board will not stand heavy usage, but pressboard pamphlets, while more expensive, are worth the additional cost. A regular pamphlet may be provided with a pocket by pasting a strip across the outer edge of the inside back cover.

For a somewhat thicker set of parts, Smead music carriers (Smead Manufacturing Company, 309–311 Second Street, Hastings, Minnesota) may be used with considerable success, though they are not strong or thick enough for heavier material. They may be had in various styles and sizes. The two types most convenient for library use are large red rope folders, 13 × 10¼ and 14½ × 12 with a horizontal pocket on each side. The pocket has no gusset or re-inforcement and tends to tear at the outside edge if the content is too heavy, but for most violin and piano works and many trios and quartets a Smead binder serves very well.

Like the photomount pamphlet binder the Smead carrier too easily absorbs dirt and stain. The next step is sure to be a plastic cover with pocket, suitable for chamber music. Perhaps someone has already developed this. One firm has expressed an interest but is unwilling to experiment while a shortage of materials makes it impossible to handle orders.

And there is a drawback about plastic covers. Where the shelves are tight, plastic bound volumes are likely not only to bend but to stick to each other because of the tape edge. However, interfiled with other bindings they work out very well. And of course the fact that the original cover can be seen is a helpful and often attractive feature.

Chamber music parts of considerable weight and thickness require special treatment. Few libraries can now afford specially made, cloth-covered box portfolios with matching flexible bindings for the parts, or a piano part in boards with the string parts in a pocket on the inside or outside of the back cover.[3]

However, cloth-covered standard size portfolios can be made at a more reasonable rate if ordered in quantity. Elizabeth Ohr of the Indianapolis Public Library showed an attractive small portfolio some years ago, and other libraries have worked out similar but varying styles with local binders. Miss Ohr reports that the National Library Binding Company of Indiana (546 South Meridian Street, Indianapolis 25), will make portfolios of any size, even those large enough to hold a set of orchestral parts. The price, of course varies, but the average is about $2.00. This particular firm is willing to sell assorted sizes. However, since some libraries do their own binding and others are obliged to employ local firms, a discussion of various possibilities may be helpful.

A practical style is of cloth-covered board with an expanding vertical gusset pocket of lighter material on the right side covered completely by the left flap when closed. A one-half or three-quarter-inch spine at the hinge is adequate for lettering. A more capacious style, with an inch and a half spine or a curved back and a more extended pocket, will serve for collections of Beethoven Quartets, Haydn Trios, or Mozart violin and piano sonatas. The gusset should not be so stiff as to form a wedge that will damage the parts in case the pocket is not full. Heavy flaps may be used instead of a pocket. They adjust easily to the size of the contents, but do not hold up so well. Tying with tapes is generally unnecessary and inconvenient.

Let me offer a warning about material. One binder unexpectedly provided an excellent, strong, oily, pebbly material on which it was practically impossible to do satisfactory lettering either by pen or stylus. The lining paper was also oily, so that pocket and dating slips fell off at once and it was necessary to sandpaper the spot where they were to be pasted. One should ask the binder to use uncoated, unembossed material. Plasti-Lac sprayed over the entire spine will protect both the lettering and the cloth.

Incidentally, a square edged back is easier to letter and looks better on the shelf, but the sharp edges show greatest wear. A rounding back adjusts itself more readily to the size of the contents and has no edges to fray.

Having worked out the portfolio best suited to its needs a large library may want to keep two widths and two heights on hand, but smaller collections will probably have to try out one size at a time or join with a neighboring institution in purchasing. Eventually it may be possible to order in small quantities.

Chamber music parts can usually be adequately protected by a simple manila folder. A piano part may need extra re-inforcement or a Plasti-Kleer cover. In some cases (Beethoven or Mozart Violin and Piano Sonatas) it may even be wise to have the parts bound in cloth, but they are still best circulated in a portfolio if the library can afford it, since the cover helps to keep the matching parts together.

A word should be said about the time involved in preparing music. Each of the operations mentioned above involves a great deal of staff time. If there is a library bindery and if there is someone in charge who understands the needs of music and will make sure that violin and piano parts are not carefully bound up in one back, the music librarian may have no problem. If, however, the music section is given the job of preparing its own material under the direction of the special librarian, the head of the library should take this into consideration in assigning the staff, for the number of hours consumed by such necessary but often misunderstood or unconsidered operations is very large, and extra personnel must be provided.

NOTES

[1] Today's actual figures may vary, but Miss Chamberlain's proportions remain accurate.–*Editor.*

[2] See also the fine discussion by Catharine Miller in the MLA *Manual,* pp. 58–63.–*Editor.*

[3] For an extended discussion of the handling of chamber music parts see Harry Kownatsky, "Performance parts and sheet music," in the MLA *Manual,* pp. 99–106.–*Editor.*

V

PHONOGRAPH RECORDS, TAPES, ETC., WITHIN THE MUSIC LIBRARY

SELECTED BIBLIOGRAPHY

There is probably more literature on the selection, processing, and circulation of records in libraries than any other phase of music librarianship. The bulk of it, however, is too paraochial to cite here; the following articles or books were selected for their historical value, as representative, and for their currency. It is essential that the reader use this *Selected Bibliography* in conjunction with that in the MLA *Manual,* pp. 75, 96–98, on which it builds.

GENERAL DISCUSSIONS OF RECORDS IN LIBRARIES:

223. Chamberlain, Gladys. "Phonograph records in public libraries," *Music Journal,* 4 (May–June, 1946), 31, 34–35.

Recognition of a record listening facility as a viable public library service.

224. Davis, Chester K. "Record collections, 1960; *Library Journal's* survey of fact and opinion," *Library Journal,* 85 (October 1, 1960), 3375-3380.

Report of an *LJ* survey of ca. 500 libraries of various types and sizes with record collections.

225. Sragow, Jeannette LaPorte. "Organization of the recordings collection of a medium-sized county public library system." M.S.L.S. thesis, Catholic University of America, 1962. "Bibliography": *ll.* 72–77.

226. Hanna, E. F. "First steps toward a record collection," *Illinois Libraries,* 44 (February, 1962), 134–150.

Precedes the MLA *Manual* article; includes a good bibliography.

227. Pearson, Mary D. *Recordings in the public library.* Chicago: American Library Association, 1963. "Bibliography": pp. 148-149.

228. Stevenson, Gordon. "Don't ignore the gifted listener," *Library Journal,* 88 (February 1, 1963), 519–522.

229. Stevenson, Gordon, ed. "[Special issue on recordings in libraries]" *Library Journal,* 88 (May 1, 1963), 1809–1840.

Contents:

Lang, Paul Henry. "The LP and the well-appointed library," 1809–1812.
Myers, Kurtz. "The record review," 1813–1817.
Stevenson, Gordon. "The practical record selector . . . ," 1819–1822; reprinted below, pp. 270–273.
Miller, Philip L. "Buried treasures," 1823–1825.
Hall, David. "CRI: A sonic showcase for the American composer," 1826–1829.
Wedgeworth, Robert. "Jazz," 1830–1832.
Cushman, Jerome. "Folk music in the library," 1833–1834.
Silber, Irwin. "A basic library of U.S. folk music," 1835–1838.
Yurchenco, Henrietta. "Folk music around the world: A basic library collection," 1838–1840.

230. Stevenson, Gordon, ed. "[Recordings]" *Library Journal,* 88 (October 15, 1963), 3783-3804.

231. *Suggestions for organizing and administering a disc record library.* North Chicago: Jack C. Coffey Co., 710 17th St., 1967.

232. March, Ivan. *Running a record library.* Blackpool, Lancs.: Long Playing Records Library, 1965.

Although philosophically sound, it reflects the British situation. It may be less *au courant* than the Currall 2nd edition, 1970, below.

233. International Association of Music Libraries. United Kingdom Branch. *Phonograph record libraries; their organisation and practice.* Edited by Henry F. J. Currall. With a preface by A. Hyatt King. 2nd edition. Hamden, Conn.: Archon Books, 1970.

234. Langridge, Derek Wilton. *Your jazz collection.* London: Bingley, 1970.

235. Leavitt, Donald L. "Some practices and problems in American record libraries," *Fontes artis musicae,* 18 (1971/1-2), 22-27.

SPECIALIZED COLLECTIONS AND ARCHIVES OF RECORDS IN LIBRARIES:

236. Spivacke, Harold. "The Archive of American Folk Song in the Library of Congress in its relationship in the folk-song collector," *Southern Folklore Quarterly,* 2 (March, 1938), 31-35.

The Archive's services to folklorists to the end of achieving "a great centralized collection of American folk songs" (Carl Engel).

237. ——. "The Archive of American Folk Song in the Library of Congress." In Music Teachers' National Association *Studies in musical education, history and aesthetics,* pp. 123-127. Hartford: 1941.

238. "Tape-recording of Archive of Folk Song completed," *LC Information Bulletin,* 28 (October 16, 1969), 552-553.

239. Moore, Jerrold N. "The purpose and scope of the Historical Sound Recordings Program," *Yale University Library Gazette,* 38 (January, 1964), 92-110.

Description of a sound archive.

240. Miller, Philip L. "Archives of Recorded Sound; Lincoln Center will soon welcome the Rodgers and Hammerstein Archives of Recorded Sound—newest addition to a proliferating body of invaluable public record collections," *High Fidelity/Musical America,* 15 (June, 1965), 38-41, 99.

241. Allen, R. B. "New Orleans Jazz Archive at Tulane," *Wilson Library Bulletin,* 40 (March, 1966), 619-623.

The Archive includes records, sheet music, memorabilia, photographs and miscellany of Nick LaRocca's band.

* * * * *

242. Colby, Edward E. "Sound recordings in the music library, with special reference to record archives," *Library Trends,* 8 (April, 1960), 556-565.

243. Spivacke, Harold. "A national archives of sound recordings?" *Library Journal,* 88 (October 15, 1963), 3783-3788.

244. Saul, Patrick. "A documentation policy for a national sound archive," *Fontes artis musicae,* 12 (1965/2-3), 152-155.

245. Leavitt, Donald L. "Association for Recorded Sound Collections [Conference, 1968, Los Angeles]" *LC Information Bulletin,* 27 (December 5, 1968), 734-736.

The common plight of serious record collectors and archivists has led to the formation of the Association for Recorded Sound Collections, a group devoted "to the exchange and dissemination of information on all aspects of the gathering and preservation of recorded sound." To date, ARSC has addressed itself to the recommendation of standards for the manufacture of discs and tapes for long-term preservation and service, record reviewing criteria, discographic format and content, the application of data processing to recorded sound collections, the technology of restoring sound on early recordings, and the legal and "fair use" concepts of such great concern to record archivists.

Leavitt's report of the Los Angeles conference is cited here because it summarizes a discussion of out-of-print records, legal ownership of recorded sound, and "fair use." See the next item.

246. "Ownership and copyright of sound recordings; transcript of panel discussion, UCLA ARSC Conference—November 22, 1968," *ARSC Journal* (Summer, 1969), 9-23.

Points out that in Justice Holmes' opinion, which has been perpetuated in the current copyright law—passed in 1909—sound produced by records is not copyrighted or protected.

247. Miller, Philip L. "Association for Recorded Sound Collections," *Fontes artis musicae,* 16 (1969/3), 146-147.

248. *ARSC Journal,* 1970– New York: Association for Recorded Sound Collections, Rodgers and Hammerstein Archives of Recorded Sound, 111 Amsterdam Ave., 1970–

Irregularly issued. David Hall, editor.

249. Leavitt, Donald L. "International Association of Sound Archives," *ARSC Journal,* 2 (Spring/Summer, 1970), unpaged.

DISCOGRAPHY, INCLUDING SOME EXAMPLES OF SPECIALIZED ONES:

250. Clough, Francis F. and Cuming, G. J. *The world's encyclopedia of recorded music.* 3 vols., 1952–1957. Reprint (3 vols.) Westport, Conn.: Greenwood Press, 1970.

See annotation in Duckles 2nd ed., 1256.

251. ——. "Problems of an international gramophone record catalogue; with an introduction and conclusion by V. Britten." In International Congress of Libraries and Documentation Centres. [*Conference, 1955, Brussels*] v. 2. Also in *Fontes artis musicae,* 3 (1956/1), 95–108.

A discussion of the difficulties encounted in compiling WERM. Valuable to record librarians for its description of the record industry's practices of re-issuing the same recorded information with a new number, or on a new label; issuing an anthology or recital by artist X without a list of contents, etc.

252. Waters, Edward N. "Notes for *Notes:* Letter from Messrs. Clough and Cuming announcing suspension of work on any further volumes of *The World's Encyclopedia of Recorded Music,*" *Notes,* 22 (Fall, 1965), 695–696.

253. Clough, F. F. and Cuming, G. J. "Phonographic periodicals; a survey of some issued outside the United States," *Notes,* 15 (September, 1958), 537–558.

A "brief assessment of the scope and utility" of record journals published outside the US, excluding Eastern Europe. Most entries include publication information and subscription rates to US residents.

254. The Sunday Times, London. *A basic record library,* by Desmond Shawe-Taylor, Iain Lang, *et al.* London: 1959.

255. Douglas, John R. "The composer and his music on record; a checklist for librarians who feel that their collections should preserve or have available for listening, examples of the composer conducting or playing his own works," *Library Journal,* 92 (March 15, 1967), 1117–1121. With discography.

256. Lissner, J. "Pop / folk / jazz: Guideposts to a basic record library; with discography," *Library Journal,* 94 (January 15, 1969), 158–161.

257. Louisiana. State Library, Baton Rouge. *Dimensions in listening; recordings spoken and musical.* Baton Rouge: Louisiana State Library, 1970.

Discography of recordings in the Louisiana State Library which are available to all state residents by mail or their local branch library. Includes jazz, spoken, and language records as well as 'classical' type records.

258. Bauer, Roberto. *The new catalogue of historical records, 1898–1908/09.* 2nd edition, 1947. Reprint. London: Sidgwick & Jackson, 1970.

Arranged by performer, then year of the recording. Not indexed by composer or composition title.

259. Roach, H. *Spoken records.* 3rd ed. Metuchen, N.J.: Scarecrow, 1970.

Annotated bibliography, short essays on spoken recordings, historical background essays. For those who must handle, including acquisition, spoken records. Probably the best tool available.

CATALOGUING AND CLASSIFICATION:

260. Lyman, Ethel Louise. "Arrangement and care of phonograph records," *Library Journal,* 62 (1937), 150–154.

Includes the Smith College record classification scheme.

261. Spivacke, Harold. "The cataloging of folk-song records," *Notes,* 1st series, no. 5 (November, 1937), 9–16.

262. U.S. Library of Congress. Descriptive cataloging division. *Rules for descriptive cataloging in the Library of Congress; phonorecords.* Prelim. ed. Washington, D.C.: 1952.

263. Morsch, Lucile M. "Printed cards for phonorecords: cataloging," *Notes,* 10 (March, 1953), 197–198.

The beginning of LC cards for records.

264. Angell, Richard S. "Printed cards for phonorecords: Subject headings," *Notes,* 10 (March, 1953), 198–200.

More on the beginning of LC cards for records.

265. U.S. Library of Congress. Descriptive Cataloging Division. *Rules for descriptive cataloging in the Library of Congress; phonorecords.* 2nd prelim. ed. Washington, D.C.: 1964.

266. Drake, H. "Cataloging recordings," *Illinois Libraries,* 46 (February, 1964), 145–152.

How to, with both a Dewey classification for records and many sample catalogue cards reproduced.

267. Scholz, Dell DuBose. *A manual for the cataloging of recordings in public libraries.* Rev. ed. Baton Rouge, Louisiana: Louisiana State Library, 1964.

Simplified, LC-oriented practice.

268. Carey, John T. "Visible index method of cataloging phonorecords," *Library Resources & Technical Services,* 13 (Fall, 1969), 502–510.

269. Phillips, Don. "Expandable classification scheme for phonorecord libraries," *Library Resources & Technical Services,* 13 (Fall, 1969), 511–515.

270. DeLerma, Dominique-René. "Philosophy and practice of phonorecord classification at Indiana University," *Library Resources & Technical Services,* 13 (Winter, 1969), 86–92.

271. Sunder, Mary Jane. "Organization of recorded sound," *Library Resources & Technical Services,* 13 (Winter, 1969), 93–98.

272. Saheb-Ettaba, Caroline and McFarland, Roger B. *ANSCR; the alpha-numeric system for classification of recordings.* Williamsport, Pa.: Bro-Dart Publ. Co., 1969.

MANUALS FOR RECORD LIBRARY PERSONNEL:

273. California. University. Library. *Manual for the phonorecord librarian.* Berkeley: 1953. "Sample catalog cards illustrating the cataloging of phonorecords in the University of California Libraries": 35p. at end.

Exceptionally complete. Based on LC practices and thoroughly oriented to the University of California at Berkeley, it is an excellent example of the contents and organization of an operational manual. Especially valuable is the section on analytical entries (pp. 20–24) which illustrates an essential alternative to the Anglo-American rules no. 250 and 251.

274. ——. *Duties of the clerk assigned to phonorecord cataloger.* Berkeley: 1953. "Glossary": pp. 41–50 [of terms essential to the clerk's duties]

Companion to **273**. Includes mechanical information. Contents: I. Introduction–II. Qualifications.–III. Description of work–IV. Typing rules.–Appendices.

275. Gross, Jean. "A selected, annotated bibliography for the phonorecord librarian of book, pamphlet and periodical literature in the English language published since 1955." M.S.L.S. thesis, Catholic University of America, 1964.

Fairly comprehensive bibliography, limited by its dates. Valuable for the novice record librarian beginning to learn the literature.

EQUIPMENT: See especially the periodicals and their appropriate departments cited on p. 97 of the MLA *Manual* to keep current with developments in electronic equipment.

276. Kubiak, Leonard P. "Cassette tape recorders–A new breed," *Electronics World,* 81 (June, 1969), 23–27.

277. Ehle, Robert C. "Audio installations in libraries," *Music Journal,* 28 (January, 1970), 42, 62–64.

278. "Cassette tape recorders for libraries," *Library Technology Reports* (November, 1970), 2p.

List of cassette tape recorders advertised as suitable for institutional use and currently under performance tests by the LTP.

279. "The proper care and feeding of phonograph records," *Music Educators Journal,* 57 (January, 1971), 76–77.

Adapted from *Professional methods for record care and use* by Cecil E. Watts, Ltd. New Hyde Park, New York: Elpa Marketing Industries, Inc., 196_ .

COPYRIGHT AND RECORD LIBRARIES:

280. "Record archives and the law," *High Fidelity/Musical America,* 15 (June, 1965), 33.
281. "Recorded sound archives facing legal risks," *Library Journal,* 94 (December 15, 1969), 4480.
282. Krasilovsky, M. William. "Problems in the relationships between the record industry and librarians of recorded sound," *Performing Arts Review,* I, no. 4 (1970), 559-583.
    Discussion of copyright provisions, including "fair use," "single copy privilege," "limited dubbing privileges under copyright law revisions," "central clearing house concept," and "miscellaneous alternatives to seeking revision of copyright statute."

The Preservation and Reference Services of Sound Recordings in a Research Library

by Harold Spivacke

The large research collection of sound recordings is a relatively new phenomenon in the library world, one which developed during the past two or three decades. These collections, some of them numbering in the tens or even hundreds of thousands, were assembled under different circumstances and for a variety of purposes. Some of them form part of existing national libraries, some are accumulations of large broadcasting organisations, others are in large university libraries, and still others are constituted as independent institutions. It seems obvious that these libraries whose origins and functions vary so considerably will each have problems which are peculiar to themselves. But they also have certain basic problems which are common to all and it is because of this fact that I shall use the terms 'research' or 'reference' library indiscriminately to apply to all these categories of libraries.

There seems to be little uniformity in the type or extent of reference service which these large libraries can offer to the scholar. For the most part, this service is quite limited when compared with the reference services offered by research libraries with their books and manuscripts. This is due in part to the rapidity with which these collections of sound recordings were acquired and in part to the special purposes for which they were prepared. The collection in a broadcasting organisation will usually consist of recordings obtained to be used in programmes or of recordings of programmes already transmitted. The large national library will in the interests of preservation occasionally accept large accumulations of recordings prepared by other government agencies although wholly unprepared to organise or service them. Other collections will grow as the result of the activities of the ethnomusicologists, the anthropologists or the linguistics experts. But whatever the history or original purpose of these collections of sound recordings they exist and our constituency is rightfully demanding that we make them more readily available for study.

The problems which I propose to discuss are in the areas of acquisition, preservation and reference services. Not all the problems related to these areas can be covered in this paper but only those will be treated which seem most pressing at present—at least to some of us in the USA. They are based on difficulties specifically related to the research libraries although, to a lesser extent, they are also applicable to the activities of the public circulating libraries as well as the record collections in universities and other educational institutions. They are problems which must be solved by all of us about to embark on a programme involving a more extensive reference service in the field of sound recordings.

In a discussion of sound recordings, it is usually necessary to separate the published pressed discs from the various forms of instantaneous recordings. This is analogous to the separation of books from manuscripts in discussion of visual, i.e. readable materials. Although the analogy may not be wholly exact, it is close enough to utilise it for our analysis. The handling of the commercially issued discs, whether they be made of shellac, vinylite or other compounds, is usually quite different from the handling of instantaneous recordings whether they be in the form of acetate discs or magnetic wire or tape. In each section of this article, we shall discuss the problems as they relate to the pressed disc and then examine the different treatment required for the instantaneous recording.

SOURCE: Reprinted from Dr. Harold Spivacke, "The preservation and reference services of sound recordings in a research library." In *Music, libraries and instruments,* Hinrichsen's Eleventh Music Book, pp. 99–110 (London: Hinrichsen Edition, 1961), by permission of C. F. Peters Corporation.

I turn first to the subject of acquisition because it seems most logical in this sequence, but not because it is the most burning issue before us today. Some of us already have more records than we know what to do with but we keep adding to them. The urge to acquire is in the librarian's blood since he knows that if he fails to store and preserve what is immediately available he will add to the difficulties of his successors in office. In the field of sound recordings the need to acquire current publications is indeed urgent for they quickly go out of print and soon become hard to obtain. This argument for prompt action is even more cogent in the case of the material usually preserved on acetate discs or magnetic tapes.

The question of who is to have the responsibility for preserving the sound recordings will have to be solved differently in various parts of the world. Those countries which now enjoy a system of *dépôt légal* will have settled this question. In others such as the USA, this is still an open question and it is conceivable that more than one department of the government will be designated as an official repository. At any rate I am certain that we all agree on the necessity for official recognition of the responsibility in each country for the preservation of the domestic products at least and the designation of one or more institutions as the repositories for these national collections.

Along with the responsibility for the establishment of national collections of sound recordings, there exists the need for the inclusion of sound recordings in the national bibliographies. There is no need for me to belabour the point but the value of such national bibliographies is obvious. A complete list of all the recordings issued in a country would have great value both for domestic and international purposes. The existence of national bibliographies would not satisfy all the requirements of bibliographical apparatus nor could they take the place of such splendid works as the *World Encyclopaedia* of Messrs Clough and Cuming,[1] but the basic need for such national bibliographies remains. They would contain the necessary raw materials from which special bibliographies could be compiled and from which information for purchase might be obtained.

The establishment of a national collection will in itself provide a sizeable research collection in those countries where there is a large and productive phonograph industry. But few of us will be satisfied with this for long. What we desire is the same type of universal collection of recordings as the universal collections of books and scores available to us in great libraries throughout the world. It is in his efforts to achieve this goal by importing records from other countries that the record librarian begins to experience certain peculiar difficulties.

One of the dilemmas which a librarian faces is that caused by the reissue of the same recording in several countries at different times. With the limited resources at his disposal, the record librarian will naturally wish to avoid the purchase of unwanted duplicates. Yet he may import a recording from abroad only to find the same recording reissued by a domestic company a year later—a recording which he will receive without cost or at least more inexpensively. The manufacturers themselves are not always in a position to foretell their own decisions to reissue foreign recordings because this will depend on supply and demand as well as general market conditions. On the other hand, a delay in purchase of even a few years may result in a situation in which the library can no longer obtain the record because records are not kept in print for very long. This dilemma seems to emphasise the necessity for national collections so that at least one library in the world will preserve a specific work should others fail to acquire it.

Still another obstacle which is more annoying is one that can be loosely termed embargos. These prevent the movement of recordings from one country to another and have their basis either in legal restrictions or in commercial practices. Whatever the cause, the librarian will find it impossible under certain circumstances to import a recording from another country. Some of these restrictions are listed in the UNESCO publication *Trade Barriers to Knowledge.* The situation is actually even worse than recounted in that book. The commercial practices which result in embargos usually occur when a manufacturer in one country acquires the rights to all the issues of a foreign concern and then refuses to allow the importation of these recordings lest it hurt the possibility of future sale of his re-issues.

Another form of restriction is that which prevents the purchase of a single record which is not regularly offered for sale in the country of the purchaser. Record manufacturers frequently sign exclusive agreements with agents abroad for the sale of their releases. These agreements, however, usually specify a minimum number of records, two hundred or so, for a single order. A librarian who orders one copy of the record from the manufacturer in the country of origin will be referred to the agent in his country who in turn may well refuse to place a minimum order for two hundred just to satisfy only one assured purchaser.

This situation which hinders the free flow of records from country to country may be alleviated in the years to come if we bring pressure as a group. We can assuredly count on the aid of UNESCO in these efforts. In the meantime, a partial solution to the problem may be found in a network of international exchanges since a librarian can purchase domestically records wanted by his colleagues abroad. This implies the availability of funds to both parties involved in the exchange as well as the existence of sufficient staff to carry on the necessary correspondence and arrange for the shipments. This is admittedly a cumbersome and expensive method of acquiring current publications but, for the time being, it may on occasion prove to be the only method at our disposal by which we can acquire foreign recordings.

In this discussion on the acquisition of recordings, I have emphasized those problems which have international implications. There are, of course, countless others of a more domestic nature but these problems will have to be solved differently in each country. This is especially true in the case of instantaneous recordings—acetate discs and magnetic tapes. The existing programme of preserving the auditory aspects of day to day events, musical or otherwise, varies enormously from country to country. In some countries where radio and television broadcasting is centralised, there have developed some splendidly organised collections of auditory and visual documentation. In others, such as the USA, these efforts have been fortuitous and haphazard. I venture to state that future historians will have to rely extensively on the tapes of broadcasts made by the very many private individuals who collect this type of recording as a hobby. As a result of this situation, we in the United States are hardly in a position to discuss international exchange of instantaneous recordings except in a few areas where small segments of our collections are in better shape. These conditions may not prevail elsewhere and there may well exist a fertile field for international exchange between many countries of the world. Let us hope that this situation will soon become universal and that we shall all be able to inaugurate such exchanges in the not too distant future.

Let us turn now to the problem of the preservation of the collections which we have already acquired. Libraries have stored records for decades but for the most part have relied on makeshift devices limited by the available shelving facilities. For some reason, there was little if any scientific investigation to justify the practices common to the profession or to indicate how the facilities for storage could be improved. With this in mind the Library of Congress approached the Rockefeller Foundation two years ago and obtained a grant of $65,000 to study the preservation of sound recordings. This amount was by no means sufficient to cover every type of sound recording and accordingly only certain discs and tapes were studied. Furthermore the problem of preservation was limited entirely to shelf storage and not to the problems involved in the use of the recording. The actual experimentation was carried out by the Southwest Research Institute in San Antonio, Texas, and the results are now in the press[2] and should be available for general distribution shortly.

In general, the conclusions arrived at by the staff of the Southwest Research Institute seem to indicate that shellac and vinylite discs can be stored for a long time provided that certain conditions regarding their environment are met. The environment recommended, however, will not be easy to achieve because it is based on an air-conditioned atmosphere of approximately 70 degrees Fahrenheit and 50 per cent relative humidity maintained steadily with little variation. We all hope to live to see the day when all libraries will be air-conditioned if only for the benefit of the librarians but it will be a long time before most of the libraries of the world have achieved this result. I might mention at this point that for some types of recordings even lower temperatures seem to be advisable but these would not be acceptable to the people working in the area so that the conditions recommended are compromises. The necessity for this is based on certain observations noted by the experimenters. For example, thermal cycling, that is wide variations in temperature, are detrimental to vinylite recordings and will cause them to warp. This same thermal cycling within certain limits however does not seem to be as detrimental to a good genuine shellac disc, but, as we all know, the composition of the so-called shellac discs varied enormously and some of them contained no shellac at all. For this reason, the steady temperature of about 70 degrees Fahrenheit is highly desirable. Both types of recordings have poor heat resistance as we all know from sad experience and excessive heat alone will produce warping whether it is maintained steadily or intermittently.

The recommended 50 per cent relative humidity is equally important. The shellac record reacts to excessive moisture by chemical degradation resulting in serious dimensional changes. The vinylite disc seems to be unaffected by excess moisture, but indirectly may still be injured by it. The reason for this is the effects of fungi. Some types of shellac discs depending on their formation are susceptible to fungal growth. The vinylite record, on the other hand, is not susceptible to fungal growth, but is not resistant to etching. This etching is the result of the secretions of the fungi which grow on the paper containers.

The fact that all types of discs were subject to damage from abrasion was of course generally known. The fact that the discs were equally subject to something called 'imprint' was not so generally known. For example, in storing its recordings in the past, the Library of Congress, as did many other agencies, frequently made use of the corrugated boards often used for fillers in packaging discs. It was found that the corrugations had imprinted themselves on the discs although the surface of the cardboard seemed smooth. In some instances this was found to be due to the fungi which developed along the lines of these corrugations—perhaps nourished by the glue, but it was also found without fungi. For these and other obvious reasons, the authors of this report have laid great stress on a new recommended means of packaging the discs for storage. The specially designed package is to be constructed of a laminate of polyethylene, paperboard, aluminium foil, and polyethylene which would be closed airtight with a pressure-sensitive tape. They hope that such a specially designed package will have the following advantages: since it is itself protected from the agents of degradation, it will not warp, grow fungi, or otherwise aid in disc degradation; it will provide a gas and vapour barrier between the disc and the ambient stack atmosphere; it will present a smooth surface to the disc and will permit disc insertion and withdrawal without sliding contact between disc and package; it will be stiff and have some structural strength to help vinyl and shellac discs resist warping, so that it will not itself deform so as to cause surface damage to disc by high contact stresses. Such a package might be relatively expensive. In the USA the estimated cost would be between 15 and 20 cents each.

It is interesting to note that the British Institute of Recorded Sound independently developed a similar envelope for its own use. Although not as elaborate as the one recommended by the researchers of the Southwest Research Institute, it can be produced much more cheaply and will achieve some if not all of the purposes for which the more elaborate product has been designed.

The SWRI also recommends that all discs be stored absolutely vertical at a 90 degree angle. This is important to note because certain manufacturers have recently stated publicly that records could be stored satisfactorily either vertically or horizontally. The horizontal attitude was found to be quite unsatisfactory if the records were to be preserved for any length of time. The authors recommend a type of slotted shelving which they believe can be manufactured reasonably and which would hold the recordings at a 90 degree angle.

Although scientific caution prevented the authors Messrs Picket, Lemcoe and their colleagues from making any specific prophecies, one gathers on reading this report that the vinylite and shellac disc may well have a relatively long life expectancy. It is my opinion that under ideal circumstances they might even be preserved for as long as a century or two. It will depend, of course, to a great extent on the quality of the materials used in the discs and the care with which they have been manufactured. But then we have the same problems with printed books and newspapers which frequently disintegrate before our eyes because of the inferior composition of the paper. On the whole it seems safe to say that the reference library can look forward with cautious equanimity to the long-term preservation of the published products—that is the pressed recordings—provided they are stored properly.

If the results of the experiments were such as to cause the reference librarian to be optimistic about the future of his collection of pressings, it is with regret that I must report that this project indicated just the opposite outlook for the instantaneous recordings. This form of recording is, of course, common to all reference libraries and constitutes more than half the collections in many of them. The Library of Congress must have about 200,000 acetate discs so the problem is indeed acute and we have already noticed serious deterioration in some of our recordings. In some cases the coating actually had flaked off the base thereby ruining the recording, whereas in other cases there was considerable discoloration, which was found to be the result of fungal growth. The coatings used on so-called acetate discs can in themselves nourish fungus, but the fungus can and frequently does start in the paper container.

The acetate recording seems to be resistant to nothing—heat, moisture, fungus, abrasion or atmospheric contaminants. In fact, the scientists doing the research have little faith in the possibility of preserving acetate recordings even under ideal conditions. Because of the loss of plasticiser, these recordings will disintegrate on the shelf and the end will come with what they call 'catastrophic suddenness.' In other words, you can look at an acetate record and believe that it is in fair shape only to find shortly thereafter that the whole coating has flaked off with little or no warning. Among the projects recommended for future study growing out of this experiment is one involving the use of spectrometry whereby it is hoped the librarian, by subjecting sample recordings to periodic tests, will be able to have some idea of the probable life expectancy of his acetate recordings.

Another disappointment was the report that not too much may be expected from the present day tapes although here, at least, there is a ray of hope. We had thought that eventually we should have to convert all acetate discs to magnetic tape, just as there is a programme throughout the world to convert old newspapers to microfilm. Unfortunately the analogy between the microfilming programmes and the re-recording on magnetic tape is not quite sound. We were shocked to hear from the research staff that certain manufacturers stated that they could make a tape which could last longer if there was a market for it. On this point, I believe, the librarians of the world should get together and convince the manufacturers that there is indeed a market for it and a better product should be made in the immediate future! A manufacturer of one of the best products produced in the USA remarked that he did not think his tape could be properly preserved for more than fifteen years. On the basis of experience, however, we believe this to be a very pessimistic estimate since we have tapes that are over ten years old which seem to be lasting quite well. Furthermore, the improvement of magnetic tapes is occurring so rapidly and new products are coming on the market so quickly that we have every reason to believe that a good tape with a long life expectancy will be available in the near future.

As to the specific recommendations of the project, it was found that the same environmental conditions are recommended for tape as for discs —that is, air-conditioning of approximately 70 degrees Fahrenheit and 50 per cent relative humidity. A new type of package made of the same laminated material is also recommended for tape and it is also recommended that the tapes be stored vertically and wound on metal reels. There are, of course, other factors peculiar to magnetic tape which affect their longevity. For one thing the tension must not be too great and a winding tension for $1\frac{1}{2}$ mil. tape should be a constant torque of from 3 to 5 ounces at the hub of a 10-inch reel. It is very important that the tape be evenly wound and periodic rewinding is recommended. It is also recommended that there be at the end of each tape a blank portion with a burst of sound so that print-through can be measured, although the team undertaking this research did not feel that print-through as such was an insoluble problem.

The recommendations coming out of this project are of course logical in themselves but some of them may prove to be impractical for some libraries. Obviously, the best way to preserve a large collection of instantaneous recordings would be to press them on long-playing vinylite discs. With a very large collection, however, the number of recordings that can be treated in this expensive fashion will be minimal. Furthermore, even the suggestion to re-wind tapes at regular intervals already seems impossible for the Library of Congress with its relatively small collection of tapes. As it grows—and it is growing fast—the possibility of rewinding becomes more remote. On the other hand, even though it will be costly in manpower, we must all recognise that a programme of periodic inspection is more essential for the recorded collection than for books or manuscripts. We can usually assume that the book or manuscript left undisturbed in a decent environment is being well preserved. The deterioration of recordings while being stored, however, continues whether or not the record is being used and therefore periodic checks are essential. Records showing dangerous signs of deterioration will have to be re-copied quickly and this will have to be done again and again until the scientists and technologists give us a more efficient method of recording sound permanently.

In approaching the reference services that a research library of sound recordings might be expected to perform, we are forced to base our discussion in part on conjecture. There is relatively little reference service of recordings available in the world today, particularly when compared with the reference services offered by libraries of books and manuscripts. There is a growing demand for such service, however, and we must soon offer a complete reference service with our collections of sound recordings. The librari. n about to embark on such a programme is faced with many problems, one in particular. The librarian is torn between his obligation to serve his constituency and his desire to preserve his collection. We have in the sound recording an object that frequently carries within itself the seed of its own destruction. The visual act of reading a book does not in itself injure the book. On the other hand, each playing of a sound recording causes more or less deterioration of the recording itself.

The project on the preservation of recordings already described did not investigate the wear and tear on recordings resulting from their use. To my knowledge there has been no systematic study of this important problem and I hope that it can be undertaken in the not too distant future. On the other hand, what makes such a study so difficult is the rapid evolution of new types of recordings. Still, even without such a systematically organised study, we do have a body of knowledge and experience with sound recordings which enables us to analyse some of the problems facing us.

Let us examine first the wear of the pressed disc. We know that the disc whether made of a shellac compound or of the more recent vinylite compounds is capable of only a limited number of playings. Even if we accept as a fact the figure 300, which some people allege is possible, we must remember that the loss in fidelity after a few playings may, under certain circumstances, become quite noticeable. After 30 or 50 playings, we are not listening to the same recording any more. Many users of the library will require a higher fidelity of reproduction than is possible after so many playings. To a librarian in charge of a circulating library, this may seem to be no problem at all. As a record wears out, he simply orders a replacement. This simple solution is not applicable to the large reference collection. First of all, the librarian never has sufficient funds to acquire all the recordings he needs for the collection, with the result that a special fund for replacements, if established at all, will have to be very small. There is still another difference which is of even greater importance. In a circulating library, a recording which wears out due to repeated playings does so rather rapidly because of its current popularity. The librarian then experiences little difficulty in obtaining a replacement because the record will probably still be in print. If it is not, another performance of the same work might well satisfy most users of the circulating library. In the reference library, however, the user expects to find both of these performances of that work and both in good condition. If a record wears out due to extensive use, it may well be years after that same record has gone out of print and is no longer available.

Let us assume for the moment that the discs are to be made available to users of the reference library for repeated performance. The first recommendation I should make is that the reader would never be permitted to handle the recording himself. Instead the playback machines should be located right in the stacks where the records are stored and the playback machines connected with loud speakers placed in small study rooms or with earphones in the general reading room. The discs should be handled only by the attendants who are responsible for their care.

I should like to make another recommendation however that will go further towards the complete mechanisation of record playing and that is the application to library use of the mechanism used in the coin operated machine known as the 'juke box' in the USA. I envisage a library in which a user would indicate on a slip the order in which he would like to listen to a group of records. The attendant would then place the recordings in the machine in the specified order and the library user would be assigned a small study room with a desk with a series of buttons which he would press after he receives a signal from the stacks that the machine is ready to be used. Naturally a series of such mechanisms would have to be on the floors where the recordings are kept and the machines would have to be constructed in a way that subjected the discs to slight wear each time they were played. In spite of this, it would be wise for the library to require the attendant to indicate the date on the container every time a recording is used so that after a certain specified number of playings, it can be withdrawn for replacement, or if that is not possible, for copying on tape for purposes of preservation.

This may sound like a Utopian scheme to some people but I am convinced that it is perfectly feasible with our present technical knowledge. Of course there are many users of recordings such as the ethnomusicologists who wish to play certain passages over and over again. It would be perfectly feasible to incorporate in such a mechanical device, a repeating mechanism to take care of this, but I recommend against it because of the obvious wear of the recording. Such a user should be required to purchase his own record for that purpose or if not available to order a tape copy.

The physical limitations of service with the instantaneous sound recordings are of course quite different. The old wax cylinders should not be played at all but service copies should be made for this purpose. The same holds true for the more common acetate discs. Experience has shown us that there is a very noticeable fall off in fidelity after just a few playings of the acetate and the record can soon become completely useless. The results of the recently completed project on the preservation of these recordings indicate that they have a very limited life expectancy so that we are all faced with the problem of making more permanent copies within the next few years.

We now come to one of the main advantages in the use of tape. In addition to its potentialities in high fidelity recording, it can be played and replayed for what is, for practical purposes, an unlimited number of times. But here too the librarian must distrust the library user. It is not too difficult to ruin a tape. Even if the equipment is in perfect condition, an inexperienced user can do a great deal of damage to a tape, so that unless it is a duplicate made for his use, a library user should not be permitted to handle the original tape himself. Tapes also should be played by the attendants from a central point in the stacks in the same manner as recommended for discs.

So far we have discussed the playing of recordings in a library. This is analogous to the services given to the reader who comes in to the building to study a book or manuscript. There are, however, other services rendered by every large research library. All of us working in such libraries spend a great deal of time giving reference service by correspondence. In the field of phonography, this will frequently involve a reference librarian in listening to a recording in order to be able to answer the question intelligently. I hope that none of my colleagues will take it amiss if I recommend that here, too, it would be desirable to insist that all recordings be played by the technicians assigned to this type of activity and that the library's own staff be at least partially restricted from handling the material themselves. At this point it might be well for me to state that the Utopian equipment for reference service that I described is not yet in the Library of Congress, although we are planning for it should we get a proposed third building. On the other hand, even with our limited service we do not permit our own staff to play instantaneous recordings but require them to have the record played by the technicians in our Recording Laboratory. This is cumbersome, expensive and time consuming but absolutely necessary if we are to preserve our acetate discs and tapes. It is desirable to apply this method also to the published discs and we hope some day to have sufficient staff to accomplish this as well.

Still another form of service common to all libraries is that of offering copies of the material in its possession. By now it is the rare library that is not equipped to make available photostats or microfilms of the materials on its shelves. A similar service will be required of a collection of sound recordings. It will be necessary to have a recording laboratory in the library equipped to render this service. The initial investment for equipment need not be any larger or perhaps not even as large as that necessary for photographic reproduction.

Finally, we must consider the problem of inter-library loans. In the case of the old shellac recordings or the instantaneous acetates, this would be out of the question because it would be unthinkable to subject these fragile materials to the dangers of damage during shipment. On the other hand, the tape recording and the modern, unbreakable vinylite disc might well go through the mails just as readily as books do now. In the case of the vinylite disc the librarian might be reluctant to make it available for inter-library loan because of the problem of wear due to repeated playings. In the case of tapes, however, particularly those commercially issued, of which there are many copies in existence, this might not be a deterrent factor. The whole question of inter-library loan has not been a pressing one in the field of sound recordings although in the Library of Congress we have received numerous requests for such loans which we have so far declined to fill. It is a question which we must consider if only to rule out for the time being. It is conceivable that sometime in the future it may become common practice.

In this analysis of some of the problems related to reference service, I have spoken of our collections in relatively static terms. We must always bear in mind that the development of new forms of recording is proceeding rapidly. The videotape which combines the visual with the auditory is already being used in television. It is terribly expensive at present but may well become common during the next generation. The prospect of looking at the same artist making the same motions every time one listens to a record may not sound attractive. On the other hand, the perfection of audiovisual devices can be used for other purposes in music. For instance, the score of the work being heard could be projected on a small screen. Another development of interest has recently been invented in Japan. This is a magnetic sheet which it is alleged can be reproduced in quantity with the speed of a rotary printing press. There are other new developments but I mention these in passing only to indicate that the art of recording is progressing rapidly indeed. Whatever practices we adopt must be flexible enough to be adapted to these new types of recordings as they appear.

So far in this talk I have on several occasions glibly mentioned the making of tape copies in order to preserve the original recordings or for the convenience of the scholar. Just as in the case of microfilms, however, there are legal restrictions. In the case of microfilms, the problem is complicated enough but simpler than in the case of recordings. Here we are faced not merely with the question of copyright, but also with the rights of the performers and in certain cases of the manufacturers, rights which are independent of copyright. The laws of the countries vary enormously on the subject of recordings and in the United States, for instance, it is technically illegal to record a copyrighted work for personal use without the permission of the copyright owner and formalities requiring the filing of a notice of use in the Copyright Office. Our law is at present undergoing a study which it is hoped will lead to a revision but it still stands. As we all know, there are millions of tape machines in homes throughout the USA and most of them, if not all, are being used in technical violation of our copyright law. I have not heard of any lawsuits being brought against an individual for such use and this may seem like a small matter. On the other hand, the librarian is a public servant and must usually be very strict in his interpretation of the law. But this is not the end of the librarian's difficulties. In most countries copyright lasts for a specific number of years. This applies however only to the copyrighted music. The rights of the performer and the manufacturer who first made the record are still to be reckoned with after the termination of copyright protection. I know that this is a subject which is being studied by UNESCO, but I think that our organisation should take an active part in trying to achieve an equitable solution.

In conclusion, I should like to express the hope that our efforts will bring forth certain tangible results. What is needed is a study, or a series of studies, initiated by the International Association of Music Libraries aimed to solve these problems, for the individual library will find itself almost helpless in trying to cope with them. We need a committee, or committees, to work on acquisitions; on the problems of physical preservation and the development of library equipment; on the development of a code of practice relating to inter-library loans and on the availability of reproductions in the form of magnetic recordings; on the legal problems, some of them quite new, which face the record librarian. For many years we have been aware of the existence of sound recordings and we have all had the feeling that in the dim and distant future the sound recording would become an important element in the music collection. Well, the dim and distant future is now here and we must take immediate steps to preserve and service these documents which represent our civilisation so well. I have no fear of failure. On the contrary, I am confident of success if only because we have the support of the International Association of Music Libraries.

NOTES

[1] See [**250**, 253].—*Editor.*

[2] A. G. Pickett and M. M. Lemcoe, *Preservation and storage of sound recordings* (Washington, D.C.: Library of Congress, 1959).—*Editor.*

The Place of Gramophone Recordings in a University Music Library

by Vincent H. Duckles

It is important to note that this paper is concerned with the place of recordings *in* a music library, not with record libraries as such. And further, the emphasis will be placed on a particular type of music library—one which serves the needs of a university faculty of music. I wish to make these limiting conditions very clear, because the problems of administering an autonomous record library differ considerably from those connected with a library where books and discs exist in the same collection. There are at least four reasons why recordings are entitled to a place in a university music library: 1. The university library shares with the museum and the national archive some of the responsibility for protecting and preserving the significant documents of our culture, and there are few today who would dispute the fact that recordings are among such significant documents. 2. The university library shares with the public library some of the responsibility for providing recreational listening opportunities for the layman. This is particularly true of such libraries in America, where university experience reaches a much larger group of the "general public" than are reached in other countries. But these two functions are incidental, or secondary in importance, as far as the university library is concerned. I shall devote most of my time to a discussion of the ways in which recordings can further the *essential* purposes of a university music library: 3. the implementation of instruction, and 4. the service to research scholars.

In presenting these problems I must ask your forbearance if I draw much of my illustrative material from practices carried out in my own library at the University of California. It can be regarded as a fairly typical example of an American university library. First it may be well to say a word or two in defense of what may be regarded as a peculiarly American attitude toward the educational values of the gramophone; for we do believe in using recordings to implement the teaching of music from the elementary grades to the graduate level of study. This attitude has led some of our colleagues in other countries to assume that we regard record listening as a kind of painless substitute for score reading, or for participation in musical performance. Such is not the case. I am sure that you would find at the University of California, or in most of the leading American universities, a range of active music making and a type of musical discipline that would compare favorably with the work in university music departments anywhere. We can thank the radio and the gramophone for opening up new opportunities for the layman, and we can also thank them on behalf of the more advanced music student for carefully reconstructed performances of early music, and for the chance to hear and rehear the works of contemporary composers. A full discussion of the rationale of recordings in education is beyond the scope of this paper, but I can refer you to the discussion by Alfred Mann in the current issue of NOTES (June, 1951) for a further discussion of this subject.

In a university music library there is nothing to be gained in isolating recordings from books and scores. On the contrary, every effort must be made to bring the media together in a functional relationship. A glance at some of our record catalog cards will demonstrate this view. Take for example, the cards for the recent recording of

SOURCE: Reprinted from Vincent H. Duckles, "The place of gramophone recordings in a university music library," in International Association of Music Libraries. 3e congrès international des bibliothèques musicales, Paris, 22–25 juillet 1951. *Actes du congrès* . . . , pp. 65–71. Kassel: Bärenreiter, 1953, by permission of Bärenreiter-Verlag.

Haydn's *Mass in B-flat major,* the so-called *Harmoniemesse,* as prepared by the University of California Music Library:
(Cards 3″ x 5″)

Card 1

Haydn, Joseph, 1732-1809.
Mass, B flat major (1802)
Missa solemnis in B flat major (Harmoniemesse)
Record nos. TR 4001-14. 1949
14s. 12″ (The Haydn Society of the U.S., Inc. Series A. v. 1)
The Munich Cathedral choir and orchestra; with Trude Konrad, soprano; Irmgard Dornbach-Ziegler, alto; Ludwig von Haas, tenor; Heinrich Seebach, bass; Karol Otto Bortzi, organ; Ludwig Berberich, conductor.
Recorded in Europe. (Continued on next card)

Card 2

Haydn, Joseph, 1732-1809.
Mass, B flat major (1802)
Missa solemnis in B flat major . . . 1949
(Card 2)

CONTENTS

pt. 1. The records, containing: Kyrie – Gloria – Credo – Sanctus – Benedictus – Agnus Dei.
pt. 2. Miniature score (photo copy / Positive) of the original Breitkopf & Härtel edition 181 –
pt. 3. Analytical notes, by H. C. Robbins Landon.

You will note that these cards provide information as to the composer (with his dates); conventional title, or filing title; transcribed title, with disc numbers; date of the recording; the number of sides (14); record size (12″); and the issuing society (Haydn Society of the U.S.). So much for the descriptive cataloging. To this is added a series of notes giving information as to the performing choir and orchestra (Munich Cathedral); the names of the principal soloists, and the conductor; the fact that the work was recorded in Europe; the contents of the album: (1) the records, (2) a miniature score of the work, (3) analytical notes. These cards are filed under a subject-heading, "Masses," and under added entries for the name of the performing group, the conductor, and the series of which this album is a part (Haydn Society Series). This album is admittedly more elaborate than most since it includes a score of the work recorded; but if time and staff would permit we should like to see every card in the record catalog contain a note to refer the user to the best available score in our collection. The catalog is arranged alphabetically by composer and subject, and we have an additional chronological file for recordings of early music (before 1800). Cataloging practice of this kind must seem highly over-developed to some of you, but I can assure you that it is not the result of a cataloger's dream but a practical effort to meet the needs of a music department where records are regarded as essential tools for instruction. Records require not less but more detailed cataloging than books and scores. One obvious reason for this lies in the fact that one has not only to consider composer, title and imprint, but the existence of a definite performer, or group of artists, is often the thing which gives the disc its special interest or value. Our aim is to make the catalog itself a useful reference tool, although we must continue to supplement it with special lists and "Discographies" from time to time. There is a real need for an adequate set of subject headings for record cataloging. Headings applicable to books and scores do not meet the requirements in this field.

There are approximately 10,000 discs in the University of California record collection. We employ the services of one full-time record cataloger, who, with the help of a clerical assistant, catalogs all of the recordings in the university collection.[1] About 5% of these are non-musical discs purchased for use in speech or language instruction. The recordings do not circulate for home use, although they may be taken out of the library by instructors for use in the various lecture rooms in the music building. The collection is used primarily by the students, who do their assigned listening on equipment provided in the music library. Circulation statistics show that some 20,000 albums and single discs were used in the library during the academic year, 1949-50, an average of a little less than 90 items per day. There are three semi-soundproof rooms, two of small size, and one large enough to accomodate as many as twenty students at one time for group listening. These rooms are equipped with good quality speakers and turn-tables for both long-playing and standard discs. In addition to these acoustically prepared rooms there are three earphone listening sets in the library reading room. As many as four students can adjust their headsets to each of these machines and listen to recordings without disturbing others who may be reading or working near by.

It should hardly be necessary to add that discs used for teaching purposes must be regarded as expendable. There can be no sure protection for them beyond the precautions which a careful user may be expected to exercise. We have learned from experience that the average record user is not as careless and destructive as he is reputed to be; he can be depended upon to handle fragile discs with the gentleness they require. But even with the most careful use, the discs must be replaced systematically and those that are unique or of great rarity must be segregated and given restricted circulation. A simple device serves to tabulate record use; a mark is placed on the envelope each time a disc is played so that we can observe its life in the collection. It is difficult to set an arbitrary figure of so-many-times played, after which the disc should be withdrawn, because even new surfaces vary greatly in quality and durability. But those discs in heavy demand are watched closely and replaced when they show signs of deterioration. Not more than two or three percent of the total collection requires replacement during an academic year. When a record album is no longer available commercially, we do not necessarily withdraw it from general circulation. Our attitude is quite unlike that of the private record collector in this respect. It is axiomatic in a library of this kind that *interest in the disc as such is secondary to interest in the musical work recorded.* There may be a dozen or more different recordings of Mozart's *G minor Symphony,* but we do not feel obliged to purchase every new issue of such a work just because it represents some new refinement in technique or interpretation. We are satisfied with one or possibly two good examples; when Kussevitzky's version wears out we are quite willing to replace it with Toscanini's, if the former should be unobtainable.

This rather casual attitude toward some of the niceties of record collecting may seem like heresy to the specialist in rare discs, but we do not hesitate to depart from the purist's point of view in more than one instance. We have little patience with the two persistent apparitions which haunt the collector: one is the ghost of technical, acoustical perfection, the other is the ghost of absolute musical authenticity. In a new and rapidly growing field of technology, like recording, it is natural to expect new improvements to be made, and as music librarians we shall welcome them and utilize them to improve our services. But a point has been reached in the development of recording technique and playback apparatus where musicians and engineers no longer speak the same language. The situation is further confused by the claims of advertisers with their mixed jargon of sales talk and technical terminology. We are told that we may as well discard our 78 rpm discs in favor of the new long-playing records. There are some who predict that in a few years discs will be made obsolete by the new media of magnetic wire or tape. One can hardly blame the librarians, by nature the most conservative of human beings, for hesitating to enter a field which shows so little stability. It is clear that we can make no progress in record library building so long as we try to evaluate our collections in terms of the standards of electronic engineers, or allow ourselves to be swayed by the claims of those who make their profit in selling gramophone equipment. As a practical though imperfect instrument for bringing the musical past into the classroom, recordings have fully established their worth. We use discs in the university library as we use microfilm, as a means to an end, and we are grateful for the extended resources they provide.

How large should the record collection of a university music library be? The obvious answer, which sounds like a truism, is that it should be no larger than it needs to be. In other words, a good working collection of this kind need not expand indefinitely; its optimum size will depend on the character and objectives of the music faculty which it serves. There is a point, or a plateau, beyond which growth will proceed at a fairly slow rate. It is safe to say, however, that libraries which implement the historical study of music will continue to grow rapidly for some time in order to take advantage of the great wealth of early music which the record companies are just beginning to issue. The problem of selection, that effort to make an adjustment between limited funds and unlimited needs, is one of the most interesting and fascinating in this field of librarianship. But generalizations are not particularly useful here, since the problem is largely a matter of local concern and will depend upon the conditions at hand. I cannot leave this subject, however, without some mention of the great value of Kurtz Myers' *Index of Record Reviews,* which appears in each issue of NOTES. This is one of the best devices for keeping abreast of the prolific output of the record reviewers.

I have been concerned thus far with the value of discs in teaching music. They are also extremely useful for certain types of musical research, and as such fall within the orbit of the university music library. I refer, of course, to the fields of primitive and folk music where recordings have proved indispensable from the early years of the present century. A number of very important collections have developed in Europe and America since 1900. In the United States, the Music Division of the Library of Congress has taken the lead and its Archive of Folk Music[2] is one of the outstanding collections of its kind. Not every college or university music department carries on research in these fields but they are attracting increasing interest on the part of scholars. Even a comparatively young institution like the University of California has a collection of California Indian music made on wax cylinders as early as 1910. During the 1930s an extensive project for recording California folk-song was undertaken and the discs were deposited in the Music Library. About two years ago an anthropological expedition to central Africa, sponsored by the University, brought back some 200 discs of native music recorded in the field. These "instantaneous" discs, as we call them, create a special problem in any record library. They are unique and irreplaceable, and their acetate surfaces will not stand repeated playings. As teaching material they are not particularly useful, but they are extremely valuable source material for the specialist in primitive or folk music and they should be made known to scholars working in these fields. Information about such collections and their contents is difficult to secure. The production of discographies for use in the study of oriental, primitive and folk music has just begun to occupy librarians, and should prove a fruitful type of activity in the future. It is encouraging to note that such beginnings are being made on an international scale in projects like the *Archives de la Musique enregestrée,* which has the sponsorship of UNESCO.

It is a short step from the discussion of "instantaneous" discs to a consideration of the library as an active agency in the production of recordings. The association of a library with a recording studio is well known in the field of radio broadcasting, but not the usual thing in academic institutions. Yet if we are to secure the type of authentic musical reproduction we require in historical sets like *L'Anthologie Sonore,* it is obvious that there must be a closer connection between the centers of musical scholarship and the production of recordings. A number of university libraries and music departments in America have developed their own resources for the making of recordings. The well known *Vocarium* series produced by Harvard University has recorded verse readings by contemporary English and American poets and distributed them widely. The discs issued by the Library of Congress *Archive of Folk Music* has made available some of the most interesting items from a great collection. There are numerous examples of libraries where audio-visual departments with facilities for making recordings are part of the administration: the University of Oregon is one; The Detroit Public Library another. The College of the Pacific at Stockton, California, has an affiliated radio station, and in other institutions the department of engineering has recording equipment available for library use. At the University of California, the Music Department has its own equipment for disc, tape, and wire recording, and the music library is accumulating collections in all forms of recorded sound. The use of the new recording media of magnetic wire and tape has become rather widespread in America at the amateur as well as the professional level. One might venture to predict that within a few years non-commercial recording, with simple, portable wire or tape equipment may become as common as the use of the camera. There are fascinating implications for library practice in the situation. For one thing, there is the suggestion that we may have, in recorded tape, a new means of exchange, or inter-library loan, as efficient as microfilm or photostat in the visual field. It has always been difficult to exchange discs because of their fragility and the expense of producing them. Duplication on wire or tape may make it possible to exchange recorded material between libraries with comparatively little difficulty.

In conclusion, let me express a word of appreciation on behalf of those of us who are concerned with the library use of discs for the fact that AIBM[3] has seen fit to include a session on recordings in the program of the Third International Congress of the organization. That in itself is testimony to the fact that AIBM regards the handling of gramophone records as a legitimate concern for music libraries. I need not stress the fact that a few years ago such a subject would never have been placed on the agenda. It would have been considered as quite outside the domain of the music librarian. In the brief discussion this morning some very important problems have not been touched upon. Chief among them is the problem of administering a large, self-contained record library—the national archive of recorded music. Nor has much been said about the needs and resources in the field of "discography," if we may be permitted to introduce that term into the language of librarianship. Further study should be made into the possibilities of standardized record cataloging, the development of techniques of exchange, the sharing of information on types of equipment and the administration of record collections. May not these, and other considerations, justify a continuing interest on the part of AIBM in this new and provocative field of librarianship? We are in a stage of development at present where coordination is still possible; if we neglect it we may find ourselves proceeding into a future confusion of aims and a needless duplication of efforts.

NOTES

[1] See [**273, 274**; 254].—*Editor.*

[2] See [**236–238**, 252].—*Editor.*

[3] The International Association of Music Libraries, referred to throughout this *Reader* by its English title and initials: IAML.—*Editor.*

The Practical Record Selector: A "Plaine and Easie" Introduction

by Gordon Stevenson

Polymathes: *Stay, brother Philomathes, what haste? Whither go you so fast?*

Philomathes: *To seek out an old friend of mine.*

Polymathes: *But before you go I pray you repeat some of the discourses which you had yesternight at Master Sophobulus his banquet, for commonly he is not without both wise and learned guests.*

Philomathes: *It is true indeed, and yesternight there were a number of excellent scholars, both gentlemen and others, but all the propose (i.e. subject) which then was discoursed upon was music.*

Polymathes: *I trust you were contented to suffer others to speak of that matter.*

Philomathes: *I would that had been the worst, for I was compelled to discover mine own ignorance and confess that I knew nothing at all in it . . . Upon shame of mine ignorance I go now to seek out mine old friend to make myself his scholar.*

And so it was that in London, in 1597, Philomathes, bent on the acquisition of knowledge, set out to find a "master" and make of himself a scholar. This dialogue is from *A Plaine and Easie Introduction to Practicall Musicke,* by a certain Thomas Morley ("Batcheler of musick, & one of the gent. of hir Majesties Royall Chappell")—a book that is neither plain, nor easy, but which is eminently practical.

Like many people today, Philomathes knows nothing about music, and he is the first to admit it. The thing that reminds us that this took place in 1597 and not 1963, is that today Philomathes would not seek out a master, but would go to his public library in search of enlightenment. Once at the library, our friend would in all probability find a collection of phonograph records. How well this collection would serve his needs, would depend, of course, on what his needs are, and which of these needs the library has decided to serve as a matter of policy.

We now have Philomathes in the library. He finds his way to the record collection and, curious fellow that he is, he quickly strikes up a conversation with the librarian:

Philomathes: *In selecting records, where do you begin?*

Librarian: *With knowledge, of course. And with my own great love of great music. We never buy anything but the very greatest of music, and this played only by the greatest musicians.*

Philomathes: *Oh? But specifically, where do you begin?*

Librarian: *Well, in the beginning was and still is "Schwann."*

Philomathes: *Swan? What is this swan of which you speak?*

Librarian: *No, no, no. It's "Schwann," not swan. It's a list of the 30,000 LP records that are currently available. I hesitate to think what life would be like without swan. I mean "Schwann." Now you have me doing it.*

Philomathes: *But what about all those books about music I see on your shelves. I see there are books by men like Reese, Bukofzer, Lang, and many great scholars in music. Do these help in record selection?*

Librarian: *No, those books are about music, not about records. Besides, I avoid them like the plague. Music is to be listened to, not read about, and I have an ear for music. I also took piano lessons when I was in the fifth grade.*

Philomathes: *Yes, but how do you decide what records to buy?*

SOURCE: Reprinted from *Library Journal,* May 1, 1963. Published by R. R. Bowker (a Xerox Company). Copyright c. 1963, R. R. Bowker Company.

Librarian: *I buy recordings of "good" music. Why don't you go away?*

Philomathes: *But how do you know what is "good?" And for whom is it good?*

Librarian: *Everybody knows what good music is. It is great music, and I'm beginning to get bored with you.*

Philomathes: *But how do you . . . Oh well, it's obvious I'm getting nowhere; so just give me a recording of Leadbelly's "Last Session" and I'll be on my way.*

Librarian: *Leadbelly! Are you a nut or something? Where do you think you are? This is a library, my friend, not the Ethnomusicological Archives.*

Philomathes: *But isn't your motto "The right book for the right person at the right time," or something like that? And what's the difference if it's a book or a record?*

Librarian: *You can have whatever book you want, right or wrong; but you, my friend, are in the Record Department, and I decide what is good and what is not good for you when it comes to music. You might think that this fellow Leadbelly is important, but I know better. Now, how about this recording of the Budapest String Quartet playing the Beethoven Opus 135?*

So Philomathes leaves the Record Department a little frustrated, since he did not get what he wanted, and no one gave him a good reason why.

Giving people what they want may not be your idea of record selection, but I am convinced that a public library record collection is for all of its patrons, not just some of them; and that all or most of them should get something of what they want (obviously, all of them will not get everything they want). And along with what they want, you can give them quite a bit of what they should want, what you would like them to want, and what would make our musical culture better if they did want.

To this end, the following suggestions are designed to be plain, easy and practical. They deal only with recordings of music, for nonmusic records are another matter. Music specialists will be annoyed at some of these ideas; but I hope they will offer some comfort to the nonspecialist.

We talk about record collections as if they had little connection with other library services. Record services should originate and grow as part of a program of music services. There are many serious and challenging aspects of our musical culture in which the library can play an important role, and in some of these, records are of little value. Get a picture of the total musical life of your community, set up goals, *then* see where records fit into your plans.

The practical selector realizes that music, like the library itself, means many things to many people; and it behooves him to give his public credit for knowing what they like and what they don't like—for they are in somewhat of a better position to know what music means to them than he is. All of his patrons may not like the kind of music he would prefer them to like, but if in the music of their choice, people find esthetic satisfaction, relaxation, peace or amusement, then this music (regardless of where it originates or what we call it) is not without a certain nobility of purpose.

This is not to say that the librarian will not try to educate his patrons; but he should begin by finding out what music means to them and why. Lifetime listening habits are not easily changed; yet library record borrowers are generally a foolhardy lot, and will give almost anything at least one hearing.

Coordinating records with books, and people. When you provide books about music for your patrons see that they have records to go with the books. Machlis' *The Enjoyment of Music,* Grout's *A History of Western Music,* J. T. Howard's *Modern Music,* B. H. Haggin's *Music for the Man who Enjoys Hamlet,* and the like, not to mention books on biography, folk music and jazz, gain real meaning when used with recordings of the music discussed. For every book about music, there are a dozen phonograph records that will enhance the significance of the book for the reader—try to get the three of them together: the patron, the book and the record.

The "Comparison Game." In the major reviewing media this game has reached the point of absurdity. Practically all judgments are subjective, seldom are historical or musicological criteria used. This game is too expensive for the library. Concentrate on building a collection of *music,* not a collection of performances or interpretations. Don't even try to keep up with the latest darling of the opera stage or lion of the keyboard. The most important and basic function of your classic record collection will be served equally well by the Toscanini, the Reiner, the Walter, or any of the other umpteen versions of Beethoven's "Eroica" symphony.

The Standard Repertory. The S.R. is something you have to live with, so you should find out what it is and how it got that way (see Mueller's *The American Symphony Orchestra*). The S.R. was formed under circumstances that were quite different from those that prevail in our society today, yet it remains as firmly entrenched as ever. The miracle of the LP record should have made the concept obsolete, but it didn't. For many, the S.R. is the only excuse for having a record collection, for others it is a strangling, suffocating force that prevents the collection from functioning as a vital educational media and a forum for important and timely issues. You must work both with S.R. and against it. If you include nothing but S.R. titles, you won't have room for anything else—and it is this "anything else" that gives the collection vitality and one of the basic justifications for existence. If your collection is big enough (around 2,000 titles) you can see that S.R. items are well represented and still have room to do a lot of imaginative things. Smaller collections are advised to include a continually changing selection of S.R. titles, not attempting to be comprehensive. The S.R. includes practically nothing written before 1750, and very little written after 1900, and only comparatively little in between. This is a rather severe limitation to place on the collection.

Background reading for the selector. Keep an eye out for books that discuss music in the context of our society. Books like Jacques Barzun's *Music in American Life,* Cecil Smith's *Worlds of Music,* Paul S. Carpenter's *Music, an Art and a Business,* Virgil Thomson's *The State of Music,* and Lang's *One Hundred Years of Music in America;* and articles like Mueller's "The Social Nature of Musical Taste" (*Journal of Research in Music Education,* Vol. IV, No. 2), and Charles Rosen's "The Proper Study of Music" (*Perspectives of New Music,* Fall, 1962)—in other words, material that deals with music, not as an art form, but as a product of our society.

Other background reading. If you read nothing but record-reviewing magazines you will get a very distorted idea of what is going on in music in this country. Minimum monthly browsing in the "serious" field are *Musical America*[1] and the *Music Journal* (the "Current Chronicle" of the *Musical Quarterly* is excellent but very technical). If you have the interest and inclination, there are a lot more music magazines on every conceivable musical subject, from *Accordion World* to Unesco's *World of Music,* many of which should help sharpen your awareness of important issues and developments in the field of music that may influence your record selection policies.

Contemporary "serious" music. A total collection of around 1,000 titles should include at least 50 recordings by contemporary U.S. composers. Don't try to keep a "standard" group of contemporaries in the catalog, there is simply too much good material available to choose from. When a record is discarded, replace it with a new title by the same composer, or a title by a composer new to your collection. Many record reviewers seem utterly incapable of adequately evaluating contemporary music—so don't place too much faith in what the reviewers say about it. Two outstanding exceptions are Alfred Frankenstein (*High Fidelity*)[1] and William Flanagan (*Hi Fi/Stereo Review*). Arthur Cohn's *The Collector's 20th-Century Music* (Lippincott, 1961) is a most useful guide.

The local scene. Coordinate some of your purchases with local concerts, if there are any; and tie them in with your collection through displays and record lists.

When you find a good cause, support it. When recording companies do attempt to bring out titles that are of a significant cultural value, but offer little chance of commercial success, go out of your way to find out if you can use the material (e.g. Decca's recordings of the New York Pro Musica ensemble, the Yale Poet series, the Record Hunter's M.G.M. reprint series, to mention only three of dozens of notable adventures in culture).

Watch those small labels. The small record producer plays an indispensable role in bringing out music that would otherwise be lost to the record-listening public. Idealistic, bold, and imaginative, the catalogs of these small producers deserve your careful attention.

The "well-rounded" collection. Some convincing arguments have been marshaled to show why the well-rounded book collection is not practical. Records are different. Music is a virtually unknown world to the layman. Only a well-rounded collection will give him room to move around in and permit him to discover the many forms that music has taken and the various roles it plays in the lives of men.

Double check. Check your holdings from a number of different angles. Consider it historically: are major styles and periods represented? Are all important forms represented? Are various instrumental and vocal media represented? For information on these matters, turn to the books on your shelves, books like Alec Harman's *Man and His Music,* Peter Garvie's *Music and Western Man,* Peter Hansen's *Twentieth Century Music,* and specialized books like Alec Robertson's *Chamber Music.*

Don't specialize in performers: build up a variety of conductors, orchestras, singers and instrumentalists.

There is more, but this will do for a start. Oh yes, if somebody named Philomathes stops in and requests something you don't have, you might consider his request very seriously as a possible purchase.

NOTE

[1] Since 1965, *High Fidelity/Musical America.*—*Editor.*

Classification Chaos

by Gordon Stevenson

"Many librarians believe that the LP recording of music defies any logical subject or content approach to classification"

Ever since phonograph records have been widely accepted as library materials we have been trying to decide how to arrange them on our shelves so that the best interests of the library patron will be served. This report will try to show what progress has been made towards a common solution to some of the problems which have plagued us since the introduction of the LP record upset some beautiful theories of record classification.

Although there has been a consistent effort to make records accessible to their users in such a way that their full potential will be realized, there has been little agreement about how best to accomplish this. The necessity of classification has been questioned, and many librarians believe that the LP recording of music defies any logical subject or content approach to classification.

Much of our thinking has been influenced by traditional methods of arranging printed material. But whereas the physical form of the book has not changed radically in many centuries, the "record" has assumed many different shapes, sizes and speeds–it refuses to settle down. There is no reason to believe that the present form of the record will not one day give way to yet a different shape, size or speed. Any system of classification that aims to be universal must take this into account.

There are almost limitless possibilities as to how records can be arranged. A decision concerning which method to use depends on the collection, its purpose, what is in it, who is going to use it, why and how they are going to use it. Recorded sound has four uses (at least) that seem to relate to traditional functions of the library: documentation, research, education, and entertainment.

The library archive that collects and preserves all types of recorded material for research, functions quite differently from the public library. In most public libraries the record is a means to an end, and the only interest in preservation is the attempt to insure that its normal life expectancy will be reached before it is consigned to the junk heap. The use of records in a formal program of education implies still different shelving arrangements and controls.

Of course it is not all this simple, since many public and university collections serve more than one function. What is right for one library may be all wrong for another. Even one library will find that the best way to handle one collection (e.g., a student browsing collection) may not be practical for another (e.g., an historical collection of 78's).

To gather information on current trends in shelving arrangements and classification schemes, a questionnaire was sent to 473 libraries with record collections. It was obvious from the returns that an astonishing amount of initiative and imagination had been devoted to the problem. Of the 392 libraries that answered the query, only 37 indicated that their system was definitely known to be based on that of some other library.

We knew that there were at least eight ways of arranging phonograph records currently in use. What we did not know is their frequency of use, or how well they actually serve the purpose for which they were intended. Because of differences in notation and the many variable elements that may be taken into account in setting up classes and subclasses, the following tabulation can be considered no more than a general indication of what is happening in the libraries which responded.

	Open or partially open stacks	*Closed stacks*
Arrangement by accession number	89	59
By manufacturer's number	13	8

SOURCE: Reprinted from *Library Journal,* October 15, 1963. Published by R. R. Bowker (a Xerox Company).

	Open or partially open stacks	*Closed stacks*
Adaptation of Dewey D.C.	46	6
Adaptation of L.C.	4	1
Arrangement by broad subject area	51	8
Color code used as location symbols	15	0
Schedules with a letter notation	42	0
Arranged in alphabetical order by composer, author, or title	30	3
Other systems	12	5

We did not ask for information on how satisfied librarians were with their own arrangement, assuming that if they chose a system, or invented one (as many of them did), and used it, they must like it. This was a mistake, of course, but many librarians volunteered the information. Almost everyone who commented made it a point to say that even though their method might seem a bit unusual, it was ideal for their situation, their patrons were delighted with it, and they could heartily recommend it to other librarians. Many expressed astonishment that a library would even consider a basic approach different from the one that they themselves had chosen.

Only six librarians indicated dissatisfaction with their current methods, each being dissatisfied with a different scheme. Seven librarians volunteered the information that they had switched from one scheme to another, but there was no pattern. One library, for example, found an alphabetical arrangement by composers unsatisfactory and switched to manufacturers' numbers. Another library found manufacturers' numbers unsatisfactory and switched to an alphabetical composers arrangement.

The above tabulation is deceptively neat and simple. It gives no idea of the incredible lack of uniformity among libraries that had adopted any one system. Hardly any two classed approaches seemed to be exactly the same in all details. Some libraries used Dewey for nonmusic and another scheme for music records. In some alphabetical setups, Dewey numbers were used to sub-arrange a composer's works by media, the class number being used *after* the composer's Cutter number. Dewey was used in one or another of its US forms and in an adaptation of the McColvin-Reeves revision of the 780's. Two libraries assigned all records to one single Dewey number, then one sub-arranged by composer, the other by accession number. Dewey was adapted to the use of records by the addition of letters, by the omission of numbers, by the displacement of the decimal point, and by the addition of the manufacturer's number. Some schedules made mnemonic use of letters, others were arbitrary.

Color codes were used in combination with Dewey, with accession numbers and with a scheme of letters. One library used 16 different colors to identify as many subject classes. Accession numbers were used within subject classes and in combination with Cutter numbers. Some libraries arranged every LP in no order other than the order in which it was processed, so Brubeck followed Mozart, the *B Minor Mass* was shelved next to *Le Sacre Du Printemps,* and Beethoven's nine symphonies were scattered all over the place in any order.

One is tempted to call the total picture chaotic, but the illusion of total confusion is created more by differences in notational systems than by a multiplicity of basic approaches to the problem.

Once we have decided, for example, that all operas should be grouped together, whether we identify this class as LP782, 78.2, 7.82, 783, 210, PRM-ML1500, Bin #13, OP, Op, O, 061, D, LO, H, M, C, Z, Zgn, the color blue, or what have you, we have at least decided that it is to the patron's advantage if we keep all operas together in one place on the shelves. Of the 302 libraries which reported open or partially open stacks, 200, or 66 percent, favored some form of classified arrangement, though the structure of these classes and sub-classes, and their sequence, varied greatly.

The question of open or closed stacks is obviously a factor of paramount importance. It is at this point that most of the academic libraries part company with public libraries. The main trend in public libraries is open stacks with very liberal loan privileges. Generally speaking, university and college libraries consider records more of a long term investment. Their use is rigidly controlled and there are few large collections thrown wide open to the potential dangers of an omniverous student public. The main functions of a public library (self-education, recreation, and entertainment) are hardly important at all in record libraries serving institutions of higher learning. In such academic communities records for recreational or noncourse related listening are often (though not always) considered ephemeral and expendable material. As often as not they are the responsibility of a student organization or some university authority other than the library.

Whether in academic or public library, once the records are in closed stacks, there are few librarians who would recommend any attempt at subject classification (not that it isn't being done), unless it be of the most general nature.

The open stack principle remains the most favored arrangement for LP's in the public library. It is felt that nothing should separate the book or the record from the potential user. I would like to suggest that we may have been wrong in assuming that what is good for the book is also good for the record. It is interesting to compare our practices with those of British libraries in this respect. A report published this year[1] indicates that British libraries, with very few exceptions, are wedded to the "closed access" method of shelving records. Either by choice or by necessity, 90 libraries that replied to my questionnaire shelve their records in closed stacks. The relative merits of the two practices should be explored further.

At least one public library has found an interesting solution to the problem (if it is a problem), by removing the discs from their jackets, storing them in closed stacks, and placing the empty (but still attractive and informative) jackets in open bins for browsing. There is a lot to be said for this idea and it deserves serious consideration. The chief objections to it are the added expense, extra demands on staff time, and doubled space requirements.

With records on open shelves we come to the crux of the problem. Ideally, we would like to follow certain bibliographical principles: variant "editions" should be shelved together, composers and authors should be arranged alphabetically, related "subjects" should be shelved together and in a logical sequence, "listener's interest" areas, and detailed subject classifications must be considered. And, as is the case with the book, the borrower should be able to go directly to the shelves, bypassing the card catalog in his first attempt to find what he wants.

It is in the nature of the LP record that none of these procedures can be faithfully followed, and in every system there will have to be some compromise. A beautiful, logical, well-ordered, and universal theory of record classification, based on the only thing about a record that really counts (the sounds hidden in those little grooves), is not possible with the LP. The difficulty stems from the fact that most LP's of music contain more than one composition, and often two or more composers are represented. We are not classifying monographs, but "bound withs," and this is the flaw in any classed or alphabetical arrangement. Only one of the two sides of the record can be used as the basis for assigning a classification number, only one composer can be given a Cutter number, and the record can only be shelved in one place.

My own feeling is that a compromise must be accepted, since the only alternatives are accession number order (which is no order at all), or a sequence based on manufacturers' numbers. The latter is the equivalent of arranging books in alphabetical order by the name of the publisher, with sub-arrangements by the order of publication.

The use of manufacturers' numbers (the number on the label and in the Schwann catalog), has the endorsement of one of the largest archives of records in the world, the British Broadcasting Corporation. The assistant librarian of the BBC Gramophone Library writes: "The number given [by the manufacturer] is most important to the librarian—it is an identification universally understood and recognized—it is in the makers' catalogues, lists, and advertisements. With its prefix (if it has one) it indicates what type and size of record it is. No greater mistake can be made by a librarian than that of substituting his own numbering system for this universal one."[2]

Other arguments in favor of this method are: fast retrieval of specific titles; cataloging costs are reduced (the "call number" is on the record, the jacket, and on printed LC cards); the number is short and efficient; and a subject classification of sorts emerges because of the tendency of manufacturers to specialize (e.g., Folkways for folk music, C.R.I. for contemporary music). If we are talking about a closed stack collection, I cannot argue with any of this (the BBC collection of 400,000 records is not exactly a browsing collection!). At least one US librarian regretted using this method, even in closed stacks, because his collection "grows unevenly in regard to labels, and shifting is a regular necessity"—a point not to be overlooked.

Shelving by accession number order is used in all sizes and types of libraries, from the smallest to the largest, with both open and closed stack collections. Almost 38 percent of all libraries which answered my query use this method. If all types of records are collected, categories based on physical characteristics have to be set up, and a notation devised to define these classes. This can result in a very large number of classes. The General Library of the University of California (Berkeley) has developed a schedule of 36 classes for phonodiscs and four for phonotapes. Major classes are indicated by one or more letters. For example, A designates a 12 in., single acoustic 78 rpm record; DX designates a 10 in., single electric $33\frac{1}{3}$ rpm microgroove record. Other wide-ranging collections have developed similar schemes (with different letter prefixes, of course).

Most reasons for using accession number order are negative, but a few positive reasons were given: the simplicity of the numerical order (unfettered by other location symbols) makes for fast shelving and retrieval, inventory is simple, reserves can be checked fast, and a fixed location eliminates much shifting.

This popular method of shelving open stack collections of LP's was not a trend I was happy to discover. Obviously there is a serious difference of opinion among librarians on this point. The Cincinnati Public Library, for example, has shelved by accession number since 1947, and its collection has grown to over 13,000 records. How serviceable is the method for them? It is "far from desirable." On the other hand, the report from the Cleveland Public Library is opposite and unequivocal: "arrangement by accession numbers is the only practical way to arrange records." Furthermore, the Chairman of the Music Library Association's Committee on Classification reported that "it was the consensus of the Committee members that shelving by accession number was the most satisfactory method." I am inclined to believe that it is a method that will never be acceptable to the majority of public librarians as long as their records are in open stacks.

If the decision is made to classify by content, the question arises as to what relationship, if any, shall exist between the notation chosen for records and the one used for books. In *Recordings in the Public Library* (ALA, 1963), Mary D. Pearson recommends the use of the Dewey classification because it "is the most flexible and relates best to other library materials," a viewpoint shared by many librarians. But it has received some strong opposition ("Dewey numbers have little meaning to patrons, the notation is too cumbersome, etc."). I'm afraid that many librarians have lived unhappily with Dewey's 780's and will resist any attempt to carry them over into the record collection. But the point is far from being settled; and so many libraries are inextricably bound to Dewey that some sort of official recommendations for a uniform way to adapt it to records would be most welcome.

It will be impossible here to do justice to the many schedules using a notation based on a series of letters—there are too many of them, they are too diverse and some of them are too involved. I believe that the most satisfactory classification schedule (still referring to open stack collections), and one that will be useful to the largest number of libraries, will be drawn from some of these. If there is any one system, other than the mnemonic, that now shows signs of being widely adopted, I failed to find it.

I gather that mnemonic letter systems can be quickly understood by library patrons, and it makes sense to them to look under B for band music, under O for opera, etc. My own reservations stem from the lack of logical order that may result. For example, the sequence Bl (ballet), Bn (Band), Ch (chamber music), is a rather violent juxtaposition of unrelated material.

Several libraries have been very successful in using color codes. Some surprisingly detailed methods have been used, but color is most often chosen as a method to quickly sort out and identify broad subject areas, often in combination with some other system of order. One method which showed something like a stroke of genius was the idea of using color to identify various types of records within one overall accession order. The idea is that the person interested in, say, chamber music, can quickly spot the records he is interested in by looking for all albums with red tabs (or whatever color was chosen to identify chamber music).

An alphabetical arrangement by composers (using Cutter numbers) strikes me as an efficient way to organize medium-sized collections. Mary Pearson, in her book, says it should work with collections up to 5000 records. Such a system will get out of hand unless a few major divisions (jazz, folk music, spoken word, etc.) are pulled out and arranged separately. There will be no end of headaches if collections are interfiled by title. Collections can be placed at the beginning or the end, or grouped by content or performer and interfiled by these groups. One librarian strongly opposed the alphabetical composers arrangement because it may very well give the patron the false idea that all of the music of one composer is together, which it is not. There is no method, classed or unclassed, that will substitute for detailed composer analytics in the card catalog.

A factor that will definitely play an important part in shaping up classification methods is the increased use of bins or "browser boxes" of the type used in many record stores. I would think that, for libraries that use them, they should sound the death knell of accession order shelving (or is this just wishful thinking?). One librarian said her circulation of records doubled within three months after she abandoned her vertical shelves for the "browsers."

At best, shelving in vertical book-derived stacks is compact; but it can be, and I speak quite literally, a pain in the neck. Try shelf-reading a few thousand records (or try to find that one you need in a hurry) with numbers like LP-785.11 B33s92t, in lettering not much bigger than this, and all standing on end in tight rows. This is why some librarians invented color codes, letter codes, and yes, even accession numbers.

If I have overlooked any of the problems involved in classifying records, I am sorry; but if nothing else, I think I have proved that it is now time for those responsible for the destinies of our record collections to stop going their own separate ways, to get together to pool their experience (of which they have accumulated much), to thrash out their differences (which are fewer than they think), and to arrive at not more than one system of classification that can be recommended for general adoption by all libraries with open stack collections. This is a professional responsibility that all who work with records must share.

It does not make sense for every librarian who wants a record collection to have to work out his own classification schedule. It can be fascinating, even therapeutic, but it is a waste of money and time, and most of us have more important things to do. The purpose, after all, is to get the records arranged as quickly, as efficiently and as economically as possible, so we can get to the business of seeing that they are properly used.

NOTES

[1] H. F. J. Currall, *Gramophone record libraries* (London: 1963).
[2] *Ibid.*, p. 55.

Copying Phonograph Records

Some months ago we published an inquiry from a reader about the legal aspects of copying records onto tape for library use. We are very much indebted to one of our readers for giving a detailed opinion. He prefers to remain anonymous, so we'll just say "Thank you, sincerely" and publish the letter in full:

"In my last issue of *High Fidelity* I notice an inquiry concerning the legal aspects of copying of phonograph records by libraries for circulation to borrowers. While I am primarily a patent rather than a copyright man, I have just finished an article for a library periodical, on photocopying by libraries of copyrighted materials. Perhaps, therefore, the results of my investigation may have some bearing on your inquiry, though they did not directly concern phonograph records.

"My advice to a library is: Don't.

"Records, as such, are not copyrightable under our present statutes, but that is far from giving carte blanche to copy and circulate them. First, the common law of unfair competition, quite aside from copyright, has been held to protect a record upon which the manufacturer has spent a lot of money producing and promoting. Second, although the record is not copyrightable, the music or other material recorded on it may be, and if it is music, ASCAP is very astute to protect its members' interests, by actions for damages and injunction. Third, even if the recorded matter has not been statutorily copyrighted, it still may be and probably is protected by common law copyright if not 'published,' and an injunction might lie for copying a record. Whether selling or otherwise circulating a record constitutes general publication of the recorded material is a point still at issue, to be determined by the law of the state where the record was made. Two federal (federal jurisdiction required by diversity of citizenship of the parties) and a state case have held that there is publication, and therefore dedication to the public; but a decision of the U. S. Court of Appeals for the Second Circuit has construed the New York law to mean that there is no publication. The U. S. Supreme Court has not yet ruled. The commercial (not library) aspect was fully discussed in an article and a note in the *Columbia Law Review* for January and February, 1956.

"Although much classical music is so old as to be in the public domain, or was never copyrighted in this country at all, the unfair competition doctrine probably would still protect the record manufacturer from unauthorized copying. In any case, it would seem prudent for the library to abstain from what probably is unlawful copying and circulation of commercial phonograph records. This is a very brief and undocumented disquisition, but it's good law."

SOURCE: Reprinted from "Copying phonograph records," *High Fidelity*, 8 (March, 1958), 4, 6, by permission of *High Fidelity*.

VI

BUILDINGS AND EQUIPMENT APPROPRIATE FOR THE MUSIC LIBRARY

SELECTED BIBLIOGRAPHY

283. "Library-Museum at Lincoln Center," *Progressive Architecture,* 47 (April, 1966), 176–183.
A description, illustrated with plates and floor plans.

284. Wallace, Mary. "Time-space and the music library," *Notes,* 27 (September, 1970), 12–18.
A superb summary of the specific equipment and architectural features and controls required by music libraries. Includes bibliographical footnotes. See also the annotated "Music library building and equipment: Selected bibliography," (June, 1969); and "Addenda," (February, 1970), compiled by Ms. Wallace in her capacity as Chairman of the MLA Committee on Buildings and Equipment. The typewritten bibliography is available for a 15¢ handling charge from James Pruett, Chairman of the MLA Publications Committee, Music Library, Hill Hall, University of North Carolina, Chapel Hill, North Carolina 27514. One should also consult the appropriate *Library Technology Reports* for more up-to-date brands and specifications: American Library Association. Library Technology Program. *Library Technology Reports; A service to provide information on library systems, equipment, and supplies to the library profession* (Chicago: ALA, 1965-   ).

On Planning a Music Library

by Wolfgang M. Freitag

One cannot discuss an institutional library without defining the institution's purpose. For, if one looks beyond the archival function and the old library school slogan according to which it is the noblest function of any librarian to "bring books and people together," the profession derives its only *raison d'être* from the needs of the fields of human endeavor it serves and from the needs of the people who cultivate these fields.

The music librarian, as a member of one of the oldest organized branches of special librarianship, shares with other professionals in educational and cultural institutions a dual loyalty—to his profession and to the field of learning to which he applies his skills. Quite naturally the music librarian is music-oriented, and the physical quarters which are the scene of his professional activities should be geared to meet the needs dictated by subject matter and clientele.

Music libraries exist in many forms and sizes. There are music divisions in national and state libraries and music collections in university libraries. There are libraries in colleges, conservatories and music schools, music departments in countless public libraries, and even a few independent all-music public libraries. While the libraries of the first group serve archival as well as research and instructional needs, the libraries of the second group are an important indicator for the level of popular music culture in the communities and are principal instruments of informal education in music.

All these different libraries have in common their allegiance to music, and, to a varying degree, the kind of materials which they collect, catalog, preserve, and make available to their readers: materials such as manuscripts, books, periodicals, scores, sheet music. To this list, phonorecords on disc and tape and microforms have been added relatively recently.

I cannot hope to give adequate treatment to all these types of libraries in their astonishing diversity; that would require a book rather than an article. I do hope, however, that my experience with the documentation of recent library architecture can serve a useful purpose. The aim of this introduction, then, is to show how library materials which represent the recorded knowledge of one subject field, music in this case, demand similar physical facilities, modified only by the characteristics of the institutional setting.

I regret very much that the space allotted me does not permit me to say more about the differences between physical and building requirements of popular and scholarly music libraries. Simply because I am more familiar with the academic library scene, I am limiting my remarks to research and university situations. This, of course, is a rather one-sided approach. I hope that in the course of the discussion which is to follow, you will have time to deal with the planning problems of other library types. For those of you who will want to read more about the planning of library quarters for public and special music libraries, I have added a bibliographical appendix. The appendix lists papers dealing primarily with practical aspects of the planning of music library buildings not referred to in my introduction. Brief annotations are given where necessary.

In the following pages some guidelines will be established for the planning of new buildings. Let us hope that later during the discussion[1] we shall also be able to consider how the objectives of music librarianship which require unusual

---

SOURCE: Reprinted from Wolfgang M. Freitag, "On planing [sic] a music library," *Fontes artis musicae,* 11 (January–April, 1964), 35–49, by permission of the International Association of Music Libraries.

architectural features can be fulfilled in buildings not originally planned for music library purposes.

MUSIC DEPARTMENTS IN LARGE RESEARCH LIBRARIES

In large research libraries—state or national libraries, or 'public' libraries of the rank of the New York Public Library, are envisaged here—the organizational set-up for music follows a more or less standard pattern. Music holdings are fully integrated, forming part of the general collection. The Music Department, however, often has its own reading room; it controls the subject, or classified catalog, and has its own bibliography section. Sometimes listening rooms with pianos and phonographs are provided. This form of organization requires a competent department chief and a trained staff, but not much unusual equipment. Naturally, an effort will be made to sound-proof the listening rooms and to install top quality machines. Desks and reading tables should be large and, if possible, have sloped tops in order to facilitate the use of large and heavy volumes such as part-books, scores, and the various *Denkmäler* editions. It seems that in these libraries the main problem is one of communication and transportation of books between reading rooms and stacks. In American libraries where books are shelved systematically by classification it is important that the stack section, which houses the music materials, is conveniently located adjacent to the public service rooms of the Music Department, so as to allow easy access for the staff and for those readers who enjoy stack privileges. In closed stack libraries of the continental tradition, where books are shelved by size and chronologically by *numerus currens,* an efficient call system, using either pneumatic devices or some kind of electronic apparatus, plus mechanical equipment in the form of lifts and conveyors, is necessary to speed up traffic between reading room, circulation desk, and stacks.

MUSIC LIBRARIES IN UNIVERSITIES

If music is handled in the central library of a university, physical requirements are essentially the same as in the large non-university research libraries. The collection is fully integrated. The larger universities will provide ample reading room space and listening rooms. Open stack libraries will also have study carrels built into the stack area. Perhaps the music section will also have its own microfilm reading equipment, especially in departmentalized collections and in those collections where no special microtext reading room exists.

In many modern closed stack libraries, the idea of mingling readers and books has been well received. A larger part of the collection is moved out of the stacks and made openly accessibly in departmental reading rooms, which are no longer simply "reference" rooms. In addition to a richer fare available on open shelves in reading rooms, many academic libraries in Europe are establishing separate reading rooms for the younger beginning student. These rooms often combine the functions of browsing rooms and undergraduate reading rooms found in American colleges. Where this trend is followed it becomes necessary to stock the open-shelf room collections with a representative selection of music materials.

University libraries which are organized according to this pattern also maintain, as a rule, separate and quite autonomous departmental or seminar libraries outside the jurisdiction of the central library. Obviously, this form of organization results in much duplication of books and periodicals, and each university administration must decide for itself whether such an arrangement, in which the archival and the service functions of library collections are quasi-separated, is desirable in the light of the expenses incurred.

In the United States we have a tradition of decentralization in the larger and older universities. The libraries of the "classic" professional schools of law, medicine and theology, have long had their own separate libraries. Keyes D. Metcalf, who for many years has been concerned with a solution to the problems involved in the tremendous growth of libraries, has calculated that replacement of the central library building at Harvard would have required thirty million dollars—a prohibitive cost. He sees the best solution to the problem in the storage of lesser-used books under inexpensive warehouse conditions and, wherever possible, in cooperative storage libraries. He also sees another solution in an even greater decentralization of the university library.[2] Harvard has always been decentralized to some extent. The professional schools have had their own libraries, some their own buildings, and the natural sciences have had their departmental libraries in the laboratory and classroom buildings. The holdings of these independent units of the library system are usually not duplicated in the main library but are represented in the form of catalog entries in the union catalog, which is located in the central library. The humanities have long resisted this trend to separate from the main collection, but this resistance was broken, first in 1956 when the music collection was moved into its own library which was constructed as an annex to the Music Building. The fine arts collection will follow the exodus from Widener, the home of the central collection, in the summer of 1963, as soon as the new stacks which are being constructed under and near the Fogg Art Museum are ready for occupancy. The Music Library, now entirely controlled by the Music Department, maintains some coordination with the main library in cataloging and in its acquisitions policy, especially with regard to some borderline areas such as folklore and libretti. But there are no *bona fide* music materials left in the Widener building except for a mere handful of bio-bibliographical reference works. Harvard also has, in its Lamont Library, a separate undergraduate library which contains a carefully selected collection of music and music books numbering 1,711 titles. This represents a mere 1.3% of the total holdings of Lamont Library which holds 126,000 volumes. It must be borne in mind that this collection is maintained to serve those undergraduates who are taking music courses as part of their general education, rather than for music concentrators.

MUSIC LIBRARIES IN MUSIC DEPARTMENTS

Let us assume now that books about music, the sheet music itself, and the phonorecords are all placed at the most convenient possible location, in a separate music library. In a university which offers courses not only in musicology but also in a number of practical conservatory subjects the collection will, of course, be different in scope from one in an institution which has limited its education program to only one aspect of the subject.

What should precede the actual planning for a building is the plan for service. This should spell out clearly:

a. The objectives of the institution
b. The estimated number of readers to be served
c. The estimated prospective increase of the number of readers over a number of years (25 years or more)
d. The anticipated rate of growth of the collection
e. The initial size of the collection
f. The number of personnel necessary to guarantee adequate service under present and anticipated conditions.

K. D. Metcalf thinks that, "A new building ought to provide for present collections, staff, and readers, plus anticipated growth for at least twenty-five years to come, and preferably for twice that period." [3]

In the design of the library, the principle objective is to plan and design so as to produce the environment and the facilities required for the purpose of the building. If the funds for a separate music library have been appropriated, the first step in planning will be the formation of a building committee. It should include one staff member from each service branch of the library (i.e. cataloging, acquisitions, circulation, reference, and, if applicable, rare books, manuscripts and phonorecords), one or more members of the faculty, a representative of the student government and the librarian *ex officio.* The building committee functions in an advisory capacity, the responsibility for the final formulation of the library's requirements rests with the librarian. When an architect is chosen, it is wise to select one for his past accomplishments without paying too much attention to other libraries he may have designed, as no two library building tasks are the same. It is also advisable to engage a consultant whose job it is to detect mistakes in the planning of the librarian and his committee. The consultant should always be a librarian who has had experience with the planning of libraries "inside-out," from a functional point of view. The architect will probably also want to call in several consultants. For instance, he may want advice from a foundation engineer where the terrain is difficult. Most architects find it necessary to have a mechanical engineer who helps with the design of plumbing, heating, air-conditioning, elevators and similar mechanical details. If the architect who is designing a music library is not himself competent in architectural acoustics, he should be required to engage a consultant in sound-control engineering. These are precautions that must be taken if serious errors are to be avoided. On the other hand, it is very important that neither the librarian nor the library consultant try to dictate to the architect the form and aesthetics of the new building. No self-respecting professional will permit laymen to meddle with these things. Selecting the right man for a given task is a decision of greatest consequence. Once he is commissioned he must be made to feel that he has the complete confidence of his clients. Because major changes are difficult to implement once construction has started, or even after the final blueprints have been made, it is very important to tell the architect early, in no uncertain terms, which features the clients expect the new building to have. Ideally, when the architect appears on the scene, the work of the building committee should have been completed.

The site of the building to be erected is often pre-determined by its relationship to other buildings, by the amount of space available adjacent to the building which houses the lecture halls and administrative offices of the music department, and by local building codes which generally prescribe height and area limitations. For correct orientation of the library, careful consideration should be given to traffic patterns between classrooms, living quarters, and library. Road and traffic noise should be studied before a site is adopted. Public entrances should be placed at those points which students frequently pass. Artificial detours must be avoided. It is equally important to avoid making any of the library's rooms a traffic lane to classrooms and faculty offices, as this would disturb readers. The height of the building depends upon building regulation, the size of the site, the desired book capacity and the number of readers to be accommodated. Planners who are taking the long view will not only consider the initial cost but also the costs of maintenance operation including costs of staffing. Certainly, more "dead" space (entrance lobbies, corridors, stairs) results in multi-storied structures and in buildings that have several public entrances. These libraries require more control points and therefore more personnel and higher salary requirements. For reasons of economy, most planners of departmental libraries, therefore, want a one-story building or a split-level building wherein only one public entrance and one central control desk are required. Many plans also call for some kind of basement storage space where certain groups of lesser-used materials can be housed.

Although planning committees will fight for it, few budgets will actually permit construction of a finished building big enough to accomodate the anticipated growth over a period of 25 to 50 years. It should be remembered that music has a literature which is purely cumulative; it does not become obsolete and it does not permit periodic "weeding" to keep a collection from growing too fast. Hence expansion problems in music libraries are to be taken more seriously than in many other fields.

With the excellent possibilities offered by modular construction, a compromise acceptable to librarian and university planning board can often be reached if space, not immediately needed for library purposes, is temporarily partitioned off and put to other use, with the thought in mind of converting it to library space later when the need arises. One writer who favors a psychological approach suggests that, if a building which would take care of the next twenty years is not feasible now, the architect should enclose as much as possible of the total space required, even if this should result in a partly empty shell. This, he reasons, will serve as a constant reminder to the authorities controlling the purse strings that there is unfinished business to be completed.[4] In America many educational buildings, not only libraries but also laboratories for research in rapidly expanding sciences, are now being finished with a certain number of stories but the top floor is left open and only provisionally roofed to provide room for expansion.

This is the point at which the terms "flexibility" and "modular design" enter our discussion. If a building is to have flexibility, areas used for one kind of activity (reading rooms, offices, workrooms, stacks) can be adapted to other uses. This may require that all floors in the library must be capable of supporting really heavy loads at all points, and that it must be possible to take away any of the interior walls without hazard to the stability of the structure. I, for my part, like daylight in a library and do not consider windows a luxury. But one can often hear the opposite view in library circles since large wall spaces can become priceless later on for placing additional shelving and increasing book capacity. Windowless rooms are also easier to air-condition.

Modular design is a means for achieving the highest degree of flexibility. The concept of a module is that of a three dimensional unit of space which repeats itself throughout the building. It is often based on the dimensions of the most vital piece of furniture or equipment in the building. Hospital planners have adopted the dimensions of a standard hospital bed as their basic module. In a music school it may well be the footage needed for a grand piano. Librarians find it convenient to use a module of 3–4 feet (0,91–1,22 m) which corresponds roughly to the length of a standard stack section, and are designing both building partitions and furniture to suit this basic unit of measurement. In order to create as much uncommitted space as possible it is necessary to supply facilities, such as power, water, drainage and air-conditioning, in service shafts which can be placed centrally, that is away from the walls, or at the periphery in ducts outside the walls. Both solutions leave as much space as possible open and uninterrupted by columns. Many librarians have in the past adopted the principle of flexibility for public and work areas but not for the bookstacks. The initially somewhat higher cost of modular construction should not keep library planners from adopting it. Flexibility of library space is a prized commodity and modular design and construction will almost certainly save the institution money later, when it and its library grows.

Libraries have to provide space for books, for readers and for their staff. A rule of thumb—by no means the only one—for estimating space requirements for these areas is this:

a. Provide seats for 30% of the student population at from 25 to 35 square feet (2,32 to 3,25 m^2) per reader. These seats can be in the reading room or elsewhere in the building, *e.g.* as carrels in the stacks.
b. Provide one square foot (ca. 9 dm^2) for every ten volumes which will be displayed on open shelves. Estimate five volumes per linear foot of shelving in the stacks. Allow for anticipated growth. The rate of growth varies from institution to institution. Young libraries may expect to grow from a rate of five to ten percent each year, whereas mature libraries may have annual increases of as little as 2 to 2.5%.
c. Allow approximately the sixth part of the total space for workrooms and offices. Or, if you prefer, allot 125 square feet (11,6 m^2) for each staff member employed. Anticipate increase in staff.
d. Add 25% of the sum total of items just listed for general space, such as corridors, washrooms, stairs, etc.

As can be seen in the above tabulation, readers' space includes seats and table space in reading rooms but also seats that may be in the stacks or even in conference rooms. K.D. Metcalf has come to the conclusion that each reader requires a total of 50 square feet (4,64 m^2) in the building.[5] As for the requirement to provide seats for 30% of the student enrollment, Liebers quotes a British colleague who suggests reading room seats for only 20% of the students.[6]

The reference and circulation desk should be placed near the entrance to the reading room. It may be in the lobby, but it is important that it be within easy distance from the public catalog. The features demanded of a circulation desk naturally depend upon the charging system used. Therefore, I shall skip the details and say that generally these desks should not be higher than 39 inches (99 cm). This height is convenient for librarian and reader and does not give the impression of a barrier, while at the same time it is sufficient to protect and shield that area in which the librarian is working.

Close to the reference-circulation desk one may wish to place the cumulative indexing and journal abstracting services and similar reference tools which are frequently used. A good solution to the problem of their shelving is to place them on shelves above a bar-type table at which readers can sit down to look up references without having to carry the heavy tomes to their tables.

The size and shape of the catalog again depend upon local traditions. The catalog cabinet may consist of one unit in libraries which use the dictionary-catalog. Where there is a tradition of divided author and title-and-subject catalogs, or of separate classified catalogs, and separate index files for phonorecords or microfilms, several cabinet units can be used, not necessarily in close proximity to one another. For instance, the record catalog may very well be nearer to the listening room than to the control desk. It is, however, advisable to put that part of the catalog which is used most by the general reader as close as possible to the service point.

Some libraries have a small alcove-like room behind the desk where they keep the lesser-used reference literature as well as booksellers' catalogs, auction price lists and all the tools needed for the cataloging and ordering of books and music. This section which is open to the public, though not in the center of the reading room, must also be easily accessible from the catalog and order departments.

Reading tables in a music library should have

somewhat larger surfaces than those in a general library. In America it is customary to allow 30 inches (76 cm) per reader along the side of a table. Tables at which music is studied should allow even more space per reader. Table tops should be inclined because, as I have already pointed out, this makes handling of large and odd-sized volumes easier. If space permits, groups of informal upholstered furniture can be added. By surrounding these informal groupings with wooden counter-high shelving a certain amount of privacy is possible. The books on these shelves form part of the regular reading room collection, the size of which will be determined by the library's policy on open stacks and by the arrangement of books in the stacks, that is whether they are arranged chronologically and by size, or by classification.

Reading room shelving may be arranged in the classical fashion by placing it along the walls of the room. This arrangement permits additional erection later of perpendicular shelving protruding into the room forming niches. Another layout calls for a number of short stack sections which are all perpendicular to one of the walls. With modern free standing shelving there are many possible arrangements which can be changed if circumstances demand reorganization. Care should be taken that enough sloped periodical display shelves are planned. They should be constructed so as to contain storage units which can hold approximately one year, unbound back issues, for each periodical displayed.

In planning the layout of reading rooms and other public spaces librarians have used paper or wooden models in order to get a two- or three-dimensional impression of how the finished rooms will look. Two-dimensional cardboard models require first a scale plan of the rooms and next, measurements scaled down and drawn on cardboard from which cutouts are made. These facsimiles can be moved easily on the plan. Three-dimensional models which are more difficult to make look even more realistic. Some library supply firms also offer models of their products which can be used provided one has right scale planning.

The monumental reading room is a thing of the past. Today eleven or twelve feet (3,35 or 3,65 m) is considered a generous height. It is economical from the point of view of heating, ventilating and illumination.

The question, how many foot-candles intensity of light are necessary for certain reading tasks, is a bone of contention between ophtalmologists and illuminating engineers. It seems to involve hard to measure psychological factors. Levels of intensity recommended by the industry have gone up almost every year with the technical perfection of light sources. Whereas some spokesmen for industry now recommend several hundred foot-candles, many doctors claim that intensities greater than twenty foot-candles have no real significance for most visual tasks.[7] Many new libraries have settled for intensities of hundred foot-candles on table tops. This light intensity is sufficient even for reading manuscript music, miniature scores and other fine print. For illumination in the public service areas, fluorescent tubes can now be recommended without reservation, because the flicker effect has disappeared. Fluorescent tubes which can be used in a great variety of fixtures and in luminous ceilings are cheaper in the long run. In the stacks fluorescent tubes are acceptable only where they are in more or less continuous use, as in aisles and on deck landings, for instance. For lighting the spaces between the shelf ranges, incandescent bulbs may actually be better than fluorescent tubes, which don't last very long when they are switched on and off frequently in short intervals.

Adequate sound control is of special importance in the music library. Here I am not thinking of the obvious acoustical problems of auditoriums and listening facilities but of reading rooms and other public spaces in the library proper. Sound control in any reading room begins with the shape of the room; it has an important influence on the acoustical qualities. As you all know, measurable loudness alone does not give a measure of the annoyance of noise. Some inevitable background noise in reading rooms is acceptable if it does not exceed twenty decibels. (The *decibel* is the acoustical term for a relative measurement of sound. One *db* corresponds to the minimal threshold of audibility. Normal conversations have intensities of 60 db.) Much can be done to dampen noise by the use of such acoustical materials as acoustical tile ceilings and sound-absorbing wall coverings. "Masking" of noise is also possible, especially if it is noise created by mechanical equipment, air-conditioning machinery, for instance. By having two, instead of one, air-conditioning units, each humming at approximately the same frequency, the noise becomes less annoying since a sound is most effectively masked by another sound of the same frequency. Footsteps are another common source of noise in reading rooms. The best way to reduce the noise of footsteps is to control it where it starts by selecting sound-reducing floor materials. Carpets are best for this purpose and are becoming more and more fashionable in library reading rooms. They, however, are expensive and present a number of hygienic and maintenance problems. Linoleum, cork-linoleum, rubber-cork and vinyl-asbestos are quite satisfactory substitutes for carpeting.

The number of other public rooms depends on the library's physical relationship to the music building. If the library is just an annex to that building, an auditorium and perhaps also piano and phonograph listening rooms are dispensable. If, on the other hand, the library is at a distance from music headquarters, these rooms are very important. They too should have good sound insulation which can be achieved, even in modern flexible buildings, by the use of prefabricated and very thin acoustical "sandwich" walls. If typewriter booths are provided they may consist of nothing more than simple recesses in a wall. They may be without doors if the internal surfaces are all covered with sound-absorbing materials. If desired, the microfilm reading machines can be put on the periphery of the reading room, or, if one wants to store the microfilm holdings in a separate room, the apparatus can be put where the films are close at hand. This room should have proper climatization. A library which owns many rare items, manuscripts, incunabula and the like, and which is therefore interested in preserving these materials, will also want an air-conditioned treasure room. In many university situations these materials will be placed in the rare book department of the central collection. No matter how large or how small a library is, it should have one or more conference rooms where seminars can meet and where students can gather for informal discussions without disturbing others. The benefits derived from informal discussion are realized by modern educators. Librarians should do their best to help with this activity by providing readily available facilities for it.

The remainder of the library will contain work and office areas, stacks, and miscellaneous general space to be used for a wardrobe, washrooms, stairs, elevators, corridors, a room for the janitor and his tools. The requirements for office and workroom space depend upon whether the library does its ordering, cataloguing and book processing on the premises or whether some of these functions are performed in the central library. If all processing is done in the music library, workroom and office space should be planned at the rate of 125 square feet (11,61 m^2) per staff member employed. The work-flow pattern should be studied carefully before rooms for the various functions are assigned. In all libraries there will be an office for the chief librarian and his secretary and a staff room. If there is to be a catalogers' room it should be directly accessible to the card catalog or catalogs and to the bibliographies. The order department will have to be placed in a position adjoining the director's room. The room which is to be used for receiving and endprocessing will be far more valuable if it has a direct service entrance, which may also have a loading platform on the outside of the building. A library of medium size will seldom have its own photographic laboratory. But simple quick-copying machines should be available for internal and public uses. To serve this purpose, a machine can be installed behind the main desk, or in an alcove of a corridor.

With regard to workrooms and offices, Liebers thinks it remarkable that, if one compares recent European library plans with American plans, one finds that the European planners assign a much greater proportion of the total space for office and similar internal uses.[8] In the course of my visits to some new library buildings in Germany, I have, indeed, been puzzled by the cellular character of many catalog and acquisitions departments which had, in my opinion, too many little cubbyholes for each staff member. European visitors to American libraries are often stunned by our large rooms with long parallel rows of desks and with the department chief somewhere at a corner desk. Can this phenomenon be explained by the existence of a particular kind of agoraphobia on the eastern shores of the Atlantic and claustrophobia on the western shores?

THE STACKS

Planning adequate stack space is the most important and also the most difficult part of all library planning. This task is, perhaps, easier in closed stack collections where one has available better statistical information on the quantity of books in various formats. For, if the number of folios, quartos, octavos, etc. and the number added to these categories annually is taken as the basis for a mathematical projection, it should not be too difficult to predict how many volumes of a given size will be in the library twenty years hence. Calculating stack space for a classified open stack library without fixed location is much more difficult. Gordon Randall, in a recent article in *Special Libraries,* asked:

> "Just how many volumes can a library of a given size accommodate? The authorities as quoted by Louis Kaplan in 'Shelving' (volume 3, part 2, 'The State of the Library Art,' edited by Ralph Shaw. New Brunswick: Rutgers Graduate School of Library Service, 1960) don't agree. He credits Melvil Dewey as assuming ten volumes to the linear foot, F. J. Burgoyne suggested 8.5 volumes and K. D. Metcalf 6.1 volumes. Of course, these estimates ranged in time from 1887 to 1947, and one might assume that in recent years authors have become wordier, or at least their books thicker."[9]

Robert Henderson, as far back as 1934, developed a formula for translating physical book space into architectural space. He first counted the actual number of books and their average dimensions. From these calculations he created a hypothetical book which he called the "cubook." According to Henderson, the number of "cubooks" multiplied by 0.676 equals the stack volume in cubic feet; if the floor area in square feet is desired one has to multiply the number of "cubooks" by 0.09.[10] The authorities quoted in the foregoing paragraphs have estimated from six to ten volumes per linear foot. Keyes D. Metcalf estimated fifteen volumes per square foot of stack area. Since music library stacks will have to accomodate many larger volumes, it is somewhat wiser to assume an even lower number, say five volumes per standard shelf (three feet long), with seven shelves per section (seven feet, six inches high), 105 volumes in each press.[11]

If unbound back issues of periodicals are to be stored lying flat, three titles will find room on a shelf. It is, however, more advisable to conserve space by keeping these unbound periodicals temporarily bundled or in cardboard boxes vertically placed. One has a choice between two different kinds of steel shelving for the stack. The classic multi-tier installation consists of units "stacked" one on top of the other. It is rigidly constructed, entirely self-supporting and usually found in big libraries with many stack decks. Multi-tier installation is the kind of stack construction used in all the older research libraries. In newer buildings, where this type of construction has been chosen, the heavy load-bearing columns are in the center of the building and the outer curtain walls are, as the name indicates, just protective wraps with no structural function whatsoever. Rigid multi-tier bookstacks naturally have almost no flexibility. In a smaller library, especially in one which has accepted the philosophy of mingling readers' and book space, one finds a large portion of the permanent collection in the reading room and a significant number of study tables, carrels, etc. built right into the stacks. For these smaller libraries, where "flexibility" is the watchword, a less rigid type of stack is preferable. Freestanding shelves, which can be easily arranged and rearranged come in two different basic models—the bracket and the slot types. The bracket-type shelf is generally considered the sturdier and the more versatile of the two since it permits insertion of individual shelves of different widths. This type is recommended for use in music libraries.

Floors in the stack section should be made of reinforced concrete of three to four inches (7, 6–10, 1 cm) in thickness. Stack ceilings can be kept relatively low; a little more than the height of the standard stack section (7 feet, 6 inches = 2,28 cm) is adequate if one does not wish to install sections with more than seven shelves. Supply firms will gladly cooperate in equipping the standard bracket-type shelving with optional features, such as periodicals' shelving or other shelving for flat storage. It is even possible to have locker compartments or newspaper racks installed. Important are the sheet metal dividers or suspended sliding wire supports for the vertical storage of "limp" materials, unbound sheet music, pocket scores and the like.

Aisles between stack ranges in open access stacks are usually 36 inches (91 cm) wide. Ranges are installed on 54 inch (1,37 m) centers (measured from post to post). Closed stack libraries naturally require less space between ranges. In this case, aisles only twenty-four inches (60,96 cm) wide should be sufficient. The length of the stack ranges should be determined by the dimensions of the stack room and from the point of view of ease of accessibility. The validity of the old assertion that no stack range should be more than fifteen feet (4,57 m) long has been questioned by Mr. Metcalf in an article on compact shelving. The library planner who wants more information on the subject of compact shelving should refer to the works of Fremont Rider and Robert H. Muller. These works have been supplemented by Mr. Metcalf's article which I have just cited.[12]

As we have seen, shelving for music materials requires some features not present in normal, standard-type bookstacks. Individual shelves should also have greater than standard width.

Vincent Duckles reports that twelve inch wide shelves with fixed partitions, approximately eight to twelve inches apart, can also be used for the storage of phonograph records. The ordinary twelve inch record album will—because there is always one inch unoccupied space in the rear of the shelf where it meets the shelf from the opposite side of the section—project a little beyond the edge of the shelf and thus offer a convenient finger hold for taking the album from the shelf.[13]

CONCLUSION

I would like to finish this cursory treatment of a vast subject by reiterating what I said a few pages earlier. The planner must first be quite clear about his present requirements and must be able to forecast as exactly as he can in which direction the institution of which the library is an integral part will be moving in the future. He must then, with flexibility foremost in mind, draw up a statement of space requirements, sizes and general layout of rooms. It is the duty of the librarian, as chairman of the planning committee, to prepare the instructions for the architect. Even if a building is to be erected in stages, it should be planned as a whole from the beginning. If budget cuts limit the quantity of construction that can be carried out at one time, under no circumstances should the quality of materials and good workmanship be sacrificed. Today nobody is building monumental library buildings of a palatial character. Fitness to the purpose for which the building is intended should be of paramount concern to all those connected with its planning. This does not mean that cheerfulness and comfort are considered obsolete; a music library certainly does not have to capture the atmosphere of a laboratory. It should, on the contrary, have pleasant landscaping, tasteful and comfortable furniture, good lighting, clean air, excellent acoustical properties and plenty of space for books, readers, and for growth. In short, let's make the music library as attractive as possible, a place where creative thinking in the humanistic tradition will find the most congenial physical environment.

APPENDIX

A. General References of Interest to Music Library Planners

Barksdale, A. Beverly. "On the planning and arranging of music exhibitions," *Notes,* 10 (September, 1953), 565-569. [Reprinted in this *Reader,* pp. 217-220.]

Bechanan, H. Gordon. "The organization of microforms in the library," *Library Trends,* 8 (January, 1960), 391-406. [Description of the Microtext Reading Room at Harvard.]

Bukofzer, Manfred. "Forms and functions of the music library," *Notes: Supplement for Members,* No. 3 (March, 1948), 3-9. [Reprinted in this *Reader,* pp. 10-14.]

Burgoyne, F. John. *Library construction: Architecture, fittings and furniture.* London: Allen, 1897. [A library classic. The chapters on stacks, shelving and equipment are well worth the attention of today's library planner. It seems that compact shelving, telefacsimile and microreproduction were well known in Burgoyne's day and that it is only thanks to our advanced technological know-how that we now can utilize effectively some of the devices which the author recommended for use in libraries.]

Content, Edward J. "Sound control in libraries," *Architectural Record,* 100 (November, 1946), 121.

Dickinson, George S. "The living library," *Notes,* 3 (June, 1946), 247-255. [Reprinted in this *Reader,* pp. 46-52].

Duckles, Vincent H., issue editor. "Music libraries and librarianship," *Library Trends,* 8 (April, 1960), 495-626.

——, "Problems of music library equipment," *Notes,* 11 (March, 1954), 213-223. [Written when the author was planning the new music library quarters at the University of California at Berkeley.]

——. "The rôle of the public library in modern musical education," *Fontes artis musicae,* 3 (July, 1956), 37-38, 140-143. [Explains the interplay between the typical American public library and the college and university library and the relationship between formal and informal music education to an European audience. Reprinted in this *Reader,* pp. 26-30.]

Ellsworth, Ralph E. "Consultants for college and university library building planning," *College and Research Libraries,* 21 (July, 1960), 263-268.

____. *Planning the college and university library building.* Boulder, Colorado: Pruett Press, 1960.

Gierow, Krister, "Library building questions; lecture held at the IFLA Council meeting 1960," *Libri,* 10 (1960), 307-313. [It is recommended that an international committee should be formed by IFLA or UNESCO to coordinate research on library building questions which is being done on the national and local level.]

Gifford, Hilda. "Function and the library," *Journal of the Royal Architectural Institute of Canada,* 36 (April, 1959), 104-105. [Some observations on "fashions" in library styles which reflect "fashions" in the philosophy of library service. Contains some practical advice on how to use the scale ruler.]

Goodfriend, Lewis S. "Lightweight partitions," *Noise Control,* 2 (November, 1956), 49.

Herner, Saul. "The physical planning of special libraries," *Special Libraries,* 42 (January, 1951), 5-12. [Two complete plans for special subject collections making use of space in existing buildings. Although the author speaks of engineering and physics libraries, this article is basic. Contains a lucid step-by-step description of each planning phase.]

Kunze, Horst. *Bibliotheksverwaltungslehre.* Leipzig: Harrassowitz, 1956. [Chapter VIII: Das Bibliotheksgebäude, pp. 311-326.]

Langfeld, Johannes. "Aus der Büchereipraxis, eine Literaturübersicht," *Bücherei und Bildung,* 5 (June, 1953), 658-660. [Bibliographical essay. Titles on building selected for their value to the planners of public libraries.]

Mevissen, Werner. *Büchereibau–Public Library Building.* Essen: Heyer, 1958. [Comprehensive discussions of new public library buildings in Europe and America. Has an excellent chapter on furniture based on the function of each piece. Illustrated by photographs, floor plans, diagrams.]

Murphy, Richard M. "The Library in a Music School," *Notes,* 10 (September, 1953), 537-545. [Clearly sets forth the planning needs for a school that teaches practical music subjects. Reprinted in this *Reader,* pp. 53-58.]

Music Library Association. "Proceedings of the Meeting at Cambridge, Mass., June 21, 1941," *Notes,* ser. 1, no. 12 (November, 1941). [Contains two important speeches by K. D. Metcalf and E. M. White on the subject of "The Music Library and the General Administrator." The question is whether the needs of music in a university are best served by a music division as part of the general library, or in a separate music library.]

Pickett, A. G. and Lemcoe, M. M. *Preservation and Storage of Sound Recordings.* Washington, D. C.: Library of Congress, 1959.

Smith, Elizabeth E. and Watanabe, Ruth. "The Music Library in its Physical Aspects," *Library Trends,* 8 (April, 1960), 604-613. [Some practical observations by the librarian and reference librarian of the Eastman School of Music Library. Lacks building data or specifications.]

Shepard, Brooks, Jr. "Problems of Music Library Administration in the College or University," *Notes,* 11 (June, 1954), 359-365. [Reprinted in this *Reader,* pp. 41-45.]

Special Libraries Association. *A suggested Checklist for Library Planning.* New York: 1958. [A timetable for the planning of a small special library. The librarian is supposed to keep this list on hand during the planning and construction stage. Items are to be checked off as each step of the building operation is completed.]

Thompson, Anthony. "University Buildings: A selected Bibliography," *UNESCO Bull. for Libraries,* 13 (August-September, 1959), 210-216.

Tilly, Dorothy. "Maintenance Costs," *Library Journal,* 76 (October 1, 1951), 1774-1775. [Practical advice on the administration of music departments in public libraries, by the chief of the Music Department of the Detroit Public Library. Reprinted in this *Reader,* pp. 35-37.]

Wilson, Louis R. and Tauber, Maurice F. *The University Library.* 2d ed. New York: Columbia University Press, 1956. [Chapter XIV: Buildings and Equipment–Subject Division and Subject Rooms.]

Wylie, D.M. "Library Record Collections," *New Zealand Libraries,* 24 (December, 1961), 245-260. [On record collections in public libraries.]

Zabel, Klaus J. *Der Wandel im Bibliotheksbau unserer Zeit.* Diss.–Technische Hochschule Stuttgart, 1959.

B. Music Library Planning for some Specific Universities and Colleges in the U.S.A.

Antioch College, Yellow Springs, Ohio

"Olive Kettering Library," *Library Journal,* 80 (December 1, 1955), 2747-2751. [ACRL Monograph No. 11 (1954), 47-67].

University of Colorado, Boulder, Colorado

Ellsworth, Ralph E. "Colorado's Divisional Reading Room Plan: Description and Evaluation," *College and Research Libraries,* 2 (March, 1941), 103-109.

North Texas State College, Denton, Texas

Heyer, Anna H. "Music Activities at North Texas State College," *Notes,* 4 (March, 1947), 234-240. [This library contains one of the largest music libraries in the West. It is operated as a subject division within the general college library.]

Olivet Nazarene College, Kankakee, Illinois

Gilley, Ruth E. "Memorial Library Olivet Nazarene College," *Illinois Librarian,* 39 (November, 1957), 333-336. [Description of the music room on the ground floor of the main library.]

Purdue University Memorial Center, Lafayette, Indiana

Purdue University Hall of Music. Pamphlet published by the University. [The music department and the music library are housed in an annex to the Memorial Union.]

Southwestern Baptist Theological Seminary, Fort Worth, Texas

Thompson, Sara. "A Library of—and for—Music," *Pioneer,* 24 (January-February, 1961), 10-11. [The most important features of this library are the audio facilities. Each sitting place has either a record player or a tape deck permanently installed in the table, complete with full control panels for proper adjustment. There is a master control panel on the instructor's desk. By present day standards this library of the department of church music in the general library of this theological school is one of the most modern ones in the country.]

Wellesley College, Wellesley, Massachusetts

Cavanaugh, J. "The Acoustical Design of the Jewett Fine Arts Center—Wellesley College, Wellesley, Mass.," *J. Acoustical Soc. of America,* 33 (June, 1961), 837. [The building houses the music library, a 350 seat auditorium, studios, classrooms and practice rooms.]

Yale University, New Haven, Connecticut

Shepard, Brooks, Jr. "Yale's Music Library Revised," *Notes,* 13 (June, 1956), 421-423. [The story of a very successful remodeling job designed by Russel Baily. Conversion of former office and classroom space in the Music School into library space.]

C. Music Library Facilities in some Specific Public Libraries

Cincinnati and Hamilton County Public Library, Cincinnati, Ohio

Brown, Karline. "From Low Estate to Hi-Fi," *Notes,* 13 (June, 1956), 406-420. [Excellent description of the audio-visual equipment in the library.]

Plaut, Alice S. "A Promenade in the Art and Music Department of the Public Library of Cincinnati and Hamilton County," *Notes,* 13 (June, 1956), 401-405. [Divisional plan. Music materials on open shelves number 15,000 volumes, with 13,000 volumes more in the general stacks. Call service by pneumatic tubes and booklift.]

Denver Public Library, Denver, Colorado

Eastlick, John T. "Denver goes Modern," *Library Journal,* 81 (December 1, 1956), 2769-2771. [The library is organized on the subject divisional plan. Music is entirely self-contained having its own reference and circulation departments. Cataloging is done under the supervision of a general chief cataloger and departmental cards are filed in a general cataloge.]

Jackson, Mississippi, Public Library

"Jackson, Mississippi, Library is one of the South's Finest," *Pioneer,* 18 (September-October, 1955). [The second floor contains the art and music department with two listening rooms and a microfilm room.]

Liverpool Music Library Suite, Liverpool, England

Chandler, G. "Liverpool Music Library Suite," *Library Assoc. Record,* 61 (June, 1959), 160-162. [The suite consists of a central foyer, a periodicals foyer, a concert room, the library proper (40,000 vols.), a manuscript exhibition foyer, a gramophone listening room, and a stack room.]

Manchester Public Library, Manchester, England

Duck, L. W. "The Henry Watson Music Library," *Library World,* 63 (March, 1962), 132-136. Historical account of the transformation of this private independent music library into the music department of the Manchester Public Library.]

Richmond, California, Public Library

Emerson, Caryl. "Music Services in a Medium-Sized Public Library in Richmond, California," *Library Trends,* 8 (April, 1960), 595-603. [Stresses importance of basically sound architectural design which should include adequate provision for the quarters of the musical department.]

NOTES

[1] At the Sixth International Congress of the International Association of Music Libraries, Stockholm-Uppsala, August 13-18, 1962, the First Symposium: Library Building.–*Editor.*

[2] Keyes D. Metcalf, "University libraries face the future," *Library Quarterly,* 22 (January, 1952), 5-12; the same, "When bookstacks overflow," *Harvard Library Bulletin,* 8 (Spring, 1954), 205.

[3] Keyes D. Metcalf, "Selection of library sites," *College and Research Libraries,* 22 (May, 1961), 184.

[4] Brother David Martin, "Architect and Librarian," *Catholic Library World,* 33 (March, 1962), 417.

[5] Keyes D. Metcalf, "Alternatives to a new library building," *College and Research Libraries,* 22 (September, 1961), 346.

[6] Gerhard Liebers, "Baufragen bei neuen Lesesaalformen," *Zeitschrift für Bibliothekswesen und Bibliographie,* 3 (1956), 206-212.

[7] Keyes D. Metcalf, "Library lighting," *Library Journal,* 86 (December 1, 1961), 4084.

[8] Gerhard Liebers, "Entwicklungstendenzen im deutschen Bibliotheksbau," *Zeitschrift für Bibliothekswesen und Bibliographie,* 8 (1961), 225.

[9] Gordon E. Randall, "Library space and steel shelving," *Special Libraries,* 53 (February, 1962), 96.

[10] Robert W. Henderson, "Bookstack planning with the cubook," *Library Journal,* 59 (November 15, 1934), 865-868.

[11] Wallace [**284**, 281] points out that scores are, generally, thinner than books and that no figure representing the average number of scores per linear shelf foot has been published–if indeed it has ever been determined. Cf. Wallace's recommended alternative, p. 13.–*Editor.*

[12] Fremont Rider, *Compact book storage* (New York: Hadham Press, 1949); Robert H. Muller, *Evaluation of compact storage equipment* (Chicago: Association of College and Reference Libraries, 1954 [ACRL Monograph Number 11]); the same, "Compact storage equipment: Where to use it and where not," *College and Research Libraries,* 15 (July, 1954), 300-312; Keyes D. Metcalf, "Compact shelving," *College and Research Libraries,* 23 (March, 1962), 103-111.

[13] Vincent H. Duckles, "Musical scores and recordings," *Library Trends,* 4 (October, 1955), 169.

VII

MUSIC LIBRARIANSHIP

This last subdivision is more oriented to the future than either the present or past. Music librarians have yet to codify their standards for academic qualifications. The great diversity of types of collections to be administered and duties to be performed by persons generically grouped as music librarians has led to the evolution of specialists within that genus. As Dr. Spivacke points out, educational qualifications and intellectual skills must be appropriate to the performance of the required specialized tasks.

Dr. Kinkeldey's classic statement, still the best we have, was made when music librarians themselves were specialists within the genus of librarianship. Almost thirty years later Dr. Spivacke makes many of the same points, but there are still no standards for the professional education of music librarians. Mme. Clercx-Lejeune concludes her discussion with a plea for an international educational standard. M. Lesure writes of the need for somewhat independent research music libraries operating in conjunction with universities and in which the librarian is himself a scholar, working with other scholars to attain bibliographic control of contemporary publications, to coordinate the work of researchers to prevent wasteful duplication of work, and to produce their own research, as well as to publish the treasures of their libraries. Dr. Duckles addresses the new interpretation of documentation—as the automated control of information—vis-à-vis the traditional bibliographic techniques.

This *Reader* began with Dr. Sonneck's essay proposing and defending music as viable library material, progressed through the spate of publications which followed the formation of the Music Library Association in 1931, through the sophistication of music librarianship in the two decades after World War II, and ends with Dr. King's history and description of the work of the International Association of Music Libraries.

SELECTED BIBLIOGRAPHY

EDUCATION FOR MUSIC LIBRARIANSHIP:

285. Angell, Richard S. "Opportunities for special training in music librarianship," *Library Journal,* 64 (March 15, 1939), 217-218.

286. ——. "Report and resolution on music library training read at the meeting of the Music Library Association, Smith College, Nov. 19, 1937," *Notes,* 1st series, no. 7 (May, 1940), 17-18.

287. Amesbury, Dorothy G. "The special music librarian," *Notes,* 1st series, no. 11 (August, 1941), 12-18.

288. "Report of the Committee on Curricula," *Notes: Supplement for Members,* No. 3 (March, 1948), 14-15.

289. "Report of the Committee on Library Training," *Notes: Supplement for Members,* No. 4 (June, 1948), 18-20.

290. "Columbia University's courses in music library training," *Notes: Supplement for Members,* No. 5 (September, 1948), 17-18.

291. Angell, Richard S. "Librarian Education Conference," *Notes,* 6 (June, 1949), 454-456.

292. "Library Education Report," *Notes: Supplement for Members,* No. 11 (March, 1950), 18-19.

293. Marco, Guy A. "After Grove's, what?" *Library Journal,* 90 (March 15, 1965), 1259-1262.
Summarizes the findings of the questionnaire circulated to the ALA-accredited library schools by the MLA Midwest Chapter's Committee on Education (below).

294. *Explorations in music librarianship; an irregular series of occasional papers for members of the Midwest Chapter.* No. 1: *Music in the library school,* by Guy A. Marco. Kent, Ohio: MLA, Midwest Chapter, 1966.

295. Marco, Guy A. "Educational standards for music librarians," Paper read at MLA, Mid-winter meeting, Chicago, 21 January 1966. Kent, Ohio: Kent State University, n.d.

296. Weichlein, William J. "Training for music librarianship," *Fontes artis musicae,* 18 (1971/1-2), 28-30.
See also MLA *Manual,* pp. 9-11, especially notes 6 and 7.

* * * * *

297. Duckles, Vincent, comp. "An Institute on Music Librarianship," *Notes: Supplement for Members,* No. 8 (June, 1949).
Selected papers read during the Institute, October 29-30, 1948, held at the School of Librarianship, University of California, sponsored by the Northern California chapters of MLA and AMS and various agencies within the University of California.

298. Music Library Association. "Institute of international music library problems. Sponsored by the Music Library Association and the International Association of Music Libraries, American branch, September 13-15, 1961 [Reports]" *Notes,* 18 (September, 1961), 558-564.
There are three sections: 1. The International Inventory of Musical Sources [RISM].—2. The International Code for Cataloging Music [**125**, 140].—3. International cooperation among record libraries.

299. Watanabe, Ruth. "Workshops and institutes for music librarians in the United States," *Fontes artis musicae,* 18 (1971/1-2), 30-35.
An historical account.

* * * * *

300. Duckles, Vincent. "The music librarian in 1960," *Library Trends,* 8 (April, 1960), 495-501.

301. Filter, Nancy H. and Marco, Guy A. "MLA: A membership profile," *Notes,* 26 (March, 1970), 487-490.

302. "Music librarianship in the United States," *Fontes artis musicae,* 18 (1971/1-2), 3-59. Preface by Thor E. Wood.
Each article is cited in its appropriate place throughout the *Reader.*

THE MUSIC LIBRARY ASSOCIATION:

303. O'Meara, Eva Judd. "The Music Library Association," *Library Journal,* 61 (1936), 571-573.

304. Dickinson, George Sherman. "Apologia for the Music Library Association," *Notes,* 1st series, no. 6 (November, 1938), 36-37.

305. Beveridge, Lowell P. "The Music Library Association," *New York Herald Tribune,* April 2, 1944, Section IV, 6.

306. Campbell, Frank C. and Waters, Edward N. "The Music Library Association," *Music Journal,* 4 (May-June, 1946), 7, 40-46.
Resumé of the goals, services, and accomplishments—including publications—of MLA, 1931-1946.

307. Hill, Richard S. "The plight of our country's libraries; budgets are 'bad for books and impossible for music'; all of us must share blame," *Musical America,* 69 (February, 1949), 25, 162, 301.
Includes a short historical sketch of the MLA and its journal, *Notes.* Also mentions the decision to make *Notes* a broader interest journal and publish minutes of music librarians' meetings and papers in its *Supplement.*

308. Miller, Philip L. "The image of MLA," *Library Journal,* 89 (February 15, 1964), 809-811.

309. Coover, James B. "American music librarianship: The formative years and the first generation," *Fontes artis musicae,* 17 (1970/3), 109-119.

310. Morroni, June Rose. "The Music Library Association," *Fontes artis musicae,* 18 (1971/1-2), 5-18.

A slightly shortened version of her unpublished thesis, University of Chicago, 1968.

THE INTERNATIONAL ASSOCIATION OF MUSIC LIBRARIES:

311. Laufer, Robin. "Second world congress of music libraries," *Notes,* 7 (September, 1950), 519-521.

The beginnings of IAML and a list of its proposed tasks.

312. "New music association; the third and constitutive congress of the International Association of Music Libraries," *Library Journal,* 76 (November 1, 1951), 1794-1795.

Adoption of IAML's constitution and election of its first officers.

313. Wood, Thor E. "The International Association of Music Libraries," *Notes,* 25 (June, 1969), 697-699.

Training For Music Librarianship: Aims and Opportunities

by Otto Kinkeldey

Before I enter upon the discussion of my actual topic, let me ask your attention to a preliminary question which lies back of whatever ideas I may have to offer.

Why do we speak of music librarianship and why should it need a special training? A library, in its ideal form, should be a place where the accumulated and combined records of the thought and activity of the human race are made accessible to modern man. Only the largest and richest libraries can make an attempt to approach this ideal, but the larger the book organization, the greater the need for a subdivision of labor. Our modern age of specialization, hardly half a century old, lays great stress upon this division of labor and of material, and, unfortunately, I believe, has fostered a belief in the universal necessity of intensive development along a particular and ofttimes very narrow line, to the detriment of a coherent and coördinated growth of general faculties and the establishment of really broad foundations and comprehensive viewpoints. In the field of education some are beginning to be a little uneasy about the effect of exclusive specialization. But the broad foundations and comprehensive viewpoints have, by the very nature of the institution, been characteristics of the ordinary library, whether it be a large public library, a national scholar's library, or a university or college library. I do not suggest that the special library, attached to a special institution, school, or society, has no justification. Of these I shall have more to say later.

But the large library has always found it useful to have specialists on its staff. I have much sympathy with the continental system in which the staff consists almost entirely of specialists, particularly where these specialists are not narrow, hidebound pedants, but are conscious of their particular place in the larger system of books and of knowledge, and perform their work with a full realization of and in careful coördination with the life and operation of the organism as a whole.

The larger libraries, not only in modern times but in earlier days also, found it necessary to give certain types of material special treatment. Prints and maps are instances of this kind. But music is an even more striking example. Books about music, of course, present no difficulty. They need no more special treatment than books in science, in literature, or in history. But written and printed musical compositions are even more in a class by themselves than prints or maps. A special adaptability and training are required to read and to understand them. If a library proposes to deal with them in any but the smallest quantities, the specialist who possesses that adaptability and has received that training must be found.

Fifty years ago, I know that some musical compositions could be studied in the old Astor Library and in the Lenox Library. There was music in the Library of Congress also, but it was not cared for in the organized way of the present day. Twenty-five years ago one could find special music collections or music rooms in the Library of Congress, the New York Public Library, the Boston Public Library, and in the Newberry Library in Chicago. I know of no other large public music collection of that era. The Yale University Library housed the Rinck Collection, and the Harvard College Library gave space to some of the large editions of the classical composers. I know that some of the circulat-

SOURCE: Reprinted from Otto Kinkeldey, "Training for music librarianship: Aims and opportunities," *ALA Bulletin,* 31 (August, 1937), 459–463, by permission of the American Library Association.

ing libraries in New York City kept the vocal scores of the repertoire operas and the current vocal, piano, and chamber music.

A VASTLY DIFFERENT SITUATION

Today the picture is vastly different. Hardly a single larger public library is without its music section. A number of the university and college libraries and several of the great music schools have developed collections of no small dimensions. The west coast is now as assiduous in providing for the needs of musical library users as the east or the central states. The small circulating library is, in its way, performing a task as important as that of the large scholar's library. The phonograph record has become library material. The libraries have already closed their contracts with the microfilm for books, and I believe the day is not far off when the photophonographic sound film will be admitted beside the sound disc, perhaps ultimately to replace the latter.

This new situation raises problems which actually require special handling. Where are we to find the librarians who are competent in this special field and how much may we expect of them? How far can we, by a prescribed course of study and training, produce a type of librarian who will be able to handle the special problems that belong to music in a library? I do not believe the time has come to set up a complete and detailed curriculum for the exclusive training of a music librarian. It is quite possible to set up certain general principles on which future developments may be expected to rest.

MUST KNOW FUNDAMENTALS

In the first place and above all else, a music librarian should be a good librarian. I mean by that, that he or she should be a person adapted by nature and temperament to general library work. So far as systematic training goes, he should have received a large part of the general training and have acquired a large part of the knowledge which we expect of anyone who is connected with a library. A music librarian who is not thoroughly acquainted with the organization and operation of a general library as we know it today, who is not reasonably familiar with the methods of book selection, ordering, classifying, cataloging, and circulating as practiced today, who feels that his domain is a world by itself, and who is disinclined to make his work fit smoothly into the larger organism, is likely to do more harm than all the good a great special knowledge may bring. I do not believe it is possible to exaggerate the importance of this point.

As to the requirements for his special function, let me enumerate a few which seem to me of primary importance. I say nothing here about a deep interest in, and even a love for, the art of music. I cannot conceive of anyone who would want to become a music librarian without this. In the same way, I pass over the requirement of a fair knowledge of musical history. It is as necessary for the music librarian as a knowledge of the history of literature is to the general librarian. Let me come to more specific requirements. It does not seem to me necessary, in the first place, that a music librarian should be a good performer or composer. To be sure, one who sings well or plays an instrument well, and one who is able to create an actual musical composition, is more likely than another to understand the peculiar nature of the material in his charge as a librarian. But he may be a wholly adequate librarian without these accomplishments. On the other hand, a reasonable acquaintance with musical theory in the widest acceptance of the word; a knowledge of all its principles and technical terms is a fair requirement. A music librarian who did not recognize a fugue when he heard it, or saw it on paper, or who did not know the meaning of the term, double counterpoint, would be as useful as a literary librarian who did not know the difference between a sonnet and an epic, or a science librarian who could not recognize an equation of the second degree when he saw it, or who could not distinguish between a genus and a species name.

MORE THAN AVERAGE SKILL WITH LANGUAGES

In one point, which is not musical, the music librarian must be better equipped than the general librarian. That is, the matter of foreign languages. The general librarian who is not acquainted with a few of the continental European languages is always handicapped. In a college or university library, or in any large scholar's library, he is practically useless. Even in a smaller library the music librarian is faced with so many linguistic problems that never come to the general librarian, that at least an elementary knowledge of French, German, and Italian is an inevitable requisite. Although we say that music is a universal language, the foreign vernacular with which it is often associated is a great stumbling block to the linguistically deficient librarian. We still draw the greater part of our musical material from continental Europe. Not only in the field of opera and other vocal music does the foreign language assume great importance. Even the titles of instrumental works and the descriptive notes or explanations which must be drawn from foreign sources require some foreign language equipment. In fact, the librarian who has to rely for his knowledge of musical compositions and books on journals, histories, encyclopedias, and dictionaries in English only, cannot go very far.

BIBLIOGRAPHIC TOOLS DISTINCTLY DIFFERENT

In one other point the music librarian needs a special training and experience, and this is the matter of bibliography. For his general dealings with books about music he needs all the bibliographical tools, English and foreign, which belong to the general librarian. But he needs something in addition. Books about music come into being and are brought into the market through the same channels as all other books. Books containing musical compositions are created by an entirely different process. Book publishing and music publishing have been two entirely distinct branches of industry and have remained so to the present day. Rarely does a single firm combine the two activities. The house of Breitkopf und Härtel in Leipzig is, perhaps, the most striking exception. The English music house of Novello has published some books and the Oxford University Press has published some music. Nevertheless, the trade lists, which play such a large part in the librarian's life, have remained practically distinct for both fields. In fact, aside from the minute and elaborate trade lists for German musical publications, there are no good musical trade lists extending over a long series of years in any country in Europe or America.

This places an unduly heavy burden on the shoulders of the music librarian. Not only in the matter of book selection and ordering, but in the way of bibliographic description and cataloging, he must work out his own salvation, largely by slow experience. Add to this the strangely different material embodied in phonograph records and it should become clear why the music librarian's bibliographical task is a distinct and somewhat perplexing problem.

A MATTER OF CHANCE AT PRESENT

These then are some of the points to be envisaged in the formulation of a curriculum for the training of music librarians. One can hardly expect that our schools of library science should go very far in this direction at present, and it is not very likely that special schools for training music librarians will spring into being at once. For the time being, libraries that need a music specialist will have to continue to find him more or less by chance. A musician who displays a fair amount of library sense, or a library school graduate who has a musical interest and has had musical training will be placed in a position in which his native endowments may find immediate application, while he wrestles with the problems that arise from the peculiar nature of his material until with time and practice he becomes an expert.

If this practical experience can be gained in one of the existing well organized music divisions in large libraries, somewhat after the manner of the old apprentice-system, the outlook for the next generation is by no means bad. After all, the growing need for music librarians does not require that they should all be highly trained musical research scholars. There is room for such experts in every large scholar's library. But the daily requirements of the smaller public library can be very well satisfied by an intelligent and sensible library school graduate, who has a personal interest and a reasonable familiarity with the art of music, who will not shrink from the labor of reading regularly one or several good musical journals, who keeps abreast of the times by following the music pages of the daily press and the program notebooks of the larger concert organizations.

In one point our library schools can give aid to a student so inclined, and this is in the matter of bibliography. I was exceedingly gratified when, a few days before this paper was written, I received the announcement and schedule of courses for next term at the Columbia University School of Library Service. Here, for the first time to my knowledge, there is listed a separate course in the bibliography of music. If such a course can give the musically inclined library school student an idea of the more important musical bibliographical handbooks, book lists, and trade lists, and make him acquainted with the bibliographically useful encyclopedias and dictionaries, much will be gained.

Where can a librarian thus trained and equipped find a berth? The number of places for specialists who will be expected to devote themselves wholly to music and nothing but music, is, of course, comparatively small. Yet, as I intimated in my historical comment at the beginning of this paper, the situation today differs greatly from that of a quarter of a century ago. At that time, a meeting such as this in which I speak, would not have been possible. This development of two or three decades is likely to continue for some time.

There are perhaps half a dozen large historical collections, either independent or connected with a large university or public library, which really need the care of a highly trained and efficient music specialist, a professional musicologist, if you will. The growth of interest in all the arts, and music among them, in our colleges, the more emphatic introduction of music in our college curricula, has given another aspect to the question of music in our college and university libraries. Thirty years ago music, in many college libraries, was either disregarded entirely or allowed to shift for itself, as it were, with a sublime trust that somehow or other it would find its own place. Now there are many college libraries that would welcome a staff member who was generally useful, but who could also handle a greater or a smaller number of cases of music ordering, classifying, cataloging, and binding. The last problem is a particular specialty of the music librarian. I could quote you several instances of otherwise well ordered libraries in which you could have found the several instrumental parts of a chamber music composition handsomely and securely bound in one cover.

The same is true of the public libraries—even of the smaller public libraries. The increasing use of music in circulating libraries and the growing collections of phonograph records make a musical reference assistant a highly desirable addition to the staff. But there are places for music librarians other than in college and public libraries. The need for a well assorted and conveniently arranged collection of music of all kinds might be felt by every large radio broadcasting station, by the film producing laboratories, and the record manufacturers. I look for a development here like that which has taken place in the laboratories and experiment stations of our great electrical, chemical, and other scientific industries.

If we do not raise our expectations too high, there is no reason why we should not count on a steady growth of interest and opportunity in this field. In any case, if it is the kind of thing you like, there is no reason why you should not attempt to cultivate this particular talent (if you have it), by the side of that knowledge, equipment, and experience which entitle you to claim for yourself the designation of a good and generally useful librarian.

The Training of the Music Librarian

by Harold Spivacke

A paper read at a symposium on "The training of the music librarian" at the 6th International Congress of IAML in Stockholm-Uppsala, 1962.

The subject under discussion is obviously designed for future generations. I am sure that everyone here has shared my disturbed feelings when asked by a young person how best to prepare oneself for a position as a music librarian. I usually reply with a series of questions in order to ascertain the particular interests of the inquirer. The reason for this is the fact that we use the term music librarian to describe several different types of occupations which have enormous differences between them. The only thing that we all have in common is a preoccupation with music and even this is not always apparent as those of us dealing with sound recordings can attest. It is much easier to advise a young person wishing to enter the fields of law or medicine than that of music librarianship.

Before beginning to discuss the actual educational problems before us, I believe it necessary to attempt a brief and necessarily rough classification of the more common types of music libraries. Most of us work for what we might call public libraries. These may be large research institutions with extensive music collections like the British Museum, the Bibliothèque Nationale or the Library of Congress. Under this heading would also fall the large or small circulating libraries with separate music departments. The research libraries are concerned mostly with reference work and only incidentally with circulation. The opposite is true in the circulating libraries where the reference functions may take the minor role.

As a second category, we might classify the educational libraries. Under this heading I think of the university and college libraries many of which have extensive and famous music collections. They frequently combine both types of activities, that of reference and circulation. A librarian equipped to work in a public library can usually move to an academic institution without too much adjustment. But in the U.S. at least there is developing a new field—that of the school librarian working at the secondary and even the elementary level. This is a new and fast growing field about which I can report little at present but a field which we should all watch with interest.

Another category and one of great importance is that of the libraries connected with the media of mass communication. The most common is to be found in the broadcasting organizations. This form of librarianship has achieved its greatest importance in Europe. The function of the radio library varies considerably from country to country as does the duties of the librarian working for the broadcasting organization. Under this category should be placed the motion picture librarian more common in America and here too we can find enormous differences.

Still another field of librarianship is that of the orchestral librarian. I refer to those large symphony orchestras that maintain extensive libraries and have need of the services of at least one full time librarian. If you think that his duties are limited to the distribution, collection and care of orchestral parts, you underestimate the difficulties of his assignment. He must attend rehearsals and follow the score with the skill of a conductor, noting those passages which lead to misunderstandings on the part of the performers and making the necessary annotations in the parts.

Finally, mention should be made of the increasing use of librarians in the music-publishing houses. In fact, those publishers who do not employ librarians should do so, as those of us who have failed to obtain their material from them can attest. I am sure that there are other fields which use the services of music librarians—such as the relatively new independent sound recording library not connected with broadcasting—

SOURCE: Reprinted from Harold Spivacke, "Paper: The training of the music librarian," *Fontes artis musicae,* 11 (1964), 57–60, by permission of the International Association of Music Libraries.

but those mentioned are sufficient to show that the variety of types is very great.

How then can we speak of "training" a person for music librarianship when the term itself defies definition. To be frank, it is my opinion that we can discuss the subject only in terms of the duties relating to the type of position involved. In other words, the training desirable for a music librarian who is to work in a circulation library would not be the same for someone else who wishes to work for a broadcasting organization.

Let us therefore review once again these different categories in the light of their activities and training requirements. The first two categories can well be discussed together since the training problems are quite similar. I should like your indulgence, if I begin by outlining current practices in the Library of Congress because they seem to point up the basic problems.

In the Library of Congress, the Music Division is essentially a reference and custodial division. The work of cataloging and other processing activities is carried on in a different department. It has been our experience that a thorough training in musicology is more important for our work in reference work than is technical training in library science. Every professional member of the staff of the Music Division has at least a master's degree in musicology. This does not mean that we underestimate the importance of training in library science. Quite the contrary, every new member of the staff is required to study the basic principles of library science and how these principles are put into practice in our particular institution. Of course, some of our staff have had formal training in both musicology and library science and we certainly welcome this when we can find it but such individuals are rare and when we have to make a choice, we favor the musicological training.

In the sections where the cataloging is carried on in the Library of Congress, the emphasis is naturally on formal training in library science. I do not mean for a moment to imply that musicological training is not necessary in the work of the cataloger and I know of several eminent musicological scholars who are working as catalogers. But the Library of Congress, through its printed cards, catalogs for the entire country and it is obvious that a complete knowledge of cataloging rules and practices is essential for this work. A degree in library science is therefore almost universally required in the U.S. of those applying for work in what we call processing activities—cataloging, classification, etc.

In presenting our practices as an example—and what you have heard is an oversimplification—I am aware that ours is not at all a typical library. I realize that it is not identical in its operations even with the other large research libraries of the world. My purpose, however, was to bring out the dichotomy that does exist between the training necessary for reference work and that for the technical bibliothecal activities. The duties of most librarians, whether they work in a research library, a public circulating library or a university library, include both aspects of music library work. This combination of the two elements may make the training of the music librarian of the future a long and time consuming operation.

Before attempting to forecast the training of future librarians, let us continue the exploration into the various fields outlined in the categories already named. Let us turn first to the field of mass communications whether by radio, television or motion pictures. Here we come to an area that is much more highly developed in Europe than in America, but I am familiar enough with the wonderful work done in Europe to state categorically that if we were to turn loose a musicologist with a library science degree in a broadcasting organization, the results could be chaotic if not actually disastrous. He would have no understanding of his duties unless he had experience in the field of broadcasting and was thoroughly familiar with all the problems of programing and production of radio and television presentations. The duties of the librarians in the mass communications field differ so widely from organization to organization that it is almost impossible to define them. In the U.S. alone, the differences are already enormous. For instance, let me point out that in some motion picture organizations, the music librarian serves as chief of the copying staff whereas in others he is responsible for all research for copyright clearances. Obviously the training for such positions will differ materially.

I have already pointed out the special duties of librarians of symphony orchestras and publishing houses but I should like to review briefly the problems facing the librarian in charge of sound recordings. There was a time when the term "recording" simply meant a recording of music and as a result of this historical accident, the work of handling this material was assigned to the frequently overworked music librarian. Since then, however, as a result of technological improvements and the growing interest in archival preservation, there is hardly any field of human knowledge which does not use some form of sound recording whether it be in anthropology (one of the oldest to utilize these resources) or political science which has recently discovered that the *way* a man said something does make a difference. The librarian in this area must indeed resemble the renaissance man who was supposed to know a great deal of all facets of human knowledge. And even in this new field, we are witnessing the development of specialists.

In reviewing the variety of the duties and functions of what we call a music librarian, my purpose was not to confuse the issue but simply to point out the complexity of the problem which faces us. Our situation might be compared with that which faced the fields of medicine and law at the beginning of the 20th century. In the 19th century there were many good doctors and lawyers in the world who had never had the advantage of formal training in a medical college or law school. It is today impossible to practice either of these professions without the benefit of formal training in an approved institution. With the present proliferation of music libraries of all types throughout the world, I can readily see a time when it will be legally impossible for our successors to practice the profession of music librarianship without similar formal training in the field. It is our duty and responsibility to lay the groundwork for such training. What we propose today will take generations to accomplish but we must face it and come up with recommendations which can be tried and improved upon as the years go by. I for one am very pleased that this is an international effort. In the past, such efforts have been local and have suffered because later attempts to reconcile them by establishing international standards were very difficult.

In the U.S. and I am sure in other countries as well, there is a growing interest in our field so that we have an increasing number of young men and women who after achieving a doctorate in musicology then go on to take a degree in library science. This may well be a trend which indicates what the future requirements should be although I do not think that the doctorate is really essential. But as already stated, even this will not prepare a young person for work in mass communications. Still this long period of training is common in other fields such as medicine.

I am aware that in presenting the problems in this introduction to our discussion, that I have been guilty of oversimplification. I am aware that there is no real analogy between the training for medicine and law and the training for music librarianship. After all the fields of medicine and law have evolved a basic course of training whereas I am not sure that we shall ever be able to accomplish this for our profession. There are educators in the field of library science who believe that the basic library training course will equip a student for any branch of library work but I do not believe that many music librarians would agree with this viewpoint. If we had a choice to make, I believe that most of us would choose music training as the prime necessity.

Before closing, I should like to add my belief that most of us here have not come to the field of music librarianship through orthodox channels. We have come to the field through a variety of paths and many of us have become librarians partly through accident. But we all have two things in common. This is a love for music in all its forms and a love for archival documents whether in manuscript, printed scores, books or sound recordings. We also have a strong urge to serve many people with our materials. But I fear that these characteristics so essential to library work can never be taught in a school. To this extent, the librarian must be born to the profession.

The Music Librarian. His Professional Training

by Suzanne Clercx-Lejeune

I. THE PRESENT SITUATION OF THE MUSIC LIBRARIAN

Although they are grouped as members of an international society, music librarians are not engaged in a profession established and protected by statutes. The category to which they belong does not exist—officially at least—in any European country. Only certain conventions, and infinitely diverse ones at that, distinguish them from other librarians.

The very title which they have chosen for themselves might be cause for surprise: does one for example speak of a "geographer-librarian" or a "philologist-librarian?" In fact in the infinitely varied world of the librarians, one hardly thinks of singling out the specialists of this or that branch of human learning. If the music librarians have wished to assemble together and to be identified by a more specific title, it is not without reason: their profession is dependent not only on the knowledge of a discipline but also on a technique which is particular to their occupation.

In order to establish the present state of the matter, we have questioned colleagues from seventeen European countries: all of them have been so kind as to reply, and we wish to thank them at this point. It is by basing our statements on the answers received that we have been able to draw the essential ideas of this report.

As a result of our consultations it follows that the title of music librarian can legitimately be assumed in three very distinct cases:

1. The curators of collections of scholarly character, exclusively devoted to musical works. The librarians of conservatories and music schools belong in this category; they are contingently in charge of school collections or performance materials, but above all of more specifically musicological collections: manuscripts or early prints, historical sets (*Monumenta* and *Denkmäler* . . .) all of them useful tools for research.
2. The librarians of conservatories, music schools, concert societies, radio stations, and phonorecord collections. Their holdings contain exclusively musical works, orchestral materials, school books, and records. Their libraries are essentially designed for circulation. In certain countries these libraries even exist apart from any institution of learning or musical activity, and they belong to the category of public libraries.
3. The librarians or curators of music divisions in large national libraries or in university libraries.

It goes without saying that the functions and consequently the mission of these three types of music librarians are different. For some of them it is a question of maintaining much more than of lending; for the others it is the reverse. But all of them serve the cause of music under its two aspects: science (*Musikwissenschaft*) and performance. Furthermore, however diverse the collections of which they are in charge may be, the music librarians have in common their social rôle.

But to serve the cause of scholarship and to serve the musical life of a community, to maintain a collection and to lend—are these not irreconcilable attitudes? All the music librarians, however, are aware of these two aspects of their task. The curator of a "precious" collection can participate in the musical life as actively as a person in charge of lending orchestral materials or school books. The

SOURCE: Reprinted from Suzanne Clercx-Lejeune, "Le bibliothécaire musical. Sa formation professionnelle," *Fontes artis musicae,* 3 (1956), 51-56, by permission of the International Association of Music Libraries. Translated by Dr. Isabelle Cazeaux.

considerable development of radio and phonorecords requires a constant renewal of programs and repertoire: "classical" and contemporary music are not sufficient for the purpose, and the search for unpublished material applies as well to the music of our time—and even that of the future—as to old music, including the most ancient. Exotic and folk music also broaden our musical horizon and open up for the listener a sonorous area which is truly planetary. The rôle of the curator of a valuable manuscript is equal to that of the collector of the most unusual records.

This rôle is not maintained, however, without divergencies which derive from the institutions and practices of the various European countries as well as from the individuals themselves.

If a librarian is also the director of a music school, or if he teaches music, if he has an active rôle as a composer or virtuoso, if he is a university professor or a trombone player in an orchestra, or else a curator of a collection other than the music division of a large depository, the stimulus which he will bring to his library will inevitably bear the stamp of his other concerns. Not only is it not possible to alter this situation, but furthermore it would not be desirable to do so. It is well that a composer should manifest, by his acquisitions, his interest in contemporary music—even if his tastes are subjective; it is beneficial that a specialist of folklore or a mediaevalist should create or enrich a musical collection, giving it a very particular slant, without of course neglecting the general interest; it is useful that a phonorecord collection dedicated to "classical" music should, under the influence of a specialist, suddenly become oriented toward non-European music, or that a paleographer should leave, after his tenure in a library, an abundant documentation on musical notation. If the history of the great musical treasures of Europe were to be studied, the successive layers of diverse interests would reveal the particular rôle of individual librarians.[1]

But whatever may be the diversity of their aspirations, the diversity of their rôle, and even the diversity of the depositories which they direct, the music librarians have before them a multifaceted mission which it is their duty to accomplish. To inventory, classify, catalogue and buy do not constitute the only duties of a "curator;" he should also truly maintain the collection, that is to say he should be responsible for the safe-keeping or the restoration of damaged works, for the good condition of the premises, for the care and prudence in handling of rare or precious items. Now the classification and cataloguing of music books present rather special problems. It is by the hundreds that the music librarian must classify thin books consisting of two to four folios, often of very different sizes (detached works for piano, chamber music, songs, *romances* . . .) which it is not convenient to group together in collections. Very often he finds himself in the position of hesitating between the historical or practical character of certain musicological or theoretical works. And how is one to solve the difficult problem of the arrangement of thematic catalogues, which are so useful for the identification of anonymous works?[2]

But maintenance is not the only aspect of the task of the music librarian: he must also circulate materials, for music is not meant to be read in the quiet atmosphere of a library: it demands—and this is one condition of its existence—the intervention of performance. The librarian must therefore lend his books or consider means of having this music reach the concert halls; for this music, resting on its dusty shelves, all too often represents only silence. And there we are faced with a dilemma. When it is a matter of manuscripts or rare printed works, there is no question about it: the copying or photographing of the documents is the only solution to be considered. But to what degree should one remove from circulation departments certain works which are considered to be manuals and are consequently indispensable in a reading room? To what extent may complete collections be momentarily dissociated and made partially unavailable for purposes of consultation and comparison, in order to find their way to the orchestra conductor's stand or to the seminar of an institute of musicology? Finally what should be the length of one circulation? Can a musical work be "penetrated" as rapidly as a book can be read?

In fact almost all our libraries present a hybrid character by the very nature of their collections and the multiple tasks of the librarian can be accomplished only if certain fundamental conditions are fulfilled.

The first pertains to the personnel. But that is a subject of general complaint. With the exception of large depositories, the shortage of professional and non-professional staff seriously affects the performance of music libraries. The lack of understanding on the part of public authorities is, in this respect, extremely detrimental. Often the assistant chiefs and the clerks—when they exist—are recruited from the administrative ranks and they are hired following a rather succinct examination, without having their musical training taken into account. Disabled war veterans and ministry employees are thus placed under the supervision of the music librarians; and the kind of help which these assistants are in a position to offer is limited to their good will and their good sense. In several European countries, therefore, important libraries exist, whose secondary personnel is inadequate and insufficiently trained.

The second condition pertains to the actual training of the music librarian. We shall examine this matter in the second part of this report.

II. THE PROFESSIONAL TRAINING OF THE MUSIC LIBRARIAN

The profession of the music librarian is determined neither by statutes nor by general conventions, and by the same token, no control exists in relation to his training. These two conditions are, moreover, interdependent, and the arbitrariness which prevails in this field is, in itself, logical.

Now we are no longer living in an age in which the directorship of a music library was entrusted to a scholar whom one hoped to honor at the same time one had the benefit of his erudition. The university professors, eminent musicologists who have presided over the destinies of great libraries, have played a considerable rôle: by their vast knowledge they have brought advantage to the depositories of which they were in charge by their judicious acquisitions and personal actions; on the other hand this rôle, which it fell their lot to perform, allowed them to extend the circle of their disciples to include numerous researchers who came both to study documents and to consult the librarian, as well as correspondents, still more numerous, who solicited their authoritative opinions. One can assert that these scholars have done pioneer work: by their prestige they have, from the very first, placed the profession of music librarianship very high in the intellectual hierarchy.

But that era is outmoded, or almost so, for university teaching implies progressively heavier duties, and the function of the music librarian has expanded considerably. The librarian participates in the musical life much more than formerly, and his sphere of influence extends beyond a limited circle of erudites. In addition, the destruction, the scattering, or the transfer of certain collections and the development of musicological science make a general inventory of musical sources necessary not only in Europe but in the whole world. The librarian must therefore dedicate himself entirely to a mission which is hardly compatible with the duties of a university teaching position. Those who still lead this double existence today agree that only long experience allows them to manage two such absorbing activities simultaneously.

It is evident that the mission of the music librarian has very important requirements. Only a solid background will permit the incumbents to immediately fulfill the task which devolves upon them without the necessity of supplementary work of adaptation.

In this respect also Europe presents one of the most variegated of mosaics. Even in countries which own large collections and where eminent librarians are in supervisory positions, there is no teaching of music librarianship. Several types of professional training can be observed, with slight differences according to model cases or even individual cases.

In large official or scholarly depositories, the music librarian, when he exists, has received the training of a bibliographer-librarian. He has kept up with the usual hierarchy, and the random order of deaths and retirements can thus bring to the head of a music division a curator who is wanting in the prerequisite knowledge. He is then compelled to learn a discipline new to him, but the technique of which escapes him. He often runs the risk of allowing himself to be dominated by better informed subordinates. But of course these instances are extremely rare, and even theoretical: in general, although no rule so stipulates, good sense has guided the choice of public or academic authorities toward the bibliographer-librarian who has manifested, during the course of his career, a more particular interest in music.

On the other hand, in conservatories and music schools, selection is generally made of either an educated musician or a musicologist equipped with a university degree; and the latter is the more frequent choice. The incumbent therefore has the desirable knowledge: the history and science of music are familiar to him, but he must also make up his incomplete training in the fields of librarianship and bibliography. His predecessor, either retired or dead, can be of no help to him. If the library of which he is in charge has been managed according to well-established rules, he may use them as a model and carry on a task which was already undertaken by others. But it should be acknowledged that frequently he must waste precious time to discover secrets and master a method which organized instruction and an adequate training stage would have taught him opportunely.

Finally there are librarians whose only training has been musical. Furthermore, the musician who, according to circumstances, is called upon to manage a depository and to enrich a collection must be endowed with uncommon capacity for work and a faculty for adaptation.

To this necessarily schematized description it is fitting to add certain details, so as to show some of the variants: in most European countries, the important collections and the music divisions of large libraries are directed by holders of university degrees (history of music) and diplomas in bibliography and librarianship. Such is the case in England, Germany, Denmark, Austria, France, Sweden, Switzerland, Norway, and Yugoslavia. On the other hand, in the libraries of conservatories or music schools, and even important ones, the requirements are less explicit: musicologists or musicians are admitted there without regard to their technical and practical preparation. Only Italy has provided serious rules for certification of conservatory librarians: an examination bears upon general culture, Latin, two modern languages, music and its history, composition, musical paleography, and some notions of librarianship.

Now we have said it: whatever the particular character of the collection may be, the profession remains essentially the same. The school library of today may become the historical evidence of tomorrow, and a progressively distant past becomes more and more a part of current musical life. In a Europe seeking to re-establish itself, in a world trying to find itself, why not attempt, as far as possible, to make the qualifications of music librarians more similar? This rapprochement can only be achieved by the training of each individual. From the unification of principles, from the equivalence—which is preferable to equality—of diplomas and titles, a true brotherhood can arise between persons who share the same concerns and who are animated by a similar ideal.

But what should be the program of studies? Where—in what institutions—could this training be given to the future music librarian? What should be the ideal duration of studies? Is it fitting to reserve for holders of university degrees and diplomas in bibliography and librarianship not only the highest positions but also the direction of less important collections? What kind of training does one have the right to expect of assistants?

On the other hand, should the distinction which exists between scholarly libraries and popular type libraries reflect on the librarians, and should different training be considered for these two categories?

These are questions which it does not behoove us to answer. We limit ourselves to raising them here. Certainly modalities vary from one country to another, and each one will propose, depending on the country which he represents, the most adequate solution, or solutions, for the individual instances which are encountered there.

Whatever the case may be, the survey of which we present the essential results indicates that numerous European countries show a trend toward rather similar requirements for the highest positions: University degrees in musicology and diplomas in bibliography and librarianship are the dual guarantee demanded by a profession with a double aspect. From expediency to convention, the step has been taken without difficulty. The same could be done, we believe, from convention to general agreement.

NOTES

[1] We have made a brief sketch of the history of the library of the Conservatory of Brussels in an article entitled: "Le problème des bibliothèques musicales en Belgique," in *Alumni,* Brussels, (August-September 1947), pp. 229-230.

[2] Madame N. Bridgman has proposed a new filing system for these catalogues. Cf. "L'établissement d'un catalogue par incipit musicaux," in *Musica Disciplina,* v. 4 (1950), pp. 65-68.

Librarians and Musicologists

by François Lesure

The time is past when the librarian had to satisfy only the limited demands of a small number of readers. He could then devote himself in all tranquillity to his personal work; his memory was sufficient to guide readers and even to trace the location of volumes on the shelves. I am convinced that many of you consider with a certain amount of nostalgia this happy man, this dilettante scholar who really lived with the books which surrounded him and who would never have been able to bear the thought that the catalogue card should have become a veritable barrier between him and the treasures under his care.

But this man is dead indeed, and daily librarians must accept increasingly heavier duties. Today one has come to wonder whether it is possible to keep an encyclopedic library up to date in the field of music alone. Yet such is the situation in most of the music divisions of the large national libraries: during the same hour and with the same means, the librarian of one of these divisions must meet the needs of the radio station which wishes to obtain—on the very same day, for a broadcast on the subject of flowers—songs which refer to primroses and camelias; of the television network which requires a mural poster of the première of *Pelléas;* of a commercial artist who is undertaking the illustration of a record jacket; of a lecturer who needs a two-page résumé of the history of Italian opera; and of a lady singer with repertoire trouble, owing to a badly placed register; and I am considering here only serious-minded people and not the host of crotchety individuals and idle ones who always constitute the stock in trade of every library in the world, and whose peculiarities are much more dangerous. Finally this same librarian, if he has any time left, should bring all his help to the musicologist who wonders about the origins of a manuscript, tries to identify the authors of an anonymous collection, and raises thousands of complex questions which have to do with paleography, history, liturgy, linguistics, bibliography, acoustics, or archaeology. Today, if the librarian is to be allowed to fulfill his rôle properly, it is time to consider specialization on the part of certain music libraries. Just as a distinction is made between working music libraries designed for conservatories and public music libraries for reading—whose aim is to diffuse music among the masses—it is fitting from now on to think of organizing scholarly libraries which would be adapted to actual needs of research—truly specialized institutes.

I do not forget that the vital duties of every library are first of all the duties of maintenance and consultation; and they generally take up most of the time of their personnel. In a scholarly library these obligations would be a means and no longer an end, and they would be delegated to non-specialized staff. The essential duty of such a center, or such an institute, would be threefold. It would include documentation, coordination, and production.

1. If it is a question of documentation, or scholarly guidance, it will first have to be acknowledged that the librarian is the only person competent to help the musicologist with his increasingly heavy load of bibliographical information. Often more time is spent searching to find whether or not an assumed innovation has been worked on earlier by someone else than in putting this so-called innovation into shape. As early as 1935, Ortega y Gasset pointed out that ours is a strange culture, one in which, "the book has ceased to be an attraction" and in which "it is considered as a heavy burden. If each new generation continues to accumulate printed matter in the same proportion as the generations of these past years, the

SOURCE: Reprinted from François Lesure, "Bibliothécaires et musicologues." *Atti del Congresso internazionale di musiche popolari mediterranee, e Convegno dei bibliotecari musicali, Palermo, 26–30 giugno 1954.* Pages 363–367, by permission of the author. Translated by Dr. Isabelle Cazeaux.

problem which is presented by the excess of books will be truly terrifying." And the Spanish writer saw the librarian as the perfect "physician," "hygienist," the "filter interposed between man and the torrent of books."[1]

The solution to this serious problem is hardly to be found in extending and keeping up to date the subject files or analytical files, which are more and more difficult to handle as they become more complete, because they take no account whatever of the value of the things being filed. There again, in an encyclopedic music library, it would be necessary to separate general reference cards from general files containing all sorts of analytics and useful for readers already experienced in the critical use of bibliographical sources. It is surely not in an increasingly elaborate technique of the catalogue card that the future of libraries lies, but on the contrary, in its reduction. The only palliative is the specialization of the librarian who will inevitably have to be relieved of the material work with which he is overwhelmed in order to effect the indispensable choice which he must certainly make at every step of his work: in acquisitions, in analytics, and in the time he reserves for the reader.

2. If it is now a matter of coordination, the scholarly librarian will be able to exert beneficial action in the international sphere as well as in his own country. The more progress is made in musicology, the more scholarly studies and editions run the risk of being duplicated. We know, unfortunately, of instances where they are already duplicated in the most regrettable manner. The librarian is almost always the first to know about the beginnings of a piece of research, through a request for information or photographic reproduction. It is therefore up to him to draw the attention of the researcher to other works in progress and to halt useless work, within the limits of possibility; this is a rôle of liaison which should of course be undertaken in close cooperation with the university. The librarian will also have the duty of informing musicologists of the assistance they may obtain from the works of historians of civilization, "pure" historians, etc., and similarly to inform the historian of civilization of the help he may expect from musicological works. He should not neglect any aspect of the human sciences and he should establish permanent contact with institutions specializing in folklore and ethnography, esthetics, sociology, etc. In another field this rôle of coordination should be exercised to facilitate the free circulation of materials from one country to another in the form of microfilm. It will be the responsibility of the special library to issue eventual authorizations and restrictions in order to safeguard national treasures. It will also have to set up for itself a film library for the purpose of systematically supplementing its collections. Not to mention American libraries, the Bibliothèque nationale [Paris] has already partially assumed this rôle and has acceded favorably to the requests of its readers.

3. Finally a scholarly library will have to produce. It is already known that the distinctive feature of a center of documentation is not to accumulate papers but to redistribute the substance of those which it receives. It will be first of all a matter of the usual catalogues, from which more is expected than formerly, and also of scholarly bibliographies, and eventually of manuals of bibliography. The librarian will have to proceed further still and not be content to be the servant of the musicologist and hand over to him the musical document all dated and identified, like a chicken ready to be cooked. His rôle will be over, in the long run, only after he has classified the works under his care, made them available for consultation, identified them, dated them, and even published them and have them heard. This is the second time that we are faced with the problem of the relations between library and university. If the music library is encyclopedic, the university professor will hardly be able to recommend to his overworked colleague the acquisition of works which he needs for his teaching or for the projects of his students. But if the library becomes the specialized institute which is our dream, a close collaboration will have to be established between these two organizations. Since the function of the librarian does not in any way designate him for teaching, no friction or competition is to be feared between them. It would be particularly ridiculous, we repeat, to limit the librarian to mechanical work with catalogue cards, when degrees, knowledge, and competence in research are increasingly required of him. In the long run, it is indeed for this research that an important place should be reserved for him. It is still being discussed—and namely in France—whether the researcher should be distinct from the professor. The question does not arise in the case of the librarian if one acknowledges that the new responsibilities which were mentioned earlier are within his province. In France, librarians who have scholarly works to their credit participate in the voting for the establishment of the commissions of the Centre Na-

tional de la Recherche Scientifique. They may perfectly well be elected to these bodies. In order to influence a scholar there is no other alternative except to be a scholar oneself, and the librarian should not be relegated to semi-clandestinity in order to do this. The arrangement which was established on the occasion of RISM between the librarians (technical part) and the musicologists (scholarly part) in no way implies that librarians do not have scholarly knowledge or that musicologists are incapable of a good bibliographical technique. It is not necessary to recall here that in the past, music divisions of libraries have published important musicological editions—notably those which have been realized by Mgr. Anglés at the library of Catalonia, and more recently by the New York [Public] Library and the Biblioteca Governativa of Cremona. Those who have committed themselves in this direction have understood that a specialized library which does not reach out, which does not diffuse the treasures from its holdings, fails miserably in its cultural responsibility.

There is no science peculiar to libraries. There is only a technique which often boils down to rules of common sense, which the largest among these libraries had to lay down for themselves in order to make possible the regular integration of the mass of publications which might have submerged them. But let us not confuse the values. If the duty of the librarian consists only in assigning call numbers to books, in having them placed on the shelves, in making clear and precise catalogue cards for them, in making them available for consultation by readers—if the technique of librarianship must be the ultimate goal of his work, one wonders then why it is necessary to be encumbered with so many guarantees of scholarship for the recruitment of these machine-men, and one can at any rate understand why the public authorities are not very eager to grant them a better position in the scale of salaries. In fact if it is a question of a really specialized library, a true center of documentation, it is necessary to resolutely separate card work from the type of work that has just been outlined. And there are enough musicologists who do not find openings at a university, and fall back on the libraries, so that one might hope that from that source one could obtain excellent results.

These few remarks, which should be commonplace, and which apply only to the most important libraries, are especially justified in the case of Latin countries, in which music is barely accepted as a university discipline. And in a field in which the university has shown itself weak, should our large libraries not make an effort to replace it?

It is at least in these libraries and in these countries that it would be fitting to create specialized institutes which, in close cooperation with the university, could be of great service to musicology. Finally they would exert a beneficial influence on the very dignity of our function—which has been compromised by certain excesses of librarianship—by having it taken for granted that it is not possible to maintain or diffuse treasures properly without being well-acquainted with them.

NOTE

[1] J. Ortega y Gasset, *Mission du bibliothécaire,* 1935, pp. 16-21.

Music Librarian—Bibliographer—Documentalist: Secondary Report

by Vincent H. Duckles

We all agree that the topic under discussion by this panel was formulated in an unfortunate way. It suggests that there are three distinguishable specialists who have their separate spheres of activity within the music library. Of course this is not the case. I know many music librarians, quite a number of music bibliographers, but no music documentalist, unless I accept the point made by Mr. John Davies in one of the earlier panels that "documentalist" is merely a new, modern term for "reference librarian". Let documentation stand for a group of techniques, some old and some new, for recording, manipulating and communicating specialized information; in these terms every librarian is a documentalist on occasion.

Yet one thing that can be said for the term is that it belongs to the future. It directs our attention toward developments of tomorrow, and that is a healthy exercise for librarians, who are by nature the most conservative of people. But while we let our imaginations run wild with the prospects of future developments in electronic computers, it would be well to recall that other claims just as extravagent have been made in the past. We in the library field have often been misled by the lure of revolutionary processes and techniques. Not long ago we were told that microfilm and microprint would completely change our attitude toward space and its allocation in the library. Similarly we were assured that recorded tape would make our collections of discs obsolete. We have since learned to live with microfilm and tape recordings, not as vast, earth-shaking developments, but as added resources in library practice, appropriate in some areas and not in others.

I must confess that I shudder when I read a statement such as appeared in the *New Yorker* magazine a few weeks ago: ". . . Machines will take over the drugery of keeping information in mind and on paper, and man will merely have to concentrate on asking the machines the right questions . . . I expect that by 1980 we'll have taken a giant step toward freeing people from the tyranny of the printed page." As musicians we can understand "the tyranny of the bar line," or even "the tyranny of the score," but no bookman is ever going to admit that the printed page, as such, exercises a tyranny from which he needs to escape. Free a librarian of the printed page and he will not know what to do with his freedom.

The one thing that librarianship, bibliography and documentation have in common is their concern with *information* and its communication, but only in the case of documentation do we have what has been called a *science* of information, a realm of thought known as "information theory." This has led to a subtle shift in emphasis from the *content* of the information to be communicated to the *processes* and *devices* through which it can be communicated. Such changes often take place in our thinking as knowledge becomes more and more specialized, but it follows that we tend to become more interested in what can be done with the machine (device, technique) than in what the machine can do for us in improving our services or helping us to meet our objectives. This is one of the dangers of a special interest in documentation as a science. We must never forget the purpose which the device is intended to serve, and if it does not serve that purpose we should discard it.

If we look carefully at these three terms, librarian, bibliographer and documentalist, we will see that they are not equally comprehensive in scope. It is possible to think of librarianship as

SOURCE: Reprinted from Vincent Duckles, "Music Librarian–Bibliographer–Documentalist: Secondary Report," *Fontes artis musicae,* 12 (1965), 138–141, by permission of the International Association of Music Libraries.

embracing the other two, or it is possible to regard documentation as the inclusive term. The term, bibliographer, however, exists on a lower level in the logic of relationships. It cannot serve as the key term in defining either of its companions. But this is not to suggest that bibliography, as an activity, is on a lower level of value. On the contrary, I am much concerned that the new techniques of documentation we have heard described at this congress will lead to the under-rating of certain traditional approaches to bibliography. I speak for those who regard bibliography as a form of literature. Its value lies in the display of subtle relationships between materials (books, articles, scores, recordings, etc.) as grouped in the mind of a specialist who has a thorough knowledge of his subject. I am grateful to Barry Brook for pointing out in his talk the other day the vital distinction between *knowledge* and *information.* There is a great deal of bibliographical work that depends on knowledge and on sensitivity to the values and relationships existing within a subject area.

The great dream of the bibliographer is comprehensive coverage. It is a frustrating dream that can never be fully satisfied. His objective is "complete bibliographical control." He would like to create a tool so complete and so precise that anyone seeking information can find exactly what he wants. Yet there is a constant state of tension between comprehensiveness and precision. If you work for one you are likely to gain it only at the expense of the other. Here, of course, is where the documentalist and the bibliographer can join forces to their mutual advantage. The virtue of the computer lies in its ability to handle vast amounts of data with speed and accuracy. It can bring us closer to the realization of the dream of comprehensive coverage, while at the other end of the scale specialists can devote themselves to problems of selective, critical bibliography.

As these new developments in documentation change our patterns of scholarship and research, a new type of scholar and librarian will have to be trained. The problems of such training have thus far been given little attention. Let me illustrate the point by an incident described by one of our colleagues at this congress. The purchase of a new and expensive music reference tool by a certain university music library was obstructed by one faculty member. And the reason he gave was that he did not want his own students to have access to resources that were not available to him when he was a student. Now at first glance this seems an extreme statement of a reactionary point of view, an appalling position for any teacher to take. Yet it contains a grain of truth, a legitimate concern that we would all do well to consider. There is indeed a threat to our traditional methods of teaching and learning presented by the new techniques of documentation. To sit in a comfortable chair and push buttons to receive pre-sorted, predigested information, is not the same thing, as digging it out for yourself. I am not concerned here with the training of the documentalist as such but with those minds whose will be affected by the documentalist's work. There is much in the older disciplines of learning that must be guarded and preserved. The way to preserve it is obviously not to take an ostrich-like attitude toward the new techniques but to appraise them in the light of their contribution to learning as a whole, to recognize their limitations and their advantages.

What we need is a clear conception of the philosophy of documentation as it affects our work as music librarians, scholars, teachers. *Philosophy* is a pretentious word, but in this context I mean no more than an effort to think through some of the questions raised in my preceding remarks. What are the limits of effectiveness for these new techniques of documentation? What can they do, and what can they not do? What values in the traditional approaches to information service are worth preserving? What articulation can be made between the old and the new? What is the nature of the new mentality that will result from the use of the new methods? How does it affect the training of scholars and librarians? Some of these questions have already been confronted in fields outside of music, and we would do well to see what we can learn from them. One example known to me is an Institute of Library Research recently established at the University of California. In the prospectus for this Institute four principles have been set down as guides to the application of the new documentation techniques to general library problems. I leave it to you to extend this application to the domain of the music librarian.

1. The approach is based on study of *the needs for better library and information services,* not just on the question of how specific techniques, such as the computer, can be used.
2. The approach is based on a *total, integrated study of all aspects* of library services, not just on fragmented studies of isolated aspects.
3. The approach is based on the *integration of needed new services with existing ones . . .* not on development of parallel, unrelated,

and experimental services which must later be put into operation.

4. The approach is based on the view of *library services as a system problem,* encompassing a variety of individual libraries and information centers into a unified whole.

The Music Librarian and his Tasks, National and International

by Alexander Hyatt King

King, Superintendent of the Music Room of the British Museum, was President of the International Association of Music Libraries when he read this paper before the International Joint Music Congress in Cambridge, 1959. A brief appreciation of King's professional achievements appeared in a recent issue of the journal of the IAML, Fontes artis musicae, *18 (1971/1-2), 2-3.*

This is the first international congress of music librarians ever held in the United Kingdom. It could, I think, hardly be held under happier or more distinguished auspices. We are honoured by the generous welcome and good wishes which we have received from Sir Sidney Roberts, and we feel that it is especially appropriate that the Congress should take place here in Cambridge. The reasons for this reach back into the distant academic and cultural past. Let me dwell on them briefly. This University and its Colleges are exceptionally rich in old and diversified collections of music, as befits the centre of learning where in 1463 the earliest known British degree in music was awarded. The University Music School itself, which the Music Faculty has so generously placed at our disposal for our meetings, is thus the heir of a venerable but living and active tradition.

Another distinguished tradition began in 1441, the year which saw the foundation by Henry VI of the College of Saint Nicholas, usually known as King's College, whose amenities and hospitality we are privileged to enjoy during this week. For over five hundred years, music has been a splendid and vital part of the life of King's. A College inventory of 1529 lists no fewer than forty-one books of "prick-song," including music by Cambridge composers active in the mid-15th century. Such books as these though lost at the Reformation were a notable precursor of the great new music library founded in 1928, which flourishes in the College today.

There is yet another reason why this Congress is held most appropriately in Cambridge. As Professor Westrup has said, Canon Francis William Galpin was a Cambridge man, a graduate and doctor of letters of Trinity College, and the eponym of the distinguished society with whom we, as librarians, are very happy to collaborate. Those who wisely drafted our Statutes in 1951 clearly foresaw that some such collaboration as this was possible and desirable. I quote from Article II of the Statutes, which sets out the principal purposes of the International Association of Music Libraries. The seventh of these is: 'to co-operate with other national and international organisations in the fields of music, of musicology, of documentation, and of library science.'

So much by way of introduction and preamble. As a background to the purpose of this Congress, and to set it in some kind of perspective, let me remind you briefly of the origins and growth of the International Association of Music Libraries. After the war, there were many new trends in librarianship, particularly in specialised fields. There had, of course, existed general international associations of librarians for nearly half a century, but similar groups of specialists were something new. It is, I think, correct to say that music librarians were first in the field, and that they were followed, in due course, by medical and agricultural librarians.

An any rate, at Florence in 1949, the first international gathering of music librarians took place. After another meeting at Lüneburg in 1950, came our first general assembly, at Paris, in 1951. Unesco acted as a munificent foster mother to our struggling infancy, which may be said to have

SOURCE: Reprinted from A. Hyatt King, "The music librarian and his tasks, national and international," *Fontes artis musicae,* 6 (1959), 49-55, by permission of the International Association of Music Libraries.

passed into adolescence at the Brussels Congress of 1955. During these years, we found that the ideal of specialisation brings its own problems, especially when, as we thought essential, it had to be linked with as much independence and self-reliance as possible. That we achieved as much as we did during these difficult, but stimulating, years is due to the devoted labours of three men above all—Professor Valentin Denis, of the University of Louvain, who was acting President up till the time of our formal inauguration: Mr. Richard S. Hill, of the Library of Congress, who during his Presidency travelled incessantly on our behalf: and M. Valdimir Fédorov whose selfless, unremitting toil, both as secretary from 1949 to 1955, and as Editor of *Fontes* since its inception, needs no praise from me.

Broadly speaking, the aims of our Association have much in common with those of other bodies of specialists in different fields. We seek to avoid duplication of effort: we desire to raise the status of our members, to give them a sense of direction, with wider horizons and higher standards of technical proficiency, and a greater interest in their job. We have, I think, shown that progress in our field can be achieved by persuasion and co-operation, not by dictation. But this is not all. For this philosophy of action is raised, as it were, to a higher plane by what I believe to be the unique quality and status of music as a library service.

I refer to a certain vital functional quality peculiar to an art which is conceived for recreation in sound and time, and is not confined in the immobile rigidity of purely spatial dimensions, nor limited to the reading of the printed word. One music librarian may hand to a schoolgirl a copy of Beethoven's 'Für Elise': another may provide a scholarly conductor with a copy of a Petrucci edition of a motet by Josquin or with the autograph of an eighteenth century cantata for checking against a suspect edition. Both librarians are functioning as the penultimate link in a process of recreation, in bringing to life from the printed page the original impulse of communication of musical form and idea. If you accept the thesis that creative art is a species of communication, I would urge that the music librarian plays a vital part in this communication. I would go further and say that the very nature of music makes his service quite distinct from almost every other branch of librarianship.

The librarian concerned with books does indeed serve as the last link in a chain of the communication and understanding of a creative idea. But the difference between literature and music lies in the fact that the transmission of the printed notes of the music is not the last stage, whereas that of the printed word—other than plays—is so, for all practical purposes. Even the librarians serving the professional needs of the man of letters, the painter, sculptor or architect, has not the satisfaction of knowing that his work will bear such immediate fruit in bringing to life an original creative impulse. The fact that our schoolgirl may receive a rap on the knuckles from her teacher for playing wrong notes or that our scholarly conductor's interpretation of Josquin may not be regarded as definitive by his peers, is, in this context, immaterial.

Hence, this distinctive function which underlies the philosophy of our profession, briefly and inadequately as I have expounded it, gives or ought to give to much of our work a sense of purpose and immediacy which should go far to lessen its irritations and frustrations. No librarian's job is free from these, but what other, besides music, can claim such compensating satisfaction?

I come now to a general aspect of music librarianship that forms part of the growing paradox of social life in the mid-twentieth century. The higher our material standards become in terms of mechanical devices, the more we are likely to become dependent on them, whether they be cars, computers or ultrasonic washing machines, but the greater is the urge to use increasing leisure in pursuit of the arts, especially music. The stereophonic record-player does not, apparently, reduce the popularity of the recorder and the fantastic increase of music published for it, as a solo instrument or in consort. Simultaneously, demand for music and for musical literature rises steadily in libraries of many kinds. The time is surely not far distant when, as reference demands arise, every music library with a large stock will have to be equipped with some kind of punched-card system for the speedy finding of data that will answer enquiries.

Besides this demand in the countries where music-making, or listening to music, has, in some measure, been long-established, there can be seen a different growth in other countries now springing into nation-hood. In these new nations, new universities, new schools, new towns and new libraries are coming into being. In music they are faced with the problems, often unique, of serving the needs of an old cultural tradition which is striving to blend itself with European influences. Their librarians have, I believe, the need of whatever our skills and experience can give them. We in turn have need of their membership. In ten years, our membership has expanded to cover thirty-five different countries. Admittedly, this membership is small in some of them, but I am convinced that a truly world-wide membership lies in our grasp, and can be developed if only we can seek out these new countries, establish contact with them, and meet their needs half-way, by making known to them the work and aims of our Association. In the present state of music it may be an exaggeration to describe it as an "international language," but that basically it comes nearer to this concept than can ever the spoken or the written word.

Let me pass to the work of our Association. This is clearly a very varied topic, and in order to bring it, so to speak, into the sharpest and clearest possible focus, I propose to consider this work mainly in terms of the several committees which co-ordinate and direct it. The order in which I mention them is not necessarily that of their prestige or importance: the sequence is broadly related to the degree or extent of public service. First, however, I would briefly touch on our journal, *Fontes Artis Musicae,* which forms the cornerstone of the whole edifice of the Association. In it you can read, among many other matters, reports of the work of our committees. With such diverse interests as our Association has, it is still very difficult to achieve in *Fontes* a balance of subject-matter which will satisfy everyone. But with our limited resources, it was a remarkable feat to bring *Fontes* into existence at all. It remains the vital link between our scattered members. The more our numbers grow, the wider its coverage can become, and the more faithfully it will reflect the light from the many prisms of our activity.

Indisputably, the most extensive direct service is given by our public music libraries. In this context "public" is a term which may connote widely differing functions in different countries, even in different libraries in the same country. This was clearly shown, I think, by the special International Congress of these libraries held at Salzburg in the autumn of 1958. It seems from this Congress, and from the work of the Committee meetings which led up to it, that the public library of music differs, in some cases, from the research library only in the nature of its stock, which usually excludes antiquarian sources. But in range of duties, reference work, the provision and servicing of current or recent musical literature and of discs, with the essential knowledge of equipment, the public librarian's responsibilities are growing rapidly. For example, at Liverpool, music issues in 1953-54 were 71,387: by 1957-58 they had risen to 314,091, that is by nearly 450 per cent. It also seems quite clear, from the Committee's enquiries, that the material rewards are generally quite incommensurate with this range of work. Here, surely, is a vital job for our Association to do—to try to raise the standards of professional training for librarians in public music libraries, and to make the responsible authorities re-assess their service at its true worth.

If public service, given in however indirect a way, is a criterion of importance, then the radio music librarian is very important indeed. He serves, but is hardly ever seen by the millions, all over the world, who listen to broadcast music. To make some of the scarce sources, which are the basis of this service, more easily available among themselves, the Radio Librarians have published a catalogue of these special materials. As the use of music in television expands, simultaneously with the more esoteric needs of these concerned with 'musique concrète' and electrophonic music, the radio librarian, who largely covers these fields, has some interesting problems ahead of him.

It is, perhaps, a platitude to say that sound cataloguing is fundamental to good librarianship. I emphasise it because it is no secret that the cataloguing of music has mostly lagged behind the standards of book cataloguing. Though the two naturally differ in many subtle ways, music-cataloguing has equal value as an intellectual discipline. Realising this difference in standards, we have always deemed most important the arduous work of our Committee on the Code of Rules for music cataloguing. The first part of these rules has been published,[1] and we hope both this and the later parts will command wide acceptance, especially in new libraries. For uniformity of practice is essential to any kind of co-operative work, in which our Association must, in time, play its part. This work of compiling rules is, of course, rather easier for printed music than for manuscript. But the great diversity and complexity of the latter is, in my view, no reason for refusing to try to draw up a set of principles by which manuscript music of different kinds can be described in an orderly and consistent fashion. This we certainly have in mind to meet a widespread need. What is quite certain, for both printed and manuscript music, is that the rules for cataloguing will have to allow for the inclusion of thematic incipits as required by certain types of composition and in certain periods where key or text do not suffice to ensure identification.

This last proviso applies equally to music or gramophone records, to which, as library material, our Association has not been able to give all the attention it urgently needs. Here is a highly specialised branch of librarianship, which is barely thirty years old. Most collections of records form part of the stock of a general music library: their problems, on a small scale, are those of the larger, separate national collections which are coming into being—with varying degrees of slowness. These problems are growing at a formidable rate. The lack of a generally accepted set of rules is one problem to the solution of which our newly established committee has already made an effective contribution. Plainly they have much more still to do. Besides the difficulties of building up his stock and equipment, and maintaining the latter in the face of bewilderingly rapid technical progress, the librarian with national responsibilities is faced with many difficulties of conservation. For despite intensive research, so little is known about the durability of disc or tape, assuming a probable use, comparable to that of the average book, of at least a century. Again, if the national record library aims at having the same kind of international coverage as is essential in a national library of books, then our Association has a great part to play in the future exchange both of commercial and non-commercial material and of information regarding technical progress. This is, perhaps, the most challenging field of all the multifarious aims we must keep in mind.

Records have also an important part to play in the work of Universities and Research Libraries, but do not, I think, constitute their most pressing problems, which are sometimes embedded in their tradition and perhaps even engendered by it. For, however old and important their collections, these libraries may become as mausolea unless they make every effort not only to acquire new rarities, but also to develop their current catalogues so that they can give a lead to research by keeping scholars swiftly and regularly informed of important acquisitions. Research libraries have of course other urgent demands to face, not least from the fantastic increase in the general demands made upon staff and resources, due, in turn, to the phenomenal growth of the numbers of students reading for musical degrees of various kinds. Let me give you some figures, in each case comparing the academic year 1937/38 with 1957/58. At Oxford, 25 degrees increased to 46. At Cambridge 27 rose to 89. At Birmingham, a modest 4 soared to 33. For America, the figures are equally striking. It is recorded that in the whole of the 1930s there were only 25 degrees taken in music. Between 1952 and 1957, no fewer than 212 were completed. To support all this in a different way, may I quote some statistics from the British Museum. In 1952/53 we received 83 orders for the photocopying of music, involving 187 items. In 1957/58 these figures had risen to 288 orders, involving 1718 items—an increase in items handled of nearly 900 per cent, which reflects something of the worldwide growth of musical research. This increase will assuredly be found reflected again in the demands on music librarians.

I have not the slightest doubt that these figures and those for other types of work will continue to show a steep increase. The constant unearthing of musical treasures in public and private collections, easier and cheaper methods of photocopying, and the growing rapidity of inter-continental travel are but three of the factors which will augment the demands for musical sources, as of course for other humanistic subjects as well. With this in mind, our Committee in this field hopes to gather and make available data about these important libraries, all over the world—their days and hours of opening: their accommodation: their facilities for photocopying and for the reading of watermarks: their catalogues: the size, sources and age of their valuable holdings. This and much other information needs to be collected and published if we are to help the travelling scholar to make the best use of his often limited time. Similar data could profitably be collected regarding the musical museums which, in some places, exist side by side with libraries. Here is another, short-term, task in which the Galpin Society and the Librarians might co-operate.

Again, the librarians have much to do—though this is a less urgent matter—in writing and publishing the history of these fascinating and often venerable collections of music. The history of general research libraries has been studied in considerable detail, but about analogous music libraries practically nothing has been written. Here is an absorbing task which is a challenge alike to scholarship and to bibliographical enthusiasm.

Bibliography, in the proper, restricted sense of the term, is, or ought to be, very much the concern of our Association. As the musical aspects of the subject have lagged far behind the comparable study of books, it is clearly important that there should be as wide an agreement as possible on the meaning of its fundamental terms. If this can be done, it will, in time, be a boon to the compilers and users of scholarly catalogues of music libraries, for they can then be reasonably certain that terms such as issue, reissue, edition, original edition, impression, state and so on, in their equivalents in various languages, bear an identical connotation. For this reason, I believe that the expert discussion which forms part of this Congress is far from being an exercise in pedantry.[2] I see it rather as the beginning of a long overdue study in verbal exactitude, which should help to raise the status of musical bibliography to that of printed books.

I must draw your attention to another lacuna in the history of music. It is a sad fact that in no language is there a comprehensive account of music printing. How little we really know of the exact nature of the revolutionary techniques of the early 16th century, of the ways in which they developed and changed as they spread from Italy all over Europe and to South America. There is no good book where the student can learn either about these beginnings or about the technical background to the revival and adaptation of the old methods in the 18th century and to their modification by the lithographic revolutions of the 19th century and the photo-lithographic one of the 20th century. But do not be alarmed: I do not plead for another committee. I mention this as another striking instance of the way in which the study of music-printing as a library subject has lagged behind that of books.[3]

It is unfortunately true that lack of comprehensive catalogues could at present make the writing of part of such a history very difficult. But this gap at least will gradually be filled by the series in the International Repertory of Musical Sources devoted to printed works. It is expected that this catalogue will ultimately contain all the principal sources, manuscript and printed, for all periods and all countries in the world. This is surely one of the boldest pieces of long-term planning ever undertaken for the source-material of any subject in the humanistic field. From the first this has been a collaborative enterprise, in which we have worked in close and amicable co-operation with the International Society for Musicology. Some of our members have served on a joint committee with their representatives, and I am confident that this committee will continue for as many years as necessary to finish this great task. The result will be a gradual but immeasurable widening of the frontiers of musical history.

Several times in this survey I have referred to the co-operative nature of some of our work. In the context of preparing catalogues, I feel bound to express what I know to be a personal opinion, not perhaps generally held, about a danger inherent in this. I believe it would be regrettable if the tendency towards the union-catalogue were to discourage libraries with old collections of great historical interest from publishing their own catalogues. This may entail some duplication of effort and expense, but it would be a great pity if the identity of these collections were lost by being merged in the larger whole.

I have so far mostly confined myself to describing the tasks which the International Association of Music Libraries actually has in hand. I should like, before I close, to refer briefly to one or two of the fields which we have not yet touched. The first is the need for the systematic and comprehensive documentation of visual records of the performance of old music in painting, carving or plastic arts, which provide data for its revival, in the most scholarly way possible. Individual research has, I know, begun and some of it has been published, but the field is so vast and the material so scattered and requires such careful interpretation that the need is clearly for intelligent, co-operative planning. Another vast field comprises the literature needed for the study of ethnomusicology, which lies hidden in all kinds of primarily non-musical sources. To find it and catalogue it on a global scale is surely the task of an international organisation.

I have said enough to indicate that our Association must develop as a world-wide community. Music is now being printed, in staff notation, in tonic sol-fa, in various forms of numerical or alphabetical tablature, in places as far apart as Tokyo, Tibet, Iceland and Honolulu. Where music is published, performed and studied, there must in time be music libraries, and, as I suggested earlier, these libraries may need the practical support of our Association. With such a scattered membership, our progress depends to a great extent on the work of our committees, which cannot possibly solve their problems by correspondence alone, even if all their members had the time or inclination to write letters continually. I hope that in the course of this address I have answered the question that is sometimes put to me: "Are your committee meetings really necessary?" Of course they must meet, regularly: even during this crowded week they will hold meetings, and will report, in due course, to the full Executive Committee.

But committees alone cannot run an international association. We shall always depend ultimately on our membership, on its steady expansion, and above all on our national groups. For it is their enthusiasm, their competitive zeal and their ideas which will be the mainspring of our progress. Without progressive ideas continually rising up from members through the committees, to the executive committee and the Council, we may stagnate and fulfil no useful purpose. But new environments bring new contacts and engender new ideas. Partly for this reason, our various meetings in these last ten strenuous years have been so fruitful. From Florence in 1949 onwards, our gatherings, either selfcontained or in conjunction with other occasions, in Lüneburg, Paris, London, Brussels, Salzburg, Kassel, Cologne, Oxford, Vienna, Utrecht, Madrid and Basel—our deliberations in each place have taken us a stage farther along our road. We look forward to future meetings in other cities and countries which lie at present beyond our effective range, particularly those, such as Scandinavia, Czechoslovakia, Poland and Russia, where so much of western musical tradition is enshrined. Meanwhile this congress at Cambridge will assuredly prove a landmark in the growth of our Association.

NOTES

[1]See [**125**,140].–*Editor.*
[2]Hopkinson, "Towards a definition of certain terms in musical bibliography," p. 135.–*Editor.*
[3]See [**87-114,** 100–101].–*Editor.*

Index

The INDEX comprehends concepts, subjects, library names, personal names, and titles of the reprinted articles, as well as the bibliographic citations throughout the book. Editor's introductions are also fully indexed. Substantive information in NOTES is indexed; notes which are simply the citation appropriate to the textual information are not indexed. For example, see note 2, page 191 and page 185, paragraph 1, which it supplements:

The index entries for Music Library Association and *A checklist of thematic catalogues* refer only to page 185; the additional information in note 2 about the *Queens College Supplement (1966)* is indexed separately.

From the NOTES on pages 191 and 192, few composers, compilers or titles of thematic catalogues are indexed; indexing only those quoted as examples in an historical essay might confuse readers about the current quantity of thematic catalogues. For lists of thematic catalogues, readers should refer to items **145-147**, 181.

In the Rosenthal article, pages 81-89, individual antiquarians and their catalogues are indexed selectively on the assumption that readers are apt to be interested in approaching only the more contemporary names through the INDEX. The authors and titles cited in Hopkinson, pages 127-134, are also indexed selectively, entries limited, essentially, to those for items which appear elsewhere in the *Reader*. Considered, *en toto,* Hopkinson's selected bibliographical citations might more appropriately be approached through other bibliographical sources. However, the APPENDIX to Freitag, pages 291-294, is completely indexed because it consists of solely library-oriented items. Similar instances throughout the *Reader* are indexed in like fashion; that is, authors and titles within article texts are indexed selectively according to their projected use to readers.

* * * * *

The filing order is straight alphabetical, word by word, disregarding punctuation.

Boldface numbers refer to the bibliographic citations throughout the *Reader;* the roman numbers are page numbers.